Criminal Law Dealing with Hate Crimes

Schriften zum Strafrecht und Strafprozeßrecht

Herausgegeben von Manfred Maiwald
und Carsten Momsen

Band 117

PL ACADEMIC RESEARCH

Christine Marie Shavers

Criminal Law Dealing with Hate Crimes

Functional Comparative Law
Germany vs. USA

PL ACADEMIC RESEARCH

Bibliographic Information published by the Deutsche Nationalbibliothek
The Deutsche Nationalbibliothek lists this publication
in the Deutsche Nationalbibliografie; detailed bibliographic
data is available in the internet at http://dnb.d-nb.de.

Library of Congress Cataloging-in-Publication Data

Shavers, Christine Marie, 1981–
Criminal law dealing with hate crimes : functional comparative law, Germany vs. USA / Christine Marie Shavers.
pages cm. — (Schriften zum strafrecht und strafprozessrecht ; Band 117)
Includes bibliographical references and index.
ISBN 978-3-631-64220-7
1. Hate crimes—Germany. 2. Hate crimes—United States. I. Title.
K5170.S53 2014
345.43'025—dc23

2014003859

ISSN 0938-6181
ISBN 978-3-631-64220-7 (Print)
E-ISBN 978-3-653-03641-1 (E-Book)
DOI 10.3726/ 978-3-653-03641-1

PL Academic Research is an Imprint of Peter Lang GmbH.

Peter Lang – Frankfurt am Main · Bern · Bruxelles · New York · Oxford · Warszawa · Wien

This book is part of an editor's series of PL Academic Research and was peer reviewed prior to publication.

www.peterlang.com

Acknowledgements

I am indebted to my thesis supervisor, Prof. Dr. Peter Rackow, for the ongoing, attentive and always pleasant supervision of this study. I could not have wished for greater academic assistance. With the help of those indescribably beneficial discussions which regularly occurred throughout the research period enabled me to succeed in this project the way I did.

I acknowledge my dissertation committee: My peer reviewer Prof. Dr. Dieter Kugelmann for providing the second opinion in a timely manner and for acting as my chairperson. Furthermore, I am grateful for him sharing his inspiring thoughts during a doctoral seminar in the early stage of the preparation of this work. I am appreciative of the pleasant rounding of the examination procedure by Prof. Dr. Joachim Kersten on the day of my dissertation defense.

I owe my gratitude to Prof. Dr. Manfred Maiwald (emerit.), it is an honor for me to publish this dissertation in his publication series. In this regard, I would like to thank Prof. Dr. Carsten Momsen for supporting me in various ways.

I am grateful to Daniel and Betti for their eager and enduring support, it is truly appreciated!

Finally, my special thanks go to Thomas for his friendship and kindness, as well as for his everlasting support, and simply for encouraging me to not only undertake this project, but to see it through successfully. Without him I could not have produced this work.

Munich, April 2013 Christine Marie Shavers

Translation Index of Selected Judicial Terms

The translation of German legal terminology is stated as a literal quote; it is freely translated and interpreted at one´s own discretion taking the meaning into account.

Aggravated statute	Qualifikation/Qualifizierte Straftatbestände
Base offense/parallel crime/ordinary crime	Straftat, die nicht von Vorurteils-Hass motiviert ist
Collective legal good/Universal legal good/ Supra individual legal good	Kollektives Rechtsgut/Universalrechtsgut/ Überindividuelles Rechtsgut
Crimes constituted by an abstract endangerment of legal goods	Abstrakte Gefährdungsdelikte
Crimes constituted by a concrete endangerment of legal goods	Konkrete Gefährdungsdelikte
Conduct crime	Tätigkeitsdelikt
Culpability, which reasons a penalty	Strafbegründungsschuld
Culpability, which is relevant in the individual case	Strafzumessungsschuld
Disvalue of the act	Handlungsunwert
Disvalue of the result	Erfolgsunwert
Equitable culpability compensation	Gerechter Schuldausgleich
German Constitutional Court	Bundesverfassungsgericht
German Supreme Court	Bundesgerichtshof
Inbuilt (methodical) legal good doctrines	Systemimmanente Rechtgutstheorien
Individual legal good/personal legal good	Individualrechtsgut

Injury offense (= crime constituted by a violation of legal goods)	Verletzungsdelikt
Worthiness of punishment/worthy of punishment	Strafwürdigkeit/strafwürdig
Legal good	Rechtsgut
Legal good theory/legal good doctrine	Rechtsgutstheorie
Mindset/attitude	Gesinnung
Non-result-constituted offense/offense of endangerment (= crime constituted by a mere endangerment of legal goods)	Gefährdungsdelikt
Real feature of guilt/real culpability feature	Echtes Schuldmerkmal
Result-constituted offense	Erfolgsdelikt
Ruling example/aggravated or mitigated case of the base offense/aggravated exemplified rule	Regelbeispiel
System-critical (substantial) legal good doctrine	systemkritische, systemtranszendente Rechtgutstheorie
Necessitates punishment	Strafbedürftigkeit
Wrong	Unrecht

Note:

- "Race" in such terms as "racially" motivated violence or "racial" bias is used inclusively to encompass motivation based not only on race, but also on the color, ethnicity, religion or national origin of the victim; moreover gender and sexual orientation may be included as well.
- The stringent gender-differentiated spelling is renounced for the reason of better understanding.

Contents

Preface

This research deals with so-called hate crimes. This is the term for offenses that are not solely characterized by a particular motive, namely by hatred against the otherness of others, but by their different social importance in the external world. It is important to understand that these offenses are not only determined by a prejudiced offender motivation. In addition to the inner motivation of the offender they are characterized by objective criteria and adverse social impacts, not only on those who are directly attacked, but on the uninvolved public[1]. Therefore it is not about the punishment of the prejudiced perpetrator-personality, or of certain prejudiced attitudes and values[2]; the general idea of this offense category is the wrong- and culpability appropriate protection of legal goods.

This study aims to provide a contribution to the current issue[3] on whether there is a need for an explicit legal recognition of hate crimes in the German Penal Code by examining findings from the current criminal treatment of hate crimes in the United States of America and Germany with the use of the functional method of law comparison. Within the context of the exploratory analysis of hate crimes, attention is quickly drawn to those legal systems that already have explicit norms to cover these offenses and which have been involved with the similar social problem more intense, or for a longer period of time, in order to, if possible, be able to gain from their knowledge and profit from their cognition. An examination of the legal situation in the United States reveals a variety of mechanisms enshrined in the country's numerous legal texts to penalize xenophobia and discrimination. The United States, considered as the founder of the concept of 'hate crime'[4], provides a wealth of experience in terms of penalizing this form of crime. This country, a country of immigration, has always been challenged with the need to unite the coexistence of different ethnic groups. Hence, it is not surprising that a societal problem connected to human diversity, and the need for combating offenses based on disregard or contempt for each other, reaches a long way back in the United States[5].

However, Germany is currently becoming a country of immigration as well, thus is becoming to be a multicultural society. Athough the United States is historically known for xenophobic and hate-motivated acts being a common phenomenon, the German society is an example of such victimization as well,

1 Schneider, Kriminologie der Hassdelikte. Konzeptionen, Ursachen, Vorbeugung und Kontrolle, in: Bewährungshilfe, 2003, p. 117; Schneider, Politische Kriminalität: Hassverbrechen, Fremdenfeindlich-keit im internationalen Kontext, Kriminalistik 2001, p. 22.

2 Schneider, Kriminologie der Hassdelikte. Konzeptionen, Ursachen, Vorbeugung und Kontrolle, in: Bewährungshilfe, 2003, p. 117; Schneider, Politische Kriminalität: Hassverbrechen, Fremdenfeindlichkeit im internationalen Kontext, Kriminalistik 2001, p. 22.

3 View the current draft law of the Federal Council to amend the German Penal Code, April 18, 2012 (Drs.17/9345).

4 Coester, Hate Crimes, 2007, p. 82.

5 Coester, Hate Crimes, 2007, p. vii.

even if the historical background may be different[6]. After all, the comparable level of civilization, the political organization of both countries and their highly developed constitutions suggest to choose the United States as an appropriate counterpart for comparison[7] when aiming to find important prerequisites in the search for a solution to the problem of hate crime. Thereby, precisely the entirely different criminal justice systems and the possible cultural differences may be able to provide a supply of solutions for the respective other society. This comparative study focuses on the aim of possibly gaining a cognition in terms of how to legally deal with this sort of offenses by comparing the current criminal handlings of hate crimes in the United States and in Germany.

A thorough and insightful comparison with the legally chosen actions to combat hate crimes requires a preliminary examination of the term "hate crime".

The term "hate crime" bears the risk of misconception[8]. "Hate crime", "bias crime" or "hate-motivated crime" as well as "bias-motivated crime" are used interchangeably with the same meaning for the same phenomenon, yet the term "hate crime" is the common use[9]. The composition of both words, 'crime' defined as "an act committed or omitted in violation of a law forbidding or commanding it and for which punishment is imposed upon conviction"[10] and 'hate' described as a feeling of "hostility or animosity towards"[11], leads to the understanding of 'hate crime' as an act, evoked by "hostility or animosity" towards the victim, which is "committed or omitted in violation of a law forbidding or commanding it, and for which punishment is imposed upon conviction". "Hatred as an emotion of extreme dislike or aggressive impulses towards a person or group of persons"[12] can be the trigger for racial motivated violence, but is also the trigger for revenge crimes, thus for most so-called crimes of passion[13]. This literal construction of a definition would completely leave out the key element of the perpetrator's bias or prejudice toward the victim which constitutes the here relevant crime. Hate crimes are about hate, but not towards the victimized individual, but towards his or her inherent characteristics[14]. Therefore, hate crimes are best described with the

---

6 Refer to the introductory text in Aydin, Die strafrechtliche Bekämpfung von Hassdelikten, 2006.

7 Refer to the introductory text in Aydin, Die strafrechtliche Bekämpfung von Hassdelikten, 2006.

8 Perry, Where do we go from here?, p.1; Unfortunately the term Hate Crime does not explain itself. (Jacobs/Potter, Hate Crimes, Criminal Law & Identity Politics, p. 27).

9 Perry and Lawrence use bias crime (Lawrence, Punishing Hate, 1999; Perry, In the name of hate, 2001). Charkraborti, Gerstenfeld, Jennes and Grattet, and far more prefer the term hate crime, however, the distribution of the favored wording within literature more or less mirrors the designation used by the public. Even though the term bias crime would be more correctly, the term hate crime prevails. According to Perry, the reason for this is that the term hate crime branded itself on the societal memory and therefore it is difficult to change this designation.

10 http://www.thefreedictionary.com/crime - accessed 2011/09/09.

11 Further held definitions as "to dislike or wish to avoid; shrink from" or "to have strong dislike or ill will for; loathe; despise" does not make a difference for the here to be understood subject. (Neufeldt & Guralnik, Webster´s new world college dictionary (3rd Ed.), 1997, p. 617; http://www.thefreedictionary.com/hate - accessed 2011/09/09.

12 Sternberg, The Psychology of Hate, 2004, p. 37.

13 Lawrence, Punishing Hate,1999, p. 9.

14 It is elementary to emphasize that the key factor of those here relevant crimes is not the perpetrator´s hatred of the victim per se, but rather his bias or prejudice towards the victim. It is considered that hate can

explanation that such crimes "occur not because the victim is who he is, but rather because the victim is what he is"[15]. With that said, hate-based or hate-motivated conducts constitute a hate crime in the here used sense only if this hatred is connected with antipathy for a racial, ethnic or religious group[16], or for an individual because of his membership in that group[17]; accurately speaking, a hate crime is an offense that is committed because of feelings of racial animus or hate towards the victim because of his or her actual or perceived race, color, religion, national origin, ethnicity, gender, gender identity, disability, homelessness, or sexual orientation.

According to this opinion, the correct term results from common linguistic, literal and judicial usage and "hate crime" is the main denoting expression. This is why, regardless such reasons of clarity, within this work the prevailing legal terming[18] as well as the societal and medial main label is adopted[19]. Whether a designation is correctly applied is not about the literal interpretation, but about its meaning referring to its actual usage. It finally depends on how it is applied and therefore understood by the overall majority in literature[20] and especially throughout society[21], not what its label intends to mean if understood literally[22].

It is crucial to bear in mind that "hate crime" do not refer to particular offenses. It could be an act of intimidation, threat, or assault - therefore directed at a human being - as well as directed against property; in this second case forming an offense of property damage, arson or any other criminal relevant act. Thinking of terrorism, gang violence or other organized - for instance - political violence, or even war[23] it becomes obvious that all these acts are motivated by hate and prejudice, or at least group affiliations of the targets to a group which the tortfeasor wishes to harm, but such should not be addressed by the here discussed hate crime concept. So as opposed to governmental controlled acts or bias-motivated criminal acts of large political factions, hate

---

be distinguished in two forms: a rational hate and a character-conditioned hate. While rational hate grounds on a verifiable basis and bears upon the relation between the offender and his chosen victim, the character-conditioned hate misses comprehensible base. Due to character-conditioned hate an entire target group is chosen (randomly) to be the object of hate and aggression. (Fromm, Anatomy of human destructiveness. 1992; Sternberg, The Psychology of Hate, 2004, p. 38)

This makes character-conditioned hate so dangerous, neither could the victim influence his victimization in any way nor has the specific victim-selection taken place in any other rational way, thus it is not preventable, concerning this more later in this dissertation.

15 Lawrence, Punishing Hate, 1999, p. 9.

16 Race, ethnic and religion are named exemplary and do not raise any claim to completeness.

17 Lawrence, Punishing Hate, 1999, p. 9.

18 View, for instance, "Hate Crime Statistic Act" which was enacted on April, 23rd 1990.

19 Interchangeable usage with bias crime included.

20 Altschiller; Hate Crimes, 1999; Coester, Hate Crimes, p. 22; Favoring bias crime over Hate Crime: cf. Lawrence, Punishing Hate, 1999.

21 Perry states, that the terminology hate crime is in the minds of society and not able to be rejected. (Perry, In the name of hate, 2001).

22 Many crimes which are motivated by hatred are not categorized as hate crimes. Murders, for instance, are often motivated by hatred arousing from previous relationship, but these are not considered as hate crimes, unless the victim was chosen because of a protected characteristic. The term hate crime is particularly used for crimes that are motivated by hateful bias and prejudice against legally protected characteristics which the victim inheres od the perpetrator perceives the victim to inhere. Therefore, hate crime is the correct term to use for the here relevant offenses, its literal translation is not of relevance.

23 Gerstenfeld, Hate Crimes, 2004, p. 9.

crimes refer to "[...] acts, committed by individuals or small groups, in which the victim was targeted primarily because of his or her [real or perceived] group [affiliation]"[24].

For the presentation of a prefixed, broad working definition, the main featuring characterizations of hate crimes are to be presented. *Lawrence* states two broad categories of crimes, the first broad category contains all crimes committed without regard to any personal characteristics of the victim[25]. The second broad category contains all crimes committed precisely because of the victimized person himself. Since in this second category, the victim is attacked because of who he or she is, the victim is not interchangeable[26]. Such crimes are committed because of emotions, thus hate, retribution, and suchlike towards the victim and result from interpersonal relations and therefore are usually committed between socio-biographic similar persons[27]. However, the here relevant crimes differ from both categories. Unlike the first category, hate crimes are crimes in which certain identifiable characteristics of the victim are critical to the perpetrator's choice of attack. Unlike the second broad category, the here discussed criminal conducts are crimes in which the individual identity of the victim is irrelevant[28]. Therefore, the victim of a hate crime is interchangeable with any other person who shares a certain way of being[29]. The perpetrator is willing to replace his (initial) target with any other person, who - in his eyes - is of a descent or of an origin that deviates from his own, who shares religious beliefs or appears to be of a race that does not match his. This becomes clear if considering that the offender of a hate crime usually does not even know his chosen victim[30]. The fact that hate crimes are usually committed among strangers[31], furthermore, the committal is even stimulated

---

24 Gerstenfeld, Hate Crimes, 2004, p.10; Further official definitions applied in the United States of America: The FBI follows the federal general definition of hate crime to be a "criminal offense against a person or property motivated in whole or in part by an offender's bias against a race, religion, disability, ethnic origin or sexual orientation." (http://www.fbi.gov/about-us/investigate/civilrights/hate_crimes/overview - accessed: January 2012); NY CLS Penal § 485.05 defines hate crimes as specified offenses committed against persons intentionally selected "[...] because of a belief or perception regarding the race, color, national origin, ancestry, gender, religion, religious practice, age, disability or sexual orientation of a person, regardless of whether the belief or perception is correct [...]."; NY CLS Penal § 485.05 defines hate crimes as specified offenses committed against persons intentionally selected "[...] because of a belief or perception regarding the race, color, national origin, ancestry, gender, religion, religious practice, age, disability or sexual orientation of a person, regardless of whether the belief or perception is correct [...]." (Illinois 730 ILCS sec. 12-7.1 Hate Crime); The Hate Crime Statistic Act refers to "[...] crimes that manifest evidence of prejudice based on race, religion, sexual orientation, or ethnicity, [...]." (Public Law 101-275).

25 Lawrence exemplarily states random muggings, drive-by shootings as all killings out of lust to kill and most robberies and burglaries, out of a wide array of crimes, which, for instance, also includes crimes in which the choice of the victim is dictated solely by the requirements of the crime; for example, "the bank teller is assaulted as a means of robbing the bank, not because of any individual characteristics of the teller". (Lawrence, Punishing Hate,1999, p. 9).

26 This second broad category of crimes refers to most passion-crimes, thus crimes committed of revenge and hate. (Lawrence, Punishing Hate,1999, p. 9).

27 Kunz, Kriminologie, pp. 238, 239; Tschaggelar, Hate Crimes und Hasskriminalität, p. 9.

28 Lawrence, Punishing Hate, 1999, p. 9.

29 Likewise, although in-artfully expressed by Seehafer: "However, the difference lies in the fact that the victim falls into a bogeyman of the offender and therefore is attacked, thus, in this respect, it is precisely not randomly or optionally interchangeable." (Seehafer, Strafrechtliche Reaktionen auf rechtsextremistisch/fremdenfeindlich motivierte Gewalttaten, p. 69 - emphasis added by underlining).

30 The offender and his victim usually never had personal contact. (Cf. Perry, In the name of hate, p. 29)

31 Schneider, Hassverbrechen, in: Schneider, Kriminologie für das 21. Jahrhundert, p. 76.

through the anonymity between the offender and his victim[32] - as in opposite to usual passion crimes which take place among relationships[33] - additionally distinguishes hate crimes from other crimes.

A key element of hate crimes is their capacity of sending a symbolic message and thereby symbolizing the victim[34]. It is claimed that by the committal of a hate crime a message is sent to the victim and to all persons who share those for the attack relevant characteristics of the immediate victim. This message states: You all are neither welcome in 'this' society, nor safe[35]. Therefore, hate crimes are said to have the effect of denying the victim's right to full participation in society[36]. Moreover, the community sharing the characteristic of the attacked person is automatically addressed as well, yet not in the practical (physical) sense but through the message which reaches them, enunciating that they are under attack because of being likely-created beings. The victim is chosen as a symbol for the attack of far parts of society, of all those who share the victim's actual or perceived characteristic[37]. The fact that hate in this sort of crime does not occur from prior personal relations or from personal contacts, but from the perpetrator's bias towards a kind of human being or certain characteristics, leads to the circumstance that the immediate attacked target is chosen randomly by an offender to be an object of hate[38]; thus latent potential hazards are created for certain people, which could intensely disturb the peace in a society as to be examined in this work.

The ordinary concept of hate crime is a "two-tiered crime".[39] This means that it requires two elements: a criminal offense committed with a bias motivation. The criminal offense refers to an act, which on its own is penalized by criminal law; indifferent whether it is an offense against person or property[40]. This first

32 Eisenberg, Kriminologie, 2005, p. 897; Tschaggelar, Hate Crimes und Hasskriminalität, p. 9.

33 Kunz, Kriminologie, pp. 238, 239.

34 Therefore, Hate Crime are called "message-crimes". (Füllgrabe, Hassverbrechen, Kriminalistik, 2004, pp. 391-397 (394); Schneider, Politische Kriminalität: Hassverbrechen, Fremdenfeindlichkeit im internationalen Kontext, Kriminalistik 2001, p. 26; Schneider, Kriminologie der Hassdelikte Konzeptionen, Ursachen, Vorbeugung und Kontrolle, in: Bewährungshilfe, 2003, pp. 115,117; Schneider, Hasskriminalität: Eine neue kriminologische Deliktskategorie, JZ, 2003, pp. 497-504 (498); Schneider, Hass- und Vorurteilskriminalität, in: Grafl/Medigovic, (eds.): Festschrift für Manfred Burgstaller, 2004, pp. 553-568, (555); Singer, Erfassung der politsch motivierten Kriminalität, in einem neuen Definitionssystem mit mehrdimensionalen Analysemöglichkeiten, p. 34; Wallace, Victimology, 1998, p. 216).

35 Hate Crime Laws: A Practical Guide, published by the OSCE Office for Democratic Institutions and Human Rights (ODIHR), 2009; p. 17.

36 Hate Crime Laws: A Practical Guide, published by the OSCE Office for Democratic Institutions and Human Rights (ODIHR), 2009; p. 17.

37 Also refer to footnote 14. This fact makes "character-conditioned hate" so dangerous, neither could the victim influence his victimization in any way nor has the specific victim-selection taken place in a rational manner, thus this sort of victimization is not preventable.

38 Within the for bias-motivated offenses relevant form of hate, called "character-conditioned hate", target groups are chosen to be objects of hate. (Fromm, Anatomy of human destructiveness. (1992); Sternberg, The Psychology of Hate, 2004, p. 38).

39 Lawrence, Punishing Hate, 1999, p. 93.

40 Because there are small variations in legal provisions from state to state, there are some divergences in the kind of conduct that amounts to a crime; but in general most states criminalize the same type of violent acts. However, if a hate crime can be constituted, depends on the penalization of the underlying offense, thus is based on the presence of the legal prerequisite established in the penal code of the competent state (unless the federal government is competent, for requirements of federal authority view above).

element of a hate crime is referred to as the "base offense"[41]; "parallel crime"[42] or "underlying crime"[43]. The second part of a hate crime is said to result from the fact that the offender committed the criminal act for reason of prejudice or bigotry based on the victim's real or perceived membership in a legally recognized protected status, which would typically be race, ethnic origin, religion and any other similar common factor, which the legislator chooses to be in need of enhanced protection. It is significant for such a characteristic to be shared by a group that is historically and actually known for being a cause for discriminatory singling out, whereby with "historically" it is referred to the particular history of the society which is concerned. Yet, this generally understood concept of the "two-tiered" crime of a hate crime is redefined, or at least defined down, during this work. All in all, the second element of a hate crime, the bias-motivation, is not the only reason for the differentiation of hate crimes from ordinary crimes. Hate crimes are more than ordinary crimes which are modified through the bias-motivation of the perpetrator; they are different due to their changed social significance. Thus, even a behavior which, without the knowledge of the xenophobic, homophobic, etc. background, would present itself as harmless may create a criminal relevant form of threat. Hence, behavior may constitute a criminal offense, if it -due to its outward form, which it receives by reason of the offenders motivation- recognizably injures a certain part of the people of society[44].

Hate crime is more a concept than a specific crime category. The term "hate crime" neither necessarily refers to a specific type of offense, nor to special laws but to a concept of combating bias-motivated criminal activity on the legal level, and above that, even far before it reaches legal involvement. According to this conception hate crime legislation covers statutes which require authorities to collect data on hate- or bias-motivated crimes; legislation that mandate law enforcement training, prohibit the undertaking of paramilitary training, specify parental liability, provide for victim compensation and laws prohibiting the wearing of masks and hoods[45]. Within this dissertation, the focus is directed to criminal law; as the term 'hate crime law' intends, the attention is put on criminal statutes which impose penalties for harmful behavior induced by bias against the other. Consequently, "to qualify as a hate crime law, a [...] statute must criminalize, enhance penalties for, or amend existing statutes regarding [offenses] motivated by bias toward individuals or groups based on particular status characteristics [...]"[46]. In order to fulfill these requirements a law must imply one of the named state policy actions, explicitly

41 Hate Crime Laws: A Practical Guide, published by the OSCE Office for Democratic Institutions and Human Rights (ODIHR), 2009; p. 16; http://www.osce.org/odihr/36426; accessed: January 2011.

42 Lawrence, Punishing Hate, 1999.

43 Gerstenfeld, Hate Crimes, 2004.

44 This applies tp cross-burning legislation; The for others visible smearing of swastikas on own goods, etc.

45 Jenness/Grattet, Making Hate a Crime, 2001, p. 73.

46 Jenness/Grattet, Making Hate a Crime, 2001, p. 77.

refer to the subjective intention of the perpetrator[47] and it must name a list of legally recognized and by the statute protected social statuses[48].

Subsequent to this introduction the basic principles of the applied methodology are presented. Hereinafter, the political organization of the United States, with its advanced Constitution, and the foundations of the U.S. legal system are illustrated briefly in order to provide a basis for comparison and for the then following presentation of the social problem in its existence which it has in the American society. This presentation takes place by examining how the U.S. legal order currently protects its citizens from attacks motivated by "disregard or contempt because of their, determined in factual or fictional group characteristics, identity"[49]. Thereafter, the current German legal situation of combating hate crimes is analyzed, including the actual classification of such offenses by the German law and bethinking how the capturing of this sort of offense could be optimized by German law.

Legal decisions, judicature and literature were considered until December, 2012.

---

47 This refers to the motive of the offender for committing a crime. The motive must be bias or hate towards the victim's legally protected status characteristics which are specified by the statute.

48 Jenness/Grattet, Making Hate a Crime, 2001, p. 77.

49 Coester, Hate Crimes, 2007, p. viii.

Chapter 1 Methodical Introduction

A. The Term 'Comparative Law'

Comparing one's own legal system with foreign legal systems provides possibilities of learning from other legal cultures and thereby enhances the legal framework of the former[50]. There are 42 legal systems in the world[51]; hence, there is plenty of material that may be used to conduct research in Comparative Law[52].

In order to understand the term Comparative Law one must understand its component words. "To compare" means "to mark or point out the similarities and differences of (two or more things); to bring or place together (actually or mentally) for the purpose of noting the similarities and differences"[53]. Law is defined as "a rule of conduct imposed by authority"[54] or, rather, as "the body of rules, whether proceeding from formal enactment or from custom, which a particular state or community recognizes as binding on its members or subjects"[55]. This imposition of rules is an ubiquitous establishment of all societies throughout the world[56]. Since it is promulgated individually, it exists in a variety of forms, shaped by its social surrounding due to assimilating the features which the particular community asks for[57]. According to that, Comparative Law may be defined as the collation of similarities and differences between legal systems. In this respect, the term Comparative Law is misleading[58] because conducting comparative law research requires compliance with certain rules. If a study is labeled as a comparative law research, a recognized method must be followed in order to achieve the general aim of "cognition"[59].

If the essence of Comparative Law is "the research of truth"[60] through the "creation of a stock of legal solutions"[61] acquired by means of comparison, it

---

50 Großfeld, Kernfragen der Rechtsvergleichung, 1996, pp.1, 3.

51 De Cruz, Comparative Law in a Changing World, 1999, p. 3.

52 The selection of which legal systems are to be compared is limited by the skills of the comparatist. Examining a foreign legal system requires a base of knowledge "in all the important aspects of comparison that make up being a comparative lawyer" (Edge, Comparative Law in a Global Perspective, 2000, p. 10). This typically includes the respective foreign language, [the necessity of] time spent immersed in the foreign legal culture and more, in order to be able to get the substantial meaning of a legal idea behind a written word and to properly translate law from one language to another. Ultimately, the selection of a foreign legal system depends on the personal interest and the aim of the comparatist, who for logical reasons will choose a foreign legal system in which he assumes to find answers for his specific legal research. Aimless comparing of non-selective legal systems is a time-consuming task, with a chance of creating useless knowledge for the matter of cause. (Cf. Markesinis, Rechtsvergleichung in Theorie und Praxis, Munich, 2004, p. 50 et seq.; Rusch, Methoden und Ziele der Rechtsvergleichung, Jusletter 13. February 2006, p. 5.

53 The Oxford English Dictionary, Second Edition, Vol. III, 1989, p. 592.

54 The Oxford English Dictionary, Second Edition, Vol. VIII, 1989, p. 712.

55 The Oxford English Dictionary, Second Edition, Vol. VIII, 1989, p. 712.

56 Edge, Comparative Law in a Global Perspective, 2000, p. Xiii.

57 Roxin, Strafrecht AT, Band I, p. 16, marginal no. 7 et seq.

58 De Cruz, A Modern Approach to Comparative Law, 1993, p. 5.

59 Zweigert/Kötz, Rechtsvergleichung, 1996, p. 14.

60 Zweigert/Kötz, Rechtsvergleichung, 1996, p. 3 - According to Zweigert/Kötz who describe Compara-tive Law as "the research of truth" and "truth" is to be found through achieving "cognition". This results from the fact that Comparative Law as such is purposeless. Therefore, "truth" and "cognition" primarily depend on a

can be said that Comparative Law "describes the systematic study of particular legal traditions and legal rules on a comparative basis"[62].

Since comparing institutions within one's own legal framework is the everyday business of jurisprudence[63], a study in the context of Comparative Law must include rules of at least two different law systems in order to find and analyze similarities and disparities in the two by means of contrast[64]. Contrary to opinions saying that Comparative Law does not need a comparative element in the sense of comparing[65], it is assumed that a side by side holding of different legal systems reveals similarities and disparities[66] between such, which then must be explored at least to some degree, in order to establish a connection between them (e.g., one's own legal system and the one of interest). Only by analyzing similarities and differences, and perhaps even exploring the reason for such, one is able to draw a conclusion in order to gain a profit in cognition concerning the respective law as such or concerning a specific initial question. This intellectual challenge makes Comparative Law a scientific task[67]. As it is shown below, the scientific component varies in dependence on which form of Comparative Law is chosen. But regardless of a certain variety, the matter of Comparative Law as such must be correctly understood and existing rules must be strictly followed in order to achieve useful results in consequence of its application.

---

concrete aim. The general aim of Comparative Law is to somehow enhance law in whatever sector. This enhancement appears from the possibility of seeing another, until then unknown, possible way of dealing with legal situations and so being able to scrutinize accustomed manners, and so fortunately refine and thus eventually find the best way of legally handling a certain matter. What is 'best' depends on the concrete aim, the initial question. For example, if the initial aim refers to the question of how to handle a given legal problem, "the best" in this contextual meaning would stand for the ideal way of handling this legal problem in reference to the particular society.

61 Expression ascribed to Zitelmann by Rheinstein, Einführung in die Rechtsvergleichung, 1987, p. 26; Zweigert/Kötz, Rechtsvergleichung, 1996, p. 14.

62 De Cruz, Comparative Law in a Changing World, p. 3.

63 Zweigert/Kötz, Rechtsvergleichung, 1996, p. 1, 2

64 De Cruz, Comparative Law in a Changing World, 1999, p. 3; Cf. Eser, FS Kaiser, Vol. II, 1998, p. 1499 (1501).

65 Rheinstein, Einführung in die Rechtsvergleichung, 1987, p. 11.

66 For the dispute whether to emphasize similarities or differences or to strike a balance between both see Dannemann, Comparative Law: Study of Similarities or Differences? in: Reimann/Zimmermann (eds.), The Oxford Handbook of Comparative Law, 2006, p. 383 (384 et seqq.).

67 De Cruz, A Modern Approach to Comparative Law, 1993, p. 5 with reference to Watson, Legal Transplants (1974) who argues for the necessity of an intellectual content to meet the requirements of Comparative Law.

B. Classification and Derivation of Comparative Law from other Disciplines

The following deals with the question of what is the nature of comparative law[68].

1. Classification of Comparative Law as a "pure science"

Comparative Law, described as a mental process, which deals with law and contains comparison[69], does not clarify the nature of the scientific approach. The study of Comparative Law follows its own specific rules. It has its own functions, which differ from the function of law as such and exceeds the purpose of an ordinary drawn comparison. Since sociology has an impact on many approaches of law comparisons, Comparative Law has been referred to as a social science[70]. However, Comparative Law is not a social science[71]. The material collected through comparison "forms part of a separate body of knowledge"[72]: Knowledge regarding law. Therefore, Comparative Law is too interlocked with the science of law to be called a social science and necessarily too interlocked with the science of law to be called a "science pure"[73]. Since law is the object of critical scrutiny, it better matches the opinion that Comparative Law is a separate scientific discipline within the study of Law[74]. Referring to the meaning of the term 'Comparative Law' there is no need to point out that the most important ingredient of this scientific approach is law. The term as such reveals the relationship: the 'Comparative' in its adjectival function serves the noun 'Law'. Nothing else applies to the semantic level of the meaning of this term: Comparative Law serves law by aiming at enlightening the entire legal sector by drawing comparisons.

2. Comparative Law, a Part of Jurisprudence?

Jurisprudence as the science of law is the general term for many areas of law, such as public law, criminal or civil law and so on.

It is common to group the rules of a society into areas depending on their specific subject. For example, rules for combating criminal behavior belong to the branch of criminal law while rules which address the state are classified as public law. Essentially, Jurisprudence is an academic science which teaches judicial thinking[75]. It is the effort to understand law by understanding the rules

---

68 De Cruz, A Modern Approach to Comparative Law, 1993, p. 2.

69 Zweigert/Kötz, Rechtsvergleichung, 1996, p. 1.

70 De Cruz, A Modern Approach to Comparative Law, 1993, p. 3 with further reference to Saleilles, Rabel, Hall; Rheinstein, Einführung in die Rechtsvergleichung, 1987, p. 11.

71 Michaels, The functional method of comparative law, in: Matthias Reimann/ Reinhard Zimmermann (eds.), The Oxford Handbook of Comparative Law, 2006, p. 339 (342).

72 De Cruz, A Modern Approach to Comparative Law, 1993, p. 3.

73 Zweigert/Kötz, Rechtsvergleichung, 1996, p. 6 says that is how Comparative Law illustrates itself for the first instance.

74 Zweigert/Kötz, Rechtsvergleichung, 1996, p. 2, 4 – with reference to Lambert, Conception générale et définition et défintionde la science du droit compáre, Procès-verbaux des seánces et documents, Congrès international de droit comparé I (1905) 26, printed in: Zweigert/Puttfarken (eds.), Rechtsver-gleichung, 1978, p. 30.

75 Cf. Zweigert/Kötz, Rechtsvergleichung, 1996, p. 22.

of a legal system. Understanding rules includes knowledge of their meaning, their implementation and their function for the addressed society. Law must be understood in order to create it and consequently, to apply it. In order to understand law different branches of a legal system[76], usually of one's own, must be studied intensively. Besides private or civil law, one must usually delve into branches such as criminal law, public law, historical law, economic- and social law and so forth[77]. Studying and practicing in the field of law means looking at a specific problem in order to find the right solution by examining various legal regulations offered by a legal code. This solution never emanates from the implementation of a single rule but from the interaction of the right combination of rules. If trying to order Comparative Law beside the categories of public law, civil law, criminal law and so on, it can be seen that it does not fit throughout these exemplary named areas[78]. Even if interpreted as a body of law in the sense of including all areas of a legal system[79] it does not suit to be considered a category of law because it misses an own substantive type of law, a "body of rules"[80]; instead it rather affects all branches of law. If one proposes to compare the criminal law system of two countries the knowledge of criminal law of both countries is a necessary precondition[81]. Therefore, a law comparison builds up on an existing area of law. Which area depends on the chosen theme of the comparison and therefore is exchangeable. What is definite is the way of dealing and handling the chosen area of law, so Comparative Law is more a form of activity, a way of exploring law, like a working technique.

An interaction of legal regulations throughout the different areas of law enables a wider insight into law and creates general legal knowledge, which is necessary to establish a judicial understanding. Since judicial understanding is the result of intensive study of legal regulation, the focus lies first – and often only – on regulations of one's own legal system. But there is no need to point out that the more branches of law one looks into and the more various handlings of legal problems are understood, the more inner relations and universal orderliness can be sensed and therefore a generally deeper and better understanding of the subject of law can be achieved. This could happen for instance by examining actual legal solutions to a concrete problem which different legal systems provide[82], in order to then critically weigh which solution seems best to address the concrete situation of one's own society at this specific moment[83] Thereby the nationally effectuate solution is clearly outlined and the sense for the own legal system can be understood in its whole

76 Zweigert/Kötz, Rechtsvergleichung, 1996, p. 22.
77 Cf. § 18 par. 2 Bavarian Training- and Examination Rules (Bayr. Ausbildungs- und Prüfungsordnung für Juristen).
78 Rheinstein, Einführung in die Rechtsvergleichung, 1987, p. 11.
79 De Cruz, Comparative Law in a Changing World, 1999, p. 1.
80 De Cruz, Comparative Law in a Changing World, 1999, p. 2; cf. The Oxford English Dictionary, Second Edition, Vol. VIII, 1989, p. 712.
81 Edge, Comparative Law in Global Perspective, 2000, p.10.
82 Zweigert/Kötz, Rechtsvergleichung, 1996, p. 22.
83 Zweigert/Kötz, Rechtsvergleichung, 1996, p. 22.

purpose[84]. This would qualify Comparative Law as an academic pursuit or a method of study and research[85], yet neglecting all the other purposes a law comparison could aim at. Besides being an academic discipline, thereby serving as a means of understanding legal rules, Comparative Law serves as an aid to law reform by being a tool for creating new law or unifying and harmonizing various legal systems by delivering a preparatory examination and therefore serving as a preparative operation[86]; or it is a great utility to legal science by researching historical developments of various legal systems due to discovering or examining legal evolutions (evolution of laws)[87]. The examination by Comparative Law is deeper than what usual studying affords. It requires a different way of delving into law. Due to its combination of studying areas of one's own legal system and those of foreign ones and putting them into a purpose-build of whatsoever specified relation a new composition arises which, according to its individual content, deserves a separate classification. Since Comparative Law moreover can be identified by an intellectual content, it involves more than just putting two different provisions next to each other and comparing them in the usual sense of comparing. Comparative Law is not just a "systematic procedure by which a complex or scientific task is accomplished"[88], hence, not just a technique, but since it describes a certain dealing and handling with law including international elements it could be named an "international legal practice"[89] or in general "a method of Jurisprudence". A method is generally referred to as "a special form of procedure adopted in any branch of mental activity, whether for the purpose of teaching and exposition, or for that of investigation and inquiry"[90]. It is hard not to identify Comparative Law as a method[91] since it is an approach which follows its own (and therefore) special rules in the branch of law and, depending on the aim of the comparatist, even fulfills all possible elements of the definition: according to its task in academic science the purpose of teaching is made clear above. The purpose of the exposition comes easy when systematically illustrating legal systems, whereas the purpose of investigation and research are essential precepts in order to find similarities and differences.

3. Resume

Comparative Law is not to be classified as a "science pure"[92]. Since it is not based on a specific and therefore distinct body of rules, but related to a special theme of law: systematic comparison, it perfectly fits in the discipline of jurisprudence. Thereby it has the potential to create new law in existing areas

84 Zweigert/Kötz, Rechtsvergleichung, 1996, p. 22.
85 Gutteridge, Comparative Law, 1949, p. 1.
86 De Cruz, A Modern Approach to Comparative Law, 1993, p. 15.
87 De Cruz, A Modern Approach to Comparative Law, 1993, p. 5.
88 http://www.thefreedictionary.com/technique - accessed 2011/09/09.
89 Rheinstein, Einführung in die Rechtsvergleichung, 1987, p. 11.
90 Simpson and Weiner, The Oxford English dictionary , Vol. IX, 1989, p. 690.
91 Rheinstein, Einführung in die Rechtsvergleichung, 1987, S. 11.
92 Zweigert/Kötz, Rechtsvergleichung, 1996, p. 6.

and thus can be defined as "rules and practice proper to a particular art"[93] and therefore constitutes a method of Jurisprudence, a method of dealing with law.

C. Tasks and Aims of Comparative Law

The general aim of every comparative study of law, regardless of which method is chosen, is 'cognition'[94] or 'the research of truth'[95]. Driven by interest in another legal culture[96], there is always some sort of enhancement expected for the legal system of the researcher.

In order to be classified as Comparative Law, a study not just has to follow a recognizable method, it must also be in pursuit of a purpose which can be achieved with respect to one of the various functions of Comparative Law. Comparative Law is used for scholarly purposes, legislative functions[97] or for reasons of scientific research.

For the purpose of scientific research various types of studies are on hand, for instance, studies ascertaining similarities and differences between legal systems, studies investigating the causal relationship between different systems of law, and those analyzing solutions to a given legal problem which various systems offer, further studies referring to the historical development of law or evolutionary history[98].

D. Methods of Comparative Law

Comparative Law is the generic term for different ways of comparing law. There are only a few approaches that are actually acknowledged for comparing law. However, it does not depend on what method a study pretends to apply, the decisive factor is its compliance with given principles so that one of the following approved variants of Comparative Law is ascertainable.

1. Case Method and Scientific-Theoretical Comparative Law

The initial point for applying the case method is a statement of affairs, a real life situation, or a legal problem that exists in a similar way in different societies as an initial point. Proceeding from the problem that is to be solved, one compares the solutions that are offered in the respective countries. This approach is based on facts, starting with law cases one examines the available solutions that are judicial decisions[99]. In contrast to the functional method described below, the relation between law and society is irrelevant.

93 Simpson and Weiner, The Oxford English Dictionary, Vol. IX, 1989, p. 690.
94 Zweigert/Kötz, Rechtsvergleichung, 1996, p. 14.
95 Zweigert/Kötz, Rechtsvergleichung, 1996, p. 3.
96 Edge, Comparative Law in a Global Perspective, 2000, p. 11.
97 De Cruz, A Modern Approach to Comparative Law, 1993, pp. 14, 15.
98 Cf. De Cruz, A Modern Approach to Comparative Law, 1993, p. 5.
99 Markesinis, Rechtsvergleichung in Theorie und Praxis – Ein Beitrag zur rechtswissenschaftlichen Methodenlehre, 2004, pp. 6, 7.

One does not aim at further cognition regarding the reason for the found similarities and disparities[100].

The method of scientific-theoretical Comparative Law illustrates several law systems by summing up similarities and differences[101] in order to find the better law[102]. Such a work could serve as a basis for decision-making for the legislator[103] or act as stimulus for "borrowing"[104] institutions from another legal system, thus implementing "legal transplants"[105]. The better the law system of a country, the more advantage it brings for other societies. Not least because of this, there is always a competition with other nations of having the better law[106] in order to achieve a locational advantage[107]. Studies which focus on comparing the developments of various legal systems or of discovering nationwide legal evolution generally[108] may proceed in a descriptive theoretical way. If an explicit illustration of similarities and differences remains undone, such a research still qualifies as Comparative Law because mentally drawn comparisons are essential in order to come up with results according to the initially mentioned aim.

2. The Functional Method of Comparative Law

Comparative Law has many manifestations; the main one is the one of functionality[109]. The principle of functionality pervades the comparison at every step, all the way to the finish. At every step of this method of comparison, functionality reveals itself in a distinct manifestation[110].

Usually functionality is referred to as a principle[111]. However, since Comparative Law is understood as a method, speaking of functionality as a

100 Örücü, Comparative Law: A Handbook, 2004, p. 52.

101 Zweigert/Kötz, Rechtsvergleichung, 1996, pp. 11, 12.

102 If legal solutions or handlings differ from each other, or even are mutually incompatible, this can not only be seen as a proof of law being differential, but as a chance for the cognitive comparatist to evaluate one legal solution as good and the other one as unsuitable. As a result, the unsuitable solution is to be avoided or abolished, not just in one's own legal system but also in the country in which it actually is effective. This cognition comes by discovering which of the incompatible laws solves the respective problem best in regard to the specific problem or topic chosen. (For general difficulties related to the attempt of evaluating in a comparative study refer to Chapter 1, D., 2. The Functional Method of Comparative Law, especially marginal no. 23).

103 Heller/Dubber, The Handbook of Comparative Criminal Law, 2011, p.1; De Cruz, A Modern Approach to Comparative Law, 1993 p. 16.

104 Entered the discourse of A. Watson, Legal Transplants and European Private Law, Vol. 4.4 Electronic Journal of Comparative Law, (December 2000).

105 Entered the discourse of A. Watson, Legal Transplants and European Private Law, Vol. 4.4 Electronic Journal of Comparative Law, (December 2000).

106 If legal solutions or handlings differ from each other or even are mutually incompatible this can not only be seen as a proof of laws being various but this could be a change for the cognitive comparatist to value one way of legal solution as good and the other one on the contrary as bad. As a result he found the better law.

107 Voigt, Globalisierung des Rechts. Entsteht eine dritte Rechtsordnung?, in: Voigt (ed.), Globalisierung des Rechts, 2000, p. 17.

108 De Cruz, A Modern Approach o Comparative Law, 1993, p. 16.

109 Platsas, The Functional and the Dysfunctional in the Comparative Method of Law: Some Critical Re-marks, Electronic Journal of Comparative Law 12.3 (December 2008), pp. 1 et seqq. (2).

110 Platsas, The Functional and the Dysfunctional in the Comparative Method of Law: Some Critical Re-marks, Electronic Journal of Comparative Law 12.3 (December 2008), pp. 1 et seqq. (10).

111 Zweigert/Kötz, Rechtsvergleichung, 1996, p. 33.

method[112] would engender a method within a method[113], thus bereft the later of its meaning. So for the sake of conceptual clarity, "functional method" here refers to a comparative method whose subject is analyzed using the principle of functionality[114].

The premise of the functional method of Comparative Law is the notion that each society addresses similar problems, which must be solved by the law of the respective society[115]. Law and society are related in so far that law fulfills a function by offering a solution to existing problems and giving an answer to social or economic needs[116]. The functional method of Comparative Law is essentially a factual method. The starting point is a real life situation which forces a legal system to react. It is based on facts.

While problems may be similar in every society, the particular way of how they are solved is to be discovered in the process of comparison. Hence, the initial point for comparison is a certain problem[117], which exists in a similar way in the societies, whose legal systems are to be compared. With this as point of departure, the solutions offered in the respective countries are compared. Since the problem is the basis of the functional approach, the legal systems are not investigated in terms of form[118]. Non-statutory regulations are in focus, but its effects in relation to the initial problem of specific society. Therefore, rules are comparable if they fulfill the same function, i.e., solving a specific problem which is common to both societies. Function so far stands for the relation between solutions and problems[119]. Functionality itself aims at explaining the effects of solutions on problems and society.

The first step of comparison is to find a problem which is to be solved by legal institutions. It is necessary to define the specific social problem which is to be investigated; therefore the term by which the original question is phrased has to be purely functional[120]. The problem has to be named without using the legal expression of any law system. It must be especially freed of expressions from one's own system in order to detect its underlying content independent of an understanding in conjunction to a legal solution. Therefore it must be extracted from any legal context and determined in the form in which it actually

---

112 Graziadei, The Functionalist Heritage in Legrand and Munday (eds.), Comparative Legal Studies: Traditions and Transitions, Cambridge University Press, 2003, p.101.

113 For the discussion see Platsas, The Functional and the Dysfunctional in the Comparative Method of Law: Some Critical Remarks, Electronic Journal of Comparative Law 12.3 (December 2008), pp. 1 et seqq. (2).

114 Ibid.

115 Richard L. Abel, Law as lag: Inertia as a social theory of law, Michigan Law Review 80, 1982, p. 785 (789); David Nelken, Towards a Sociology of Legal Adaption, in: Nelken/Feest (eds.), Adapting Legal Cultures, 2001, p. 7 (12); Uwe Kischel, Vorsicht, Rechtsvergleichung!, ZvglRWiss 104, 2005, 10 (p. 16).

116 Uwe Kischel, Vorsicht, Rechtsvergleichung!, ZvglRWiss 104, 2005, p. 10 (16); Otto Kahn-Freund, Comparative Law as an academic subject, The Law Quarterly Review 82, 1966, 40 (p. 51).

117 Reitz, How to do Comparative Law, American Journal of Comparative Law 46, 1998, pp. 617 et seqq. (622).

118 Michaels, The functional method of comparative law, in: Reimann/Zimmermann (eds.), The Oxford Handbook of Comparative Law, 2006, 339 (pp. 370 et seqq.).

119 Michaels, The functional method of comparative law, in: Reimann/Zimmermann (eds.), The Oxford Handbook of Comparative Law, 2006, 339 (p.366).

120 Zweigert/Kötz, Rechtsvergleichung 1996, p. 33.

exists in the individual society[121]. This enables one to seek for the counterpart in the foreign society and to make sure it is truly the same or, at least, basically similar[122] to the problem existing in one's own society. The underlying assumption that the needs and problems of societies are universal qualifies the problem as the denominator of comparison, while the comparables are the institutions which are marked as solutions. It follows that function itself serves as a tertium comparationis. Tertium comparationis as "the third part of the comparison" is the quality that the two things which are being compared have in common[123]. The next step of the comparison requires choosing the legal systems for comparison. Choosing a legal system as a comparable, presupposes that one has an idea which counterpart seems most fruitful according to the specific aim of the comparatist. In principle, comparing one thing to any other thing is possible[124], yet this says nothing about the usefulness of a comparison. Partly, a distinction is made between intra- and intercultural law comparison. A different method should be chosen when comparing societies of different socio-cultural types, one which focuses more on the social context[125]. Some want to exclude certain sections of law which are influenced by moral- and religious thoughts and thus differ between societies[126]. Others prefer to compare only legal systems of societies, which are on similar levels of development[127].

With respect to the matter of functionality, the choice of the comparable legal system depends on the purpose of the comparison[128]. Do the legal systems which are to be compared share the same function, in the meaning of being functionally equivalents? Do they, in its principal coincide in remit, approach and typology with one another[129]? If not, is it able to overcome these differences in terms of transferability of possible solutions? If both countries share the same function, at least according the relevant aspects of comparison, there is a common denominator for a valid comparison.

After one has chosen the relevant societies, the next step is to search for solutions to the chosen problem provided by the compared societies. Since the starting point of all functional comparison is a problem, a real life situation, a solution can be provided not only through a legal rule (law in the books) and

121 Zweigert/Kötz, Rechtsvergleichung 1996, p. 33.

122 Edge, Comparative Law in Global Perspective, 2000, p. 12.

123 Zoller, Congruence and Proportionality for Congressional Enforcement Powers: Cosmetic Change or Velvet Revolution?, Indiana Law Journal 78, 2003, 567 (p.582).

124 Örücü, The Enigma of Comparative Law, 2004, p. 19; Platsas, The Functional and the Dysfunctional in the Comparative Method of Law: Some Critical Remarks, Electronic Journal of Comparative Law 12.3 (December 2008), p. 6.

125 Kamba, Comparative Law: A Theoretical Framework, International and Comparative Law Quarterly 23, 1974, 485 (pp. 511 et seqq.).

126 Zweigert/Kötz, Rechtsvergleichung, 1996, p. 38.

127 Schmitthoff, The Science of Comparative Law, The Cambridge Journal 7, 1939-1941, p. 94 (96).

128 Platsas, The Functional and the Dysfunctional in the Comparative Method of Law: Some Critical Remarks, Electronic Journal of Comparative Law 12.3 (December 2008), p. 4.

129 Platsas, The Functional and the Dysfunctional in the Comparative Method of Law: Some Critical Remarks, Electronic Journal of Comparative Law 12.3 (December 2008), pp. 6 et seq.

not only in their application (law in action) but through a non-legal answer[130]. This results from the fact that functional comparative law does not focus on formal requirements of the comparable in foreign law but on how foreign law operates in the area of law in question[131]. Considering this, one might have to look beyond legal rules to find possible functional equivalents[132]. Rabel had the opinion that universal problems cause common results[133]. Zweigert/Kötz[134] suggested even stronger that the comparatist shall assume that different societies have equal problems which leads to similar solutions. This praesumptio simultudinis reviews the advanced step in which the initial problem was determined: if an equivalent solution cannot be detected in another legal system, one must go back to the first step and check if the problem was not named functionally enough and the extent of the search might not have been wide enough[135]. Within this step it is suggested to build a systematic system and invent own terms by building wide general terms to cover different but functional similar terms[136].

After drawing the comparison and knowing how the respective legal systems deal with their similar problem it seems that an evaluation and the decision according which solution serves best is the logical consequence[137]. After all the comparatist experienced the subject-matter at first hand and thus seems predestined to gain the laurels of the comparative work by providing the best solution. However, evaluating which solution is best in the manner of determining the better law[138] is generally not accepted in the functional approach. Usually it is the main aim to reveal how well or not a legal rule fulfills its function in solving the specific addressed problem.[139] Therefore, it is necessary to examine whether the effect which it is aimed by a norm is achieved in society[140]. However, at this point, this effect has not been the object of study within a comparative work. Even the recourse to existing

---

130 Michaels, The Functional Method of Comparative Law, in: Reimann/Zimmermann (eds.), The Oxford Handbook of Comparative Law, 2006, p. 339 (364).

131 Zweigert/Kötz, An Introduction to Comparative Law, 1998, pp.34, 35.

132 Zweigert/Kötz, An Introduction to Comparative Law, 1998, pp.35, 38.

133 Piek, Die Kritik an der funktionalen Rechtsvergleichung, GreifRecht 2009, p. 84 (89); Rabel, Aufgabe und Notwendigkeit der Rechtsvergleichung, Rheinische Zeitschrift für Zivil- und Prozessrecht, 13, 1924, pp. 279 et seqq.

134 Zweigert/Kötz, Rechtsvergleichung 1996, p. 39.

135 Zweigert/Kötz, Rechtsvergleichung, 1996, p. 39.

136 Zweigert/Kötz, Rechtsvergleichung, 1996, p. 43.

137 Bogdan, On the Value and method of rule-comparison in comparative law, in: Mansel (ed.), Festschrift für Erik Jayme, Vol. 2, 2004, p. 1233 (1240); Piek, Die Kritik an der funktionalen Rechtsvergleichung, GreifRecht 2009, pp. 84 et seqq.

138 With the meaning of "the better law" it is referred to such cases in which legal solutions or handlings differ from each other or even are mutually incompatible and the comparatist not solely views this difference as, the proof that laws are various but also judge that one legal solution is more valuable that the other in order to serve a specific problem. However the decision of one law being favored over another can be acknowledged solely in regard to a single problem and has no validity if it is not connected to the object of investigation.

139 Capeletti, A General Introduction, in: Capeletti et. al., Integration through Law, Europe and the American Federal Experience Band 1, Vol. 1, 1985, p. 5; Piek, Die Kritik an der funktionalen Rechtsvergleichung, GreifRecht 2009, p. 84 (94).

140 Bogdan, On the Value and Method of Rule-comparison in Comparative law, in: Mansel (ed.), Festschrift für Erik Jayme, Band 2, 2004, p. 1233 (1240); Piek, Die Kritik an der funktionalen Rechtsvergleichung, GreifRecht 2009, pp. 84 et seqq.

material of empirical social research might not lead to the sufficient answer of the comparatist´s general question of which law is best. It might be that a better solution could not be chosen, because whether something is good or not often depends on value judgments or political decisions[141]. The effects of the same rule as such could differ from one society to another because such effects depend on the mentality of a society, on the culture of the people, lifestyle habits, economic and social conditions which are all influenced by the specific history of a nation and many more complex factors. Whoever wants a law comparatist "to be something of a functionalist, a sociologist, a historian, a political scientist and a contextualist[142] all at the same time"[143] certainly seems to misinterpret the sense of a legal comparative study. By accepting the possibility that a comparative work does not end with the word of advice which law to choose, a legal comparison remains in its best cause being a preparatory base[144], serving a wide range of possible solutions out of which the legal authority is able to choose. The recognition of this service of a comparative study renders a valuation at the end as superfluous[145]. Therefore, the decision as to which way of dealing with the issue at stake is best has to be made by legal authority[146].

To avoid misunderstandings, valuing at the end is welcome[147]. Moreover failure to show results from the achieved cognition would be unreasonable, but only with regard to the examined aspect of a rule, which lies in solving this one specific problem, leaving all other possible functions unconsidered. With this understanding the proposition that the valuation must "occur only upon the

141 Bogdan, On the Value and Method of Rule-comparison in Comparative law, in: Mansel (ed.), Festschrift für Erik Jayme, Band 2, 2004, p. 1233 (1240 et seqq.); Piek, Die Kritik an der funktionalen Rechtsvergleichung, GreifRecht 2009, pp. 84 et seqq.

142 Contextualism "describes a collection of views [-originally derived in philosophy-] emphasizing the importance of the context in solving problems, holding the opinion that an action, [...] expression [and so on can] only be understood relative to that context. Contextualist views [–in whatever doctrine-] hold that controversial concepts, such as "the reason for hate crime" and possibly even findings such as "being true" or "being right" only have meaning relative to a specific context". (Cf. http://encyclopedia.thefreedictionary.com/contextualist - accessed June 2011; for further information refer to Price, Contextuality in Practical Reason, 2008 and Feldman, Contextualism and Skepticism, in: Tomberlin (ed.), Philosophical Perspectives 13, Epistemology, 1999).

143 E.g. Legrand, 'How to Compare Now' (1996) 16 LS 232, at 236 citing Law, 'Introduction: Monsters, Machines and Sociotechnical Relations in Law (ed.) A Sociology of Monsters[:] Essays on Power, Technology and Domination (London 1991) 18. ; Cf. example in: Platsas, The Functional and the Dysfunctional in the Comparative Method of Law: Some Critical Remarks, Electronic Journal of Comparative Law 12.3 (December 2008), p. 1 (4).

144 Jeschek, Entwicklung, Aufgaben und Methoden der Strafrechtsvergleichung, 1955, p. 43.

145 Cf. Eser, FS Kaiser Vol. 2, 1998, p. 1499 (1522) - who states that working out possible solutions and finally making a choice are two different things.

146 Eser, FS Kaiser Vol. 2, 1998, p. 1499 (1511).

147 Markesinis, Rechtsvergleichung in Theorie und Praxis, 2004, p. 26; Graziadei, 'The Functionalist Heritage' in Legrand and Munday (eds.) (n 1) 101; Samuel, 'Epistemology and Comparative Law: Contributions from the Sciences and Social Sciences' in: Van Hoecke (ed.) (n 2) 39 noting that 'Concepts and rules need to be contextualized within a range of factual situations so that their function can become evident' and M Van Hoecke, 'Deep Level Comparative Law', in: Van Hoecke (ed.) (n 2) 167. Cf. Graziadei in the work stated in this note at pp. 110-111; Platsas, The Functional and the Dysfunctional in the Comparative Method of Law: Some Critical Remarks, Electronic Journal of Comparative Law 12.3 (December 2008), p. 1 (5).

recognition of the primacy of the principle of functionality in the comparative method"[148] stays respected.

The following opinion leads to the same result concerning the precept that a valuation which law is to be chosen within a legal comparison is not the general idea of a law comparison: It is opined that every legal rule has to justify its existence. Hence, not only the question what is the function of a rule in society is to be answered, but also if this function is being served properly, or if another rule would serve this function better[149]. This is done by illustrating the consequences which occur in case of keeping, abolishing or changing a rule[150]. However, this evaluation does not involve any opinion whether a rule should be changed, abolished or kept. That would be a matter for legal politics, but not for a law comparison[151].

Since legal institutions are only being compared in regard to their functional relation to a specific problem, a decision whether a norm shall be abolished, kept or changed cannot be made at this point. In order to make this decision, a legal rule has to be examined as a whole. This would require investigating all other possible functions of a legal institution in order to evaluate its right to exist in the present form[152]. This extent of complexity reveals that an evaluation at the end, in terms of determining which norm is to be chosen for the own legal system, is not part of a law comparison but comprises a different task, involving many other, in the comparison not yet considered, aspects. Therefore, an evaluation stating what legislative changes are to be made at the end of a legal comparison based on the alternatives worked out for a given legal problem would not be thought out well and has to be omitted. In any case such an evaluation would be useful only in regard to the narrowed area concerning the one examined problem.

Law comparison according to the functional principle can be accomplished on different levels. On an abstract level, a comparison is drawn in a wider range via a comparison done on a deeper specified level. While in the first level legal systems are compared in all points, or at least certain points are compared en bloc, the second level of comparison scrutinizes detailed legal subjects.

Comparative Law done on the macro level takes place between more general or basic legal circumstances. General dealing and handling with law is being compared for example by comparing the frame of legal systems, the overall surrounding or basic principles on which a legal systems are built on. Also different methods of law could be compared not in relation to specific problems or subjects but showing up differences within the matter of law on the whole[153].

148 The question of function precedes that of context. See Rabel's approach as described in: Glendon/Gordon/Osakwe, Comparative Legal Traditions (West Publishing, St. Paul, Minn., 1994) 11; Platsas, The Functional and the Dysfunctional in the Comparative Method of Law: Some Critical Remarks, Electronic Journal of Comparative Law 12.3 (December 2008), p. 5.

149 Rheinstein, Einführung in die Rechtsvergleichung, 1987, p. 26.

150 Rheinstein, Einführung in die Rechtsvergleichung, 1987, p. 26.

151 Rheinstein, Einführung in die Rechtsvergleichung, 1987, p. 26.

152 Piek, Die Kritik an der funktionalen Rechtsvergleichung, GreifRecht, 2009, p. 84 (96).

153 Zweigert/Kötz, Rechtsvergleichung, 1996, p. 4.

Therefore, abstract generic topics are chosen to be compared such as working techniques, tasks and functions of persons being involved in legal systems and so on.

On the micro level, specified legal dealings and handlings are compared. On this layer Comparative Law focuses on concrete problems and their legal localization. Comparison takes place on a deeper layer by specifying a concrete matter of comparison. While comparison on the macro level concentrates on different legal systems as such, comparison on the micro level concentrates on individual problems which are embedded in different legal systems. For example, when analyzing the legal handling of so-called hate crimes in a legal system, one would compare specific institutions and legal solutions to a specific problem in different legal systems and thus law comparison takes place at the micro level.

A strict separation of these two levels of comparison is not always possible because specific problems in foreign legal systems often can be understood only if the foreign legal system is examined as a whole[154]. In the example given of comparing law referring to hate crimes, the legal practice of the relevant legal systems need to be understood in order to fully compare the legal handling corresponding to the specific problem.

3. The Delineation of Comparative Law to other Disciplines

After the description of Comparative Law, one may be tempted to think of other disciplines of jurisprudence dealing with international legal systems. Comparative Law is necessarily separated from other branches which, at least, partly focus on foreign rules such as International Civil Law, International Public Law, Historical Law, Ethnological and Social Law, but especially International Law.

International Civil Law is not based on comparison. It solely answers the question which legal system is to be followed if a concrete case, which involves private individuals, includes foreign elements[155]. Therefore, it is about the implementation of national law in the case that foreign elements play a role. Comparative Law on the contrary is the examination of own and foreign law by interrelating different legal systems.

Public International Law is a cross-border stock of binding regulations among nation-states and other international parties[156]. Therefore, it is a distinct greater law of affiliated parties, addressing states not civilians.

The science of Historical Law is often utilized by Comparative Law. An examination of a historical legal system necesssarily leads to drawing a comparison between the one being explored and the one actual being in force[157]. By taking into consideration that a comparison could be drawn not

154 Zweigert/Kötz, Rechtsvergleichung, 1996, p. 4.
155 De Cruz, A Modern Approach to Comparative Law, 1993, p. 7.
156 Rogers, International Law and United States Law, 1999, p. 1.
157 Zweigert/Kötz, Rechtsvergleichung, 1996, p. 8.

only between different national legal systems, but also within the same legal system within different times[158], it becomes difficult to distinguish Comparative Law from Historical Law. Even if one requires a foreign element for law comparison[159], there is an interrelation between these two sciences[160]. It is essential to have a comprehensive understanding of a regulation in order to conduct a law comparison[161]. This understanding can be achieved by a comprehensive interpretation of a rule. There are certain specific methods accepted to achieve the full sense of a rule. One of these methods is to interpret a rule from a historical viewpoint[162]. To be able to compare law, a law comparatist may employ this method of historic examination. Actually, the comparatist uses the historical examination of a rule only in order to achieve his original goal, which is comparing law; thus he does not conduct historical research for historical exploration purposes only. This is where Historical Law and Law Comparison differ. The distinction of Historical Law and Comparative Law lies in the different setting of priorities with respect to the history of law. Historical Law focuses on researching the development of law in contemporary history, whereas the study of Comparative Law just takes the historical development of law into consideration as a necessary intermediate step on the way to the final aim. After all, historical research regarding the development of a rule in the context of performing a Law Comparison is just a means to an end.

The study of International Law describes the law of one or more foreign countries[163]. In the context of this study, one provides a monographic overview of a foreign legal system, not necessarily with regard to a special topic. If one chooses to examine law systems of more than one foreign country, the results are usually displayed by providing a synoptical illustration[164]. The difference of this procedure to Comparative Law is that the pure description of a foreign law system does not include an evaluation or any kind of comparison. The study of International Law misses the key element of interrelating different legal systems[165]. The lacking element of comparing provides the criterion for demarcation. This study of International Law is a way of gaining and imparting foreign legal knowledge to one's own system without drawing a conclusion. International Law is a separate subject, but a necessary first step before

158 Different opinion stated by De Cruz, A Modern Approach to Comparative Law, 1993, p. 7 - where Comparative legal history is described as vertical comparative law whereas the comparison of actual legal systems is referred to as horizontal comparative law.

159 De Cruz, A Modern Approach to Comparative Law, 1993, p. 3; Zweigert/Kötz, Rechtsvergleichung, 1996, p. 2.

160 Zweigert/Kötz, Rechtsvergleichung, 1996, p. 8.

161 De Cruz, A Modern Approach to Comparative Law, 1993, p. 7.

162 Legal interpretation methods.

163 Rheinstein, Einführung in die Rechtsvergleichung, 1987, pp. 22, 28.

164 Rheinstein, Einführung in die Rechtsvergleichung, 1987, p. 22.

165 De Cruz, A Modern Approach to Comparative Law, p. 4 referring to Watson, Legal Transplants, 1974, pp. 6,7; Zweigert/Kötz, Rechtsvergleichung, 1996, p. 6.

dealing with Comparative Law[166]. Only when one knows about the foreign law to which a comparison is aimed at, one is able to compare[167].

Legal Sociology is concerned with how legal rules affect society[168]. Especially in certain principles of Comparative Law, in particular the functional principle, the study of Comparative Law does not only focus on exploring similarities and differences between legal handling, but if such are found, also tries to seek the reasons for such[169]. Such an analysis must be accomplished by considering the social surrounding in which a legal rule came into effect once upon a time and how social conditions affected it then and now[170]. Considering this, both sciences are aiming at the extent to which law influences behavior and therefore its effects on society. However, when Comparative Law aims at more than just understanding one's own legal system, it tries to clarify the function of law as such, therefore the boundary of legal sociology is crossed[171]. Some opinions even claim that the method of Comparative Law and Legal Sociology are similar in some ways[172]. How much the Sociology of Law and Comparative Law have in common depends on which of the above named variant of Comparative Law one follows, this again depends on the individual aim of comparison and must be decided in connection with the topic that is explored.

---

166 Rheinstein, Einführung in die Rechtsvergleichung, 1987, p. 22.
167 Edge, Comparative Law n Global Perspective, 2000, pp. 10, 11.
168 Zweigert/Kötz, Rechtsvergleichung, 1996, p. 10.
169 Rheinstein, Einführung in die Rechtsvergleichung, 1987, p. 28.
170 Rheinstein, Einführung in die Rechtsvergleichung, 1987, p. 28.
171 Rheinstein, Einführung in die Rechtsvergleichung, 1987, p. 28.
172 Zweigert/Kötz, Rechtsvergleichung, 1996, p. 10.

Chapter 2 Preparatory Country Report

A. Choosing the Appropriate Reference Country

The selection of legal systems that are to be compared is limited due to the skills of the comparatist. Examining a foreign legal system requires a base of knowledge "in all the important aspects of comparison that make up being a comparative lawyer"[173]: the respective foreign language, the legal culture, and an awareness of the mindset of the foreign society in order to capture the effects and consequences of legal rules. It is therefore beneficial if time is spent immersed in the respective legal culture and society in order to get the full sense and the substantial meaning of a legal rule to be able to properly translate law from one language to another.

Since potential language and cultural barriers are surmountable, the selection of a foreign legal system ultimately depends on the personal interest and the aim of the comparatist, who for logical reasons, will choose a foreign legal system in which he assumes to find answers for his specific legal research question. Aimless comparing of non-selective legal systems is a time-consuming task, with a chance of creating useless knowledge for the matter of cause[174].

If legal enhancement is the aim, it may be helpful to choose a basis of comparison which, at least at first sight, seems ahead of one's own legal system or holds a leading role regarding the examined subject. For the examination of legal solutions to the phenomenon "hate crime" in Germany by Law Comparison, an intent look into American criminal law seems particularly promising. With the United States leading the way in fighting crimes labeled as "hate crimes" through legal institutions, which are released with varying markedness, in every state, the District of Columbia and the Federal Government[175], it seems appropriate to avail oneself of the rich source of experience in science and jurisdiction which necessarily has been created by decades-long involvement[176] with this sort of crimes. In addition, the U.S. jurisprudence has an universal importance which, excluding the Roman law, no other national legal system has ever achieved[177]. Since U.S. "states lead the world in enlightened criminal law codification"[178] and the fact that the anglicizing term of the issue at stake already expects its origin in the U.S.

173 Edge, Comparative Law in a Global Perspective, 2000, p. 10.

174 Cf. Markesinis, Rechtsvergleichung in Theorie und Praxis, 2004, pp. 50 et seqq.; Rusch, Methoden und Ziele der Rechtsvergleichung, Jusletter 13. February 2006, p. 5; Piek, Die Kritik an der funktionalen Rechtsvergleichung, GreifRecht, 2009, p. 84 (96).

175 Pearlman, Sanctioning Bias Crime, 2008, p. 1.

176 The date of founding of the U.S. concept of hate crime legislation is attributed to the Civil Rights Act of 1964 (Coester, Hate Crimes, 2008, p. 82). Anyhow the first Regulation explicitly named hate crime law was released in 1990 which was the Hate Crimes Statistic Act (Jacobs/Potter, Hate Crimes, Criminal Law & Identity Politics, 1998, p. 4). According to that the United States America is concerned with legally fighting "hate crimes" for several decades.

177 Schünemann in: Dubber, Einführung in das US-amerikanische Strafrecht, 2005, p. VII Preface.

178 Robinson in: Heller/Dubber; The Handbook of Comparative Criminal Law, p. 565.

jurisprudence, the idea of choosing the U.S. criminal law as a basis for comparison suggests itself.

In order to get started, it is essential to be aware of the way the respective systems work their law. Therefore, a brief introduction into the American and the German legal systems in form of a summary of the legal framework of the respective societies is provided in order to offer a fundamental understanding of the different legal systems. In the following the source of law of the respective societies is reflected to then view the polity of the societies. Hereinafter it is turned to the relevant field of criminal law. The knowledge which is gained from the following illustration according the legal systems of the German and the U. S. society enables one to achieve a fundamental understanding of the current law established in both societies. This, thereby established basis, enables one to be fully aware of the subsequent discussion about hate crime in its legal specifics.

B. The U.S. Legal System

A brief summary of the U.S. legal system with focus on criminal law, is provided in the following by beginning with the source of law. The constitutional extracts are introduced in order to generate the necessary preunderstanding which enables one to follow the features of hate crimes and the difficulties arising from hate crime legislation in the United. Moreover, a basic overview of the U.S. criminal law and the legislative procedure is essential in order to allow one to not only make up ones own opinion about the pros and cons concerning hate crime legislation in general, but specifically to enable one to conceive the comparison with the German legal situation, which is drawn later in this dissertation.

1. The Common Law System

There are three major legal families[179] in the world: the Roman-Germanic law, the Law of the socialistic legal systems and common law[180]. The law of the United States structurally belongs to the legal family of common law[181]. Common law is a "body of law, derived from judicial decisions, rather than

179 Each sovereign community has its own legal regulation. Which law is applicable must not necessarily be answered with referring to the political borders. Even within a country different legal regulations could be effective in different parts of such. Due to that there is an infinite multiplicity of legal orders throughout the world which provokes an aim to somehow summarize these different legal orders by building an umbrella term or finding a common determinator. Through historical research one comes to the conclusion that all the different legal orders originate from only a few prototypes and just differentiated from each other over time due to the fact that law lives on separately in different territories. These few original sources are referred to as "legal families". So by referring to the root of a legal order and thus classifying it to its original base from which it once derived, i.e. categorizing it to a legal family, the summary succeeds.(Cf. Neumayer, Grundriss der Rechtsvergleichung, in: David/Grasmann, Einführung in die großen Rechtssysteme der Gegenwart, 1988, pp. 46 et seqq.; Zweigert/Kötz, Einführung in die Rechtsvergleichung, 1996).

180 Will, Das Common Law in: Rene/Grasmann, Einführung in die großen Rechtssysteme der Gegen-wart, 1988, p. 431-542; Coester, Hate Crimes, 2008, p.501.

181 Will, Das Common Law, in: David/Grasmann, Einführung in die großen Rechtssysteme der Gegen-wart, 1988, pp. 431-542 (508).

from statutes or Constitutions"[182]. Common law[183] once started with a judicial decision. Therefore, back in the days the judge had to decide a dispute with common sense[184] based on central ideas as equity, fairness and morality. His so rendered judicial decision contains law. It arises through deciding the case and becomes directly enforceable law through proclaiming the sentences. This is explained by the concept that through a verdict a specific legal regulation corresponding to this particular case is expressed for the first time, and from there it evolves into a binding force for all judges who have to decide a later similar case[185]. Whether a case is similar, and the decision, which failed once, fits a later legal dispute, depends on the reasons which made the judge decide the case the way he did. For that, decisions are not to be followed by construing the words of a judgment. It is necessary to examine the exact circumstances of the former and the actual case to distinguish differences or to detect equality in its entirety[186]. "Thus it was the principle of the case, not the words which went into common law"[187]. This causes a legal principle not to be an abstract device; it is closely linked to the case in which it was first expressed to solve a specific problem[188]. Consequently a rule can only be understood, if one knows every single fact of the case for which the rule was once created[189]. With this, common law[190] is developed from the collection of judicial decisions. According to this, law is found in judicial decisions and from these accrued maxims.

1.1. Origin and Development of the Common Law in the United States of America

English courts originally developed "common law" in the abovementioned way[191], implying that the jurisdiction of English courts resulted in lawmaking. Simply by collecting their judicial decisions, which as such embodied the law

---

182 Garner, Black´s Law Dictionary, 2009, 9th Edition, p. 293.

183 The description of common law is based on Garner, Black´s Law Dictionary, 2009, 9th Edition, p. 293; Devlin, The Judge, 1979.

184 Will, Das Common Law, in: David/Grasmann, Einführung in die großen Rechtssysteme der Gegen-wart, 1988, pp. 431-542 (499).

185 This is the doctrine of "stare decisis". Inferior [and judicial authority of the same instance] are bound by the legal precedents established by prior decisions of superior courts [or courts of the same instance] (Cf. Hay, The Law of the United States, 2010, p. 9).

186 Will puts it straight to the point stating: "[Common Law] is a workmanship of lawyers who do not construe but distinguish" - own translation of Rene/Grasmann, Einführung in die großen Rechtssysteme der Gegenwart, 1988, p. (477).

187 Devlin, The Judge, 1979, p. 177.

188 Will, Das Common Law, in: David/Grasmann, Einführung in die großen Rechtssysteme der Gegen-wart, 1988, pp. 431-542 (475).

189 Will, Das Common Law, in: David/Grasmann, Einführung in die großen Rechtssysteme der Gegen-wart, 1988, pp. 431-542 (475).

190 Common law system here is used to distinguish Anglo-American law as a legal family from the legal family of "civil law" which exists, for instance, in Continental Europe. Regardless of other, finer distinctions between common law and case law, common law within this work shall be used as a synonym for case law (encompassing all decisional or judge-made laws) and is meant to describe all law derived from courts in opposition to statutory law, statute law, legislative law or ordinary law. For difference between case law and common law and further information concerning the terminology refer to: Hay, Law of the Unites States, 2010, p. 6; Hay, Civil Law, in: Smelser/Baltes, International Encyclopedia of the Behavioral and Social Sciences 1865, 2001.

191 Will, Das Common Law in: David/Grasmann, Einführung in die großen Rechtssysteme der Gegen-wart, 1988,p. 431, 435.

for England and, adding a systematic application, the English legal system was created. American colonies then adopted this law from England as it existed[192] and it was brought to U.S. territory by English immigrants in the 17th century[193]. Not only was the body of English law adopted as it existed, but the way of creating law was also carried into the legal conception of the early American colonies.

After implementing English law, American Courts autonomously took over the role of further developing this "received" English law for American country[194]. In doing so, the once adopted law was fitted into the American society and territory and consequently altered[195]. Alteration occurs because law is released in particular, shaped by its social surrounding in the process of incorporating the features the particular community asks for[196]. The adopted English regulations were made for England; whereas, the situation in the American territory in which English principles were about to place themselves was totally different from the one in England[197]. Different countries, especially according to such different types of societies[198] (referring to England and the United States in the 17th century), require different legal solutions. If the same law is enacted in different sovereign countries it will live on separately in each territory[199] and therefore potentially develop differently. Likewise, if a law, which was made for a specific society, is adopted by another society, it necessarily has to be adjusted to individual needs which occur among the independent-minded people of the respective society.

So from the beginning, a territorial, social, cultural and economic adaptation of English principles to specific requirements – which the American society asks

192 Robinson in: Heller/Dubber; The Handbook of Comparative Criminal Law, p. 564; Wengler, Die Anpassung des englischen Rechts durch die Judikatur der Vereinigten Staaten, in: FS Rabel, Vol. I, Tübingen, 1954, pp. 39-65.

193 Will, Das Common Law, in: David/Grasmann, Einführung in die großen Rechtssysteme der Gegen-wart, 1988, pp. 431-542 (502).

194 Robinson, in: Heller/Dubber; The Handbook of Comparative Criminal Law, p. 564; As Hay states: "American courts gave an 'American gloss' to the received English common law" (Hay, Law of the United States, 2010, p. 2).

195 The English system with its lots of judicial decisions and the multiplicity of courts was too complex to be adopted unmodified by Colonialists, who faced a lack of legal scholar and very own, new problems which result from the fact of different people clashing together in a new territory. (Cf. Ramsey states in: Katz, The Oxford International Encyclopedia of Legal History, Vol. 2, 2009, pp. 287-295 (287)).

196 Roxin, Strafrecht AT, Band I, p. 16, marginal no. 7 et seqq.

197 Many variant factors play a role while the once for England created law could not fit the American territory as it existed by adoption. Such as geographical characteristics, regional distinctions, the impact of American mindset, then the fact that handling case law requires experience jurists and legal knowledge among society which did not exist in the new American society, etc. causes the need of alteration of the English law in form and content. (Cf. Will, Das Common Law, in: David/Grasmann, Einführung in die großen Rechtssysteme der Gegenwart, 1988, p. 431, 502; but esp. Pound, The Formative Era of American Law, 1938).

198 The law in England was created by and for a feudal system, whereas the American territory was a land settlement society. The differences of both types of societies could not be bigger (Cf. Will, Das Common Law, in: David/Grasmann, Einführung in die großen Rechtssysteme der Gegenwart, 1988, p. 431, 502). Therefore, it is obvious that one and the same law cannot live up to serve both in the same -satisfying-way. (For further information refer to Pound, The Development of American Law and its Derivation from English Law, in: 67 Law Quarterly Review, England, 1951, pp. 49-66).

199 Neumayer, Grundriss der Rechtsvergleichung, in: David/Grasmann, Einführung in die großen Rechtssysteme der Gegenwart, 1988, pp. 1-78 (46).

for as distinct from the English society[200] – took place in the American legal system, leading to steadily increasing alteration between the originally adopted English common law and the common law established in the U.S. back then and nowadays[201]. A further cause for the increasing departure from English law was that, in addition to the alteration of already implemented legislation, no further adoption of English principles followed since 1776[202]. Instead, independent lawmaking adapted to fit the needs of the United States transpired. As a result, in the present day not only single legal principles of the common law in England and the common law in the U.S. differ from each other, but also the American conception of legality changed due time and the legal structure deviated from the original English sample. Accordingly, common law in England and such in the United States are only egalitarian but certainly not equal. However, American law has its source from English law causing both laws to be clannish. Both laws are cast in the same mould, both spring from a verdict, principally sharing the same idea of legal creation[203] and conception[204].

So despite all modifications and alterations which the law of the United States has experienced since its transplantation, its derivation from the English source and thus its affiliation to the legal family of common law is beyond dispute[205].

1.2. Common Law in the United States of America as of today

Even though the U.S. Law system undisputedly belongs to the legal family of common law[206], U.S. jurisprudence in principle could not and cannot turn a

200 Back in the 17th century, the common law of England was (partly) not applicable for the American situation. Common Law is based on a deep understanding of legal decisions and knowledge of legal scholar which wasn't represented in the new territory. One component of law is a systematic application of rules. Existing legal rules without knowledge of how to apply it does not qualify as "law". At least, the best legal rules remain impractical. In addition, new problems occurred during the colonization of the new territory for which the common law provided no solutions. There were no regulations in the English legal repertoire for the situation in which labor shortages and the clash of Europeans with Indians and Blacks in a new "world" had to be managed. (Cf. Ramsey in: Katz, The Oxford International Encyclopedia of Legal History, Vol. 2, 2009, pp. 287-295 (287); For further information why English common law had to be altered and could not fit into the American situation, refer to: Pound, The Formative Era of American Law, 1938; Pound, The Development of American Law and its Deviation from English Law, in: 67 Law Quarterly Review, England, 1951, pp. 49-66; Will, Das Common Law, in: David/Grasmann, Einführung in die großen Rechtssysteme der Gegenwart, 1988, pp. 431-542 (502, 503).

201 Hay, Law of the United States, 2010, p. 2.

202 Will, Das Common Law in: Rene/Grasmann, Einführung in die großen Rechtssysteme der Gegen-wart, 1988, pp. 431-542 (505).

203 The American opinion of law, in accordance with the definition of common law, is that law is basically court law. This leads to the fact, that statutes are not truly established until they became applied and construed by courts. (Cf. Will, Das Common Law, in: David/Grasmann, Einführung in die großen Rechtssysteme der Gegenwart, 1988, pp. 431-542 (475, 477, 508).

204 In line with the general conception of common law, the U.S. Conception agrees that law is not primarily directed to find justice but more aimed at the correctness of the proceedings in a law suit (cf. p.445). In contrast to this, the roman conception of law is that the commitment to ethics goes beyond any legal regulation and its compliance. (p. 475) Will, Das Common Law, in: David/Grasmann, Einführung in die großen Rechtssysteme der Gegenwart, 1988, pp. 431-542 (445 and 475).

205 Hay, Law of the United States, 2010, p. 1; Will, Das Common Law, in: David/Grasmann, Einführung in die großen Rechtssysteme der Gegenwart, 1988, pp. 431-542 (508).

206 Will mentions the commonalities (such as the same language and the originally English people who populated America) between England the United States of America as the reason for the strong binding to

blind eye to the advantages of systematically codified law. While the United States certainly shares the same idea of law as judge-made law, consequently having the same understanding of a legal rule[207] as an English jurist and decently counting their own legal system in the family of common law, their method of legislation nowadays matches more the one of Roman law[208]. Local conditions[209] in the United States led to a certain freedom in handling, causing the prevailing principle of stare decisis to lose some of its strictness[210]. As statutes gain credence among the judiciary[211], legislation further converges with manners of Roman law whereby rules become systematically ordered in written form. By converging to Roman law in these two basic points the U.S. judiciary eliminates from common law such which was originally unclassified court law.[212] While the idea of codes being equal to court law coming to the fore[213] concerns new law, there have also been several attempts[214] to bring the already existing law (court law) into a systematic order by publishing Restatements[215] in several fields of law. While the way of arranging existing

---

the common law system of the U.S.. Cf. David/Grasmann, Einführung in die großen Rechtssysteme der Gegenwart, 1988, pp. 431-542 (505).

207 There is a difference between the understanding of "legal rule" in systems of common law and systems following Roman law. Therefore, a translation on the semantic level from German into English and back is not possible. The translation "on the wording level" of "legal rule" into German would be "Rechtsnorm", but the meaning of such differs: In the U.S. legal understanding a legal rule is never abstract; it is a concrete regulation for solving a specific case. Necessarily, if a rule is enacted by the legislative (statute law) without any relation to a specific legal case, it requires a court to connect it to a legal problem by applying it and thus giving it a "tangible" content, a meaning. Therefore, the effect of a legal rule is only comprehensible when one knows the relevant case to it. In continental law system a rule exists to solve a variety of cases, therefore it is abstract. A connection to a specific case is never required and a legal rule must be construed to get the sense of it and to be sure if it fits the case in question. This difference not only leads to different measures of abstraction, but also to further distinctions as different legal working techniques (distinguishing via construing), different valuations of codes. A code is of secondary importance; by itself it cannot provide a legal solution. Further material (judicial decisions) is required. (Cf.: Will, Das Common Law, in: David/Grasmann, Einführung in die großen Rechtssysteme der Gegenwart, 1988, pp.431-542 (457-480, 508).

208 The method of Roman jurisprudence is to follow norms which have been enacted by the legislature and which are organized in a certain manner within a Code. (Will, Das Common Law, in: David/Grasmann, Einführung in die großen Rechtssysteme der Gegenwart, 1988,pp.431-542 (505).

209 Next to the courts of a state there are federal courts and also courts of other states; the decisions of one local territory – in general – is not binding to another. This fact led to the existence of a great unmanageable mass of case law, which is often conflicting.

210 American lawyers seem to start thinking less in terms of decisions but more towards "jurisprudence", thus like a German jurist. (Cf. Buckland/Mc Nair/Lawson, Roman & Common law, 1952, p. 9) As Will states: In law schools the comprehension of law is achieved by a comprehensive search of the better, i.e. the true justice. (Cf. Will, Das Common Law, in: David/Grasmann, Einführung in die großen Rechtssysteme der Gegenwart, 1988, pp.431-542 (520)).

211 Will, Das Common Law, in: David/Grasmann, Einführung in die großen Rechtssysteme der Gegen-wart, 1988, pp.431-542 (520).

212 Common law consists of a steadily increasing accumulation of variant types of judicial decisions including legal proceedings and solutions which ensure a solution for each concrete case in opposite to Roman law in which a Code is provided, which serves a certain, almost stare number of abstract solutions for a multitude of legal cases and which is arranged in a systematic order.

213 Will, Das Common Law, in: David/Grasmann, Einführung in die großen Rechtssysteme der Gegen-wart, 1988, pp. 431-542 (520).

214 The work in hand refers to attempts of codification due to the American Law Institute (ALI) only. The American Law Institute is a non-governmental initiative which aimed at bringing the rules of common law into a systematically order. Therefore, it has undertaken research and drafts projects to bring rationality into the American Law system. Further information about ALI can be found on http://www.ali.org/ - accessed 2011/09/09.

215 Drafts released by private Institutes to arrange existing law in a reasonable order are referred to as "Restatements". The difference between a Restatement and a Code under Roman laws is that a Restatement is accomplished by private authors, not by the legislative; in other words, it is a written

codes in an alphabetical order[216] seems to be the easiest form of ordering, it is not what a jurist accustomed to Codes of Roman law would consider as systematic statement of the law in force. In contrary to early beginnings[217], nowadays there are drafts suggesting different orders depending on the field of law[218]; such are in no way inferior to Codes of Roman Law systems in regards to its systematical clarity. Nevertheless, a Restatement is not a code. In case a Restatement is cited in a judicial decision, it is not meant to qualify the Restatement as a legal basis. Such a citation only names the place where a judicial decision or a rule or both originates from, which again itself determines the law in the above explained peculiar sense of common law.

One must be sensible about the fact that with the nationwide launch of Restatements on all areas of law an idea, which roots in Roman law and is actually unfavorable to the "lively"[219] common law, caused a changeover or at least a sensitization in the minds among U.S. jurists towards the technique of codification[220]. All in all the American legal system is "heavily influenced by statutory law"[221]. Today this qualifies the American legal system more as a "mixed system"[222] than a true common law system even though codes often just recite the former common law rules without serving any systematic meaning. While nowadays several areas of law are still characterized by decisional law on the one hand, and even statutes are subject to court construction on the other hand[223], some fields are exclusively regulated by

---

summary of law not a Code, therefore a judicial decision can never be determined by a restatement (Cf. Will, Das Common Law, in: David/Grasmann, Einführung in die großen Rechtssysteme der Gegenwart, 1988, pp. 431-542 (531).

216 Robinson states that "The major contribution of early codifiers frequently was to organize the offenses in alphabetical order. Alphabetical listings were the prototypes of the original American codes in 1800s". (Robinson, United States, in: Heller/Dubber, The Handbook of Comparative Criminal Law, 2011, pp. 563-592 (564, 565)).

217 According to Robinson in times before the 1960's. (Cf. Robinson, United States, in: Heller/Dubber, The Handbook of Comparative Criminal Law, 2011, pp. 563-592 (564)).

218 Volumes concerning preset areas of law (for instance, contract, agency, conflict of laws, torts, property, security, trusts, and judgment) are divided into two parts: The Restatement of the Courts illustrates the judicial decisions which refer to a sentence which is displayed in the restatement. The second part regarding "State Annotations" presents the extent to which a sentence, which is displayed in the Restatement, is followed by which state. (Will, Das Common Law in: Rene/Grasmann, Einführung in die großen Rechtssysteme der Gegenwart, 1988, pp. 431-542 (531).

219 Common law is stated as to be more flexible than legal systems which statutes are ordered in a code. Rules which become effective through long legislations procedures and then are codified are not made for changing. Whereas common law, which has been developed through courts, always fits the actual situation and so can be easily steadily altered.

220 Will holds the opinion that the American common law is no longer in line with the English legal family of common law - in terms of its method. According to the method American law nowadays is said to come even closer towards the method applied in Roman legal systems. (Cf. Das Common Law, in: David/Grasmann, Einführung in die großen Rechtssysteme der Gegenwart, 1988, pp. 431-542 (505)). However, since the statutory text of a norm after all has different meanings to a Jurist located in the legal family of Roman law compared with the meaning such has to an American Jurist, this statement can not be followed completely. If the appreciation of statutory law differs from each other, necessarily different working and application habits follow. According to the legal family of Roman law a norm is followed by a jurist as soon as it is enacted, whereas a jurist used to common law yearns for judicial interpretation before viewing a norm as fully integrated into a legal system. With this concept of American jurists in terms of the handling statutory law, the bond to common law remains.

221 Hay, The Law of the United States, 2010, p. 7.

222 Hay, The Law of the United States, 2010, p. 7; Some opinion thinks about whether America should be counted to Roman Law systems. (Cf. Radin, Handbook of Roman Law 1 (1927)).

223 Hay, The Law of the United States, 2010, p. 9.

statutes. Regardless of whether statutes are merely reciting the former common law rule or truly being enacted by the legislature, the field of criminal law is strictly codified and courts are not authorized to create new law or change existing regulation[224]. With regard to this, state and federal statutes are compiled in statutory codes that group the statutes by subject. That makes the American legal system neither a purely case law system, nor does such exclusively consist of statutes or codifications[225]. With the exception of the Constitution of the United States, which is understood as an applicable law without court interpretation[226], the understanding of law today conforms to the English way of viewing the value of statutory law in respect of its binding effects and its application method. Therefore, the entire statutory regulation pertaining to the mentioned sector of criminal law does not lead to a different attitude among American jurists towards the general opinion of statutes[227]. A statute is not fully integrated into law until a court has applied and, therefore, construed it[228]. The meaning which the court has bestowed on a norm will grow into the legal system. This shows that nowadays, even though the American legal system is pervaded with statutory law in many sectors, the basic structure remains to be such of common law[229], as it was once adopted from England[230]. For conceptual clarity, it is best to refer to American common law as "the body of judge-made law that developed during and after the United States colonial period, esp. since independence"[231].

2. The U.S. Constitution

Speaking of the U.S. Constitution, one refers to the 'Federal Constitution of the United States of America', which is continuously effective since April 1, 1789[232], and known as the oldest sustained written Constitution in the world[233].

2.1. Structure and form of the U.S. Constitution

The U.S. Constitution begins with a preamble which, like an introduction, provides the reason for the establishment of itself. The preamble is followed by Articles (Articles I-VII, partially divided into sections), in which the form and organization of the nation is set. By determining the legislative, executive and

---

224 Robinson, United States, in: Heller/Dubber, The Handbook of Comparative Criminal Law, 2011, pp. 563-592 (565).

225 Hay, The Law in the United States, 2010, p. 7.

226 The federal Constitution has been valid, fully accepted and binding in practice since day one of its enactment; even without a court applying it for the very first time; therefore such stands in opposite to all other law, which in order to be fully accepted by jurists shall be applied and thus construed by a court before it is fully incorporated into the present legal order.

227 Will, Das Common Law, in: David/Grasmann, Einführung in die großen Rechtssysteme der Gegen-wart, 1988, pp. 431-542 (538).

228 Will, Das Common Law, in: David/Grasmann, Einführung in die großen Rechtssysteme der Gegen-wart, 1988, pp. 431-542 (538).

229 Hay, The Law of the United States, 2010, p. 7.

230 Will, Das Common Law, in: David/Grasmann, Einführung in die großen Rechtssysteme der Gegen-wart, 1988, pp. 431-542 (508); Hay, Law in the United States, 2010, p. 9.

231 Garner, Black's Law Dictionary, 2009, 9th Edition, p. 293.

232 The Constitution was ratified between December 1787 and July 1788 (Cf. Bernstein in: Katz, The Oxford International Encyclopedia of Legal History, Vol. 2, 2009, pp.147-156(147).

233 Bernstein in: Katz, The Oxford International Encyclopedia of Legal History, Vol. 2, 2009, pp.147-156 (147); Hay, The Law of the United States, 2010, p. 19.

judicial powers in Articles I-III the principle of horizontal separation of power is regulated; by defining the limitations of the federal government in relation to the states of the United States (Article IV) the vertical separation of power is established[234]. Articles V-VII deal with matters referring to the Constitution as such, while Article V describes the procedure which would be necessary to change the Constitution and Article VI provides the requirements of the ratification of the Constitution and further demands that the Constitution is the highest of all laws and inferior legislation must conform to Constitutional provisions.

This relation between the federal governments in proportion to the states on the one hand, and to the citizens[235] on the other hand, is codified in a more detailed way in the Amendments, which are attached after Article VII of the Constitution. These Amendments have been referred to as "explicit textual additions"[236] because of their concrete terms and their subsequent order[237]. The first ten Amendments are called "Bill of Rights", because they define concrete fundamental, inviolable rights of all citizens of the United States.

Such Amendments are based on Article V of the Constitution, which provides the conditions for an Amendment to be proposed[238]. The first Amendment of the Constitution guarantees a person's freedom of speech, and thus obviously causes the necessity of accomplishing a balancing act between hate crime laws, which include expressions and comments indicating prejudices based on race, religion and further characteristics of another and the within here guaranteed right. When speaking of basic rights, attention is further directed to Amendments XII, XIV and XV, which guarantee that certain rights of citizens of the United States are not to be "denied or abridged"[239] and especially to Amendment XIV Section 1 which promises equal protection of the laws to all the people living under the U.S. government (Equal Protection Clause) and therefore, at first sight, could seem to possibly disagree with existing hate crime laws. At least if one assumes that by these laws certain groups are legally protected differently from others.

The American understanding of "Constitution" back in 1787 agrees with the understanding of Constitution today, which relates to a "fundamental and organic law [...] that establishes the apparatus of a government, defines governmental sovereign powers, and guarantees civil rights and civil liberties"[240]. This deserves additional mentioning since the United States is

234 Will, Das Common Law, in: David/Grasmann, Einführung in die großen Rechtssysteme der Gegen-wart, 1988, pp. 431-542 (532).

235 Citizens in reference to Amendment XIV Section 1 of the Constitution are "All persons born or naturalized in the United States [...]".

236 Levinson, in: Katz, The Oxford International Encyclopedia of Legal History, Vol. 2, 2009, pp.156-160 (160).

237 The original text of the Constitution was ratified in 1787 (1788) and consisted of Articles only. As the denoting expression of "Amendment" reveals additional Codification, such were gradually added afterwards leading to an extent of nowadays Constitution counting twenty seven Amendments.

238 Refer to Article V of the Constitution; Levinson, Article V in: Tanenhaus, Encyclopedia of the Supreme Court of the United States, 2008, pp.106 et seq.

239 Refer to Amendment XV of the Constitution.

240 Garner, Black´s Law Dictionary, 2009, 9th Edition, p. 330.

engendered by common law. Despite the fact that American jurists have been guided by the idea of codes being written instruments embodying vague guidelines which necessitate interpretation through courts in the field, they have always considered the Constitution as the most fundamental law of the United States[241], i.e. that the Constitution out of itself regulates all other legal areas and all laws. Accordingly, all legal rules are subject to the Constitution, thus must conform to all provisions of the Constitution. So in opposite to the principle of law being what the court says it is the Constitution provides the standards of what is to be considered as law. Judicial decisions of the entire nation must be in line with the Constitution; otherwise a court's decision is unconstitutional and must be revoked[242]. This shows that even the system of common law as such derives its legitimation from the Constitution[243]. This makes up the principle of constitutional verifiability of all legislation, in addition to the policy that all legal regulation must be compliant with the Constitution, as stated in Article VI of the Constitution.[244].

2.2. Separation of Powers

The United States is a federal and presidential democracy. As the highest legal norm, the federal Constitution stands above all, and by laying down rules, it could convey the impression of a federally created sovereignty apparatus. This again contradicts to its contained human rights, which serve as a protection of the people against all sorts of state interference. It is the endeavor of any democratic society to guarantee each individual citizen – under indeed state leadership – the highest level of freedom and independence. Thus a Constitution has to cope with the combination of ensuring a governmental claim to power without infringing certain guaranteed rights of citizens, namely basic human rights.

To secure "Constitutional rights and liberties"[245] the principle of horizontal and vertical separation of powers, firmly established in Article I-IV U.S. Constitution, serves as a limitation and control of governmental power. This fundamental power separation pervades the entire governmental sector of the United States[246].

The principle of horizontal separation is satisfied by a separation of powers, which used to be implemented by separating the judiciary from other state

---

241 Levinson even states that the American culture views "the written Constitution as an almost sacred text". (Cf. Levinson, Article V in: Tanenhaus, Encyclopedia of the Supreme Court of the United States, 2008, p. 106).

242 "However the Court may interpret the provision of the Constitution, it is still the Constitution which is the law and not the decision of the Court". Cf. Corwin, The Constitution of the United States of America, 1952, p. X; The Supreme Court in United States History, III, 470-471 (1922) 1988, p. 431-542 (533).

243 Will, Das Common Law, in: David/Grasmann, Einführung in die großen Rechtssysteme der Gegen-wart, 1988, pp. 431-542 (535).

244 Will, Das Common Law, in: David/Grasmann, Einführung in die großen Rechtssysteme der Gegen-wart, 1988, pp. 431-542 (532, 533).

245 Hay, The Law of the United States, 2010, p. 34; Amar, The Bill of Rights: Creation and Reconstruction, 2000; Hickok, The Bill of Rights: Original Meaning and Current Understanding, 1991; Monk, The Bill of Rights: A User's Guide, 2004.

246 As Corwin states: "[...] constitutional law as a system of restraints on governmental action in the United States, [...]" in: Corwin, The Constitution of the United States of America, 1952, p. XI.

institutions[247]. The bisectioning in the past results from the fact that American law appertains to the legal family of common law, in which judiciary and legislature were coalesced. Nowadays one would expect – at least in legal areas in which courts generally no longer have the role of refining and developing law[248] – a strict three-part division into a legislative, an executive and a judicial branch. In fact the legislative branch and the executive branch often share their tasks and assume to be combined[249]. Therefrom occurring concerns , considering the precept of power separation, are minimized due to the fact that a delegation of authority from the legislative to the executive branch only occurs in such cases in which necessary operational reasons require such[250].

The vertical separation is implemented through the constitutionally grounded federal structure of the United States consisting of the Federal Government and the individual states – each having an own government – and the District of Columbia[251].

The strong understanding of federalism is expressed in the federal U.S. Constitution by explicit distinguishing between the addressed audiences, sometimes addressing the federal government only, yet sometimes just the states[252]. The question of whether the Bill of Rights affects the states, since Amendment I U.S. Constitution beginning with "[The] Congress shall [...]", expressively refers to the 'Congress' as the federal legislature organ[253] was not so clear. This idea seems awkward since the Bill of Rights should serve as a protection of the people against all sorts of governmental interference. Protection would not be sufficient if the federal government as such has to respect specific rights, yet its constituent units do not. However, this thought becomes reasonable when one considers the strong impression which the constitutionally implemented principle of federalism has on the minds of people

247 Hay, Law of the United States, 2010, p. 18.

248 For instance, in the field of criminal law.

249 The circumstance that the two federal branches are compartmentalized but do not work isolated from each other, thus their fields of function are rather interpenetrative, is "[...] known as the system of checks and [balances]". Under the U.S. Constitution and the state constitutions, federal and state governments are comprised of a mutual control and equalization system among the legislative, executive, and judicial branches. The power of statutes over other forms of laws, however, is not complete. As the system of checks and balances plays out, the executive and judicial branches have the opportunity to fashion legislative statutes within certain limits.(Law of the United States, 2010, p. 18; Chandler/Enslen/Renstrom, The Constitutional Law Dictionary, Vol. 2,1987, pp. 56, 57).

250 Moreover the legislative must determine a specific scope in which the executive is authorized to act. Chandler/Enslen/Renstrom, The Constitutional Law Dictionary, Vol. 2, 1987, p. 179; For further information refer to: Corwin, The Constitution of the United States of America, 1952, p. XVII.

251 D. C. as for District of Columbia, is not part of any U.S. State, it is an independent city which is not administered as a part of another local government. It is the capital of the U.S., founded July 16, 1790. It has a government of it's own but in several respect falls within the jurisdiction of the federal government. Washington D. C is not part of any U.S. States. Certain parts of the United States are territories which are not established as states, exemplarily Puerto Rico and several dependent oversee territories and areas, such as Virgin Islands and Guam. Special structures and forms of government and administration of the D. C. and such of U.S. territories and Indian tribal reservations are being spared out within this enterprise.

252 Article V, Amendement I, XIII, XVI Sec. 2, etc. refers to the federal government only, Art. 6, Amendment XIV, XVII, etc. explicitly refer to the states.

253 Paulsen, ZStW 77 (1965), p. 145; Barron v. Baltimore, 32 U.S. 243, 8 L. Ed. p. 672 (1833); Trüg, Lösungskonvergenzen trotz Systemdivergenzen im deutschen und U.S.-amerikanischen Strafver-fahren, 2003, p. 34.

of the entire United States[254]. Ultimately, Amendment XIV[255] and its Due Process Clause, in the way it was interpreted by the judiciary in the 1960s[256], made sure that the Bill of Rights in most sectors[257] has a binding force on the states[258]. So, to the present day, it is unquestionable that the U.S. Constitution as the highest norm has a binding force on all U.S. territory despite the strong preoccupation of federalism. Therefore, the Constitution affects all U.S. state law. Therefore the Constitution of each state, as well as all lower laws, must conform to the federal Constitution.

2.3. Constitutional Powers

Speaking of separation of powers on the horizontal level, one must also consider take the vertical separation and distinguish between the horizontal discussion on federal and state matters. On the federal level, the Congress is the responsible organ of the legislative branch. In line with Article I Section 1 of the U.S. Constitution the Congress consists of two chambers, the Senate and the House of Representatives[259]. The executive power is vested in the President[260], including the ministries and agencies reporting to him. The judicial power is covered by Article III of the U.S. Constitution and the judicial branch consists of the Supreme Court and inferior federal courts[261]. The United States Supreme Court has the exclusive jurisdiction in matters of Constitutional law[262].

Due to the federal structure of the United States resulting from accomplishing the task of vertical separation, each respectable state has its own government. The constitutional obligation to provide a separation of powers pervades through every level of governance so that the horizontal separation must again be implemented in every respectable state. In order to accomplish this precept, the governmental structure of each state equals the structure of the federal government[263]. While there are huge distinctions between each state regarding the forms of local government, the following section referring to state matters, provides a description in general terms. State Constitutions are not required by the federal Constitution[264]. However, each respective state has its own fundamental law. Similar to their federal counterpart, state governments

---

254 Trüg, Lösungskonvergenzen trotz Systemdivergenzen im deutschen und US-amerikanischen Strafverfahren, 2003, p. 34.

255 When Amendment I came into effect, Amendment XIV, which transmits the process clause to the states, did not exist. When it came into force the discussion occurred if the guarantees of the Bill of Rights has a binding force on the states due Amendment XIV or if Amendment XIV expresses own (i.e. independent of the first ten Amendments) rules for the states. For further information refer to Trüg, Lösungskonvergenzen trotz Systemdivergenzen im deutschen und US-amerikanischen Straf-verfahren, 2003, p. 35.

256 Trüg, Lösungskonvergenzen trotz Systemdivergenzen im deutschen und US-amerikanischen Strafverfahren, 2003, p. 35.

257 For further information which explicit rights are not included refer to: Trüg, Lösungskonvergenzen trotz Systemdivergenzen im deutschen und US-amerikanischen Strafverfahren, 2003, p. 35.

258 La Fave/Israel, 1992, p. 60; Israel/La Fave, 1991, p. 15; Israel/Kamisar/La Fave, 1995, p. 43 et seq.

259 Hay, The Law of the United States, 2010, p. 20.

260 Refer to the opening clause of Article II of the Constitution.

261 Hay, The Law of the United States, 2010, p. 20.

262 Hay, The Law of the United States, 2010, p. 18, 19.

263 Hay, Law of the United States, 2010, p. 31.

264 Chandler/Enslen/Renstrom, The Constitutional Law Dictionary, Vol. 2, 1987, p. 61.

have their own legislative body, which in most states, like the federal Congress, uses the two-chamber system[265].

The federal Constitution defines the legislative competence of the federal government (Article I Section 8 U.S. Constitution), expressly leaving the authority to issue law, in all the matters which are not mentioned, vested in the states[266]. However, the "Interstate Commerce Clause" of Article I Section 8 hands the competency over to the federal government in certain cases. The federal Congress therefore has the power to tax, the war power, the legislative jurisdiction in civil rights matters[267] and the power of regulating such areas which require uniform nationwide regulation[268]. Therefrom the authority to issue law in the field of criminal law is vested in the states. However, the authorization of the Congress to legally regulate tax matters and the Interstate Commerce Clause is used by the federal legislator to enact criminal norms in wide sectors, which is legitimate whenever it is deducible from the Constitution[269].

The executive branch in the different states consists of a Governor as the Head of the State and of the state's executive branch[270]. The court system of each state, usually providing three levels of courts, forms the judicial branch.

The vertical separation of powers at the state level is realized through a separation in departments of inferior governmental units, such as – in descending order – counties, cities, and other localities with legal personality, such as villages[271]. Conformable with the horizontal principle of separation, again a separation of departments has to be ensured on these lower levels of governance. However, it is to be ensured that the constitutional obligation of power separation pervades through the entire governmental structure of the United States and therefore being accomplished even on the lowest level of governance.

2.4. Summary

With the constitutional doctrine of federalism, demanding the distinction of powers of government among several of its constituent parts in order to prevent a concentration of power in any one part[272], is ideal; implemented through horizontal separation by means of independent branches (legislative, executive and judiciary), and vertical separation by means of territorial partitioning. One must keep in mind that the principle of vertical separation of

265 Hay, Law of the United States, 2010, p. 31.

266 Will, Das Common Law, in: David/Grasmann, Einführung in die großen Rechtssysteme der Gegen-wart, 1988, p. 431-542 (510); Hay, Law of the United States, 2010, p. 7.

267 Hay, Law of the United States, 2010, p. 300.

268 Art. I Sec. 8: "The Congress shall make all laws which shall be necessary and proper for carrying into execution the foregoing powers, [...]". After all the United States is a federal organized commonwealth and therefore a unit. (Analogous, although in different context: Will, Das Common Law, in: David/Grasmann, Einführung in die großen Rechtssysteme der Gegenwart, 1988, pp. 431-542 (513)).

269 Will, Das Common Law, in: David/Grasmann, Einführung in die großen Rechtssysteme der Gegen-wart, 1988, pp. 431-542 (510).

270 Hay, The Law of the United States, 2010, p. 31.

271 Hay, The Law of the United States, 2010, p. 34.

272 Chandler/Enslen/Renstrom, The Constitutional Law Dictionary, Vol. 2, 1987, p. 56.

powers demands that each part, which arises through a realized separation, is equipped with sovereignty, and again, with the precept to fulfill the doctrine of federalism within itself.

3. U. S. American Criminal Law

Since hate crime legislation is part of criminal law, the following provides an overview of the sector concerning federal and – in generalized terms – state criminal law.

3.1. Constitutional Base of Criminal Law

Article I Section 9 U.S. Constitutio compraises substantive criminal law. In consequence to forbidding "ex post facto law" according to Article I Section 9, criminal legal norms are constitutionally demanded as an essential fundament for punishment. Thus individualized regulation and verbally retroactive penal legislation is prohibited[273].

Article I Section 9 also imposes a judicial process ("bill of attainder") based on the violation of a legal norm existing at the time of the act as a stringent necessity for punishment. Several constitutional provisions concern the judicial process. Starting with the Fourth Amendment, which prohibits "unreasonable searches" and discretionary arrests, the Fifth Amendment continues the provision of Article I Section 9 by enhancing the demand of a previous judicial process for the reason of sanctioning, as for any kind of disturbance of a person's integral domain. In addition, the requirements of such a necessary judicial process are stated. Accordingly "no person shall be held to answer for a capital" without a judicial process based on an "indictment of a grand jury"[274]. The institution of a jury, which decides prior to the start of a main trial if there is a probable case, is considered to be the materialization of democracy, according to the American mindset[275]. America's society is averse to governmental power and therefore tries to diminish it wherever possible[276]. On the judicial level this aim is implemented by not letting the judge, as a governmental institution, fail the verdict, but a group of civilians. This idea occurs through the fact that a jury is an institution independent from the prosecutor, which in contrary to the prosecutor has a certain distance to the indictment. Overall it implies that the more serious the interference to one's basic rights appears, the more impartial, in the sense of independent, and therefore just, the structuring of a trial must be. This explains why the more serious the indictment is, the more stringently required the presence of a jury is[277].

---

273 Hay, The Law of the United States, 2010, p. 38.

274 Refer to Article 9 U.S. Constitution.

275 Trüg, Lösungskonvergenzen trotz Systemdivergenzen im deutschen und US-amerikanischen Strafverfahren, 2003, p. 12.

276 Trüg, Lösungskonvergenzen trotz Systemdivergenzen im deutschen und US-amerikanischen Strafverfahren, 2003, p. 57.

277 Offenses which are punished with one year or above require a grand jury on federal level, unless the accused waive a jury. For the case that the imposition of the death penalty stands in question, a grand jury

Further, the guarantee against "double-jeopardy"[278] and the right against self-incrimination are constitutional established in Article 9 U.S. Constitution.

The Sixth Amendment concerns the criminal trial itself by setting provisions which secure -in general terms: a fair trial; including, for instance, the accused right to counsel, the right to obtain a witness and the right to trial by jury, also a speedy and public trial is guaranteed. Finally, Article I Section 9 Sentence 2, known as the habeas corpus clause, allows all arrested persons to seek judicial review of the legality of their internment, and if it should emerge that an unconstitutional instance has been involved somewhere during the entire judicial procedure, redress is adjudged from the locally competent federal court[279]. With that, the field of criminal law, especially the criminal procedure, is regulated by the Constitution of the United States of America in general.

The reason why the criminal sector, and in a wide range the sector of criminal procedure law[280], is being established in the U.S. Constitution, is to limit and to control governmental intervention[281] which infringes people's elementary rights: such are naturally endangered by governmental punishment at its most. The Bill of Rights, constituting human rights, constitute the establishment which to ensure and secure these rights and therefore such must demand the situations in which these basic rights can be constitutionally restricted[282]. With recognizing that the main function of the U.S. Constitution is to limit governmental power and secure people against governmental abuse[283], one recognizes that the U.S. idea of governmental guarantees is the protection of the individual against the state. Regarding the relation to the people, the government has a restrained position. Colloquially "less government, more people" penetrates through every sector of governmental participation, leading to the fact that within the sector of criminal law, governmental interference is more responsive and not so much preventive[284]. This refers to the idea prevalent in U.S. penal law theory. According to which the limit of the legitimate ambit of criminal law is based on the assumption that there is a fundamentally protected personal sphere of the individual, in which the criminal legislator must not intervene[285]. The establishment of inviolable human rights within the federal Constitution of the United States of America implies the duty of securing their realization in practice. Criminal law has the

---

is imperative (Trüg, Lösungskonvergenzen trotz Systemdivergenzen im deutschen und US-amerikanischen Strafverfahren, 2003, p. 46).

278 The prohibition of double-jeopardy stated in Amendment V of the Constitution says that not any person shall be prosecuted or punished twice for the same offense.

279 Hay, The Law of the United States, 2010, p. 37.

280 The Bill of Rights contains twelve matters referring to the criminal procedure (Cf. Trüg, Lösungskonvergenzen trotz Systemdivergenzen im deutschen und US-amerikanischen Strafver-fahren, 2003, p. 13).

281 Zalman/Siegel, Criminal Procedure, 1991, p. 30; Trüg, Lösungskonvergenzen trotz System-divergenzen im deutschen und US-amerikanischen Strafverfahren, 2003, p. 13.

282 Trüg, Lösungskonvergenzen trotz Systemdivergenzen im deutschen und US-amerikanischen Strafverfahren, 2003, p. 13.

283 Zalman/Siegel, 1991, p. 30.

284 Trüg, Lösungskonvergenzen trotz Systemdivergenzen im deutschen und US-amerikanischen Strafverfahren, 2003, p. 13.

285 Mill, On Liberty, 1859; West, Mill´s case for liberty, pp. 22 et seqq., in: Ten (ed.), mill´s On Liberty, 2008.

highest potential to infringe these rights. Therefore, in the concept of law in the American view, substantive law, but especially the general conditions of the criminal procedure, must be provided in the U.S. Constitution. Difficulties in securing the basic rights of men resulted from the wording of the Constitution, which in terms of the Bill of Rights refer to the federal government only. Due to federalism and the division of legislative powers between the states and the national government, these rights would be meaningless if they would not refer to the several autonomous political entities in same way as they bind the national government. Nowadays, since the enactment of Amendment XIV and its juridical interpretation, the Bill of Rights binds the states to the same extent as they bind the federal authority. The U.S. Constitution, which on its merits is orientated towards the federal government, ultimately demands that all laws, whether federal or state, must be in harmony with the federal Constitution. Consequently, every single criminal norm, whether state or federal, must meet the constitutional standards.

3.2. Legislative Competence and Institution

As seen above, the federal government and the states are independent from each other. Each governmental subject has own governmental authorities and its own territory in which it has carte blanche to rule within the constitutional frame. However, within a federal commonwealth, the member states usually somehow suffer a loss of sovereignty[286]. Even though the states have their own criminal law, federal criminal law exists in the United States and must in some matters come into effect. In so doing, a point of contact between the federal government and the state takes palce. Consequently, the question of the competency of legislation between the federal government and the state rises. The answer to the question of competency, distributed between the federal government and the states referring to the enactment of law, is provided by the tenth Amendment of the U.S. Constitution. While the Constitution explicitly defines the legislative competencies of the federal government, the tenth Amendment reserves all other competencies not mentioned to state legislative power[287].

3.2.1. Federal Matters

Federal law refers to all legislation which came into effect under the authority of the federal government, consisting of the U.S. Constitution[288], federal statutes[289], federal treaties (Article VI U.S. Constitution) and constitutional case law.

3.2.1.1. Federal Legislative Competence

286 Neumayer, Aufgaben der Rechtsvergleichung, in: David/Grasmann, Einführung in die großen Rechtssysteme der Gegenwart, 1988, pp. 1-78 (46).

287 Refer to Amendment X of the federal Constitution of the United States of America; Hay, The Law of the United States, 2010, p. 7.

288 When referring to the law of the U.S. Constitution, the constitutional case law of the federal courts is included (Cf. Hay, The Law of the United States, 2010, p. 7).

289 Federal statutes include regulations issued by federal administrative agencies in conformity with the federal statutes. (Hay, The Law of the United States, 2010, p. 7).

With regards to Amendment X U.S. Constitution, one realizes that the legislative power of the federal government to enact law is the exception and only exists in areas provided for by the U.S. Constitution. When referring to the field of criminal law, federal legislative competence for legal regulation is not explicitly mentioned. The federal legislative department is concerned with lawmaking in the field of criminal law. Thus the Constitution must provide competencies for such. If one searches the U.S. Constitution for a legal basis of the federal government to enact law in general, one will find it in Article I Section 8[290]. The matters enumerated in Article I Section 8 U.S. Constitution do not seem to be explicitly designed for assigning legislative power within the field of criminal law, even less such do not provide a constitutional basis for federal authority to regulate the field of criminal law in its entirety. Yet the federal government has released far reaching criminal legislation throughout the entire sector of criminal law, regarding substantive criminal law as well as the release of rules for criminal procedure. The main source for this federal activity is the Commerce Clause of Article I Section 8 U.S. Constitution. This rule gives the federal government the authority to regulate the national – "among the several states" – and the international trade[291]. Therefore, the term "trade" is understood very generously: it includes all areas of law which in some way could affect the trade. By adding economic, social and educational matters as components, due to arguing that these areas constitute the success of the trade of a country in a wider sense[292], the federal lawmaking competencies are extended to all of these areas as well. As a result, in the field of criminal law,[293] the federal government widely released penal norms. These punish behavior for the reason of such being a disturbance of national and international trade[294]. This is in opposition to other sectors of law in which, pursuant to the general restraint in common law against codifications, the federal government has abstained from its legislative powers[295]. A parallel can be drawn to the law of the European Union. In the relationship of the EU with its member states the EU adopts rules based on the goal of creating a better development of economic life in a possible harmonized economic space. Other common legislative competencies used to regulate the field of criminal law through the U.S. federal legislator are the power to tax, the war power and the jurisdiction in civil right matters[296]. Thus, according to the U.S. Constitution, the

290 The federal government has the power to enact law regarding all subjects mentioned in Article I, Section 8 of the U.S. Constitution, which respectively are for instance, the power to collect taxes, duties, impost, excises, provide for the general welfare, etc. and - in general - cases in which it is necessary and proper for the Congress to have the legislative authority to enforce its competences. (Cf. Will, Das Common Law, in: David/Grasmann, Einführung in die großen Rechtssysteme der Gegenwart, 1988, p. 513).

291 Dubber, Einführung in das US-amerikanische Strafrecht, 2005, p. 5.

292 The authority to regulate the trade provides far reaching powers for law enforcement to the federal government due to the expansion of the term "trade" to including economy. By this expansion federal laws regarding economical areas aiming at social improvements are in line with the Constitution. (Cf. National Labor Relations Board v. Jones and Laughlin Steel Co., 301 U.S. 1 (1937); Will, Das Common Law, in: David/Grasmann, Einführung in die großen Rechtssysteme der Gegenwart, 1988, pp. 431-542 (535)).

293 Dubber, Einführung in das US-amerikanische Strafrecht, 2005, p. 5.

294 Dubber, Einführung in das US-amerikanische Strafrecht, 2005, p. 5.

295 Will, Das Common Law, in: David/Grasmann, Einführung in die großen Rechtssysteme der Gegen-wart, 1988, pp. 431-542 (510).

296 Hay, The Law of the United States, 2010, pp. 300.

federal government primarily criminalizes those acts that affect interstate commerce[297]. The fact of missing explicit constitutional empowerment of the federal legislature, in combination with far reaching existing federal criminal law, is an indication of quite an amount of creativity when it comes to constitutional traceability of a legislative basis for federal law enforcements. Expressively this creativity is in demand when it comes to establishing a necessary connection between the legally prohibited circumstance and the harmful effect of this circumstance for the interstate commerce. Then, finally, it depends on the judgment of the U.S. Supreme Court if a federal norm presents a sufficient nexus. In the 1960's, for instance, the United States Supreme Court interpreted the phrase "interstate commerce" very broadly[298]. This broad way of interpretation seems to have become restricted since 1995[299], when the Court struck down the Gun-Free School Zone Act, which made it a federal crime to possess a gun within a school zone[300]. According to the Court there was no sufficient nexus between gun ownership and interstate commerce[301]. Admittedly, the reason for declaring the law as unconstitutional was the Congresses' failure to reveal the harmful effects of carrying a gun near a school for commerce. If just any nexus between the commerce and the aimed at prohibition would have been determined by the Congress, the constitutionality of the law would have probably not been denied[302]. The fact that there is no explicit constitutional provision empowering the federal legislature to enact criminal law does not only limit the federal legislature's ability for handling, but also creates a huge portion of uncertainty towards the legitimation of federal legal activity. In this context, also the federal government's power to punish bias-motivated crime is highly in question[303]. Clearly the federal legislature may criminalize bias-motivated crimes which affect interstate commerce. However, with this limitation the federal laws could only address a small percentage of bias-motivated crimes. An indication of a lack of competence of the federal legislator to enact hate crime norms could be seen in the verdict of United States v. Morrison[304]. The Violence Against Women Act, a federal norm, allowed rape victims to sue rapists in federal court. This portion of the Act was declared as unconstitutional by the Supreme Court because – among further reasons – the law exceeded Congress's authority under the commerce clause[305]. The fact that the federal government

297 Gerstenfeld, Hate Crimes, 2004, p. 12.

298 Trüg, Lösungskonvergenzen trotz Systemdivergenzen im deutschen und US-amerikanischen Strafverfahren, 2003, pp. 32, 33; Dubber, Einführung in das US-amerikanische Strafrecht, 2005, p. 5.

299 Trüg, Lösungskonvergenzen trotz Systemdivergenzen im deutschen und US-amerikanischen Strafverfahren, 2003, pp. 32, 33; Dral & Phillips, Commerce by another name: The impact of United States v Lopez and United States v. Morrison; Tennessee Law Review, 68, (2001), pp. 605 – 633.

300 United States v. Lopez, 514 US 549, (1995).

301 Dral & Phillips, Commerce by another name: The impact of United States v Lopez and United States v. Morrison; Tennessee Law Review, 68, (2001), pp. 605 – 633; Gerstenfeld, Hate Crimes, 2004, p. 13.

302 Dubber, Einführung in das US-amerikanische Strafrecht, 2005, pp. 5, 6.

303 Hasenstab, Is hate a form of commerce? The questioned constitutionality of federal "Hate Crime" legislation, St. Louis University Law Journal, 45, (2001), pp. 973 – 1017; Peek, Where are we going with federal Hate Crime legislation? Congress and the politics of sexual orientation. Marquette Law Review, 85, pp. 537-577; Gerstenfeld, Hate Crimes, 2004, p. 13.

304 United States v. Morrison, 2000.

305 United States v Morrison, 2000; Gerstenfeld, Hate Crimes, 2004, p. 13.

has the power to release Civil Rights Acts based on civil rights matters jurisdiction leads to the idea[306] of subsuming bias-motivated offenses under Civil Rights Acts legislation. These laws, in general, allow a person to sue a state or a local government employee or an individual in federal court, if such interferes with his or her constitutional rights. But the discussion[307] whether the federal government could use the laws of the Civil Rights Acts[308] to punish bias-motivated crimes, says little about its competence to release explicit hate crime laws; the matter of Civil Rights Acts being linked to the matter of hate crimes is discussed more deeply later on in this dissertation.

Federal substantive and procedural criminal legislation is applied whenever federal courts are called into action. Therefore, the federal government not only has its own legislation regarding substantive criminal law but also regarding the criminal procedure[309]. By using the seemingly small federal legislative competence to release abundant criminal legislation[310], the principally provided distribution of power between state and federal lawmaking in the field of criminal law appeared to have changed without the need of a formal change of Constitution[311].

3.2.1.2. Federal Legislative Institution

The Congress is the legislative branch of the federal government and it consists of two chambers: the Senate and the House of Representative (Article I Section 1 U.S. Constitution). While there are two sources of law in the United States - common law and statutory law – the Congress is responsible for the statutory law, while leaving the common law matter to the courts. Except from the constitutional case law of the federal Supreme Court there is no further case law on the federal level[312]; thus at federal level, only the legislature adopts laws. The following legislative process is applied whenever a new law is enacted[313]: The process begins with an introduction of a legislative proposal of a member of Congress. This proposal, named bill,- after surviving the legislative committee process - must be approved by both houses of Congress[314]. Finally it must be ratified by the President. With his

---

306 Gerstenfeld, Hate Crimes, p. 13.

307 Gerstenfeld, Hate Crimes, p. 13.

308 The Civil Right Acts, passed in 1871 by the Congress, was the first civil rights legislation. These laws permit the federal government to prosecute people who have deprived others from their civil rights, either in concert with other perpetrators or in their capacity as government employees. In general Civil Right legislation allows a person to sue a state or a local government employee or a individual in federal court if such interferes with his or her constitutional guaranteed rights.

309 Article III, Section 2 U.S. Constitution. (For further information concerning federal procedural law view Chapter 2, B., 3., 3.4., 3.4.1., 3.4.1.1. Federal Courts and Chapter 2, B., 3., 3.4., 3.4.1., 3.4.1.2. Applicable Federal Law).

310 Hay, The Law of the United States, 2010, p. 300.

311 Trüg states that the entire federal competence regarding legislation and court authority has been expanded since the New Deal Program of the 1930thies (Trüg, Lösungskonvergenzen trotz Systemdivergenzen im deutschen und US-amerikanischen Strafverfahren, 2003, pp. 32, 33).

312 For the existence of federal common law refer to the following Chapter 2, B., 3., 3.2., 3.2.2., 3.2.2.1. State Legislative Competence.

313 For the legislative process refer to Hay, The Law of the United States, 2010, p. 8.

314 When a bill becomes law, the various provisions in the bill are called statutes. The term statute denotes the elevation of a bill from legislative proposal to law.

signature, the bill becomes a law[315]. Treaties, on the contrary, become effective upon ratification by the President after the adoption of a two-thirds majority of the Senate – the adoption by the House of Representatives omitted. Since treaties have the same force and effect as federal statutes, although the prerequisites for adoption are diminished, possibilities for their enactment must be limited in order not to revoke the legislative rights of the House of Representative. Therefore, their adoption is legitimate only in terms of international matters[316].

3.2.2. State Matters

The term 'state law' refers to the summary of rules and legislations enacted by the individual state[317]. According to the federal structure of the United States, each state is a sovereign governance and has its own statutory law and its own collection of decisional law in such matters where decisional law – understood as construal of norms – becomes relevant concerning the criminal legal sector[318]. The statutory law of each particular state consists of its own Constitution, its statutes and the enactments of its constituent inferior departments[319].

3.2.2.1. State Legislative Competence

Substantive criminal law is expressly directed to state legal authority. Due to the fact that the police power is enshrined in the Constitution as state law, the authority of sentencing primarily lies in the authority of the particular state[320]. "Police" in this sense, is understood in the old meaning of welfare[321]. Because of this, each state is authorized and duty-bound to protect the welfare of its people[322] and, if necessary, release sentence acts. As a result, every state has its own criminal substantive law and criminal procedure, which is eagerly called into action, whenever a legally punishable act is committed. Most criminal prosecutions are conducted by the states, due to the limited legal resources of the federal legislative and judicial branches[323]. State law must not only be in harmony with the federal Constitution, it must also not interfere with interstate handling. The fact that states are empowered to enact criminal provisions says little about their authority to enact their own decisional law. Decisional law, even nowadays, comes into effect if a case, for which there is no applicable statutory norm, must be decided; whereas this, in practice does not refer to criminal law anymore. The situation that a statute is too vague to take effect without judicial determination of its legal prerequisite, stays relevant

315 Hay, The Law of the United States, 2010, p. 22.
316 Hay, The Law of the United States, 2010, p. 7.
317 Hay, The Law of the United States, 2010, p. 8
318 Hay, The Law of the United States, 2010, pp. 8, 12.
319 Hay, The Law of the United States, 2010, p. 8.
320 Dubber, Policing Possesion: The War on Crime and the End of Criminal Law, 91. J. Crim. L. & Criminology 829, 2001; Dubber, The Police Power: Patriarchy and the Foundations of American Government, 2004.
321 Wüst, Die „gute Policey“ im Rechtskreis: Zur frühmodernen Normensetzung in den Kernregionen des alten Reiches, 2001; Dubber, Einführung in das US-amerikanische Strafrecht, 2005, p. 5.
322 Dubber, Einführung in das US-amerikanische Strafrecht, 2005, p. 5.
323 Gerstenfeld, Hate Crimes, p. 13; Kamisar/LaFave/Israel/King, 1999, p. 2.

for the subject of criminal law even nowadays[324]. This incident, which in the eyes of an U.S. jurist refers to common law whereas a Roman jurist would call it "construal of a norm through court", raises the question which interpretation in a case of diverging construction takes effect, such of the state or that of the federal court. As soon as the question regarding the competency of legislation between the federal government and the state is answered, then the follow-up question, whether common law is the legal order of the federal government or such of the states, rises[325]. The difficulty of the - either federal or state - nature of common law occurs from the fact that there are federal courts and courts of the states and their respective competencies do not go in line with the distribution of power of law-making[326]. Federal courts are able to take action in legal cases, even if it is not within their range of authority, for instance, if a legal matter requires common, nationwide handling[327]. To cite as a reason, it is enough if the parties are citizens of different states and the law case has a certain importance. If speaking of criminal law, as stated earlier, neither the creation nor the change of criminal law is subject to courts any longer. But, since it was until the second half of the 20th century[328], each state still has its own distinct laws nowadays. In addition, with the existing sovereignty of courts, further new distinctions regarding the interpretation of norms accrue in the judiciary. In such doing, new differences between the sovereign parts develop within decisional law even today. Even if all states would once adopt uniform laws and the legislature would not introduce any changes and amendments to the once adopted version of law, due to the particular state's judicial interpretation and application such would diverge and so over time would cause distinctions between the former legal uniformity. For all intents and purposes, however, courts have to interpret a law enacted by the legislature (statutes). Due to this, there are differences in the legal handling among the states and the federal level. So the question arises which "interpretation" (of which court) is to be followed in cases of distinctions. After all there is no superior judicial authority at the federal level that could coordinate divergent state judicial practices[329]. While it was once uncertain whether federal courts should be able to apply their federal common law over the distinct common law of a particular state, it is beyond dispute that common law is within the authority of each state[330]. Consequently a federal court must apply the common law of the concerned state, which is the state in which it is locally based and to which it has the concurrent jurisdiction. But since each state is bound to the Constitution and thus bound to the case law of the federal

324 Hay, The Law of the United States, 2010, p. 12.

325 Will, Das Common Law, in: David/Grasmann, Einführung in die großen Rechtssysteme der Gegen-wart, 1988, pp. 431-542 (509).

326 Will, Das Common Law, in: David/Grasmann, Einführung in die großen Rechtssysteme der Gegen-wart, 1988, pp. 431-542 (511).

327 Will, Das Common Law, in: David/Grasmann, Einführung in die großen Rechtssysteme der Gegen-wart, 1988, pp. 431-542 (511).

328 Dubber, Einführung in das US-amerikanische Strafrecht, 2005, p. 7.

329 Hay, The Law of the United States, 2010, p. 9.

330 "There is no federal general common law" Swift v. Tyson is overruled (Cf. Will, Das Common Law, in: David/Grasmann, Einführung in die großen Rechtssysteme der Gegenwart, 1988, pp. 431-542 (514)).

Supreme Court, state courts usually follow the decisional law of the federal Appellate Courts in cases, in which their legislation – statute law or decisional interpretation of statute law – or certain applications of their provisions are found to be noticeably different and thus possibly unconstitutional. So a conflict in criminal law, regarding the matter of whether the decisional interpretation of the federal court or such of the state court is to be applied, hardly occurs.

3.2.2.2. State Legislative Institution

When referring to the institutions for lawmaking, one must differentiate between case law and statutory law. Whereas statutory law is enacted by the legislature, case law becomes effective through a verdict of a court; therefore the legislative institution in the second case is a court - however, this distinction in the area of criminal law is obsolete.

The course of court proceedings in state courts is not specified in the Constitution., but the states in general mirror the handling of the federal government[331].

3.2.3. Summary

Federal statutes are subject to limitations, legally and practically[332]. Legally, according to the U.S. Constitution, the Federal Government is able to criminalize acts which affect interstate commerce, but all in all its authority is restricted to certain areas. In addition to the legal limitations, further potential practical limitations might occur from constitutional construal, dependent on the Supreme Court. This refers to the matter of how strict the United State Supreme Court interprets the phrase "interstate and commerce". Until the 1960's the interpretation through the Court took place very broadly[333]. In more recent years it seems that the United States Supreme Court is to set an end to the spread of criminal norms based on the commerce clause[334]. However, the criminal law of the United States is predominantly state law[335]. Despite the far reaching federal legislation in the field of criminal law, it is noted that the main control in the range of punishment and the most frequent application of the criminal law is done by the states. Only between one and three percent of criminal offenses are brought to a federal court[336].

---

331 Hay, The Law of the United States, 2010, p. 31.

332 Gerstenfeld, Hate Crimes, 2004, p. 12.

333 Gerstenfeld, Hate Crimes, 2004, p. 12; Trüg states, that the entire federal competence regarding legislation and court authority has been expanded since the New Deal Program of the 1930thies (Trüg, Lösungskonvergenzen trotz Systemdivergenzen im deutschen und US-amerikanischen Straf-verfahren, 2003, pp. 32, 33).

334 United States v. Lopez, 514 US 549 (1995).

335 Dubber, Einführung in das US-amerikanische Strafrecht, 2005, p. 4.

336 Kamisar/LaFave/Israel/King, 1999, p. 2; Trüg, Lösungskonvergenzen trotz Systemdivergenzen im deutschen und US-amerikanischen Strafverfahren, 2003, pp. 33, 34.

3.3. Manifestations of Criminal Law in the United States of America

Departing from the convention that law in the United States is essentially (at least based on) common law, criminal law today strictly follows a code. In the area of criminal law, courts no longer have the authority to change or create law[337]. They have to interpret an existing code in order to pass the adjudictation which the code provides for the specific case. Nevertheless, the relatedness to common law comes to light even in criminal matters, where law seems entirely codified. There are statutes which are too indefinite to come into effect without court assistance. Courts have to imply a legal meaning to such a statute by naming the concrete requirements for culpability in accordance with the precedence systematic of common law[338]. Thereby, despite the codification of all regulations, common law lives on in the sector of criminal law[339].

With respect to the above discussed federal structure of the United States and the therefrom resulting partition in federal and state matters, one realizes that Americans are used to organizing their legal affairs under two sets of laws followed by two sets of courts: federal and state[340]. Keeping that in mind, one can say that there is no U.S. criminal law as such, but many, exactly fifty two[341], criminal laws which exist independently next to each other. Whereas each state has its own legislations, the federal government has its own criminal law in addition. Whereas an exact distinction between the criminal laws of each state cannot be discussed in this dissertation, the federal and state dealing with criminal law – in general terms – is shown in the following.

3.3.1. Federal Criminal Law

Next to the criminal laws enacted in each state, the federal government has released laws in separate matters wherever the U.S. Constitution provides a legal basis for such. When noted that state and federal legislation is compiled in codes this says nothing about the participation of the legislature in the creation of this codified law, nor is a code an indication for a systematic order of law. Often the rules, which were once created by courts, were directly transferred into a code. So even it appears that the federal government established a code, it must be realized that such does not provide any systematical grouping, nor a form and content which is assumed when referring to the term "code" in European legal systems. The Federal Penal Code does not have a general part with general regulations determining the general applicability of the following rules or which provide general elements

337 Robinson in: Heller/Dubber; The Handbook of Comparative Criminal Law, pp. 563-592 (565).

338 Dubber, Einführung in das US-amerikanische Strafrecht, 2005, pp. 12, 13.

339 The judiciary has the power to review statutes and thereby determine whether they are valid under those constitutions. Whenever a court strikes down a statute, it in effect creates a law of its own that applies to the general public.

340 Weinberg in: Katz, The Oxford International Encyclopedia of Legal History, Vol. 2, 2009, pp. 255-262 (258).

341 The law of the 50 states, the law of the District of Columbia and the law of the federal government (Trüg, Lösungskonvergenzen trotz Systemdivergenzen im deutschen und US-amerikanischen Straf-verfahren, 2003, p. 32).

that refer to every offense, such as an act, attendants, circumstances, mental states, modes of culpability and prima facies[342]. Furthermore, rules regarding sentences are scattered all over the code. In fact, the federal code consists of fifty headlines containing various offenses in a confusing order. Offenses are also to be found in enormous collections of ordinances, released by lower departments[343]. While there has been talk of reform since after the Second World War[344], the Federal Penal Code implemented little of system.

3.3.2. State Criminal law

In the present day, criminal law is developed by legislative branches, and states are independent legal systems. Thus nearly every state has its own Penal Code as its primary source of criminal law[345]. This gives an idea of how many different crime legislations exist in the United States. Not only does statutory law exist on both levels, federal and state[346], but the fact that in the respective state level, criminal law is further enacted by lower governmental units (e.g., counties, cities, and other localities with legal personality such as towns and villages[347]) which again varies between the respective states, makes it difficult to localize and to restrict; which would significantly simplify the comprehension of the matter[348]. This makes it clear that all the benefits which a high level of sovereignty brings at the same time entail disadvantages. The fact that a state has an independent legal system, which leads to an individual realization of governmental regulation on every level of power, reveals that local authority for lawmaking is not only a decisive criterion for sovereignty. This also leads to varied legislation in one nation, even though, a federally organized commonwealth is essentially one unit. Therefore, the United States as a federal government must reconcile the interests of a single state with the interests of the whole nation. These tasks must be accomplished in similar ways by the European Union in regard to its Member States. If the European Union enacts policies, such must meet the interests of all Member States in equal measures, thus European policies must be universally applicable and valid, despite local and individual differences of the Member States, whereas the unity-promoting factor of the European handlings stays paramount.

342 Dubber, Einführung in das US-amerikanische Strafrecht, 2005, p. 24.

343 Called 'Code of Federal Regulations' cf. Dubber, Dubber, Einführung in das US-amerikanische Strafrecht, 2005, p. 25.

344 Herrmann, Strafrechtsreform in den Vereinigten Staaten, in: Kaiser/Vogler (eds.), Kolloquium Straf-recht und Strafrechtsvergleichung, 1975, p. 25; Wechsler, The Challenge of a Model Penal Code, harv. L. Rev. 65 (1952), 1097, note 1.

345 Robinson, in: Heller/ Dubber; The Handbook of Comparative Criminal Law, pp. 563-592 (564).

346 Hay, The Law of the United States, 2010, p. 7.

347 As mentioned in the previous chapter, Chapter 2, B., 2. The U.S. Constitution, a delegation of authority from the legislative to the executive branch takes place occassionally. This causes criminal rules to be frequently found in communiques of the executive, for instance, in the area of Environmental- and Tax matters. Therefore, there is a large number of norms enacted by different legal authorities in every state. (Cf. Dubber, Einführung in das US-amerikanische Strafrecht, 2005, p. 3).

348 Dubber, Einführung in das US-amerikanische Strafrecht, 2005, pp. 2, 3; Hay, The Law of the United States, 2010, p. 8.

Regardless of the dimensions of diversity of the distinct sector of law in the United States, uniform laws have been introduced by non-profit organizations[349] in many areas of law in order to bridge the differences in the entire U.S. nation[350]. For reasons of clarity and comprehensibility public sponsored and private organizations[351] in the 20th century started promoting nationwide unity of legislation in the United States by launching suggested legal handlings, subjecting several sectors of law. Whereas in other areas of law the above mentioned Restatements of the American Law Institute could render clarity and comprehensibility to many sectors of law[352], within criminal law a restating of existing law was refused[353].

In 1953[354], it became apparent that in general the existing rules in the area of criminal law were condemned, and thus could not serve as a solid base for a Restatement. The gap between the laws of the states was too big for summarizing. Rules as such were deficient all too frequently, so that instead, a model of a code was provided[355]. This codification of criminal law officially worked out in 1962[356], named the Model Penal Code, ranges at the highest level of systematic clarity. With regard to its systematic order, it is claimed to be even superior to, for instance, the German Penal Code (StGB)[357]. Anyway, it is certainly not less systematic than codes of Roman law, even though American jurists – in contrary to Roman jurists - have not been used to organizing their legal matters in systematic codes at all times. Now these uniform laws or model codes still must be adopted by the respective states in order to bring uniformity[358]. While the adoption, and therewith the success, of uniform laws has been uneven[359], the Model Penal Code as such has been a huge success. The revised edition from 1985[360] triggered an impulse for a nationwide reform of existing criminal law. For the majority of the various legislators throughout the United States of America the Model Penal Code not only served as an impetus for legislation to renew ailing criminal rules, but served as a leading example for all legal reform efforts in the field of criminal law[361]. Most states[362] adopted the suggested provisions or reformed their

349 The organization which is responsible for publishing uniform laws is the National Conference of Commissioners on Uniform State Laws (NCCUSL). It is a non-profit Association, consisting of members of each state. Its aim is to detect the areas of law in which uniformity of law among the states is required, due to the fact that existing legislation is deficient or the law of the states has become too various in certain sectors. In these areas the Association launched model drafts which were suggested to be adopted by the states. (For further information refer to http://www.nccusl.org/ - accessed 2011/09/09). Regarding the sector of Criminal law in particular, the American Law Institute, a private organization, has contributed to the success in creating uniformity of law among the states.

350 Hay, The Law in the United States, 2010, p. 8.

351 The National Conference of Commissioners proposes Uniform Laws in collaboration with the American Law Institute. (Hay, The Law of the United States, 2010, p. 8).

352 Robinson, United States, in: Heller/Dubber, The Handbook of Comparative Criminal Law, p. 565.

353 Robinson, United States, in: Heller/Dubber, The Handbook of Comparative Criminal Law, p. 565.

354 Robinson, United States, in: Heller/Dubber, The Handbook of Comparative Criminal Law, p. 565.

355 Robinson, United States, in: Heller/Dubber, The Handbook of Comparative Criminal Law, p. 565.

356 Dubber, Einführung in das US-amerikanische Strafrecht, 2005, p. 1.

357 Schünemann, Geleitwort, in: Dubber, Einführung in das US-amerikanische Strafrecht, 2005, p. VIII.

358 Hay, The Law of the United States, 2010, p. 8.

359 Hay, The Law of the United States, 2010, p. 8.

360 Robinson, United States, in: Heller/Dubber, The Handbook of Comparative Criminal Law, p. 565.

361 Robinson, United States, in: Heller/Dubber, The Handbook of Comparative Criminal Law, p. 565.

existing laws along the lines of the Model Penal Code[363]. States in which legislation has not been changed due to the launch of the Model Penal Code were at least influenced through their judiciary, which followed the suggestions of this draft[364]. Whereas the criminal reform based on the Model Penal Code was implemented on the federal level at the least[365], the federal judiciary orientates itself towards the specifications of the Model Penal Code despite the lack of adjustment of the terms[366]. Thus with the nationwide introduction of the Modal Penal Code reasonable order was brought into the once common law ruled American criminal law[367]. Because of the highly systematic configuration of the Model Penal Code most criminal law in the United States nowadays uses an analytic structure that is easily compatible with the German scheme[368], which presents a prefixed general part which refers to all following norms.

The success of the Model Penal code is understandable if one incorporates the view of law which is inherent in a common law jurist. Since the American legal system still primarily is a common law system, as discussed above, this fact still influences the law of the country[369]. Therefrom it results that a statute does not develop their full legal validity until a court has defined its meaningfulness. With the definition which is bestowed upon a norm by the respective court, such becomes truly legally relevant and constitutes binding applicable law for the next case. Because of this, it is clear that statutes are still subject to binding - and authoritative - interpretation by the courts[370].

However, if the case law develops in a direction not intended by the legislature, the legislative branch can always pass new legislation to bring about a correction[371]. It is revealed that in sectors in which the need for legislative intervention is especially urgent a statute is accepted at its best[372]. With respect to the "unsound and ill"[373] criminal law, the appreciation and the readiness for a reform of the sector of criminal law was high; in fact, the suggestions of the Model Penal Code came in handy. So the success of the criminal law reform throughout the entire nation is attributable to the need for an improvement in the field of criminal law on the one hand, and the highly developed legal structure of the Model Panel Code on the other hand.

---

362 Forty out of fifty adopted the suggested provisions or reformed their existing laws along the lines of the Model Penal Code. - according to Dubber, Einführung in das US-amerikanische Strafrecht, 2005, p. 16.

363 Dubber, Einführung in das US-amerikanische Strafrecht, 2005, p. 16.

364 California, for instance, has hardly managed to renew their laws along the lines of the Model Penal Code. (Dubber, Einführung in das US-amerikanische Strafrecht, 2005, p. 17).

365 Dubber, Einführung in das US-amerikanische Strafrecht, 2005, p. 17.

366 Dubber, Einführung in das US-amerikanische Strafrecht, 2005, p. 17.

367 Robinson, United Sates, in: Heller/Dubber; The Handbook of Comparative Criminal Law, p. 565.

368 Dubber, Comparative Criminal Law, in: Reimann/Zimmermann, The Oxford Handbook of Comparative Law, 2006, p. 1319.

369 Hay, The Law of the United States, 2010, p. 12.

370 Cf. Hay expresses that statutes are subject to a "judicial gloss". (Hay, The Law of the United States, 2010, pp. 9, 12).

371 Hay, The Law of the United States, 2010, p. 12.

372 Similar: Will, Das Common Law, in: David/Grasmann, Einführung in die großen Rechtssysteme der Gegenwart, 1988, pp. 431-542 (541).

373 Robinson, United States, in: Heller/Dubber: The Handbook of Comparative Criminal Law, p. 565.

3.3.3. Summary

In many areas, the laws of the different states may be very similar. Nevertheless the distinctions require a common determinator. In order to fulfill the main subject of this undertaking, an appropriate basis for comparison is needed, which necessarily has to consist of one stringent way of dealing in the respective chosen subject in order for that subject to serve as a suitable basis for comparison. This one stringent way of handling in the sector of criminal law in the United States then serves as an appropriate basis, when comparing it with one other way of handling, such – with respect to the chosen matter – is the German way of handling in the sector of criminal law. Choosing the one criminal law from the multitudes of criminal orders which exist in the United States, reveals to be difficult. It is searched for that one stringent way of criminal handling, which could serve as a basis. The precept of "one law" would relate to one criminal legal order as it actually exists in the United States in one of the states – leading to the fact of leaving all other American criminal laws behind, which causes the problem that the chosen law would not serve as a valid base for comparison due to the lack of objective criteria. From one particular law, one may not refer to the actual legal treatment throughout the country, since one legal order does not represent the entire criminal law sector of the United States.

If there is a common determinator in the criminal law of the United States it is the Model Penal Code[374]. When speaking of a common denominator to encompass the entire U.S. criminal law, it is referred to the Model Penal Code[375] because it serves as the principal source of penology in the entire United States[376].

3.4. Jurisdiction and Competence of Criminal Courts

In respect to the strict obedience of federalism[377] there are two parallel proper channels of jurisdiction for each lawsuit, one on the state level and one on the federal level. Both are separate and independent from each other[378].

3.4.1. Federal Matters

A legal case is a federal matter if a federal court is competent to decide the case. A federal court is competent to decide a case whenever a claim arises from federal law; whenever a subject requires even treatment and whenever

374 Dubber, Einführung in das US-amerikanische Strafrecht, 2005, p. 16.

375 Dubber states: "Without the influence of the Model Penal Code it would not make sense to speak of the American law." Own translation of: Dubber, Einführung in das US-amerikanische Strafrecht, 2005, p. 29.

376 About three-quarter of the states modeled their Penal Code like the MPC, which demonstrates the impact of the MPC on the entire U.S. criminal law. Cf. Dubber, Einführung in das US amerikanische Strafrecht, 2005, p. 2, 16; Robinson, United States, in: Heller/Dubber; The Handbook of Comparative Criminal Law, p. 564.

377 Trüg, Lösungskonvergenzen trotz Systemdivergenzen im deutschen und US-amerikanischen Strafverfahren, 2003, p. 36.

378 Will, Das Common Law, in: David/Grasmann, Einführung in die großen Rechtssysteme der Gegen-wart, 1988, p. 431-542 (521).

the relevant parties have diverse citizenships[379], either from different states or from different nations[380]. Since federal courts apply federal rules, there must necessarily be federal trial law. Yet, the legislative basis for such federal legislation must be traceable to the U.S. Constitution. However, federal courts do not have exclusive jurisdiction in the field of criminal law. They have parallel jurisdiction with state courts on all judicial levels (with the Supreme Court as an exception), hence, in all of their criminal cases[381]. Consequently there are two parallel proper channels for each lawsuit. As a corollary to the strict obedience of federalism[382], such necessarily leads to the fact that both channels are independent from each other, consequently courts of one channel do not overrule courts of another channel, expressly a federal court does not function as an appellate or superior court of a state court[383].

3.4.1.1. Federal Courts

The U.S. Constitution demands one Supreme Court and an undefined number of inferior courts[384]. From the federal perspective, the realization of this constitutional demand led to the establishment of three instances of federal courts. The legal path starts with a claim arising under the court of first instance (trial court), which in federal matters, is an U.S. District Court and is represented in every state at least once[385]. Larger states are parted into regions; in this case, each region has its own District Court[386], which results in an overall of ninety-one established District Courts in the United States of America[387].

If a claim reaches the second instance, the Court of Appeal is competent to conduct a review. There are thirteen Courts of Appeal in the United States. The number thirteen is fixed; it accrues from the number of regions, named "circuits", in which the country is divided. Each region supplies one Court of Appeal which is in charge for that entire region. Since a circuit crosses national state borders and comprises several states, a Court of Appeal is cognizant for

379 A federal court is competent for adjudicating upon legal problems resulting from interstate matters in whatever combination Such combination, expressly, would be controversies between two or more states, between a state and a citizen of another state, between citizen of different states. (Article III, Section 2 of the U.S. Constitution).

380 This refers to all jurisdictions which have any kind of international connection: For example cases affecting ambassadors, public ministers or consuls, cases of admiralty or maritime jurisdiction and between a state or a citizen thereof and foreign states, citizens or subject. (Cf. Article III, Section 2 U.S. Constitution).

381 Federal courts do not have exclusive jurisdiction except in a very few areas, such as maritime matter and in bankruptcy trials (Hay, The Law of the United States, 2010, p. 57).

382 Trüg, Lösungskonvergenzen trotz Systemdivergenzen im deutschen und US-amerikanischen Strafverfahren, 2003, p. 36.

383 Hay, The Law of the United States, 2010, p. 55.

384 Article III Section 1 U.S. Constitution.

385 Trüg, Lösungskonvergenzen trotz Systemdivergenzen im deutschen und US-amerikanischen Strafverfahren, 2003, p. 36.

386 Hay, The Law of the United States, 2010, p. 55.

387 Trüg, Lösungskonvergenzen trotz Systemdivergenzen im deutschen und US-amerikanischen Strafverfahren, 2003, p. 36.

several states. Each circuit is identified by number; this number is also the designation of the respective Court of Appeal[388].

The highest Court in the federal judicial system is the U.S. Supreme Court. There is only one exception to the statement that federal courts, no matter on which level, do not function as appellate or superior courts for state courts[389]: The U.S. Supreme Court, the highest court in the United States, which, as the guardian of the U.S. Constitution, is vested with the charge of being the point of verification of all jurisdiction[390]. Therefore, as a federal court, the U.S. Supreme Court does function as a final review instance for state court decisions.

The U.S. Supreme Court has competence on the first level and on the last level of legal proceedings, but practically only the last level is of importance[391]. This results from its power of discretion, due to which the Justices of the Court are able to decide which claims to accept for jurisdiction. Generally, cases which refer to essential federal matters or cases with major importance for the U.S. nation are to be heard[392].

3.4.1.2. Applicable Federal Law

In a federal case, federal courts apply federal law. As stated before, the federal government has its own set of statutory law and applies its own rules created by the federal legislature.

Something else occurs, if federal law, which is required to solve the pending legal case, does not exist. If a federal rule does not exist, a court would – in respect of the common law tradition of the United States – create law. However, to such creation federal courts are not competent[393]. Federal common law must not exist[394]. This question, as seen before, does not apply within the field of criminal law, because since the 21st century, criminal law is entirely codified. However, what refers to criminal law is the possibility that statutory federal and state law differ from each other or that just the interpretation of law through federal courts and such of the respective state court differ. In case a criminal rule is too indefinite to be applied just as it has been enacted by the legislature, a court has to construe the meaning, which occurs individually, by the court concerned. Whatever occurs individually, leads to diversity between the respectively dealing departments. So if a federal court deals with a criminal case and has to apply a rule which is construed in a

---

388 For instance, it is referred to the "court of Appeals for the Second Circuit"; or more laxly just to "the second circuit" (Hay, The Law of the United States, 2010, p. 55).

389 Hay, The Law of the United States, 2010, p. 55.

390 Refer to Article III, Section 1 U.S. Constitution.

391 Will, Das Common Law in: David/Grasmann, Einführung in die großen Rechtssysteme der Gegen-wart, 1988, p. 522.

392 Will, Das Common Law, in: David/Grasmann, Einführung in die großen Rechtssysteme der Gegen-wart, 1988, p. 522.

393 Erie Railroad Co. v. Tompkins, 304 U.S. 64, 58 S. Ct. 817, 82 L. Ed. 1188 (1938); Will, Das Common Law, in: David/Grasmann, Einführung in die großen Rechtssysteme der Gegenwart, 1988, pp. 431-542 (513 et seq.).

394 "there is no federal general common law". Erie Railroad Co. v. Tompkins, 304 U.S. 64, 58 S. Ct. 817, 82 L. Ed. 1188 (1938).

different way in the federal courts, then it is due to the state court, to which it has concurrent jurisdiction, the question rises, which interpretation is to be followed, the federal or the one of the state? As discussed above, in diversity cases a federal court must apply the law of the state in which it is located[395]. Would a federal court apply its own law in the case of the double court hierarchy, the chances of decisional disparity would be high. If considering the possibility that a federal and a state court both adjudicate over a case and thereby apply their own concurrent case law and thus pass different verdicts, it becomes apparent that this could lead to unrest; therefore the primacy of state law is reasonable. Of course, all courts, including state courts, are bound by decisions of the U.S. Supreme Court that interpret a particular federal rule at issue and so are forced to interpret their potentially same rule in the same "federal", i.e. constitutional, way. This so far concerns statutory law, but also included the dealings with common law matters occurring during a criminal trial.

Regarding the criminal procedure, Federal law, is shaped by the federal Constitution and is further based on the Federal Rules of Procedure, Federal Rules of Appellate Procedure and the special rules promulgated for criminal legal procedures[396]. Such a special rule regarding the federal criminal procedure is the mandate of a jury trial for serious crimes[397]. This is imperative, unless the defendant has waived this right in writing with the consent of the court and the prosecutor. However, such a waiver is not legal in case a crime is punishable by the death penalty, irrespective of the sentence which in the end is imposed[398]. The task of the jury is to pass the verdict in correspondence to the guilt of the offender[399]. If the defendant is found guilty on all or some charges, a sentence – based on the judgment of the jury - is pronounced by the judge.

In case of a lack of federal regulation concerning a legal matter the federal court may apply state law. If federal law, regarding the criminal procedure, conflicts with state procedural law and claims applicability[400], it preempts state law in proceedings in federal courts, even when the claim is based on state law, which could occur in diversity jurisdiction cases[401]. After all the "Supremacy Clause" of Article VI U.S. Constitution determines that federal law overrides state law. This rule is relevant in the case that a behavior meets the legal facts of a state offense and such of a federal offense likewise. Given that

395 Hay, The Law of the United States, 2010, p. 57.

396 Hay, The Law of the United States, 2010, pp. 54, 55.

397 "Serious" in this context surely refers to crimes punished with one year imprisonment and above in a federal prison, fine or death penalty (felonies). However, the Supreme Court has stated that any crime punishable by imprisonment in excess of six months triggers the right to a jury trial, irrespective of the sentence eventually imposed. (Blanton v. North Las Vegas, 489 US 538, 109 S. Ct. 1289, 103 L. Ed. 2d 550 (1989); for further information see Duncan v. Louisiana, 391 US 145, 161, 88 S, Ct. 1444, 20 L. Ed. 2d 491 (1967).

398 Dubber, Einführung in das US-amerikanische Strafrecht, 2005, p. 6.

399 Trüg, Lösungskonvergenzen trotz Systemdivergenzen im deutschen und US-amerikanischen Strafverfahren, 2003, p. 50.

400 Applicability in this case is given when uniform treatment of an issue is needed.

401 Hay, The Law of the United States, p. 58.

the federal law is made in pursuance of the Constitution, the "Supremacy Clause" comes into effect whenever state law and the law of the federal government differ from each other. Even though there are several criminal laws which the federal government may use to punish crimes, federal courts do not often play a role in the prosecution of crimes. The majority of the criminal proceedings are conducted in the states[402].

3.4.2. State Matters

State courts have criminal jurisdiction over all claims regarding criminal law. This means that a claim which arises under federal law may be brought to a state court, as well as it may be brought to a federal court[403]. The jurisdiction of the state court depends on the territory where the crime was committed or where it produced effect[404].

3.4.2.1. State Courts

Like in every sector of the U.S. governmental regime, the arrangement of legal power of the states mirrors that of the federal handling. So state law – in general – provides for three levels of courts[405], just as the federal government does, even though it is not constitutionally demanded for either one. For the first instance, there are lower courts which mainly decide over misdemeanors[406], which are crimes punishable not above one year of imprisonment[407]. On the same level there are higher courts which function as a first instance for felonies and more serious crimes.

The next instance provides the intermediate appellate court, which reviews the decisions of the lower courts[408].

The highest court is a constitutional court of the respective state, mirroring the federal Supreme Court[409].

3.4.2.2. Applicable State Law

States have their own statutory, procedural and common law which they apply. If a claim arises under federal law, the respective state court decides the case within its concurrent jurisdiction by applying its own legal rules. State procedural law derives from the federal Constitution, state statutes and the state Rules of Procedure, state Rules of Appellate Procedure and the special rules promulgated for criminal legal procedures. It usually regulates formalities

402 Only 1 – 3% of offenses are brought to federal court, cf. Trüg, Lösungskonvergenzen trotz Systemdivergenzen im deutschen und US-amerikanischen Strafverfahren, 2003, pp. 33, 34; Gerstenfeld, Hate Crimes, 2004, p. 13.

403 Hay, The Law of the United States, p. 60.

404 Hay, The Law of the United States, p. 300.

405 Hay, The Law of the United States, 2010, p. 59.

406 Trüg, Lösungskonvergenzen trotz Systemdivergenzen im deutschen und US-amerikanischen Strafverfahren, 2003, p. 37.

407 Dubber, Einführung in das US-amerikanische Strafrecht, 2005, p. 6.

408 Trüg, Lösungskonvergenzen trotz Systemdivergenzen im deutschen und US-amerikanischen Strafverfahren, 2003, p. 37.

409 Hay, The Law of the United States, 2010, p. 59.

as time limitations, organizations of trials and so on[410]. Many states have adopted rules based on the federal example. As in a federal court, state courts provide jury trials for serious crimes. The task of the jury, as in a federal proceeding is to pass the verdict of guilt. If the defendant is found guilty on all or some charges, the sentencing procedure which follows is usually performed by the judge. However, in some states this is taken over by the jury as well, in contrast to the norm[411]. Thus, the main goal of U.S.s of reducing the risk of the abuse of governmental power becomes even more evident[412].

Each state has its own appellate courts; a federal court does not review decisions of state courts. As an exception to the strict separation of the federal and state judicial branch, state courts are bound by decisions of the U.S. Supreme Court which interprets the particular federal rule at issue. As a consequence, state courts must interpret their corresponding legislation in the same, "federal", constitutional way. The compliance of this demand must somehow be supervised. This is done by the U.S. Supreme Court. Thus it becomes apparent that state courts may in principle be overruled by a federal court. However, this is possible through the Supreme Court only, which has an exceptional position. As a rule of thumb it must be said that if a claim arises under state law and the parties do not have diverse citizenships, federal courts are not competent to decide the case. There are two main sources of cases coming before a federal court: "federal question" jurisdiction, and "diversity" jurisdiction, apart from those, state courts in principally handle the criminal case until up to a certain instance. The Supreme Court – as a federal court – functions as an appellate court for all courts of the United States of America[413]. In case of the Supreme Court functioning as a court of first instance, which could happen if a "writ of certiorari" would be conceded[414], the competence of the Supreme Court interferes with the principle of exclusive state competence regarding criminal trials.

3.4.3. Summary

Corresponding to the two sets of law there are two sets of courts: state and federal.

State courts have jurisdiction over criminal trials. Since the courts of each state are independent and sovereign from courts of other states and from federal courts, each state court applies its individual statutory law and moreover produces its own common law, which in the field of criminal law emerges from judicial interpretation of rules. So every state court has access to its own state-based set of law and consequently it decides the pending case. If the claim

410 Hay, The Law of the United States, p. 55.

411 Kamisar/LaFave/Israel/King, 1999, p. 30.

412 Trüg, Lösungskonvergenzen trotz Systemdivergenzen im deutschen und US-amerikanischen Strafverfahren, 2003, p. 57.

413 The Supreme Court functions as an appellate court for state courts, for instance, regarding the legal question concerning the habeas corpus-remedy. (Hay, The Law of the United States, p. 342).

414 If a legal question is of major importance for the whole nation, the U.S. Supreme Court would take the case for adjudication, regardless if the claim arises under state law or federal law. (Will, Das Common Law in: David/Grasmann, Einführung in die großen Rechtssysteme der Gegenwart, 1988, pp. 522, 523).

arises under federal law, federal courts have jurisdiction over criminal matters in addition to the basic competence of state courts. Besides, federal courts have concurrent jurisdiction with state courts in state law cases, if the relevant parties are from diverse states or nations ("diversity jurisdiction")[415].

According to the Supremacy Clause of the U.S. Constitution, federal law overrules state law due to the fact that states are bound to decisional law of the U.S. Supreme Court. Other than that, when it comes to common law, federal courts inferior to the Supreme Court must apply the specific case law of the respective state in the case of diverse jurisdiction.

C. The German Legal System

The law in Germany is based upon the law of the ancient Romans. Therefore, a brief introduction to the coalescence of German and Roman law is provided, which forms the basic understandings and regulations in German jurisprudence in every field of law.

1. The Roman - Germanic Law System

Roman law, once created by the Romans, an Italian tribe[416], and Germanic law, which due to the invasion of Germanic peoples was brought into the Roman Empire, forms the basis of the apprehension of law in Germany[417].

Both demographic groups, the Romans and the Germans, who were located in one territory when they converged with each other and thus, near the end of the 15th century, the territory was not only "named" the Holy Roman Empire of the German Nation but also "understood" as such[418], so that consequently both legal systems (which were separate until then) coalesced[419], building the Roman – Germanic law. This law forms a basis not only for present-day German law, but also for legal systems all over continental Europe. Yet Roman – Germanic law is the fundamental component of laws today, not the existing law in present-day societies. From the formation of Roman – Germanic law back then to the form which the law is effective in Germany today, there has been a long process of change. Legal ideas of other legal concepts, adoptions and enhancements over time[420] led to several different legal formations of the initial legal concept of the Roman - Germanic people. Since the different legal opinions throughout Europe derive their origin from the law of the Roman – Germanic people, those systems due to the mentioned alterations necessarily do not have the same legal orders, but these legal orders are related to each other due to their common root. Due to this common denominator of legal orders throughout Europe, and even in other parts of the

415 Hay, The Law of the United States, 2010, p. 60.
416 Tilch/Arloth, Deutsches Rechts – Lexikon, Vol. 3, 2001, p. 3584.
417 Garner, Black's Law Dictionary, 2008, 9th edition, p. 1355.
418 Kotulla, Deutsche Verfassungsgeschichte, 2008, p. 7.
419 Müller-Gugenberger, Die römisch-germanische Rechtsfamilie, in: David/Grasmann, Einführung in die großen Rechtssysteme der Gegenwart, 1988, p. 83.
420 Müller-Gugenberger, Die römisch-germanische Rechtsfamilie, in: David/Grasmann, Einführung in die großen Rechtssysteme der Gegenwart, 1988, p. 79.

world[421], Roman – Germanic law is not just left to describe the historical legal concept of Italy, but it serves as a legal family[422].

If one wants to describe Roman – Germanic law today from the viewpoint of a German jurist stressing the signification for German jurisprudence, one can say it is a "construct developed through European sciences, which provides jurists a frame, a legal vocabulary and, most of a all, a method to help find the most just solution"[423].

1.1. Origin and Development of Roman – Germanic Law in Germany

Roman law is an ancient cultural artifact of high rank[424]. Nevertheless, it is of importance in the present-day because of its historical impact on existing regulations. Although, due to its alterations, Roman law in its original form has come to an end in Germany, the Roman legal mindset continues to have an effect on legal norms today[425].

Roman – Germanic law emerged in continental Europe, where it still has its central area of validity nowadays[426]. In the late Middle Age the process of adopting Roman law in Germany began, which caused a wide field of present-day law to be of Roman descent[427]. Thus not only does the German legal system have its roots in Roman law, but its legislation today is also strongly influenced by rules created by Romans back in the days. This statement especially refers to the field of civil law. Hence, a lot of today's effective regulations are understandable and therefore correctly applicable due to the understanding of the historical Roman conception of law. Yet, the basic concept of the Roman conception of law not only refers to the area of civil law, but affects the basic approach of law in general.

What constitutes the concept of Roman – Germanic law and so unifies the discipline of the Roman – Germanic legal system[428] is the way of understanding a legal norm and thereby the handling of law. The goal of jurists belonging to Roman – Germanic legal families is to arrange the legal togetherness of people among a society with the lowest possible number of regulations as accurately as possible. This occurs from the fact that real life

---

421 Africa, parts of Asia and even parts of the United States of America have legal systems which are part of the Roman-Germanic family. A few parts of the United States of America, namely: Louisiana, Quebec and Puerto Rico, which once were under foreign (Spanish or French) supremacy, belong to the legal family of Roman-Germanic law. (Müller-Gugenberger, Die römisch-germanische Rechtsfamilie, in: David/Grasmann, Einführung in die großen Rechtssysteme der Gegenwart, 1988, p. 121).

422 Refer to the meaning of the term "legal family" in the prior chapter, Chapter 2, B., 1.The Common law System. (For further information view Müller-Gugenberger, Die römisch-germanische Rechtsfamilie, in: David/Grasmann, Einführung in die großen Rechtssysteme der Gegenwart, 1988, pp. 79 et seqq.).

423 Own translation of: Müller-Gugenberger, Die römisch-germanische Rechtsfamilie, in: David/Grasmann, Einführung in die großen Rechtssysteme der Gegenwart, 1988, p. 91.

424 Söllner, Einführung in die römische Rechtsgeschichte, 1996, p. 13.

425 Söllner, Einführung in die römische Rechtsgeschichte, 1996, p. 13.

426 Müller-Gugenberger, Die römisch-germanische Rechtsfamilie, in: David/Grasmann, Einführung in die großen Rechtssysteme der Gegenwart, 1988, pp. 81, 82.

427 Söllner, Einführung in die römische Rechtsgeschichte, 1996, p. 13.

428 Enneccerus/Nipperday, § 30 I: "The full rules of law. The law governs the human community by commandments, prohibitions, and grants."; Grasmann, Die römisch-germanische Rechtsfamilie, in: David/Grasmann, Einführung in die großen Rechtssysteme der Gegenwart, 1988, pp. 145 et seq.

brings a multitude of indefinable possible situations and thus problems which, if they should be legally subsumed, either result in a confusing quantity of norms, or lead to a special system which encompasses such with a restricted number of rules. In choosing a system of subsumption, the necessary result is a certain measure of abstraction[429]. A certain degree of abstraction demands even more for sane principles and regulations in order to capture the matter of subject. Therefore, the Roman – Germanic legal systems have a common technique to handle law; this technique is based on the developed specific mindset regarding the sense of a rule. Such is based on the idea that one rule must fit a variety of legal problems. Therefore, the understanding of a legal rule is abstract and detached from a particular case. Without any relation to a specific occurrence a rule is designed to capture a particular problem in a variety of formations; thus by isolating concrete circumstances a varying kind of manifestations are able to be compromised. Since, according to this, one rule fits a multitude of situations, such must be construed[430] in order to get the true sense of it in regard to the particular aim and ascertain if it fits the concrete case in question. The interpretation of a rule requires a juridical armamentarium and the mastery of the recognized legal technique of construal. This refers to the requirement of knowledge regarding accepted legal interpretation methods[431], the knowledge of how to imply the legal context surrounding the respective norm in a code[432], the inclusion of definitions in combination with ways of consulting the spirit of the law, and more[433]. Overall, there is a generally accepted approach in order to find out if an abstract norm fits a concrete case, and such has to be mastered by every application of German law. The applicability of this approach requires a particular arrangement of rules in a code in reference to their subject matter, because such is based on the inclusion of the settings of a relevant norm; only with regard to this ordering it is possible to conceive the full meaning of a rule and to subsume a concrete case under an abstract legal devise. By following this juridical recognized approach, any legal expert must be able to solve a legal case on his own, just by finding the relevant rule combined with the application of his legal tools of the trade. From this, it is clear that the decision of one court does not make a precedent binding if the same questioned issue arises again. Every court, like every lawyer, may work out its own judgment by consulting and applying the correct norm, and thus come to his own decision; but, if the norm and the techniques are applied properly, in relation to the same problem everyone has to come up with the same legal decision. This,

429 Will, Das Common Law, in: Rene/Grasmann, Einführung in die großen Rechtssysteme der Gegen-wart, 1988, pp. 431-542 (476).

430 In the German opinion every legal rule requires to be construed in order to be applied. The reason for construal is the need of clarification in regard to the meaning of a rule concerning a specific case and thereby also detect whether a rule needs to be adapted due to changed societal needs or altered legal opinions. (Cf. Wessels/Beulke, Strafrecht AT, p. 15).

431 Larenz, Methodenlehre der Rechtswissenschaft, 1991, pp. 312-360.

432 Sometimes legal devices attain their meaning and their constitutive legal effect only due the connection with other legal norms, therefore an application of such a norm without regard to further norms concerning the particular context is impossible. (Cf. Larenz, Methodenlehre der Rechtswissenschaft, 191, p. 257; Bierling, Juristische Prinzipienlehre, p. 222; Somló, Juristische Grundlehre, p. 186).

433 For further information cf. Larenz, Methodenlehre der Rechtswissenschaft, 1991, pp. 312-360.

basically, makes the institution of a doctrine such as stare decisis redundant. In practice, however, the problem of conflicting judgments exists nonetheless. To ensure the consistency of jurisprudence, or to prevent different judgments, there are special provisions in the code for court proceedings that regulate how to proceed in the case of irreconcilable judgments[434].

It is however clear that even though judgments of courts do not force binding precedents, a certain bond of future decisions to spoken sentences occurs[435]. But this is no more than the consideration of general expert opinion regarding the law on the point[436].

This particular application of the law dissociates the Roman-Germanic legal families from other legal systems and the common law system respectively. In Roman – Germanic law a norm is traditionally understood by itself by applying the technique of construal, whereas in common law, where a norm exists to decide a concrete case[437]. The meaning derives from the content which a court assigns to such, thus the norm derives the meaning in reference to a concrete case. Consequently according to the German understanding a legal norm is generally binding, not viewed in connection to one specific case, but in regard to the abstract characteristics which are listed in the norm. If a concrete case fits the abstract statement of facts which are described in the norm, a court must examine by construing the legal prerequisites of the relevant norm.

The reason for the distinct understanding of a norm in the Common and the Roman-Germanic Legal family relates to its distinct way of incurrence. The specific, now German, technique of how to understand a rule in its full meaning and the way of how to establish a connection between a concrete case and an abstract norm emerged through the centuries – long[438] scholarly activity of universities[439]. In the scope of sciences, it was the task of universities to develop regulations which fit into the properly organized society and which existence comes naturally due to its logical fairness[440]. The proof of scientific achievement regarding the legal scholarship resulted in the creation of a code[441]. A code contains the acquisitions of legal schools. It presents their educationally developed law in a summarized depictive representation[442].

434 Gerichtsverfassungsgesetz (GVG) - Courts Constitution Act - is the name of the code in which regulations are established to regulate court proceedings in case of conflicting judgments (view Section 132 Courts Constitution Act).

435 Buckland/Mc Nair/Lawson, Roman & Common law, 1952, p. 9.

436 The consultation of an expert is followed by taking verdicts of higher courts into account and, as a lower court, orientate towards their decisions.

437 Grasmann, Die römisch-germanische Rechtsfamilie, in: David/Grasmann, Einführung in die großen Rechtssysteme der Gegenwart, 1988, p. 146.

438 From the thirteenth until the nineteenths century legal principles were defined by universities. (Grasmann, Die römisch-germanische Rechtsfamilie, in: David/Grasmann, Einführung in die großen Rechtssysteme der Gegenwart, 1988, p. 213).

439 Grasmann, Die römisch-germanische Rechtsfamilie, in: David/Grasmann, Einführung in die großen Rechtssysteme der Gegenwart, 1988, p. 213.

440 Müller-Gugenberger Die römisch-germanische Rechtsfamilie, in: David/Grasmann, Einführung in die großen Rechtssysteme der Gegenwart, 1988, p. 91.

441 Müller-Gugenberger, Die römisch-germanische Rechtsfamilie, in: David/Grasmann, Einführung in die großen Rechtssysteme der Gegenwart, 1988, p. 110.

442 Grasmann, Die römisch-germanische Rechtsfamilie, in: David/Grasmann, Einführung in die großen Rechtssysteme der Gegenwart, 1988, p. 213.

Thus, by codifying this source of legal knowledge, the achievements were made available to the practice. Simultaneously, with the publication of a code not only were the implemented rules provided to everyone, who was occupied with law, yet actually not being part of an actual scholarship program; but by the systematic organization of the law in such a code, a technique for a special way of applying law was provided. As a result courts were actually able to make use of the maturely and soundly created knowledge[443]. In the process, the law of academics was transformed into (practicable, thus applicable) positive law[444]. The scientific achievements and (until then only) theoretical principles, were realized to solve real life problems. For the record, with courts applying academically made law, the law of the society was to date determined by legal schools. From the moment when codes were introduced into the legal public[445] the code took over the place, which until then was the task of universities: it provided the law. Setting this studious (scholarly) Law in comparison to the judge-made law of the United States, it shows why the law is developed in abstract through savant masters: to provide comprehensive, generally applicable methods to solve legal problems[446].

A legal unity of the revived Roman-derived law existed in Europe far into the modern period[447]. Not until the launch of codifications the legal development began to part from each other[448]. Along with the advantages of a code came the disadvantage that law became star and stiff. One thought a code provides the faculty of reason for all times, with the result that universities stopped developing law and searching for better legal solutions. They switched from their role as research scientists to just representing the actual state, i.e. the status quo of the law and how it is being applied[449].

1.2. Roman - Germanic Law in Germany as of today

Today the aging of the Codes soothes the strict law positivism[450]. One knows about the importance of the task of science and the importance of judicial

443 Müller-Gugenberger, Die römisch-germanische Rechtsfamilie, in: David/Grasmann, Einführung in die großen Rechtssysteme der Gegenwart, 1988, pp. 110, 111.

444 Müller-Gugenberger, Die römisch-germanische Rechtsfamilie, in: David/Grasmann, Einführung in die großen Rechtssysteme der Gegenwart, 1988, p. 110.

445 This was at the time of the 19/20. Century: In France after the French Revolution 1789, in Prussia with the release of the Prussian Civil Code of 1794, in Austria with the launch of the Austrian General Civil Code in 1811 (Müller-Gugenberger, Die römisch-germanische Rechtsfamilie, in: David/Grasmann, Einführung in die großen Rechtssysteme der Gegenwart, 1988, pp. 111; 113, 114).

446 In the United States the respective judge at trial did not aim at solving a problem in general, but at solving his specific case only. While sole "decision-collecting" , without the development of overriding principles for the conception of a superior relation in order to gain independence from the concrete case, could never provide an abstract method equal to the German procedure, this would have been essentially superfluous, since the common lawyer has his own operating principles incorporating the relevant case to fit his specific problem - namely, those arising from the doctrine of stare decisis. Thus, the American jurisprudence developed a juristic method without previous university research.

447 Söllner, Einführung in die römische Rechtsgeschichte, 1996, p. 14.

448 Söllner, Einführung in die römische Rechtsgeschichte, 1996, p. 14.

449 Müller-Gugenberger, Die römisch-germanische Rechtsfamilie, in: David/ Grasmann, Einführung in die großen Rechtssysteme der Gegenwart, 1988, p. 112.

450 Translated from the German: "Gesetzespositivismus". (Müller-Gugenberger, Die römisch-germanische Rechtsfamilie, in: David/Grasmann, Einführung in die großen Rechtssysteme der Gegenwart, 1988, p. 114).

implementation when it comes to creating and developing law[451]. Even in the field of criminal law, in which the basic principle of legitimacy seems to justify a stronger binding to a once-enacted law, growing judgment and discretion is allowed, especially when it comes to imposition of sanctions and their enforcement[452]. The adaptability in the field of criminal law is illustrated by the fact that there have been not less than four huge reformations of the entire criminal law since 1970[453].

Nowadays, the task of law and those who are concerned with jurisprudence is to concretize the prevailing ideas of justice of the people and realize such within their society[454]. Obviously, the development of new law, which becomes necessary due to the constant adjustment to social needs, can only be achieved by observing the developments of mindsets not only in the respective society, but of foreign countries by the help of comparative law[455]. The modern way of legislature does not stick to the once codified ideal[456]. Instead of a code which regulates all legal questions finally, the legislature creates new laws solving individual problems of communal life[457]. Such laws which are created for a certain period of time, thus not for the eternity, leave gaps, which have to be completed by jurists. Since, in contrast to common law systems, these gaps should not be completed by decisional law. It requires that everyone who is concerned with legal handlings bethink oneself of the systematic and the conception of law, which itself guarantees the legal certainty and with that finally constitutionality[458]. The systematic and dogmatic, which are therefore necessary, have been mainly developed in Roman law[459]. Since the Romans knew about the necessary incompleteness of legal norms[460], the delivery of methodical instruments corresponding to this matter took place as well. Even nowadays the Sections 6 and 7 AGBGB[461] mention the legitimacy of

---

451 Müller-Gugenberger, Die römisch-germanische Rechtsfamilie, in: David/Grasmann, Einführung in die großen Rechtssysteme der Gegenwart, 1988, p. 114.

452 Müller-Gugenberger, Die römisch-germanische Rechtsfamilie, in: David/Grasmann, Einführung in die großen Rechtssysteme der Gegenwart, 1988, p. 114.

453 In the years of 1970 and 1998 the 3rd – 6th reform of criminal law were implemented.

454 Müller-Gugenberger, Die römisch-germanische Rechtsfamilie, in: David/Grasmann, Einführung in die großen Rechtssysteme der Gegenwart, 1988, p. 115.

455 Müller-Gugenberger, Die römisch-germanische Rechtsfamilie, in: David/Grasmann, Einführung in die großen Rechtssysteme der Gegenwart, 1988, p. 115.

456 Söllner, Einführung in die römische Rechtsgeschichte, 1996, p. 13.

457 Söllner, Einführung in die römische Rechtsgeschichte, 1996, p. 13.

458 Söllner, Einführung in die römische Rechtsgeschichte, 1996, p. 13.

459 Söllner, Einführung in die römische Rechtsgeschichte, 1996, p. 13.

460 Cicero, de inventione 2, 151: multis in legibus multa praeterita esse, quaw idcirco praeteita nemo arbitetur quod ex ceteris, de quibus scriptum est, intellegi possint. (Honsell, Römisches Recht, 2010, p. 14).

461 AGBGB = Ausführungsgesetz zum BGB = Implementation Act to the German Civil Code. Basically, in the area of substantive criminal law an analogy to the detriment of the accused may not be imposed. The analogous application of existing law usually applies when a legal regulatory gap occurs during the application of law. Such may occur if a circumstance was not considered by the legislature when establishing the law. While in other areas of the law (e.g., in the are of civil law) this gap may be closed by the meaningful and purpose-related appliance of another legal rule, which in regard to its content and its policy fits the legal issue, such would be a breach of the constitutional rights of the accused (a breach of Article 2, Section 1 Basic Law). Accordingly, the analogous application of rules for these cases constitutes a recognized legal method of law-application due to the German dogmatic; yet, in the area of criminal law, the analogous application of a rule must not lead to the detriment of the accused. The analogy-ban derives from the principle of "nulla poena sine" (which stipulates that no punishment may be imposed without law) and is further enshrined in Article 103, Section 2 Basic Law, and in Section 1 Penal Code (which reads:

analogy[462], due to which – as long as the analogy is in harmony with the Constitution – a norm is able to provide answers for cases to which it does not explicitly refer to. Overall, Roman law is described as a feature of an especially good method to accomplish practical problems, thus an especial legal technique[463] which guides the manner of the German legal approach in every juridical situation.

Today, lawyers are challenged by correctly fulfilling the requirements of this legal technique; especially when it comes to adjusting the law and creating new law when societal needs requires such. The balance between strict obedience to once-created norms by simultaneously respecting the spirit of a law must be mastered. This emanates from the fact that once created, a rule requires strict obedience in every single aspect. This causes an extreme formalism and an anxious, strictly speaking pedantic bond to the word. This bond is also found in the construction of law[464], whereby a rabulistic interpretation of words is sought[465]. The anxious adherence to the word in principle benefits the legal circumvention[466]. Such is identified if one complies with the words of a norm, but at the same time bypasses the spirit of the norm[467]. In the end, both a strict obedience to the word and the spirit of the law, must be accomplishable. These are the challenges of today's German legislators when enacting new law. The task is to keep up the once represented idea of abstractness of a legal rule and continuing the system of subsumption by following an elaborated legal technique. In order to master this goal, one has to meet the challenge of finding the optimal degree of generalization of a norm, and at the same time not to stick to thoughtless legal positivism[468]. In the present-day the law in Germany derives from legal norms which were enacted by the competent legislator. But in reference to the science regarding the source of law[469], it is recognized that finding the law is a task which has to be fulfilled by all legal experts and thus all legal departments together[470].

2. The German Constitution

The Constitution of Germany, named 'Grundgesetz', has been effective since May 23, 1949[471]. The term "Constitution" refers to the same meaning in

"An act may only be punished if criminal liability had been established by law before the act was committed"). Therefore, as a method "analogy" is legitimately accepted within criminal law as well, but only if its application is for the beneficiary of the accused.

462 Cicero, de inventione 2, 151: multis in legibus multa praeterita esse, quaw idcirco praeteita nemo arbitetur quod ex ceteris, de quibus scriptum est, intellegi possint. (Honsell, Römisches Recht, 2010, p. 14).

463 Söllner, Einführung in die römische Rechtsgeschichte, 1996, p. 13.

464 Further information cf. Honsell, Römisches Recht, 2010, p. 10.

465 Further information cf. Honsell, Römisches Recht, 2010, p. 11.

466 Honsell in: 1. Festschrift Kaser, 1976, p. 111 et seqq.; Honsell, Römisches Recht, 2010, p. 11.

467 Honsell in: 1. Festschrift Kaser, 1976, p. 111 et seqq.; Honsell, Römisches Recht, 2010, p. 11.

468 Article 20, Section III Basic Law.

469 "Rechtsquellenlehre".

470 Grasmann, Die römisch-germanische Rechtsfamilie, II. Titel, in: David/Grasmann, Einführung in die großen Rechtssysteme der Gegenwart, 1988, p. 220.

471 It is controversial whether the German Constitution came into effect at the end of the day of its promulgation (Mai, 23rd 12 o'clock p.m.) or with the start of the day subsequent to its promulgation (Mai, 24th 12 o'clock a.m.). For the opinion Mai, 23rd cf. BVerfGE 2, 237, 258; 4, 331, 341; Jauering, JZ 1989,

Germany as it does in the United States of America, which is the understanding of Constitution as the legal fundamental order of a society[472]. This understanding of Constitution makes it easy to follow the German choice of words naming their Constitution "Basic Law". To avoid conceptual confusions, one has to be aware that the description "Basic Law" is used in Germany as a byword for "Constitution", so applied synonymously in this approach, even though the official German term for "Constitution" is "Basic Law". Usually one speaks of the "Basic Law of the Federal Republic of Germany" when referring to the German Constitution. The German Basic Law comprises the form of legal organization of German society, including its political structure and attached to this, the administration of governmental power and the relations to its subject[473]. If referring to the relation between the administration of governmental power and the thereby affected parties, who are the citizens of the respective government, the interest quickly diverts to the 'Grundrechte' (Basic Rights), expressly speaking, to the fundamental rights of citizens, which are part of the German Constitution in a similar way as they are part of the Constitution in the United States of America ("Bill of Rights").

2.1. Structure and Form of the German Constitution

Germany is a federal, democratic republic with a president as representative at the head of government. Whereas Germany (the "old" Federal Republic of Germany) consisted of eleven federal states, in the present day it consists of sixteen federal states, because the five eastern states, hereinafter labeled as GDR[474], which before formed a sovereign state and were affiliated to the Russian federation, rejoined the German nation in October 3, 1990. As a consequence thereof, the Constitution, which is valid today, encompasses entire Germany[475]. When speaking of the time before the reunification of the eastern and the western part of Germany, one refers to the "old" Federal Republic of Germany which comprised eleven states, only the western part of Germany. These eleven states were affiliated to the three victorious powers England, France and the United States, whose military governors presented the Minister-Presidents of each of the eleven states on January 1, 1948 three documents[476], whose contents laid the foundation of today's German Constitution[477]. The first document contained the relevant sources for forming a federal democratic nation out of the German government by providing elementary principles which the German nation must implement in their

615 et seqq. For the opposite view refer to the commentary literature regarding Article 145 Basic Law. With the accession of the former German Democratic Republic (GDR/East Germany) on the 3rd of October 1990 the German Constitution came into force in this acceding territory. Particular questions, esp. such concerning the approximations of laws, were answered in the Unification treaty of August, 31st 1990. Due to constitutional amendment of Article 146 Basic Law, the Constitution from then on applied to the entire German people. (Cf. Degenhart, Staatsrecht I, Staatsorganisationsrecht, 2010, p. 7).

472 Kotulla, Deutsche Verfassungseschichte, 2008, p. 1.

473 Kotulla, Deutsche Verfassungseschichte, 2008, p. 1.

474 GDR as for German Democratic Republic.

475 Since the reunion on October 3rd in 1990 both parts of Germany are in the Constitution of the entire German people.

476 Referred to as "Frankfurter Dokumente".

477 Maurer, Staatsrecht I, 2009, p. 79.

governmental, political and legal structure. *Maurer* mentions three basic declarations relevant to the enactment of the present-day German Constitution: The Minister – Presidents of the states had to call a meeting to enact a Constitution until the January 9, 1948. For the Constitution to be enacted it had to be a democratic Constitution; implementing the principle of federalism by providing a considerable amount of sovereignty to the states by also creating a central authority and implementing the guarantee of basic rights and freedom to its people[478]. Finally it refers to the commencement of this future Constitution by determining that its legitimacy requires the approval of the governors of the military powers and of a majority of the people in at least two-thirds of the states[479].

With a number of alterations, especially regarding the direct approval through the German people[480], the Constitution in the old Federal Republic of Germany, referred to as FGR, was formed.

The German Constitution begins with a preamble which, in the way of an introduction, paves the way for the following principles. It states that the Constitution is based on the will of its society; refers to the responsibility towards god; formulates the goal of being an equal part of Europe and serving the peace in the entire world; mentions the unity of (east and west) Germany[481] and finally determines the area of its validity[482].

The preamble is followed by what is called "Bill of Rights" in the U.S. Constitution, but what is called basic rights in German language use, such are understood as fundamental rights for the defense of citizens against their government, moreover referred to in the sense of basic rights for the entitlement to governmental benefits and as rights of the individual citizen to participate in governmental activity[483]. Most democratic Constitutions choose to contain a catalogue of fundamental rights of the nation's citizens, because thereby, not only is the relation between the government to its citizens and to the economy determined, but moreover is the basis for a government set[484].

The next part consists of provisions which are called 'basic – rights – alike' rights, followed by the last part, which is a huge complex containing provisions regarding the polity of the German nation in all of its aspects.

The basic rights are organized in Article 1 – 19, while the 'basic – rights – alike' provisions are scattered all over the Constitution (Articles 20, 33, 38, 101, 103,

---

478 Content of 'Frankfurter Dokumente'; Maurer, Staatsrecht I, 2009, p. 79.
479 Maurer, Staatsrecht I, 2009, pp. 79, 80.
480 The German Minister-Presidents had chosen that instead of the people, the state parliament was to elect the organs for the meeting to create the Constitution; moreover they decided that the state parliament also was the relevant organ to give the required approval to the once created Constitution; instead of letting the people approve it directly. (Maurer, Staatsrecht I, 2009, p. 80).
481 At the time when the Constitution was enacted (1949), the preamble contained two goals, the second was the goal of the reunion of both German parts to one. In 1990, when this goal was achieved, the preamble was changed to only one state goal: the goal of being an equal part of Europe and serving the peace in the entire world.
482 Maurer, Staatsrecht I, 2009, pp. 129-133.
483 Hufen, Staatsrecht II, 2011, pp. 51 et seqq.
484 Maurer, Staatsrecht I, 2009, p. 134.

104 Basic Law). The law concerning the polity of the German nation is determined in Article 20 and the following; containing general provisions in Article 20 – 29 and Article 34, and the organization of the German territory, named as law of internal organization, is set in Article 38 until 69, by defining the relation between the federal government in proportion to the states on the one hand (Article 30 – 32, 35 – 37, Articles 70 et seq.), and marking down the individual competences of the particular governmental departments in relation to each other on the other hand. In conjunction with each other, all these Articles imply the inviolability of the human dignity; ensuring it, because all governmental powers are bound to the constitutionally determined basic rights and the constitutional law in general, and further through the accurate definition of basic structural principles, such as constitutional democracy, republic, federalism and welfare state, which constitutes the German governmental organization. Finally the Constitution provides rules for the case that a state of defense occurs. It ends with temporary and closing provisions[485].

The German appreciation of "Constitution" agrees with the understanding of Constitution as the fundamental law of the nation[486]. It provides the conditions which must be stringently complied with by all constituent parts of the nation; expressly speaking, of all governmental departments and the people. Because an all over compliance with the Constitution is a must, the nation is organized and therefore able to function as a government. The Constitution, functioning as the basic law for all German people, requires extra explanation, since at the time of its formation; it served only the western part of Germany. In 1947, as it turned out that the four victorious powers, Soviet Union, England, France and the United States, could not achieve a consensus about the future of Germany, a division of Germany was decided[487]. Because of this, the part later named GDR was separated from the rest of Germany. The Constitution formed in the western part of Germany and therefore only took effect in the old FGR. But at the time of its enactment it provided an easy extension to the separated parts of Germany, thus to the former GDR. Therefore, the Constitution was prepared for the eventuality of the reunion of all German parts (Article 23 Section 2 Basic Law old version), which was aimed at all times[488]. On the 3rd of October 1990, the GDR and the old FRG were reunited and became the Federal Republic of Germany, after the GDR submitted the necessary declaration of enrollment and the old FRG provided their assent to the extension of their Constitution to the joining parts[489]. Since then, the Constitution of 1949 – its alterations notwithstanding – is the highest ranking

485 Maurer, Staatsrecht I, 2009, pp. 133, 134.

486 Maurer states that "the majority of the German people accepts the constitution of 1949 as the fundamental legal order of Germany". (Cf. Maurer, Staatsrecht I, 2010, p. 85).

487 Decision of the four victorious powers, including the Benelux states (Belgium, Netherlands, and Luxembourg). Maurer, Staatsrecht I, 2010, p. 79.

488 The German separation was from the beginning on and always seen as a temporary state, the goal was to achieve back the unity of the German nation. (Cf. Maurer, Staatsrecht I, 2010, p. 80).

489 For the unification of the two parts of Germany the Unification Treaty was contracted between the GDR and the old FRG, which contained the substantial provisions necessary for the governmental unity. (Maurer, Staatsrecht I, 2010, pp. 102; 99 et seqq.).

law in Germany. Superior law always supersedes lower-ranking law. This applies to all law, e.g. statutory norms, legal decrees, regulations under public law - in descending order - must comply with the Constitution; as it is the case in the United States of America. This provision is fulfilled by the compliance of the precept that each lower-ranking norm must comply with the next superior norm[490], causing – in case every norm is correctly enacted - a complete chain of constitutionality traceable through all levels of law.

2.2. Separation of Powers

Whereas the structuring of democracy is diverse throughout different societies, the German way of embodiment is similar to that of the United States, considering that a separation of power is implemented to ensure the just handling of all involved parties that have some sort of power, and therefore to minimize any abuse of power[491]. Despite the general implementation of the principle of a separation of powers on the vertical and the horizontal level, and the therefore mentioned "matchableness" of both societies, the realization of this principle took place differently in Germany from how it did in the United States. While, as stated in the discussion of the system of the United States, the American society chose a presidential system, the German system, in contrast, is a parliamentary democracy[492]. The result is that both systems have the same power separation on the vertical level, with its constitutional organs of legislative, executive and judiciary, and the same separation on the horizontal level, which contains elements of federalism. Yet the particular institutions on the vertical level are hardly comparable to each other[493], nor is the federalism as strongly marked in Germany as it is in the United States[494].

The separation of power is implemented on the horizontal level by a strict separation between the legislative, the executive and the judicative branch. Among the three branches, the lawmaker (legislative organ) has precedence; the judiciary and the executive departments solely ensure the proper execution of the law[495].

Germany is a federal commonwealth (Article 20, Section I Basic Law), which means that Germany as a nation is formed by sixteen states, which - sovereign from each other - in their entirety form the federal government. The

490 Avenarius, Die Rechtsordnung der Bundesrepublik Deutschland, 2001, p. 9.

491 "The democracy that is established by the German Basic Law, is a constitutional democracy, and that means especially a power separated democracy in relation to the state organs among each other." (BVerfGE 68, 1 (86)); Schnapp, in: von Münch/Kunig, GG, Art. 20 marginal no. 56 et seq.; Degenhart, Staatsrecht I, 2012, pp. 115 et seqq.

492 Schnapp, in: von Münch/Kunig, GG, Art. 20 marginal no. 18 et seqq. (19).

493 Neither is the U.S. Congress similar with the German Bundestag, nor has the federal President of the United States of America the same function as the German Bundeskanzler.

494 Lösche, Merkmale der Präsidialdemokratie, in: Bundeszentrale für politische Bildung, Informationen zur politischen Bildung, Heft 283, Politisches System der USA, 24.10.2008.

495 The specific order of the distribution and balance of state power, that is to be ensured by the Basic Law, must not be undermined by a falsely understood monism of power in form of a need of approval by the parliament in all areas. (BVerfGE 49, 89 (124 et seqq.). Even the principle of parliamentary responsibility necessarily requires the existence of a core area in which the executive part of the government is responsible. (BVerfGE 67, 100 (139); BVerfGE 68, 1 (86)); Schnapp, in: von Münch/Kunig, GG, Art. 20 marginal no. 61, 65 et seq.; 73 et seqq.

term "sovereign" is to be used restrictively, referring to the fact that such is not absolute; the constituent state's sovereignty is restricted in several areas of law or policies, which therefore are reserved as being outside of a state's control. Since the federal constitution is the highest law of the German nation, all parties are bound to its provisions. Even if it is a federally enacted law, it is beyond dispute that it refers to the single states in same way that it does to the federal state. No differentiation is made within its lines between federal and state in respect to the addressed audience. Therefore, the people must have accepted the federal law as their superior law[496]. The principle of democracy requires the approval of the people, not such of the government of the constituent state, to acknowledge the federal law as the super ordinate law, because it is demanded that the state authority is executed by the people (Article 20, Section II, sentence 1 Basic Law). This percept, though, is only realized indirectly in the German system. "Indirectly" refers to the circumstance that the people, avoiding personal appearance, do not act in person, but they choose representatives, who fulfill their will for them (Article 20, Section II, sentence 2 Basic Law)[497]. These representatives[498] of each state[499] then gave their approval to the nowadays effective federal constitution, and thereby acknowledged it as the highest norm of the German nation, which had a binding effect on all governmental parties as a result, and thus the states. The Constitution, being essentially a federal norm, defines the competence of the individual states in relation to the federal state. With that, the division of powers depends upon whether the federal government takes action to regulate a legal area. While this federal regulation might create the impression, at least from the American point of view, that the federal central authority has too much power, the distribution becomes acceptable, when consulting the borders of Article 79, Section III Basic Law, due to which no law can be constitutionally passed without the participation of the states[500]. Although the states have already contributed to the creation of the Constitution, their participation must continue in every future federal lawmaking.

---

496 Acceptance of the people in democratic societies usually refers to a "democratic majority" which in the case of the German constitution would have been a majority of two third of the people; Cf. "Principle of majority rule". (Maurer, Staatsrecht I, 2010, p. 80 – with referral to the Frankfurter Dokumente, Dokument Nr. 1).

497 The direct will of the people must be implemented by periodically recurring elections and votes (Article 20, Section II, sentence 2 Basic Law; BVerfGE 1, 14 (33); BVerfGE 30, 56; BVerfGE 95, 335 (349 et seqq.); These votes must be based on a free process of opinion formation. (BVerfGE 44, 125 (139); BVerfGE 97, 350 (369); BVerfGE 70, 324 (358); BVerfGE 89, 155 (185)); All governmental actions must ultimately find their basis in a decision of the people, they must be based on an uninterrupted chain of democratic legitimacy. (BVerfGE 47, 253; BVerfGE 83, 60 (72 et seq.); Schnapp, in: von Münch/Kunig, GG, Art. 20 marginal no. 23).

498 The representatives elected by the people of a state in their sum constitute the legislative body of the respective state. The legislative body of each state contributed to the enactment of the federal constitution, or at least accepted it. Inherent in this concept of the enactment of the Constitution is its binding force on the member states.

499 The only state which did not approve the today valid constitution on October 8, 1949, the day of its voting, was Bavaria. Despite the refusal, the Bavarian state subjected to the constitution referring to the principle of "democratic majority" (according to which a decision is valid to the entirety if it is failed by a majority of two-third), articled in 144, Section I Basic Law which concerns the approval of the constitution.

500 Degenhart, Staatsrecht I, 2010, p. 177.

Speaking of Germany as a federal state, federalism is understood in the sense of a "cooperative federalism"[501]. The general sense of federalism is the sovereignty of those parts, which in their entirety constitute the country. This as a starting point leads to the aim of reducing the amount of sovereignty for reasons of functionality by keeping up the idea of parts forming a union. So, by basically holding on to the federal organization of the nation one aims at a preferably high amount of cooperation between the constituent states themselves and the federal state[502]. With this idea, one must bear in mind that the respective states do not solely function as purely executive organs of the federal government, which would contradict the federal principle[503], especially since the actual situation in Germany shows that the federal government mainly sets the law, while the respective states are mainly busy with administrative work[504]. Moreover, the Basic Law of Germany demands that the government of each state be bound to the basic democratic principles (Article 28, Section I sentence1 Basic Law), consequently, the states are only able to shape their own governmental order within these federal defined limits[505]. However, the statehood of each of the German states is constitutionally guaranteed[506], thus they are authorized to build their own governmental institutions on every horizontal level[507]. As a result each state has its own governmental institutions in concurrence to the institutions of the federal state; as in opposite to the system of the United States where each state has its own governmental institutions parallel to the ones of the federal state. The relation between the distribution of authority between the states and the federal government in Germany is determined in Article 30 Basic Law. It shall be deemed that the administration of government is in the authority of the constituent states, as long as the Constitution does not explicitly mention federal competence to a subject matter. This rule is repeated in Article 70 Basic Law specifically for the legislative branch, Article 83 Basic Law revisits this principle for the executive branch and Article 95 Basic Law does so for the judicative branch[508]. The fact that lawmaking in the majority takes place on the federal level anyway results from the far reaching powers which are given to the federal government.

Article 72, Section III Basic Law – and the precept of Article 31 Basic Law which demands that in the case of diversions of state regulation and federal

---

501 Tilch/Arloth, Deutsches Rechtslexikon, Band 1, 2001, p. 1655 "Förderalismus".

502 Tilch/Arloth, Deutsches Rechtslexikon, Band 1, 2001, p. 1655 "Förderalismus" with further references to Kisker, Kooperation im Bundesstaat, 1971.

503 Avenarius, Die Rechtsordnung der Bundesrepublik Deutschland, 2001, p. 179; BVerfGE 34, 9, 19 et seq.

504 Degenhart, Staatsrecht I, 2010, p. 178.

505 BVerfGE 60, 175, 208; Degenhart, Staatsrecht I, 2010, p. 178.

506 Article 20 Section I Basic Law refers to the federal organization of the German nation, while Article 79, Section III Basic Law guarantees the constancy of this purpose. (Cf. Degenhart, Staatsrecht I, 2010, p. 179).

507 The states all have the same status, this applies in relation to each other and to the federal government. BVerfG 1, 299 (315); BVerfG 12, 205 (255).

508 Degenhart, Staatsrecht I, 2010, p. 178.

regulations, the federal rule outdo the state rule[509], supports the lawmaking of the federal government.

2.3. Constitutional Powers

The principle of power separation demands a separation between the three known branches. However, nothing is said about how this separation is implemented within a government. The power vested not only in one organ but in several, led to the formation of, in generalized terms, four constitutional powers at the federal level, the states mirroring this setup one-on-one.

On the federal level[510] the legislative power to begin with is the Bundestag (Congress), which is the federal legislative branch. As mentioned above, the federal government must integrate the legislative branches of each state when forming new federal law[511]. This precept is realized through the creation of another federal legislative department referred to as Bundesrat (Federal Council/ Assembly), which despite the fact that it is a federal institution, consists solely of the representatives of the states[512]. Both institutions work together when federal law is to be created.

The executive branch is the *Bundesregierung* (Federal Government) and all administrative agencies are under the federal authority.

Speaking of the President of the United States as the executive branch, it must be mentioned that Germany does have the institution of a President as well, but with a very different function. The President in Germany can only be carefully counted to the squad of constitutional powers[513]. He mainly has a representative function, like representing the German nation in the world (Article 59 Section I Basic Law). Aside from other functions, which cannot be discussed in detail here, he must approve every law which enactment is aimed at by the federal government. As stated, the institutions of each of the respective states mirror those of the federal government, of course, with exception of the '*Bundesrat*'. The position of the federal president is taken by the governor of each state[514].

2.4. Summary

Due to the limited - when set in comparison with the U.S. - extent of federalism in Germany the states and the federal government almost seem to be coalesced with each other. The advantage of this strong bond is a huge amount of homogeneity in all entities, which again benefits to consistency and thus stability of a nation, which after all is a unity.

---

509 Ipsen, Staatsrecht I, 2011, p. 196.
510 For further information refer to: Maurer, Staatsrecht I, 2010, p. 373 et seqq.; Degenhart, Staatsrecht I, 2010, p. 232; Ipsen, Staatsrecht I, 2011, pp. 63 et seqq.
511 BVerfG 1, 299 (315); "cooperative federalism" - Sachs, GG, Art. 20, marginal no. 58.
512 Sachs, GG, Art. 20, marginal no. 61.
513 "The German Basic Law equipped the president solely with few direct constitutional competences." Cf. Degenhart, Staatsrecht I, 2010, p. 293.
514 For further information, refer to: Avenarius, Die Rechtsordnung der Bundesrepublik Deutschland, 2001, p. 51.

3. German Criminal Law

Criminal law, as it is effective in Germany today, is distinguished between substantive criminal law, which regulates the requirements for punishment and its consequences, and criminal procedural law, which deals with the inquiry and sentencing of punishable acts, thus with the imposition of the norms of substantive criminal law and the law regarding the execution of sentence, which serves the enforcement of the criminal verdict[515].

3.1. Constitutional Base of Criminal Law

The right of the legislator to punish is codified in Article 74, Section 1 Basic Law. The here determined fact of criminal law being a part of the concurrent legislative power reveals that the existence of a legal punishment is constitutionally presumed[516]. However, nothing is said about how behavior must be in order for it to be legitimately punished by the legislator. With that, it is referred to the question of the substantial content of criminal relevant behavior[517]. This answer is sought by taking the task of criminal law into account, which in Germany is understood to be the subsidiary protection of legal goods[518]. The premise that a criminal norm must always aim at protecting a legal good, serves a criminology criterion to the legislator for what to punish[519].

The formal basis of criminal law in the German Basic Law is provided in Article 103, Section II Basic Law, which demands that only a written law is able to constitute a crime and legitimate punishability. In the same way that Article I, Section 9 of the U.S. Constitution prohibits "ex post facto law", thus retroactive legislation or even individualized sentencing regulation, Article 103, Section II Basic Law lays the foundation for substantive criminal law in Germany[520]. As seen above[521], the entire criminal investigation proceedings up to and including the criminal trial itself are established in the U.S. Constitution in order to control governmental intervention at the constitutional level. Since the Constitution is not only the provider, but also the conservator of the civil rights, the placement of such regulations within the Constitution seems to be the appropriate place for establishment. Unlike in the United States, the German Basic Law does not provide any detailed regulations and provisions of how to lawfully proceed if someone is incriminated of an offense. Germany is a written law country and therewith the respective legal Code shall present its law as a unified whole, containing both general and abstract rules and principles which can be applied to every legal problem. This character of German law as a code and statute-based legal system reveals itself to its utmost in the sector of

515 Avenarius, Die Rechtsordnung der Bundesrepublik Deutnschland, 2001, p. 157.
516 Roxin, Strafrecht AT I, p. 13, § 2, marginal no. 1.
517 Zipf, 1980, pp. 106 et seqq.; Roxin, Strafrecht AT I, p. 13, § 2, marginal no.1.
518 Roxin, Strafrecht AT I, p. 13, 14, § 2, marginal no. 1.
519 View hereto: Chapter 2, D., 2.1. Content of the German Legal Good Theory and Chapter 2, D., 2.2. Result of a Critical Understanding of the Legal Good Theory.
520 The latin policy of "nullum crimen, nulla poena sine lege scripta", thus the principle of legality, refers to any democratic society, although the way of implementation might differ from society to society.
521 Cf. Chapter 2, B., 2. The U.S. Constitution.

criminal law. Consequently, the Penal Code must contain any legal fact which constitutes a crime, in order to legally determine a behavior as criminally relevant. This requirement results from Article 103 Basic Law and its doctrine of nulla poena sine lege[522]. In accordance with the traditional division[523], Criminal Law is separated from Public Law. Nevertheless, Public Law[524], in the sense of Constitutional Law and Basic Rights, has a strong effect on German Criminal Law and its code. In the German opinion the Constitution sets the frame of all law, including criminal law, and surely provides and therefore secures the fundamental rights. Yet, the true structuring of the relationship between the state and its citizen is made by subconstitutional law. In Germany, the formal elevation of fundamental criminal maxims towards the constitutional level is not deemed to be necessary; yet the substantial foundations are set in the Basic Law. From this it follows that elementary laws referring to the criminal procedure, such as investigation proceedings, court handlings and the final imposition of sentence, as opposed to the U.S. constitutional arrangement, are not established in the German Basic Law, but are enacted within an extra code, the Code of Criminal Procedure[525]. This law, for instance, demands that similar to Article I, Section 9 U.S. Constitution, a criminal prosecution can only take place if someone has been criminally charged by a public prosecutor[526]. Remarkably, the German criminal trial does not provide the institution of a jury. Compensating the principle of the autonomy of the court, the judge and his decisional power are expressly held up high. The idea of civilians without any sort of judicial knowledge and understanding being able to decide prior to the start of a main trial if such must takes place or not, and even are appointed to pass a verdict at the end of a trial seems utterly misguided. Therefore, the judge in Germany is the only one authorized to pass the verdict and adjudicate sentence, as opposed to an American trial, where the judge generally is competent to solely assess and pronounce the sentence, according to what the jury has previously decided. However, Penal Courts in Germany are frequently courts of lay assessors. A court of lay assessors is a court in which volunteer judges do jury service, which is the case if a lower court (Amtsgericht) deals with criminal proceedings where it is about the imposition of a penalty of up to four years imprisonment and in the trial chambers at the higher District Courts (Landgerichte). I.e., the judge is not responsible as an individual for the decision, but he shares the decision-making power with the volunteer judges, these are honorary judges who participate independently and are equipped with the same voting rights as the professional judge at trial. They fully judge over the guilt or wrong of an accused person and bear the same responsibility for the passed sentence as

522 "No penalty without law" – this principle is repeated in Section1 Penal Code.

523 Public Law, Civil (Private) Law, Criminal Law.

524 Constitutional Law, Basic Right and also General and Particular Administrative Law are summarized under the term Public Law, due to the common fact that the addressee of the Code is the government.

525 "Strafprozessordnung" (StPO).

526 Section 152 Criminal Trial Law.

the professional judges[527]. Either way, all these regulations are not set in the German Basic Law, but since concerning the criminal trial, are established in the German Criminal Code of Criminal Procedure/Trial Code (StPO). However, the civil rights in connection with the basic principle of legality in Article 103 Basic Law constitutionally influence the German criminal law. Since all law must be compliant with the Constitution, and the German Basic Law in principle establishes inviolable civil rights and thereby sets the frame for criminal law, the German way of stating provisions regarding the criminal procedure as subconstitutional law, instead of listing it in the Constitution, does not serve any cause for concern. Regardless of the level of establishment, both societies, Germany and the United States, follow similar, strict, fundamental, codified principles in criminal prosecution. Whenever dealings regarding legal issues are uncertain and an answer cannot be found in the German Criminal Law, one refers to the Constitution and its Basic Rights. Summarized, the sources of German criminal law primarily lie in the Penal Code, but such, after all is subject to the German Federal Constitution of 1949 and its various legal rules[528] as well as constitutional principles[529], as Article 20, Section 3 Basic Law states, the legislature shall be bound by the constitutional order, whereas the judiciary is bound by law and justice[530]. Case law[531], as well as legal science[532], does have a great impact on the application of the precepts of the Penal Code. Even though they are not binding, in the end, German criminal law is influenced by all three separate sources. Wheras the German legal system is not bound by precedents like common law[533], previous decisions of higher courts are observed and considered in practice anyway.

The primary source of sentencing is the German Penal Code. Such is divided into a general and a special part; the general part states basic principles, e.g. principles of criminal liability and culpability; mitigating and aggravating factors which apply to all offenses; the territory of validity of the criminal law; the doctrine of crime and its legal consequences, etc. The German way of applicating law takes place correlating the provisions stated in the general part to the norms established in the special part. The German tradition of legal abstractness asks for the establishment of such a general part in a code as a

---

527 The legal basis for courts of assessors can be found in Sections 30 et seqq. Judiciary Act (GGV), Section 44 German Judiciary Act (Deutsches Richtergesetz).

528 In particular: Art. 103, Section 2 Basic Law (nulla poena sine lege); Art. 102 Basic Law (abolition of capital punishment); Art. 46, Section 1 Basic Law (indemnity of Member of Parliament).

529 For instance, the principle of culpability; the constitutional principle of proportionality; moreover, the legislative, executive and the judicial branch must respect the constitutional guaranteed Civil Rights of every citizens (Article 1, Section 1-3 in connection with Articles 2 – 19 Basic Law).

530 Krey, Deutsches Strafrecht, Vol. I, p. 129; marginal no. 153.

531 Apart from Section 31, paragraph 1 BVerfGE and several other exceptional rules, there is no binding case law in Germany (Article 20, Section 3 Basic Law); but judicial verdicts are of importance to all legal fields, so also to the courts. (Krey, Deutsches Strafrecht, Vol. I, p. 129; marginal no. 155).

532 A typical German criminal law phenomenon is the mutual recognition of criminal scholars and court decisions. Legal science has a strong influence on case law; particularly the BGH orientates itself by publications of legal scholars, whereas the latter orientates itself by decisions of the Supreme Court. (Krey, Deutsches Strafrecht, Vol. I, p. 131; marginal no. 156).

533 View hereto: Chapter 2, D., 3.4. Competence and Jurisdiction of Criminal Courts. This chapter presents the Federal Supreme Court and the precepts of its decisions for future judicial handlings.

prefix, which provides leading principles and general concepts relating to the following norms[534]. The special part of the German Penal Code contains specific criminal offenses (murder, assault, larceny, etc.), arranged according to the protected legal good, for instance, into categories as offenses against life or physical health, offenses against property, offenses against the environment and so on, and thereby set the general frame of punishment according to the respective wrong of the offense.

3.2. Legislative Competence and Institution

Just as the U.S., Germany is a federal republic. Federalism in Germany and in the U.S. includes the federalist element of an unity of many politically independent entities. These political entities are called states in the United States and "Länder"[535] in Germany. The division of legislative powers between a national government on the one hand, and its constituent states, on the other, is implemented by the former being a government of enumerated powers, while the latter are governments of residual powers. The direct operation, of each of these centers of government takes place for the most part in their own assigned sphere and takes effect upon all persons and property within the respective territorial limits. The supremacy of the national government is in force in the case of conflicting state power[536]. In as much as all these elements are equally realized in both societies, the provision - as it is effective in the American system, stating that each center must be equipped with the complete apparatus of law enforcement (legislative, executive and judicial department) - does not fully apply to the German federal system. As mentioned above, Germany implemented a "cooperative federalism"[537]. From this it follows that the German system does not have a parallel panel through the entire apparatus of law enforcement in the way the American system has. The system according the legislative responsibilities is better described as a system of concurrent panel, in which the states compete with the federal government. If the national government regulates a field of law, in most cases, the states are not authorized to release norms any longer. At first sight, the distribution of legislative powers of the federal government (*Bund*) and its constituent states (*Länder*) as stated in Article 70 Basic Law empowers the state to enact law. According to Article 70, Section I Basic Law the federal government may only take over state powers and pass laws, if the Basic Law expressly permits for such. In fact though, most of the legislative responsibilities lie with the federal government, so that in practice of the majority of lawmaking takes place on the federal level[538]. This is due to Article 70 Section 2 Basic Law which reveals the true distribution of power in the field

534 E.g., view the principle of culpability in German Criminal law, established in Sections 19 et seqq. Penal Code, determines cases in which the defendant is not legally blameworthy for a committed crime. Since these precepts apply regardless of the nature of the crime to any offender, they are arranged in the general part und thus are valid for all offenses codified in the special part.

535 The German wording "Länder" is translated into "states" in the following.

536 Corwin, Constitution of the United States of America, 1952, Federalism, p. XI.

537 Badura, Staatsrecht, 2010, p. 399.

538 Degenhart, Staatsrecht I Staatsorganisationsrecht, p. 67.

of lawmaking, by leading the focus towards the requirements of Articles 71-74 Basic Law. Thereafter it is to demarcate between the exclusive federal authority to enact law (Articles 71, 73 Basic Law)[539] and the concurrent authority[540]. As the designation implies, in the areas of exclusive legislation (Article 73 Basic Law), the federal lawmaker is the only legal organ which is competent to promulgate law. According to those subject matters which are stated in Article 74 Basic Law the states are authorized to enact law as long as the national government does not make use of its power to do so[541]. However, the federal legislator did enact law for the area of criminal law in accordance with Article 74 Basic Law; consequently the states are no longer authorized to enact criminal norms. In the example of criminal law, it can be shown that Germany is not as pervaded by federalism as the United States is. Due to the existence of areas of concurrent legislation, the German order requires a norm like Article 74, Section I, No. 1 Basic Law, which states that the competence to enact law lies within the states unless the federal government takes action. Due to an enhanced sovereignty of the states, thus a missing establishment of concurrent legislative competence, this norm has no counterpart in the United States[542]. When the federal government of Germany releases criminal law it is binding on the entire nation. There is one code in Germany, which provides the substantive criminal law for the entire country. Thus it is equally effective for the federal government and the states. The same applies for the federally enacted criminal procedural law. Since there is only one code[543] providing the law for all, such problems as conflicting laws do not exist in Germany. Questions which occur in the United States, whether the government is competent to enact hate crime legislation despite that the states have the power to enact criminal law, in consequence, are not relevant in Germany.

---

539 Exclusive legislative jurisdiction means that the federal government has the exclusive right to make laws. The states in this case, have the power to enact law only if they are expressly authorized by federal law (Article 71 Basic Law).

540 In the area of concurrent legislative power of the federal government (Article 72 Basic Law), the state may only enact law to the extent to which the federal government did not exercise its legislative powers. The criminal law, for example, is an area of concurrent legislation. Article 74 Basic Law lists the areas which fall under the concurrent legislative jurisdiction of the federal government. (Detterbeck, Oeffentliches Recht, p. 56, marginal no. 138 et seqq.).

541 There are three situations in which the federal government can make use of the concurrent legislative competence: Basically, the federal government can act without the need of additional conditions being met (Article 72, Section 1 Basic Law). In certain areas the federal government has the right to legislate, but only if and insofar as the establishment of equal living conditions throughout the federal territory or the maintenance of legal or economic unity requires a federal regulation (Article 72, Section 2 Basic Law - "necessity clause"). In the third aspect, finally, the Federal Government does have the legislative power, but the states have a deviation of competence (Article 72, Section Basic Law); Detterbeck, Oeffentliches. Recht, p. 55, marginal no. 135 et seqq.

542 Trüg, Lösungskonvergenzen trotz Systemdivergenzen im deutschen und US-amerikanischen Strafverfahren, 2003, p. 32.

543 The statement of Germany having one code, which provides the entire criminal legislation for the country refers to the main penal code (Strafgesetzbuch) only. Such provides the basic substantial criminal law, thus the "main" criminal law. However, there are several criminal law statutes in addition to those stated in the German penal code. So called side-criminal regulations (medical criminal law, environmental criminal law, etc.) are established in various codes, but are negligible with respect to this topic. Criminal procedural law is established in an own code (Strafprozessordnung) which deals with the legal proceedings of criminal lawsuits.

A bisectioning into federal and state matters, as it took place in regard to the American presentation, is not required in the following.

3.3. Competence and Jurisdiction of Criminal Courts

Whereas there is one Penal Code in force, and therefore the problem of conflicting state and territorial criminal laws does not exist, the problem of diverse jurisdiction could occur anyway. This even more depends on whether there is only one proper channel for criminal procedures.

Germany's territory is divided in twenty-four districts. Each of the sixteen states is subdivided in several districts, the number depends on its size. Each district provides an own appellate tribunal for criminal trials. The normal channel of a criminal trial starts with a claim arising under a state court. Therefore, a criminal trial, in simplified terms, starts with a suit at the "*Amtsgericht*", which is the lowest ranking court in Germany for criminal trials, and which is addressed in cases where a sentence is not to exceed four years of imprisonment. The next higher court, the court of appeal is the "*Landgericht*", followed by the highest regional court, the "*Oberlandesgericht*" [544]. Contrary to this normal channel, where the "*Landgericht*" functions as an appellate court for several lower courts[545] of first instance, namely for the "*Amtsgerichte*", and the "Oberlandesgericht" serve as the appellate tribunal for the "*Landesgericht*", the "*Landesgericht*" itself and even the "*Oberlandesgericht*" may function as entry-point for a lawsuit, depending on the seriousness of the crime. Whereas until this level of appeal the jurisdiction has been a purely state based jurisdiction, the highest appellate court is a federal court, the Federal Supreme Court[546], settled in Karlsruhe. So there is parallel jurisdiction on the state level, after all each state provides its own stages of appeal, but the final authority is a joint federal facility. In contrast to the American criminal trial there is no parallelism between the jurisdiction of federal courts and state courts.

German criminal courts primarily operate under state authority, but because of the supreme jurisdiction being subordinate to the federal government, and state courts also uniformly apply federal law, court decisions can not drift apart too far. Since in case of appeal, the final verdict may be passed by a federal court, such sets nationwide even construal measures for the future and thereby promotes homophonous standards across the states due to the fact that the lower state courts will orientate themselves towards the determinations and precepts published by the pronounced decision[547]. The Federal Supreme Court is not to be equated with the Constitutional Supreme Court. Although both are located in Karlsruhe, they have different functions

544 "Oberlandesgericht" is the highest Court of Appeal under state authority. Depending on the number of districts per state, a state may have one or more "Oberlandesgericht(e)".

545 Only in one case ("Landgericht I" for "Amtsgericht Muenchen") it occurs that one Court of Appeal (Landgericht) functions as appellate court for just one lower court, usually one Court of Appeal serves as an appellate court for several "Amtsgerichte".

546 "Bundesgerichtshof".

547 Unlike to the stare decisis doctrine of the U.S. jurisprudence, the measures set in the Supreme Court decisions do not have a binding effect on the decisions of lower courts in the future, but the precepts which led to such decisions are adopted and adjusted to the individual case, however enable reasoned deviation.

and thus are different courts. The here addressed Federal Supreme Court is the highest federal court in civil and criminal matters. It serves as an appeal[548] and a revisal[549] court at the same time. Whether it has jurisdiction as an appellate court or as a revisal court depends on the individual case, on the matter in dispute and on the previous courts which dealt with the case. The Federal Constitutional Court in contrast decides a case, if legal questions arise directly from the Constitution and its Basic Right catalogue. Its jurisdiction is independent of any judicial appeal stages, it is, a limited jurisdiction court which is extracted from the normal channel. Its task is to watch over the constitutionality of governmental actions and it therefore ensures that the legal measure of a public agency, a law or a judgment does not violate any constitutional precepts.

3.4. Manifestation of Criminal Law

The structure of crime according to German criminal law is tripartite: The act of the offender, the unlawfulness/illegality of the committed act, and the culpability of the offender manifested in the act. The "act" and the "unlawfulness" of the offense constitute the penalized wrong of the behavior, whereas "culpability" refers to the liability of the offender for the concrete realized wrong. An act is unlawful in the formal sense, if it breaches an effective legal prohibition or commandment[550]. It is substantially unlawful, if a legal good is violated by it in a socially damaging way, which cannot be sufficiently combated by other non-criminal legal devices[551]. Under the valuation aspect of the norm, the substantial wrong presents itself as a violation of a legal good, and the need of the relevant behavior to be legally addressed. The substantial content of wrong therefore has importance not just for the offense type, but also for the unlawfulness of an act[552]. The quantity and the quality of the substantial wrong are moreover crucial for the degree of culpability. If an offender realizes wrong and criminal law constitutes the preventive necessity to prosecute him, the offender must also have burdened himself with guilt. Depending on what function the term 'culpability' refers to, it is to distinguish between the "culpability, which reasons a penalty"[553] and the "culpability, which is relevant in the individual case[554][555]. The "culpability, which reasons a penalty" depends on the committed degree of wrong; such is

548 Within an appeal the entire case is rolled up again and is re-examined with respect to all legal questions.

549 In case of revisal, the Federal Supreme Court must only decide with regard to procedural errors or other errors of law, the case will not be reopened and re-examined.

550 Hörnle, Das Unwerturteil und der Schuldvorwurf, in: Hefendehl, Empirische und dogmatische Fundamente, pp. 105 – 134 (105 et seqq.).

551 Roxin, Strafrecht AT I, p. 602, § 14 B, marginal no. 4.

552 Only if the constituted wrong occurs to be unlawful such shall be punished. "From the point of illegality, the substantive wrong of the violation of a legal good can be excluded in the case when there is a collision between two legal goods and the higher rated legally protected good is preferred to be worthy of protection to the disadvantage of the lower rated good. The substantive illegality allows to graduate the wrong". (cf. Roxin, p. 602, § 14, marginal no. 4 – 6).

553 "Strafbegründungschuld".

554 "Strafzumessungsschuld".

555 Achenbach, Historische und dogmatische Grundlagen der strafrechtssystematischen Schuldlehre, 1974, pp. 2 et seqq.; Lenckner/Eisele, in: Schönke/Schröder, StGB, Vorbem. §§ 13 et seqq. marginal no. 107.

determined by the relevant offense category. Thus the "culpability, which reasons a penalty" embraces guilt as epitome of the subjective premises for imputation, which reasons the imposition of punishment[556]. Considered in connection with the culpability of the individual offender, thus the "culpability, which is relevant in the individual case", enables one to impose the concrete sentence[557]. Therefore, the wrong and the culpability together define the degree of the concrete penalty[558]. Whereas the legislator determines the general penalty frame "relatively" (except for Section 211 Penal Code)[559] by considering the wrong committed and the thereon based general culpability, the concrete penalty - in respect to the individual offender - is to be meted out during the sentencing process of the court. The path how to determine the culpability, which is relevant in the individual case, is shown in general for all offenses in Section 46 Penal Code. Accordingly, a court reasons the concrete degree of penalty which is to be imposed, by starting off within the frame that is provided by the legislator in the codified offense. The facts that are taken into account in accordance with Section 46 Penal Code are the same that were taken into account by the legislator when determining the general penalty frame[560]. The difference is solely that the court considers such concretely, in relation to the case and the individual perpetrator's personality. Insofar culpability is the starting point for imposing a penalty, by asking if one is blameworthy for the wrong committed, and asking if there are any concrete reasons (mitigating circumstances) which exclude (diminish) the criminal liability[561].

3.4.1. Enhancing Criminal Penalties according to German Criminal Law Doctrine

As mentioned, the threat of punishment in German norms is determined "relatively", by setting up the range of punishment, the law determines the maximum - and the minimum limit and therewith serves the points for orientation in sentencing[562]. For the average case, the middle of the range of punishment is to be imposed as the concrete sentence[563]. In other cases, they are to be aligned in reference to the concrete degree of wrong - and culpability of the offender[564]. The maximum degree of punishment comes into

556 Roxin, Strafrecht AT I, p. 876, § 19, marginal no. 54; Lenckner/Eisele, in: Schönke/Schröder, StGB, Vorbem. §§ 13 et seqq., marginal no. 111.

557 Roxin, Strafrecht AT I, p. 877, § 19, marginal no. 54.

558 Roxin, Strafrecht AT I, p. 603, § 14, marginal no. 7.

559 "Relatively" means that the law predetermines a frame of penalty within which the judge assesses the concrete penalty for the individual case.

560 Stree/Kinzig, in: Schönke/ Schröder, StGB, Vorbem. §§ 38 et seqq. marginal no. 52.

561 Sections 19 and 20 Penal Code govern reasons for excluding criminal liability. While Section 19 Penal Code negates the criminal responsibility of children under the age of 14, Section 20 Penal Code refers to mental disorders, which lead to the circumstance that the offender was unable to perceive the wrong of his act or to act in accordance with this insight at the time when he committed the act.

562 Stree/Kinzig, in: Schönke/Schröder, StGB, Vorbem. §§ 38 et seqq. marginal no. 42.

563 The average case is not to be euquated with the ruling case, i.e. the repeatedly occuring case. (Fischer, StGB, § 46 marginal no. 17; BGHSt 27 4 with note of Bruns, JR 77, 146).

564 Stree/Kinzig, in: Schönke/Schröder, StGB, Vorbem. §§ 38 et seqq. marginal no. 42.

consideration for acts whose severity level is considered to be at the top of the frame and which the offender committed in full responsibility[565].

The concrete sentence within the limits legally determined by a norm is to be meted out by the judge in an arbitrary decision, according to Section 46 Penal Code as adjudication. The assessment of penalty in Section 46 Penal Code though, is a decision to be made in equity and good conscience, bringing with it all the intricacies which come with personal decision making[566]. Moreover, the possibility of verifying the just imposition of sentence through a higher court is restricted[567]. It can be reviewed considering the misuse of discretionary power, but not according to justness of the decision[568]. This must be taken into account when arguing in support of a general penalty enhancement for certain aims or motives of the offender, but favoring such to be implemented within the actual forming of Section 46 Penal Code.

On various occasions, the legislator constricts the breadth of judicial discretionary power by adding aggravating or mitigating circumstances to an offense[569]. These are circumstances which usually would play a role in the process of determining the correct sentence through the judge. The determination of aggravating or mitigating cases applies in various legal modes by statutory law:

3.4.1.1. Aggravated Statute[570]

A new range of punishment may be imposed for an act by final legislative determination, due to adding altering facts towards an already existing law[571]. If one of the cases determined in the norm occurs, the judge must impose the modified sentence. This modification can either change the character of the offense from a misdemeanor to a crime (as for example in: Sections 226, 315 Paragraph 2 Penal Code), change the amount of wrong (Section 244 Penal Code) or change the culpability, or even both[572].

3.4.1.2. Aggravated Ruling Example[573]

With such, the law indicates the most important cases of when to alter a sentence, even though the list is not intended to be exhaustive. These are rules for determining the sentence, but these do not change the statement of facts. If the precepts of a case are fulfilled, the sentence is to be imposed according to the amended sentence. Thus, the judge is able to pass a verdict

565 Stree/Kinzig, in: Schönke/Schröder, StGB, Vorbem. §§ 38 et seqq. marginal no. 42.
566 Bruns, StrZR, pp. 87 et seqq.
567 Section 46, Paragraph 2 Penal Code requires that the court considers the circumstances that weigh for and against the offender. According to Section 267, Paragraph 3, Sentence 1 Code of Criminal Procedure only those facts are to be stated in the verdict which were considered to be decisive for the imposed penalty by the respective court. Therefore, not all sentencing considerations are listed, but only those determined for the judgement. Consequently, only those which are listed in a verdict can be included in the assessment process of evaluating the just of a penalty in a judicial verification process of a court of appeal.
568 BGH VRS 21, 54; Zipf, Strafmaßrevision, pp. 164 et seqq.
569 "Strafschärfungs- und Strafmilderungsgründe".
570 "Qualifizierter Straftatbestand".
571 Sections 224, 244, 250, 260, 315 Paragraph 2 Penal Code.
572 Stree/Kinzig, in: Schönke/Schröder, StGB, Vorbem. §§ 38 et seqq. marginal no. 42a.
573 "Regelbeispiele".

in line with the exemplified case and in accordance enhance the sentence for an offense, though he does not have to. The indicative effect of the circumstances determined in such a norm can be compensated by mitigating circumstances. It is up to the judge at trial to decide on which of the circumstances surrounding the act the focus must be drawn to. Therefore, it is for him to decide himself in which conditions he views the offense to constitute an aggravated case. His position therefore is no different than if the legislator would simply enhance the range of punishment of the base offense[574]. It is important to consider that the classification of an aggravated or privileged [mitigated] case does not have to be quoted in a judgment[575]. An aggravated and mitigated case is reviewed by the next higher court only in regard to the question if the reason which is stated to define an altered case makes sense at all. A verdict would be repealed if it generally fails to provide essential facts or considerations which led to the judgment, and thus lacks justification[576].

3.4.1.3. Transfer of the General Penalty Enhancement Methodology to the matter of Hate Crime

According to German criminal dogmatic there are three recognized possibilities to implement possibly desired sentence enhancements for hate crimes[577]: Possibly a new, independent offense could be enacted, which refers to certain bias-motivated acts. Moreover, one could implement alterations for hate crimes connected to previous established offenses, thus constitute aggravated norms or ruling examples in the special part and place them with the offense in question; further, one could establish a sentence modification in the general part of the Penal Code which, as a prefix, would then be applicable for all those in the special part named offenses.

3.4.2. Classification of Offenses

It is distinguished between a misdemeanor and a crime, depending on the severity of the possible to be imposed punishment[578]. Whether a criminal offense is classified as a felony or as a misdemeanor is determined in an abstract manner, according to the statutory minimum sentence, the punishment actually imposed in the concrete case is irrelevant for the classification. It is important to keep in mind that the mitigation or the aggravation of offenses does not change the nature of the act, categorized as felony or as misdemeanor. Pursuant to Section 12, Paragraph 3 Penal Code, mitigations in less serious cases are irrelevant for classifying the criminal act in question as felony or as misdemeanor; likewise aggravations in extremely serious cases do not “upgrade” a misdemeanor to a felony. The legal relevance of the distinction between felonies and misdemeanors lies in the fact

---

574 Stree/Kinzig, in: Schönke/Schröder, StGB, Vorbem. §§ 38 et seqq. marginal no. 46.

575 Stree/Kinzig, in: Schönke/Schröder, StGB, Vorbem. §§ 38 et seqq. marginal no. 50.

576 Stree/Kinzig, in: Schönke/Schröder, StGB, § 46 marginal no. 65.

577 In regard to the terminology "hate crime" and the concern of hate crime criminal laws refer to: Preface (and the herein contained explanations prior to Chapter 1).

578 According to the severity of the imposed punishment all offenses are divided into crime and misdemeanor, Section 12 StGB. (Wessels/Beulke, Strafrecht AT, p. 7, marginal no. 17).

that the attempt to commit a felony is always punishable, whereas the attempt of commiting a misdemeanor is not. The attempt to commit a misdemeanor only leads to punishment, if the law explicitly provides for such (Section 23, Paragraph 1 Penal Code). The different ways of establishing a criminal offense refers to the fact that the necessary first step of establishing a norm relies on the the legal good which requires protection, while the second step focuses on the direction of attack. A norm must determine how the behavior must be constituted in order to defend the legal good principally worthy of protection against exactly this form of behavior, i.e., it must determined how an act must take place in order for it to be legitimately branded as criminal.

German criminal law differentiates between several offense categories. According to the relation between a punished act and the harmful effect it causes, one distinguishes between result-constituted offenses and non-result-constituted offenses[579].

Based on the damage to the concerned victim, the criminal law differentiates between offense of causing an injury and conduct offenses, which are simply fulfilled by commission. Result-constituted offenses[580] require a measurable damage towards society, which entails a causal connection between the act and the result[581]. This result must be negative, i.e., socially harming; thus leading to an injury of a protected legal good. The objective elements of facts of an offense causing an injury require a causation of harm to the victim, thus the occurrence of a measurable loss of value. In addition, the result must be objectively attributable to the offender as his act.

Non-result-constituted offenses[582] do not require an actual harmful outcome. The punishable wrongdoing is already realized when a person acts in the way it is described and codified in a criminal norm[583]. In other words, regardless of whether an offender has achieved his goal or not through his behavior, the mere act is already punishable by law. Conduct crimes solely require the causation of a situation which endangers the legally protected good[584]. Insofar, concrete and abstract crimes constituted by mere endangerment of legal goods must be distinguished[585]:

Crimes constituted by concrete endangerment of legal goods[586] are result-constituted offenses. The legal elements of these offenses require the existence of a concrete danger to life, limb, property or another legal good of

579 Translated from German: "Erfolgsdelikte/schlichte Tätigkeitsdelikte". (Krey/Esser, Strafrecht AT, marginal no. 218 et seq.; Rönnau, Jus 2010, p. 96; Wessel, AT, p. 7, marginal no. 22).

580 Result-constituted offenses are, for instance: manslaughter (Sections 212, 211 Penal Code; physical assault (Sections 223 et seqq. Penal Code; Section 303 et seq. Penal Code).

581 Wessels/Beulke, Strafrecht AT, p. 8, marginal no. 23; Krey, Deutsches Strafrecht Vol. I Grundlagen/Basics, 2002, p. 151, marginal no. 183.

582 "Schlichte Tätigkeitsdelikte/Gefährdungsdelikte".

583 Krey, Deutsches Strafrecht Vol. I, 2002, p. 151, marginal no. 184; Roxin, Strafrecht AT I, § 10, marginal no. 103; Wessels/Beulke, Strafrecht AT, marginal no. 24. Examples for such offenses are "perjury", established in Section 154 Penal Code; "Driving while under the influence of drink or drugs", established in Section 316 Penal Code.

584 Wessels/Beulke, Strafrecht AT, p. 8, marginal no. 27.

585 Krey, Deutsches Strafrecht Vol. I, 2002, p. 153, marginal no. 186.

586 "Konkrete Gefährdungsdelikte".

the victim[587]. In this respect, a danger is concrete, if the occurrence of damage is probable, according to the circumstances of the case at hand[588]. More precisely: if the respective object of the act (e.g. another human being or another person's property) is in such a threatening situation that it is only a question of coincidence whether or not an actual violation could occur, the situation - causing behavior may constitute an offense[589].

The situation is different in the case of crimes constituted by an abstract endangerment of legal goods: They are mere conduct crimes (non-result constituted offenses). Their legal elements demand neither a violation, nor a concrete endangerment of a legal good. Rather, the legal elements of crimes constituted by abstract endangerment of legal goods are already fulfilled once the legally required conduct (e.g. drunk driving) has been committed[590]. Their typical dangerousness is merely the legislator's motive for the criminalization of such acts[591], not a statutory requirement.

Whenever a norm is enacted, the legislator must determine the legal good, whose protection is the aim, and then establish the offense's variation, by which it seems advisable to acknowledge that the more abstract the protected legal good presents itself, the clearer the prohibited behavior must be determined; thus, the modalities of the act must be clear.

3.5. Sense and Purpose of Penalty according to the German Legal Doctrine

According to the German understanding there is a difference between the question of the legitimacy of penalty and the sense and purpose of punishment[592]. Prior to legitimating a concrete norm, the sense and the purpose of punishment must be determined. Before searching for a legitimate legal good which is protected by the relevant norm, one must ask what is the purpose of penalty[593]. Penal theories provide various possibilities of giving meaning to penalty. Since hate crime laws imply a sentence enhancement, such must be justified as punishment[594].

587 Krey, Deutsches Strafrecht Vol. I, 2002, pp. 155; 157, marginal no. 190.

588 Lackner/Kühl, StGB, § 315c marginal no. 22.

589 Lackner/Kühl, StGB, § 315 c marginal no. 22; Roxin, Strafrecht AT I, § 10, marginal no. 123; Krey, Deutsches Strafrecht Vol. I, 2002, p. 155, marginal no. 187.

590 Drunk driving: Section 316 Penal Code.

591 Roxin, Strafrecht AT I, § 10 marginal no. 123; Wessels/Beulke, Strafrecht AT, marginal no. 29 with further references.

592 Jescheck/Weigend, Lehrbuch des Strafrechts AT, 1996, § 8, p. 66.

593 Jescheck/Weigend, Lehrbuch des Strafrechts AT, 1996, § 8, pp. 66 et seqq.; Roxin, Strafrecht AT I, § 3, pp. 69 et sqq.; Baumann/Weber/Mitsch, Strafrecht AT, § 3, marginal no. 24 et seqq.; Stree/Kinzig, in: Schönke/Schröder, StGB, Vorbem. §§ 38 et seqq.; marginal no. 1 et seqq.

594 In regard to the terminology "hate crime" and the concern of hate crime criminal laws refer to: Preface (and the herein contained explanations prior to Chapter 1).

3.5.1. Absolute Penal Theory

According to the Absolute Penal Theory, punishment has no purpose. It solely serves the retribution of a wrong committed (Retribution Theory)[595]. Punishment is legitimate for the pure reason that a crime has been committed. Only through retribution, expressed as penalty, the social-ethical behavior of the offender is disapproved and justice thereby restored[596]. According to the Absolute Penal Theory a sentence is solely constituted by the wrongdoing committed, the culpability of the offender is not taken into account.

According to this, enhanced or additional penalties for hate crimes would be legitimate, if they constituted a greater wrong compared to the relevant base offense. Yet, the constitutional precepts require that the guilt of the offender is crucial to determine punishment[597]. Considering the formation of the German Penal Code, the consideration of the culpability of the offender is essential for imposing the correct penalty[598]. Consequently, this theory in its pure form does not apply in German criminal law[599].

3.5.2. Relative Penal Theory

Even though the advantage of the Absolute Penal Theory lies in the fact that the penalty is determined in accordance with the committed act, this theory misjudges that the sole orientation towards the past does not contain any value for the future. The modern Relative Theories therefore are orientated preemptively, the main reason for punishment must not lie in the aim of retaliating wrong committed, but to prevent future offenses[600]. In the preventive function of penalty it is distinguished between the function of individual prevention and general prevention.

3.5.2.1. General Prevention Theory

The Theory of General Prevention does not aim at the effects of penalty towards the offender, but to its effects towards the general public, this is considered to take place in two ways, negatively and positively. Basically, according to the idea of general prevention, penalty is imposed on an offender in order to keep the community from committing an act in the punished form. In

---

595 The Theory of Retribution has been elaborated by Immanuel Kant (*1724-†1804); Metaphysik der Sitten, Rechtslehre, third edition, 1919, pp. 158 et seqq.; and Georg Wilhelm Friedrich Hegel (*1770-†1831), Grundlinien der Philosophie des Rechts, 5th edition, 1996, § 99, pp. 158 et seq.

596 This theory is based on the idea of equality of crime and punishment. (Kant; Metaphysik der Sitten, Rechtslehre, 3rd edition, 1919, p. 159; view also: Roxin, Strafrecht AT I, § 3, pp. 71, 72).

597 Article 103, Section 2 Basic Law; For further constitutional provisions in this regard view: Roxin, Strafrecht AT I, § 3, pp. 91 et seqq. (92).

598 Jescheck/Weigend, Lehrbuch des Strafrechts AT, 1996, § 8, pp. 77, 78; The legal determination that the culpability of the offender is the basis for sentencing finds it´s implementation in the German Penal Code in Section 46, Paragraph I.

599 The criminal politically also discussed "atonement theory" aims at compensating the weaknesses of the retribution theory regarding the missing consideration of the culpability by assuming that the perpetrator wants to reconcile with the law through punishment, he thus expiate the crime. Atonement requires culpable commission of a crime and the respective consciousness of the perpetrator in regard to his wrongdoing. (Heinrich, Strafrecht AT I, marginal no. 15). But also this theory has no practical relevance in German criminal law.

600 Jescheck/Weigend, Lehrbuch des Strafrechts AT, 1996, § 8, pp. 71 et seqq.

the Theory of negative General Prevention it is considered that the potential of penal consequences deter unwanted behavior[601]. Therefore, offenses are prevented by the fact that the threat of punishment serves as deterrence for all humans, i.e., the general public, in order not to commit certain behavior[602]. Used positively[603], it is considered that, due to the imposition of punishment on the offender. The sense of right and wrong and the general confidence of the people towards the law of the society is strengthened, because if wrongdoing in a society is punished, the members of society are motivated to observe the law[604]. The confidence in the inviolability of the law, which is won thereby, causes the citizens to behave in a law-abiding manner in general[605]. In summary, it is acknowledged that even though general preventive purposes might detain other offenders from committing a crime. This purpose fails when an offense is committed spontaneously or when the offender decides to commit a crime without evaluating the consequences of his action. Moreover, even an unlimited penalty imposed on an offender could not achieve to prevent all criminal acts. After all, it is not the most strict but the most fair penalty that can function as a "morally-forming power" on the public[606].

Imposing a disproportionate penalty on an offender in order to state a negative general preventional signal to society contradicts the culpability principle codified in the German Penal Code[607] as an expression of the constitutionally guaranteed protection of the dignity of men. Therefore, penalty cannot be based on the purpose of general prevention alone. Enacting increased penalties for hate crimes with the intention of abolishing xenophobic criminal behavior would not be legitimate according to the German Constitution if the penalty is not based on relevant facts from the concrete behavior of the offender and his individual amount of culpability when committing the crime.

3.5.2.2. Specific Prevention Theory

---

601 Stree/Kinzig, in: Schönke/Schröder, StGB, Vorbem. §§ 38 et seqq.; marginal no. 2, 12; Ambos/Steiner, JuS 2001, pp. 9, 12.

602 Such, by the imposition of penalty aimed at "psychological coercion" towards the general public, is considered to deter and thereby educate the people so that they do not commit punished behavior. ("Education through psychological coercion": Roxin, Strafrecht AT I, § 3, pp. 78 et seqq. (80)); The theory of psychological coercion stems from Paul Johann Anselm von Feuerbach (*1775 – †1833): Feuerbach, Lehrbuch des gemeinen in Deutschland gültigen peinlichen Rechts, 1832, § 13, pp. 15 et seq.; Momsen/Rackow, JA 2004, pp. 336 et seqq. (336).

603 The Theory of positive General Prevention does not have a counterpart in the United States in this formation. If it is referred to the variant of integrating the Theory of General Prevention in the American discussion, it is referred to the "Moral Educational Effect of criminal law". (von Hirsch, Der Rechtsgutsbegriff und das "Harm Principle", in: Hefendehl/von Hirsch/Wohlers, Die Rechtsgutstheorie, 2003, p. 13-64, p. 13 with reference to: Andenaes, Punishment and Deterrence, 1974).

604 This refers to the key term "Positive General Prevention" (compare to BVerfGE 45, 187, 256; BVerfGE 2004, 2073, 2075; Stree/Kinzig, in: Schönke/Schröder, StGB, Vorbem. §§ 38 et seqq.; marginal no. 12; Ambos/Steiner, JuS 2001, pp. 9, 12; Heinrich Strafrecht AT I, marginal no. 17; Roxin, Strafrecht AT I, p. 80).

605 Momsen/Rackow, JA 2004, pp. 336 et seqq. (pp. 337, 338).

606 Jescheck/Weigend, Lehrbuch des Strafrechts AT, 1996, § 8, p. 75.

607 The applicable principle in German criminal law "nulla poena sine culpa" determines that no one may be punished for an act if not being blamable for it (culpability principle). The principle of culpability leads to the precept that legal punishment not only presupposes guilt, but also draws on such, it therefore constitutes the basis for the sentence. This finds expression in the law in Sections 19, 20, and 21 Penal Code and is constitutionally enshrined in Article 103, Section 2 Basic Law.

In contrast to the general prevention theory, the theory of individual prevention, at its core, is based on the effects caused by penalty on the individual[608]. This theory focuses purely on the effect of punishment on the individual offender, who - as the central figure of the event - requires the main focus of consideration. Hence, penalty should be imposed to mainly achieve a rehabilitation of the offender, in order for him to lead a non-criminal life in the future; this refers to those offenders who are mendable[609]. Secondly, those offenders, who are not in need of becoming better, shall be deterred from committing punished behavior[610]. Lastly, in cases in which the offender is not mendable, the society may be protected from him by defanging him[611].

This theory in its plain form is criticized as well and is not applied within the German Penal Law because the principle of culpability is neglected. Since the punishment is solely imposed for the betterment of the offender and the protection of society, the concrete criminal act is not considered. Moreover, the intention of social rehabilitation fails for those acts which are committed only once in a specific given situation.

3.5.3. Unification Theories

Since in its pure form none of the above mentioned theories is convincing enough to substantiate the legitimate purpose of punishment, the prevailing view of German legal scholars nowadays considers a fusion of the mentioned aspects[612], which is codified in Section 46 Penal Code[613]. Therefore, the starting point for penalty is the general preventive purpose, i.e., the inhibition of the committal of criminal acts by the general society due to the imposition of punishment. This aspect, pointing towards the protection of the general society, serves the idea of protecting a legal good in order to legitimate penalty in its best. The fact that justice or law succeeds in protecting legal goods is expressed towards the general society[614]. But this aspect alone is not enough to provide a legitimate interpretation and meaning to punishment by

608 The Theory of Specific Deterrence goes back to Franz v. Liszt (*1851-†1919), Der Zweckgedanke im Strafrecht, Vol. I, 1905, pp. 126, 176.

609 Technical term in German: "Positive Spezialprävention".

610 Technical term in German: "Negative Spezialprävention".

611 Momsen/Rackow, JA 2004, pp. 336 et seqq. (p. 338), with reference to: v. Liszt, Strafrechtliche Aufsätze und Vorträge, Erster Band, Berlin 1905 (Reprint Berlin 1970), p. 166.

612 Technical term in German: "Vereinigungstheorie" (Summation of "culpability compensation, prevention, rehabilitation of the offender atonement, retribution... " (Momsen/Rackow, JA 2004, pp. 336 et seqq. (p. 339)); BVerfG NJW, 1977, 1525, 1531; Stree/Kinzig, in: Schönke/Schröder, StGB, Vorbem. §§ 38 et seqq.; marginal no. 20, with further references).

613 Section 46 "Principles of Sentencing" reads: "(1) The guilt of the offender forms the basis for sentencing. The effects of the sentence, which can be expected for the offender's future life in society, shall be taken into account. (2) When sentencing the court shall weigh the circumstances in favor of and against the offender. Consideration shall in particular be given to the motives and aims of the offender; the attitude reflected in the offence and the degree of force of will involved in its commission; the degree of the violation of the offender's duties; the modus operandi and the consequences caused by the offence to the extent that the offender is to blame for them; the offender's past, his personal and financial circumstances; his behavior after committing the offense, particularly his efforts to restitute for the harm caused by him, as well as the offender's efforts to reconciliate with the victim. (3) Circumstances which are already statutory elements of the offense must not be considered."

614 Stree/Kinzig, in: Schönke/Schröder, StGB, Vorbem. §§ 38 et seqq.; marginal no. 2; Roxin, Strafrecht AT I, p. 80.

simultaneously respecting the human dignity of the offender[615]. In addition, the culpability of the offender must be punished only if the confidence of society in the functioning of the law would be destroyed in case the offender is not punished, which is due to the severity of the act.

Therefore, criminal sanctions must be imposed after a careful consideration and only as an instrument of ultima ratio[616], which requires a consideration of all aspects of the individual case, because a penalty serves it's general and individual purposes only if it is just[617].

This requirement of justice is fulfilled if the guilt of the offender is commensurate to the severity of the penalty[618], which is the case if the offender deserves it due to his wrongdoing. An offender deserves an individual penalty if such must be imposed in regard to his concrete wrongdoing and his personal responsibility[619]. Therefore, according to German criminal law, retribution means that "the penalty is an answer towards the guilty wrongdoing and therefore must be just, according to the principle of retributive equity"[620]. After all, the culpability is the starting point for retribution.

The history of German criminal law reveals that the legislator, as well as the court, intends to impose enhanced penalties for general preventive reasons[621]. Meanwhile, it is agreed that a penalty must not exceed the degree of culpability[622]. The culpability principle prohibits imposing a penalty on the offender which exceeds his guilt, for instance, for the reason of general deterrence[623]. Therefore, it is generally agreed that a sentence enhancement for hate crimes can only be implied if it is proportional to the culpability of the offender[624]. The general justification of enhanced sentences for hate crime offenses - as compared to the penalties determined in the relevant base offenses - could be based on the modified gravity of wrongdoing, which results

---

615 The recognition of culpability as a requirement of just punishment derives from Article 1 Basic Law. (BVerfGE 80, 244 (255); BVerfGE 50, 205 (214). Accordingly, the offender is not treated "as a subject in the determinants of legal compulsion, but as an object defined in heteronymous interest" as long as he is punished for the purpose of prevention only and not additionally demand that he gets the punishment he deserves. By the latter the human dignity would become denied. (Köhler, Über den Zusammenhang von Strafrechtsbegründung und Strafzumessung, Erörtert am Beispiel der Generalprävention, 1983, pp. 16, 37, 38, 42; Seehafer, Strafrechtliche Reaktion, 2003, p. 69).

616 The Ultima Ratio Principle of criminal law defines that penal provisions are only legitimate if less restrictive means are not sufficient to protect a legal good. (Wessels/Beulke, Strafrecht AT, marginal no. 9; BVerfGE 90, 145, 172 et seqq.; BVerfGE 39, 1, 47).

617 That is if the penalty is in accordance with the rule of law and the principle of proportionality, which defines that penalty must be appropriate in relation to the severity of an act and to the content of culpability.(BVerfGE 45, 187; 50, 5).

618 BVerfG NJW 93, 3255; BVerfGE 105, 154.

619 Stree/Kinzig, in: Schönke/Schröder, StGB, Vorbem. §§ 38 et seqq.; marginal no. 3.

620 Jescheck/Weigend, Lehrbuch des Strafrechts AT, 1996, p. 66 with reference to: Bockelmann, HWB Soz. W., p. 212.

621 Stree/Kinzig, in: Schönke/Schröder, StGB, Vorbem. §§ 38 et seqq. marginal no. 13.

622 Stree/Kinzig, in: Schönke/Schröder, StGB, Vorbem. §§ 38 et seqq. marginal no. 13; BGH 17 324; NJW 66, 1276.

623 BVerfGE 80, 244 (255); BVerfGE 50, 205 (214).

624 The applicable principle in German criminal law "nulla poena sine culpa" determines that no one may be punished for an act if not being blamable for it (culpability principle). The principle of culpability leads to the precept that legal punishment not only presupposes guilt, but also draws on such, it therefore constitutes the basis for the sentence. Therefore, any penalty must only be imposed if it corresponds to the culpability of the offender in regard to his perpetrated wrong (Article 103, Section 2 Basic Law).

in a severe offense type and/or leads to greater culpability on the part of the hate crime perpetrator in comparison to the perpetrator of the relevant base offense. Thus, the perpetrator of a hate crime may receive an enhanced penalty, if his act reveals an enhanced level of culpability, even though his offense does not constitute a greater degree of wrong than the base offense which is committed by a not hate- or otherwise motivated perpetrator.

In view of the action-directing aspect of punishment, the sense of justice of the community at large must play an important role within the respective normative framework when considering the question of a commensurate penalty, because an undeserved punishment neither creates nor reinforces any general preventive aspect for the purpose of affirming a general sense of right and wrong[625]. Assuming that the general sense of right and wrong of the society at large implies that the perpetrators of hate crimes deserve more severe penalties than the perpetrators of the relevant base offense[626], a respective sentence enhancement fulfills this perception and the general confidence in the justice of law of the society is strengthened. Yet, even though the empirically verifiable sense of justice may aim at a penal aggravation for hate crimes - a penalty may be imposed only if it is appropriate to the culpability of the offender[627], that is if the normative requirements are on hand.

3.5.4. Summary

From a dogmatic view the importance of the wrongdoing is the main aspect for determining the punishment. In the end though, the guilt of the offender defines the concrete sentence. This finding matches the practice implemented in the Penal Code and its legal consequences. The theory of positive general prevention is the prevailing theory acknowledged in German criminal law.

625 Cf. Kunz, ZStW, Vol. 98, (pp. 823-838), p. 832.

626 Assumption based on the U. S. American society due to scientific studies. Findings reveal that the (American) people assume that the perpetrator committing a hate crime deserves an enhanced penalty in comparison to the perpetrator committing the respective parallel crime. Thus, for the public the perpetrator of hate crimes deserves a severe punishment. (Saucier/Brown/Mitchell/Cawman, Effects of Victim's Characteristics on Attitudes Toward Hate Crimes, in: Journal of Interpersonal Violence 21, 2006, pp. 890-909).

627 With this it is referred to the necessary compliance of penal law to the culpability-principle of sentencing, which is set in Article 103, Section 2 Basic Law.

D. Determination of the Legitimate Ambit of Criminal Law in Both Countries

In a democratic society, the binding determination of what is to be punished must be exclusively determined by the legislator[628]. As shown, this is true for the traditionally Common Law - shaped America in the field of criminal law as well. However, this says little about the right of a legislator to establish a specific law. Logically the legislator is only allowed to interfere with the constitutionally guaranteed "liberty rights of an Individual"[629] in a way which upholds these Basic Rights. But the basic question here is not one of the constitutionality of criminal norms in the actual German or American legal system[630] because even if the Constitution gave the legislator the right to establish a certain law, it could be inappropriate for the legislature to exercise its constitutional authority in a certain fashion. In such a case, the legislator would have acted constitutionally but not legitimately. It rather refers to a valid principle of what is to be legitimately punished according to German penal theory compared with the American penal theory. From the – perhaps constitutional – authorization one must distinguish the much more interesting question whether the legislator is justifiably authorized to prohibit certain human acts[631]. Expressly speaking, what opinion is held by German and American jurists regarding the justification of criminal law, and how does the respective currently prevailing penal doctrine justify punishability of a particular criminal norm. The following presents the search for criteria which legitimately constitute state punishment; it is presumed to find the answer to the question of what sorts of conducts may the state rightly make criminal.

The existence of criminal law as such is a potential legal interference into the activity of every citizen. Focusing on statutory prohibitions, whose compliance is enforced with penal sanctions, one can imagine what an immense destructive impact such norms may have on human interests in cases where behavior diverges from the regulatory content stated in the norm. This leads to the question of legitimacy of the existence of a criminal law as such. The fact that the existence of criminal law is reasoned likewise in every liberal-democratic society spares the distinction between Germany and the United States: The fundamentals of the accrual of legally protected interests, legal norms and criminal offenses and thus, the roots of criminal law, lie in the socially and ethnically conditioned moral values of a legal society[632]. Since the interest of a state community in preserving their fundamental values and to safeguard legal peace in their society can only be fulfilled if a legal order

628 Wohlers, Deliktstypen des Präventionsstrafrechts, 2000, p. 213; Worms, Bekenntnisbeschimpfung, p. 79.

629 Schünemann, GA 1995, pp. 201, 213.

630 This results from the fact that the following arguments are addressed to an ideal legislature, not to an ideal Supreme Court. Moreover, according to Feinberg, constitutional statutes may not be legally valid and some legally required statutes may not be constitutional (Feinberg, Harm to others, Vol. 1, p. 4 et seqq.).

631 Roxin, Rechtsgüterschutz als Aufgabe des Strafrechts?, in: Hefendehl, Roland, Empirische und dogmatische Fundamente, pp. 135 – 150 (135).

632 Wessels/Beulke, Strafrecht AT, marginal no. 9; Günther, JuS 1978, 8 et seq.; Kaufmann, JuS 1978, p. 361.

prohibits certain socially harmful behaviors by the threat of punishment, the justification of the existence of criminal law is already implied through its necessity for a thriving and peaceful communal life among human kind[633].

1. Purpose of Criminal Law according to the American Penal Theory

Pursuant to the prevailing U.S. opinion, the "[...] purpose for which power can be rightfully exercised over any member of a civilized community, against his will, is to prevent harm to others"[634]. Accordingly, the purpose of criminal law is to prevent harm to persons other than the actor[635]. The reasoning for penal legislation is the elimination or at least the reduction of harm to citizens. While the prevention of harm refers to the prevailing view of the purpose of criminal law, further possible reasons for sentence are discussed, so that the general answer to the question pertaining to the purpose of law which is held by the American opinion, is the prevention of a certain exterior impact that is damaging or infringing and originates from human behavior. This aim should be achieved by penalizing its triggering incident, which is a certain human act. However, of what nature the exterior impact must be, in order to legitimately punish its triggering behavioral incident, is partly debatable. Nevertheless, the "harm-principle" as the general principle concerning the proper range of criminal law is generally accepted in the U.S. view of criminalization. Thus, the prevailing view in the U.S. regarding the purpose of statutory prohibitions enforced by penal sanctions is the prevention of harm to others.

1.1. Content of the American Penal Theory: Harm Principle

The question of criminalization, referring to the prevailing American opinion, is usually answered by drawing on the Harm Principle[636]. Similar to the legal good doctrine in German penal theory, the Harm Principle[637] serves as an instrument to determine and constrain the legislator's authority to enact criminal norms[638]. The Harm Principle is based on the idea that criminal law is the primary instrumentality for preventing people from harming one another, hence its function is not to prevent harm as such, but to counteract any acts of harming[639]. Herein lays the universal consent in the American opinion: legitimate criminalization must be based on the U.S. appreciation of harm, or at least on the contingency of the occurrence of harm by someone other than the one induced it through his certain behavior. In short, it is legitimate or proper for the state to prohibit conducts that causes harm to someone due to an actor.

---

633 Stree/Kinzig, in: Schönke/Schröder, StGB, Vorbem. §§ 38 et seqq. marginal no. 1; Wessels/Beulke, Strafrecht AT, marginal no. 5; HK-GS-Rössner, Vorbem. § 1 marginal no. 7; Günther JuS 1978, pp. 8 et seqq.

634 Mill, Über die Freiheit, 1988, p. 16; Mill, On Liberty and other Writings, p. 13; Feinberg, Harm to others, Vol. 1, p. 31.

635 Wittig, Rechtsgutstheorie, „Harm Principle“ und die Abgrenzung von Verantwortungsbereichen, in: Hefendehl/v. Hirsch/Wohlers, Die Rechtsgutstheorie, 2003, pp. 239-243 (239).

636 Hirsch, Der Rechtsgutsbegriff und das Harm Principle, GA; 2002, pp. 2-14 (3).

637 Also called "the harm to other principle" (Feinberg, Harm to others, 1984, p. 11).

638 Hirsch, Der Rechtsgutsbegriff und das Harm Principle, GA; 2002, pp. 2-14 (3).

639 Feinberg, Harm to others, p. 31.

1.1.1. Liberty-Limiting Principles

While it is agreed that the Harm Principle is a valid principle for determining the legitimate invasions of liberty and thus a legitimate instrument to constrain and determine the legislator's authority to enact criminal norms, and moreover that this is the leading doctrine in American penal theory, it is controversial whether the "Harm Principle" is the only valid principle[640]. Other reasons discussed for legitimate penalization are the offense-principle, legal paternalism and legal moralism[641]. All these discussed principles have in common their aim of providing reasons for legitimate penalty. These reasons, if found, called "liberty-limiting principles or equivalently coercion-legitimizing principles"[642], are based on the idea of the harm-principle, as they all relate to various negative effects caused by human behavior. While only one of these other reasons for punishability is well-recognized besides the harm-principle, the others are incompatible with the understanding of human dignity according to democratic Constitutions.

1.1.1.1. Offense-Principle

Whereas one opinion argued in effect that the Harm Principle is the only valid principle for determining legitimate invasions of liberty and that no conduct which fails to satisfy these terms can appropriately be made criminal[643], another view states that in addition to the generally agreed upon question that the state is able to legitimately prohibit conducts that cause harm, the offense-principle is to be a valid reason for criminalization as well[644]. As stated, harm as valid reason for prohibiting its triggering behavior is generally accepted, but beside this, it is discussed if "offenses" alone, instead of harm, can be a sufficient reason to punish (its triggering) behavior. Offenses, in this context, are seen as disliked states of mind and therefore as phenomena distinguishable from harm[645]. Therefore, an act should be legitimately punishable, if it is irritating enough to be considered as interference into the right of others (wrongful offensive conduct), and the interests of the one feeling aggrieved are to be considered worth protecting to the disfavor of the actor, which must be figured out by a balancing test[646]. As a result such behavior, which causes unwanted emotions, can be penalized, if these emotions are sufficiently intense, their appearance is common and the act, which causes these feelings, is performed in public in a way which makes it difficult for others to evade it. The reason for penalization of behaviors, which under

640 Feinberg, Harm to others, 1984, pp. 11, 12.
641 Feinberg, Harm to others, 1984, pp. 12 et seqq.
642 Feinberg, Harm to others, 1984, p. 9.
643 Mill, Über die Freiheit, p. 16 et seqq.
644 Feinberg, Harm to others, 1984, p. 14.
645 Feinberg, Vol. 2, pp. 3 et seqq.
646 The key element to make intense annoying behavior a punishable offense is the disrespectful and reckless treatment of others caused by it. If such a treatment takes place, it is further to be evaluated, whether the necessity of a prohibition of such behavior can be stated. This evaluation is made through the balancing-test for which Feinberg provides an instrument, what he calls "Mediating Principles", in which the extent and intensity of the harassment and the possibility of bothered persons to avoid such, plays a role. These principles should enable a categorization of behavior whether it is bothering enough to be criminal relevant and therefore punishable. (Feinberg, The Moral Limits of the Criminal Law, Vol. 2, p. 25 et seqq.).

certain circumstances have the tendency to treat other persons with disrespect and are reckless, therefore does not cause harm, but unwanted emotions of others[647]. If sole disrespect for others serves as a sufficient reason for legitimate criminalization is to be discussed and, however that may be, it is not generally accepted in the U.S. view of legitimate penal law. What seems to be worth keeping in mind, especially concerning the matter of hate crimes discussed here, is that even though a given hurt may not qualify under the criteria to be discussed in the following as harm, and will not therefore warrant preventive coercion under the Harm Principle, it is nevertheless an evil of its own kind, and perhaps in some circumstances a sufficiently serious evil to warrant protective intervention under an alternative principle of criminalization[648]. We can interpret the offense-principle as authorizing legal coercion to prevent "offenses" in the widest possible interpretation of that term, in which it includes offenses proper (e.g. revulsion and disgust), hurts (e.g. "harmless" throbs and pangs), and "others" (e.g. shame and embarrassment). Surely, if "offenses proper" (e.g., those caused by racial slurs) can rightly be punished by the criminal law, then any intense pains that somehow fail to qualify as harms might also be preventable by similar means[649].

1.1.1.2. Legal Paternalism

Other principles are discussed beside the offense principle and the harm-principle, but are declined in the end. A criminal legislation justified by paternalism is not compatible with the autonomy of the individual. A liberal society must not force values relevant for a good life upon its members by state, but must leave it to the particular individual to find his own conception of what is good within the frame set through the freedom of the other citizens[650]. Consequently, every member of society is only responsible towards society for his acts if they affect society. If an act does not concern the society, one's liberty is absolute. This is why in the prevailing American opinion of penal law no one can be punished for doing or not doing something which causes harm (only) to himself[651].

1.1.1.3. Legal Moralism

Comparable with the grounds for the U.S. approval of "legal paternalism", "legal moralism" as a justification for penal legislation is to be scrapped as well. Within this view, it is accepted that a determination of criminal relevant behavior requires drawing on normative considerations[652]. While taking such normative values into account is legitimate for the determination of wrongful harms and wrongful offenses, such cannot be equated with the enforcement of

---

647 Hirsch, The Offense Principle in Criminal Law, King's College Law Review 11 (2000), 78; Simester/v. Hirsch, Rethinking the Offense Principle, Legal Theory 8, 2002, 269.
648 Feinberg, Harm to Others, p. 48.
649 Feinberg, Harm to Others, p. 48.
650 Feinberg, The Moral Limits of the Criminal Law, Vol. 3, pp. 52 et seqq.; 57 et seqq.
651 Mill, Über die Freiheit, p. 16 et seqq.
652 Feinberg, The Moral Limits of the Criminal Law, Vol. 4, pp. 11 et seqq.

specific moral values for their own sake[653]. A person can never be punished by mankind because the prevailing view conceives it would be better for him to act in a certain way. Within a democratic mindset it is nowadays universally agreed that conduct must not be prohibited solely on moral grounds[654].

1.1.1.4. Summary

With the focus lying on the result which might be caused by a certain behavior, all these American opinions have in common that their yardstick for sentencing a certain behavior depends on the (potential) occurrence of an unpleasant circumstance, which is evoked by the actor through his behavior. They solely differ from each other when it comes to deciding what unpleasant circumstance justifies the criminalization of certain behavior.

1.1.2. Result: Harm-Principle as Main Principle among Possible Others

Agreed upon the fact that an act has to be performed by somehow having an exterior impact, which is incompatible with the rights of others, it is further clear that not just any behavior which seems inappropriate to the majority can be legitimately punished, necessary is that it tends to cause a sufficient negative impact on others. While the idea of negative impacts arising from moral grounds is to be rejected in its totality, it is controversial if harm as an impact is the only valid reason for legitimately punishing behavior or if it is just the main reason among further possible legitimate reasons. In principle, it is the only one which is generally agreed to be a legitimate reason for penalization. Thus, without any claim to the truth or falsity of other principles that have been proposed, the Harm Principle, with its precept that behavior can be legitimately penalized if it causes harm to others than the actor, is the generally valid theory of criminalization in the U.S. opinion.

Since the 19th century, the Harm Principle plays the major role in justifying criminal sanctioning in the United States[655]. Constitutive are the achievements of Mill, who laid the foundation of the American penal theory, now known as the Harm Principle[656]. Based on the value of freedom of the individual as the norm, it is concluded that coercion always requires a special justification[657]. Liberty is understood as freedom of the individual (civil liberty); expressly specifically, as freedom of the individual being a member of society (social liberty)[658]. Starting off from this, one must find general principles which allow an interference with the basically guaranteed liberty of the individual[659]. The subject-matter, therefore, is the question about the nature and the limits of power, which can be legitimately exercised over the individual[660]; in short, the

653 Feinberg, The Moral Limits of the Criminal Law, Vol. 4, p. 12; Wohlers, Deliktstypen des Präventionsstrafrechts, 1999, p. 259.
654 Jäger, Strafgesetzgebung und Rechtsgüterschutz bei Sittlichkeitsdelikten, 1957, p. 39.
655 Hirsch, Der Rechtsgutsbegriff und das Harm Principle, GA; 2002, 2-14 (3).
656 Hirsch, Der Rechtsgutsbegriff und das Harm Principle, GA; 2002, 2-14 (3).
657 Feinberg, Harm to others, 1984, p. 9.
658 Mill, Über die Freiheit, p. 5.
659 Such principles are called "liberty-limiting principles" or equivalently "coercion-legitimizing principles" as stated in Feinberg, Harm to Others, p. 9.
660 Mill, Über die Freiheit, p. 5.

question applies to the proper range of criminal law. With this, the search for reasons which have universally valid weight when balanced against the presumptive case of liberty starts. "Harm to others" is generally accepted to be such a reason to weigh against the liberty of the actor as stated in the leading principle – the Harm Principle – of U.S. penal theory, with the result that statutory prohibitions enforced by penal sanctions, which are released to prevent harm to parties other than the person interfered with, are legitimate. The challenge now, is to examine the essence of the Harm Principle.

1.1.2.1. Word Meaning of 'Harm' in the Context of the Harm Principle

An act, which causes harmed states or conditions or – in contrast to Mill[661] – has the tendency to do so, is said to be a proper target of prohibitory legislation[662]. Harm in this context is defined as setback of interests that are wrongs[663], and which at the same time must necessarily violate the victim's right[664].

a) Setback of Interests

Before going into detail about the understanding of the harm-principle, it must be pointed out that within the framework of this dissertation the prevailing view of penal theorist who favors a liberal model of state interference with individual liberty is followed[665]. Instead, those who espouse this view insist that it is the task of legal prohibitions to prevent social harm as in opposite to individual harm; corresponding to the opinion of those, who among the German penal theory have the opinion that the task of legal prohibitions is to promote the collective good, this opinion is refused in the American view of criminalization in the same way as it is refused in the German discussion: The relationship between the collective and the individuals and between the state and its citizen according to a liberal democratic Constitution allows no other opinion than the idea of individuals being the beneficiaries of all law[666].

Criminally relevant interests are neither just wishes and inclinations (passing wants) nor instrumental wants, nor focal aims, but solely welfare interests[667]. Welfare interests are considered as "minimal, but not ultimate goods". Without their fulfillment, a person is lost[668]. They are the "basic requisites of a man's well-being"[669]. If such an interest is infringed through an invasion by a human being (by self or others) its possessor is harmed in the non-normative sense of simple setback of interest; if harm is also caused in the legal sense, it depends on the following aspects.

661 Hirsch, GA 2002, pp. 2-14 (5).
662 Feinberg, Harm to others, 1984, p. 31.
663 One person wrongs another when his indefensible (unjustifiable and inexcusable) conduct violates the other's right. (Cf. Feinberg, Harm to others, 1984, p. 34).
664 Feinberg, Harm to others, 1984, p. 36.
665 In the sense of John Stuart Mill.
666 Hörnle, Offensive Behavior and German Penal Law, p. 259.
667 Feinberg, Harm to others, 1984, pp. 37 et seqq.
668 Examples for such goods are life, physical health, the capacity to engage normally in social intercourse, a tolerable social and physical environment, and many more. (Feinberg, Harm to others, 1984, p. 37).
669 Rescher, Welfare: The Social Issue in Philosophical Perspective; Pittsburgh: University of Pittsburgh Press, 1972, p. 6.

b) The Need to "Wrong" the Other

The requirement of wrongfulness eliminates acts from being legitimately penalized. Namely through this corrective those acts, which infringe on the interest of others but are not "wrong", cause no harm in the here meant sense[670]. Therefore, the necessity of wrongdoing in the term of the definition of the harm – principle functions as a kind of necessary normative tool[671]. Whenever an actor acts excusably or justifiably or the other has no right to have an interest respected the requirement of wrongdoing is not fulfilled [672]; positively expressed, an indefensible conduct, which violates the other's welfare-interests, is a wrongful doing by the actor, therefore wrongs the other[673]. However, the indefensibility is to be determined, which requires an elaborate set of "mediating maxims, interest-rankings, principle of justice and the like"[674] in order to legitimately make out the wrongfulness of certain behavior. The aim of the harm-principle at preventing only those harms that are wrongs, demands a supplement of normative tools before it can be applied to real legislative problems[675].

c) Violation of Rights

This feature, referring to the necessity of the violation of a victim's right, refers to two premises. First of all, the respective behavior must cause interference to the interest of others, which is legally recognized as a right. If this is the case, it must be answered in the abstract. However, it must be observed that rights, in the view of Feinberg, can be violated without harm to (substantial[676]) interests. In such a case the law must recognize a proprietary interest[677]. In this prerequisite it is solely important that the damage affects a legally recognized "something" – which, in connection with the other characteristics of the definition, must be a legally recognized welfare interest. Secondly, it is focused on the particular person whose right is supposedly to be harmed. If the victim agrees to be harmed, no harm – as in the sense of the harm-principle – is caused. This refers to the word "violation", which suggests the element of wrongfulness of the infringing behavior[678] in the above mentioned sense of wrongfulness. The Harm Principle with its subjectivistic orientation[679]

---

670 "Only setbacks of interests, that are wrongs and wrongs that are setbacks of interests, are to count as harms in the appropriate sense." (Feinberg, Harm to others, 1984, p. 36). For explanation Feinberg provides the following example: Natural events like earthquakes cause harm in purely interest-affecting sense, but this is not a wrongful violation interests.

671 Feinberg, Harm to others, 1984, p. 34.

672 Feinberg, Harm to others, 1984, pp. 34 et seqq.

673 Feinberg, Harm to others, 1984, pp. 35, 52.

674 Feinberg, Harm to others, 1984, p. 36.

675 Feinberg, Harm to others, 1984, p. 36.

676 "Substantial" in the meaning of "tangible and of material kind" .

677 E.g. in the case of the so-called harmless trespass on another's land, the landowner's property rights are violated, thereby wronged, even though his land as such is not harmed. The law recognizes a proprietary interest in the exclusive possession and enjoyment of one's land, and for whatever it is worth, the trespass do invade that interest. (Cf. Feinberg, Harm to others, p. 35).

678 Feinberg, Harm to others, p. 52.

679 Hirsch, Der Rechtsgutsbegriff und das „Harm Principle", in: Hefendehl/v. Hirsch/Wohlers, Die Rechtsgutstheorie, 2003, pp. 13-25 (22); Hirsch, GA 2002, pp. 2-14 (8).

fundamentally focuses on actual damages in reference to the victim[680]. This again takes the autonomy of the individual into account.

1.1.2.2. Summary: Word Meaning of 'Harm' in the Context of the Harm Principle

According to its definition the term 'harm' in the context of the Harm Principle does not refer to a material damage as pecuniary injury, but to an invasion of an interest, which must have been legally recognized as an interest. Therefore, 'harm' in this context has two components; one is a certain deleterious effect on one's interests and the other the violation of the victim's rights (a wrong to him)[681].

As a consequence, prohibition of consensual activities is not justified, even if such acts are likely to thwart the interests of consenting parties, because the aim of the Harm Principle is to prevent only setbacks of interests that are wrongs, and wrongs that are setbacks to interest and setbacks of solely such interests which are legally recognized as rights[682].

1.2. Summary: Content of the American Penal Theory: Harm Principle

Assuming the case that the welfare interests of one or more persons are wrongfully damaged and the respective behavior at the same time violates the victim's rights, this in principle refers to the kind of harm, relevant for criminal sentencing. An automatic legitimizing of criminal sanctions in cases of the presence of such kind of harm, which is considered as a valid reason for criminalization, does not apply. The limitation of liberty caused through penalization shall require a weighing of interests, which leads to the determination of wrongfulness of behavior. The balancing of interests and the thereon based determination of wrongfulness of behavior takes place by examining the setback by several mediated maxims in order to distinguish the harmful setbacks from the harmless in the requisite sense[683].

Essentially, coercion-legitimizing principles (as liberty-limiting principles[684]) are said to be a always morally relevant reason in support of penal legislation, but never claims to be a necessary condition for the justification of criminal statutes or a sufficient or conclusive reason to enact such[685]. Consequently, the Harm Principle as a subcategory of so-called coercion-legitimizing principles[686] must also purport not to be a sufficient condition for justified state

680 Despite the individualistic orientation of the harm-principle, acts which cause collective harm can still be legitimately prohibited under the Harm Principle, due to a direct or indirect connection of collective harm to the harm of the individual (Hirsch, GA 2002, pp. 2-14 (8)).

681 Feinberg, Harm to others, 1984, p. 52.

682 Feinberg, Harm to others, 1984, p. 36.

683 Feinberg, Harm to others, 1984, pp. 187 et seqq., 218 et seqq.

684 Both principles used as synonyms (Cf. Feinberg, Harm to others, 1984, p. 9).

685 Feinberg, Harm to others, 1984, pp. 9, 10.

686 The Harm Principle is easily to be classified as a subcategory of the liberty-limiting principles if one follows the opinion that there are more principles which legitimize penal coercion, however, it can be called the "main category" instead. If assuming that the harm-principle is the only reason for legitimate state sanctioning, the umbrella term of "liberty-" or "coercion-legitimizing-principles" seems superfluous (Cf. Terms used by Feinberg, Harm to Others, p. 9).

coercion[687]. However, it is basically legitimate for a government to prohibit conduct that causes serious private harm, or the unreasonable risk of such harm, or harm to important public institutions and practices[688] in the U.S. prevailing opinion of criminalization. In short, state interference seems to be morally justified when it is reasonably necessary to prevent harm or the unreasonable risk of harm to parties other than the person interfered with[689]. The need of a weighing of interests includes normative elements in the determination process and thus shows that - similar to the German penal theory - a clear, absolute principle, that constitutes which behavior is to be punished, does not exist in the American view. The Harm Principle does not name the basic requirements of welfare completely in order to enable an answer to the question what – if harmed – legitimates penalty[690]. A referral to the specific conduct is compelling. Anyway, the harm-principle serves as a suitable guideline for determining the legitimacy of criminal norms within the American penal theory. Additionally, the offense principle is acknowledged to punish conducts which cause intangible adverse effects to others.

2. Purpose of Criminal Law according to the German Penal Theory

While the general question regarding the legitimation of the existence of criminal law as such is likewise accepted in German and American scholars, the reasoning differs[691]. The prevailing view among the German penal theory pursues its own approach by referring to the protection[692] of legal goods[693].

According to the prevailing opinion among the German perspective the question of criminalization depends on whether the behavior in question violates a legal good[694]. Accordingly, the function of criminal norms is to protect legally defined goods against threat or harm[695]. "According to this, important, elemental community values are the basis for a orderly cohabitation" and the task of criminal law is to protect those important

---

687 Feinberg, Harm to others, 1984, p. 187.

688 For the inclusion of collective interests into individual interests view Feinberg, Harm to others, 1984, p. 63.

689 Feinberg, Harm to others, 1984, p. 11.

690 Seelmann, Rechtsgutskonzept, „Harm Principle" und Anerkennungsmodell als Strafwürdigkeits-kriterien, in: Hefendehl/v. Hirsch/Wohlers, Die Rechtsgutstheorie, 2003, pp. 261-267 (262)

691 The following overview is based on the scheme of Grützner, Die Sanktionierung von Submissionsabsprachen, pp. 420 et seqq. and Wohlers, Deliktstypen des Präventionsstrafrechts, 1999, pp. 215 et seqq.

692 Criminal law is a "protective law". (BVerfGE 21, 391, 403 et seq.; BVerfGE 27, 18, 29; BVerfGE 39, 1, 46; Appel, Verfassung und Strafrecht, p. 62 et seqq.; Wessels/Beulke, Strafrecht AT, § 1, p. 2, marginal no. 6.

693 Lagodny, Strafrecht vor den Schranken der Grundrechte, p. 145.

694 Legal good translated from German: Rechtsgut. Lagodny, Strafrecht vor den Schranken der Grundrechte; Roxin, Strafrecht AT I, § 2 C, pp. 16 et seqq.; Roxin, Rechtsgüterschutz als Aufgabe des Strafrechts?, in: Hefendehl, Roland, Empirische und dogmatische Fundamente, pp. 135 – 150; Grützner, Die Sanktionierung von Submissionsabsprachen, p. 420, footnote 402: Maurach/Zipf Strafrecht AT Tb 1 § 19 marginal no. 4 et seqq.; Rudolphi, SK-StGB, Vor § 1 marginal no. 2; Jescheck/Weigend, Lehrbuch des Strafrechts AT, § 1 III 1; Lenckner/Eisele, in: Schönke/Schröder, StGB, Vorbem. §§ 13 et seqq., marginal no. 8 et seqq.; Baumann/Weber/Mitsch, Strafrecht AT, § 3, marginal no. 10 et seqq.; Bockelmann/Volk, Strafrecht AT, p. 10; Hassemer, in: AK-StGB, Vor § 1 marginal no. 247; Lackner/Kühl, StGB, Vor. § 13 marginal no. 4; Jescheck, in: LK, Vor §§ 13 et seqq. marginal no. 5 et seqq.; Otto, Grundkurs AT, § 1 marginal no. 22; Stratenwerth/Kuhlen, Strafrecht AT I, marginal no. 53 et seq.; Naucke, Strafrecht, § 6, marginal no. 62 et seqq.; Stree/Kinzig, in: Schönke/Schröder, StGB, Vorbem. §§ 38 et seqq., marginal no. 1 et seqq.; BVerfGE 25, 269, 286; BVerfGE 50, 142, 153.

695 Roxin, Strafrecht AT I, § 2, marginal no. 9.

community values[696]. While this view refers to most parts of German perspectives[697], another opinion states that the direct function of criminal coercion is more likely to be the "counterfactual stabilization of norms"[698]. At least, it could not be the direct purpose of criminal law to protect legal goods from violation since the application of criminal law requires a previous harm to such[699]. This opinion after all chooses the starting point for explaining the purpose of criminal law with an already existent criminal norm, while the starting point for answering this issue starts logically and necessarily earlier, which is the point of accrual of a norm[700]. The answer rather lies in the reasons chosen at that time for creating the norm[701]. Moreover, the orientation of the penal legislator towards the preventive aspects of punishment are neglected, since the impostion of punishment on the offender creates a deterrent effect towards future offenders[702]. However, this opinion ultimately acknowledges the theory of the purpose of criminal law lying in the protection of legal goods, at least indirectly, by accepting that the stabilization of norms cannot end in itself, but serves as a device to protect "elementary socio-ethical values", which protection includes the protection of the individual legal good[703]. Similar it represents itself in the opinion which considers that a norm precedes the criminal law[704]. Penalization is therefore directed against disobedience, or against the non-compliance with a norm. This understanding can not distinguish between the breaches of different norms, thus rating differences in terms of disobedience are impossible[705]. So, to define crimes and in order to differentiate such from each other[706] one turns towards the material element, which is viewed to be the purpose of the norm[707]. The purpose of a norm is to ensure the integrity of legal goods, to protect them from unwanted injury or threat; the legal good is the substantive core of the crime[708]. And since, according to this oppinion, legal goods are constituted by a value judgement of the legal community[709], the committal of an offense means the violation of the interest of the legal community[710].

---

696 Hefendehl, Kollektive Rechtsgüter im Strafrecht, § 3, p. 44.

697 Grützner, Die Sanktionierung von Submissionsabsprachen, p. 420.

698 Welzel, Das deutsche Strafrecht, p. 3; Welzel, in: Gierke-Festschrift, p. 290 (297); Wohlers, Deliktstypen des Präventionsstrafrechts, p. 215; Grützner, Die Sanktionierung von Submissionsabsprachen, p. 420.

699 Welzel, Das deutsche Strafrecht, p. 3; Welzel, in: Gierke-Festschrift, p. 290 (297); Wohlers, Deliktstypen des Präventionsstrafrechts, pp. 215 et seq.; Grützner, Die Sanktionierung von Submissionsabsprachen, p. 420.

700 Binding, Normen I, pp. 98 et seqq.

701 Binding, Normen I, pp. 98 et seqq.

702 View Chapter 2; C; 3.5.2.1. General Prevention Theory; Wohlers, Deliktstypen des Präventionsstrafrechts, p. 215.

703 Welzel, Das deutsche Strafrecht, pp. 4 et seqq.; Wohlers, Deliktstypen des Präventionsstrafrechts, p. 216; Grützner, Die Sanktionierung von Submissionsabsprachen, p. 420.

704 The subject of a criminal attack is the norm which precedes the criminal law, at least conceptually. (Binding, Normen I, pp. 3 et seqq., 7, 42, 45; Anastasopoulou, Deliktstypen, pp. 16 et seqq.).

705 Wohlers, Deliktstypen des Präventionsstrafrechts, p. 216; Grützner, Die Sanktionierung von Submissionsabsprachen, pp. 421, 422.

706 Binding, Normen I, pp. 98 et seqq.

707 Binding, Normen I, pp. 54, 353 et seqq.

708 Binding, Normen I, p. 365; Anastasopoulou, Deliktstypen, pp. 16 et seqq.

709 Binding, Normen I, p. 357.

710 Binding, Normen I, p. 359.

As opposed[711] to the notion of 'legal goods' one German opinion being discussed describes the matter of criminalization as "general prevention of crime by practicing the approval of norms"[712]. However, the characterization of the purpose of criminal law as being the stabilization of the code of conducts might be agreeable if the question refers to the function of criminal law as an institution[713]. It is not sustainable if the focus lays on the function of the particular criminal norm[714], especially since not every breach of a rule leads to sentencing, much less to undifferentiated punishment[715]. Instead – for reasons of legitimacy – each penalty is to be assessed depending on the breach of the particular norm. Thus penalty cannot be remitted without reference to the content of the norm, which leads to the protected "something" [716]. So here we are again: not able to neglect the relevance of the legally protected good when it comes to answering the question of what justifies criminalization in the opinion of German scholars. As a result of this, in line with the prevailing viewpoint in German penal theory, the function of German criminal law is to protect legal goods[717].

2.1. Content of the German Legal Good Theory

According to the "legal good" doctrine, it is incumbent upon criminal law to protect the legal order of the society's entire legal system[718], in order to protect the orderly and peaceful cohabitation of the societies´citizen. Through the legislature's decision to protect goods, criminal law conduces to the preservation of peace and the fruition of public welfare[719], by protecting the therefore necessary important community values[720]. Thereby a criminal norm serves the protection of a legal good due to the fact that the committal of criminal behavior being the interference with a legal good is the reason for

711 For criticism regarding the concept of "legal goods" refer to Jakobs, Strafrecht AT, 2, pp. 16 et seqq., pp. 22 et seqq.; partially referable to Naucke, Strafrecht, § 6 III 5; Maurach/Zipf Strafrecht AT Tb 1 § 19, marginal no. 12 et seqq.

712 "General prevention through practice of standard recognition". (English translation of: Jakobs, Strafrecht AT, 1/15); Jakobs, Staatliche Strafe: Bedeutung und Zweck, 2004, pp. 29 et seq.).

713 Wohlers, Deliktstypen des Präventionsstrafrecht, p. 217; Grützner, Die Sanktionierung von Submissionsabsprachen, p. 421.

714 Wohlers, Deliktstypen des Präventionsstrafrechts, 1999, p. 217.

715 Grützner, Die Sanktionierung von Submissionsabsprachen, pp. 421 et seq.

716 Wohlers, Deliktstypen des Präventionsstrafrechts, 1999, p. 217. If the imposition of penalty is just, the respective penalty must be assessed by determining the degree in which sentencing is legitimate, such is based on the breach of the norm. The eligibility check (the legitimacy of the concrete sentence) can only be accomplished if one draws a connection to the content of a norm by asking what is to be protected by such and as a result of this valuate the severity of a violation.

717 View footnote 693: Otto, Grundkurs AT § 1 marginal no. 21 et seqq.; Baumann/Weber/Mitsch, Strafrecht AT, § 3 marginal no. 10; Stree/Kinzig, in: Schönke/Schröder, StGB, Vorbem. §§ 38 et seqq., marginal no. 1; § 19 II marginal no. 4 et seqq.; Roxin, AT I, § 2 marginal no. 2 et seqq.; Rudolphi, in: SK-StGB, Vor 3 1 marginal no. 2; BVerfGE 96, 245 (249); Jescheck/Weigend, Lehrbuch des Strafrechts AT, § 1 III 1; Jescheck, in: LK Vor § 13 marginal no. 5 et seqq.; Naucke, Strafrecht § 6 III 5 a; Schmidhäuser, Strafrecht AT Lb 2/30 et seqq.; Wessels/Beulke, Strafrecht AT, marginal no. 6; Lackner/Kühl, StGB, Vor § 13 marginal no. 4; Maurach/Zipf, Strafrecht, AT Tb 1 § 7 marginal no. 1 et seqq.

718 Grützner, Die Sanktionierung von Submissionsabsprachen, p. 422: The German Supreme Court made clear, that the major aim of penalty it to protect the society of social harming behavior and to secure the elementary values of communal life (cf. BVerfGE 45, 187 (254)).

719 Wessels/Beulke, Strafrecht AT, marginal no. 6; Roxin, Rechtsgüterschutz als Aufgabe des Straf-rechts?, in: Hefendehl, Empirische und dogmatische Fundamente, p. 138.

720 Hefendehl, Kollektive Rechtsgüter im Strafrecht, § 3, p. 44.

sentencing, in other words, sentencing takes place if an act breaches a criminal norm[721]. With that, it is important to note that according to the German conception, this notion of 'legal good' operates at a high level of abstraction[722]. The criminalization of a protected something takes place in the abstract, in the form of a general criminalization, detached from the individual will of the person in possession of the legal good. From the German viewpoint, it does not matter whether the person who is concerned of the legislator's decision to protect a legal good actually desires protection in a specific situation[723]. What matters is the legislature's decision to protect goods as a "condition generally rated positively"[724]; thereby the liberty of the individual remains. It solely comes to an end where it infringes the integrity of a legally protected good. According to Article 2, Section 1 Basic Law it is valid to limit the basic right of freedom of action, as far as it is clarified under what criteria a legal right of others, thus a legal good, is to be rightfully acknowledged as a conditioned worth being protected by criminal law. However, even this section requires that milder devices would not achieve a similar accomplishment of goals[725]. The legislator must observe limits depending on the choice of which good is to be considered as a value worth serving legal protection; the liberty of citizens cannot end at the point of interference of just any good. With this the problem of legitimacy of criminal norms is shifted over to the search for valid legal goods[726]: by answering the question whether a norm is linked to a legitimate legal good, the legitimacy of a norm could be determinable. In so far the precept of a required legal good serves as a tool to determine the legitimacy of exercised governmental power[727]. Thereby the power of governmental intervention and civil liberty could be brought into a balance which provides the individual as much protection as necessary but also grants as much freedom as possible[728]. The fact that a legal good must be determined by the legislator in a legitimate manner raises the question of what constitutes a good to be protected by criminal sentencing, since not all goods are protected by criminal law[729] and especially not every good is protected in its entirety[730], the protection of

721 Grützner, Die Sanktionierung von Submissionsabsprachen, p. 422; Maurach/Zipf, Strafrecht AT Tb 1, § 7 marginal no. 4; § 19 II marginal no. 4 et seqq.; Rudolphi, in: SK-StGB, Vor 3 1 marginal no. 2; Jescheck/Weigend, Lehrbuch des Strafrechts AT, § 8 I 2; Stree/Kinzig, in: Schönke/Schröder, StGB, Vorbem. §§ 38 et seqq., marginal no. 1.

722 Hörnle, Offensive Behavior and German Penal Law, pp. 255-278 (259).

723 Hörnle, Offensive Behavior and German Penal Law, pp. 255-278 (259).

724 Hörnle, Offensive Behavior and German Penal Law, pp. 255-278 (259).

725 The Ultima Ratio Principle of criminal law defines that penal provisions are only legitimate if less restrictive means are not sufficient to protect a legal good. (Wessels/Beulke, Strafrecht AT, marginal no. 9; BVerfGE 90, 145, pp. 172 et seqq.).

726 Wohlers, Rechtsgutstheorie und Deliktsstruktur, GA, 2002, pp.15-20 (15).

727 "The prohibition of a behavior under threat of punishment, which can not rely on a legal good, would be state tenor [...]". (Hassemer, in: Hefendehl/von Hirsch/Wohlers, p. 57, supra note 1, p. 64; Roxin, Rechtsgüterschutz als Aufgabe des Strafrechts?, in: Hefendehl, Empirische und dogmatische Fundamente, pp. 135, 137).

728 Roxin, Rechtsgüterschutz als Aufgabe des Strafrechts?, in: Hefendehl, Empirische und dogmatische Fundamente, p. 135, 138; Grützner, Die Sanktionierung von Submissionsabsprachen, p. 423.

729 Only goods which are believed to be worthy of protection are protected by criminal norms.

730 Maiwald, in: Maurach-Festschrift, p. 9 et seq.; Grützner, Die Sanktionierung von Submissionsabspra-chen, p. 423.

criminal law therefore is fragmentary[731]. The provision of constructing a legal good requires the protection of a human or common interest, which qualifies as a criminal legal good[732]. Such a qualification results from the fact that certain goods of life, social values and legally approved interests of individuals or of the community have a special importance to society and thus are in need of legal protection[733]. However, what is said intensifies the issue of which standards are to be held true when it comes to determining the group of legal goods worthy of protection.

Since in the prevailing view in Germany the acknowledgement of the "legal good" doctrine is agreed upon with its demand that the substantial part of a criminal act must occur from harming a legal good and, therefore, criminal norms without a connection to a legal good must not exist legitimately, its proponents disagree when it comes to the understanding of the definition of a 'legal good'[734]. Considering the diverse opinions existing in Germany, the term 'legal good' is described at random[735]. Therefore, the following provides a brief overview of the controversy by presenting the main opinions according to the understanding of the legal good concept and finally a wrap-up, corresponding to the actual leading German theory, is served.

2.1.1. Inbuilt or System-Critical Understanding of the Legal Good Doctrine

In the context of the prevailing legal good doctrine and its discussion regarding the term 'legal good' the research does not revolve around the question whether a related behavior can be accepted as a legitimate cause for governmental intervention[736]. Instead, it is sought after a definition of the term 'legal good', in order to thereby achieve a universally valid answer to the question of what is legitimately punishable[737]. Such a definition then shall be able to provide a guidance by setting clear characteristics and standards to identify what constitutes a legal good. By that, the legal good serves as an instrument in determining and constraining the legitimate area of application[738]. As a consequence the discussion is not about the positive determination of what is to be acknowledged as a legal good worthy of protection, it is rather asked: Where are the limits for the German legislator when applying criminal

731 Jescheck/Weigend, Lehrbuch des Strafrechts AT, p. 52 et seq.; Hefendehl, Der fragmentarische Charakter des Strafrechts, JA 2011, number 6, pp. 401-406; Maiwald, in: Maurach-Festschrift, p. 9 et seq.; Wessels/Beulke, Strafrecht AT, marginal no. 9;

732 Maiwald, Maurach-Festschrift, p. 11; Roxin, Strafrecht AT I, § 2, marginal no. 2 et seqq.; Kasper, Erheblichkeitsschwelle, p. 16; Rudolphi, in: SK – StGB, vor § 1 marginal no. 5 et seqq.; Hassemer, in: AK-StGB, vor § 1 marginal no. 196.

733 Wessels/Beulke Strafrecht AT, marginal no. 7.

734 Roxin, Strafrecht AT I, § 2B, marginal no. 2 - 4; Stratenwerth, in: Lenckner-FS, 1998, p. 377.

735 "vulnerable, protectable states" ; "good which is legally at least worthy protection"; "valuable state of the external reality of life"; "criminal protected interests"; "spiritualized, intangible value" and others. (View summary in Roxin, AT I § 2B, marginal no. 3, with reference to: Köhler, AT, p.25; Freund, in: MK, StGB, Vor § 13, marginal no. 43; Maurach/Zipf, Strafrecht AT/1; § 19, marginal no. 4; Baumann/Weber/Mitsch, AT, § 3, marginal no. 18).

736 Wohlers, Deliktstypen des Präventionsstrafrechts, 1999, p. 254. This is rather the strategy of the American approach.

737 Marx, Zur Defintion des Begriffs Rechtsgut, 1972, pp. 62 et seqq.

738 Hirsch, Der Rechtsgutsbegriff und das Harm Principle, 2002, pp. 2-14 (3).

coercion? If such limits could be defined, the field of legal goods which are legitimately worthy of protection, could be determined subsequently.

There are different approaches on hand, two in particular, to answer the crucial question regarding what standards are to be applied to determine the ambit of legal goods worthy of criminal protection[739]. Both theories aim at providing standards for determining the group of legal goods worthy of criminal protection, however by choosing different assessments. The theories in point are the concept of the inbuilt (methodical) legal good doctrines (*systemimmanenten Rechtgutstheorien*) which equate the term 'legal good' with those objects presented in the German Penal Code; and the system-critical (substantial) legal good doctrines (*systemkritischen, systemtranszendeten Rechtgutstheorien*)[740] which aim at equipping the term 'legal good' with substantial content in order to determine the worthiness of protection of a matter autonomously from the legislator's decision[741]. Therefore, the difference lies in the requirements for the substantive criteria[742].

2.1.1.1. Inbuilt Understanding of the Legal Good Doctrine

The inherent legal good doctrine defines the term 'legal good' from the sum of objects codified in the German Penal Code[743]. This doctrine emanates from the given order of legal goods and does not exceed this frame of the existing legal selection, thus, it is inbuilt[744]. By doing so, this understanding does not challenge the assortment of protected objects chosen by the legislator. It rather answers the question of what qualifies as a 'legal good' by enumerating the legal goods presented in the German Penal Code[745]. This inbuilt doctrine querys the systematic arrangement of the given protected objects, it serves the methodical working up of the encountered legal situation[746]. Thereby the cognition of this approach does not aim at challenging the protected content of the norms summarized by the legislature[747]. The inbuilt theories therefore provide a valuable content solely regarding the systematic of the de lege lata effective norms or in respect of classifying specific dogmatic differences by descriptively illustrating such[748]. So, in regard to the relevant question of what is to be punished legitimately by the German legislator, the inbuilt theories will

739 Wohlers, Deliktstypen des Präventionsstrafrechts, 1999, p. 218; Baratta, FS für Arthur Kaufmann, pp. 393 et seqq.; fundamental hereto: Hassemer, Theorie und Soziologie des Verbrechens; pp. 19 et seqq.; Marx, Zur Defintion des Begriffs Rechtsgut, 1972, p. 9; Müssig, Rechtsgüterschutz, p. 9; Stächelin, Strafgesetzgebung, pp. 30 et seqq.

740 The designation "system - critical" must be understood in the sense of "legislation - critical", because the term "legal good" moves within the constitutional system but wants to set limits to the legislature. (Roxin, Strafrecht AT I, § 2C, p. 18, supranote 27).

741 Hassemer, Theorie und Soziologie des Verbrechens; pp. 19 et seqq.; Wohlers, Deliktstypen des Präventionsstrafrechts, 1999, pp. 218, 219.

742 Müssig, Rechtsgüterschutz, p. 9.

743 Hassemer, Theorie und Soziologie des Verbrechens, pp. 19 et seqq.; Grützner, Die Sanktionierung von Submissionsabsprachen, pp. 423 et seqq.

744 Müssig, Rechtsgüterschutz, p. 9

745 Grützner, Die Sanktionierung von Submissionsabsprachen, p. 424.

746 Müssig, Rechtsgüterschutz, p. 9.

747 Hassemer, Theorie und Soziologie des Verbrechens; pp. 20 et seqq.

748 Roxin, Strafrecht AT I, § 2B, marginal no. 4,5; Wohlers, Deliktstypen des Präventionsstrafrechts, 1999, p. 218.

not provide any further cognitions[749]. As a result, these doctrines are deemed useless in determining the term 'legal good' as far as one aims at a cognition beyond a systematic understanding[750].

2.1.1.2. System-Critical Understanding of the Legal Good Doctrine

The supporters of the critical legal good doctrine do not accept the legal goods stipulated in the Penal Code as legitimate without questioning. The proponents of the critical 'legal good' doctrine aim at determining the term 'legal good' substantially and independently from the decision made by the legislator in order to be able to answer the question of which goods are worthy of criminal protection and thus to be able to distinguish the ones worthy of protection from those that are not[751]. In this theory, the German Penal Code is examined by using one´s own measurements, which shall independently define the characteristics, states and conditions that are to be considered worthy of protection in order to determine those objects that are considered to be legitimately constituted as legal goods[752]. With such an aim, this theory is capable to satisfy the desire for an independent tool for determining which good is to be legitimately protected by criminal law. This theory is willing to set the parameters for outlining a legitimate area for punishing by setting the borders for the appliance of criminal law. The aim of preventing the legislator from adjudicating just anything to be a good worthy of protection through criminal sentencing just because he is interested in its maintenance and therefore potentially constrain the freedom of the individual in an illegitimate manner, can be satisfied if the intention of defining the criteria for determining a legitimate scope for the use of criminal law succeeds. In this case, the ultimate goal of limiting the legislator in the application of criminal law is achieved[753]. After all though, the critical theory, at first glance, does not actually serve any clear guidance of which goods to legitimately protect. It must be further examined whether the critical theory is able to fulfill its aim; specifically, if it actually formulates criteria due to a critical understanding, which enables one to determine the group of goods which are to be protected by criminal law.

2.1.2. Intermediate Result: System-Critical Understanding of the Legal Good Doctrine

Due to the missing meaningfulness of the term 'legal good' regarding the question what is legitimately punishable, one follows the critical approach of the legal good theory and realizes that, up to here, it does not offer any clear statements in order to define constituting elements of a 'legal good'. Insofar, by

749 Fischer, Öffentlicher Friede, p. 539 et seqq.; Frisch, Strafbarkeitsvoraussetzungen, p. 203; Worms, Bekenntnisbeschimpfung, p. 24; Wohlers, Deliktstypen des Präventionsstrafrechts, 1999, pp. 218, 219; Grützner, Die Sanktionierung von Submissionsabsprachen, p. 425.

750 Wohlers, Deliktstypen des Präventionsstrafrechts, p. 219.

751 Wohlers, Deliktstypen des Präventionsstrafrechts, p. 219 with further references: Appel, Verfassung, pp. 342 et seq.; Hassemer, in: NK-StGB, Vor § 1 marginal no. 261.

752 Hassemer, Theorie und Soziologie des Verbrechens; p. 24.

753 Hassemer, in: AK-StGB, vor § 1 marginal no. 259, 261; Lenckner/Eisele, in: Schönke/Schröder, StGB, Vorbem. §§ 13 et seqq., marginal no. 10.

the use of the term 'legal good', one can not generally determine what is to be made punishable by referring to the protection of the legal good. At this point it is solely clear that the 'legal good' is not equated with the interest of the legislator, which might have caused him to create a norm[754]. So, what can be legitimately protected by criminal law, and thus serve as a legitimate legal good according to the German perspective, must be further examined in order for the legal good theory to serve as a valuable criterion to distinguish the legitimate from the illegitimate[755].

2.1.3. Individual- and Collective Goods

In order to determine and thereby limit the legitimate application scope for applying criminal law, within the system-critical understanding of the legal good doctrine it is tried to achieve a definition of the term 'legal good' by distinguishing between collective legal goods and individual legal goods[756]. Life, physical integrity, personal freedom and ownership of the individual are traditionally considered as individual goods, while the existence of the government and its liberal-democratic basic order, the ensuring of state secrets, the judicature, the incorruptibility of officials, the security of monetary transactions and the dependability of legal dealings are declared as collective goods[757]. The subdivision into collective and individual legal goods usually takes place through the separation of the legal entity[758]; collective legal goods as so called described interests or interest of the general public therefore stand as a counterpart to the interest of the individuals[759]. While in the framework of a critical understanding the so-called dualistic legal good concepts (*dualistische Rechtsgutskonzeptionen*) acknowledge the individual and the collective legal goods as equal subcategories, therefore view both types, despite their separation, as criminal legal goods[760], the proponents of the monistic approaches[761] conceive legal goods as either being originated solely from the state, stated as monistic state legal good doctrines (*monistisch etatischen Rechtsgutslehren*), or from the individual, stated as monistic personal legal good doctrine (*monistisch personalen Rechtsgutslehren*)[762].

754 Since such an understanding would meet the concept of an inbuilt (methodical) legal good doctrine.

755 Wohlers, Deliktstypen des Präventionsstrafrechts, 1999, p. 221.

756 Hassemer, in: NK-StGB, Vor § 1 Rdnr. 261; Rudolphi, in: FS für Honig, Göttingen 1970, p. 154; Grützner, Die Sanktionierung von Submissionsabsprachen, pp. 426 et seqq.

757 Roxin, AT I, § 2C, marginal no. 9.

758 With the help of discretionary power concerning the legal good, one wants to pay attention to the fact that the consent of a person to a violation of a legal good shall be valid to remove the wrongdoing of a behavior, but only if the person is the only legal entity of the respective legal good. (Cf. Hassemer, in: NK-StGB, Vor § 1 marginal no. 269 et seqq.; Jescheck, in: LK, Vor § 13 marginal no. 6; Maurach/Zipf, Strafrecht AT, Band I, § 19, marginal no. 10; Schmidhäuser, Strafrecht AT, 2 /33).

759 Jescheck/Weigend, Lehrbuch des Strafrechts AT, p. 259 et seq., Maurach/Zipf, Strafrecht AT, Vol. I, § 19, marginal no. 11; Wessels/Beulke, Strafrecht AT, marginal no. 7.

760 Grützner, Die Sanktionierung von Submissionsabsprachen, p. 428; Tiedemann, Tatbestandsfunktio-nen, pp. 118 et seqq.

761 Grützner, Die Sanktionierung von Submissionsabsprachen, p. 428 with reference to: Hassemer, AK-StGB, vor § 1 marginal no. 271, 275; Kasper, Erheblichkeitsschwelle, pp. 17 et seqq.

762 The representatives of the monistic theories follow "the idea that individual- and common goods are together in a relation of derivability", the dispute between the dualistic and the monistic theories is mainly about how deep the distinction are to be confirmed theoretically. Due to the lack of cognition for the here

Whereas the first approaches are incompatible with the effective German basic order due to their underlying concept of the state[763], the monistic - personal legal good doctrines can not be dismissed easily. Its representatives refuse to accept collective legal goods as a separate, independent category of objects worthy of criminal protection. They accept the protection of collective legal goods as a legitimate reason for the existence of a criminal norm only in so far, as collective goods serve the personal development of the individual[764]. Thus, for evaluating the legitimacy of legal goods, one starts with determining the importance of collective goods for human interests.

The strict division between collective and individual interests is barely possible[765]. During the presentation of the Constitution it has already been shown that the personal freedom of the individual demands the guarantee of basic preconditions which are required for the exercise of personal freedom (*status positivus*). Consequences therefore are that a single member of society, being an individual, has a collective interest in the guarantee of the existence of such institutions and preconditions which are necessary for his freedom[766]. After all, the main task of criminal law, which is the maintance of a state of peace[767], is an individual aim due to living in a collective.

This connection to the sphere of the individual is neglected if collective interests in the existence of legal goods, which refer to the entire social community, are considered as interests of the state community or - in the opinion of the representatives of the monistic state legal good doctrines[768] - as legal goods of the state[769]. The protection of collective legal goods finally serves for the protection of those requirements which are essential for human co-existence, induced by the communal life, and thus can be considered as the individual interest of those human beings living with these institutions[770].

---

stated question, a presentation of the controversies opinions is omitted. (Grützner, Die Sanktionierung von Submissionsabsprachen, p. 428).

763 The "monistic" approaches derive the individual legal goods from the governmental functions; accordingly they consider them as "goods of the entirety of the state". (For further information view: Grützner, Die Sanktionierung von Submissionsabsprachen, pp. 426 et seqq.; Cf. Honig, Einwilligung, p. 115; Oetker, ZStW 17 (1897), pp. 493 (508); Maurach/Zipf, Strafrecht AT Tb 1, § 19 marginal no. 8). These approaches envisage the derivation of individual legal goods from the universal legal goods, therefore set the state and not the people at the center of legislative action. Such an understanding of the government contradicts to the constitutional understanding of government, which is determined in the Basic Law, according to which the states exist for man's will and not man for state's sake. (cf. BVerfGE 7, 198 (205); Grützner, Die Sanktionierung von Submissionsabsprachen, p. 429).

764 Roxin, Rechtsgüterschutz als Aufgabe des Strafrechts?, in: Hefendehl, Empirische und dogmatische Fundamente, p. 140; Hassemer, in: NK-StGB, Vor § 1 marginal no. 271; Wohlers, Deliktstypen des Präventionsstrafrechts, p. 221.

765 Wohlers, Rechtsgutstheorie und Deliktsstruktur, GA 2002, pp.15-20 (16).

766 Hefendehl, Kollektive Rechtsgüter, pp. 73 et seqq.; Hörnle, Grob anstößiges Verhalten, p. 93; Wohlers, Deliktstypen des Präventionsstrafrechts, p. 222; Rawls, Theorie, p. 300.

767 Goehrs, Der Rechtsfrieden, p. 2.

768 The "monistic state" theories consider individual goods as "goods of the entirety or of the state" (cf. Honig, Einwilligung, p. 115; Oetker, ZStW 17 (1897), 493 (508); Maurach/Zipf, Strafrecht AT Tb 1, § 19 marginal no. 8).

769 Wohlers, Deliktstypen des Präventionsstrafrechts, p. 222.

770 Hefendehl, Kollektive Rechtsgüter, pp. 73 et seqq.; Hörnle, Grob anstößiges Verhalten, p. 93; Wohlers, Deliktstypen des Präventionsstrafrechts, p. 222; Rawls, Theorie, p. 300; Roxin, Rechtsgüterschutz als Aufgabe des Strafrechts?, in: Hefendehl, Empirische und dogmatische Fundamente, p. 140; Hassemer, in: NK, Vor § 1 marginal no. 271; Wohlers, Deliktstypen des Präventionsstrafrechts, p. 221.

Since in this opinion it is not considered that collective legal goods are independent state interests which consequently do not serve for the interests of the individual, the strict division between individual and collective legal goods is not followed[771]. In consequence, the qualification of being a legal good can neither be denied for individual nor for collective goods. The idea of constraining the legitimate application area of criminal norms through a division into individual and collective legal goods fails because a clear classification into purely individual interest in order to distinguish such from purely collective interests is not possible. The idea is rejected because a principal exclusion of collective goods from the criminal legal order can not be reasonably placed, since the legislator aims at fulfilling his purpose of securing the peaceful co-existence of its citizens when protecting collective legal goods and the need for this securing, in turn, only occurs due to the collective.

In summary, it can be said that a division of individual- and collective legal goods does not serve any further cognition for determining the term 'legal good' and its capability of serving a guidance of what is to be legitimately protected by criminal law[772].

2.1.4. Substantiality of the Term Legal Good

According to the critical theories it is agreed upon the fact that the material content of a norm cannot be equated with the interest of the legislator which caused him to create the respective norm[773]. This leads to the question: what is the content of a legal norm? Creating the follow-up question of how tangible a legally protected object must be. To answer these questions, it is sought after the concrete, material substrat of a norm, seeking for the extent of substance that the term 'legal good' must bear in general bear[774]. Basically there is a discussion between those doctrines that prefer a tangible legal good concept[775] and those that follow an intangible legal good concept[776]. Among all views, it is agreed upon the fact that legal goods with substantial, tangible objects, indisputably belong to the group of legal goods which are legitimately worthy of protection through criminal law. However, this cognition only serves to a small aspect of goods which seem to be worthy of criminal protection. Therefore it is questionable whether a norm must refer to a tangible basis like providing something substantially typified, or whether an ideal or spiritual value could be seen as an object being legitimately protected by criminal norms as well[777]. There are various dematerialization approaches[778] to determine the

771 Hassemer, Theorie, p. 231 et seqq.; Wohlers, Deliktstypen des Präventionsstrafrechts, p. 222.

772 Grützner, Die Sanktionierung von Submissionsabsprachen, p. 432; Wohlers, Deliktstypen des Präventionsstrafrechts, p. 222.

773 Grützner, Die Sanktionierung von Submissionsabsprachen, p. 432.

774 "Decisive, [therefore], is the search after the "something" which caused the legislator to release a particular norm." (Grützner, Die Sanktionierung von Submissionsabsprachen, p. 432; Stratenwerth, Lenckner-FS, p. 377 (379 et seq.); Wohlers, Deliktstypen des Präventionsstrafrechts, pp. 219 et seqq.).

775 Marx, Zur Definition des Begriffs Rechtsgut, 1972, pp. 9 et seq.; 62 et seqq.

776 Jescheck, AT, § 26 I 2, p. 232; Wessels/Beulke, Strafrecht AT, § 1, p. 2; Baumann-Weber, AT, § 12 II 3, p. 140; summary at: Müssig, Rechtsgüterschutz, pp. 50 et seqq.

777 Wohlers, Deliktstypen des Präventionsstrafrechts, p. 220.

778 Müssig, Rechtsgüter, pp. 50 et seqq.

legal good term[779]. The "spiritualization of the legal good concept"[780] has developed to the extent that legal goods are defined as "mental structures"[781], "ideal goods"[782] or simply as "values"[783]. At least a legal good should be tangible in some way, yet it must be discussed whether it must be prehensile. According to the critical understanding, it is partially recognized that a legal good must provide a certain content of materiality[784]. That is considered to be fullfilled if legal goods can be described as "violable, defendable states"[785], which again are understood as "definable, (...) able to be harmed through external acting, valuable conditions"[786]. Nevertheless, within the framework of these views it is either pointed out that legal goods do not necessarily have to present something tangible or it shows conclusively by adjudicating the quality of a legal good to certain conditions, such as the freedom of decision-making[787]. Under the terms set by a critical understanding, it seems unconvincing to require a constraint of the legal good term to objectively consolidated legal goods within a modern society because it is not possible to embrace all issues relevant to life in society as a pure accumulation of concrete goods[788]. Even though, within the framework of a system-critical understanding of the legal good doctrine, one logically cannot urge the argument that this opinion is not in conformity with the actual German legal situation. But, constraining the term 'legal good' purely to physical – substantial objects would lead to the fact that even established criminal norms, whose existence is indisputably legitimate, would lose their justification[789]. And it would be proven to be a mistake to exclude a priori legal goods from the group of legal goods potentially worthy of criminal protection which support the goal of a peaceful communal life, just because they are insubstantial phenomena[790]. Defining the term 'legal good', therefore, cannot solely depend on a proven substantial interference but, rather, on the assumption that interference meets the "prevailing rational structure of a society" or that it is

779 For example, the legal good doctrine is transferred in the theory of social harmfulness. According to that, behavior is punishable if it is generally suitable to disorganize society. Legal goods therefore are phenomena that are violable in the way that it comes to socially harmful effects on society. (Amelung, Rechtsgüterschutz, 1972, pp. 361 et seqq. (388).

780 Müssig, Rechtsgüterschutz, p. 50 with reference to Blei, AT, § 24 II, p. 89, Jescheck, AT, § 26 I 2, p. 232.

781 Blei, AT, § 24 II, p. 89; Müssig, Rechtsgüterschutz, p. 50.

782 Schmidhäuser, Strafrecht AT, 5/27; Müssig, Rechtsgüterschutz, p. 50.

783 Jescheck, AT, § 26 I 2, p. 232; Wessels/Beulke, Strafrecht AT, § 1 I 2, p. 2 – according to: Müssig, Rechtsgüterschutz, p. 50.

784 Grützner, Die Sanktionierung von Submissionsabsprachen, p. 437.

785 Wohlers, Deliktstypen des Präventionsstrafrechts, p. 225; Jäger, Rechtsgüterschutz, p. 13.

786 Roxin, Täterschaft und Tatherrschaft, 1. Auflage, 1963, p. 413, supra note 63; Grützner, Die Sanktionierung von Submissionsabsprachen, p. 433.

787 Roxin, Täterschaft und Tatherrschaft, 1. Auflage, 1963, p. 413.

788 Anastasopoulou, Deliktstypen, p. 42; Hefendehl, Kollektive Rechtsgüter, pp. 75 et seqq; Müssig, Rechtsgüterschutz, pp. 155 et seqq.; Wohlers, Deliktstypen des Präventionsstrafrechts, p. 226, Grützner, Die Sanktionierung von Submissionsabsprachen, p. 435.

789 Usually the object of attack is considered as the "tangible" something. However, one must differentiate the protected legal good from the object of attack. But even the object of attack is not always "tangible" since norms, which protect the "honor" or "free will", are considered to be legitimate. (Worms, Rechtsgutstheorie und Deliktsstruktur, GA, 2002, pp. 15-20 (16); Worms, Bekenntnisbeschimpfung, p. 52; Wohlers, Deliktstypen des Präventionsstrafrechts, p. 228).

790 Wohlers, Deliktstypen des Präventionsstrafrechts, p. 228.

790 Hassemer, Theorie, p. 237 et seqq.

consistent with such, as the case may be[791]. Even in the case of missing a concrete, physically prehensile object of attack, punishability is legitimately possible according to the German prevailing understanding of the legal good theory. As a result, the constraint of the group of legal goods worthy of protection cannot be achieved by the criterion of substantiality[792]. The requirement of palpability does not serve as a valid explanation of what constitutes a legal good.

2.1.5. Intermediate Summary

Even though it is generally recognized that the material substrata of a crime must accrue from the interference of a legal good, and consequently penal provisions without a connection to a legal good legitimately must not exist[793], one is not able to ultimately define what a legal good is in order to determine what is to be legitimately protected by penal law[794]. As a result, it must be stated that the critical legal good doctrine does not provide precise criteria - except for the necessity of a sufficient clear contouring of the protected object – to differentiate legally protected goods which deserve to be acknowledged as worthy of criminal protection from those which do not adjudge criminal protection[795]. The problem of the lack of criteria for a conceptual term remains[796]. According to that, in so far there is no generally accepted definition in German law to describe the term 'legal good' within the frameworks of the prevailing legal good theory. What is worked out so far is solely that the critical approach among the legal good doctrine is followed to examine the legitimacy of criminal norms and that it is agreed upon the fact that neither impalpable nor collective goods can be excluded a priori, or in other words: tangible personal interests are surely regarded as legal goods and thus are rightfully protected by criminal norms. It remains indeterminate what else may serve as a legal good worthy of criminal protection.

2.1.6. Linking the Legal Good Theory to the Social Theory

The previous presentation was based on discovering criteria to determine the term 'legal good'. The now following approach aims at enriching the legal good theory by linking it to the social theory. Instead of purely holding on to the legal good theory built on conceptual criteria[797], the legal good doctrine is connected

791 Hassemer, Theorie, p. 237 et seqq.
792 Wohlers, Rechtsgutstheorie und Deliktstruktur, GA, 2002, pp.15-20 (16).
793 Grützner, Die Sanktionierung von Submissionsabsprachen, pp. 436, 437; Stratenwerth, in: Lenckner-FS, p. 377.
794 "The question of what contentual quality a behavior must be in order to be subject to punishment of the government will always be a central problem, not only for legislators, but also for the science of criminal law." (Roxin, Rechtsgüterschutz als Aufgabe des Strafrechts?, in: Hefendehl, Empirische und dogmatische Fundamente, pp. 135 et seqq.; Stratenwerth, in: Lenckner-FS, p. 377 (378 et seq.).
795 The self defined aim of the system-critical legal good theory which is to serve the legislature a plausible criterion to make up the decision of which norms are legitimate and at the same time develop an external standard of review for the justice of a norm failed. (Wohlers, Rechtsgutstheorie und Deliktsstruktur, GA, 2002, pp. 15-20 (pp. 15, 16)); Grützner, Die Sanktionierung von Submissionsabsprachen, p. 437).
796 Wohlers, Rechtsgutstheorie und Deliktsstruktur, GA, 2002, pp. 15-20 (p. 16).
797 Jakobs, Strafrecht AT, 2/15.

to a social theoretical base[798]. This connection shall enable a normative enrichment of the legal good doctrine by increasing its suitability as a device for determining the legitimacy of criminal norms. It is opined that the criteria for constituting legal goods cannot be found within the term 'legal good', but must be found within the social order of the respective society and be integrated into the term[799]. Legal goods are said to not arise by spontaneous developments, they are always relative to historical, geographical, economic and cultural contexts of a society[800]. However, this approach on its own cannot bring a final decision whether a norm is legitimate or not, either. Such an approach will show which conditions of human coexistence must be protected to obtain an actual social environment, but it cannot make out if the actual state of an environment is to be maintained or if it would be better to transform a certain social system or to arrest a certain imminent change in society with the device of criminal law[801]. The potential of the binding of the legal good doctrine to the social theory lies in the possibility of sorting out illegitimate cases in which a norm either relays on protecting a good which is not existent, or cases in which a norm aims at protecting a good, but this aim is impossible to be fulfilled with the chosen device[802]. The insight that lies herein is rather that the function and the design of the concept of the legal good doctrine can only be measured against the respective socio-political background[803].

2.1.7. Constitutional Guideposts

Even though the legal good theory, according to what has been stated, is based upon the idea of criminal norms having substantial substrates, there are increased efforts noticeable which try to concretize the potential of the critical legal good theory through a normative enrichment of the term 'legal good'. This is supposed to be achieved by shifting the dispute about the content and the scope of legal goods within criminal law[804] over to the field of constitutional law[805]. Concerning this, it is to say that even though there are points of contact between the legal good system of criminal law and the value order of the Constitution, only limited cognition can be received from the Constitution in respect to the question of what interests constitute a legal good worthy of

---

798 Roxin, JA 1980, 545 546/547; Amelung, Rechtsgüterschutz und Schutz der Gesellschaft, 1972; Hassemer, Theorie und Soziologie des Verbrechens, 1973.

799 Jakobs, Strafrecht AT, 2/22.

800 Anastasopouou, Deliktstypen, p. 12; Hassemer, in: NK-StGB, Vor § 1, footnote 283; in that sense also Rudolphi, FS für Honig, p. 164.

801 Wohlers, Rechtsgutsheorie und Deliktsstruktur, GA, 2002, pp. 15-20 (17).

802 Roxin, Strafrecht AT I, § 2C, marginal no. 10; Wohlers, Deliktstypen des Präventionsstrafrechts, pp. 240, 241; Grützner, Die Sanktionierung von Submissionsabsprachen, p. 439.

803 Anastasopouou, Deliktstypen, p. 12.

804 Stuckenberg, Grundrechtsdogmatik statt Rechtsgutslehre - Bemerkung zur heutigen Diskussion um Strafe und Staat, GA, 2001, pp. 653 – 661 (654); Roxin, AT, § 2I, marginal no. 91; for summarized presentation view Jakobs, Strafrecht AT 2, 2/7 et seqq.

805 Grützner, Die Sanktionierung von Submissionsabsprachen, pp. 446, 447; Tiedemann, Tatbestandsfunktionen, p. 29; Vogel, StV 1996, 110.

criminal protection. The German Constitution does not serve a sufficient content to enable a definite determination of the term 'legal good'[806].

As far as a consent exists, it solely reaches to the effect that at least extremely private or esoteric interests are to be legitimately excluded from the group of concerns worth of protection[807]. Yet, the argument that the legislature is bound by law to penalize solely such behavior which, for instance, is damaging to a legal good, is not compatible with the freedom of action of the democratic legislator – as long as it cannot be translated into a compelling constitutional argument[808]. "So unpleasant it may be, it could hardly be constitutionally justified to ban a parliamentary majority to penalize "simply immoral"[809] behavior"[810].

The full limits of the legitimacy of protecting certain legal goods by criminal law cannot be articulated definitively[811], just as little as the legislator can be required to apply the instrument of criminal law for the protection of certain goods. Even though the German Constitutional Court (*Bundesverfassungsgericht*) decided that the legislator may be constitutively obliged to enact criminal norms in order to fulfill his state duty of protection[812], the court set this precept under the provision of the discretionary power of the legislator[813]. With regard to the incest - judgment of the Constitutional Court, one even assume a "rejection of the criminal legal good doctrine by the Constitutional Court"[814]. Consequently, the legislator has a wide discretion regarding the enactment of criminal norms[815].

806 Lagodny speaks of "(...) basic rights functioning as a directive" ("Richtlinienfunktion der Grundrechte" - Lagodny, in: Hefendehl/v. Hirsch/Wohlers, 2003, pp. 79); Roxin, Strafrecht AT I, § 2, marginal no. 94; Others speak of the constitution solely serving as a guiding principle according to which the legislator must orientate himself when developing criminal legislation. (Cf. Wohlers, Deliktstypen des Präventionsstrafrechts, p. 248; Woesner, NJW 1966; p. 1729).

807 Roxin, Rechtsgüterschutz als Aufgabe des Strafrechts?, in: Hefendehl, Empirische und dogmatische Fundamente, p. 135; Roxin, Strafrecht AT I, § 2C, marginal no. 17, 21 et seqq., 32; Grützner, Die Sanktionierung von Submissionsabsprachen, p. 451.

808 Stuckenberg, Grundrechtsdogmatik statt Rechtsgutslehre, pp. 653-661 (659); Zabel, Kriminologische Aspekte des modernen Rechtsgüterschutzes, Monatsschrift für Kriminologie und Strafrechtsreform, 2009, pp. 395-412.

809 Appel, Verfassung und Strafe, p. 356.

810 Appel, Verfassung und Strafe, pp. 198 et seqq. (200); Stuckenberg, Grundrechtsdogmatik statt Rechtsgutslehre, pp. 653-661 (656); Zabel, Kriminologische Aspekte des modernen Rechtsgüterschutzes, Monatsschrift für Kriminologie und Strafrechtsreform, 2009, pp. 395-412 (395); Grützner, Die Sanktionierung von Submissionsabsprachen, p. 451.

811 "A legal good theory itself sets no limits to the legislator." („Eine Rechtsgutstheorie setzt für sich genommen dem Gesetzgeber keine Grenzen") cf. Stächelin, Strafgesetzgebung, 1998, p. 67.

812 The legislator can be compelled to protect the living by the use of criminal law in an extreme case, if the protection that must be provided according to constitutional precepts can not be achieved in any other way. (Cf. BVErfGE 39, 1, 45).

813 BVerfGE 39, 1 (47); BVerfGE 88, 203 (257 et seqq.).

814 Stuckenberg, Grundrechtsdogmatik statt Rechtsgutslehre - Bemerkung zur heutigen Diskussion um Strafe und Staat, GA, 2011, pp. 653 – 661 (655); Incest - judgment of the Constitutional Court: BVerfGE 120, 224.

815 The task of criminal law, according to the Bundesverfassungsgericht (German Supreme Court), is "to protect important, elementary common goods". („Schutz gewichtiger, elementarer Gemeinschaftsgüter ist" BVerfGE 45, 187, (253); 80, 244 (255 et seq.)); 88, 203 (257); 90, 145 (184). However, it acknowledges a wide discretion to the legislator concerning the question whether a common matter fulfills these criteria of being important and elementary in order to be worthy of criminal protection. (Vogel, StV 1996, 110 (112 et seq.).

The Constitution does not provide a sufficient answer regarding the question what is to be protected legitimately with the instrument of criminal law, moreover the full-fledged critical potential of the legal good theory is narrow, as well as the constitutional dimension of the legal good doctrine is[816], but still no further perimeter is found in the understanding of the term 'legal good' according to the German Federal Constitutional Court[817]. The reference to the Constitution is beneficial for the critical understanding of the legal good doctrine insofar that it helps to filter out those goals pursued by the legislator with the enactment of criminal norms, which a priori evidence themselves as illegitimate[818]. In the end it is the Constitution that sets the confines for the legitimate selection of goods worthy of criminal protection and which the legislator must obey when penalizing certain behaviors[819]; insofar it does provide a control measure[820]. With that, a normative description of the legal good term is indispensable. Due to the fact that the society is not static, but provides a dynamic structure, a completing definition of the substantial content of the term 'legal good' is not possible[821]; legal goods are only the enumeration of social conditions, whose determining require the evaluation of the decisive constitutional appreciatory value aspects[822]. Consequently, the content of the term 'legal good' is to be determined under continuous concretization with the support of these constitutional aspects[823], a rigorous specification of protectable aspects can not be given because of the "colorfulness of life"[824]. By that, the legitimacy of a legal good must be defined for the given social situation appropriately.

With that said, it can be stated that the protection of a good by criminal law must always take place when it concerns an integral component of society, which at the same time is an inevitable requirement for a thriving cohabitation of liberal human beings in a society[825] and its protection by criminal law proves to be necessary to ensure the essential requirements for a free development

---

816 The reason for this is its "conceptual and content indigence" (Stuckenberg, Grundrechtsdogmatik statt Rechtsgutslehre, GA, 2001, pp. 653 – 661 (656)).

817 BVerfGE 50, 142, 162; 90, 145, 173; 120, 224, 240; 124, 300, 331; Vogel, StV 1996; 110, 112.

818 Grützner, Die Sanktionierung von Submissionsabsprachen, p. 423; Wohlers, Deliktstypen des Präventionsstrafrechts, p. 279.

819 BVerfGE 27, 18 (30); BVerfGE 80, 244 (255); BVerfGE 90, 145 (173); BVerfGE 96, 10 (25 et seq.);Therewith, the principle of prohibition of excess ("Übermaßverbot") as a benchmark for the review of the legitimacy of criminal norms is of particular importance. (BVerfGE 90, 145 (172); BVerfGE 92, 277 (326); BVerfGE 96, 10 (25); BVerfGE 27, 18 (30); BVerfGE 73, 201 (212); BVerfGE 45, 272 (289); BVerfGE 51, 60 (74)).The Constitution rather only sets the framework for constitutional legislation. (Hefendehl, Kollektive Rechtsgüter im Strafrecht, § 3, pp. 47, 48; Günther, JuS 1978, 8 (13); Otto, NJW, 1979, 681 (683); BVerfGE 39, 1 (42 et seq.)).

820 "[...] influence of the Constitution as control measure, [..]." (Hefendehl, Kollektive Rechtsgüter im Strafrecht, § 3, p. 44).

821 "The roots of the criminal law are lying in the social and ethical values of the legal community" (Wessels/Beulke, Strafrecht AT, § 1, marginal no. 9), and these "social and ethical values" are subject to change.

822 Cf. Grützner, Die Sanktionierung von Submissionsabsprachen, p. 448.

823 Rudophi, in: SK-StGB, Vor § 1 marginal no. 7 et seq.; Grützner, Die Sanktionierung von Submissionsabsprachen, p. 448.

824 Jakobs, Rechtsgüterschutz?, 2012, p. 14; Binding, Normen I, p. 353.

825 Rudophi, GA 1969, 129 (pp.139 et seqq.); Rudophi, in: SK-StGB, Vor § 1 marginal no. 8.

of the respective citizens[826]. What good qualifies to be protected with the strongest means of criminal law, is dependent on which value is attributed to such[827]. The higher the value of a legal good is adjudged by the constitutional order, the more likely it is to be protected by criminal law. On the other hand, the lower the priority of the respective good, the more appropriate it seems to solely grant protection by criminal norms against particular attacks, which contain a special amount of social degradation[828].

It is not possible to make clear criteria to conclude what requires legitimate criminal protection by the legal good doctrine by referring to the terminological approach, neither with the legal doctrine linked to social theoretical grounds, nor with the legal good doctrine in connection with the constitutional value order. At best, all these approaches serve to limit the legal good term, but they do not lead to its constitution[829]. The question in German scholars of what sorts of conducts may the state rightly make criminal is to be answered by referring to the prevailing legal good doctrine with the aid of normative valuating aspects, which orientates themselves by the mind of the present society and their constitutional value order.

Whether the German legislator would observe constitutional limits when enacting or refusing to enact a criminal norm regarding hate crimes decisively depends on the underlying legal good of such a norm. To what in particular such a protective interest of a legislator must and/or could refer to, is clarified in the following.

2.1.8. Result of a Critical Understanding of the Legal Good Theory

While the main opinions try to define the justifiable ambit of criminal law by the term 'legal good', others try to incorporate constitutional values or attach importance to social conditions for determining the legitimate area of statutory prohibitions. Beyond those generally recognized individual legal goods, whose protection is considered to legitimate a criminal norm, no further consent is achieved according to the question of what criteria establishes a legal good.

2.2. Result according the Content of the German Legal Good Theory

Based on the findings above, it is clear that an abstract definition of the term legal good, which is generally applicable for determining the legitimacy of legal norms, is not available in German legal scholars because of its dependency on individual circumstances which do not exist statically[830]. The succes of the legal doctrine therefore must neither be ascribed to its fixed guidance, nor to

826 Rudophi, in: SK-StGB, Vor § 1 marginal no. 1; Grützner, Die Sanktionierung von Submissionsabsprachen, p. 448.
827 Hassemer, Theorie und Soziologie, p. 147; Müssig, Rechtsgüterschutz, pp. 58/59.
828 Otto, NJW 1979, pp. 682 (683); BVerfGE 39, 1 (42 et seqq.).
829 Hefendehl, Kollektive Rechtsgüter im Strafrecht, § 3, p. 47: claiming that most approaches refer to the linking of the legal good theory to the constitutional value order only for the reason of limiting the legal good term.
830 Rudolphi, SK-StGB, Vor § 1 marginal no. 7.

its "chameleon-like changeability"[831], but to its ability to adapt to social needs. The changeability of society and normative standards forces the content of the legal good term to go along with them. For the problem of legitimacy of criminal norms there are no patent remedies in German scholars, but one still follows a quite concrete argumentation concerning the dogmatic reasoning of what constitutes penalty. This is the violation of a legal good which has been chosen by the legislator. Such must be defined by the legislator in dependence on the actual societal situation with reference to the consequences that the relevant behavior has for a peaceful and liberal communal life and by assessing the risk of the occurrence of such harmful consequences. Even the legal good doctrine does not provide detailed answers to legislative questions and cannot ultimately serve the answer of what sorts of conducts may the state rightly make criminal, it does provide a coherent and plausible set of principles to guide the legislator by locating the constraints that limit his options. It may fail as an approach to distinguish legitimate from illegitimate legislative purposes as a foregone conclusion[832], but by being an useful instrument to sort out illegitimate choices among those alternatives that do fall within the legislator's idea as a value worthy of protection, it sets proper limits to a legislator who then must consider the social utility and practical wisdom of his various options himself[833].

3. Purpose of Criminal Law according to the American and the German Penal Theory

In order to name the legitimate substantial content of a criminal norm, one seeks for the substantial goal of criminal law at its beginning[834]. This refers to the condition "in which every human being compliant to the principle of egalitarianism has a basic stock of elementary liberty rights with a corresponding territory and the possibility of self-determination."[835] For the achievement of such a condition, an "optimal legal good protection"[836] is required, which aims for determination[837]. How to determine such requirements in order to achieve such an ideal condition, the German penal view concentrates primarily on the legal good doctrine, whereas the prevailing American penal view refers to the harm-principle.

The harm principle and the legal good doctrine, in their penal law-limiting configuration, are both based on the mindset of enlightenment and political liberalism[838]. The cognition that the American theory refers to the concrete object of attack, while the German penal theory pays attention to an abstract

831 "The success of the legal good doctrine is not based on its fixed direction, but on its chameleon-like changeability [...]". (Jakobs, Rechtsgüterschutz?, 2012, p. 16).
832 Wohlers, Rechtsgutstheorie und Deliktsstruktur, GA, 2002, pp. 15-20 (pp. 15, 16).
833 Roxin, Strafrecht AT I, § 2 I, marginal no. 93.
834 Wohlers, Deliktstypen des Präventionsstrafrechts, 1999, p. 49.
835 Kratsch, Festschrift für Oehler, p. 67, 68.
836 Kratsch, Verhaltenssteuerung, p. 351 et seqq; Kratsch, GA 1989, p. 49, 55; Kratsch, Festschrift für Dietrich Oehler, p. 69 et seqq.; Kratsch, JuS 1994, 372, 377.
837 Wohlers, Deliktstypen des Präventionsstrafrechts, p. 213.
838 Wittig, Rechtsgutstheorie, „Harm Principle" und die Abgrenzung von Verantwortungsbereichen, in: Hefendehl/v. Hirsch/Wohlers, Die Rechtsgutstheorie, 2003, pp. 239-243 (239).

legal good, unrelated to the object which is affected through the protection of a legal good, reveals the propensity of German jurisprudence to abstractness. The harm principle with its subjectivistic orientation[839] focuses on actual damages in reference to the victim[840], which takes the autonomy of the individual into account and in a good way underlines the democratic opinion in an anthropocentric perception, whereas German penal theorists see the abstraction of legal goods from human interests as an advantage[841]. The idea bears resemblance to the comparison of the common law tradition to the Roman-Germanic law system. The comparison of legal systems, a system whose norms belong to individual cases in opposition to a system whose norms impose rules universally valid/unrelated to a specific case, reveals distinct measure of abstractness; thus this different concept of legal treatments according abstractness pulls all through.

One idea is sticking to a single approach in comparison to sticking to one approach with various formations. In Germany, one valid penal doctrine must be able to explain all prohibitions, whereas the American approach permits possible further principles to justify criminal norms; therefore not all criminal norms are to be explained solely by the harm-principle, but by another principle, deriving from the harm-principle, the highly accepted offense-principle[842]. Yet, both liberal legal doctrines answer the question of why a certain behavior can be legitimately prohibited by statutory norms enforced by penal sanctions with the fact that it causes a specific external effect on society, which is harming or endangering the concrete interests of others or legal goods[843]. Thus also both concepts present similar problems in the approach to answer the question what the state may legitimately make criminal. The respective theories show similar deficits when it comes to naming the requirements of upon what the regulatory content of statutory prohibitions must be based and thus reveal the limits of determining the ambit of legitimate criminal norms to quite the same extent. What remains to be asked in both theories is which interests must be protected by criminal law. None of the Constitutions serve an answer for that question. The criteria which determine a group of legal goods are uncertain[844], as uncertain as the measurements in order to determine legally relevant interests.

Both concepts are historically and systematically aligned to provide protection for personal rights and exhibit problems in justifying penalty beyond personal

839 Hirsch, Der Rechtsgutsbegriff und das „Harm Principle" , in: Hefendehl/v. Hirsch/Wohlers, Die Rechtsgutstheorie, 2003, pp. 13-25 (22); Hirsch, GA 2002, pp. 2-14 (8).

840 Despite the individualistic orientation of the harm-principle, acts which cause collective harm can still be prohibited under the harm principle, due to a direct or indirect connection of collective harm to the harm of the individual (Hirsch, GA 2002, pp. 2-14 (8)).

841 Seher, Liberalismus und Strafe: Zur Strafrechtsphilosophie von Joel Feinberg, 2000, pp. 71-72; Hörnle, Offensive Behavior and German Penal Law, p. 259.

842 Feinberg, Offense to Others, Vol. 2, 1985; Hirsch, Der Rechtsgutsbegriff und das „Harm Principle" , in: Hefendehl/v. Hirsch/Wohlers, Die Rechtsgutstheorie, 2003, pp. 13-25 (22).

843 Wittig, Rechtsgutstheorie, „Harm Principle" und die Abgrenzung von Verantwortungsbereichen, in: Hefendehl/v. Hirsch/Wohlers, Die Rechtsgutstheorie, 2003, pp. 239-243 (239).

844 Roxin, Strafrecht AT I, Band I, § 2 arginal no. 5; For further information refer to: Sina, Die Dogmengeschichte des strafrechtlichen Begriffs „Rechtsgut" .

rights, especially, when it comes to justifying the protection of collective goods[845]. But even within the circuit of individual goods neither the German nor the American views serve a clear criterion for demarcation on what is to be set up as an interest worthy of criminal protection. According to the harm principle, a conclusive determination of what constitutes welfare interests, thus what are the basic requirements for the realization of one's own life planning and what emotions seems to be worthy of protection within the weighting against the interests of the actor, is missing[846]. Likewise, in the legal good doctrine, a clear statement about what demands protection by criminal norms beyond the protection of clear substantial personal goods is not recognizable. There is no selectivity to make out within the varying kind of views. Both theories show a lack of criteria for selecting the legal protected interests. While the Harm Principle names "welfare interests" as criterion without naming the therefore relevant basic requirements of welfare, the legal good doctrine answers the question even more inexactly by choosing the abstract circumlocution of every good being worthy of criminal protection, which protection conduces for the preservation of peace and the fruition of public welfare[847].

Nevertheless, this is acceptable so far, because the decision regarding of what conduct is to be made criminal must be made by the legislator in the end. Whereas the answer to the question which behavior must be punished in legitimate manners is searched for in the doctrines of two different legal systems; the proportionality criterion, according to which the ultimate decision of what must be made punishable and what is to be left unpunished, in turn, must be made by the legislature. Both legislature have this discretion in common. Based on constitutional standards and on common cultural fundamental convictions of the respective country, the legislator must ascertain what sort of protection one's own society asks for in the actual situation, in order to maintain a peaceful coexistence of its citizen in opposite to the illusive idea of abstractly determining a static and for all times valid precise number of objects worthy of criminal protection by one or another legal doctrine.

845 Seelmann, Rechtsgutskonzept, „Harm-Principle" und Anerkennungsmodell als Strafwürdigkeitskriterien, in: Hefendehl, v. Hirsch, Wohlers, Die Rechtsgutstheorie, pp. 261-267 (262).

846 Seelmann, Rechtsgutskonzept, „Harm-Principle" und Anerkennungsmodell als Strafwürdigkeitskriterien, in: Hefendehl, v. Hirsch, Wohlers, Die Rechtsgutstheorie, p. 261-267 (261).

847 Wessels/Beulke, Strafrecht AT, marginal no. 6.

Chapter 3 Hate Crime in the United States of America

The American legislature finds and determines that criminal acts involving violence, intimidation and destruction of property based upon bias and prejudice have become more prevalent in the United States of America[848]. The legislature addresses their increasing appearance and the seriousness of such "crimes and threats against persons because of their race, color, religion, ancestry, national origin, gender, sexual orientation, or mental, physical, or sensory handicaps". The basic idea of hate crime legislation is that such acts are more damaging to society than "ordinary" offenses motivated by other base motives. They do not only wound the particular victim to a greater degree, but they also "threaten the safety and welfare of all citizens" in such an extreme way that they "tear at the very fabric of free society" and thus dangerously harm democracy[849]. Since hate crimes are considered to be different due to their wider and deeper repercussions on particular victims and on society in comparison to "usual" crimes, they must be treated differently. Intolerance and discrimination played a huge role in determining the harmfulness of such crimes. The legislature of the United States embodied the unified opinion that ordinary "law does not adequately recognize the harm to public order and individual safety that hate crimes cause".[850] Accordingly, hate crimes are prosecuted and punished with severity, resulting in harsher sentences in comparison to other parallel crimes.

A. Course of Action

This research will focus on statutes contained in criminal codes which penalize bias-motivated behavior. In this regard, a distinction shall be made between legislation directed towards understanding and determining the extent of the phenomenon "hate crime", which shall include legislation aimed at establishing proper fact-finding procedures during a criminal investigation to enable a proper prosecution of hate crimes, and those laws which directly penalize and/or enhance punishments for hate-motivated offenses. To the first category, one would count all laws regulating the capturing of statistical data concerning hate crimes by investigative authorities, as well as legislation which focus on improving the investigation and detection of hate-motivated offenses. Statutes which prescribe training for judicial authorities concerned with hate crimes in order to teach how to detect and handle this sort of crime (e.g., police training laws) are intended to facilitate and ensure more correct acquisition of data through proper detection and recognition of relevant surrounding indicators which classify crimes as hate crimes. Proper detection

848 Assessment given in: NY State Penal Code § 485.00; Wash. Rev. Code § 9A.36.078.

849 NY State Penal Code § 485.00.

850 NY State Penal Code § 485.00; "The legislature finds that the state interest in preventing crimes and threats motivated by bigotry and bias goes beyond the state interest in preventing other felonies or misdemeanors [...], or other crimes that are not motivated by hatred, bigotry, and bias and that prosecution of those other crimes inadequately protects citizens from crimes and threats motivated by bigotry and bias". (Wash. Rev. Code § 9A.36.078).

and classification of hate crimes thus serve the aim of proper criminal prosecution as well.

The focus shall lie on legislation intended to penalize acts of hate violence. However, it is important to understand that laws aiming at penalizing the criminal behavior of hate crime comprise only one component of the legal incorporation. Thus, legislation surrounding these criminal statutes shall be illustrated broadly in order to encompass the whole subject of hate crime as it is effective in the United States, which on the one hand contains data collection law and legal devices for detecting hate crimes properly, and on the other hand imposes severe penalties on perpetrators of hate crimes. Anyway, it is not the concept, but rather the term "hate crime", understood as an umbrella term for such criminal offenses which reveal a racial[851], bias- or hate-related trigger[852]. Therefore, effective hate crime statutes enshrined in U.S. penal codes are illustrated in the following in order to be analyzed using German criminal standards in the aftermath.

The aim of this enquiry is to bring about mutual knowledge: The American discussion can benefit from thoughts concerning their legitimation practice towards hate crime laws, whereas German jurisprudence has the chance of acquiring knowledge and understanding of possible ways of explicitly dealing with such crimes by making a foray into the American supply of hate crime statutes.

By comparing the legal handling of bias-motivated conducts in the American legal system with such of the German legal system, the starting point shall be the underlying social problem which leads to the relevant legislation. Such is the phenomenon of bias-motivated incidents, broadly expressed, which constitutes a threat to the concerned society. Therefore, assuming that this problem exists in a similar way in both societies, the different approaches to this problem shall be compared in an inquisitorial manner. Even if the "exact" same social problem probably exists in both societies, that is xenophobia and crimes motivated by it, such differ in its extent, prevalence and according the magnitude of its effects. Therefore it must be carefully identified whether it really exists and, if it does, how it develops in the respective society.

B. Emergence of the Hate Crime Concept in the USA

With the abolition of slavery, the democratic doctrine of equality, and harsh criminal legislation to preserve the given order, one would assume that the American society is well prepared for egalitarianism. Nevertheless, since around 1980,[853] notable changes in criminal legislation have taken place to address racism, xenophobia, homophobia, misogyny and other forms of

851 "Race" in such terms as "racially" motivated violence or "racial" bias is used in this work inclusively, not exclusively, to encompass motivation based not only on the race, but also on the color, ethnicity, religion, national origin, gender and sexual orientation of the victim.

852 Glet, Sozialkonstruktion und strafrechtliche Verfolgung von Hasskriminalität in Deutschland, 2011, p. 9.

853 Around 1980, the first hate crime laws occurred. (Gerstenfeld, Hate Crimes, p. 9) It is said that the first hate crime law was enacted in California 1978. (Coester, Hate Crimes, p. 84).

discrimination in the American society. The perception[854] that ordinary legislation in form of general criminal statutes, which do not take prejudice, bias or hate as motives for committing a crime into account, is not enough to defend social equality, caused changes in criminal codes on both governmental levels (federal and state).

Criminal law is a device of last resort[855]. This implies that criminal law is a legitimate instrument to solve societal problems only if other devices are not equally suitable to achieve the goal of ensuring peaceful coexistence among people of a democratic society. Therefore, before hate crimes could be enshrined explicitly into American criminal law, such offenses had to pose a problem to the American society which is of such an alarming extent that no other solution seems capable to cope with it. A circumstance is considered to be a problem to society that is worthy of criminalization, if the underlying behavior of a hate crime proves to be socially damaging by violating statutory rights in such an outrageous manner that retaliatory actions must be eminently urgent and the imposition of punishment is the only effective device to protect such rights of these particular infringements[856]. So for criminal legislation to be enacted to address hate crimes, hate crimes must have constituted such a described social problem to the American nation.

Since the 80s, the term hate crime has been on everyone's lips in the United States. However, there is a debate, whether the problem of hate-motivated acts (actually) increased at an alarming rate during the last decades or whether this increase was merely "constructed" by social movements and the works they compiled surrounding the matter. There is talk of a hate crime epidemic or of a professed hate crime epidemic[857].

854 "Beginning in the late 1970s [...] some people and advocacy groups began to argue that [...] special hate crime laws should be passed." (Gerstenfeld, Hate Crimes, p. 15).

855 Ultima ratio principle of criminal law - cf. Jareborg, Criminalization as Last Resort, Ohio State Journal of criminal law, Vol. 2, pp. 521-534; accessed Nov. 2011; Roxin, Strafrecht AT I, p. 45, marginal no. 97.

856 Roxin, Strafrecht AT I, p. 45, marginal no. 97.

857 Aydin, Strafrechtliche Bekämpfung von Hassdelikten in Deutschland und den Vereinigten Staaten von Amerika, p. 34; Jakobs/Potter, Hate Crimes Criminal Law & Identity Politics 4 (1998); "[...] what they perceived to be an escalation of racial, ethnic, religious, and other forms of inter group conflict [...]". (Jenness/Grattet, Making Hate a Crime, 2001, p. 33).

1. The Hate Crime Concept and the Role of Social Movements

Those who subscribe to the idea of the problematic increase of crimes being committed against minorities as being more of a "social construct" rather than a true phenomenon argue that the works of social movements and the identity politics that are incited by them are the reason for

a. the existence of the social problem referred to as "hate crime";
b. the propagation of the term "hate crime" among American society;
c. the existence of hate crime legislation within the United States of America in general and for the particular wording and composition of these statutes[858].

1.1. Social Movements rumored to be the Author of the Social Phenomenon Hate Crime

The following refers to the debate whether hate crimes indeed constitute a social problem in the American society, potentially worthy of being addressed by criminal legislation or if the problem of hate crimes is merely constructed.

The U.S.A. has been dealing with prejudice and discrimination in a variety of forms and degrees ever since its founding[859]. Thinking of Native Americans who were slaughtered in the conquest of new territory, Africans who were captured and enslaved, the inhuman exploitation of the Chinese and other immigrant workers who built the railroad tracks across the Midwest, hostility against Jews[860] – just to name a few – it is evident that "bloodshed based on race or creed is interwoven with the fabric of American culture from the first arrival to the present day"[861]. Violence against selected individuals or groups because of certain characteristics is therefore not a new phenomenon; it has always existed and continues to do so. The question, rather, is why hate crime legislation suddenly emerged, thus establishing "new" criminal elements for age-old of offenses[862]. Transforming the historically given into a new phenomenon demands newfound attention to an age-old behavior[863]. This attention to hate crimes is often said to be brought by the works of social movements[864]. In that framework, it is claimed that groups of disadvantaged individuals began to protest against their unequal situation, invoking equal

858 Miller/Holstein, Constructionist Controversies: Issues in Social Problems Theory, 1993; Jenness/Grattet, Making Hate a Crime, 2001; Maroney, The Struggle against Hate Crime: Movements at a Crossroads, New York University Law Review 73(2), 1998, pp. 564 – 620.

859 Pearlman, Sanctioning Bias Crime, 2008, p.1.

860 Jenness/Grattet, Making Hate a Crime, 2001, p. 18.

861 Newton/Newton, Racial and Religious Violence in America: A Chronology, 1991, p. ix.

862 Volker Baldus, Hate Crime: Gesetze zur effektiven Bekämpfung von Rechtsextremismus und Fremdenfeindlichkeit in Deutschland?, 2003, p.3; Jennes/Grattet, Making Hate a Crime, 2001, p. 1.

863 Jennes/Grattet, Making Hate a Crime, 2001, p. 1.

864 Jennes/Grattet, Making Hate a Crime, 2001; Pfahl/Traughber, Ursachen rechtsextremistisch motivierter Gewalt, Kriminalistik, 2001, pp. 38-43.

protection under the law to all persons[865]. They created public attention in an attempt to achieve change for their particular situation[866]. The formation of such groups of citizens, their supporters all fighting for a certain aim, is called an interest group[867]. The members of such a group feel a sense of togetherness because of their common identity and consequently, they lobby as a group against certain social conditions, in most cases aiming at equal treatment for their kind as a result of the fact that they feel, or more often indeed are, discriminated in society[868]. In order to receive the treatment which they seek after, they demand a change in society oriented towards enhancing the legal, social and economic status and welfare of specific minorities or minorities in general in the United States. By generating enough public attention, such interest groups are called social movements because of their impact on the minds of people of their society[869]. Hand in hand with attracting public attention and influencing social views is the politicization of their aim; the work of such interest groups is therefore called "identity politics"[870]. The first movement of such a kind that became famous under the name Civil Rights Movement was the American Civil Rights Movement of the 1950s and 1960s which struggled for equal rights for African-Americans; soon multiple "modern"[871] social movements flourished[872]. The most influential ones which are related to the hate crime subject were the Civil Rights Movement, the Women's Movement and the Gay and Lesbian Movement, each of whose supporters fought for equal rights for their selected groups[873]. What these movements had in common was that each movement portrayed a particular group as systematically victimized by society and created far reaching attention to their cause[874]. On the other hand there was the Crime Victim Movement, which focused on individuals being targets of crimes. Victims are considered as persons who have been unjustly harmed or damaged by forces beyond their control[875] and thus are easily viewed as deserving support and protection among the public mind[876].

---

865 "The aspirations and demands of blacks fed back into the minds of members of other disadvantaged groups legitimized their rejection of socially prescribed places and roles". (Goldberg, 1991, p. 198).

866 As pioneers the African-American struggle facilitated the mobilization of other oppressed, for instance, such of the later established Civil Rights movements consisting of women, gays and lesbians. (Jenness/Grattet, Making Hate a Crime, 2001, p. 23).

867 Coester, Hate Crime, pp. 48 et seq.

868 Haselbach, Multikulturelle Apartheidpolitik, in: Kommune. Forum für Politik, Ökonomie und Kultur, 1997, p. 17.

869 Coester, Hate Crime, p. 49.

870 Jenness/Grattet, Making Hate a Crime, 2001, pp. 13 et seq.; Haselbach, Multikulturelle Apartheidpolitik, in: Kommune. Forum für Politik, Ökonomie und Kultur, 1997, p. 17; Coester, Hate Crime, pp. 48 et seq.

871 Morris calls the Civil Rights movements emerging in the mid-1950s "the modern" Civil Rights movements because they are the result of a political struggle that began in the Reconstructions period of the 1860s. (Morris, 1984, p. IX; Jenness/Grattet, Making Hate a Crime, 2001, p. 21).

872 Jenness/Grattet, Making Hate a Crime, 2001, p. 20.

873 Jenness/Grattet, Making Hate a Crime, 2001, pp. 13, 21, 31 figure 2.2.

874 Coester states that "the logic of identity politics is that being viewed as disadvantaged and victimized is strategically beneficial" – own translation of: Coester, Hate Crimes, 2007, p. 49.

875 Miller/Holstein, Rethinking Victimization: An international approach to Victimology, 1990, pp. 103-122; Jenness/Grattet, Making Hate a Crime, 2001, p. 9.

876 With the example of the Crime Victim Movement and the condolence and sympathy it provokes for its members, the effect of organizational work is easily understood. The Crime Victim Movement logically achieved public attention and, even more importantly, considering a preferably high magnitude of

Starting from the question what "made" crimes against particular victims an appalling problem in American society one must explain how hate crimes emerged to be a social problem[877] and why now, in order to then comprehend the specific legal treatment of such. Insofar social movements, particularly the Anti-Hate Crime Movement, are said to be the trigger for the change in attitude towards bias-motivated violence – from being long established and judicially ignored to being explicitly labeled at first and finally to being addressed in legal terms[878].

Following the development of movements in the United States described above, the emergence of the social problem of hate crimes is attributed to a convergence of the Civil Rights Movement fighting for justice for disadvantaged minorities and the Crime Victims' Movement[879]; both in combination constituted the Anti-Hate Crime Movement. Such emerged in the late 1970s[880] and is said to have laid the foundation for the hate crime policy effectuated in the United States today[881]. The reason for the Anti-Hate Crime Movement developing out of two social movements is that hate crime victims represent the overlap between both subjects[882]. The Civil Rights Movements "called attention to the personal costs of minority groups' political victimization" and the Victim Rights Movement "called attention to the political context of personal victimization"[883]. Together these two succeeded in instigating the public discussions about discrimination that manifests as violence[884] and in so doing aroused such widespread attention that a "social problem" occurred as a result of one's own doing.

1.2. Propagation of the Term "Hate Crime" among American Society

The term hate crime used throughout the world[885] to describe "criminal acts, committed by individuals or small groups (as opposed to governments or large political factions), in which the victim was targeted primarily because of his or her group"[886], originates from the United States. It is said that the term "hate crime" simultaneously came into existence with the emergence of the social

influence, extensive public support was gained. By drawing attention to the harsh fates of individuals, sympathies for such were felt. "The so-called Victim Rights Movement seemed to be making faster progress than any previous Civil Rights thrust in United States history". (Curtis J. Sitomer, New Civil Rights Thrust: Aid for Victims in: Christina Science Monitor, April 5, 1983, p. 1).

877 A social problem is a deviation of a standard that is considered to be a social problem. (Dollinger/Raithel, Einführung in die Theorien abweichenden Verhaltens, 2006, p. 21).

878 Clearly the change from the pure fact of existence of racial violence to the recognition of such as a social problem is the crucial point for the development of the concept followed by the USA. (Coester, Hate Crimes, 2007, p. 48).

879 Jenness/Grattet, Making Hate a Crime, 2001, p. 31.

880 Gerstenfeld states that the late 1970s were the begin of advocacy groups arguing that Hate Crimes laws are required. (Cf. Gerstenfeld, Hate Crimes, p. 15).

881 Jenness/Grattet, Making Hate a Crime, 2001, p. 18.

882 Jenness/Grattet, Making Hate a Crime, 2001, p. 31.

883 Maroney, 1998, p. 579.

884 Jenness/Grattet, Making Hate a Crime, 2001, p. 31.

885 "The ten international Synopsys the World Society for Victimology have recognized the concept in all parts of the world". (Schneider, Kriminologie der Hassdelikte. Konzeptionen, Ursachen, Vorbeugung und Kontrolle, in: Bewährungshilfe, 2003, pp. 115 et seqq. (115); OSCE/ODIHR, Hate Crime Laws: A Practical Guide, 2009).

886 Gerstenfeld, Hate Crimes, p. 10.

issue in the United States. The subject of hate-motivated violence is said to have been brought to the limelight of disputes by several interest groups and since then is consistently being discussed in public[887]. The term "hate crime" was then invented to designate the general subject in its core and thereby facilitate the discussion[888].

1.3. Hate Crime Legislation as Problem-Solving Approach induced by Social Movements

The first step for legislators to concern themselves with bias-motivated conducts, and thus develop a concept, is the existence of a social problem concerning these types of crimes. After all, as stated above, this social problem must develop the necessary degree of severity of the injury to statutory rights to legitimate criminal legislation combating it. Thus, it is stated that "the interpretative processes that constitute what comes to be seen as oppressive, intolerable or unjust conditions"[889] are the relevant causes for the existence of hate crime laws within the United States. These interpretative processes are said to be led and controlled through organizational works of interest groups and so, consequently, social movements are claimed to be the determiner for the existence of hate crime legislation in the United States.

1.4. Influence of Social Movements on the Wording and the Composition of Hate Crime Laws

Even though the basic framework addressing the fight against hate crime is set in the United States, and the federal government, as well as the majority of states, follows a similar concept in general, i.e. penalizing attacks motivated by bias against particular persons or properties with enhanced sentences, and tracking these incidents for statistical data collections, the material content of effective laws, in contrast, differs. In particular the characteristics that are protected by the laws vary[890]. This raises the question: why is it that characteristics such as disability and gender identity or expression were not enshrined in legal devices until October 1, 1995[891]? And why are not, for instance, police officers, the elderly or children protected by hate crime laws? Some views answer this question also with the influence of social movements[892]. As early as 1988, Representative John Conyers Jr. declared in

887 If one divides the formation of a problem into steps, the naming of facts by "collective acteurs" is the first of six steps. (Cf. Dollinger/Raithel, Einführung in die Theorien abweichenden Verhaltens, 2006, p. 27; Schetsche, Wissenssoziologie sozialer Probleme. Grundlegung einer relativistischen Problemtheorie, 2000, pp. 30 .et seqq.; Glet, Sozialkonstruktion und strafrechtliche Verfolgung von Hasskriminalität in Deutschland, 2010, p. 29).

888 Frequent hearing of a catchphrase logically enhances awareness.

889 Miller/Holstein, Constructionist Controversies: Issues in Social Problems Theory, 1993, p. 4; Jenness/Grattet, Making Hate a Crime, 2001, p. 9.

890 The breadth of protected classes differs across the nation. (Perry, In the Name of Hate, p. 7 et seqq.).

891 Substitute House Bill No. 5657, Public Act No. 04-135; effective October 1, 2004; Jenness/Grattet, Making Hate a Crime, 2001, p. 42.

892 Grattet/Jenness, The Birth and Maturation of Hate Crime Policy in the United States, American Behavioral Scientist, Dec 1, 2001, pp. 668-696; Jacobs/Potter, Hate Crimes: A Critical Perspective. In: Tonry (ed.) Crime and Justice, Band 22. Chicago, London, 1997, pp. 1 -50 (pp. 2,3); Jenness/Grattet, Making Hate a Crime, 2001.

a congressional hearing that hate crimes motivated by intolerance need to be distinguished from other crimes motivated by other factors“[893]. The question of what criteria a legal device shall provide in order to make up such a distinction could not be answered conclusively[894]. When one considers the laws in effect at present, the question remains of what led some traits to be enshrined in statutes while others are not protected[895]. Advocates of the idea that social movements constructed the hate crime issue state that the reason why one characteristic (race, religion, etc.) is legally protected by hate crime laws, and another is not, is simply because of the fact that one group has a lobby of decisive size, whereas the other does not[896]. To be more precise: the interests of a legally recognized group were taken into account in the legal hearing on a bill because of the sufficient impact of an advocacy group promoting the necessity of legal protection for their own kind, whereas the interests or characteristics of other legally unprotected groups, who lacked support from society a.k.a. organizational works, lacked recognition by Congress. This is said to be the reason why "federal hearings have yet to be held on hate crimes devoted exclusively to the problem of violence directed at children, the elderly, or police officers"[897].

2. Clarifying the Role of Social Movements

Hate crimes emerged as a social problem around the 1980s. Whether the number of hate-motivated acts provided by the statistical data of social movements[898] in the beginnings of legal involvement is evidence of an "epidemic" of bias-motivated criminal incidences, and thus highlights the problem underlying such offenses; or it merely makes up such a (nonexistent) problem, is controversial. While social movements may be perceived as

---

893 Congress 1988c, 8 ; Jenness/Grattet, Making Hate a Crime, 2001, p. 42.

894 Jenness/Grattet, Making Hate a Crime, 2001, p. 42.

895 This question is not to be confused with the issue of which traits are to be legitimately recognized as worthy of protection. It merely refers to the status quo of legal statutes. A substantive judgment as to which characteristics are to be legally enshrined into legislation shall be discussed later in this dissertation (G.1.10.2 Protected Characteristics).

896 The works of the ADL in particular are highlighted because the ADL is addressed as one of the most influential organizations when it comes to rationalizing the way legal devices on hate crimes are embodied in the United States (view hereto: Chapter 3, D., 2.1. The Launch of a Model Law). It is stated, that the ADL's data collection work did not go unnoticed in federal hearings on hate crime. The data from the ADL is claimed to have been the primary source of information on hate crime to which lawmakers referred when formulating the first hate crime laws. As proof for this thesis, it is provided that the concept of the ADL favored race and religion over other statuses and early legislation reflected exactly those characteristics – race and religion – indicating that the substantive character of hate crime in the beginnings of federal law addressing bias-motivated conducts was defined and institutionalized through the significance of the presented works of an interest group. (Cf. Grattet/Jenness, The Birth and Maturation of hate crime Policy in the United States, American Behavioral Scientist, Dec 1, 2001, pp. 668-696; Seehafer, Strafrechtliche Reaktionen, 2003, p. 46; Jenness/Grattet, Making Hate a Crime, 2001, pp. 48, 53).

897 In a 1988 congressional debate on the inclusion of sexual orientation to the list of status provisions, Representative Conyers explained why the provisions protected some groups and not others: "We did not include octogenarians who are assaulted [...] because there was no testimony that suggested that they ought to be, as awful as the crimes visited upon them are, and the reason we did not account for policemen killed in the line of duty, although police organizations do, is that there was no request that they be separated out from the uniform crime statistics". (Congressional Record 1988, 11403) – stated in Jenness/Grattet, Making Hate a Crime, 2001.

898 With the statistical data collection of the ADL leading the way, it is said that the formation of early legislation mainly leaned on statistical data of interest groups which registered incidents of hate-motivated offences all over the United States to reveal the extent of the problem of bias-motivated conducts.

having created a nonexistent social problem, hate crimes therefore not being a real threat to American society, it is equally conceivable that, since hate crimes have been denounced, the problem in fact exists and was merely uncovered through the works of social movements by bringing the facts to the minds of society and politics[899].

2.1. Social Problem "Hate Crime" - Real or Constructed?

The matter of a social problem necessarily raises the question of its objectivity or its constructivity[900]. To answer the question there are two recognized views, one that holds the opinion that social problems exist without being recognized[901], whereas the other opinion assumes that the social definition and not the objectivity of a given societal condition determines whether it exists as a social problem[902]. If one examines the history of the United States of America[903] one may assume that the problem of hate crime has in fact always existed (in the form of a remarkable number of bias-motivated offenses with certain destructive effects on society) and still exists today as a matter of fact[904]. Whether it was recognized as an unacceptable part of reality and thus constituted a social problem or was merely a construct of the work social movements and with such an ongoing process, does not need to be determined. Since the true existence of a considerable number of hate-motivated offenses cannot be denied, it is up to the parties involved to decide whether these constitute a social problem[905].

As to the question why hate crime legislation was not enacted before the 1980s, it may be that American society was ready to recognize hate crimes as an issue demanding legislative attention just at that point in time, i.e. the 1980s. Along with an increasing degree of civilization, it might be that the problem of hate crimes could be recognized just at that point. Possibly the receptivity of society did not allow a recognition of prevailing circumstances

---

899 The literature speaks of exogenous factors which provide the impetus for criminalization. These factors include a diverse array of social actors. Such actors either create or highlight a social condition which requires solving; which is why criminal issues are spoken of as "social constructs". Jenness/Grattet, Making Hate a Crime, 2001, pp. 20; 75 – with further references.

900 Coester, Hate Crimes, pp. 50 et seqq.

901 Coester, Hate Crimes, p. 50 with reference to Blumer, 1975, p. 105.

902 Coester, Hate Crimes, p. 50 with reference to Peters, 2002, p. 23.

903 Regarding this, view the following historical presentation, which shows that the disenfranchisement of citizens of certain races remained after the Civil War and the abolition of slavery. Several federal and constitutional demands, e.g. the adoption of the Fourteenth Amendment to the U.S. Constitution in 1868 specifying equal protection under the law to all persons did not serve equality of all mankind in the United States; but rather was lawful slavery replaced with institutionalized racism and bias-motivated violence to oppress minorities and retain the claim of power to former slaveholders.

904 Hate Crimes are still - extremely - prevalent in the USA according to the annual hate crime report published by the FBI which provides an impartial and neutral picture of the magnitude of the hate crime problem in the USA since 1991 (http://www.fbi.gov/about-us/cjis/ucr/ucr - accessed 2011/09/09). View the hate crime Statistics for 2010, which states an increased number of reported hate crimes when compared with figures reported for the same time in 2009. (Cf. http://www.fbi.gov/about-us/cjis/ucr/hate-crime/2010/narratives/hate-crime-2010-incidents-and-offences - accessed in 5. January 2012).

905 A criminal phenomenon such as hate crime can be real or constructed because all issues are interpreted through social actors. (Glet, Sozialkonstruktion und strafrechtliche Verfolgung von Hasskriminalität in Deutschland, 2011, pp. 2; 28; Hacking, Was heißt soziale Konstruktion?, pp. 18, 123; Dollinger/Raithel, Einführung in die Theorien abweichenden Verhaltens, 2006, pp. 27, 28; Schetsche, Wissenssoziologie sozialer Probleme, 2000, pp. 30 et seqq.).

earlier. In the civilization process, the sensitivity of society regarding the use of violence increases[906]. During the time when slavery was lawful, there was a different, if at all any, awareness of racial discrimination[907]. Yet, democratic development leads to changed cognitive ability. Finally, cognitive ability changes depending on the prevalent point of view, which can vary at different times[908]. So in reference to the problem of hate crimes, it may be assumed that the recognition of such a social problem requires a highly developed democracy to begin with. Such an initial situation, perhaps, could not be attributed to American society until the second half of the 20th century[909] - because despite the abolition of slavery, physical representation of social inequality remained in this society for decades[910]. With the awareness of these inequalities, hate crime legislation appeared[911]. While one must distinguish between the earlier abolished de jure segregation[912] and the later disestablished de facto segregation[913], only the significantly later de facto abolishment can influence cognitive ability. Hate crimes have always been present indeed, but American society was not ready to recognize it as a serious social problem before the 80s[914], which as such constitutes the foundation for criminal legislative actions. However, one must admit that, as always in history, democratical proceedings are accelerated by social

---

906 Elias, Über den Prozess der Zivilisation, 1939.

907 The starting point for a social problem that is recognized as such, is formed by the values and standards that apply in a society. (Dollinger/Raithel, Einführung in die Theorien abweichenden Verhaltens, 2006, p. 23 with reference to R. K. Merton, Soziologische Diagnose sozialer Probleme, in: K.O. Hondrich, Menschliche Bedüfnisse und soziale Steuerung, 1975, pp. 113-129).

908 Althoff, Die soziale Konstruktion von Fremdenfeindlichkeit, p. 92; Glet, Sozialkonstruktion und strafrechtliche Verfolgung von Hasskriminalität in Deutschland, 2011, p. 27; "What constitutes a social problem, and what does not, is [...] subject to change". (Cf.Dollinger/Raithel, Einführung in die Theorien abweichenden Verhaltens, 2006, p. 22).

909 Until 1964, racist Jim Crow laws were effective (despite the decree of the Fourteenth Amendment). Until the second half of the 20th century, legal disenfranchisement of minorities was general accepted. Only through the enactment of the Civil Right Act of 1964 it was made "[...] clear to all, that race has no place in American life or law". (Parts of President John F. Kennedy's speech in Congress, when Civil Rights laws were sent to Congress on June 19, 1963. - Johnson, The laws that shaped America, 2009, p.306; Morris, The Origin of the Civil Rights Movement: Black Communities Organizing for Change, New York: The Free Press, 1986, pp. 1-2).

910 Refer to racial segregation.

911 During the Jim Crow Era, however, the call for hate crime legislation would have been misplaced. The starting point of hate crime laws in effect nowadays is said to lie within the Civil Rights Act of 1964 (Coester, Hate Crimes, p. 82). Admittedly, 20 years as a period for transformation is hardly worth mentioning - speaking of the time range from Jim Crow Laws becoming ineffective to the time when hate crime legislation came into effect (Civil Right Acts was effectuated in 1965 countering Jim Crow legislation and the introduction of the first hate crime bill was in 1985).

912 The ending of de jure segregation started with a series of Supreme Court decisions, starting with Brown v. Board of Education in 1954. Yet, the end was not articulated clearly until the enactment of the Civil Rights law of 1964. (Refer to John F. Kennedy's speech in Congress according Civil Right laws on June 19, 1963, stating that these laws for the first time made " [...] clear to all, that race has no place in American life or law". (Johnson, The laws that shaped America, 2009, p. 306).

913 De facto segregation "in fact" persists - to a variable extent - probably until today. Visible to anyone, racial segregation today is best detectable by looking at American neighborhoods; such have been shaped by mortgage discrimination, public policies leading to or aimed at geographical groupings of racial groups, colloquially known as "black ghetto"; "china town"; etc. (for further information view Massey/Denton, American apartheid: segregation and the making of the underclass, 1993).

914 "Laws - especially criminal laws - are an expression of society's values." (OSCE/ODIHR, Hate Crime Laws: A Practical Guide, 2009, p. 7). The question of the reason for the lack of hate crime Laws in a value system that is characterized by racial segregation in earlier times, yet their later introduction can be plainly explained with the changing value system of the respective society.

movements, wherein groups of citizenry feel bound in honor stand up and demand a change. Through the works of social movements, attention was drawn to the problem of hate crimes at a faster pace.

First and last the reasons for the emergence of the new offense category in the U.S. in the mid 80's are complex. Some people draw the radius for explanations further[915]: Except that racial, religious and ethnic minorities gained strength in the 20th century due to distinct civil right movements and thereby the pressure on the held-down, unconscious people to not let their victimization become known decreased; further, the end of the Cold War and the collapse of the Soviet Union is cited as evidence that the suppression of ethnic conflict ended[916]. Thus the hatred between communities became an ubiquitous global phenomenon. "With the increased "migration movement" in many parts of the world in the late 20th century several societies became more heterogeneous, more dissimilar, more multiethnic, more religious, and more racial. Thereby numerous group conflicts in pluralistic societies increased"[917]. Based on this, the "real" problem of hate crime in fact increased at that time. While this reasoning is put in a larger, more global context with claimed effects on the U.S. society, the result broadly remains the same: In any case the American population at this time became more sensitive to violence that is based on blind, fanatical hatred and prejudice[918].

So, contrary to the claim that groups of the oppressed and their defenders had to pave the way in order for discriminatory violence to be recognized[919] bias-motivated conducts may be viewed as having been present all the time; however, in order for it to be seen not as a social condition but as a societal problem, society as such had to recognize the need for action by itself through continuing evolution[920]. In this case, hate crime laws would have been enacted nowadays either way as a result of the spirit of the time[921]. The change in perspective of those (judicially, politically and socially) responsible for interpreting the given facts and circumstances[922] was rather the reason for the

915 Schneider, Politische Kriminalität: Hassverbrechen, Fremdenfeindlichkeit im internationalen Kontext, Kriminalistik 2001, pp.21-28 (22).

916 Schneider, Politische Kriminalität: Hassverbrechen, Fremdenfeindlichkeit im internationalen Kontext, Kriminalistik 2001, pp.21-28 (22).

917 Schneider, Politische Kriminalität: Hassverbrechen, Fremdenfeindlichkeit im internationalen Kontext, Kriminalistik 2001, pp.21-28 (22).

918 In parallel, also the problem of hate crime in fact increased. "An increasing number of hate groups, ideological cults arose in all parts of the world." (Schneider, Politische Kriminalität: Hassverbrechen, Fremdenfeindlichkeit im internationalen Kontext, Kriminalistik 2001, pp. 21-28 (22)).

919 Jenness/Grattet, Making Hate a Crime, 2001, pp. 20; 75.

920 As there was no democratic situation constituted within society before, referring to the pure attempts of creating equality among human beings due to legislative, executive and judicial treatment, which the Thirtheenth and Fourtheenth Amendment and the Federal Civil Right legislation since 1866 aimed at, an endeavor to hate crime legislation could have not take place.

921 It is said that social phenomena and their definitions are "constructed" in collective dialogues and within the frame of social processes. (Althoff, Die soziale Konstruktion von Fremdenfeindlichkeit, p. 92). The construal and the defintion depends on the particular existent of the surrounding social, historical and cultural conditions which again themselves are influenced by perceptions, experiences and individual backgrounds, which vary from time to time. With that the reality follows the "social construction" or in other words: the reality is constructed by society. (Glet, Sozialkonstruktion und strafrechtliche Verfolgung von Hasskriminalität in Deutschland, 2011, p. 26 et seqq.(27)).

922 Which are, for instance, criminal policy-makers, police, and justice.

legislation which followed such incidents. The problem became palpably evident when the extent of hate crimes was released to the public through statistical data material gathered by organizational works. However, the recognition and perception of a problem must not, as such, be equated with the actual existence[923]. So what may be granted as to be the "effect of social movements" is the steering of attention to existing conditions, due to the aroused attention such conditions then were recognized as a problem. The terms "construct"; "construction of hate crimes" and the like therefore, are used solely in the sense that all issues experience interpretation through social actors[924].

2.2. Propagation of the Term "Hate Crime" among American Society

The term hate crime appeared in legal wording for the first time in 1985, and at least since then has been on everybody's lips[925]. Introduced in 1985 to Congress[926], the hate crime Statistics Act[927] was the first piece of legislation to bring national attention to the problem of hate-motivated violence[928]. Obviously, when coining the term "hate crime", the correct dogmatic coverage of the problem in question was not considered, but rather it was about being easily embedded into the minds of people. For the simplification of a public discussion the memorability of a catchphrase is more important than the dogmatical correctness of a terminology[929]. Whether formed by social movements or rather through the general public discussion which, as conceded, was (further) stimulated by social movements is irrelevant, since in any case this terminology was launched officially through the introduction of the first federal hate crime bill and from then on was effectively launched in general.

923 In no way shall the true existence of bias-motivated behavior be in doubt. Nor shall the existence and the efforts of several social movements concerning hate crimes be in doubt. Only the attributed effect of their works, which are said to be solely accountable for the enactment of criminal law, is criticized and for the most part declined.

924 Hacking, Was heißt „soziale Konstruktion“ ? pp. 18; 123; For a deeper understanding of how social phenomena occur refer to: Schetsche, Wissenssoziologie sozialer Probleme. Grundlegung einer relativistischen Problemtheorie, 2000; Glet, Sozialkonstruktion und strafrechtliche Verfolgung von Hasskriminalität in Deutschland, 2011, p. 26 et seqq

925 It is agreed that 1985 was the year when the term first appeared (Bleich/Hart, Quantifying Hate: The Evolution of German Approaches to Measuring 'Hate Crime', German Politics, 2008, pp. 63; Coester, Hate Crime, p. 19; Aydin, Strafrechltiche Bekämpfung von Hassdelikten, p. 34).

926 The bill was introduced by three members of Congress: John Conyers (D-Michigan), Barbara Kennely (D-Conn.), and Mario Biaggi (D-N. Y.). (Cf. Aydin, Strafrechtliche Bekämpfung von Hassdelikten, p. 34, fn. 74).

927 Hate Crime Statistics Act, 28 U.S.C. § 534. (View hereto: Chapter 3, D., 1.2. Hate Crime Statistics Act of 1990).

928 Jenness/Grattet, Making Hate a Crime, 2001, p. 53.

929 A designation simplifies a public discussion concerning a criminal phenomenon. Thus, for the introduction to a subject, a term which encompasses the subject easiest is required. "The performance of the defintion [...] will decide whether and how a situation is interpreted as a problem." (Cf. Dollinger/Raithel, Einführung in die Theorien abweichenden Verhaltens, 2006, pp. 24, 28; Glet, Sozialkonstruktion und strafrechtliche Verfolgung von Hasskriminalität in Deutschland, 2010, p. 29).

2.3. Hate Crime Legislation as a Problem – Solving Approach

It is not the work of social movements which legitimate legal devices, but social conditions. If at all, going one step back, social movements, in a manner similar to the one discussed above, highlighted these social circumstances by bringing such to people's minds at a faster pace; and in so doing indirectly caused legislators to take action against such at that specific time. It is also possible that this provided the foundation for legislators to become legally active by serving material which highlighted criminally relevant conditions and thereby legitimated the enactment of legislation[930]. Dogmatic reasons for legal action, for example, could have been the findings of legislators (even if these findings were provided through the gathered material of social movements) that hate-motivated violence has consequences beyond the pain and suffering of the individual victim, because it terrorizes entire communities. If bigoted violence primarily is a form of crime which directly victimizes only particular groups of minorities – Jews, immigrants, blacks, gays and lesbians, women and persons with disabilities –, a starting point for legitimate legal involvement directed towards the protection of certain characteristics is conceivable, the construction of a "new" type of crime being the consequence. Hardly could lobbyism by several movements cause legal changes in criminal law in a democratic society without the existence of any dogmatically legitimate basis for such. Those opinions which state that the existence of hate crime laws can be attributed simply to the political impact of social movements neglect that such movements provided reasons in the data material they provided, which as such could possibly serve as dogmatic material to legitimate punishability due to revealing a social problem that requires legal solving[931]. Therefore, social movements could influence legislators indirectly, by accelerating their handlings.

With that said, in the concept currently followed by U.S. jurisprudence, criminal statutes are rather the result of the cognition received from previously enacted data collecting legislation which serves to encompass the problem. Prosecuting these crimes in their specific way required by hate crime law in effect nowadays, is the outcome of long discussions by legal experts[932] which,

930 According to Jenness/Grattet, social movement communities organize around the pursuit of legal reform, by providing their collective data material in order to prove the extent of harm caused to their members and further interacting with policy maker's interpretative and discursive practices to give meaning to hate crimes statutes as they develop and stabilizes. (Jenness/Grattet, Making Hate a Crime, 2001, pp. 42 et seqq.).

931 Referring to findings within statistical data proving, for instance, the extent of harm caused to victims of minorities due to bias-motivated conducts, highlights the existence of the social problem of hate crimes. Further gained cognition, e.g. that victimization which arises from racially motivated violence is different from other victimization, could serve as a legitimation base for law.

932 Crediting the relatively recent legislative recognition of bias crime to social movements of that time and the preceding decades (instead of to judicial findings), especially also to the works of the Anti - Defamation League of B´nai B´rith (as done by Jenness/Grattet, Making Hate a Crime, 2001, pp. 32 et seqq.; 42 et seqq. 48, and many others) is criticized in this opinion, since the so claimed "one of the most influential organization" Anti Defamation League of B´nai B´rith, was founded as early as in 1913, and already then had the mission "[...] to stop, [...] by appeals to law unjust and unfair discrimination against and ridicule of any sect or body of citizens". (Anti-Defamation League, 2012, http://www.adl.org/combating_hate/ especially: http://www.adl.org/about.asp?s=topmenu - accessed January 2012). So these views claiming the decree of law refers to interest groups and their lobbying fail to explain why the enactment of such

as a result, found that a special treatment of hate crimes by classifying them in their own criminal category[933], by including the offender's motive for committing a crime to a special degree, is envisaged from a legal point of view[934]. Therefore, in the present day, hate crime is no more just a social problem in the U.S., but a theoretical concept[935].

2.4. Influences on the Wording and the Composition of Hate Crime Laws

The same holds true for the wording and the material content of hate crime laws. These depend on the legislator's decision of which legal goods require what sort of protection.

Perhaps the works of social movements caused a sooner and more urgent legal debate. However, there have been legal approaches to capture bias-motivated violence by the enactment of Civil Rights Laws for over a century[936]. Moreover, one must take into consideration that the first hate crime law, which was enacted on federal grounds in the 80s, is not a law which stipulated new penalties for bias-motivated offenses; nor did it alter any criminal consequences for offenses motivated by bias. It merely required the collection of empirical data[937], which was considered necessary to develop effective policy[938]. This shows that the legislator did not solely depend on data provided by social organizations, nor did the legislature enhance penalties on the basis of material collected by interest groups. Consequently, the legislator did not base the enactment of criminal legislation on the interpretation of lobbies and opinions at second hand only. Legislative research was done before criminalization through specific criminal laws took place[939]. Therefore, this

---

legislation did not happen in 1913. Legislation on that part was not enacted before 1985. Howsoever, what started to be discussed as a result of social movements in the United States, is accredited today in the entire international literature, which is not be influenced by U. S. American interest groups. (Aydin, Die strafrechtliche Bekämpfung von Hassdelikten, 2006; Schneider, Internationale Handbuch der Kriminologie, Vol. II, pp. 297 ff; Adler/Müller/Laufer, Criminology and the Criminal Justice System, 2007, sixth edition, pp. 272, 273; Bartol/Bartol, Criminal Behavior, 9th edition, 2010, pp. 18 – 20; Siegel, Criminology, eleventh edition, 2011, pp. 306 – 308; Conklin, Criminology, eleventh edition, 2011, pp. 58, 59; Barkan, Criminology, 5th edition, 2011, pp. 287 – 289; Vito/Maahs, Criminology, 3rd edition, 2012, pp. 312 – 316; Arrigo, Criminal Behavior: A System Approach., 4th Edition , 2006, pp. 125, 126; Riedel/Welsh, Criminal Violence, Patterns, Causes, and Prevention. 2008, pp. 138 – 157).

933 Levin/Mc Devitt, The rising tide of bigotry and Bloodshed, 1993; G. M. Herek/K. T. Berill, Hate Crimes – Confronting Violence Against Lesbians and Gay Men, 1992.

934 While movements at the beginnings might have generated social awareness for necessary legislative response to hate crimes, meanwhile the "[...] legislative efforts and academic debate have gone on independent of the views of ordinary citizens". (Tereylyn/Pearlman, Sanctioning Bias Crime, 2008, p. 1).

935 Schneider, Kriminologie der Hassdelikte. Konzeptionen, Ursachen, Vorbeugung und Kontrolle, in: Bewährungshilfe, 2003, p. 115.

936 View hereto: Chapter 3, D., 1.1. Civil Rights Legislation.

937 Under the Hate Crime Statistics Act of 1990, the FBI has been reporting hate crimes based on perceived race, religion, ethnicity, and sexual orientation. Since 1994, their reports have included disability.

938 Those supporting this statute argue that involving the police in identifying and counting hate crimes could help law enforcement officials to measure trends, fashion effective responses, design prevention strategies and develop sensitivity to the particular need of victims of hate crimes, thus it was designed as an evaluating instrument of how hate crimes are to be combated best, which finally led to the here to be examined penalty enhancement laws within the criminal law sector.

939 The FBI, as independent governmental authority, has been collecting hate crime statistics under the Federal Hate Crime Statistics Act (HCSA) since 1991. Within that report own, autonomous findings are made, in order to create an own picture of the magnitude of the hate violence problem in the United States of America. (http://www.fbi.gov/about-us/cjis/ucr/ucr - accessed 2011/09/09).

collection of data was a notable and necessary intermediate step before explicit criminalization of bias-motivated behavior was established[940]. It served for the evaluation of the extent and the content of the problem and thereby served as the basis for the enactment of legislation which meets its needs.

The idea that the choice of which groups are protected by law nowadays is the result of the successful portrayal of these groups as victims by organizations[941], which were particularly influential, and this again is addressed to its numbers of supporters, cannot be parsed. To begin with, it could be argued that there is a potential connection between the numbers of supporters of a movement (i.e., the power of an interest group due to its size)[942] and the actual existence and extent of a social problem, whose change is the aim of the movement. Logically, an interest group might have a high number of advocates because the need for change in society pertaining to their represented subject is one of the greatest[943]. On the other hand, characteristics like race, ethnicity and religion, which are provided in early legislation, are the very characteristics for which one became singled out and have his/her rights deprived according to the historical context of the United States. Lynching took place against certain races (blacks), not against homosexuals. Native Americans, as an ethnic group, were attacked and discriminated, but not so much the disabled. In addition, in the U.S. Constitution these characteristics are explicitly constituted as features to which the U.S. government is constrained to not accept any acts of discrimination. In this respect the abolition of discriminatory behavior towards race, ethnicity[944] and religion suggests itself, at least, more obviously than discriminatory behavior towards gender, gender identity, disability, or sexual orientation. Since discrimination based on race, ethnicity and religion is explicitly defined as unconstitutional, the transfer of this constitutionally prescribed valuation to inter-social acts was not far off. This does not mean, however, that other groups actually protected by hate crime laws - even if historically they are not notably persecuted – do not deserve criminal protection. The aim is merely to unravel the connection between the demands of an interest group and the indeed legal enshrinement of such demands into law, since the idea of

---

940 By collecting data, the seriousness of the problem becomes evident or as Perry states: "In the absence of empirical information about bias-motivated violence, it is difficult to construct conceptual frameworks." (Perry, Where do we go from here?, p. 16).

941 Jenness/Grattet, Making Hate a Crime, 2001, pp. 44 et seqq.

942 Coester points out the problematic nature of the relation between the size of an interest group and successfully achieving an aim, e.g. of legal, social or political change (cf. Coester, Hate Crimes, pp. 48, 49).

943 Huge organizations are said to be very powerful when it comes to achieving political actions. However, such organizations, which are said to have strongly influenced certain matters due to their size, might have achieved far reaching implementation of their aims, because the need for change in this subject matter was at its greatest.

944 Moreover, constitutional precepts could work as counter-argument to the idea of early legislation containing race, ethnic and religion as characteristics since these traits are constitutionally granted and therefore must be protected by the government, thus supported by legislation if endangered. Race and ethnicity easily encompass further characteristics as color, and national origin. This argues against the opinions that claim that those features became legally enshrined solely because such were promoted by larger social-movements at that time, notably through the ADL (cf. Jennes/Grattet, Making Hate a Crime, pp. 42 et seqq.).

lobbyism forming legal devices in a democracy is misguided because there are in fact well-prescribed barriers in the legislative process[945]. After all, there are reasons why certain groups are visibly protected in legislation over others; other than just the preference for such characteristics by one or several interest groups, which legislators are then said to carry out blindly by following the objectives of lobbyists without closer examination. For example, why the elderly or police officers are not presently identified as groups deserving protection could depend on insufficient criminal reasoning[946].

3. Conclusion: Emergence of the Hate Crime Concept in the USA

The phenomenon hate crime occurred in the United States of America through the interpretation of the given social situation that offered the actual existence of offenses motivated by bias. According to this interpretation, in the late 1970s legal action was found to be required to combat the social problem of hate crimes. Whether the situation indeed presented a social problem or was more socially constructed is consequently immaterial, since the answer to this depends on the construal of the interpretation processes concerned[947]. There is no need for a general decision on this matter because interpretations and views do not serve the general public, but are in the eye of the beholder, which in this case is the legislator of the United States. Although, the numbers of hate crime incidents presented by statistical data, federal data being foremost[948], continually hint at the true existence of bias-motivated offenses. Nonetheless, the severity of the phenomenon, specifically the question whether the registered incidents of hate crimes committed in the USA harm the society in a particularly intolerable way or whether the registered harm caused by such crimes is intolerable enough to be classified as a social problem, as stated, is subject to the perception of the interpreters involved. Hence general examination will not suffice to determine the tolerability of the harm[949]. Without prejudice to the generality, it depends on the view of the concerned people of the United States if hate crimes constitute a social

---

945 If examining how a bill becomes a law (view Chapter 2, B., 3., 3.2., 3.2.1., 3.2.1.2. Federal Institutions, marginal no. 75) one realizes that a bill, once introduced by members of Congress, runs through several audit instances before finally being ratified by the President. One should be allowed to assume that a purely by interest groups proposed law would lack approval at some point of the ratification process.

946 View hereto: Chapter 4, G., 1.10.2 Protected Characteristics, which addresses the topic of which characteristics must be protected by a hate crime law, in accordance to the here followed understanding.

947 Hacking, Was heißt „soziale Konstruktion"? pp. 18; 123; Glet, Sozialkonstruktion und strafrechtliche Verfolgung von Hasskriminalität in Deutschland, 2011, p. 28.

948 According to the Hate Crime Statistics Act under the authority of Section 534 of Title 28, United States Code, the Attorney General shall acquire data, for each calendar year, about crimes that manifest evidence of prejudice based on race, religion, disability, sexual orientation, or ethnicity, including where appropriate the crimes of murder, non-negligent manslaughter; forcible rape; aggravated assault, simple assault, intimidation; arson; and destruction, damage or vandalism of property. (28 U.S.C. § 534 Section 1(b) (1) as amended November 2010 by the U.S. Department of Justice-Federal Bureau of Investigation). In 2009, for instance, 2,034 law enforcement agencies reported 6,604 hate crime incidents involving 7,789 offenses. For detailed information and statistics according incidents, location type, offenses, victims, and known offenders by bias motivation view the latest published numbers of 2009 at: http://www2.fbi.gov/ucr/hc2009/data/table_01.html.

949 Compare to Glet, who holds the opinion that the phenomenon hate crime is a construct which extent and manifestation depends on internalized associations, individual perceptual- and interpretative patterns, and of the selective strategies of involved law enforcement authorities. (Glet, Sozialkonstruktion und strafrechtliche Verfolgung von Hasskriminalität in Deutschland, 2010, pp. 25, 27, 40).

problem in their nation. As their decision stands, hate crimes exist in the United States and are considered to constitute a social problem which is to be acknowledged as real by the world at large.

The terminology "hate crime" arose from the social discourses of that time, officially traceable to the introduction of a bill by members of Congress.

Whereas the reasons for the emergence of the new offense category in the U.S. in the mid 80's are complex, the formation of the legislative concept of hate crimes valid today, at least, can not rely solely on interpretation processes, because legislative action requires dogmatic reasoning in addition to the (real) existence of a social problem. This dissertation will examine the existence and forms of such dogmatical reasoning which could possibly justify hate crime legislation. Despite the fact that opponents of hate crime laws wanted them to be abolished because they claim that such laws are merely social constructs (constructs understood as "made up)", the body of international literature today acknowledges that crimes of this sort deserve to be codified in an own criminal category[950]. Hate crimes, which began to be discussed as an issue created by social movements in the United States, nowadays are considered to cause far more damages than their counterparts which are not motivated by bias or hate, i.e., "ordinary" crimes, as discussed in the course of this work[951]. This fact could constitute a legitimate base for their existence.

After all it must be said that the work of social movements is precisely a part of democracy. Especially Civil Courage is necessary in the fight against xenophobic and similar behavior[952]. "It is often not sufficient, if politicians, intelligence agencies, police and judiciary keep their eyes open to social problems, each citizen is required to counter open and hidden forms of [bias-motivated violence]. The best protection of a democratic Constitution is the willingness of the citizens to stand up for their democratic system and a tolerant interaction with each other"[953]. Not more than that is represented by the work of social movements.

---

950 Aydin, Die strafrechtliche Bekämpfung von Hassdelikten, 2006; Schneider in continuous academic literature: 1996; 2001a, 2001b; 2003a; 2003b; 2003c; 2004; 2006a; 2006b; Adler/Müller/Laufer, Criminology and the Criminal Justice System, 2007, sixth edition, pp. 272, 273; Bartol/Bartol, Criminal Behavior, 9th edition, 2010, pp. 18 – 20; Siegel, Criminology, eleventh edition, 2011, pp. 306 – 308; Conklin, Criminology., eleventh edition, 2011,pp. 58, 59; Barkan, Criminology, fifth Edition, 2011, pp. 287 – 289; Vito/Maahs, Criminology, 3rd edition, 2012, pp. 312 – 316; Arrigo, Criminal Behavior: A System Approach., 4th edition, 2006, pp. 125, 126; Riedel/Welsh, Criminal Violence, Patterns, Causes, and Prevention. 2008, pp. 138 – 157).

951 View Chapter 4, G., 1., 1.1., 1.1.1.

952 According to the quote of Mr. Otto Schily in the preface to the Annual Constitution Report of 1999, as stated in: Scholzen: Rechtsextremismus, Gefahr erkannt, Gefahr gebannt?; in: Kriminalistik. 2001, pp. 314 – 316 (316).

953 Quotation of Mr. Otto Schily in the preface to the Annual Constitution Report of 1999, as stated in: Scholzen, Reinhard: Rechtsextremismus, Gefahr erkannt, Gefahr gebannt?; in: Kriminalistik. 2001, pp.314 – 316 (316).

C. Beginnings of Hate Crime Legislation

Historically, crimogenic conditions flourish with active encouragement or connivance by systems of governance. Especially the criminal justice system supplied for the omnipresence of race-motivated violence in the United States[954]. In response to the Thirteenth Amendment to the U.S. Constitution, which abolished slavery throughout the United States, various states enacted legislation intended to limit the Civil Rights of newly freed slaves[955]. In addition to such sorts of governmental discrimination came government-promoted or civil discriminatory violence. The following period of Reconstruction[956] was marked by an excessive increase[957] of racist crimes,[958] hence, the required additional protection of former slaves against their former owners was not only warranted, but proven every day by horrible criminal acts in form of lynching, burning of churches etc. to terrorize entire segments of society. Since 1868 the Fourteenth Amendment to the U.S. Constitution determined that no state "shall make or enforce any law which shall abridge the privileges or immunities of the citizens of the United States... [or] deprive any person of life, liberty, or property without due process of law, [or] deny to any person within its jurisdiction the equal protection of the laws"[959]. By this, all "Black Codes" were countered by the Constitution[960]. However, states enacted all sorts of laws with similar discriminatory content, so-called "Jim Crow" laws[961] which the Supreme

954 Maroney, 1998, pp. 564-565.

955 Southern legislatures enacted "Black Codes" in reaction to the abolition of slavery and their defeat in the Civil War in the 1860s. These laws mandated legal racial segregation in all public facilities. Since these laws were enacted in southern states only, one ought not to think that there were constitutional circumstances prevailing in northern states. Northern segregation similarly took place, just without explicit legal base. As these laws were enacted under state authority, the Supreme Court approved such laws adding the fictional requirement of the "separate but equal" doctrine (Plessy v. Ferguson, 163 U.S. 537 (1896)). That landmark decision stated that segregation is constitutional, thus state and local governments are legitimately authorized to segregate all public facilities, "[...] providing, of course, that they were "equal" (which they hardly ever were)." (Johnson, The laws that shaped America, 2009, p.296; On the history of Jim Crow laws, view: Woodward, The Strange Career of Jim Crow, 3rd rev. Ed. (New York: Oxford University Press, 1974, 1955)). Black Codes were overruled by the Civil Rights Act of 1866, "which established citizenship for "all persons born in the United States" regardless of race or prior condition of servitude, required equal protection under state laws, and set up enforcement mechanisms." (Cf. Lawrence, Punishing Hate, p. 121). However, soon after the adoption of the Fourteenth Amendment to the U.S. Constitution in 1868, the states sought after new laws in order to keep the disenfranchisement up: "Jim Crow" laws took over the oppression, regardless of constitutional or federal standards.

956 The term "Reconstruction Era" used within this dissertation refers to the time after the American Civil War, 1865 until 1877.

957 Gerstenfeld states "this was the era in which the Ku Klux Klan was born". (Gerstenfeld, Hate Crimes, 2004, p. 10).

958 Jacobs, The Emergence and Implications of American Hate Crime Jurisprudence, 1993, p. 150.

959 Amendment XIV, Section five to the U. S. Constitution gives power to the Congress to enact any legislation necessary to enforce the Amendment.

960 "Black Codes" - ′by law′ - theoretically have already been countered by the prior enacted Civil Rights Act of 1866 which established equal rights for former slaves and slave owners.

961 These Jim Crow laws are to be distinguished from former Black Codes: Black Codes where in force after the American Civil War in reaction to the Thirteenth Amendment, whereas Jim Crow laws were more of a reaction to the Fourteenth Amendment and were effective during the years of 1868 and 1964. Jim Crow laws were enacted after the Fourteenth Amendment countered all "Black Codes" and were overruled by the Civil Right Act of 1964. By all means, both types of legislation restricted the Civil Rights and liberties of African Americans.

Court approved by pronouncing the "equal but separate"[962] doctrine. The everyday societal reality was that the United States was traversed by discrimination and hounded by hate offenses. Since every day life constituted an unconstitutional reality despite constitutional determinations, further federal legal intervention was required. In order to implement the constitutional demand of the Fourteenth Amendment to the U.S. Constitution, Congress enacted numerous Civil Rights statutes[963]. "A civil right is an [...] enforceable [...] privilege" based on constitutionally guaranteed rights, "which if interfered with by another, gives rise to an action for injury"[964]. Discrimination occurs when the Civil Rights of an individual are denied or interfered with because of their membership in a particular group or class. Civil Rights legislation therefore aims at protecting the Civil Rights of the individual. Early Civil Rights legislation started with the specific combat against government workers depriving individuals of their constitutional rights and with specifically addressing conspiracies of two or more individuals to commit an offense[965]. The federal Civil Rights laws of 1871[966], for instance, enabled the federal government to penalize people who interfere with the constitutionally guaranteed rights of others, either in concert with other perpetrators (18 U.S.C. § 241)[967] or in their capacity as government employees (18 U.S.C. § 242)[968].[969] These early laws reflect their trigger, which is the cognition of the federal government that local authorities, due to racial motivation, acted corruptly and

962 In Plessy v. Ferguson, 163 U.S. 537 (1896) the United States Supreme Court ruled that state laws which required segregation in public conveyances and public schools, provided that they are equal, are constitutional. The separation led to diverse medical treatment, diverse financial support and diverse accommodations for minorities; all usually inferior to those provided for white Americans, further systematizing a number of economic, educational and social disadvantages included.

963 After the Civil War, the federal government enacted comprehensive Civil Rights protections (Civil Rights Act of 1866, 14 Stat. 27 (1866); Civil Rights Act of 1870 (The Enforcement Act), 16 Stat. 140 (1870); Civil Rights Act of 1871, 17 Stat. 13 (1871); Civil Rights Act of 1875, 18 Stat. 335 (1875)), only to have those laws negated by court rulings. The domination of whites over blacks (and any other minority) was comprehensive and persuasive, and had an impact on every area of life: Even in the present day the country still has to recover from the economic oppression of minorities: minorities were consigned to low-paying, non-skilled, dirty jobs. The domination of a white power structure was carried on by political oppression; through intimidation, barriers to voting and political participation, poll-taxes and more. Further the domination was held up high through the denial of personal freedom and dignity to all non-whites. Segregation was overall present, Jim Crow laws popped out everywhere. (For the most absurd laws and an overview of the re-emergence of the white power structure after the Civil War view: Johnson, The laws that shaped America, 2009, pp. 293 et seqq.).

964 Examples of Civil Rights are "the right to vote"; become a member of jury; "freedom of speech, press, and assembly"; and "the right to equality in public places". Public establishments include places of public accommodation (e.g., hotels, motels, and trailer parks), restaurants, gas stations, bars, taverns, and places of entertainment in general. (America: What are Civil Rights?, view at: http://tntalk.wordpress.com/america-what-are-civil-rights/ - accessed: January 2012).

965 These laws addressing organizational conspiracy were enacted to fight hate-motivated activities of groups, since the Ku Klux Klan and other racist groups became big in the era of Reconstruction. (Gerstenfeld, Hate Crimes, 2004, p.10).

966 Civil Right Act of 1871 was later amended and placed in U.S. Code (42 U.S.C.) as section 1983.

967 Conspiracy Against Rights of Citizens (18 U.S.C. § 241).

968 Deprivation of Rights Under Color of Law (18 U.S.C. § 242).

969 These two laws, especially section 242, have been used to punish people in wide areas, even unrelated to xenophobia or bias towards a certain groups. (Gerstenfeld, Hate Crimes, p. 10). The difference between these former laws and the hate crime legislation today is that hate crime law nowadays is primarily not directed towards so-called hate groups (organizational violence ensuing from, for instance, the Ku Klux Klan) but against bias-motivated criminal behavior of individuals. (Jacobs, The Emergence and Implications of American Hate Crime Jurisprudence, p. 151).

rarely prosecuted offenders of the white supremacy class for victimizing minorities[970]. Especially the skepticism of Northerners about local authorities in the South prosecuting whites for attacking blacks properly led to federal legislative action[971]. According to the wording of these laws, such were enacted to abolish discriminatory inequality among humankind by eliminating unequal treatment by governmental workers and conspiracies to racist violence; they did not provide specific criminal legislation for crimes based on xenophobia and bias committed among societal members themselves. Unless committed by group offenders (view 18 U.S.C. § 241), these early Civil Rights Laws did not encompass bias-motivated, violent behavior of individuals. Yet, until today, things change in Civil Rights Legislation, which is illustrated in the following. Far-reaching legislation addressing hate-motivated violence has been built upon these early Civil Rights Laws which arouse through the federal idea of punishing discriminatory racist behavior on the ground that it is contradictory to constitutional provisions, such as in the Fourteenth Amendment.

D. Effective Hate Crime Laws in the United States of America

To begin with, one must distinguish between federal and state legislation. Legislation intended to punish acts of hate violence can be either federal (dealing with violations of constitutional rights) or state (resulting from violations of a particular state law)[972]. Due to limitations in federal competence in criminal jurisdiction, criminalizing bias-motivated behavior primarily lies within the competence of a particular state. Nevertheless, as a result of the expansion of competencies pursuant to the prosecution of hate crimes in the year 2009, the federal government has issued a nationwide procedural directive towards the eradication of hate crimes and watches over state compliance.

The following illustrates the concept of hate crime in its effectual shaping on federal and state levels. While the concept as such consists of legislation intended to capture data on the hate crime problem (data collection laws); laws to ensure the correct prosecution of offenders committing a hate crime (all sorts of training laws); and finally of legislation defining or modifying penalties for committing hate crimes, the focus of this paper lies on laws pertaining to the penalty for hate crimes.

970 The Act of 1871 intended to provide a federal remedy for private conspiracies of the sort practiced by the Ku Klux Klan against African Americans and other minorities. By 1871 it was apparent that local and state courts were ineffective in prosecuting Klan violence and such corrupt handlings of their own kind. Local and state law enforcement officials, including judges, were often sympathetic to Ku Klux Klan activities or were subject to intimidation by the group, as were trial witnesses. Therefore, the Civil Rights legislation of 1871 enabled victims of group violence (referring to Klu Klux Klan violence) to take their case to a federal court where they would supposedly receive a fairer trial.

971 Many Northerners feared that the local authorities participated in these attacks themselves (Cf. Gerstenfeld, Hate Crimes, 2004, p. 10).

972 Public Policy and the Law: How Hate Crimes are prosecuted and interpreted, p. 171.

1. Federal Hate Crime Laws

The federal government initiated the step to criminalize hate crimes; and proceeded from one state handling to another so that until today it has made sure that the states follow its lead. This way, the federal government ultimately dictates which groups are to be protected and has the power to make sure that crimes are prosecuted nationwide to federal satisfaction.

1.1. Civil Rights Legislation

Since state governments, particularly the southern states, refused to acknowledge constitutional rights of anyone who is not of Caucasian race long into the 20th century, Civil Rights legislation primarily endeavored to create constitutional conditions in the American nation[973]. Civil Rights Laws, in general, allow a person to sue a state or a local government employee in federal court, if the latter interfers with his or her constitutional rights. As discussed above, the federal authority must ensure the actual implementation– thus, the real existence – of the constitutionally guaranteed rights of every citizen. Therefore, the federal government aimed at forcing the states to act in conformity with the constitutional regulations by embodying the constitutionally established doctrines at the sub-constitutional law level and simultaneously established federal jurisdiction over state and local government employees or agents who breach the law. The original, early idea of Civil Rights legislation addressing bias-motivated offenses was to set up an enforcement mechanism so that governmental and institutional discriminatory[974] violence may not remain legally ignored. The decisive change regarding Civil Rights laws, which were enacted earlier, came with the Civil Rights Act of 1964[975], strictly speaking, with the Civil Rights Act of 1968 and its Section 18 U.S.C. § 245[976] – which was intended to be a follow-up to the Civil Rights protections of 1964 – and which is considered to be the start of criminal legislation addressing bias-motivated behavior[977]. The key modification is referred to lie within the reach of the Fourteenth Amendment which no longer encompasses governmental

973 Several federal Civil Rights laws, for instance, Civil Right Act of 1965 (42 U.S.C. A. § 2000), and Voting Rights Act of 1965 (42 U.S.C. A. § 1973) aimed at combating governmental discriminatory actions.

974 Civil Rights Acts in 1871, for instance, 18 U.S.C. § 241 "Conspiracy Against Rights" makes it a punishable offense if two or more persons conspire to commit a crime in any U.S. territory based on the aim to withdraw one's constitutionally or federally provided rights (aimed at stemming the problem of the Ku Klux Klan activity which spread during the Reconstruction Era); and "Deprivation of Rights Under Color of Law", 18 U.S.C. § 242 is connected to discriminatory acts, committed in a feigned legal function. This law was mainly addressed to police officers who were trampling on human rights of minorities. It was used in the attention-getting case - due to the fact, that the crime was videotaped and published afterwards - of four police officers attacking Rodney King 1992 in Los Angeles. (Stacey C. Koon v. United States/Laurence M. Powell v. United States, No. 94-1664, 518 U.S. 81).

975 Pub. L. 88-352, 78 Stat., launched on July 2nd, 1964.

976 Civil Rights Act of 1968 (42 U.S.C. A. § 3601) and its section 18 USC § 245, named "Federally Protected Activities" states "[...] (b) whoever, whether or not acting under color of law, by force or threat of force willfully injures, intimidates or interferes with, or attempts to injure, intimidate or interfere with - [...] (2) any person because of his race, color, religion or national origin and because he is or has been - (A) enrolling in or attending [...] (B) participating in or enjoying any benefit service, privilege, program, facility or activity provided or administered by any State or subdivision thereof; [...] shall be fined under this title or imprisoned for any term of years or for life, or both, or may be sentenced to death."

977 Coester, Hate Crimes, 2007, p. 82.

actions only, but reaches to certain situations in which individuals discriminate others and in so doing aim at depriving them of their constitutional rights. Implemented in 18 U.S.C. § 245[978], this statute is considered to be the starting point of criminal hate crime legislation established nowadays in penal codes throughout the United States. Because they address every citizen of the nation, these laws, for the first time, are said to have made [...] "clear to all, that race has no place in American life or law"[979]. However, one must bear in mind that federal criminal legislative power is constitutionally limited[980]. According to 18 U.S.C. Section 245 in its actual effective form, federal prosecution is authorized if the relevant criminal behavior was motivated by race, color, religion, or national origin and in addition, the offender must have intended to deprive the victim of a federally protected right[981]. That said, whenever reference is made to "federal hate crime legislation", the matter deals with violations of constitutional rights. This necessary double requirement in order for hate crimes to be punishable by federal jurisdiction, i.e., crime committed because of bias towards the victim's protected characteristic and willful interference because of the victim's participation in a certain activity protected by the Act (in order to be classified as federal)[982], combined in one statement of facts, limits the possibility of application and overstrains any prosecution efforts.

From a legal standpoint, according to the U.S. Constitution, Congress may criminalize primarily those acts of individuals that affect the Commerce Clause of Article I, Sec. 8 U.S. Constitution[983]. Therefore, if one cannot prove how a bias crime affected interested commerce, the federal authority simply does not

978 An example of violating this statute would be a rather common case in which a restaurant operator denies entry to a person because of his race. In case that this restaurant is "administered by any State or subdivision thereof" (18 USC § 245 (b) (2) (B)), eating in such is a federally protected activity, consequently if access to such is denied by force, 18 U.S.C. § 245 would apply. In Heart of Atlanta v. United States (1964) and Katzenbach v. Mc Clung (1964), the Supreme Court held that activities of restaurants could be federally regulated, even if most of the guests were local residents.

979 Parts of President John F. Kennedy's speech in Congress, when Civil Right laws were sent to Congress on June 19, 1963. (Johnson, The laws that shaped America, 2009, p.306; Morris, The Origin of the Civil Rights Movement: Black Communities Organizing for Change, New York: The free Press, 1986, pp. 1-2); Through the enactment of the Civil Rights of 1964 all former Jim Crow laws and legal disenfranchisement of minorities became overruled.

980 Federal criminal law may be enacted mainly due to the Commerce Clause of Article I, Sec. 8 U.S. Constitution, further competence being used to enact such originate from the power to tax, the war power and from the here relevant jurisdiction in Civil Right matters (Hay, The Law of the United States, 2010, p. 300).

981 In order to punish actions of individuals, Congress must use its power to regulate interstate commerce. This leads to the fact that hate crimes can only be federally prosecuted if such are committed because the victim was engaging in one of six legally encompassed, thus federally protected, activities and the offender willfully interfered with such or attempted to do so.

982 Victims must be engaged in a protected activity - including activities such as going to school, serving on a jury and eating in a lunchroom.

983 In order to serve interstate commerce Civil Right Laws usually protect federal establishments by punishing certain behaviors connected to bias in or near public establishments. Therefore, laws as "Damage to Religious Property, Obstruction of Persons in the Free Exercise of Religious Beliefs" (18 U.S.C. § 247); "Freedom of Access to Clinic Entrances" (18 U.S.C. § 248); "Prevention of Intimidation ´Provision of Fair Housing Act´" (42 U.S.C. § 3631; "Use of Fire or Explosive in the Commission of a Felony" 18 U.S.C. § 844 (h)) can be used for prosecuting hate crimes through arson or burnings of several symbols. In 1985, the U.S. Supreme Court held that arson of an apartment building affected interested commerce (United States v. Russell, 1985).

have the power to address most bias-motivated crime[984]. Nevertheless, the fact that the federal government has the power to release Civil Rights Acts based on Civil Rights matters jurisdiction leads to the idea[985] of subsuming bias-motivated offenses under Civil Rights Acts legislations. But, if one examines the nature of Civil Rights Laws, one recognizes that their application area is too narrow to address hate crimes in its core;[986] but yet, the strict observance of federalism in the United States bars them from being enhanced. Federal Civil Rights laws could only serve as a stopgap solution in combating hate crimes. For legally combating hate in society, devices may not be restricted to state-operated racial abuse of power (18 U.S.C. § 242) nor is there a sense in limiting hate crime legislation to group activity (18 U.S.C. § 241); whereas the groundbreaking 18 U.S.C. Section 245, which pertains to the punishable coverage of hate crimes committed by individual perpetrators, protects only specifically defined (federal/constitutional concerning) activities on the part of a victim. Due to the fact that federal Civil Rights Laws cannot encompass most hate-motivated crimes, and U.S. Congress does not have the legal power to enact federal criminal statutes specifically designed to combat hate crimes, the enactment of criminal statutes in order to punish hate-motivated offenses are a matter of state concern.

The federal government, however, tries, as far as constitutionally possible to compensate for the lack of initiative of the states and takes up every available power to enact hate crime laws. The established federal laws, which are categorized as hate crime law, are illustrated in the following[987].

1.2. Hate Crime Statistic Act of 1990

Introduced in 1985 to Congress[988], the Hate Crime Statistics Act[989] was the first piece of legislation to bring national attention to the problem of hate-motivated violence[990]. Its purpose is the development of an effective criminal combat of hate crimes[991]. It assigned the Attorney General to acquire data

984 The federal government's power to prohibit bias-motivated crime is highly in question. (Hasenstab, Is hate a form of commerce? The questioned constitutionality of federal "hate crime" legislation. St. Louis University Law Journal, 45, (2001), 973-1017; Peek, Where are we going with federal hate crime legislation? Congress and the politics of sexual orientation, Marquette Law Review, 85, pp. 537-577; Gerstenfeld, Hate Crimes, 2004, p. 13). Clearly the federal legislative may criminalize such bias-motivated crimes which affect interstate commerce, but the problem with this legal limitation is that due to it, federal laws are able to encompass only a small percentage of bias-motivated crimes.

985 Gerstenfeld, Hate Crimes, p. 13.

986 "These laws were enacted under specific circumstances and with the purpose of addressing specific problems (e.g. the activities of the Klan during Reconstruction)." (Gerstenfeld, Hate Crimes, 2004, p. 13).

987 For the reserved but effective tactic of federal legislation, view the regulation system established in the following described Matthew Shepard and James Byrd, Jr. Hate Crimes Prevention Act (Chapter 3, D., 1., 1.5. Matthew Shepard and James Byrd, Jr. Hate Crimes Prevention Act). According to this, the federal government may prosecute Hate Crimes only in the case a state refuses to do such, thus leave the main competence of criminal prosecution to the states.

988 The bill was introduced by three members of Congress: John Conyers (D-Michigan), Barbara Kennely (D-Conn.), and Marios Biaggi (D-N. Y.). (Cf. Aydin, Strafrechtliche Bekämpfung von Hassdelikten, p. 34, fn. 74; President George H. W. Bush signed the Public Law 101-275, the Hate Crime Statistics Act of 1990, (28 U.S.C. 534) on April 23, 1990.

989 Hate Crime Statistics Act, 28 U.S.C. § 534.

990 Jenness/Grattet, Making Hate a Crime, 2001, p. 53.

991 Aydin, Strafrechtliche Bekämpfung von Hassdelikten, p. 34.

about crimes bearing a relation to bias against race, religion or ethnicity[992]. At the time the bill was introduced, hate crimes were considered as being motivated by prejudice based solely on these three defined target groups. In 1990, when President George Bush signed the bill into law, a "sexual orientation clause" was added to its list of status provisions[993]; thus the law provided a narrow legalistic definition of hate crime: "[...] crimes that manifest evidence of prejudice based on race, religion, sexual orientation or ethnicity"[994]. Today, the U.S. Justice Department is mandated to gather data for each calendar year pertaining to "[...] murder, and non-negligent manslaughter, forcible rape, aggravated assault, simple assault, intimidation, arson, and destruction, damage or vandalism of property" if such "manifest evidence of prejudice based on race, religion, disability, sexual orientation, or ethnicity [...]". This law does not stipulate new penalties for bias-motivated crimes; it merely requires the collection of empirical data necessary to develop an effective hate crime policy[995]. Seen as a necessary intermediate step for criminalizing bias-motivated behavior[996], it is illustrated in this description as one stride towards the enactment of criminal hate crime legislation.

1.3. Violence Against Women Act

In 1994, the Congress passed the Violence Against Women Act[997]. The act created a civil remedy for victims of violent crimes motivated by gender until 1999; this was when it was declared unconstitutional by the U.S. Supreme Court because of an insufficient nexus to interstate commerce[998]. This act defined hate crime as "a crime of violence committed because of gender or on the basis of gender, and due, at least in part, to animus based on the victim's gender". Since this law bears upon civil remedy it does not stipulate new penalties for hate crimes, nevertheless it served a definition and shows the incorporation of gender into the concept of hate crime.

---

992 Prior to that time, the only data available were those provided by organizations like the Anti-Defamation League and the Southern Poverty Law Center. (Woods, Sometimes it's personal: Hate Crime Prosecution in California, 2008, p. 6; Jacobs & Potter, 1997).

993 Under the Hate Crime Statistics Act of 1990, the FBI/U.S. Department of Justice has been reporting hate crimes based on perceived race, religion, ethnicity, and sexual orientation. Since 1994, their reports include disability.

994 Perry, In the name of Hate, 2001, p. 7.

995 Those supporting this statute argue that involving the police in identifying and counting hate crimes could help law enforcement officials measure trends, fashion effective responses, design prevention strategies and develop sensitivity to the particular need of victims of hate crimes, thus it was designed as an evaluating instrument of how hate crimes are to be combated best and which finally led to the here to be examined penalty enhancement laws within the criminal law sector.

996 By collecting data, not only does the seriousness of the problem become evident due to fact finding, but gathered information also increases the ability of policy makers to solve the matter - as Perry states it: "In the absence of empirical information about bias-motivated violence, it is difficult to construct conceptual frameworks." (Perry, Where do we go from here?, 2003, p. 16).

997 42 U.S.C. 13981; Public Law 103-322.

998 "The act was declared unconstitutional by the U.S. Supreme Court in Brzonka v. Morrison. The court held that the act was an impermissible extension of federal authority, according to such criminal activities can be regulated if they have a sufficient nexus to interstate commerce. The majority opinion argued that "gender-motivated crime of violence is not - in any sense of the phrase - economic activity. This hate crime provision was subsequently left out of the renewal of the Violence Against Women Act in 2000" . (Gerstenfeld, Hate Crimes, 2004, pp. 13 et seqq.).

1.4. Hate Crime Sentencing Enhancement Act of 1994

Also in 1994, Congress passed the Hate Crime Sentencing Enhancement Act[999] which assigned the United States Sentencing Commission to enhance the sentence for a crime if such is a hate crime. This piece of law identifies eight predicate crimes - murder; non-negligent manslaughter; forcible rape; aggravated assault; simple assault; intimidation; arson; and destruction; damage; or vandalism of property - for which judges are required to impose penalties of "not less than three offense levels [above the penalty for the parallel crimes] for offenses that a finder of fact at trial determines beyond a reasonable doubt are hate crimes"[1000]. This led to an automatic increase of sentences imposed on a perpetrator who commits a federal violent hate offense.

The legal background of the Hate Crime Sentencing Enhancement Act dates from 1984, the year in which Congress enacted the Comprehensive Crime Control Act (Sentencing Reform Act)[1001] in order to reform the sentencing guidelines. This law demanded the formation of the United Sentencing Commission ("Commission") that, as an independent agency in the judicial branch, creates the sentencing policies and practices for the federal criminal justice systems[1002]. Within its task the Commission releases guidelines for federal judges, prosecutors, probation and parole agents[1003]; especially judges are able to rely on such in order to impose the appropriate sanction for a crime[1004]. Since the U.S. Congress mandated the United Sentencing Commission to modify the sentencing guidelines; more precisely, to bring forth a penalty enhancement for hate crimes, the Commission proclaimed a penalty enhancement for hate crimes in May 1995, the amendment took effect on November the 1, 1995[1005]. Within its Section 3 A 1.1 (a) of the adjustment of the United States Sentencing Guideline the Violent Crime Control and the Law Enforcement Act provide a modification of penalty concerning the victim after which the penalization of all federal offenses is to be increased if the crime - "beyond a reasonable doubt" - is a hate crime[1006].

---

999 Named: Violent Crime Control and Law Enforcement Act, (Pub. L. No. 103-322, tit. XXVIII, § 280003, 108 Stat. 1796).

1000 Public Law 103-322; 28 U.S.C 994.

1001 Pub. L. No. 98-473; §§211-239, 98 Stat. 1987 et seqq.; incorporated in 18 U.S.C. § 3551 et seqq.

1002 28 U.S.C. § 991 (a), 28 U.S.C. § 991 (b) (1), went into effect 1.1.1987; amended through November 2000.

1003 The Sentencing Reform Act of 1984 (Title II of the Comprehensive Crime Control Act of 1984) provided for guidelines which support the basic purposes of criminal punishment, such are quoted to be: deterrence, incapacitation, just punishment, and rehabilitation. The Act delegated broad authority to the Commission to review the federal sentencing process and therefore contained detailed instructions as to how this determination should be made. By that the Commission was directed to determine categories of "offense behavior" and "offender characteristics" which are the two elements relevant for establishing the range of penalty. According to the guidelines the sentencing range that specifies an appropriate sentence for each class of convicted persons is to be determined by coordinating the offense behavior categories with the offender characteristic categories. (Cf. United States Sentencing Commission, Guidelines Manual, (= U.S.S.G.), Chapter 1, Part A – Introduction and Authority, pp. 1, 2). [November 1, 2010].

1004 28 U.S.C. § 991 (a) (1).

1005 U.S.S.G. § A 1.1 a).

1006 U.S.S.G. § 3 A 1.1 (a).

The application of this enhancement of the gravity of a crime in case such is a hate crime is performed as follows: To begin with, judges who establish a sentence refer to the federal guidelines, which determine the base offense levels for every federal offense, applicable in every district court. Thus, once the relevant offense is made out, the base offense level which is subject to this offense is the starting point for determining the correct sentence[1007]. That base level determines the number of points that a crime rates. According to the protected legal interest of the violated norm, these differ from 1 (slight) to 43 (severe crime)[1008]. To the number of points set for base offense level, points are then added or subtracted according to the gravity of the crime which is to be made out through referring to the adjustments of the Sentencing Guidelines, which include crime-relating factors like the behavior of the accused referring to the "defendant's role in the offense" in case of several perpetrators[1009]; "obstructing or impending the Administration of Justice"[1010]; "multiple counts"[1011]; "acceptance of responsibility"[1012]; and, ahead of all named amendments, the victim – related adjustments which are due to the implements of the Hate Crime Enhancement Act subdivided into "Hate Crime Motivation" and "Vulnerable Victim"[1013]. Thus, once the offense level of the underlying offense is ascertained a modification in reference to the victim takes place according to which the court at sentencing increases the offense level in all cases in which the defendant intentionally selected the victim because of his or her bias towards the victim's legally protected characteristic[1014] or in cases in which the victim chosen by the offender provides an increased vulnerability[1015]. The guidelines determine that "if the defendant knew or should have known that a victim of the offense was a vulnerable victim" the offense level is to be increased by two levels[1016]. A vulnerable victim refers to a person "[...] who is unusually vulnerable due to age, physical or mental condition, or who is otherwise particularly susceptible to the criminal conduct"[1017]; but also to "official victims", such as government employees or, especially in case of a victim being a police officer; if "the offense of conviction against such was motivated by such status" the level shall be increased by three levels[1018].

1007 According to the relevant protected legal interest (or in other words, according to the relevant underlying offense) the correct base offense level must be determined. In order to make out the underlying protected legal interest of a hate crime it can be helpful to take a look in the appendix of the Sentencing Guidelines Manual. (U.S.S.G. § 1B1.2 and Appendices).

1008 If the underlying crime is a Civil Right offense, Chapter 2 of the guidelines manual, part H – "Offences Involving Individual Rights" is applicable for sentencing.

1009 U.S.S.G. § 3 B.

1010 U.S.S.G. § 3 C.

1011 U.S.S.G. § 3 D.

1012 U.S.S.G. § 3 E.

1013 U.S.S.G. § 3 A.

1014 According to U.S.S.G. § 3 A 1.1 (a).

1015 U.S.S.G. § 3 A 1. (b).

1016 U.S.S.G. § 3 A 1.1 (b) (1).

1017 Application Note 2. to U.S.S.G. § 3 A 1.1.

1018 U.S.S.G. § 3 A 1.2 (a).

The increase of the base level offense for crimes which evidence to be hate crimes, effectuated federally through the Hate Crime Sentencing Enhancement Act, states as follows: "If the finder of fact at trial or, in the case of a plea of guilty or nolo contendere, the court at sentencing determines beyond a reasonable doubt that the defendant intentionally selected any victim or any property as the object of the offense of conviction because of the actual or perceived race, color, religion, national origin, ethnicity, gender, gender identity, disability, or sexual orientation of any person [...]" the base level is to be increased by three levels[1019].

Whenever faced with the choice of whether to apply the hate crime modification provided since 1995 or the longer established modification which refers to the vulnerability of the victim, it is proper to follow the guidelines for determining a hate crime. The legislative history of the Hate Crime Sentencing Enhancement Act states: " [in] order to constitute as a hate crime, the selection of a victim [...] must result from the defendant's hate or animus toward any person bearing one or more of the characteristics set forth in the definition of hate crime. Any other reason would link the imposition of unacceptable duplicative punishments upon the defendants for substantially the same offense"[1020]. With this, it is clear that a sentence modification according to hate crimes is applicable only if an offense was committed because of feelings of racial animus or hate towards the victim because of his or her actual or perceived race, color, religion, national origin, ethnicity, gender, gender identity, disability, or sexual orientation; but it does not apply in cases in which the victim happens to be colored but the offender's trigger for crime committal was a different fact about the victim[1021]. Briefly worded, a modification according to U.S. S. G. § A 1.1 (a) is solely but always applicable, if the crime is a hate crime. Thus, in cases where both victim-related modifications (i.e., hate-crime motivation and vulnerable victim) are applicable, the modification according Hate-Crime motivation has priority[1022].

The ultimate total of points assigned to the accused is therefore based on the crime-relevant base offense level and the respective amendments enhancing (or lowering) it - especially when he or she committed a hate crime, the gravity of the crime is increased by at least two levels - and from the points occurring from the criminal history of the offender. The latter plays an important role according to the federal guidelines in determining the sentence range. According to their illustration "the offense level (1-43) forms the vertical axis of the Sentencing Table. The Criminal History Category (I-VI) forms the horizontal axis of the Table. The intersection of the Offense Level and Criminal

1019 U.S.S.G. § 3 A 1.1 (a).

1020 H. R. Rep. No. 103-244, 1993, p. 5.

1021 E.g. In the case, in which the victim is colored, but the offender chose to attack him or her because of him or her being rich, sentencing modification would not apply. (See also United States v. Boylan, 5 F. Supp. 2d 274, 283 (D. NJ. 1998); Aydin, Strafrechtl. Bekämpfung von Hassdelikten, 2006, p.66.

1022 U.S.S.G. § 3 A 1.1, Commentary 3: "The adjustments from subsections (a) and (b) are to be applied cumulatively. Do not, however, apply subsection (b) in cases in which subsection (a) apply unless a victim of the offences was unusually vulnerable for reasons unrelated to race, color, religion, national origin, ethnicity, gender, gender identity, disability, or sexual orientation."

History Category displays the Guideline Range in months of imprisonment" from which the respective judge imposes the sentence. The exact sentence which is to be imposed from the range determined by the point total is made out in accordance with the general application principles provided in the guidelines under § 1 B 1.1.

The Hate Crime Sentencing Enhancement Act of 1994 is the kind of legislation that is in the focus of this work. It is a piece of criminal law which refers to hate-motivated conducts and imposes or alters penalties for crimes in which the victim was selected because of his or her actual or perceived membership in a particular group or in which the defendant acted out of hatred towards the victim's actual or perceived group status.

1.5. Matthew Shepard and James Byrd, Jr. Hate Crimes Prevention Act

In 1999[1023], the bill for the Hate Crimes Prevention Act, today also known as Matthew Shepard Act, was introduced to Congress for the first time[1024]. This bill was introduced to even up differences between effective hate crime legislation launched by the respective states. To assure even-handed criminal prosecution of hate crimes, federal involvement should become authorized. However, the bill died in committee, as it did – until 2009 – several times, after being reintroduced.[1025] Finally on October 28, 2009 President Barack Obama signed the Matthew Shepard and James Byrd, Jr.[1026] Hate Crimes Prevention Act (HCPA) into law which extended federal jurisdiction in hate crimes, enabled nationwide even protection against hate crimes, and simultaneously laid down an expansion of protected group statuses.[1027]

1023 Prior hereto, in 1997, another specialized, federal hate crime law was passed: the Church Arson Prevention Act (110 Stat. 1392 Public Law 104-15-July 3, 1996). This law was a reaction to an increase of church burnings and arson of places of religious worship that serve predominantly African-American congregations. The law contains provisions increasing the sentencing for damaging places of worship. Congress found that destruction and vandalism of places of worship "[...] pose a serious national problem." And that "[...] changes in Federal law are necessary to deal properly with this problem." (Church Arson Prevention Act of 1996 18 USC 247 note; Sec. 2 "Findings").

1024 106th Congress, H. R. 1082. It was proposed earlier in 1998, "but was then put aside as Congress became busy with the impeachment hearings of then- President Clinton." (Gerstenfeld, Hate Crimes, 2004, p. 29).

1025 The Hate Crime Prevention Act before was "bouncing around Congress for several years". It was originally proposed in 1998, but was then put aside; similar proposals of this bill in 1999, 2001, and 2002 died in committee. (Gerstenfeld, Hate Crimes, 2004, p. 29).

1026 The Act is named after Matthew Wayne Shepard, a gay college student who was brutally murdered eleven years ago (pronounced dead on October 12, 1998) in a bias-motivated attack in Wyoming. The murder was motivated by the hate of the offenders towards gays. (Brooke, Witnesses Trace Brutal Killing of Gay Student, in: New York Times, Published: November 21, 1998). The offenders could not be charged with a hate crime, because no Wyoming criminal statute provided for such a charge. At that time, neither under federal law (referring to Civil Right legislation), nor under Wyoming state law crimes committed on the basis of sexual orientation were prosecutable as hate crimes. James Byrd, was chained to a pickup truck and dragged to his death by three members of a white supremacist gang in 1998, in Texas, view CNN News, July, 6, 1998; http://edition.cnn.com/US/9807/06/dragging.death.02/) Two of the offenders went to death row, one was sent to life prison term (CBS news on September 22, 2011). Alarmed by these horrible hate crimes, both could not be prosecuted as such due to missing legislation, Congress finally proceeded to action. (FOX News: "Obama Signs Defense Policy Bill That Includes 'Hate Crime' Legislation", published October 28, 2009.

1027 The prior version of the bill did not provide authority for the federal Department of Justice to investigate and prosecute bias-motivated crimes based on the victim's actual or perceived sexual orientation, gender, gender identity, or disability. So in addition to race, religion, and national origin the Matthew Shepard and

If one takes a look at the legal actions of the several states to combat hate crimes it is observed that most states have released laws in their own manner, protecting distinct groups in distinct ways. Almost all states, including the District of Columbia have some sort of hate crime laws, but only thirty states and the District include sexual orientation and disability in their law; only twenty-six states and the District include gender; only twelve states and the District include gender identity[1028] as characteristic which, if shared by a person and caused his or her victimization, constitutes a hate crime. In order to ensure penalization and enhanced criminal actions against all such sorts of hate crimes which was found by the federal government to constitute a hate crime. Federal intervention was provided for by this act. While states continue to play the primary role in the prosecution of bias-motivated violence[1029], the federal government by this piece of law became jurisdiction to address those limited cases in which local authorities are either unable or unwilling to investigate and prosecute[1030]. Thus, the prior requirement of a victim's engagement in federal activity and the offender's intention of interfering with such, for authorized federal legal involvement, dictated by 18 U.S.C. Section 245, can be now circumvented whenever a local government does not prosecute a hate crime in its legally[1031] dictated manner[1032].

In summarized terms, the HCPA of 2009 extended federal competence to prosecute hate crimes[1033] and by that simultaneously served for nationwide uniformity according the criminalization of hate crimes; and it expanded legal protection - in addition to race, religion and national origin - the HCPA authorizes the Department of Justice to investigate and prosecute hate crimes based on the victim's actual or perceived sexual orientation, gender, gender identity, or disability[1034].

James Byrd, Jr. Hate Crimes Prevention Act contains further protected groups statuses and thereby authorizes the Department of Justice to investigate and prosecute far more bias-motivated crimes.

1028 Anti-Defamation League, 2012, (http://www.adl.org/combating_hate/ - accessed January 2012) especially: http://www.adl.org/combating_hate/What-you-need-to-know-about-HCPA.pdf (accessed January 5, 2012).

1029 Harry Reid, a Nevada Democrat who is Senate majority leader is quoted to be said that "states will still bear primary responsibility for prosecuting most hate crimes, which is important to me as a former state prosecutor." (Kimball, Hate-crimes bill would expand federal jurisdiction, in: Richmond Times; Published: June 13, 2009) (http://www2.timesdispatch.com/lifestyles/2009/jun/13/i-hate0531_20090611-212807-ar-40471/; accessed January 2012).

1030 The Hill's "Congress Blog" November 9, 2009.

1031 "Legally" in this case, also refers to such manners which does not reflect federal interests in dealing with hate-motivated violence; e.g. in cases in which a state statute does not encompass all federal chosen protected groups.

1032 Emily Kimball, Hate-crimes bill would expand federal jurisdiction, in: Richmond Times; Published: June 13, 2009 (http://www2.timesdispatch.com/lifestyles/2009/jun/13/i-hate0531_20090611-212807-ar-40471/; accessed in January 2012).

1033 As stated in the Civil Right Acts of 1964, federal involvement in hate crimes investigation and prosecution was due to the constitutional requirement of affected Commerce only authorized if the victim of a bias-motivated crime was attacked because he or she was engaged in a specified federally-protected activity. Today, federal hate crime prosecution takes place whenever such is committed within the field of federal competence (Civil Right matter jurisdiction) or when the state's efforts to investigate and prosecute such a crime are too lax.

1034 Prior federal law, speaking of the Civil Rights Act of 1965, 18 U.S.C. § 245, did not provide authority for involvement in these last four categories of cases at all.

With the current legal federal formation of criminal handlings according the combat against hate-motivated violence, the HCPA serves as an acceptable instrument among hate crime law supporters[1035].

1.6. Conclusion of Current Federal Hate Crime Legislation

The former federal legislation a.k.a. Civil Rights Acts required an intentional interference, by force or threat of force, with the enjoyment of a federal right or benefit on the basis of race, color, religion, or national origin in order to be applicable. Prior to 2009, the possibility to legally prosecute hate crimes through federal jurisdiction - referring to Civil Rights laws and to the application field of the Sentence Enhancement Act which increases sentence for offenses motivated by prejudice against legally protected groups only in such rare cases in which a hate crime constituted a federal crime - was narrow. Within federal hate crime statutes, i.e. Civil Rights Legislation, the prosecutor not only had to prove that the offender was motivated to commit the crime because of the victim's membership in a protected group[1036], in addition, a federal hate crime must have been committed „because – not while – the victim was engaging in a federally protected activity"[1037]. Without the engagement in a federally protected activity therefore, the federal prosecutors were powerless to intervene in bias-motivated crimes. With the current federal legal situation though, federal hate crime laws can be considered a supportive assistance in form of a filler of gaps of state legislation addressing hate crimes. Through limited jurisdiction for federal law enforcement officials to investigate and prosecute certain bias-motivated crimes in states in which current law is inadequate[1038], the HCPA provided the possibility of nationwide even (because federally balanced) response to hate crimes[1039].

Taking the federally limited competence in the field of criminal law into account, the greater ability of the federal authorities today to engage in hate crime investigations that local authorities choose not to pursue[1040] is constitutional because the fundamental competence of prosecuting hate

---

1035 View the opinion towards the enactment of the HCPA, for instance, of the ADL. (view at: Anti-Defamation League, 2012, http://www.adl.org/combating_hate/, particulary http://adl.org/combating_hate/What-you-need-to-know-about-HCPA.pdf (accessed January 2012).

1036 Refer to "racial animus model" – requiring that the defendant acted out of hatred for the victim's racial group (Lawrence, Punishing Hate, 2003, pp. 29 et seqq.).

1037 Anti-Defamation League, 2012 (http://www.adl.org/99hatecrime/federal.asp - accessed January 5, 2012); this form of double requirement reminds one of the similar qualifications required in the Civil Right law discussed above, 18 U.S.C. § 245, which limits the potential of successful prosecution.

1038 Inadequacy of current law refers to hate crime legislation of a particular state which does not protect characteristics mentioned in the federal piece of law. Usually statuses like sexual orientation, gender, gender identity or disability are missing protection by state hate crime legislation. In case of the committal of a hate crime motivated through the hate of the offender towards the victim's sexual orientation in a state, which legislation does not protect sexual orientation as status characteristic, federal jurisdiction would apply.

1039 Anti-Defamation League, What-you-need-to-know-about-HCPA, 2012. (http://www.adl.org/combating_hate/What-you-need-to-know-about-HCPA.pdf - accessed January 5, 2012).

1040 "Because the FBI doesn't have sole responsibility for hate crime investigations, these cases can be worked jointly or concurrently. Or we may follow the state or local investigation to make sure the federal interest has been served." (http://www.fbi.gov/news/stories/2007/april/crossburn_043007 - accessed January 2012).

crimes remains within state jurisdiction[1041]. The federal jurisdiction has the potential to legally address hate crimes only in cases in which a particular state fails to prosecute such or in Civil Rights matter jurisdiction, consequently its authority is in conformity with constitutional precepts according its limited criminal authority.

2. State Hate Crime Laws

According to the legislature in Washington state, for example, it is found that protecting citizens from threats of harm due to bias and bigotry is a compelling state interest[1042]. The state legislature finds that state interest in preventing crimes and threats motivated by bigotry and bias exceeds the state interest in preventing other felonies or misdemeanors that are not motivated by hatred, bigotry, and bias[1043]. Based on this view, many states enacted broad hate crime legislature with the result that to the present day almost all states, including the District of Columbia, have their own particular hate crime legislation. By the 1980s and 1990s most state legislature passed at least one piece of legislation designed to deal with violence born of bigotry. Today, these laws cover crimes committed because of race, religion, color, ethnicity, (protected by nearly all hate crime statutes) ancestry, national origin, sexual orientation, gender, alienage[1044], age, disability[1045], creed[1046], political affiliation[1047], involvement in civil or human rights movements[1048] and service in the armed forces[1049]. The extremely wide and different version of the laws, especially in relation to the width of the different protected groups stems from the fact that the multitude of legislative bodies adopts laws which relate to their individual needs. Thereby a hate crime law is considered "a useful, additional tool" to protect any group, according to which it turns out that the prejudice-motivated hatred is aimed at them as a group from parts of society[1050]. So if, for instance, the respective state legislature is of the opinion that there is a need to protect people who serve in the armed forces against the prejudice-

1041 Harry Reid, a Nevada Democrat who is Senate majority leader is quoted to be said that "this bill strengthens federal jurisdiction over hate crimes as a backup, but not a substitute, for state and local law enforcement." (Kimball, Hate-crimes bill would expand federal jurisdiction, in: Richmond Times; Published: June 13, 2009 (http://www2.timesdispatch.com/lifestyles/2009/jun/13/i-hate0531_20090611-212807-ar-40471/ - accessed January 2012).

1042 Wash. Rev. Code § 9A.36.078.

1043 Wash. Rev. Code § 9A.36.078.

1044 Conn. Gen. Stat. § 46a-58 criminalizes deprivation of rights "on account of religion, national origin, alienage, color, race, sex, blindness or physical disability." Also covers damage to religious objects, symbols or houses of worship, and cross burning.

1045 N.J. Stat. § 52:9DD-9 covers efforts to "promote prejudice reduction and prevent and deter crimes based upon the victim's race, color, religion, national origin, sexual orientation, ethnicity, gender, or physical, mental or cognitive ability."

1046 Mont. Code Anno., § 45-5-222 describes enhanced sentences for offences committed because of victim's "race, creed, religion, color, national origin, or involvement in Civil Rights or human rights activities or that involved damage, destruction or attempted destruction of a building regularly used for religious worship."

1047 Iowa Code § 729A.1 prohibits violence or intimidation against persons or property based on "race, color, religion, ancestry, national origin, political affiliation, sex, sexual orientation, age, or disability."

1048 See fn. 75 Mont. Code Anno., § 45-5-222.

1049 The fact that these laws cover crimes committed because of "service in the armed forces" is mentioned by Jenness/Grattet and could not be confirmed. (Jenness/Grattet, Making Hate a Crime, 2001, p. 73).

1050 Winnie Stachelberg in: Timothy Lynch and Winnie Stachelberg, Hate Crime Laws, Morning Show on C-SPAN's Washington Journal, March 13, 2012.

motivated hatred which derives from parts of the society, such a law would be considered a legitimate piece of hate crime legislation protecting the characteristic of being a soldier; because it thereby serves a governmental interest in protecting the community against bias-motivated threats to public safety and order[1051]. The same applies to laws banning the wearing of masks and hoods, yet the enactment of such mainly aims at combating the activities of the KKK[1052]. The legislation started with the punishment of homicide offenses. The first hate crime law is said to have been enacted 1978 in California[1053], stating that killing is classified as first degree murder if "the victim was intentionally killed because of his or her race, color, religion, nationality, or country of origin"[1054]. During these early beginnings of the legal process within state legislature the supportive role of the Anti Defamation League of B´nai B´rith (ADL), lobbying the necessity of hate crime laws and suggesting their model piece of legislation in the early 80's to state legislatives, is to be highlighted.

2.1. The Launch of a Model Law

There are several interest groups which are to be mentioned in the combat of hate crime: In particular the National Association of colored people (NAACP), founded in 1909 – the peak period of lynchings and violence against minorities - to ensure racial justice[1055]; the Southern Poverty Law Center (SPLC), founded in 1971, especially noteworthy in view of judicial achievements, helping to ensure "that the promises of the civil right movement"[1056] becomes a reality among the judiciary[1057]; and the Anti Defamation League of B´nai B´rith (ADL) -founded in 1913 to combat racial discrimination against Jewish people. These and far more organizations[1058] are well known for their joint effort against the unequal application of criminal law in cases in which the victim belongs to a minority. They all track hate crime incidents across the United States with partially slightly different focus[1059], but with the same goal of abolishing all sorts of discriminatory treatment of minorities, the strengthening of minority rights in general and the improvement of living conditions of those

1051 Reasoning in regard to cross-burning legislation according: R.A.V., Petitioner, v. City of St. Paul, Minnesota; 505 U.S. 377 (112 S.Ct. 2538, 120 L.Ed.2d 305); No. 90-7675; argued: December 4, 1991; decided: June 22, 1992.

1052 Lawrence, Punishing Hate, p. 20; Seehafer, Strafrechtliche Reaktionen auf rechtsextremistisch/ fremdenfeindlich motivierte Gewalttaten, p. 45.

1053 Coester, Hate Crimes, 2008, p. 84.

1054 8 Penal Code of California 190.2.

1055 http://www.naacp.org.

1056 http://www.splcenter.org.

1057 View footnote 1065 for an exemplified verdict achieved by the legal assistant of the SPLC.

1058 E. g. the American-Arab Anti-Discrimination Committee; the American Jewish Committee; the Center for Democratic Renewal; the Center for the Prevention of Hate Violence; the Committee Against Anti-Asian Violence; the National Coalition of Anti-Violence Programs; the National Gay and Lesbian Task Force; the National Institute Against Prejudice and Violence; the Simon Wiesenthal Center.

1059 For instance, the National Institute Against Prejudice and Violence (NIAPV) broadly focuses on what now is termed "ethno violence". "Ethno violence" is defined as "an act in which the other is an ethnic group, an ethnic member, or a person perceived to be an ethnic group representative or identified with an ethnic group. Ethno violence is a subset of group violence." (Cf. Howard J. Ehrlich, 1989, p. 71). While others, such as the Committee Against Anti Asian Violence, or the National Gay and Lesbian Task Force already imply by their designation what there focus is or at least originally was.

who suffer. Alarmed by what they tracked and frustrated with the existing legal situation with respect to federal and state laws the ADL's Legal Affairs Department[1060] drafted a model hate crime bill in 1981, which it wanted to be established in state legislatures, at least it was introduced to inspire and guide the U.S. state legislature towards enacting hate crime penal law. Their engagement that led to a legislative model is so noteworthy, because the second paragraph of this draft suggested the elements of facts of an offense entitled "intimidation"[1061] whose formation is one of the two basic embodiments of today´s effective hate crime criminal legislation[1062]. This second paragraph of the model legislation today has been altered by adding gender to its list of protected groups in 1996, based on the conclusion that gender-based crimes could not be easily distinguished from other forms of hate-motivated violence and its title has been changed to "Bias-motivated Crimes"[1063]; it therefore reads:

> *"Bias-Motivated Crimes:*
> *A. A person commits a Bias-Motivated Crime if, by reason of the actual or perceived race, color, religion, national origin, sexual orientation or gender of another individual or group of individuals, he violates Section ... of the Penal code (insert code provisions for criminal trespass, criminal mischief, harassment, menacing, intimidation, assault, battery and or other appropriate statutorily proscribed criminal conduct).*
> *B. A Bias-Motivated Crime under this code provision is a ... misdemeanor/ felony (the degree of criminal liability should be at least one degree more serious than that imposed for commission of the underlying offense)."*[1064]

This second paragraph of the ADL's model statute implements the two ingredients considered necessary for the presence of a hate crime: A violation of some existing criminal statute by reasons of the victim's imagined or actual group membership. If both elements - violation of a criminal statute by reasons of bias towards the victim - are present, a person is found guilty of a bias-motivated crime which increases the severity of a penalty of at least one degree. Therefore, the core of this legal approach is penalty enhancement for already penalized behavior when it is committed because of the victim's race, religion, ethnic origin and the further.

1060 While in the early beginnings the ADL's work was said to mainly focus on the victim status of those harmed by violence because of their race and religion (Jenness/Grattet, Making Hate a Crime, 2001, p. 33), the ADL today itself makes clear that its concerns lie on all hate crimes, not just on anti-semitic violence.

1061 Gerstenfeld, hate crimes, 2004, p. 24; Aydin, Strafrechtliche Bekämpfung von Hassdelikten, 2006, p. 39.

1062 Coester states that back in 1981, the term hate crime was not present yet, therefore early statutes were named "crimes of intimidation". (Coester, Hate Crimes, 2008, p. 85, fn. 343).

1063 Anti-Defamation League, 2012 (view at: http://www.adl.org/issue_government/ADL_model.asp - accessed in 01/05/2012).

1064 Anti-Defamation League, 2012 (view at: http://www.adl.org/99hatecrime/text_legis.asp - accessed: January 2012).

In total, the model statute contains four provisions. The first provision, entitled Institutional Vandalism, criminalizes offenders who target places of worship (churches, cemeteries, even community centers, etc.). The third paragraph of the model statute creates a civil cause of action for victims of paragraph one and two, victims of bias-motivated crimes or of institutional vandalism, shall be able to sue their offenders. This provision is considered an effective instrument to eradicate hate crimes committed by offenders with an institutional or wealthy background. It appeared that civil actions are a particularly useful strategy to affect hate groups and their leaders as also provided for through federal Civil Rights Legislation; in several legal cases such caused high financial losses on the part of perpetrators of hate crimes[1065]. By hitting racist organizations where it hurts the most, adjudicating victims of hate crimes high sums of compensation, a racist group has been forced to turn over their headquarter to satisfy a judgment and so the organization became bankrupt[1066]. The last section of this model statute dictates reporting and analyses of bias-motivated crimes by state police or other appropriate state law enforcement agencies and also mandates training of police officers in identifying, responding to, and reporting of bias-motivated crimes.

Since the constitutional distribution of competence mandates that the particular state is the authority to address hate crimes, the ADL together with above named allies laid their efforts on encouraging the states to enshrine legislation similar to this model statute within their penal codes[1067]. Thus, these organizations support the legislative process in the states in which they delivered data collection material and model examples of laws that is intended to help combat unequal application of the law and the lack of criminal prosecution of hate crime. Regardless of the implementation of the exact wording of the draft served by the ADL, state legislature became active on their own in the fight against hate crime[1068]: by 1994, 34 states and the District of Columbia had some kind of penalty-enhancement type law for hate crimes, by 2000 only seven states did not have legislation punishing hate crimes[1069]; and today forty-five states and the District of Colombia have hate crimes laws[1070] which, referring to penalty enhancement for already penalized

1065 Gerstenfeld, Hate Crimes, 2004, pp. 24, 25.

1066 The elaborate legal strategy requires that an organization be held responsible for the crimes of individual members. This strategy helped to produce a $7 million judgment for a hate crime victim's mother in Mobile, Alabama, in 1987. This verdict bankrupted the United Klans of America and resulted in its national headquarters being sold for $ 52,000 to help satisfy the judgment. (Donald vs. United Klans of America: United States District Court, Southern District of Alabama, Southern Division; Civil Action No.: 84-0725-AR; Beulah Mae Donald, as Executor of the estate of Michael Donald (Plaintiff) vs. United Klans of America, inc. Knights of the Klu Klux Klan; Bennie Jack Hays; Henry F. Pays; Jas Llewellyn Knowles, Jr. ; Frank Cox; Thaddeus O. Betancourt; William O'Connor (Defendants)) (http://www.splcenter.org/sites/default/files/downloads/case/beulahvunklan_judgment.pdf).

1067 Gerstenfeld, Hate Crimes, 2004, p. 24.

1068 "[...] in seemingly no time at all, a hate crime jurisprudence had sprung up." (Maroney, 1998, pp. 567-568).

1069 Gerstenfeld, Hate Crimes, 2004, p. 25.

1070 Anti-Defamation League, 2012 (view at: http://www.adl.org/combating_hate/Introduction-to-Hate-Crime-Laws.pdf - accessed in 01/05/2012).

behavior, the Supreme Court ruled constitutional in the landmark case Wisconsin v. Mitchell in 1993[1071].

2.2. Legal Formation of State Law

Today the majority of states have enacted laws analogous to the ADL model. Nearly all states have adopted at least one hate crime statute that recognizes, defines and responds to discriminatory violence[1072]. Basically, in conformity with the federal preconditions and along with the wording of the ADL model statute, several states define four kinds of acts as hate crime legislation:[1073]

2.2.1. Hate Crime Reporting Statutes

According to the federal pendant, the "Hate Crime Statistic Act" of 1990, such laws require the collection of empirical data and analysis of information relating to crimes that are committed because of the victim's specific beliefs or further characteristics. Such legislation is often referred to as Data Collection Laws[1074]. Training for law enforcement personnel, such as Police Training Laws[1075] could be included within this section since they aim at a better recognition of bias-motivations within investigations for reasons of correct classification of such crimes, but also for reasons of reporting and acquisition of hate crimes, finally for statistical returns[1076].

1071 Wisconsin v. Mitchell, 508 U.S. 476 (1993).

1072 A few states might have a single statute which could be considered as a reserved approach to a hate crime statute, e.g. Georgia criminalizes vandalism of places of worship in O.C.G.A. § 16-7-26, but do not criminalize hate crimes, nor do they prosecute or punish hate crimes in any other kind of way with enhanced severity. Only four states besides Georgia -Arkansas, Wyoming, Indiana and South Carolina – do not have state hate crime laws.

1073 Jacobs, The Emergence and Implications of American Hate Crime Jurisprudence, pp. 154 et seqq.

1074 Tex. Gov't Code § 411.046 provides for the establishment and maintenance of a central repository for the collection and analysis of information relating to crimes that are motivated by prejudice, hatred, or advocacy of violence; Rev. Code Wash. (ARCW) § 36.28A.030 provides for creation of central repository for the collection and classification of information regarding crimes of bigotry or bias.; Idaho Code § 67-2915 provides for statistical report of malicious harassment crimes; R.R.S. Neb. § 28-114 provides for the establishment of central repository for the collection and analysis of information regarding criminal offences committed against a person because of the person's "race, color, religion, ancestry, national origin, gender, sexual orientation, age, or disability."; ORS § 181.550 mandates the reporting of crimes "motivated by prejudice based on the perceived race, color, religion, national origin, sexual orientation, marital status, political affiliation or beliefs, membership or activity in or on behalf of a labor organization or against a labor organization, physical or mental handicap, age, economic or social status or citizenship of the victim."

1075 Rev. Code Wash. (ARCW) § 43.101.290 mandates training in identifying, responding to, and reporting crimes of bigotry and bias.; Cal Pen Code § 13519.6 covers hate crimes training for peace officers.; ORS § 181.642 mandates training on the investigation, identification and reporting of crimes "motivated by prejudice based on the perceived race, color, religion, national origin, sexual orientation, marital status, political affiliation or beliefs, membership or activity in or on behalf of a labor organization or against a labor organization, physical or mental handicap, age, economic or social status or citizenship of the victim."

1076 Article 18B of New Mexico's Penal Code deals with the matter of hate crime. While within Article 31-18B-4. of New Mexico's Penal Code the demand of data collection is regulated with the prescription that "every district attorney and every state, county and municipal law enforcement agency, to the maximum extent possible, shall provide the federal bureau of investigation with data concerning the commission of a crime motivated by hate [...].", the following Article 31.18B-5 "Hate Crimes; law enforcement training" dictates that law enforcement training "concerning the detection, investigation and reporting of a crime motivated by hate" shall be provided by the New Mexico law enforcement academy. In so far training legislation serves the matter of reporting and insofar also, though not conclusively, requires data collecting.

2.2.2. Paramilitary Training Laws

These laws criminalize paramilitary training camps[1077]. It is crucial for the training to be unlawful that the person who conducts it must "[knowingly] or having reason to know or intending that the same will be unlawfully employed for use in, or in furtherance of, a civil disorder within the United States"[1078]. Therefore, "training or teaching of the use of weapons to be used for hunting, recreation, competition, self-defense or the protection of one person or property, or other lawful use" is not prohibited by the law[1079]. This type of law obviously aims at fighting Hate Groups and larger hate based structures, such as organized crime.

2.2.3. Legislation for Criminalizing Bias-Motivated Behavior

The core of hate crime criminalization in the U.S. legislature is penalty enhancement. However, to achieve this result, criminal statutes are put into various forms. In the following, the focus will lie on statutes punishing criminal relevant hate-motivated behavior and on the way such embody this behavior in order to justify punishing it. This refers to such legislative action which according to the ADL model statute is captioned as “Bias-Motivated Crimes”. Such effectuated in the particular states vary in their formation which is caused by the individual enactment of each state respecting different societal needs and the uneven efforts put into the enactment of statutes by the particular legislator. The most widest enshrined sentence mechanism for hate crimes in U.S. penal codes applies to a person found guilty of violating some existing law, thus committed an offense, and “intentionally selected” the victim, “based on”, “by reason of” or “because of” the victim’s imagined or actual group membership[1080]. Frequently encountered are statutes proscribing criminal penalties for Civil Rights violation, specific “ethnic intimidation” and “malicious harassment” statutes.

2.2.3.1. Substantial Hate Crime Statutes

1077 Tschaggelar, Hate Crimes und Hasskriminalität, 2003, p.23.

1078 Florida Statute, Title XL VI, Chapter 790, Section 29 – "Paramilitary training; teaching or participation prohibited." - states in its Paragraph one - three: "(1)This act shall be known and may be cited as the "State Antiparamilitary Training Act. (2) As used in this section, the term "civil disorder" means a public disturbance involving acts of violence by an assemblage of three or more persons, which disturbance causes an immediate danger of, or results in, damage or injury to the property or person of any other individual within the United States. (3)(a) Whoever teaches or demonstrates to any other person the use, application, or making of any firearm, destructive device, or technique capable of causing injury or death to persons, knowing or having reason to know or intending that the same will be unlawfully employed for use in, or in furtherance of, a civil disorder within the United States, is guilty of a felony of the third degree, punishable as provided in [...]. (b) Whoever assembles with one or more persons for the purpose of training with, practicing with, or being instructed in the use of any firearm, destructive device, or technique capable of causing injury or death to persons, intending to unlawfully employ the same for use in, or in furtherance of, a civil disorder within the United States, is guilty of a felony of the third degree, punishable as provided in s. [...]."

1079 Florida Statute, Title XL VI, Chapter 790, Section 29, Paragraph (4) states "Nothing contained in this section shall be construed to prohibit any act of a law enforcement officer which is performed in connection with the lawful performance of his or her official duties or to prohibit the training or teaching of the use of weapons to be used for hunting, recreation, competition, self-defense or the protection of one's person or property, or other lawful use."

1080 Pearlman, Sanctioning Bias Crime, p. 3.

Substantial hate crime laws[1081] are also termed pure bias crime laws[1082], or "freestanding" statutes[1083] all of which refer to the same meaning of statutes presenting own statement of facts in order to criminalize bias-motivated behavior[1084]. These autonomous norms - best described as formally "freestanding"[1085]- must itself be subdivided into various forms:

The main distinction is that some are based upon already penalized behavior while others criminalize behavior which as such is not penalized on its own yet[1086].

a) Substantial Hate Crime Statutes refering to previously Penalized Behavior

This category encompasses legislation which either explicitly refers to already established norms by listing such and dictating an increase of sentence up to several degrees in case the perpetrator intentionally selects his victim based on his perception of the victim's membership to a legally protected group; or to such statutes which do not explicitly refer to already established norms, but which describe already criminalized behavior and by connecting such to a bias motivation of the offender impose a new, higher sentence. Accordingly, the only difference between the two possibilities of drawing a connection to already criminalized acts is that statutes, which provide their own description, do not rely on previously established norms explicitly, but describe similar behavior in their own terms. In this way several penal codes defined new substantial offenses, providing new names for "old" crimes by adding the requirement of bias-motivation for committal and stipulating new sentence[1087]. Under such legislation the perpetrator, when convicted of a hate crime, is usually found guilty of two parallel offenses: the conduct which it is referred to in the hate crime statute and the actual hate crime. "The defining feature of statutes in this category [...] is that they directly distinguish hate- or bias-motivated violence from other forms of violent crime"[1088], and by this serve

1081 Jacobs/Potter, Hate Crimes, Criminal Law & Identity Politics, p. 33.

1082 Lawrence, Punishing Hate, p. 92.

1083 Jenness/Grattet, Making Hate a Crime, 2001, pp. 73 et seqq., 80.

1084 Such "pure" bias crime statutes proscribe specified racially motivated behavior directed at a person or property. (Lawrence, Punishing Hate, pp. 82, 83).

1085 Jenness/Grattet, Making Hate a Crime, 2001, p. 83.

1086 According to this, the first would be considered as a sentence enhancement law (aggravating statute), whereas the latter would be considered as an independent penal law.

1087 Based on opinion of Jenness/Grattet, Making Hate a Crime, 2001, pp. 73 et seqq.; frequently all sorts of property damage laws are taken and reformed to statutes for explicit penalization - usually for vandalism of places of worship. These reformed statutes are explicitly enacted to combat bias-motivated acts in addition to the underlying general property damage laws: Nev. Rev. Stat. Ann. § 206.125 criminalizes damage to places used for religious worship or other religious purpose, schools or community centers, or property contained therein; S.C. Code Ann. § 16-11-110 covers church burning.; S.C. Code Ann. § 16-11-535 covers willful injury to any place of worship; Nev. Rev. Stat. Ann. § 62.226 covers unlawful acts involving graffiti or defacing religious property; describes penalty.; Va. Code Ann. § 18.2-138 covers destruction of property within places of worship.; Va. Code Ann. § 18.2-127 covers willful or malicious injury to places of worship.; Tex. Penal Code § 28.08 covers graffiti or other markings on place of worship.; Tex. Penal Code § 28.03 covers damage or destruction to place of worship.; N.M. Stat. Ann. § 30-15-4 criminalizes desecration of a church.; Tenn. Code Ann. § 39-17-311 covers desecration of venerated objects.

1088 Jennes/Grattet, Making Hate a Crime, p. 81.

their purpose as specific hate crime laws. However, they are "substantive" and "freestanding" in their formal sense only.

Statutes relying on established criminal norms are usually named as "ethnic intimidation"[1089] or "malicious harassment"[1090].[1091] The respective legislator created new substantive statutes by criminalizing malevolent behavior that causes distress or discomfort, aimed at an individual because of her or his status characteristics (which are specified by the statute). Statutes of this sort require two essential components. To begin with, the statute specifies conduct and activities which in the classical sense qualify as menacing, harassment and intimidation (for example, bodily injury, property damage, trespass, threats, and most recently applied: invasion of privacy[1092]). Secondly, it stipulates that the defendant acted to intimidate or harass the victim because of the victim's real or imagined membership in a legally protected status. By this, these laws criminalize ethnic intimidation or malicious harassment by drawing on already established crimes in criminal codes and adding hate or bias as required motives for their commission[1093].

b) "Real" Substantial Hate Crime Statutes

The following, organized as a second category of substantial hate crime laws, illustrates substantial hate crime statutes which do not rely on already criminalized behavior.

Not only in the United States[1094], but also in European literature[1095], it is broadly opined that the concept of hate crime is a two-element crime without

---

1089 ORC Ann. 2927.12 defines the offense of "ethnic intimidation" to cover certain offences committed by reason of the victim's race, color, religion and national origin.

1090 Rev. Code Wash. (ARCW) § 9A.36.080 describes "malicious harassment" as follows: "A person is guilty of malicious harassment if he or she maliciously and intentionally commits one of the following acts because of his or her perception of the victim's race, color, religion, ancestry, national origin, gender, sexual orientation, or mental, physical, or sensory handicap: (a) Causes physical injury to the victim or another person; [...]" etc.

1091 Jennes/Grattet, Making Hate a Crime, p. 80.

1092 Invasion of privacy is punished within New Jersey Code of Criminal Justice in its section 2C:14-9, section 1. a. and forbids observing another person without that person's consent and under circumstances (sexual activity) in which a reasonable person would not expect to be observed. As applied in the case of New Jersey vs. Dharun Ravi, on March 16, 2012, Ravi was found guilty of invasion of privacy because of filming his gay room mate in their shared dorm room without his knowledge, while him kissing another man. Yet, the crime of bias intimidation requires that the offender intimidated his victim by reasons of him or her being, for instance, gay. While during the trial it was considered as proven that the victim (Mr. Clementi) was intimidated by Ravi violating the privacy invasion statute, the jury concluded that Mr. Ravi had not knowingly or purposely intimidated the men. But it found him guilty of the charge of bias intimidation, because it was proven that Mr. Clementi "reasonably believed" he had been made a target because he was gay. (Zernike, Kate, Jury Finds Spying in Rutgers Dorm Was a Hate Crime, The New York Times, N.Y. Region, March 16, 2012) Therefore, as in typical hate crime laws being based on intimidation, the prima facie evidence of intent to intimidate a person or group of persons is sufficient for their appliance.

1093 Exemplified in Washington's "malicious harassment" statute: A person is penalized if he or she commits one of the criminal acts provided in Washington's Code (several acts are inserted) against a victim "because of his or her perception of the victim's race, color, religion, ancestry, national origin, gender, sexual orientation, or mental, physical, or sensory handicap: [...]". (RCW 9A.36.080 "Malicious harassment") – Since this statute requires a conviction of the offender for the committal of another crime already established in the Revised Code of Washington for its appliance, the bias-motivation of the offender for committing this relevant crime serves for a prosecution under the additional enacted criminal statute "malicious harassment".

1094 Lawrence, Punishing Hate, pp. 93 et seqq.; Perry, In the Name of Hate, 2001, p. 8.

1095 OSCE/ODIHR, Hate Crime Laws: A Practical Guide, 2009, pp. 16 et seqq.

exception. The here held view is different. In contrary to the opinion that there is no substantial distinction between pure hate crime laws and sentence enhancement laws, because pure hate crime laws create a free-standing prohibition only formerly since the conduct they describe is a previously established crime of its own, according to this opinion, certain behaviors, which are currently unpunished, are perceived to become criminal due to their racial bias element and by that are to be considered as constituting a "new" offense, thus a hate crime[1096]. This, however, contradicts the ordinary "two-tiered" crime concept[1097] of hate crimes criminalizing already punished behavior severe due to a bias motivation of the offender.

aa) Cross Burning Legislation

When *Lawrence* states that two tiers being inherent in every bias crime and demands that every hate crime contains a parallel crime, also called underlying offense and base offense against person or property, and therefore it is concluded that pure hate crime laws are "free-standing in appearance only"[1098], cross-burning statutes and intimidation statutes are chosen to contradict this idea. The cross-burning statute of Virginia as an example for the non-existence of an always present underlying offense provides as follows:

> *"It shall be unlawful for any person or persons, with the intent of intimidating any person or group of persons, to burn, or cause to be burned, a cross on the property of another, a highway or other public place. Any person who shall violate any provision of this section shall be guilty of a Class 6 felony.*
> *Any such burning of a cross shall be prima facie evidence of an intent to intimidate a person or group of persons[1099]."*

Usually cross burning legislation contains trespass and vandalism as so-called base offenses. Yet, supposing that the cross is burned outside the victim's property line, and, additionally, supposing that there is no local ordinance banning the burning of non-toxic materials on a public street in the respective state, the parallel offense would be "menacing"[1100]. Whereas statutes termed "intimidation"[1101], or "threatening"[1102] possibly serve as base offense as well -

---

1096 For further explanation view Chapter 3, D., 2., 2.2., 2.2.3., 2.3.3.1., b).

1097 Lawrence, Punishing Hate, pp. 93 et seqq.

1098 "Pure Bias Crime laws, however, are freestanding in appearance only. If there is any distinction between pure bias crime laws and penalty enhancement laws, it is that the former rely upon other criminal statutes implicitly whereas the latter rely explicitly." (Lawrence, Punishing Hate, p. 93). What all statutes enacted across the nation are claimed to be sharing "is an emphasis on the legal definition of "crime". That is, the term 'hate crime' assumes the commission of a criminal offense, a violation of an existing criminal norm. The hate crime designation may be applied only where a "predicate offense", or underlying crime, is committed as a result of bias or prejudice". (Perry, In the Name of Hate, 2001, p. 8).

1099 Va. Code Ann. § 18.2-423.

1100 Oregon's menacing statute ORS § 163.190 Menacing: "A person commits the crime of menacing if by word or conduct the person intentionally attempts to place another person in fear of imminent serious physical injury."

1101 Montana's intimidation statute: Section 45-5-203. Intimidation: "A person commits the offense of intimidation when, with the purpose to cause another to perform or to omit the performance of any act, he communicates to another, under circumstances which reasonably tend to produce a fear that it will be carried out, a threat to perform without lawful authority any of the following acts: [...]".

even though intimidation statutes focus upon coercion, while "the gravamen of menacing is the specific intent to cause fear"[1103] - not every legislator has chosen to enshrine plain intimidation or menacing statutes in the Penal Code of the respective state. Thus, the plain behavior, which intends to cause threat, does not serve as a base offense for a hate-motivated threatening behavior in every state. In such cases, an enacted cross burning statute would not rely on an existing criminal statute, thus it cannot be referred to "intimidation" as the parallel crime of an enacted hate crime statute. In that case, the underlying behavior of the hate crime is punished "in and of itself", because "cross burning is clearly intimidation"[1104].

This shows that in several states which enacted cross burning statutes but do not penalize the parallel "pure" intimidating behavior in a plain intimidation or menacing statute, a base offense for the relevant hate crime statute is not provided, yet, the hate crime is a real substantial hate crime law. Insofar it must be enough if the prima facie evidence intent to intimidate a person or group of persons, which then is required within the elements of facts of the respective hate crime statute. With that, the option for punishment, even though it cannot be relied on an underlying criminal behavior, is provided. However, the reversal of the burden of proof, referring to the intent of the perpetrator to intimidate his victim, proves that within such laws it is more about sanctioning the cross burning as racist activity.

bb) Intimidation Statutes

The fact of behavior being punished that is not established as a criminal conduct somewhere else in the relevant code, can be further revealed in New York's aggravated harassment legislation, however, arguing from a different perspective:

New York's Penal law does have a harassment statute enshrined in their penal code[1105]. Nevertheless, aggravated harassment punished by another statute is a "pure" hate crime law, since it newly punishes certain activity unrelated to the previously enacted "ordinary" harassment statute. In N. Y. Penal Law §§ 240.31, one commits a class E felony if one acted "with intent to harass, annoy, threaten or alarm another person, because of a belief or perception regarding such person's race, color, national origin, ancestry, gender, religion, religious practice, age, disability or sexual orientation, regardless of whether the belief or perception is correct [...]." Now, specific additional behavior is listed, especially referring to its subsection 3 until 5 penalizing one for somehow placing "a swastika, commonly exhibited as the emblem of Nazi

1102 Connecticut's threatening statute: Section 53a-62. Threatening in the second degree: Class A misdemeanor: "A person is guilty of threatening in the second degree when: (1) By physical threat, such person intentionally places or attempts to place another person in fear of imminent serious physical injury, (2) such person threatens to commit any crime of violence with the intent to terrorize another person, or (3) such person threatens to commit such crime of violence in reckless disregard of the risk of causing such terror".

1103 Lawrence, Punishing Hate, 2003, p. 98.

1104 De Vries, Lloyd, High Court Upholds Cross-Burning Ban, CBSNews, May 7, 2009.

1105 N.Y. Penal Law §§ 240.26.

Germany, on any building or other real property" or setting "a cross on fire in public view". Whereas the requirements of intent to harass, annoy, threaten or alarm another person are said to be based on prior enacted law, the underlying behavior though, thus the relevant objective facts of the crime are newly made up and punished. Insofar, new behavior which previously was unpunished became criminal due to a hate crime law.

This critical view which contradicts the prevailing literary opinion[1106], based on the nature of most hate crime laws as aggravating the sanction of already sanctioned behavior, will be considered during the classification of hate crimes as a separate crime category in the German approach[1107].

cc) State Civil Rights Laws

Another category which is to be considered as a part of this section, because it neither explicitly nor conclusively relies on statutes previously enacted within the particular penal code, are statutes which typify an infringement of a Civil Right. Even though such could be presented separated from this illustration because such laws are only applicable in the surrounding of Cilvil Rights, such legislation, however, autonomously penalizes certain behaviors, expressly, wilful intimidation or the interference with the Civil Rights of another, because of the person's race, religion, ethnic origin and the further.

According to the federal counterpart of Civil Rights Acts these laws criminalize people for depriving others of their civil or constitutional rights[1108]. Laws that criminalize the interference with Civil Rights aim at unjustifiable conducts that, by force or threat of force, interfere with or intimidate others in the exercise of their constitutional guaranteed Civil Rights. State laws, in opposite to federal Civil Rights Legislation, do not name a list of protected statuses, but usually protect the exercise of Civil Rights in general[1109]. As in opposite to Congress, which has the competence to penalize only specific statuses connected to federal activity, state legislators are authorized to penalize all sorts of interference with another one´s Civil Rights. Substantially, through these kinds

---

1106 The prevailing view considers hate crime as a "two-tiered" crime, an offense which is based on already punished behavior. (Lawrence, Punishing Hate, 2003, p. 93; Perry, In the Name of Hate, 2001, p. 8; "hate crimes always comprise two elements: a criminal offence committed with a bias motive.[...]. If there is no base offence, there is no hate crime." -according to: OSCE/ODIHR, Hate Crime Laws: A Practical Guide, 2009, pp. 16 et seqq.

1107 View hereto Chapter 4., G. Eligibility Check of Hate Crime Legislation according to German Criminal Law Doctrine.

1108 S.C. Code Ann. § 16-5-10 criminalizes conspiracies to deprive others of civil or constitutional rights.; S.C. Code Ann. § 16-17-560 covers assault or intimidation on account of exercise of civil or constitutional rights.; .R.S. Neb. § 28-110 states the right to live without violence, intimidation, or damage to property, regardless of "race, color, religion, ancestry, national origin, gender, sexual orientation, age, or disability."; Tenn. Code Ann. § 39-17-309 criminalizes the act of damaging the real or person property of others with the intent to intimidate them from exercising their constitutional or Civil Rights.

1109 According to S.C. Code Ann. § 16-5-10 "it is unlawful for two or more persons to band or conspire together or go in disguise upon the public highway or upon the premises of another with the intent to injure, oppress, or violate the person or property of a citizen because of his political opinion or his expression or exercise of the same or attempt by any means, measures, or acts to hinder, prevent, or obstruct a citizen in the free exercise and enjoyment of any right or privilege secured to him by the Constitution and laws of the United States or by the Constitution and laws of this State."

of laws hate crimes are equalized with the Violation of Civil Rights; though violated by individuals.

This type of law is considered as "real" substantive legislation in this illustration, since it is not just formally freestanding, but indeed has the potential to punish until yet unpunished behavior if it infringes the Civil Rights of a person.

dd) Conclusion "Real" Substantive Hate Crime Statutes

"Real" substantive hate crime statutes therefore do not rely on already criminalized behavior, but focus on acts which usually are committed to expose bigotry and hate towards certain people based on their race, religious beliefs, gender and the further are frequently enacted. Surely, usually this exposure of xenophobic bigotry causes threat – threat therefore being the base offense, however the legislature had to recgonize what behavior is eligible to cause such due to its racist component and based on that determine which behavior – even though previously unpunished - creates anxiety and threat only because of that component.

In any case, these laws criminalize the use of fear in order to achieve racial exclusion[1110]. Independent of hate crime laws, many states[1111] have some sort of assault law that proscribes the creation of fear or terror in a victim[1112]. Decisive within hate crime laws which criminalize bias-motivated acts creating fear in a victim is that they pick out specific behavior historically known to be designed to instill serious fear in minorities. Therefore, laws imposing punishment for the use of certain symbols and the burning of crosses are enacted to criminalize behavior which evidences racist motivation and qualifies as real threat[1113].

1110 "[L]ighting a cross has been passed down as a tradition. If it's lit in somebody's yard, they're doing something you don't like or that you want stopped – like living in your neighborhood." (Statement of a perpetrator of a cross burning law during police inquisition, according to: Levin/Mc Devitt, America's War on Those Who Are Different, 2002, p. 174; Jones, Racially Motivated Violence: An Empirical Study of a Growing Social Problem, National Urban League Report, May 1989.

1111 The Montana Intimidation Act, for example, provides as follows: "(1) A person commits the offense of intimidation when, with the purpose to cause another to perform or to omit the performance of any act, he communicates to another, under circumstances which reasonably tend to produce a fear that it will be carried out, a threat to perform without lawful authority any of the following acts: (a) inflict physical harm on the person threatened or any other person; (b) subject any person to physical confinement or restraint; or (c) commit any felony. (2) A person commits the offense of intimidation if he knowingly communicates a threat or false report of a pending fire, explosion, or disaster which would endanger life or property." (Mont. Code Ann. 45-5-203 [2005]).

1112 These laws are variously enacted as intimidation, menacing, and threatening statutes. Whereas menacing statutes focus on the specific intent to cause fear, intimidation statutes focus upon coercion. The main point about these statutes is that it is not focused on a certain behavior of the defendant (e.g. they may be violated through the defendant's words alone), important is solely that he or she purposely or knowingly acts in any kind of way to produce fear of serious harm and that the threat is real. Similar to these statutes are terroristic threatening statutes in that they criminalize the use of fear to achieve certain results. (Lawrence, Punishing Hate, 2003, p. 98).

1113 In "Washington state legislature findings to hate crime legislation" it is stated "that in many cases, certain discrete words or symbols are used to threaten the victims. Those discrete words or symbols have historically or traditionally been used to connote hatred or threats towards members of the class of which the victim or a member of the victim's family or household is a member. In particular, the legislature finds that cross burnings historically and traditionally have been used to threaten, terrorize, intimidate, and harass African Americans and their families. Cross burnings often preceded lynching, murders, burning of

Substantive hate crime statutes which do not rely on already criminalized behavior according to the respective penal code, but criminalize a certain behavior solely by the particular hate crime statute are based on the will of the legislator to abolish racist acts through the instrument of criminal law as established in N.J. Stat. § 52: 9DD-9, referred to as "the Duties of council" in its Section 2. a. who may develop policy proposals to "promote prejudice reduction and prevent and deter crimes based upon the victim's race, color, religion, national origin, sexual orientation, ethnicity, gender, or physical, mental or cognitive ability."

The constitutionality of these laws is most questioned, since their potential to violate the First Amendment of the U.S. Constitution is the highest. However, they don't interfere with the First Amendment, if they constitute fighting words acts. Fighting words refer to such expressed opinions which are likely to make the person to whom they are addressed to commit an act of violence. Fighting words are not protected by the First Amendment, because, like other unprotected categories (for example, defamation, obscenity, etc.) they are not an exposition of ideas but clearly harrassing[1114].

2.2.3.2. Sentencing Enhancement Laws

According to the federal counterpart "Hate Crime Enhancement Act" these laws increase penalty – the fine or term of incarceration - for certain offenses committed because of[1115] the "actual or perceived race, color, religion, national origin, physical or mental disability or sexual orientation of the victim was different from that characteristic of the perpetrator"[1116]. Enhanced penalty

---

homes, and other acts of terror. Further, Nazi swastikas historically and traditionally have been used to threaten, terrorize, intimidate, and harass Jewish people and their families. Swastikas symbolize the massive destruction of the Jewish population, commonly known as the holocaust. Therefore, the legislature finds that any person who burns or attempts to burn a cross or displays a swastika on the property of the victim or burns a cross or displays a swastika as part of a series of acts directed towards a particular person, the person's family or household members, or a particular group, knows or reasonably should know that the cross burning or swastika may create a reasonable fear of harm in the mind of the person, the person's family and household members, or the group". (Rev. Code Wash. (ARCW) § 9A.36.080).

1114 For further information on the constitutionality of hate crime legislation see Chapter 3, F. The standards set by the U.S. Supreme Court. In Chaplinsky v. New Hampshire, 315 U.S. 568 (1942), the Supreme Court constituted the doctrine of fighting words, which is an exception to the First Amendment's protection of free speech. This exception is explainable by the fact that such words usually are not part of a "dialogue or exposition of ideas". Fighting words refer to such expressed opinions "which are likely to make the person to whom they are addressed commit an act of violence". (For further information on fighting words and the history of Supreme Court decisions in regard to this doctrine view the broad overview at: Silver/Stein/Surman/Thompson; Fighting Words, at: http://www.bsos.umd.edu/gvpt/gvpt339/fightingwords.html; Chaplinsky v. New Hampshire, 315 U.S. 568 (1942); Cohen v. California, 403 U.S. 15 (1971); Hess v. Indiana, 414 U.S. 105 (1973); R.A.V. v. City of St. Paul, 112 S. Ct. 2538 (1992); Wisconsin v. Mitchell, 113 S. Ct. 2194 (1993).

1115 "Because of" refers also to "by reason of" legislation. However, the clear wording of Enhancement Laws being considered constitutional by the Supreme Court (Wisconsin v. Mitchell § 508 U.S. 476) refers to the § 939.645 Wisconsin statute, which decrees an enhancement of penalty whenever the defendant "[i]ntentionally selects the person against whom the [...] is committed or selects the property that is damaged or otherwise affected by the crime [...] in whole or in part because of the actor's belief or perception regarding the race, religion, color, disability, sexual orientation, national origin or ancestry of that person or the owner or occupant of that property, whether or not the actor's belief or perception was correct."

1116 Nev. Rev. Stat. Ann. § 193.1675 enhances penalty for crimes committed because the "actual or perceived race, color, religion, national origin, physical or mental disability or sexual orientation of the victim was

statutes are said to differ from statutes creating separate crimes since they do not reprocesses statement of facts; they step in after a conviction on a charge of an established crime has taken place, and increases penalty, if that criminal act “evidences” or “demonstrates” prejudice or bigotry based on the victim’s real or imagined membership in a legally recognized protected status[1117]. Penalties are increased in two ways: either a new, higher range of sentences for a crime is determined in case of its committal by reasons of hate or bias[1118]; or the underlying offense is upgraded, broadly speaking, for instance, through the conversion of a misdemeanor into a felony; more practical: a class C misdemeanor is treated as a class B misdemeanor, a second degree felony becomes a first degree felony, and so on[1119]:

If a statute dictates that the sentence for the underlying crime is cumulated with the sentence of a newly defined hate crime[1120], then it surely determines a penalty enhancement as a result, but it does not stipulate a certain sentence; it merely clears the mode of operation in the case of more than one statute being applicable to a hate crime. Consequently it is not to be considered as a sentence enhancement statute; rather this mechanism reveals the legislator’s choice to create substantial hate crime statutes.

Louisiana’s law, for instance, provides a penalty enhancement statute which dictates a higher range of sentences for several crimes in case the offender selected his or her victim or target because of the racial, religious, etc. nature of the person, property or institution. La. R.S. 14:107.2 B rules: “[...] if the underlying offense is a misdemeanor, and the victim is selected in the proscribed manner[1121], the offender may receive an additional consecutive sentence of imprisonment for not more than six months, or fine of not more

different from that characteristic of the perpetrator."; R.R.S. Neb. § 28-111 enhances penalty for offences against a person or a person's property because of the person's "race, color, religion, ancestry, national origin, gender, sexual orientation, age or disability."; Tex. Penal Code § 12.47 enhances penalty for offense committed because of bias or prejudice.

1117 Jenness/Grattet, Making Hate a Crime, 2001, p. 82.

1118 For instance, on conviction of a Class A felony that was found to have been motivated by bias towards the victim, the sentence shall not be less than 15 years; On conviction of a Class B felony, in terms of bias-motivation, the sentence shall not be less than 10 years; and so on. (Code of Alabama 1975, Section 13A-5-13 (c), referring to felonies in (1) and misdemeanors in (2)); Mont. Code Anno., § 45-5-222 demands additional sentence for hate crimes by ruling: "A person who has pleaded guilty [...] of any offense, [...], that was committed because of the victim's race, creed, religion, color, national origin, or involvement in Civil Rights or human rights activities or [...], in addition to the punishment provided for commission of the offense, [...], may, [...] be sentenced to a term of imprisonment of not less than 2 years or more than 10 years [...]."

1119 Iowa Code § 712.9 "A violation of sections 712.3 through 712.8, which is also a hate crime as defined in section 729A.2, shall be classified and punished as an offense one degree higher than the underlying offense."; Tex. Penal Code § 12.47 "Penalty If Offense Committed Because of Bias or Prejudice“ states: "If an affirmative finding under Article 42.014, Code of Criminal Procedure, is made in the trial of an offense [...] the punishment for the offense is increased to the punishment prescribed for the next highest category of offense."

1120 In Rev. Code Wash. (ARCW) § 9A.36.080 it is stated under passage five of the statute "Every person who commits another crime during the commission of a crime under this section may be punished and prosecuted for the other crime separately."

1121 RS 14:107.2 (§107.2. "Hate Crimes") "It shall be unlawful for any person to select the victim of the following offences against person and property because of actual or perceived race, age, gender, religion, color, creed, disability, sexual orientation, national origin, or ancestry of that person or the owner or occupant of that property; [...]."

than five hundred dollars, or both."; and La. R.S. 14:107.2 C.: regulates that in cases in which "the underlying offense is a felony, and the victim is selected in the proscribed manner, the offender may receive an additional consecutive sentence of imprisonment with or without hard labor for not more than five years, or fine of not more than five thousand dollars, or both." Attention must be drawn to the fact that this sentence shall run consecutively to the sentence for the underlying offense. Whether the base offense is a misdemeanor or a felony. An additional and consecutive sentence is to be imposed for hate crimes which, as a result, serve as a sentence cumulation.

Several laws modificate an established statute by adding a clause that reclassifies the crime if it was committed for reasons of hate or bias against the victim's legally recognized protected group status characteristic. In such forms of hate crime legislation, additions referring to hate- or bias-motivated behavior are inserted in any chosen criminal norm; established norms are extended instead of new ones being created.

2.2.3.3. Overview of Various State Laws and their provided Definition of Hate Crime

Hate crimes are defined in various ways, and legally encompassed differently from state to state. The following several statutes are exemplified to encompass the actual U.S. legal situation concerning the criminalization of hate crimes.

a) Alabama

"The Legislature finds and declares that it is [...] the right of every person, regardless of race, color, religion, national origin, ethnicity, or physical or mental disability, to be secure and protected from threats of reasonable fear, intimidation, harassment, and physical harm caused by activities of groups and individuals."[1122] Therefore, Section 13A-5-13, Code of Alabama 1975, stipulates that „[u]nder existing law, additional penalties are imposed against a person if the offense committed is motivated by the victim's race, color, religion, national origin, ethnicity, or physical or mental disability, sexual orientation, or gender identity or expression."[1123]

Additional penalties are imposed by making clear that the offender has to be found guilty of a (base-) crime and that he had to - beyond a reasonable doubt - be motivated by the victim's actual or perceived race, color, religion, national origin, ethnicity, physical or mental disability, sexual orientation, or gender identity or expression; due to which the sentence for the (base-) offense found to have been motivated by the victim's actual or perceived membership in a legally protected group shall be served a sentence which "shall not be less than [...]".

1122 SB27By Senator Dial; RFD Judiciary; Rd 1 07-FEB-12; a bill is to be entitled as an act to amend Section 13A-5-13, Code of Alabama 1975, relating to hate crimes in order to impose additional penalties for the following crimes: arson, burglary, and criminal mischief in any degree when committed against religious property.

1123 Amendment to Section 13A-5-13, Code of Alabama 1975, §13A-5-13. (b).

b) California

Under Title 11.6 Civil Rights, Chapter one "Definitions" of California Penal Code in Section 422.55 (a) a prevenient definition of hate crimes in sort of a previous general part is provided with the following meaning[1124]: "Hate crime" refers to a criminal act committed, in whole or in part, because of one or more of the following actual or perceived characteristics of the victim: disability; gender; nationality; race or ethnicity; religion; sexual orientation; association with a person or group with one or more of these actual or perceived characteristics.

Further a penalty enhancement is enshrined in the act demanding that "[...] a person who commits a felony that is a hate crime or attempts to commit a felony that is a hate crime, shall receive an additional term of one, two, or three years in the state prison, at the court's discretion."[1125]

c) Connecticut

"A person is guilty of intimidation based on bigotry or bias in the first degree when such person maliciously, and with specific intent to intimidate or harass another person because of the actual or perceived race, religion, ethnicity, [or] disability, sexual orientation or gender identity or expression of such other person, causes serious physical injury to such other person or to a third person."[1126]

d) Georgia

The state of Georgia, as the exception, has only one criminal act that qualifies as a hate crime. According to their legislation: O.C.G.A. § 16-7-26 implies aggravate punishment for criminal defacement and vandalism of churches and religious insitutions, thus protects places of worship. It is remarkable that Georgia, the birthplace of Ku Klux Klan activity and home of former slavery protectionists, does not have the kind of widescale statutory protection that 48 other states and even the federal government – by challenging its competencies – provide to protect people from victimization because of what they are[1127].

e) Louisiana

A far-reaching hate crime concept is followed by Louisiana which defines hate crimes, provides for training of law enforcement officers, and requires reporting in the Louisiana Uniform Crime Reporting System. Louisiana's Crime Reporting System publishes results of collected data relating to hate crimes, as defined by R.S. 14:107.2 occurring within the state in an annual report to the governor and the members of the legislature as required by R.S. 15:1204.2(B)(8). In Louisiana, in its Title 14, referring to criminal law in §

1124 Section 422.55-422.57 of California's Penal Code is addressed to hate crimes.
1125 Cal Pen Code § 422.75.(a).
1126 Gen. Stat. Ann. § 53a-181j (West Supp. 1994).
1127 Monroe, Hate Crimes in Georgia, October 16th, 2010. (View at: http://www.merlinusmonroe.com/2010/10/16/hate-crimes-in-georgia/).

107.2. - “Hate Crimes”, hate crimes are defined as certain enumerated criminal offenses in which the victim is selected because of that person's race, age, gender, color, religion, ancestry, national origin, disability, creed or sexual orientation. Further *Louisiana* provides a penalty enhancer for hate crimes, distinguishing between misdemeanors[1128] and felonies[1129]. It is important to keep in mind that this sentence shall run consecutively to the sentence for the underlying offense, whether the base offense is a misdemeanor or a felony.

f) Virginia

Virginia´s hate crime reporting statute defines hate crimes for purposes of this section in the following: "hate crime" means (i) a criminal act committed against a person or his property with the specific intent of instilling fear or intimidation in the individual against whom the act is perpetrated because of race, religion or ethnic origin or that is committed for the purpose of restraining that person from exercising his rights under the Constitution or laws of this Commonwealth or of the United States, (ii) any illegal act directed against any persons or their property because of those persons' race, religion or national origin, and (iii) all other incidents, as determined by law-enforcement authorities, intended to intimidate or harass any individual or group because of race, religion or national origin[1130]."

g) Washington

Washington hate crime laws penalize an offender for “[...] malicious harassment if he or she maliciously and intentionally commits one of the following acts” [acts like physical injury to the victim, destruction of the victim’s property and threat are numbered in the following] “because of his or her perception of the victim's race, color, religion, ancestry, national origin, gender, sexual orientation, or mental, physical, or sensory handicap: [...]”.[1131] Thus, legislation is not termed hate crime law or something similar, but “malicious harassment”. This section punishes conducts in terms of bias motivation separately from other laws, with the result that in the case of a conviction under this law the sentence for the underlying offense and the sentence for malicious harassment are added together and by this lead to increased punishment in case the punished act constitutes a hate crime[1132]. It is also worth mentioning that the law contains a reversal of the burden of proof for the committal of a hate crime to the disadvantage of the offender in the case of committing certain acts, e.g. if the offender “(a) Burns a cross on property of a victim who is or whom the actor perceives to be of African American heritage;”

1128 La. R.S. 14:107.2 B. "[...] if the underlying offense is a misdemeanor, and the victim is selected in the proscribed manner, the offender may receive an additional consecutive sentence of imprisonment for not more than six months, or fine of not more than five hundred dollars, or both."

1129 La. R.S. 14:107.2 C. In cases in which "the underlying offense is a felony, and the victim is selected in the proscribed manner, the offender may receive an additional consecutive sentence of imprisonment with or without hard labor for not more than five years, or fine of not more than five thousand dollars, or both."

1130 Va. Code Ann. § 52-8.5; 1988, c. 838; 2002, cc.588; 623.

1131 Revised Code of Washington (RCW) 9A.36.080 "Malicious harassment - Definition and criminal penalty."

1132 RCW 9A.36.080 "Malicious harassment - Definition and criminal penalty." imposes under its passage (5): "Every person who commits another crime during the commission of a crime under this section may be punished and prosecuted for the other crime separately."

or "(b) Defaces property of a victim who is or whom the actor perceives to be of Jewish heritage by defacing the property with a swastika."[1133] "Unless evidence exists which explains to the trier of fact's satisfaction that the person did not intend to threaten the victim or victims, the trier of fact may infer that the person intended to threaten a specific victim or group of victims because of the person's perception of the victim's or victims' race, color, religion, ancestry, national origin, gender, sexual orientation, or mental, physical, or sensory handicap [...]". Considering the sentencing enhancement provided for hate crimes[1134], this idea of placing the onus for not committing a hate crime on the offender is remarkable, but consequential since in such cases the bias-motivation of an act is perfectly obvious. If one of the cases stated under (a) and (b) are not relevant, the state's ability to prosecute a person for "malicious harassment" is not restricted to such if the facts of another case implies bias motivation[1135].

3. Ambiguity of Hate Crime Laws in the American Nation

After working through the particulars of the statutes of several states and the federal hate crime laws and finally concentrating on the body of law to which the attention of this dissertation is drawn, i.e., "bias-motivated crimes", it can therefore be concluded that there are two identifiable and distinct ways of how U.S. legislatives formally formed hate- or bias-motivated conducts in a legislative mode:

1. penalty enhancements laws and
2. substantial laws being divided in
   a) statutes punishing bias-motivated committal of criminal acts and
   b) intimidation statutes.

1133 RCW 9A.36.080 (2) (a) and (b) "Malicious harassment - Definition and criminal penalty." The fact that cross burnings and defacing property by Jewish swastika are punished in particular is reasoned by the legislature of Washington as follows: "[...] The legislature finds that the state interest in preventing crimes and threats motivated by bigotry and bias goes beyond the state interest in preventing other felonies or misdemeanors such as criminal trespass, malicious mischief, assault, or other crimes that are not motivated by hatred, bigotry, and bias, and that prosecution of those other crimes inadequately protects citizens from crimes and threats motivated by bigotry and bias. [...] The legislature also finds that in many cases, certain discrete words or symbols are used to threaten the victims. Those discrete words or symbols have historically or traditionally been used to connote hatred or threats towards members of the class of which the victim or a member of the victim's family or household is a member. In particular, the legislature finds that cross burnings historically and traditionally have been used to threaten, terrorize, intimidate, and harass African Americans and their families. Cross burnings often preceded lynching, murders, burning of homes, and other acts of terror. Further, Nazi swastikas historically and traditionally have been used to threaten, terrorize, intimidate, and harass Jewish people and their families. Swastikas symbolize the massive destruction of the Jewish population, commonly known as the holocaust. Therefore, the legislature finds that any person who burns or attempts to burn a cross or displays a swastika on the property of the victim or burns a cross or displays a swastika as part of a series of acts directed towards a particular person, the person's family or household members, or a particular group, knows or reasonably should know that the cross burning or swastika may create a reasonable fear of harm in the mind of the person, the person's family and household members, or the group." (RCW 9A.36.078 Malicious harassment - Finding.).

1134 RCW 9A.36.080 passage (7) provides: "Malicious harassment is a class C felony."

1135 "This subsection does not restrict the state's ability to prosecute a person under subsection (1) of this section when the facts of a particular case do not fall within (a) or (b) of this subsection." (RCW 9A.36.080 (2)).

Civil Rights legislation, as mentioned, was enacted to ensure an uniform application of all laws and to constitute the safeguard of fundamental rights for all citizens in equal measures and may be considered as truly substantial hate crime law.

Each legal strategy can contain varying combinations of conduct and status provisions so that the wealth of variations offers numerous forms of existing bias-motivated offenses. To qualify as a "criminal" hate crime law, "a statute must criminalize, enhance penalties for, or amend existing statutes regarding crimes motivated by bias toward individuals or groups based on particular status characteristics"; in order to fulfill these requirements, a statute must imply a state policy action, explicitly refer to the subjective intention of the perpetrator[1136] and it must name a list of legally recognized and by the statute protected social statuses[1137].

The task of organizing the multitude of laws by common features in order to find a common determinator under which one may examine the effectuated American hate crime statutes in unison has failed. Instead of an examination in unison of all laws, these laws are discussed in conjunction with each other. Yet, the reason for the failure and the result of the attempt to group the statutes shall be provided briefly.

- Various Definitions

The definition of what is to be considered as a hate crime varies between the different laws throughout the American nation. These laws protect differing characteristics; only certain basic characteristics are evenly protected by all laws. Such are race, national origin or ethnic and religion. However, which groups must be legitimately protected has been determined by the federal government since 2009 through the Matthew Shepard and James Byrd, Jr. Hate Crimes Prevention Act, such are race, color, religion, national origin, religion, gender, sexual orientation, gender identity, and disability. It is up to the individual local legislature to protect additional characteristics.

- Uneven Statement of Facts

Legal embodied motivations vary[1138]. Moreover, the difference between the wording "because of" and "by reason of" in the statutes is unclear. The requirements for the intent of the offender are not the same. In summary, there are two types of hate crime statutes that have been enacted. One is based on the "animus" model, and requires hostility on the part of the perpetrator to the victim's group. The other is based on the "discriminatory selection" model (upheld by the U.S. Supreme Court in Wisconsin v. Mitchell[1139]); this punishes the selection of victims on the basis of group characteristics, independently of any animus towards the group. "The mental state of the perpetrator is critical in

1136 This refers to the motive of the offender for committing a crime. It must be bias or hate towards the victim's legally protected status characteristics which are specified by the statute.

1137 Jenness/Grattet, Making Hate a Crime, 2001, pp. 77, 78.

1138 Aydin, Strafrechtliche Bekämpfung von Hassdelikten, 2006, pp. 71-78.

1139 508 U.S. 476 (1993).

distinguishing these statutes"[1140]. Either the perpetrator must willfully attack a person because the person embodies a true or perceived legally protected characteristic or "intentionally select" a victim based on his protected group membership.

Statutes based on "discriminatory selection" have different requirements for the affirmation of the existence of a hate crime. In contrary to the core of hate crime being animosity or hatred towards a legally protected group, it is considered to be sufficient if a perpetrator chooses a victim based on its features, which are established in the law. By strictly following the "discriminatory selection" model, a burglar who chooses targets of a particular group simply because he believes they are richer would constitute a hate crime. This applies even though the target is chosen in view of the crime intended and not because of the perpetrator's sentiment towards the chosen target group. For instance, if a perpetrator decides to burgle a house, he assumes – due to his prejudice – that all Jews are rich; therefore he chooses to burgle the house of Jews. Indeed, his prejudice led him to choose a certain group of people to victimize, but the true selection is based on his intention to successfully commit his planned crime, whereas a true hate crime offender is not driven by the urge to choose an appropriate object for committing an already aimed at offense, but only commits an offense because of hate towards the chosen target group. However, the discriminatory selection model has a point to proponents of the vulnerable victim idea supporting hate crimes. Other than the 'animus' model, the 'discriminatory selection' model would involve cases in which a perpetrator chooses targets of a particular group simply because he believes the probability of apprehension is lower (because e.g. the police/law enforcement authorities are less concerned) or because they are easier targets (e.g.: the elderly are less able to defend themselves when robbed). Whereas these motives might become blurred for hate crime perpetrators - because of their idea that certain humans have a lower value, they could possibly assume that this idea is shared by the society and thus the law enforcement authorities will not be interested in elucidation. This motive at least could become relevant when perpetrators choose in particular the homeless, or the disabled, and (at least back in the days) certain races – but in truth their reason for attacking certain groups is less the idea of encountering less resistance, but only their animus against such. Today, all criminal law scholars agree on the fact that hate crimes protect all human groups evenly, therefore the vulnerable victim theory has no place in justifying hate crime laws. Anyway, the 'discriminatory selection' model is applicable since upheld by the U.S. Supreme Court[1141].

The need to fulfill the requirements of the underlying base offense, in reference to which a hate crime law is constituted, is unclear. Whether such an enacted hate crime law must fulfill all so called "base" requirements/requirements of the base offense or just some varies from

1140 Lawrence, Punishing Hate, 2003, p. 29.
1141 Wisconsin v. Mitchell 508 U.S. 476 (1993).

statute to statute. This lack of clarity results from the various intimidation statutes which somehow constitute new elements of facts but also mingle up the ordinary elements of a menacing offense. Their frequent use and their unknown extent seems to be the attempt of the legislature to overcome the inconsistencies mentioned above and in the following.

The difference between new, separate statement of facts and aggravating statements of facts of an already criminalized behavior is uncertain, at least not easy to make out in every law. Frequently, states have enacted both kinds in parallel.

The answer to the question whether the general penalty enhancement is based on the assumption of an increased wrong of the act or on the increased culpability of the offender is not detectable by analyzing the wording of the law. Penalty enhancements for hate crimes therefore are based on one or both facts. Accordingly, American hate crime laws impose increased penalties in accordance with the wrongfulness of the perpetrator's actions or on the ground of 'greater culpability' on the part of the perpetrator. A few scholars refer to normative standards stating that hate motivation is morally more blameworthy than other motivations for crime[1142]. To the German understanding, the approach which refers to an increased wrong of the act could justify separate substantive offenses/penalty enhancement laws/aggravated offenses for hate crimes, since the penalty frame of the base offense in this case would possibly not be sufficient to encompass or reach the amount of wrong fulfilled by a hate crime. The reasoning with 'greater culpability', though, tends to lead to the adjustment of the sanction for hate crime offenders within the established penal frame of the base offense during the judicial sentencing process.

One disagrees whether the bias-motivated hate of the offender is part of the intent/ subjective element of facts or if it is a motivation. However, what is clear is that the presence of the motivation that constitutes the hate crime must be proven beyond a reasonable doubt. Since it increases the penalty, it is an aggravating fact, and therefore, in the same way as any other prerequisites of an offense, it´s presence must be proven in legally determined manners during trial. Thus, the presence of the hate crime motivation of the offender must be proven beyond a reasonable doubt by the jury or whoever is the trier of fact (since not all states have the implementation of a jury - the constitution requires a jury only for federal courts - the decision according the presence can be made by judges in local cases) during the trial.

1142 For general cause why motives shall play a role in determining a defendant's sentence (in contrast to motives being considered within liability determinations) view: Gardener, The Mens Rea Enigma: Observations on the Role of Motive in the Criminal Law Post and Present, 1993, Utah L. Review 635, pp. 747 - 749.

E. Brief Look at the American Justification of Hate Crime Laws

Many criminal law scholars[1143] adopt a retributive perspective, which *Dillof* terms the "wrongfulness/culpability paradigm"[1144]. This approach focuses on setting penalties in accordance with the wrongfulness of the perpetrator's actions[1145]. Using the wrongfulness/culpability paradigm, supporters of hate crime laws make at least one of the following claims, which then are amplified by respective studies: The first is that hate crimes involve 'greater culpability' on the part of perpetrators in that hate motivation is more morally blameworthy than other motivations for crime[1146]. The second is that hate crimes involve a 'greater wrong', either to the victim (by causing greater physical or psychological harm) or to third parties (by instilling fear in other members of the out-group, or through the possibility of retaliation) or towards the society at large[1147].

Therefore, proponents must manage hate crime laws within the context of traditional moral theories and orthodox First Amendment concerns[1148].

1143 Stated differently by Lawrence, who claims that the Dentological justification is espoused by "most supporters" of bias crimes laws. (Lawrence, Punishing Hate, 2003, p.61). This 'Dentological' justification, which is based on the criminal's mental state in order to justify hate crime legislation in the core states, that on some accounts, mental states are relevant to blameworthiness not because they imply greater responsibility for a harm, but because they reflect the flawed character that is the underlying cause of the crime. By rejecting the equality principle - "one of the most deeply held tenets in our legal system and our culture" – the bias criminal reveals his character to be more deeply flawed than that of the ordinary criminal. (Lawrence, Punishing Hate, 2003, p. 61; Dillof, Michigan Law Review, Vol. 98, pp. 1678-1703 (1681).

1144 Dillof, Punishing Bias: An Examination of the Theoretical Foundations of Bias Crime Statutes, Northwestern Law Review 91 (4), (1997), pp. 1015-1081; Dillof, Michigan Law Review, Vol. 98, pp.1678-1703.

1145 Dharmapala/Garoupa, Penalty Enhancement for Hate Crimes: An Economic Analysis, Georgetown University Law Center, Working Paper Series in Business, Economics, and Regulatory Law Working Paper No. 268644, 2001, p. 5.

1146 For further information on, according to U.S. understanding of what acts may the state rightly make criminal, view Feinberg's, 3rd Volume of "The Moral Limits of the Criminal Law" in which the principle of legal moralism is explained, according to which it is necessary to prevent immoral conduct whether or not it harms anyone. (Feinberg, Harmless Wrongdoing the Moral Limits of the Criminal Law, Michigan Law Review Volume: 88, Issue 6, (1990), pp. 1415-1429).

1147 Hagan, Introduction to Criminology, 4th edition; Nelson/Hall, 1998, p. 244; Lawrence, Punishing Hate, 2003, p. 40, 63; with reference to: Henneberger, "For Bias Crimes, a Double Trauma" , Newsday, 113 (Jan. 9, 1992); Kleinfield, "Bias Crimes Hold Steady, But Leave Many Scards" , New York Times, A – 1 (Jan. 27, 1992); Levin, "U. S. Supreme Court Upholds Stiffer Sentences for Hate Crimes", Intelligence Report, 166 (Sept. 1993); Weiss, "Ethnoviolence: Impact upon the Response of Victims and the Community", in: Bias Crime: American Law Enforcement and Legal Response, pp. 182, 183 (1993); see also Weiss/Ehrlich/Larcon, "Ethnoviolence at Work" , 18 Journal of Intergroup Relations, p. 18 (Winter 1991 - 1992) – according to this study of violence in the workplace it was found that victims of bias-motivated violence reported a significantly greater level of negative psychological symptoms than did such victims of non bias-motivated violence. Hate crime victims have been compared to rape victims according the fact that the physical harm associated with the crime, however great, is less significant than the powerful accompanying sense of violation. (Weiss, "Ethnoviolence: Impact upon the Response of Victims and the Community", in Bias Crime: American Law Enforcement and Legal Response, pp. 174, 182 (1993). Furthermore, hate crime are said in particular to leave an unwelcome dent in the harmonious functioning of society. (Anti-Defamation League, An Introduction to Hate Crime Law, 2012, view at: http://www.adl.org/combating_hate/Introduction-to-Hate-Crime-Laws.pdf - accessed January 2012).

1148 Dillof, Punishing Bias: An Examination of the Theoretical Foundations of Bias Crime Statutes, Northwestern Law Review 91 (4), (1997), pp. 1015-1081; Dillof, Michigan Law Review, Vol. 98, pp. 1678-1703.

F. The Standards set by U. S. Supreme Courts

Much of the legal literature on hate crime legislation has focused on their constitutionality, particularly with respect to the First Amendment[1149]. However, as of today, the Supreme Court ruled these laws constitutional, if certain guidelines are respected.

In RAV v. City of St. Paul[1150] a white male erected and burned a cross in the fenced front yard of an African American family. The perpetrator was charged with two counts, one of which was the violation of the St. Paul Bias-Motivated Crime Ordinance[1151], which basically punished fighting words actions[1152]. The trial court dismissed this charge based on the ground that the ordinance was "substantially overbroad and impermissibly content-based", but the State Supreme Court reversed. It rejected the overbreadth claim because the phrase "arouses anger, alarm or resentment in others" is capable to limit the ordinance's reach to "fighting words" according to the doctrine set in Chaplinsky v. New Hampshire[1153]. Nevertheless, it was ruled partially invalid, therefore unconstitutional, because even if narrowly construed, it does not solely "impose special prohibitions on those speakers who express views on the disfavored subjects of race, color, creed, religion or gender" but, furthermore, addresses contents which goes beyond the actual subject of hate crime[1154]. However, by this State Supreme Court decision it was made clear that cross burning laws are constitutional and does not violate First Amendment Rights if a law is narrowly tailored to reach only fighting words and thereby serve a governmental interest in protecting the society against bias-motivated threats to public safety and order[1155].

Wisconsin v. Mitchell[1156], in this groundbreaking decision in favor of the constitutionality of hate crime legislation, the Supreme Court upheld the

1149 Gellman, Sticks and Stones Can Put You in Jail, but Can Words Increase Your Sentence, UCLA Law Review 39, (1991), pp.333-396.

1150 505 U.S. 377 (1992).

1151 The law established: "Whoever places on public or private property, a symbol, object, appellation, characterization or graffiti, including, but not limited to, a burning cross or Nazi swastika, which one knows or has reasonable grounds to know arouses anger, alarm or resentment in others on the basis of race, color, creed, religion or gender commits disorderly conduct and shall be guilty of a misdemeanor." A city (as opposed to a state or the federal government) may enact law if it forms a municipality. "A municipality, such as a city, town, village, or borough, is a political subdivision of a state within which a municipal corporation has been established to provide local government to a population in a defined area." A piece of law, passed by a municipal government, is named an ordinance, e.g. "St. Paul Bias-Motivated Crime Ordinance". "The power of municipal governments to enact ordinances is derived from the state constitution or statutes or through the legislative grant of a municipal charter. The charter in large part dictates how much power elected officials have to regulate actions within the municipality." (West's Encyclopedia of American Law, "Ordinance", Edition 2, 2008; view at: http://legal-dictionary.thefreedictionary.com/ordinance.)

1152 For further information on fighting words and the history of Supreme Court decisions in regard to the doctrine of fighting words view footnote 1113; and the broad overview at: Silver/Stein/Surman/Thompson; Fighting Words, at: http://www.bsos.umd.edu/gvpt/gvpt339/fightingwords.html.

1153 315 U.S. 568 (1942) – view footnote 1113.

1154 R.A.V., Petitioner, v. City of St. Paul, Minnesota; 505 U.S. 377 (112 S.Ct. 2538, 120 L.Ed.2d 305); No. 90-7675; argued: December 4, 1991; decided: June 22, 1992; pp. 391-393.

1155 R.A.V., Petitioner, v. City of St. Paul, Minnesota; 505 U.S. 377 (112 S.Ct. 2538, 120 L.Ed.2d 305); No. 90-7675; argued: December 4, 1991; decided: June 22, 1992.

1156 508 U.S. 476, 476 (1993); pp. 391-393.

general idea of taking an inner connection between the act and a motivation into account when defining penalty; and therefore ruled that a state may legitimately punish the circumstance that a crime was committed or initially motivated due to a perceived or actual characteristic of the victim and its membership in a protected group[1157]. A group of African American teenagers went outside, being incited by a movie they watched shortly before, which portrayed the racist past of America with its locally prevailing open racism, lack of cooperation from the local police authorities and the generally unconstitutional living conditions for black people in the town Mississippi. Everyone being enraged, the perpetrators saw a white passer-by across the street and agreed quickly to beat him up, out of revenge for the happenings just seen in the movie. They also stole his shoes. Since this act constitutes a hate crime the local Crime Sentencing Enhancement Statute increased the penalty up to four years[1158]. In contrast to RAV v. City of St. Paul[1159] the Supreme Court upheld the lower court's decision of increasing the penalty in accordance with the hate crime statute because the underlying act was constituted by handlings not by expressed opinions; thus, it was the perpetrator's behavior which was addressed by the legislation. The fact that the motives, on which this behavior was based, caused a penalty enhancement was not considered as violating the First Amendment of the Constitution[1160]. If such a correlation between motive and action verifiably exists, then it may find its expression in the underlying sentence. Thereby "the statute prohibits intentional conduct, not belief or expression"[1161]. Therefore, it was ruled that hate crime Laws do not unconstitutionally infringe free speech. Moreover, the most famous Supreme Court decision with regard to the constitutionality of hate crime legislation also proves that hate crime laws are not established in order to protect only certain races, nor solely minorities, since in this decision African Americans were sent to court under hate crime legislation for attacking a white person.

The following decision refers to the longtime unanswered question whether all sentence-range maximizing facts must be proven beyond a reasonable doubt during trial or whether such can be dependent on judicial sentencing[1162]; which

1157 Todd Mitchell, one of the defendants was found guilty by jury of aggravated battery and a hate crime provision of Wisconsin law that permits enhancement of the maximum penalty for an offense. This penalty-enhancement statute can be implemented whenever the defendant "[...] intentionally selects the person against whom the crime is committed because of race, religion, color, disability, sexual orientation, national origin or ancestry of that person".

1158 § 939.645 Wisconsin statute established an increasing of penalty whenever the defendant "[i]ntentionally selects the person against whom the crime under par. (a) is committed or selects the property that is damaged or otherwise affected by the crime under par. (a) in whole or in part because of the actor's belief or perception regarding the race, religion, color, disability, sexual orientation, national origin or ancestry of that person or the owner or occupant of that property, whether or not the actor's belief or perception was correct." T. Mitchell was sentenced for aggravated battery and this sentence was enhanced due to this norm because he intentionally selected his victim on account of the victim's race.

1159 505 U.S. 377 (1992).

1160 Tolmein, Rassistisch motivierte Gewaltdelikte, ZRP, 2001, pp. 315-319, p. 315 with reference to Butler, Haß spricht - Zur Politik des Performativen, 1998, pp. 67-97.

1161 Written opinion of Justice Shirley S. Abrahamson, who became chief justice of the Supreme Court in 1996, according State v. Mitchell 169 Wis. 2d 153 (1992).

1162 See Jones v. United States, 526 U.S. 227, 251-52 (1999).

was the case in a New Jersey hate crime law. In this hate crime law, the existence of bias was treated as a sentencing factor, instead of an offense element to be proven at trial. This, however, concerns the manner in which states from then on were required to establish the implementation of bias motives within hate crime laws, not the constitutionality of bias-based penalty enhancements generally. The New Jersey Supreme Court[1163] reviewed a law that made bias a sentencing factor that increases the maximum sentence to which a defendant is subject. According to the defendant, this law violated the Due Process Clause's guarantee that every sentence increasing fact must be found by a jury under the reasonable doubt standard. The New Jersey Supreme Court rejected this contention based on its interpretation of Supreme Court precedent[1164]. In Apprendi v. New Jersey[1165] the decision by the Supreme Court was made: the Supreme Court considered it a violation of the right to fair trial, if a judge, after the jury determined the factual prerequisites of the base crime, then - independently - as part of the sentencing process, applies the regulation for penalty enhancement[1166] which has not been discussed with the jury in the trial before. According to the Court, the jury must determine on its own whether the racist motivation, which is reflected in the crime, is present[1167]. As the standard of proof must apply here, any reasonable doubt as to the racist motivation of the act must be eliminated. This decision was not about the fundamental admissibility of aggravating penalties for hate crimes, but to the procedural circumstances, it may have an impact towards the substantive side of hate crime laws. Since only elements of an offense must be determined by a jury, hate crime legislators who form their laws by establishing motives as a part of the elements of a statute are on the safe side, according to Supreme Court's precepts.

It can be concluded that these decisions do not provide the final answer to the question regarding the uncertain legal implementation practice of how to incorporate the bias motive into a legal device. Some commentators, who have argued against the consideration of motive for liability determinations, have argued that the motive should play a role in determining a defendant's sentence. As a defendant's motive is a reflection of his character, "which could only be evaluated by discretionary moral judgment"[1168], these opinions are whether proved wrong nor right. In Wisconsin v. Mitchell, the Supreme Court confirmed that a defendant's motive for committing an offense is "one important factor" that a trial judge may consider in deciding what sentence to

1163 State v. Apprendi, 731 A.2d 485 (N.J.), cert. granted, 120 S. Ct. 525 (1999).
1164 State v. Apprendi, 731 A.2d 485 (N.J.), at 493-95.
1165 US Supreme Court No. 99-478 v. June 26, 2000.
1166 N.J.Stat.Ann § 2C:44-3(e) (West Supp 2000).
1167 Tolmein, Rassistisch motivierte Gewaltdelikte, ZRP, 2001, pp. 315-319 (315).
1168 Hall, General Principles of Criminal Law, 1947, (153), pp. 162-163 ("the determination and evaluation of the motives of criminal behavior are allocated to administration; in the first instance, to judicial discretion in the selection of a proper sentence"; noting that a sentencing judge's discretion "is very great"); Gardner, The Mens Rea Enigma: Observations on the Role of Motive in the Criminal Law Post and Present, 1993, Utah L. Review 635, pp. 747 - 749; Hessick, Motive's Role in Criminal Punishment, Southern California Law Review, Vol. 80, 2006, p. 15.

impose[1169]. In Apprendi v. New Jersey it is ruled that the presence of the necessary connection between the act and the relevant motive must be found pertinent by a jury; this refers to the organization of the American criminal process, which is bisected: the sentence is imposed by the judge, whereas the hate crime increasing fact, e. g. the motive, must be determined by the jury. Once, the presence of the necessary connection between the act and the relevant motive is found by a jury, the judge then may take such into account when imposing the penalty. Therefore, nothing is said about whether a hate crime motive is a part of the elements of a statute, i.e. part of the intent/subjective element of facts or whether it is a motivation, thus the reflection of the defendant's character.

In the present day it is clear that hate crime laws do not infringe the Right of Free Speech, however, some legislation might be open to challenge on other constitutional grounds. The quite newly enacted Matthew Shepard and James Byrd, Jr. Hate Crimes Prevention Act is especially claimed to be unconstitutional because the federal legislature is said to exceed its competence in the field of criminal law by the enactment of this piece of law.

G. Conclusion: Hate Crime in the United States of America

The hate crime concept followed by the U.S. contains a mix of data collection and penalty enhancement laws. This procedure model aims at comprehending the nature of hate crimes on the one hand, and by the thereby achieved cognition, be able to abolish hate crimes through clear and authoritative criminal response on the other hand.

The preferred manner of penalizing hate-motivated behavior varies from state to state: some states prefer to respond to hate-motivated violence with statutes proscribing criminal penalties for Civil Rights violations, or specific "ethnic intimidation" and "malicious harassment", others chose provisions for enhanced penalties for a selection of offenses[1170]. These laws cover crimes committed because of race, religion, color, ethnicity, (protected by nearly all hate crime statutes) ancestry, national origin, sexual orientation, gender, alienage[1171], age, disability[1172], creed[1173], political affiliation[1174], involvement in civil or human rights movements[1175] and service in the armed forces[1176].

1169 508 U.S. 476, 485 (1993).

1170 Jenness/Grattet, Making Hate a Crime, 2001, p. 73.

1171 Conn. Gen. Stat. § 46a-58 criminalizes deprivation of rights "on account of religion, national origin, alienage, color, race, sex, blindness or physical disability." It also covers damage to religious objects, symbols or houses of worship, and cross burning.

1172 N.J. Stat. § 52:9DD-9 covers efforts to "promote prejudice reduction and prevent and deter crimes based upon the victim's race, color, religion, national origin, sexual orientation, ethnicity, gender, or physical, mental or cognitive ability."

1173 Mont. Code Anno., § 45-5-222 describes enhanced sentences for offences committed because of victim's "race, creed, religion, color, national origin, or involvement in Civil Rights or human rights activities or that involved damage, destruction or attempted destruction of a building regularly used for religious worship."

1174 Iowa Code § 729A.1 prohibits violence or intimidation against persons or property based on "race, color, religion, ancestry, national origin, political affiliation, sex, sexual orientation, age, or disability."

1175 View footnote 1173: Mont. Code Anno., § 45-5-222.

Furthermore, "many states have statutes that prohibit institutional vandalism and the desecration or the defacement of religious objects, the interference with or disturbance of religious worship, cross burning, the wearing of hoods or masks, the formation of secret societies, and the distribution of publications and advertisements designed to harass select groups of individuals"; this last group of laws, which do not rely on already penalized activity, but, rather, prohibits a behavior which – without the connection to the offender's will to harass a select group because of their characteristics – would not be suspect to prosecution, can be confidently termed as "real" hate crime law, which together with the sum of all hate crime laws build a new offense category of its own; the diversity of approaches used by the states reflects their struggles to respond to hate-motivated violence while also attending to civil-liberties-related concerns and remaining sensitive to the sociopolitical particularities of each state[1177].

1176 "Service in the Armed Forces" as a legally protected group status is mentioned by Jenness/Grattet, Making Hate a Crime, 2001, p. 73.

1177 Jenness/Grattet, Making Hate a Crime, 2001, p. 75.

Chapter 4 Hate Crime in Germany

The internationally launched term "hate crime" is literally translated into German from time to time, but - at least since the reform of the police data collection system in Germany took place in 2001 – it is applied in the basics of its original American meaning, independent from English or translated German usage[1178]. Since that time hate crimes are understood as acts which originate from the dislike of a perpetrator towards the, usually unchangeable, identifying characteristics of a victim[1179]. Therefore, the social problem, freed from any involvement in idiosyncratic socio-political and legal conceptions, is acknowledged in both countries in a similar fundamental meaning. However, this applies only to the understanding which is followed in the detection mode, as it is revealed in the following. In order to reach the identical core of this social problem, the country-specific classifications of the phenomenon must be understood. Then one is able to extract the individual surroundings and recognize the comparability of the problem, coexisting in both countries, named hate crime.

Meanwhile in German literature it is widely acknowledged that criminal acts, which are motivated by hate against certain characteristics and based on the bias of an offender towards certain human features, require special criminal attention[1180], and moreover, constitute a separate offense category[1181]. This recognition is gained from knowledge established in U. S. studies that the harm resulting from hate crimes towards the individual victim and the entire society is larger than such caused by comparable non-hate-motivated criminal acts[1182]. The fact that "hate crime" is acknowledged as a distinct part of

1178 The usage of the term stems from the data collection system of the police and its subcategory hate crime in the field of politically motivated crime.

1179 Bannenberg et al., in Egg: Extremistische Kriminalität, p. 18.

1180 Several publications in Germany and the German catchment area deal with anchoring of hate crime legislation in Germany: Eisenberg, Kriminologie, pp. 896, 897; Schneider, in a variety of publications, view, for instance: Schneider, Hassverbrechen, in: Schneider, Kriminologie für das 21. Jahrhundert, 2001, pp. 70-90 – with further references; Seehafer, Strafrechtl. Reaktionenen auf rechtsextremistisch/ fremdenfeindlich motivierte Gewalttaten – Das amerik. „Hate Crime" Konzept u. seine Übertragbarkeit auf das deutsche Rechtssystem; Peucker, „The Hate Crime Concept in Germany and how to improve the Knowledge on the Extent of Hate Crimes" , 2006; Aydin, Die Strafrechtliche Bekämpfung von Hassdelikten in Deutschland und den Vereinigten Staaten v. Amerika, 2006; Krupna, „Das Konzept der Hate Crimes in Deutschland" ; Bleich/Hart, "Quantifying Hate: The Evolution of German Approaches to measuring Hate Crime", 2008; sparsely: Baldus, Hate Crime: Gesetze zur effektiven Bekämpfung von Rechtsextremismus u. Fremdenfeindlichkeit in Deutschland, 2003.

1181 That hate crime constitute a distinct crime category is acknowledged in German and European literature: H. J. Schneider, in a variety of publications; 1996, 2001a; 2001b; 2003a; 2003b; 2003c; 2004; 2006a; 2006b; 2009; with further references; Adler/Müller/Laufer, Criminology and the Criminal Justice System, 2007, sixth edition, pp. 272, 273; Bartol/Bartol, Criminal Behavior, 9th edition, 2011, pp. 18 – 20; Siegel, Criminology, eleventh edition, 2011, pp. 306 – 308; Conklin, Criminology, eleventh edition, 2011, pp. 58, 59; Barkan, Criminology, fivth edition, 2011, pp. 287 – 289; Vito/Maahs, Criminology, third edition, 2012, pp. 312 – 316; Arrigo, B. A., Criminal Behavior: A System Approach., fourth edition, 2006, pp. 125, 126; Riedel/Welsh, Criminal Violence, Patterns, Causes, and Prevention, 2008, pp. 138 – 157; Schwind, Kriminologie – eine praxisorientierte Einführung mit Beispielen, 19. Auflage, Heidelberg, 2009, p. 154.

1182 Herek/Berill, Hate Crimes, 1992; Craig, Journal of interpersonal Violence, 1999, 138 – 151, (14); Martin, Criminology, 1995, 303 – 326, (33); Levin/Mc Devitt, Hate Crimes, 1993; Levin/McDevitt, America's War, 2002; Martin/Chase, 2001. For further studies dealing with the concept of Hate Crime view: Lyons, Soc. Sci. J., 2008, p. 107-131; Grattet et al., ASR, 1998, p. 286 – 307; Martin, 1995; 1996; Levin, 1999; Mc Devitt et al., 2001; Herek et al., 2002; Boeckmann/Turoin – Petrosino, 2002; Green/McFalls/Laurence, Hate Crime: An Emergent Research Agenda, 2001; Perry, In the name of Hate, 2001; Mc Laughlin, Rocks

politically motivated crimes in data collection reveals that those who are responsible in the German criminal-political area acknowledge that hate crime are somehow different from "ordinary" crime; thus that the offenders are different not the victims. Also legal endeavors reflect that the German judiciary recognizes that these offenses constitute a serious threat to the peace and welfare of society, not just to that of the United States, but also to Germany's own domain[1183]. Questionable therefore is, why, if it is recognized that hate crime constitute a criminal idiosyncrasy[1184], the German hate crime concept insofar is limited to categorizing and recording committed hate crime incidences by a police data collection system[1185]. An explicit inclusion of the term hate crime in the overall judiciary area[1186], most notably in the Penal Code, like the American model exemplifies, has not (yet) happened. It is to pursue whether the non-implementation of hate crime legislation into the German legislation provides a legal loophole. After all, despite from the recognition that hate crime is a criminal matter[1187], there have not been any amendments to the Penal Code in order to address such.

To begin with, the attention shall be drawn to the social and criminal-political context, the political environment and the existence of the problem hate crime in Germany.

and Hard Places, 2002; Hall, Hate Crime, 2005; Levin, Understanding and Defining Hate Crime, 2009; Chakraborti, Hate Crime. Concepts, Policy, Future Directions, 2010. U. S. literature approving these studies: Lawrence, 1999; Perry, 2001, p. 19; Berk/Boyd/Hammer, 2003; disapproving: Jacobs/Potter, 1997; 1998; contrary Dillof – however, with successful processing of the favorable opinion, in: Michigan Law Rev., Vol. 98, No. 6, 2000, "The Importance of Being Biased Punishing Hate: Bias Crimes under American Law by Frederick M. Lawrence", pp. 1678-1703.

1183 Evidenced by the repeated amendment of a bill through a political subject in order to change the German Penal Code by implementing hate crime legislation. At last in April 2012: BT-Drs. 17/ 9345 (view at: http://dipbt.bundestag.de/dip21/btd/17/093/1709345.pdf).

1184 Bill of Baden-Wuerttemberg BR-Drs. 564/00 dated 21.09.2000; bill of Brandenburg BR-Drs. 577/00 dated 26.09.2000; bill of Mecklenburg-Vorpommern BR-Drs. 759/00 of 16.11.2000. The development in the 90ies, with its disastrous increase in the number of recorded right-wing extremist crimes led to a recognition of the priority of criminal prosecution of hate crimes by the German justice system. (Glet, Sozialkonstruktion und strafrechtliche Verfolgung von Hasskriminalität in Deutschland, 2011, p. 17; BT-Drs. 12/6853, p. 18; Bleich, Hate Crime Policy in Western Europe: Responding to Racist Violence in Britain, Germany, and France. In: American Behavioral Sc., Volume 51, No. 2, 2007, pp. 149 – 165). The recognition of a modified wrongfulness of hate crime compared to their un-, or otherwise motivated counterparts was recently repeated in the draft of the German Bundestag, 18 April, 2012, BT-Drs. 17/9345, p.1, where it is written: "These so-called hate crimes inhere an increase of wrongfulness compared to other violent crimes".

1185 The answering starts with the reason of the complexities to legally encompass the phenomenon of hate crime, which as stated by Bleich and Glet - already starts with the uncertainty in Germany to come up with a clear description of such "complex societal realities". (Glet, Sozialkonstruktion und strafrechtliche Verfolgung von Hasskriminalität in Deutschland, 2011, p. 56; Bleich/Hart, Quantifying Hate: The Evolution of German Approaches to Measuring 'Hate Crime', pp. 63-80).

1186 "Because [in Germany] the term hate crime is used primarily as a working definition of the police, it is not implicated in the general practice of law enforcement." (Glet, Sozialkonstruktion und strafrechtliche Verfolgung von Hasskriminalität in Deutschland, 2011, p. 50).

1187 Police, Consitutional Protection and Justice considere right-wing offenses as "an urgent problem since years". (Scholzen, Rechtsextremismus, Gefahr erkannt, Gefahr gebannt?, in: Kriminalistik. 2001, pp.314-316 (314).

A. Historical Background of Hate Crime in its Social and Criminal Political Context (Brief Overview)

While the Holocaust Era, also termed as "Nazi – Germany", is discussed in details in designated historic literary works, one might refer to such in order to refresh the xenophobic, anti-Semitic and overall misanthropic orientation of the German society, including their legal system at that time. Here the focus lies on the nowadays democratic system of Germany, and the problems of Bias- and hate crimes existing therein.

According to the classification of hate crime in the official police statistic, such – due to constituting a subcategory of politically motivated delinquency - are considered as a part of the so named politically motivated crimes[1188]. Accordingly, the hate crime concept in Germany, unlike that in the USA, is implemented into the superior topic of politically motivated crime, which as such focuses on left-wing-, and right-wing terrorism in equal measures. The part which refers to right-wing violence again has an own section for hate crimes, as it is shown in the following[1189].

The historical development[1190] of politically motivated crime in the Federal Republic of Germany brings to mind the major issues resulting from left-wing terrorism in the seventies and eighties, recalling the crimes of members of the Red Army Faction, the "June 2 Movement", and the "Revolutionary Cells", which as such required the full commitment of all departments involved in the criminal process, ranging from police force to judiciary to deal with the threat resulting from this form of political motivated violence, and endangering the entire democratically German system by neglecting its constitutional values and Basic Rights of each member of society. For a long time, it felt like left-wing violence was the main issue to focus on in the German society. But as early as in the 60s German jurisprudence already had to deal with hate crimes. Because of a series of anti-Semitic offenses[1191] and several judicial scandals[1192], and especially based on international efforts[1193], the German

---

1188 „Politisch motivierte Kriminalität" (PMK); BT-Drs.17/508 (http://dip21.bundestag.de/dip21/btd/17/050/1705082.pdf (accessed June 2012).). For more detailed information on this topic view: Gelt, Sozialkonstruktion und strafrechtliche Verfolgung von Hasskriminalität in Deutschland, 2011, pp. 79 et seqq.

1189 The hate crime concept in Germany - at this point - by name officially solely exists in the federal data collection system implemented since 2001 in police agencies to gather statistical data regarding committed offenses, therefore, the explanation of hate crime refers to the police classification of such crimes.

1190 Inspired by the summary provided on the website of BMI (Federal Ministry of the Interior) and the brief introduction on "political motivated crime". (View at: http://www.bmi.bund.de/DE/Themen/Sicherheit/Extremismus/PolKriminialitaet/PolKriminal_node.html (accessed June 2012)).

1191 "At the end of the fifties it could not be overlooked that there was an anti-Semitic protest potential in society." (Reichel: Vergangenheitsbewältigung in Deutschland., 2001, p.147.

1192 Reichel: Vergangenheitsbewältigung in Deutschland, 2001, pp.144 - 157.

1193 At international level the Declaration of the United Nations General Assembly according "The Elimination of All Forms of Racial Discrimination" was stated in 1963. In December 21st, 1965 followed the adoption of the "International Convention on the Elimination of All Forms of Racial Discrimination", which was signed by the FRG on January 1st, 1969 and therefore became effective. (BGBl. 1969 II, S. 961, 2211.). According to this agreement, Germany commits itself to Art. 4 (a) CERD, which stipulates "States Parties condemn all propaganda and all organizations which are based on ideas or theories of superiority of one race or group of persons of one color or ethnic origin, or which attempt to justify or promote racial hatred

legislature drafted legal amendments to the Penal Code as early as in 1959, which focused on the penalization of attacks against humanity and the legal peace. In January, 1959 the Federal Government for the first time introduced a draft bill for a new version of Section 130 Penal Code[1194]. Even back then one refused to name the true aim of this amendment by naming certain characteristics worthy of protection which do not refer to racial, religious or similar characteristics. This was reasoned - similar to such reasoning of the U.S. discussion[1195] - with the fact that the general legislation is sufficient to address the problem of xenophobic crimes and that by explicitly naming certain characteristics in a law, certain minorities would become denounced as legally privileged[1196], which led to the fact that in 1960 the amendment of the legal text of Section 130 Penal Code was not implemented by the words "incitement to racial hatred", but with the attack on the "human dignity of others"[1197].

It thereby becomes evident that the German legislator dealt with the problem of hate crimes already back then. At that time, despite the low explanatory power of the implemented amendment of Section 130 Penal Code towards the true problem, one agreed on the fact that this change of law was necessary for the prosecution of attacks on humanity and public peace[1198].

Yet, the high rise of dangerous crimes in the 90's[1199] committed by parties of the right-wing or, if committed by individuals were categorized as equivalent with right-wing criminality due to the police definition system at that time, proved that, after all, the internal problem with hate crimes has not been eliminated in the German society[1200]. Xenophobic, anti-Semitic and other prejudice-motivated violence, which in Germany was generally considered as crimes committed by the 'extreme right' and thus termed synonymously, proves the danger of hate crime to its fullest. Sad examples for the danger of

and discrimination in any form, and undertake to adopt immediate and positive measures designed to eradicate all incitement to, or acts of, such discrimination and [...] (a) shall declare an offence punishable by law all dissemination of ideas based on racial superiority or hatred, incitement to racial discrimination, as well as all acts of violence or incitement to such acts against any race or group of persons of another color or ethnic origin [...]". View hereto also: Seehafer, Strafrechtliche Reaktionen, 2003, pp. 15 et seqq.

1194 Partsch, EuGRZ 1994, 429; Reichel: Vergangenheitsbewältigung in Deutschland, 2001, pp.152 et seqq.

1195 In the U.S. discussion opponents of hate crime legislation state that hate crime laws promote inequalities as well.

1196 Reichel, Vergangenheitsbewältigung in Deutschland, 2001, p.153.

1197 Adolf Arndt, a member of the political party SPD, was of the opinion that not a law, but judges who apply the existing law, are missing in order to combat hate crime. He meant that discrimination against minorities violates legal equality and thereby attacks the human dignity of every human. The idea of not enacting a special law for the exclusive protection of minorities was remarkably supported by the Jewish community in particular. This led to the result that the violation of human dignity was made punishable, however not the incitement of hatred against racial groups. (Reichel, Vergangenheitsbewältigung in Deutschland, 2001, pp. 152, 153).

1198 Partsch, EuGRZ 1994, pp. 429 et seqq.

1199 Kubink, Rechtsextremistische und fremdenfeindliche Straftaten, ZRP 2002, p. 308; Partsch, EuGRZ 1994, p. 429.

1200 "In the second half of 2000 right wing extremism constituted the predominant theme." (Scholzen, Rechtsextremismus, Gefahr erkannt, Gefahr gebannt? in: Kriminalistik. 2001, pp. 314-316 (314); Cf. Bleich/Hart, Quantifying Hate: The Evolution of German Approaches to Measuring 'Hate Crime', pp. 63-80 (63).

this form of crime caused in Germany are attacks and pogroms[1201] of Hoyerswerda (in 1991), Rostock-Lichtenhagen (1992), Moelln (1992) and Solingen (1993)[1202]. Not ending since the German reunification the outbursts went on in 1994 with Magdeburger Himmelfahrtskrawalle, Hetzjagd in Guben (1999), Nagelbomben-Attentat in Cologne (2007), the violent clashes in Muegeln (2007)[1203] and the unimaginable murders of the Zwickauer Terror Cell, which were revealed to the public in 2011, and suspected to have been committed by a right-wing group that selectively killed people with immigrant backgrounds, in this case, nine suspected victims originate from the Bosporus (Turkey and Greece).

B. The Hate Crime "Concept" in Germany

The understanding of bias- and hate-motivated violence refers to its implementation in the official data collection system of the police named "Kriminalpolizeilicher Meldedienst-Politisch motivierte Kriminalität" (KPMD-PMK) and its manner of categorizing bias- and hate-motivated offenses. Because, strictly speaking, hate crime is embedded in the German criminal system solely due to data collection. At this point, hate crime does not constitute a separate offense category in penal law.

1. Early Beginnings of Data Collection

The old concept of collecting hate crime data was mainly based on the term 'extremism'. Accordingly, hate crime was categorized to the subject of (political orientated) "right-wing-extremist" violence. This led to difficulties in organizing offenses which were obviously not motivated by the aim to overthrow the government[1204], but by hateful biases directed against certain individuals.

Hate crime does not necessarily constitute an attack on the democratic order of Germany, in the sense that it receives through the categorization. There are cases in which the offender massively attacks certain groups of people, but does not want "another State". "Hate crimes are often an expression of fear of unwanted immigration or "hyperxenesis"."[1205] Such hate crimes therefore lack the intent of "overthrowing the governmental system"[1206]. The findings of an

1201 "Pogrom", that is the outrage against national, religious or racial groups. (Schneider, Politische Kriminalität: Hassverbrechen, Fremdenfeindlichkeit im internationalen Kontext, Kriminalistik 2001, pp. 21-28 (22, 23).

1202 Singer, Erfassung der politisch motivierten Kriminalität. In einem neuen Definitionssystem mit mehrdimensionalen Analysemöglichkeiten, Kriminalistik, 2004, p. 34, with reference to: Kaiser, Kriminologie, 1996, § 36, marginal no. 49.

1203 Spiegel Article, "Racism Alive and Well - After Attack on Indians, Germany Fears For its Reputation", 08/22/2007. (http://www.spiegel.de/international/germany/racism-alive-and-well-after-attack-on-indians-germany-fears-for-its-reputation-a-501352.html).

1204 Kubink,Rechtsextremistische und fremdenfeindliche Straftaten, ZRP 2002 No. 7, p. 308, 311.

1205 Singer, Erfassung der politsch motivierten Kriminalität. In einem neuen Definitionssystem mit mehrdimensionalen Analysemöglichkeiten, Kriminalistik, 2004, p. 34.

1206 Singer, Erfassung der politsch motivierten Kriminalität. In einem neuen Definitionssystem mit mehrdimensionalen Analysemöglichkeiten, Kriminalistik, 2004, p. 34.

empirical study[1207] shows that right-wing violence is less to be categorized as right-wing delinquency, but rather as bias crimes[1208]. The violence of hate crime is not motivated by an extreme right-wing ideology, but is based on different motives, which in general are attributed to misanthropic and dehumanizing attitudes, thus it is a misanthropic form of violence[1209].

But, despite that the orientation towards the extremism term leads to problematic acquisition deficits[1210], one has to acknowledge that due to the German National Socialist past and the committed genocide Germany pays great attention to right-wing-extremism[1211]. What can not be denied is that National Socialism inherits this special misanthropic element that is significant for bias-motivated attacks[1212]. It does not matter whether the contempt for mankind is directed against Jews in particular, or against foreigners, the homeless, the disabled, the old, the homosexuals, etc.

Until recently, the perception and problematization of xenophobic and misanthropic aggression and violence in Germany has mainly been influenced by the events of their history[1213]. Thus the cognition that hate- and bias-motivated conducts present a multifarious appearance did not yet exist in Germany in earlier times. Consequently, data collected according to official guidelines did not differ between the motivation of hate crime offender and such of political offenders.

Even though, in 1992 the separate collection of data on xenophobic crimes began and in 1993 a special category was implemented in the collection system to gather data of anti-Semitic violence[1214], it is not possible to provide a clear acquisition of hate crime data prior to the point of renewal of the police data collecting system in 2001[1215].

2. Data Collection in the Present Day

In order to resolve the failures in taking the bias- and hate related motives of the offender into account during the prosecution of certain violent offenses which do not evidence extremism[1216] the data collecting system was reformed

1207 Krüger, Zusammenhänge und Wechselwirkungen zwischen allgemeiner Gewaltbereitschaft und rechtsextremen Einstellungen. Eine kriminologische Studie zum Phänomen jugendlicher rechter Gewaltstraftäter, 2008.

1208 Krüger, Rechte Gewalt als Vorurteilskriminalität, in: Bewährungshilfe, 2011, pp. 161-168 (161).

1209 Krüger, Rechte Gewalt als Vorurteilskriminalität, in: Bewährungshilfe, 2011, pp. 161-168 (161).

1210 Singer, Erfassung der politsch motivierten Kriminalität. In einem neuen Definitionssystem mit mehrdimensionalen Analysemöglichkeiten, Kriminalistik 2004, pp. 32-37 (33).

1211 Reichel, Vergangenhheitsbewältigung in Deutschland, 2001; Glet, Sozialkonstruktion und strafrecht-liche Verfolgung von Hasskriminalität in Deutschland, 2011, pp. 17 et seqq.

1212 Glet, Sozialkonstruktion und strafrechtliche Verfolgung von Hasskriminalität in Deutschland, 2011, p. 18; Coester, Hate Crimes, p. 353.

1213 Glet, Sozialkonstruktion und strafrechtliche Verfolgung von Hasskriminalität in Deutschland, 2011, p. 18.

1214 Compare to: BT-Drs. 14/5773, pp. 2 et seqq.

1215 Glet, Sozialkonstruktion und strafrechtliche Verfolgung von Hasskriminalität in Deutschland, 2011, p. 79; Compare to: Holzberger, Bürgerrechte & Polizei/CILIP (68/1), 2001.

1216 Report on current and planned actions and activities of the Federal Government against right-wing extremism, xenophobia, anti-Semitism and violence acc. Section 21 of the decision of the German Bundestag of 30th March 2001 (BT-Drs. 14/5456), Singer, Erfassung der politsch motivierten Kriminalität. In einem neuen Definitionssystem mit mehrdimensionalen Analysemöglichkeiten, Kriminalistik 2004, pp.

by separating data for hate crime from other right-wing-extremist crime data in 2001 and named "Kriminalpolizeilicher Meldedienst - Politisch motivierte Kriminalität" (KPMD-PMK)[1217]. The specific term 'hate crime' has been implemented into the police definition system, according to which the detection and fight against crimes "directed against a person because of his political beliefs, national origin, ethnicity, race, color, religion, belief, national origin or because of his physical appearance, disability, sexual orientation or social status (so-called hate crimes), including such acts that are not committed directly against a person, but committed against an institution in the context mentioned above"[1218] is a main focus. Accordingly, the definition which has been in use until 2001 and which focused on "extremist motivated security offenses"[1219], was replaced by "politically motivated offenses", which then display several subcategories, precisely such referring to hate crime. Thus, "politically motivated offenses" include all extremist motivated security offenses, "even if in the individual case, a political motive cannot be found"[1220]. Contrary to the conceptuality of "politically motivated", hate crimes accordingly are recognized as crimes which are detached from any political orientation of the offender and so meet up to the universally valid understanding[1221], therefore the umbrella term "politically motivated offenses" has no influence on the conception of its subcategory hate crime.

This data collecting system of the police in the present day requires all police agencies to compile a national report of incidents triggered by motives revealing hate or bias towards foreigners or Jewish believers. The rewarding progress is that this system for the first time concentrated on the triggering

---

32-37; Glet, Sozialkonstruktion und strafrechtliche Verfolgung von Hasskriminalität in Deutschland, 2011, p. 79.

1217 The "Kriminalpolizeilicher Meldedienst - Politisch motivierte Kriminalität" (KPMD-PMK) refers to the following Sections of the Penal Code to gather politically motivated crimes:113, 114, 125, 125a, 177, 178, 211, 212, 213, 216, 222, 223, 224, 225, 226, 227, 231, 234, 239, 2391, 239b, 249, 250, 251, 252, 253, 306, 306a, 306b, 306c, 307, 308, 315, 315b, 316a, 316c Penal Code. (Glet, Sozialkonstruktion und strafrechtliche Verfolgung von Hasskriminalität in Deutschland, 2011, p. 81).

1218 Bundesministerium des Innern, Bekämpfung politisch motivierter Kriminalität, 2009-2012. (http://www.bmi.bund.de/DE/Themen/Sicherheit/Extremismus/PolKriminialitaet/PolKriminal_node.html - accessed Mai 2012).

1219 "Specifically, the following offenses are regarded as state security offenses [in here referred to also as extremist motivated security offenses]: Sections 80-83, 84-86a, 87-91, 94-100a, 102-104a, 105, 108e, 109, 109h, 129a, 129b, 234a and 241a Penal Code. Considered as relatively common examples, incitement (Section 130 Penal Code) and propaganda offenses (Sections 86, 86a Penal Code), but also the formation of a terrorist organization (Section 129a Penal Code) and treason (Sections 81, 82 Penal Code) are to be named." (http://www.bmi.bund.de/DE/Themen/Sicherheit/Extremismus/PolKriminialitaet/PolKriminal_node.html)

1220 Bundesministerium des Innern, Bekämpfung politisch motivierter Kriminalität, 2009-2012 (http://www.bmi.bund.de/DE/Themen/Sicherheit/Extremismus/PolKriminialitaet/PolKriminal_node.html - accessed Mai 2012). Non-political motives, e.g. such which in first sight result as if constituted of relationship conflicts, are concluded in the statistic as long as such express the image of constituting a social enemy or incite hatred. (Kubink, Rechtsextremistische und fremdenfeindliche Straftaten, ZRP 2002 No. 7, p. 311).

1221 Xenophobic offenses result from diversified and wide-spread causes, which are not necessarily linked to extremism. Compare to: Jens Peter Singer, Erfassung der politisch motivierten Kriminalität. In einem neuen Definitionssystem mit mehrdimensionalen Analysemöglichkeiten, Kriminalistik 2004, pp. 32-37, p. 34.

motivation of a criminal act[1222], regardless of the intent of the perpetrator or the external shape of an offense revealing an intent of the perpetrator to overthrow the governmental system or the fundamental democratic order of Germany[1223]. It therefore ensures data gathering that is more intensive and more complete according to the definition of hate crime used in the United States and therefore enables a higher expressiveness regarding the ratio of numbers if set in comparison to incidents registered in the U.S. [1224]. Thus, it seems capable of providing useful data regarding the magnitude of committed hate crimes in Germany. It collects data nationwide and does not concentrate on the intentions of the perpetrator to attack the democratic Constitution, but on the main fact of the triggering motivation of the offender to commit the act[1225], which must not necessarily originate from political motives, e.g. extremism, but from hate or bias towards certain characteristics[1226] and thereby shares the conceptual understanding of the term 'hate crime' used in the U.S. definition[1227]. Thus, in the present day, the data collecting has moved away from the orientation to the extremism term when classifying a crime as a hate crime[1228]. Due to the change of meaning, a transformation "from an ideological (class warfare) extremism tendency of the term to a "comprehensive" coverage of, in the broadest sense, all such politically tinged motives"[1229] has been achieved.

What triggered the review and the updating of old definitions and collecting methods, was a media report in September, 14th 2000 in two main German newspapers, which published a list presenting ninety-three fatal victims of hate

---

1222 The PMK in its present application places the motive of the offender - regardless of the feature of 'overthrowing the democratic system' - in the center for defining. (Glet, Sozialkonstruktion und strafrechtliche Verfolgung von Hasskriminalität in Deutschland, 2011, p. 81). Confusing therefore Keiser: "[...] Political crime is detected due to a special defining system for the Police Crime Statistic. Thereby the mental attitude of the offender is, in contrary to Section 46 Paragraph 2 of the Criminal Cod, irrelevant." (Statement of lawyer Keiser in: "Public Hearing of the Legal Committee of the German Bundestag on 06/13/2012 to so-called Hate Crime", p. 3) – this applies not to the subcategory "hate crime".

1223 Xenophobic offenses result from diversified and wide-spread causes, which are not necessarily linked to extremism. Compare to: Singer, Erfassung der politisch motivierten Kriminalität. In einem neuen Definitionssystem mit mehrdimensionalen Analysemöglichkeiten, Kriminalistik 2004, pp. 32-37, p. 34.

1224 The acquisition of data according racist motivated offenses according to the new definition started reactive from January 1, 2001. The main improvement is the launch of the category "politically motivated right-wing offenses" with its two subcategories xenophobic and anti-Semitic crimes. Before ideologically motivated crimes where only recorded by the police if "the perpetrator showed intentions of disturbing fundamental democratic principles of the state". (Glet, Sozialkonstruktion und strafrechtliche Verfolgung von Hasskriminalität in Deutschland, 2011, p. 79; Wiecej; Opferperspektive e.V., Studie: Monitoring Hate Crimes and victim assistance in Poland and Germany, 2009, p.7; (German or English abridgement can be viewed at: http://www.stiftung-evz.de/publikationen/studien/).

1225 Glet, Sozialkonstruktion und strafrechtliche Verfolgung von Hasskriminalität in Deutschland, 2011, p.79 et seqq.

1226 This way of registering data matches the original conceptual understanding of the term "hate crime" as it occurred and is used nowadays in the United States, which encompasses offenses motivated by hate – and bias of the perpetrator against certain characteristics of the attacked victim, not relevant is the political view or aim of the offender.

1227 It is referred to "Politically Motivated Offenses" "[i]f the circumstances of the offense or the attitude of the offender indicate that the offense is directed against a person because of his political opinion, nationality, ethnicity, race, color, religion, ideology, origin, sexual orientation, disability or physical appearance, or his social status." (Printed Matter of the German Parliament No. 14/5456 dated 03/30/01. p. 64).

1228 Singer, Erfassung der politsch motivierten Kriminalität. In einem neuen Definitionssystem mit mehrdimensionalen Analysemöglichkeiten, Kriminalistik 2004, pp. 32-37 (33).

1229 Kubink, Rechtsextremistische und fremdenfeindliche Straftaten, ZRP 2002 No. 7, p. 311.

crimes since the German reunification. Official statistics first presented significantly lower numbers. But after these news reports were published, the official count was increased from 25 fatal victims of hate crimes previously to 36 victims murdered by bias-related offenses, or "fatal victims of right-wing violence" as they were called[1230]. It goes without saying that the validity and correctness of official data collection of the police was doubted officially[1231], as it has already been doubted by the commission of the safety report itself[1232]. Due to the sustained criticism of the official counting of racist-motivated offenses and the discrepancies between the statistics of different collection systems[1233], the implementation of the currently effective data collection system by the police was decided[1234] in May 10, 2001.

3. Comparison

In comparison with the U.S. understanding of the term hate crime, one recognizes that the German police definition stresses certain biases or hate motives. The clear outline of politically motivated violence, xenophobia and Jewish related hostility refers to specific social experiences of Germany and its society. In Germany, xenophobia is referred to as the core of hate crimes[1235] and by considering the fact that such violent acts are committed against all foreigners as such, and are often committed by followers of the right-wing-extremism, the conceptual genesis, with its emphasis on the named, becomes

---

1230 Jansen, "Rechte Gewalt. Seit der Einheit 93 Tote", in: Der Tagesspiegel, 13.09.2000 and Elsässer, in: "Frankfurter Rundschau" reported for the period 1990 to July 2000, a number of 93 fatal victims of right violence, while from the public side of the federal government in the same period only 25 fatal victims were reported of being victimized by right-wing violence. With regard to this the former periodic safety report reads: "Due to the significant discrepancy between the figures calculated by the journalist and those data managed by the KPMD-S a detailed review of the listed cases has been caused. The issues were treated and evaluated by the competent police authorities of the states on the basis of the test-related findings. As a result, it should be noted that the number of fatal victims of right-wing violence has increased by 25 people to a total of 36 deaths victims. In the remaining 57 cases a right-wing motivation of the perpetrator could not be detected." (Periodical Report, July 2001, p.273; (http://www.bmi.bund.de/SharedDocs/Downloads/DE/Veroeffentlichungen/erster_periodischer_sicherheitsbericht_langfassung_de.pdf?__blob=publicationFile).

1231 Falk, Anmerkungen zum polizeilichen Lagebild Rechtsextremismus, Antisemitismus und Fremdenfeindlichkeit. BKA, Herbsttagung. Wiesbaden. 2000, pp. 51-73.

1232 Periodical Report, July 2001, p.272; (http://www.bmi.bund.de/SharedDocs/Downloads/DE/Veroeffentlichungen/erster_periodischer_sicherheitsbericht_langfassung_de.pdf?__blob=publicationFile).

1233 Wiecej; Opferperspektive e.V., Studie: Monitoring Hate Crimes and victim assistance in Poland and Germany, 2009, p.7; (German and English abridgement can be viewed at: http://www.stiftung-evz.de/publikationen/studien/).

1234 BMI/BMJ, 1. PSB, pp. 262 et seqq.; 2. PSB, p. 134 et seqq.

1235 It must be noted that this "new" understanding of the term hate crime relies on the reformed understanding of bias-motivated offenses, which refers to the American (today international valid) conceptual approach. In earlier times, from 1992 until 2001, the term which was used in the data collection system of the police referred to xenophobic offenses which are "committed against persons, to whom the perpetrator (based on his intolerant attitude) due to their nationality, race, color, religion, belief, national origin or due to their appearance denies the right to stay or residence in his home environment or in Germany" (Police against xenophobic violence. Information supplied by the interior ministry of North Rhine-Westphalia, 2. Ed, 1995, p.1/Polizei gegen fremdenfeindliche Gewalt. Informationsbroschüre des Landesinnenministeriums NRW, 2. Auflage, 1995, p. 1.) Therefore, in the former German consideration "Xenophobia [was] understood as a negation of the right of local residency of foreign victims." Thus, xenophobic violence was considered to aim at ending the residency of an individual. (Literal translation of: Kubink, Rechtsextremistische und fremdenfeindliche Straftaten, ZRP 2002 No. 7, pp. 308, 309).

clear[1236], after all, according to the German experiences in the "Nazi Era", xenophobia was connected to political concerns.

With regard to the understanding of the term, it must be noted that xenophobic or bias-related aggression has not been identical to what in the United Sates is called hate crime; nor was the official data kept to monitor hate crimes comparable to U.S. definitions before 2001[1237]. This has changed. Despite German societal specifics and the German emphasis on terms like "right-wing-extremism" and "xenophobia" it must be noted that in the present day a deeper analysis reveals that a purely xenophobic – and thus erroneous – restrictive term association or an understanding of hate crime according to its classification as "politically motivated offenses" is not followed in Germany. Correspondingly, the understanding of the term hate- and bias-motivated crimes applied in the hate crime concept of the United States and in the German data acquisition system is understood as the combination of phenomena such as xenophobia, Anti-Semitism, anti-foreigner bias, etc. - with the recognition of societal specifics, such as right-wing radicalism in Germany and specific acts such as cross burnings and mask wearing in the United States - which are put into a larger context in order to come up with the basic mechanism of such occurrences[1238].

Still, in the present day, it has been said that hate crime investigation focuses on the right-wing extremist background of an offense too much, which leads to the problem that hateful and biased motivated criminal behavior committed by an individual offender is categorized as "hate crime" too rarely[1239]. Surely, the high record of hate crimes committed by right-wing-extremists is related to the externality of these acts, thus to their ostensible capability of recognition, but connected to this, must be the result of an high estimated number of unreported non-political affiliated hate crimes committed by individuals[1240]. In contrary though, it must be emphasized that combating right-wing extremism is an order of special priority in the criminal-political discourse of Germany in the light of German history[1241]. German law enforcement practices have been

1236 Also victimized in Germany are homeless persons, social welfare recipients, punks and people affiliated to the political left-wing and homosexuals. (Periodical Report, July 2001, p.274; (http://www.bmi.bund.de/SharedDocs/Downloads/DE/Veroeffentlichungen/erster_periodischer_sicherheits bericht_langfassung_de.pdf?__blob=publicationFile).

1237 Watts, Aggressive Youth Cultures and Hate Crime Skinheads and Xenophobic Youth in Germany, American Behavioral Scientist December 2001 vol. 45 no. 4, pp. 600-615 (600).

1238 Schneider, Internationales Handbuch der Kriminologie, Bd. II, p. 298.

1239 Glet, Sozialkonstruktion und strafrechtliche Verfolgung von Hasskriminalität in Deutschland, 2011, pp. 90, 91; It is claimed that in Germany solely obvious xenophobic violence is categorized as such, which usually is the case if the offense hints towards right-wing extremism due to used official signs and pictures. Therefore, hate- and bias-motivated crimes committed without a connection to right-wing extremism are not recognized as bias crimes. (Coester, Hate Crimes, p. 406.); Seehafer, Strafrechtliche Reaktionen, 2003, p. 2003, p. 37, fn. 292.

1240 Human Rights Watch interviewed victims-support-organizations in Berlin, Lower Saxony, North Rhine-Westphalia, Saxony, Saxony-Anhalt and Thuringia, during which it was revealed that victims sometimes hesitate to report hate crime to the police. (Die Reaktion des Staates auf „Hasskriminalität“ in Deutschland Human Rights Watch-Hintergrundpapier, Dezember 2011, pp. 13-15; with further references to the way of how the findings were gathered in footnotes 21 et seqq.).

1241 Glet, Sozialkonstruktion und strafrechtliche Verfolgung von Hasskriminalität in Deutschland, 2011, p. 18; with reference to: Kohlstruck et al.; BFG 2007 (30/8), 11.

occupied with battling against right-wing extremism since the beginning, from the said scandals in the 60s to today's failed detection of a nationally active right-wing-operated terrorist cell[1242]. With that it becomes evident that the focus must especially lie on violent crimes committed by these kinds of (political) perpetrators. Nevertheless, the political motivation of an offender must never be crucial to whether a committed offense is to be categorized and prosecuted as a hate crime or not.

So, as long as the German way of classifying hate crime as a subcategory of politically motivated crimes does not lead to a neglect of hate crimes which do not reveal an obvious "political" context[1243], this way of categorization is acceptable. If the police guidelines are followed properly, which impose that police officers monitor "offenses, which according to the circumstances of the offense and/or the motivation of the offender provides evidence that the act is directed against a person because of her/his political view, national origin, ethnic, race, skin color, religion, nativity, outward appearance, disability, sexual orientation, societal status and the act is causal to such or committed in connection to such against an institution/subject or an object"[1244]. The understanding of the term 'hate crime' matches the understanding of hate crime adopted in the American discussion, which is that "hate crimes are acts of violence committed against a person or against an object solely or primarily because of race, religion, ethnicity, gender, political orientation, sexual orientation, age, disability of that person or the owner of an object."[1245]

4. Operation of the Data Acquisition System

According to the German data collection the police must register crimes which are considered to constitute a hate crime by categorizing such under the subsection termed "politically motivated offenses". Hence, the individual estimation of what constitutes a crime to be worthy to be registered as hate crime plays a huge role[1246]. A motivation which is kept to oneself will not constitute an offense and therefore cannot be criminally relevant[1247]. In order for the internally formed motivation to constitute a hate crime in police data, it must project outward, i.e., it must be reflected in the objective facts or in the factual circumstances. This occurs from the necessity that it must be possible to detect the relevant bias, and, furthermore, prove the bias motive whenever

1242 "Nationalsozialistischer Untergrund" (abbr. "NSU") is a German right-wing terrorist group that become publicly known in November 2011 and until then acted in the underground undetected by the German authorities for years.

1243 Conclusion could be drawn if referring to Glet, who revealed that during the "capturing of violent xenophobic crimes, the focus is drawn towards (the) phenomenon which reveals right-wing-extremist characteristics and parallels to German National Socialism." (Glet, Sozialkonstruktion und strafrechtliche Verfolgung von Hasskriminalität in Deutschland, 2011, p. 19).

1244 BKA, Information to the police definition system of politically motivated crime, 2010, p. 5.

1245 Schneider, Politische Kriminalität: Hassverbrechen, Fremdenfeindlichkeit im internationalen Kontext, Kriminalistik 2001, pp. 21-28 (22); with further references to: Reid, Crime and Criminology, ninth Edition;, Burr Ridge/Il, Dubuque/IA, Madison/WI u. A. 2000, 36/37, pp. 188-191; Conklin: Criminology, eleventh Edition, p. 135/136; Reiss/Roth: Understanding and Preventing Violence, Band 1, 1993m, p. 77/78.

1246 BMI/BMJ, p.1; PSB, p. 266; Glet, Sozialkonstruktion und strafrechtliche Verfolgung von Hasskriminalität in Deutschland, 2011, p. 83.

1247 For difficulties with the investigation of the motives of an offender, view: Morsch, The Journal of Criminal Law and Criminology 82 (1991) p. 659.

penal policies shall refer to such. So it is referred to certain objective facts in order to provide guidelines for the police and all instances dealing with evaluating whether a crime constitutes a hate crime or not. In order to enable a uniform crime reporting system, thus for the police to correctly classify an offense as a hate crime and uniformly record such offenses, the Federal Office for Constitutional Protection in Germany provided detailed information for the police authorities of the counties how to classify a hate crime in the correct and especially even manner[1248]. Such are similar to instructions provided by the American Federal Hate Crime Guidelines in its section "Objective Evidence that the Crime was motivated by Bias", which aim at a careful encompassment of the overall circumstances of the crime, especially uncovering the course of events[1249].

If one bears in mind that the recognition of the motivation of the offender and the first classification of an offense as hate crime is done by the police at a very early stage of the prosecution process, one realizes what a huge role the police plays in the overall acquisition management. Despite on the police level, there is no other explicit regulatory hate crime management in the entire prosecution process; not only the "statistical degree" of the hate crime problem depends on the police, but additionally the actual criminal detection and legal

---

1248 BMI, Bundesverfassunsschutzbericht 2002, p. 31; Glet, Sozialkonstruktion und strafrechtliche Verfolgung von Hasskriminalität in Deutschland, 2011, p. 87: with the note that the content of these instructions are only intended for the internal use of the police.

1249 "1. The offender and the victim were of different race, religion, disability, sexual orientation, and/or ethnicity/national origin. For example, the victim was black and the offender was white.
2. Bias-related oral comments, written statements, or gestures were made by the offender which indicates his/her bias. For example, the offender shouted a racial epithet at the victim.
3. Bias-related drawings, markings, symbols, or graffiti were left at the crime scene. For example, a swastika was painted on the door of a synagogue.
4. Certain objects, items, or things which indicate bias were used. For example, the offenders wore white sheets with hoods covering their faces or a burning cross was left in front of the victim's residence.
5. The victim is a member of a racial, religious, disability, sexual-orientation, or ethnic/national origin group which is overwhelmingly outnumbered by other residents in the neighborhood where the victim lives and the incident took place. This factor loses significance with the passage of time; i.e., it is most significant when the victim first moved into the neighborhood and becomes less and less significant as time passes without incident.
6. The victim was visiting a neighborhood where previous hate crimes were committed against other members of his/her racial, religious, disability, sexual-orientation, or ethnic/national origin group and where tensions remained high against his/her group.
7. Several incidents occurred in the same locality, at or about the same time, and the victims were all of the same race, religion, disability, sexual orientation, or ethnicity/national origin.
8. A substantial portion of the community where the crime occurred perceived that the incident was motivated by bias.
9. The victim was engaged in activities promoting his/her race, religion, disability, sexual orientation, or ethnicity/national origin. For example, the victim was a member of the NAACP or participated in gay rights demonstrations.
10. The incident coincided with a holiday or a date of particular significance relating to a race, religion, disability, sexual orientation, or ethnicity/national origin, e.g., Martin Luther King Day, Rosh Hashanah.
11. The offender was previously involved in a similar hate crime or is a hate group member.
12. There were indications that a hate group was involved. For example, a hate group claimed responsibility for the crime or was active in the neighborhood.
13. A historically established animosity existed between the victim's and the offender's groups.
14. The victim, although not a member of the targeted racial, religious, disability, sexual-orientation, or ethnic/national origin group, was a member of an advocacy group supporting the precepts of the victim group." (U.S. Department of Justice, Federal Bureau of Investigation, Criminal Justice Information Services Division, Hate Crime Data Collection Guidelines, Revised October 1999, p. 4-6).

prosecution is based on the police categorization above-average[1250]. Because if the police categorize a crime as a hate crime due to their stipulations, it is reasonable that a prosecutor recognizes it as such[1251], if a prosecutor recognizes a crime as hate crime, a judge may give the subject attention[1252].

A proper classification at the start significantly indicates the further direction of whether a crime is correctly recognized as a hate crime[1253]. This refers to whether hate crimes are established as a crime category in explicit statutory requirements in a Code, or if, like at present, the judiciary considers the motive in the part of sentencing by drawing on such facts found by the police[1254]. However, at the current time, solely the police regulations of investigating and categorizing hate crimes provide a compulsory, or as to say "explicit" necessity to pay attention to the bias motive that surrounds the crime. Therefore, a "high sensibility" of police officers[1255] is essential and reveals that training laws for police officers, as enacted in the United States, are exemplary in the entire hate crime concept of a country[1256]. Training programs for police officers enhance the assurance of correct detection and uniform classification[1257]. The

1250 One statistic showed that offenses which due to the judgment were based on a hate crime motive and for which the motive was considered during trial where solely such offenses which were committed by an offender who, according to the police registering, was categorized to the area of PKM-right/extremism. (Glet, Sozialkonstruktion und strafrechtliche Verfolgung von Hasskriminalität in Deutschland, 2011, p. 228).

1251 The judges seem to follow the prosecutor's previous evaluation of the motive. It has been revealed that in such proceedings in which bias motives played a role and have been expressly named during the trial it was in such cases in which a xenophobic background has already been assumed from the beginning. (Glet, Sozialkonstruktion und strafrechtliche Verfolgung von Hasskriminalität in Deutschland, 2011, p. 228).

1252 The fact that the judges always - but apparently only - if the prosecutor had already made observations to the prejudice related motive take such into account as an aggravating factor during penal assesment deserves special attention. (Statement of Keiser, in: "Public Hearing of the Legal Committee of the German Bundestag on 06/13/2012 to so-called Hate Crime", p. 5, with reference to Glet, Sozialkonstruktion und strafrechtliche Verfolgung von Hasskriminalität in Deutschland, 2011, p. 222). More information according to the point of judicial dealings with hate crime motives during trial view Chapter Four, D., Judicial Dealing with Hate Crime.

1253 The judges seem to follow the previous estimates of the prosecutor regarding the motive. In proceedings in which bias motives play a role and called by its right name the trial had already been based on a xenophobic background. (Glet, Sozialkonstruktion und strafrechtliche Verfolgung von Hasskriminalität in Deutschland, 2011, p. 228).

1254 View Chapter Four, D., Judicial Dealing with Hate Crime.

1255 Glet, Sozialkonstruktion und strafrechtliche Verfolgung von Hasskriminalität in Deutschland, 2011, p. 90; with further reference to: Ziercke, in: Egg, Extremistische Kriminalität: Kriminologie und Prävention, 2006, pp. 61-106 (66).

1256 The police, by concentration on risk factors and adequate reaction to Hate offenses can help control hate crimes. (Schneider, Kriminologie, Bd. 2, p. 328; Sherman/Eck, Policing for Crime Prevention, in: Sherman/Farrington//Welsh/Mac Kenzie (eds.): Evidence-Based Crime Prevention., 2002, pp. 295-329).

1257 There are known examples of incidents where the police indeed stopped racial attacks, though, however, failed to initiate the necessary steps for investigation. Before the officers record a prejudice-motivated incident, and, in conformity with the lawful division of powers, let the prosecutor decide whether the relevance of the incident due to the public interest requires an indictment, the police officers on their own, rather mentally categorize hate offenses as "bar room wrangling", and thereby prevent any possibility for an act to become recognized as a hate crime. (Article published in Saarkurier Online „Polizeiausbildung ist Schlüssel zur Eindämmung von Hasskriminalität„ , 12 Dezember, 2011 (View at: http://www.saarkurier-online.de/?p=58150); Interview of Hugh Williamson (Head of Department for Europe and Central Asia at Human Rights Watch), printed in: taz magazine, on 10.12.2011, titled: „Menschenrechtsexperte zur Polizeiausbildung" - „Es fehlt der Fokus auf Hass als Motiv" (view at: http://www.taz.de/!83472/). With such police handlings the hate crime offender never receives a proper penalization, the victim never receives justice and to the society it is expressed that hate crimes are not worthy a judicial involvement. (For deficits of the police during investigating hate crimes in general view the study of Human Rights Watch of December 2011, Hintergrundpapier „Die Reaktionen des Staates auf „Hasskriminalität" in Deutschland" ,

prevention and prosecution of crime by the police is vested in the local counties, which leads to local distinctions in categorizing crimes as hate crimes according to the nationally uniform definition[1258]. This again reveals the difficulties of the police to correctly and uniformly record hate crimes in Germany.[1259] "One does not have to refer to the acts of the Nazi Underground[1260] to notice that there are deficits in investigations"[1261]. If the police denies a hate crime, although the suspect was previously noticed by his xenophobic attitudes and the victim fits the expressed image of an enemy[1262], deficiencies in investigative actions are indicated and show that an increased awareness of a possible right-wing extremist - namely misanthropic - background of the action is necessary[1263]. In addition to the indisposition of hate crime victims, leading them not to file a report, comes the incorrect recording at the crime scene, which is possible because a hate crime is not recognized as a legal criminal problem. After all, the Penal Code does not expressly address hate crime, so a hate crime may as well be classified as a minor dispute among equals, instead of a serious crime among unequals. If the regulations accruing from the police definition of hate crime according to the acquisition system are neglected and a hate crime is committed but not handled as such, the perpetrator misses the complete message of criminal law, which is that his offense is not tolerated since every person is equally valuable[1264].

---

at: http://www.hrw.org/de/news/2011/12/09/die-reaktion-des-staates-auf-hasskriminalit-t-deutschland, pp. 11-22; similar hereto view reports of hate crimes victims explaining their experiences with the police after a hate crime incident, at: www.opferperspektive.de; www.mobile-opferberatung.de).

1258 Glet, Sozialkonstruktion und strafrechtliche Verfolgung von Hasskriminalität in Deutschland, 2011, p. 90, 91.

1259 According to studies in Germany, it can be assumed that the Police in many cases do not take hate crimes as seriously as they are, or serious at all. "One must not refer to the acts of the Nazis Underground, to notice that there are deficits in investigations." (Stolle, in: "Public Hearing of the Legal Committee of the German Bundestag on 06/13/2012 to so-called Hate Crime"; Stoltenberg, Verpflichtung der Ermittlung und Berücksichtigung rassistischer Motive bei der Strafzumessung, ZRP 2012, 119). For betterment, there are training programs offered for police officers in the United States, for "developing and maintaining respect and appreciation for the growing diversity in society". Therefore, accordingly, the goal of such a course is not only to recognize hate crimes and to investigate them correctly, but also to respond to them in appropriate manners. (View: Schneider, Kriminologie, Bd. 2, p. 328).

1260 The "Nazi Underground" refers to Nationalsozialistischer Untergrund" (abbr. "NSU") also known as "Zwickauer Terrorzelle", is a German right-wing terrorist group that became publicly known in November 2011 and until then acted in the underground undetected by the German authorities for years.

1261 Rechtsausschuss – Stellungnahme Stolle, 08.06.2012, zum Entwurf eines Gesetzes zur Änderung des Strafgesetzbuches, BT-Drs. 17/8131; 17/9345; 17/8796; Stoltenberg, Verpflichtung der Ermittlung und Berücksichtigung rassistischer Motive bei der Strafzumessung, ZRP 2012, 119.

1262 Die Reaktion des Staates auf „Hasskriminalität“ in Deutschland Human Rights Watch-Hintergrundpapier, Dezember 2011, pp. 18, 19; with further references to the way of how the knowledge been gathered view footnotes 35-38.

1263 Jansen/Kleffner, Der Tagesspiegel-online, October 05, 2001.

1264 Whether it is referred to explicit statutory law or, like at present, the judiciary must investigate a hate crime on its own, a legal prosecution process is based on the facts which have been presented by the police. In any case, the classification of offenses as hate crimes must take place uniformly. A reform in the German Penal Code which explicitly refers to hate crimes would not lead to legitimate justice in the field of prosecuting hate crimes without proper police training ensuring correct recording. This applies especially in the case of hate crime because an investigation of hate crimes even more requires efforts in securing relevant evidence. (FAZ Article "Deutschland: Polizeiausbildung verbessern, um Hasskriminalität zu bekämpfen. Brief an die Bundesjustizministerin, den Bundesinnenminister sowie die Justiz- und Innenminister der Länder", 12 April, 2012 (view at: http://www.hrw.org/de/news/2012/04/12/deutschland-polizeiausbildung-verbessern-um-hasskrinimalit-t-zu-bek-mpfen).

5. Hate Crime Situation in Case Numbers[1265]

According to the data collection system of the police for categorizing crimes as hate crimes, all investigated offenses motivated by xenophobia, disability, anti-Semitism, racism, societal status, disability, religion and sexual orientation are gathered, and so are meant to provide an overview of the actual situation on hate crimes in Germany since 2001. After a high rise of hate crimes in Germany in the 90s[1266], the official number of hate crime incidents stated for the year of 2001 is 5,456[1267]. In 2002 and 2003 the numbers decreased to 5,257 in 2002 and 4,325 in 2003. Violent hate crimes on the other hand rose to 774 in 2002 from 714 in 2001. While the number of biased crimes was stable between 2004 and 2006, a new rise occurred in 2006 to 5,367 offenses. Violent crimes also counted up to 644 cases. In 2008, 4,756 cases were registered, 561 were violent crimes, with two fatal victims. Again in 2009 a fatal victim was registered among 418 violent crimes with a total of 3.981 hate crime offenses. The number reported by the police for 2008 was a total of 4,759 offenses, including 561 violent offenses.

If switching to other recognized official statistics concerning the problem such present 467 violent xenophobic acts for the year 2010[1268]. This high number of hate crimes will not decrease in the year 2011, which is shown by the response of the federal government to an enquiry by the Left Party[1269]. "For the month of January 2011 [...][1270] a total of 820 crimes were reported, which are assigned to the phenomenon of "Politically motivated criminality - right". Among them were 40 violent crimes and 563 propaganda offenses. 176 offenses, including 45 propaganda offenses and 18 violent crimes were assigned to the subject of "hate crime". In 110 crimes, including 25 propaganda offenses and 17 acts of violence, a xenophobic background could be detected[1271]. The comparison of the individual states reveals high differences in the amount of recorded incidents: whereas in Saarland[1272] not a

1265 Numbers provided are in accordance with those reported by the Federal Criminal Police Office (BKA). The BKA is the supreme authority of the Federal Police and reports to the Federal Ministry of the Interior. For more profound information about the situation in Germany regarding hate crimes (extremist crimes) view: Ziercke, in: Egg, Rudolf (ed.). Extremistische Kriminalität: Kriminologie und Prävention, in: KrimZ, 2006, pp. 61 et seqq.; Glet, Sozialkonstruktion und strafrechtliche Verfolgung von Hasskriminalität in Deutschland, 2011; First and foremost the study of Bannenberg et al. in: BMJ/DFK, Hasskriminalität - Vourteilskriminalität, 2003, which directs the attention to the issue of "hate- and bias-motivated criminality in Germany" and attempts to encompass the problem of hate crime in the actual situation in Germany (pp. 18 et seqq.).

1266 Registered hate crime acts raised above 10.000 per year; view hereto the Constitutional Protection Reports of the years 1990 until 1999 on: www.verfassungschutz.de; Seehafer, Strafrechtliche Reaktionen, 2003, p. 10; Glet, Sozialkonstruktion und strafrechtliche Verfolgung von Hasskriminalität in Deutschland, 2011, p. 104.

1267 The numbers of the Federal Criminal Police Office have also been cited in: Glet, Sozialkonstruktion und strafrechtliche Verfolgung von Hasskriminalität in Deutschland, 2011, p. 104; Seehafer, Strafrechtliche Reaktionen, 2003, p.10.

1268 The Constitutional Protection Report of the Federal Ministry of the Interior for the year 2010 recorded 762 acts of violent hate crimes nationwide. The numbers stated in this report are based on the prior outlined numbers of the BKA, however they do not provide a specific outline of hate crime.

1269 The numbers are preliminary numbers and based on numbers provided in BT-Drs. 17/4839 and BT-Drs.17/5082.

1270 It is referred to the time period of January 1, 2011 until 21 February 2011.

1271 BT-Drs.17/5082 (http://dip21.bundestag.de/dip21/btd/17/050/1705082.pdf).

1272 Saarland is one of the smallest states in terms of area and population.

single hate crime was counted, in North Rhine Westphalia 23 hate crimes and 2 violent hate crimes have been recorded[1273].

6. Significance of these Numbers

Unfortunately it is not possible to draw a conclusion from these figures on the actual existence or the extent of a hate crime problem in Germany. The provided data cannot prove the precise extent of the social problem of hate crimes in Germany. If at all, it is valid material to evaluate certain trends, but it cannot examine the current threat caused by such or encompass their effects on the German society. This is due not only to statistical deficits.

Whereas the main focus for classifying crimes in the data collection system which is valid since 2001 is put on the inner motivation of the offender, the detecting officer himself still might be orientated towards external evidence only, which could lead to the fact that possibly either an existing motive is not detected, or as it may happen when investigating propaganda offenses, from the outer appearance it is drawn to the political nature of an offense, without the motive of the perpetrator being questioned at all[1274].

In addition to such deficits of acquisition, the discussed issue of the construction of crime phenomena is particularly pointed to police scopes. The discretionary power of the policemen at the crime scene to categorize a crime as a hate crime and further falsifications of the reported numbers could control the extent of a problem in one or another direction, and so represent - in the worst case - a theoretical reality that is far from the actual situation.

But, the published caseloads could provide a first indication of the principal incidence of hate crimes and thereby hint at the existence of similar problem areas. However, one cannot derive any evidence from these for the existence of an unbearable, only by means of criminal law to combat, social problem.

What in so far has been shown is that these numbers are a cause for concern. An initial examination of the above statistics suggests that the German society, as well as the U.S. society, is more or less threatened by hate crimes. However, a clear decision as to whether or not the provided statistical data prove the existence of a socially harming problem requiring legal action is not necessary. The empirical uncertainty does not affect the normative level. The legislator's prerogative for assessment allows him to recognize hate crime as an intolerable social problem or to assess it as insignificant for social life. The legislative scope requires no clear empirical evidence, information concerning the matter must be sufficient.

1273 BT-Drs.17/5082 (http://dip21.bundestag.de/dip21/btd/17/050/1705082.pdf).

1274 Keiser differently: "The mental attitude of the offender [...] does not matter at all [for classifying an offense as a Hate Crime]." In: statement of lawyer Keiser in: "Public Hearing of the Legal Committee of the German Bundestag on 06/13/2012 to so-called Hate Crime", p. 3.

7. Result: German Hate Crime "Concept"

Comparable to special laws which are adopted in the U.S. to combat Ku Klux Klan activity[1275] and which are also termed "hate crime laws", specific features addressing right-wing extremism - in politics also called, "the struggle against the Right"[1276], "resistance of the decent"[1277] - are included in the German discussion about how to deal with hate-motivated violence. Since hate crimes are subjects of statistical detection, a basis for examining trends and developments in hate-motivated violence is provided by the police data recording system. After all, the U.S. hate crime concept started similarly. Considering the U.S. way of collecting and analyzing data as the first step of the nowadays applied "concept", Germany reveals that a component of legal attack is set up.

A comparison of the German implementation of hate crime in their all over political, social and legal area with such of American handling at the present time highlights that the German hate crime "concept" consists of federal data collecting by police agencies only; further "tools", with regard to the American standards, like legal measures, uniform and reliable data collecting which in particular focus on hate crime only, training programs for all authorities involved in the matter, and foremost legal requirements and penal laws are not existent. Thus, the German handlings do not earn the designation "concept", when referring to societal and criminal – political standards in the field of hate crime. After all, the question of an implementation of a necessary legal "concept" is the reason for this examination.

C. Legal Dealing with Hate Crime

With regard to the substantial structure of the German Penal Code and the unnamed offense category "hate crime", there were several legislative initiatives in Germany since the year 2000. According to the definition system of the German police, as the only, or at least "first" implemented part of a German hate crime "concept", the prevailing legislative aspirations in Germany were primarily circulating around the terms "right-wing extremism" and "xenophobia". But nonetheless, the reference to the actual core of hate crimes becomes evident: The lack of tolerance towards strangers to such an extent that it turns into hatred, which is relieved by violating a legal good and therewith becomes objectified in the contempt of constitutional values; this

1275 To combat activities of the Klu Klux Klan, several states in which this hate group was active, e.g. in Georgia - the state where it was founded - enacted anti-mask legislation. Such statutes penalize the wearing of masks or hoods in public, they also banish typical KKK activities such as cross-burnings. (G. A. C. Ann. 16-11-38 (a)).

1276 Such keywords are used by media and politics in reference to all sorts of programs and activities of fight right-wing extremism and therewith connected right-wing violence which always necessarily constitute hate crimes. For example: http://www.spiegel.de/politik/deutschland/kampf-gegen-rechts-kabinett-beschliesst-bundesweite-neonazi-datei-a-809782.html (accessed in Jan. 2012).

1277 This keyword emerged as the then Chancellor Schroeder of Germany in 2000 after an arson attack on a synagogue called for defense measures against right-wing violence. View example in the media for the usage of this keyword: http://www.spiegel.de/politik/deutschland/0,1518,96537,00.html -accessed in Jan. 2012.

generated hatred can be directed against disability, gender, political opinions, etc. - and is not limited to xenophobia[1278]. Assuming that hate crimes contain a greater degree of injustice in comparison to other offenses, several legal initiatives have been taken to amend the German Law in order to cover hate crimes. Numerous drafts, presented in the following, contain amendments of the German Penal Code, but also of the Code of Criminal Procedure, and concerning the Juvenile Court Law.

1. Draft Bill of Baden-Wuerttemberg Drs. 564/00, dated September 21, 2000

The draft bill of the state of Baden-Wuerttemberg[1279] was the first in the series of debates on the fight against hate crimes held in the German political arena. Entitled, "Resolution of the Federal Council to improve the fight against xenophobia and right-wing violence" this proposed law did not (yet) aim at a clear combat against hate crimes by, for example, the establishment of a separate law offense, it was more about specific actions in individual areas, which peripheral affect the area of hate crime. Even though, the introduction emphasized the appalling acts of violence against foreigners, and also arouse attention towards the impact on similar target groups victimized by hate-motivated violence, the draft only aimed at "legislative action in the field of juvenile justice, as well as contemplating measures especially in the field of international cooperation: Strengthening of Europol, harmonization of laws, combating Internet crime."[1280] The amendment of the law was primarily about punishing German hate crime offenders, who harm the image of the FRG[1281], by committing corresponding propaganda offenses abroad. The punishing of committing offenses abroad should be made possible under less stringent conditions. In addition to expanding international cooperation, one pursued changes to the juvenile justice system, in order to be able to respond more adequately to the blame of juvenile hate crime offenders.

2. Draft Bill of Brandenburg Drs. 577/00, dated September 26, 2000

This draft, submitted by Baden Wuerttemberg, proposed that the current criminal law is sufficient to punish hate crime, but the almost simultaneously issued proposal of Brandenburg[1282] raised concerns. The bill had the aim to ensure that "propaganda offenses and incitement to hatred committed by German perpetrators abroad can be prosecuted in Germany" (extension of Section 5 Penal Code to Sections 86, 86a and 130 Penal Code); included further actions on international cooperation; new remand reasons; and proposed for changes in the juvenile justice relating to the introduction of a ban

---

1278 The German typical term-restriction referring to xenophobia of right-wing extremism affiliates occurs only "apparently" due to the categorical subordination of the hate crime term under the category of politically motivated crimes.

1279 BR-Drs. 564/00.

1280 BR-Drs. 564/00; attachment p. 1.

1281 "Such recently committed horrifying acts of violence against foreigners harm [...] also the international reputation of the FRG. In this context right-wing extremism and xenophobia are strongly to be combated." (BR-Drs. 564/00; attachment p. 1).

1282 BR-Drs. 577/00.

on driving for right-wing extremist offenders[1283]. Moreover though, the draft especially targeted at an enhancement of penalty for hate crime offenders: by creating a new offense, the specific content of wrongdoing in racially motivated crimes was to be legally recognized[1284].

"Based on the base offense of assault, a new provision, Section 224a Penal Code, should stipulate that a term of imprisonment of one to ten years shall be imposed on whoever commits a bodily injury because of hatred against segments of the population; or against a national, racial, religious group; or against such characterized by its ethnic customs; or because of other base motives"[1285]. While the first alternative clearly belongs to the matter of fighting hate crime, the second alternative relates to an extension of punishment for vague cases[1286]. This formation of a law would lead to the unpleasentness that hate crime sentencing becomes mixed up with the punishment of various other despicable offender convictions. If the reasoning of the bill itself stresses that the term "base motives" insofar should follow the meaning which it "received in decades of jurisprudence of the Supreme Court"[1287], according to Section 211, Paragraph 2 Penal Code, it is clear that an offense, worded in the respective form, would affect assault offenses which do not relate to racist violence. Thus, the establishment of this proposal in the German Penal Code would have caused an overall enhancement of penalty in relation to certain offenses of bodily injury[1288]. Whereas it can be assumed that the legislature, with reference to the title of the drafted bill stating: "a draft bill to improve the combat against extremist violence and other extremist criminal acts"[1289] and by citing particularly serious examples for low motivation in Subparagraph 2 and pointing towards the "wanton lust for physical abuse", or "the for the victim in particular degrading way of committing a crime[1290], in particular had such base motives in mind, which typically describe hate crimes, it must be acknowledged that these modalities of committing a crime are transferable to other, not by bias-motivated, assault offenses. Hence, the conclusion "that

1283 Planned changes: insertion of a No. 16 in Section 5 Penal Code, new Section § 224a Penal Code; extension of Section 112, Paragraph 3 Code of Criminal Procedure because of Section § 224a, Paragraph 1 and 2 Penal Code; Amendment of Article 10 Basic Law through insertion of criminal offenses according to Section 130 Penal Code.

1284 "The state government of Brandenburg believes that crimes committed with such a [despicable] misanthropic motivation are often characterized by an extreme brutality of the offender and therefore must be punished more severely than acts that do not exhibit these characteristics. This must be made clear by the legislature." (Schelter, in: Plenarprotokoll Bundesrat – 754. Sitzung – 29. September 2000, pp. 367, 368).

1285 Schelter, in: Plenarprotokoll Bundesrat – 754. Sitzung – 29. September 2000, p. 368.

1286 "The 1st Variant thereby takes constituent elements of Section 211 Penal Code, the other such from Section 130 Penal Code"- or vice versa. (Tolmein, Neue strafrechtliche Reaktionsmöglichkeiten auf rassistisch motivierte Gewaltdelikte, ZRP 2001, pp. 315-319 (316)).

1287 Reasoning of the Law, p. 5; Scheffler, Körperverletzung aus niedrigen Beweggründen, NJ 1/2001, pp.13-15 (13).

1288 Tolmein, Neue strafrechtliche Reaktionsmöglichkeiten auf rassistisch motivierte Gewaltdelikte, ZRP 2001, pp. 315-319 (316).

1289 BR-Drs. 577/00.

1290 BR-Drs. 577/00, Legal Reasoning, p. 6.

Section 224a Penal Code would go far beyond the fight against extremism"[1291] is obvious.

With the enactment of Section 224a, Paragraph 1 Penal Code, in addition to Section 224 and Sections 226, 227 Penal Code, there would be a third independent aggravation law, based on simple assault (Section 223 Penal Code), established in the Penal Code[1292]. The second Paragraph of the to be enacted Section 224a Penal Code contains both[1293], a sentencing rule, ("not less than three years"), as well as the technique of inserting "aggravated exemplified rules"[1294] ("if the offense is jointly committed by several perpetrators, by a life threatening or an abusive treatment of the victim")[1295]. In order to avoid that a "simple assault, such as a simple slap in the face constitutes a crime"[1296], Section 224a Penal Code would provide a Paragraph 3, which lowers the basic minimum sentence of one year back to six months[1297].

Considering the intent of the legislature, this proposed law[1298] hits the core of hate crimes: it acknowledges violent offenses - which are committed because of hate or prejudice against another - as a distinct, separate crime category, and criminally oppose their increased wrongfulness by modifying the offense character[1299], thereby simultaneously increasing the penalty framework for violent hate crimes[1300].

The penalty enhancement is further justified with the more serious impacts on victims[1301]. Moreover, - expressed in terms of the American doctrinal

---

1291 Scheffler, Körperverletzung aus niedrigen Beweggründen, NJ 1/2001, pp.13-15 (13).

1292 Scheffler, Körperverletzung aus niedrigen Beweggründen, NJ 1/2001, pp.13-15 (13).

1293 The draft of Section 224a, Paragraph 1 reads: "In particularly serious cases, punishment of less than three years' imprisonment must not be imposed. A particularly serious case is usually constituted if the act is committed jointly by several perpetrators, by means of a life threatening treatment or cruel abuse of the victim."

1294 "Regelbeispieltechnik".

1295 "We are taking the aggravating criteria of Section 211 Penal Code and implement them in the scheme of physical assault offenses". (Kurt Schelter, in: Plenarprotokoll Bundesrat – 754. Sitzung – 29. September 2000, p. 368; view at: http://www.bundesrat.de/SharedDocs/Downloads/DE/Plenarprotokolle/2000/Plenarprotokoll-754,templateId=raw,property=publicationFile.pdf/Plenarprotokoll-754.pdf).

1296 Instead of constituting a misdemeanor.

1297 Reasoning of the Law, p.10; Scheffler, Körperverletzung aus niedrigen Beweggründen, NJ 1/2001, (pp. 13-15 (13).

1298 For dogmatic criticism of the idea of enacting a norm punishing bodily assault out of base motives, view further literature, especially: Scheffler, Körperverletzung aus niedrigen Beweggründen, NJ 1/2001, (pp.13-15); Tolmein, Neue strafrechtliche Reaktionsmöglichkeiten auf rassistisch motivierte Gewaltdelikte, ZRP 2001, (pp. 315-319), for criticism or a proposed solution to combat hate crimes in general, refer to the final discussion of this work.

1299 According to the draft bill, bodily injury caused by a hate crime would generally constitute a crime (instead of a misdemeanor).

1300 Krupna's appropriate statement: "With this step, one called after a normative adjustment of the Penal Law towards the specific realized wrong for the first time." (Krupna, Das Konzept der Hate Crimes in Deutschland, p. 62).

1301 One has drawn a comparison between the consequences of victimization through a hate crime and those consequences which are caused by the victimization through a serious injury as it is established in Section 226 Penal Code and therefrom concluded that the impacts on the victims of hate crime are more serious (Appendix to BR-Drs. 577/00, p. 9).

reasoning perspective[1302] - it is pointed towards the vulnerability of the victims of hate crime, or towards the weaker position of the victim, which is typical for hate crime attacks, since the perpetrators are usually either numerically or otherwise[1303] superior in a hate crime attack. Furthermore, the causation of a generally higher degree of harm in several individual areas is pointed out, which derives from the nature of these acts, which are characterized by a particularly inhumane execution[1304].

3. Draft Bill of Mecklenburg-Vorpommern Drs. 759/00, dated November 16, 2000

The state of Mecklenburg-Vorpommern based its bill to fight hate crime on the reason to protect the human dignity, and therefore did not aim at the establishment of a separate offense, but at a clarifying regulation[1305] in the General Part of the Penal Code, which would have effects on all offenses anchored in the special part and thus, in general encompass all committed hate crimes, independently of the particular form of offense. This dogmatic approach was related to changes in Sections 46, 47 and 56 Penal Code[1306]. Section 46 Penal Code provides general principles of sentencing for courts on how to impose the individual penalty. On this basis, the draft mainly suggested the insertion of a 4th half sentence in Section 46, Paragraph 2 Penal Code which read as followed: "When sentencing, the court shall weigh the circumstances in favor of and such against the offender. Consideration shall in particular be given to the motives and aims of the offender, especially also person-despising, racist or xenophobic ones, the attitude reflected in the offense and the degree of force of will involved in its commission; [...]." With this, an express declaration would be anchored into law that courts must consider the motives of a hate crime offender when fixing the penalty. This dogmatic approach, with its range of possibilities to legally address hate crimes, gained new relevance and huge support by the draft bill newly submitted this year, dated April 18, 2012[1307], from the middle of the Federal Council, which is discussed in the following[1308]. With this former draft it should

1302 According to the the equality thesis, the state must remove the inequalities that derive from race, religion, gender, and sexual orientation (Harel/Parchomovsky, On Hate and Equality, 109 Yale L.J., 1999, pp. 510, 511; Aydin, Die strafrechtliche Bekämpfung von Hassdelikten, pp. 109, 110). View also Chapter 4, F. Brief Review.

1303 It is given the example that the victim in these kinds of attacks is typically inferior with regard to his equipment. (Appendix to BR-Drs. 577/00, p. 5).

1304 Appendix to BR-Drs. 577/00, p. 5.

1305 BR-Dr 759/00, "It must be expressed that, on the part of the state, there will be a response to such in politically motivated (violent) crime lying disregard of all values that carry our system of fundamental rights, as they are centrally reflected in respect for the universal human dignity (Article 1 Basic Law), for the right to life and physical integrity (Article 2, Section 2, Clause 1 Basic Law), for inviolability of the individual liberty (Article 2, Section 2, Sentence 2 Basic Law) and for the protection of minorities from persecution and discrimination (Article 3, Section 3, Sentence 1 Basic Law), due to a general preventative intent and for the reason to defend those values." ("Act to improve the legal protection of human dignity" - BR-Drs. 759/00, p. 2).

1306 In addition, the bill proposed an expansion of the accelerated procedure that is established in the Code of Criminal Procedure; the introduction of the driving ban as a primary penalty for juvenile hate crime offenders and an extension of Section 86a, Paragraph two, Sentence 2 Penal Code regarding to "modified symbols".

1307 Proposal BT-Drs. 17/8796; Draft Bill of the Federal Council Drs. 17/9345.

1308 View hereto: Chapter 4, C., 6. Draft Bill of the Federal Council Drs. 17/9345, dated April 18, 2012.

also be clarified that, contrary to Section 47 Penal Code, overwritten with "short terms of imprisonment as the exception", an offense according to this new 4th half sentence in Section 46, Paragraph 2 Penal Code, forms a reason for imposing a short prison sentence as a rule. Hence, committing a hate crime do not allow a court to suspend a prison sentence. Instead of imposing a suspended sentence, imprisonment must be served[1309]. Section 56 Penal Code regulates several cases according to which a custodial sentence may be suspended so that the offender is placed on probation instead of being imprisoned. Section 56 Paragraph 3 Penal Code provides that a sentence by more than six months should be enforced to imprisonment, if this is necessary to "defend the legal system". By altering Section 47 Paragraph 1 Penal Code it would be regulated that "[i]n cases of an imposed imprisonment of at least six months, the enforcement must not be suspended if the defense of the legal system require it." In defense of the legal system, imprisonment instead of probation is usually required in case the crime constitues a hate crime[1310]. Thereby the imposition of a suspended sentence for the committal of a hate crime would be declared to constitute an exception. The state of Mecklenburg-Vorpommern was of the opinion that, in principle, the increased incidence of certain crimes sensibly should not result in changes of statutory law, but that in the case of hate crimes this premise necessitated an exception because such crimes are directed against the constitutional state in an incomparable way[1311]. The demands towards law enforcement agencies stipulating that bias-motives must be noticed during crime investigation in general, and moreover constrain the court at trial to consider such motives as punishment increasing facts, due to - dogmatical not compelling[1312] - legally binding precepts, would lead to a documentation of the judicial handling of hate crime motives during trial. Clarifications in the general part of the Penal Code could have a greater meaningfulness regarding the message that the legislature does not tolerate hate crimes, and therefore have a greater effect on the entire law than changes of individual offenses in the special part of the Code would be able to have. Insofar this draft complies with its concern[1313] of an overall clarifying function.

4. Draft Bill of Brandenburg/Sachsen-Anhalt Drs. 572/07, dated August 20, 2007

In 2007, the states of Brandenburg and Saxony-Anhalt together proposed a draft, which "[I]n order to close the identified gaps in protection [provide for] enhancements in the general legal sanction system of the Penal Code[1314]".

1309 "Usually the imposition of a prison sentence is essential to defend the law, if the act was influenced by dehumanizing, racist or xenophobic motives or objectives."

1310 Moreover the draft provides the introduction of the ban as a major penalty in the Penal Code and in the Juvenile Court Act and specifies the provisions for the application of the accelerated procedure by indicating a maximum period of six weeks in Section 418, Paragraph 1 Code of Criminal Procedure.

1311 Sellering, in: Plenarprotokoll 757, Bundesrat – 757. Session – 1. December 2000, p.553.

1312 For a critique of this solution regarding the criminal acquisition of hate crimes in German criminal law see the final discussion of this work.

1313 BR-Drs. 759/00, p. 5.

1314 BR-Drs. 572/07, p. 3.

Thereby they considered "a comprehensive and sustainable" legislative action, based on the "number of offenses motivated by bias and hatred against individuals or segments of the population, especially the rise of right-wing violence", as mandatory[1315]. Similar to the previously discussed draft, this proposal suggested an explicit inclusion of the mentioned motives into Section 46, Paragraph 2 Penal Code, in the sense of a norm-application-order[1316], in order to force courts and law enforcement authorities, concerned with hate crime, to impose an appropriate penal enhancement[1317]. Further, the scheme of Section 47, according to which short prison sentence are to be suspended in the event of hate crime, should be applied and vice versa, so that the sanction for a hate crime principally is imprisonment, regardless of its imposed duration[1318]. This means that, in principle, a suspension of enforcement is also not considered for these cases in the event of a positive social prognosis (accordingly, Section 56, Paragraph 3 Penal Code must be amended)[1319]. The aggravated sentence for hate crimes is rationalized with the - by these offenses - special dimension of the realized wrong, which must be opposed by particular criminal sanction[1320]. However, the reasoning does not fit the aimed at amendment, since the special dimension of wrong would correctly be considered in the culpability, which reasons a penalty[1321] and not in the specific culpability, which is relevant in the individual case[1322], since such is open only for valuation regarding the individual guilt of the perpetrator, and not regarding the principal dimension of guilt in connection to the committed wrong, which must be pre-determined in the codified offense through the legislator. If the wrong of a hate crime is greater compared to the base offense - as it is assumed in the draft bill[1323] - it must be decided whether the given penalty frames of the base offenses capture such anyway, or reasons must be stated, which allow the punishment to stay behind that, which corresponds to the wrong inflicted, because - as already said - in the context of sentencing, only the basic degree of wrong of this type of action is to be determined in the law, not the individual culpability levels. In any case, the states wanted a raise of awareness of law enforcement authorities for inhuman crimes due to aggravating the law in context to this sort of crimes. It was further reasoned that the sanctions system - despite the paramount importance of human dignity in the German Constitution - does not provide a sufficient protection against such criminal behavior.

5. Draft Bill of the Federal Council Drs. 458/08, dated July 4, 2008

The proposal of the states of Brandenburg, Mecklenburg-Vorpommern, Saxony, Saxony-Anhalt, Thuringia agrees to the above discussed bill in its

1315 BR-Drs. 572/07, p. 1.
1316 "Normanwendungsbefehl".
1317 BR-Drs. 572/07, p. 3.
1318 BR-Drs. 572/07, p. 4.
1319 BR-Drs. 572/07, p. 4.
1320 BR-Drs. 572/07, p. 4.
1321 "Strafbegründungsschuld" - view hereto: Chapter 2, C., 3.4 Manifestation of Criminal Law.
1322 "Strafzumessungsschuld" - view hereto: Chapter 2, C., 3.4 Manifestation of Criminal Law.
1323 BR-Drs. 572/07, p. 4.

core points, likewise it is based on normative deficiencies of the German Penal Code in relation to hate crimes: "The general criminal law in its present configuration, inadequately expresses the central precept of the Constitution - directed to all governmental powers - that any form of disrespect for the human dignity must be opposed in those cases, in which persons are victimized by criminal behavior due to inhumane motivation or aims."[1324] So again, it is intended to insert the words "particularly inhumane, racist or xenophobic" in Section 46, Paragraph 2, Sentence 2 Penal Code, after the words "aims of the offender"[1325]. The change would affect the prosecution process of "right-wing motivated" and hate crime offenders in so far as the examination of political or bias related motives or goals of action would explicitly be required for the sentencing of every offense. By amending Section 47 Penal Code, the imposition of short prison sentences would constitute to be the standard for those cases in which an offender is convicted for committing an offense by the reason of bias. This is contrary to the current handlings in which short terms of imprisonment are the exception, because a court shall impose a fine instead. Accordingly, the 'standard-exception relation'[1326], which is actually embodied in Section 47 Penal Code, would be applied vice versa. In addition, the suspension of a prison sentence should be more difficult to apply (Section 56 Penal Code); therefore, if committing a hate crime, one would have to expect a prison sentence.

6. Draft Bill of the Federal Council Drs. 17/9345, dated April 18, 2012

The initiators of the two latest identically worded legislative proposals, one initiated by the Federal Council[1327], the other by the Social Democrats (SPD)[1328], request for change of the German Penal Law in order for it to take the increased wrongfullnes of hate crime into account explicitly. Therefore, both bills aim at an amendment of Section 46, Paragraph 2 Penal Code by adding human-contemptuous and racist motives and aims of an offender as aggravating circumstances, which are to be taken into account as aggravating facts during sentencing. Further, several representatives and the political fraction Alliance 90/The Greens called for 1.) the federal government to generally affirm the special public interest in prosecuting an offense whenever it reveals that the offender was motivated by misanthropy[1329]; 2.) further they

1324 BR-Drs. 458/08, p. 3.
1325 BR-Drs. 458/08.
1326 In Section 47, Paragraph 1 Penal Code it is stipulated that the court shall not impose a term of imprisonment of less than six months unless special circumstances exist either in the offence or the person of the offender that strictly require the imposition of imprisonment either for the purpose of reform of the offender or for reasons of general deterrence. Accordingly the court shall impose a fine unless the imposition of a sentence of imprisonment is strictly required pursuant to the aforesaid. By the implementation of the following sentences: "Indispensable to the defense of the law is the imposition of a prison sentence usually if the act was influenced by dehumanizing, racist or xenophobic motives or goals", the imprisonment for less than 6 months for the committal of political right-wing motivated offenses should become the norm.
1327 BT-Drs. 17/9345.
1328 BT-Drs. 17/8131.
1329 "Request offense" refers to an offense that (transl. of: Antragsdelikte, Section 77 Penal Law) may only be prosecuted upon a request of the victim to prosecute. Thus, if the victim does not file a request to prosecute, the offense may not be prosecuted, regardless of the will of a prosecutor to do so. Most of the

asked the Federal Government to submit a law that extends Section 130 Penal Code through adding all groups, which are to be protected against the respective behavior, in particular those, which due to their sexual identity, gender, belief or age are victimized by seditious acts; and 3.) for the assignment of a study on the application mode of Section 46, Paragraph 2 Penal Code with respect to such cases in which the offender of an offense was motivated by group-focused enmity[1330].

Again, it is established that the particular dimension of wrong, resulting from these resentments, occurs from the fact that the actions constituting a hate crime not only address the victim as an individual, but beyond the infliction of suffering of the actual victim are suitable to insecure much of the population and to undermine their confidence in the inviolability of the law. Thereby, bias-motivated offenses do not just contradict the liberal democratic constitutional polity, but directly attack it[1331]. Therefore, the public interest in prosecuting such an act is always assured. The request for an amendment of Section 130 Penal Code reveals which groups are considered to be most likely endangered by hatred actions. Since the question whether hate crime are criminally considered by aggravating sentencing is a matter of court handlings, the petition asks the federal government to contract to launch a study to investigate the actual practice with regard to Section 46, Paragraph 2 Penal Code in order to finally find out, whether at all the German criminal procedure acknowledges the particular injustice of these crimes: "There is still no sufficient empirical legal research on how group-focused enmity as a motive for crime commission is considered during sentencing purposes. For some forms of prejudice-motivated crime there is virtually no legal factual research, such for example, in the area of homophobic violence"[1332].

The German Federal Parliament has sent the two draft laws mentioned above[1333] and the motion of several representatives and the political fraction Alliance 90/The Greens[1334] to the Legal Committee, to the Committee for Internal Affairs and to the Committee for Human Rights and Humanitarian Aid for deliberation. After discussion, the Committee recommended the rejection of the two identically worded bills and of the motion in the meeting, held on 17th October 2012[1335]. The rejection is reasoned with the general view that,

"request offenses" in German law are prosecutable upon request of the victim and also liable to public prosecution in case the prosecutor affirms a special public interest in prosecuting the offense (mixed request offenses, transl. of: "Mischantragsdelikte"). Therefore, the law enforcement office may clear up an offense due to public interest in prosecution even though the victim did not request upon prosecution. The request of this bill therefore aims at the general affirmation of a special public interest in prosecution whenever an offense reveals that the offender was motivated by the respective motivation. This would affect those criminal cases in which a request of the victim to prosecute is required for criminal prosecution, but the victim does not file the request, because the prosecutor now must investigate anyway, due to the general special public interest in prosecution if the crime appears to be a hate crime; and thereby make sure not to let hate crime offenders go unpunished.

1330 BT-Drs. 17/8796.

1331 BT-Drs. 17/8796, p. 2.

1332 BT-Drs. 17/8796, p. 2.

1333 BT-Drs. 17/9345; BT-Drs. 17/8131.

1334 BT-Drs. 17/8796.

1335 BT-Drs. 17/11061, p. 4.

although the fight against inhuman crimes is an important concern, the submitted templates would not lead to the desired results[1336]. It is opined that the concern of the templates - to counter inadequate criminal investigation and consideration of inhuman motives of offenders during criminal investigation and trial, as well as the idea that an explicit inclusion of inhuman motives in the catalog of Section 46, Paragraph 2, Sentence 1 Penal Code would be able to spell out the increased disvalue, i.e. the unworthy of action[1337] - cannot be achieved by a change in the law for two reasons:

a) The dogmatic structure of Section 46 Penal Code cannot provide for these aims.

b) Section 46 Penal Code applies only to the courts, but not to the police and the prosecutors, among which the problem of insufficient consideration of the respective motives is considered to be more prevalent than among courts[1338].

7. Descriptive Summary and Evaluation of the Draft Laws

In summary, the above named bills[1339] have in common that they try to close a potential "gap" in the statutory design of the Penal Code in relation to the prosecution of hate crimes. The approaches vary between criminal aggravation, which is to be implemented in the context of judicial sentencing and codified in the general part, and the approach of creating a specific offense in the form of an aggravation norm for bias-motivated violent crimes. In the reasoning it is focused on both, on the increased wrong of these acts, as well as on the increased guilt of the perpetrators who commit such an offense. Although the sentence does not have the task to compensate culpability for its own sake, a sentence is only justified if it proves to be in necessary means to fulfill the preventive protective role of criminal law[1340]. Further justification approaches provide potential to legitimize a possible reform of the Code: The reasons include, on the one hand, the increased impact on victims, the message broadcast by hate crime committal, the lack of regard towards the protection of the human dignity in the frame of the current design of the law, and on the other hand, the necessary request to the legislature to take a position and to make clear that hate crimes are prosecuted with vigor by the German legal system. The latter citation is equivalent to the call for symbolism. Therefore, according to the here followed opinion of the ultima ratio principle of criminal law and its necessity to be used for the protection of legal goods[1341],

---

1336 BT-Drs. 17/11061, p. 5.

1337 BT-Drs. 17/8131; BT-Drs. 17/11061, p. 5 – stated view of the Social Democrats (SPD).

1338 BT-Drs. 17/11061, p. 5.

1339 And further bills of individual parliamentary parties, such as the bill of the Social Democrats (SPD) Drs. 17/8131 of December 14th, 2011, and identical hereto: BT-Drs. 17/8796, which is submitted by Representatives and the FDP parliamentary group. This legislative proposal suggests to consider "inhuman, especially racist or xenophobic motives and objectives of the offender as circumstances in Section 46 Paragraph 2 Penal Code as an aggravating factor in sentencing" in order to abolish "the current, unsatisfactory legal situation." (Drs. 17/8131, pp. 1,2).

1340 BGHSt 24, 42; Stree/Kinzig, in: Schönke/Schröder, StGB, Vorbem. §§ 38 et seqq., marginal no. 18a.

1341 BVerfGE 96, 249: "Criminal Law is ultima ratio in the protection of legal goods"; Stree/Kinzig, in: Schönke/Schröder, StGB, Vorbem. §§ 38 et seqq., marginal no. 1; Hefendehl, Der fragmentarische Charakter des Strafrechts, JA 2011, number 6, pp. 401-406.

offers little to legal reasoning. The other references do apply to the previously mentioned requirement of criminal law, that is that criminal law is applied as a necessary mean for the protection of legal goods.

In recent years the legislative initiatives are rather turned towards a clarifying insertion in Section 46 Penal Code by which it shall be achieved to compel, in particular, the judiciary and the law enforcement authorities involved, to rightfully convict hate crime offenders. Thereby the legislature turned away from the protection of the legal good of the human dignity, but oriented itself more towards indicating the judiciary that the motives of a hate crime act must be acknowledged guilt-increasing. Nevertheless, by that the legislature continues to leave the principle decision on the specific content of wrong and guilt fulfilled by these acts with the courts, and put it to their prey to recognize such, through proclaiming the sentence.

Therefore, the anticipated gain, according an amendment which addresses hate crime, is ultimately seen in an intensive clarification that the offenders are not tolerated, but labeled as hate crime criminals[1342], moreover the symbolic content and expressive power of such an amendment, is considered to raise the awareness of the jurisdiction to release reasonable judgments[1343]. However, such a symbolic effect will not automatically be fulfilled by just any legal implementation; it further depends on the actual naming of the problem. Thereby it seems necessary that a legal device clearly names the attacked problem[1344]. Resultant from the prevailing social issues concerning right-wing violence, the groups which are concerned by the phenomenon, i.e. the condemning motives, must be listed individually, instead of just implementing the word "misanthropic", which could possibly embrace all sorts of inhuman intents. Perpetrators, who - because of their racist, or anti-Semitic motives, because of their disgust against the homeless, or any other social Darwinist motives; because of their hate towards certain sexual orientation and/or gender, or disability - attack others, may pose an additional threat to the public peace and other legal goods, which could be expressed and stemmed if they are addressed directly by the legislature through providing a clear statement in form of a law[1345]. Yet, the idea of using "misanthropic" as a circumscription, after all, makes clear that the legislator has recognized the core of hate crimes. That is, that the motives and aims of the perpetrators, which namely are "the denial of the right of physical integrity and life" of certain human beings, are crucial in weighing the harmful effects of committed behavior, and that people are not attacked because they are "strange" to the perpetrators, but because of the perpetrator's inner idea of viewing certain persons as

---

1342 Seehafer, Strafrechtliche Reaktionen, 2003, pp. 103, 104.

1343 The social function of possessing a "certain moral-building power" is attributed to criminal law, this necessitates that the criminal law set value-based signals. (Herzog, Präimplantationsdiagnostik – im Zweifel für ein Verbot?, in: ZRP, 2001, pp. 393, 397).

1344 Schneider, Politische Kriminalität: Hassverbrechen, Fremdenfeindlichkeit im internationalen Kontext, Kriminalistik 2001, p.26.

1345 "Gemeinsame Stellungnahme zum Gesetzesentwurf "Hasskriminalität"" der Opferperspektive vom 06/06/2012 (view at: http://opferperspektive.net/Home/Publikationen/Strafschaerfung/1114.html - accessed June, 2012).

inferior and unequal, which after all does refer to the human dignity of all human beings and attacks crucial constitutional demands. Therefore, such an expression in the general part of the German Penal Code through a supplement in Section 46 Penal Code could have an awareness-rising effect towards the entire judiciary, and to all law enforcement authorities involved. So, the symbolic impact on victims and perpetrators, which expresses that these acts are not tolerated in our democratic community, would, after all, be democracy-promoting.

The recommended decision of the Parliamentary Committee to reject the proposals of 2012 in its meeting, held on October 17th, 2012[1346] was influenced by the fact that an explicit mentioning of hate crime motives in Section 46 Penal Code will not necessarily lead to an aggravated consideration of those motives by a court. The doctrine of Section 46 Penal Code precisely does not allow a generalized aggravated consideration of therein specified motives, possible is even a consideration of such in the norm specified motives in favor of the offender[1347]. Against this background, it is agreed to the decision of the Committee against the implementation of a generalized legal regulation for an aggravated consideration of certain motives in the context of Section 46 Penal Code. Section 46 Penal Code is the wrong legal instrument to capture biased motives which lead to crime committal, due to its dogmatic structure[1348].

Section 46 Penal Code relates to the individualized sentencing. Yet, when it comes to hate crime, it is about the general increase of the range of sentence, for which the legislature is responsible. In the Committee one located the problems with not considering the motive of hate crime in the criminal investigation process and not so much in the main court proceedings[1349]. Therefore, one opined, that an amendment of Section 46 Penal Code, which applies primarily to the courts, is not the correct tool to ensure correct prosecution of hate crime. Against this opinion it must be noted that with following this view, one insufficiently considers the fact that the investigating authorities especially draw their attention towards those facts, which knowingly play a role in court proceedings. Voicing the remark that "these motives are already not adequately investigated during crime recording" as an argument against a legal amendment, ignores the causal connection of the current legal configuration for the investigative activities of the police and the prosecutors and thus for the investigative deficits in the area of hate crime. If a police officer, due to the legal situation, would be aware of the importance of the motive, which it has for the criminal case, he would hardly be able to not record such. So, would the courts evidentually value the enlightenment of bias related motives during trial, in order to incorporate their existence into sentencing, such would necessarily be investigated more intensive during preliminary proceedings – so it´s a cycle, in which one forgot that on the level

1346 BT-Drs. 17/11061, p. 4.

1347 BT-Drs. 17/11061, p. 5.

1348 View hereto Chapter: 4.; D.; 3. Hate Crime in the Light of Section 46 Penal Code and Chapter: 4.; G., 2.3. The Enactment of a Rule for Judicial Assessment.

1349 BT-Drs. 17/11061, p. 5.

of preliminary proceedings, namely in police handlings, first express steps have already been taken to make hate crime recognizable[1350]. Yet, on the legal level, not at all. Each level of separation of powers has to ensure that hate crimes are legitimately considered during criminal proceedings, an assignment of the identified problem to another level does not lead to an all-encompassing solution on all levels of law enforcement. The fact that the problem of insufficient legal consideration of certain motives is shifted towards the police and prosecutors, and it is seen not to be prevalent or even existent in trial or within court proceedings, leads the Committee to believe that – because sentencing is an individual decision of the courts – "one is able to and must trust the courts in respect of this matter" [1351]. Against this idea, it is opined that law is less based on trust, but more on effective control, traceability and transparency. And precisely this trust, especially due to a lack of control, traceability and transparency according judicial handlings in the area of hate crime and due to a potential lack of a thoroughly legitimate imposition of penalty in the case of hate crime, is impaired.

Although one admitted the need of action on the level of preliminary proceedings[1352] one rejected the fundamental duty to investigate every hate crime. In case of request offenses, the prosecution office will investigate only if the immediate victim requests an investigation[1353], therefore the special general public interest to prosecute hate crime is declined.

Contradictory to the rejection of the motion of several representatives and the political fraction Alliance 90/The Greens regarding point 3.) which requires legal factual research on court dealings with hate crime[1354], is the finding of the Committee that due to the lack of sufficient legal factual findings regarding the judicial practice, it cannot be answered unequivocally whether a trust in the courts here in this case is appropriate, and therefore whether for the solution of the problem, legislative action actually is necessary[1355]. So even though, the Committee rejected the request Drs. 17/8796 in all points, it comes up with the result that with regard to the judicial practice in dealing with hate crime, further factual legal research is required.

In summary, the Committee saw the solution of the discussed initial problem, which is described that hate crime "motives of offenders are often not adequately investigated and considered in criminal investigations and in the judicial trial"[1356], not in the need to ensure an appropriate legal enlightenment of hate crime offenses. It is suggested that the real issue is not a legal one, but the general lack of awareness for inhuman motives of society. Cliché-like, it is

1350 With renewing the Police Data Collection System hate crime became an own crime category, view hereto Chapter 4; B; 2. Data Collection in the Present Day.
1351 BT-Drs. 17/11061, p. 5 – opinion of the FDP fraction.
1352 BT-Drs. 17/11061, p. 5 – acknowledgement of the Social Democrats (SPD) and the Alliance 90/The Greens.
1353 Point 1.) of the application Drs. 17/8796.
1354 BT-Drs. 17/8796.
1355 BT-Drs. 17/11061, p. 5 – opinion of the CDU/CSU fraction.
1356 BT-Drs. 17/11061, p. 5.

argued that we must improve the legal status of foreigners in total, so that this would increase their acceptance in society, which then would lead to an overall awareness of society for inhuman motives[1357].

8. Symbolic Reasoning of Hate Crime Law

Ultimately, it must be noted that the reasons given by these drafts in terms of raising an awareness of the law enforcement bodies, addresses the function of a hate crime norm.

In the United States of America hate crimes are said to be less controlled by the high sentence but more by the symbolic effect which is sent by these norms which points out to society that these offences are not tolerated and the constitutional- and human rights of the victimized groups are protected[1358]. Supporters of such effects can be found in German literature, where it is suggested that "hate crime are message crimes, which require a strong counter message of non-tolerance. The victims need a strong signal to still their fears. It is completely inappropriate to [...] hope for spontaneous regression through non-intervention"[1359]. Theorists of symbolic interactionism insist that crime is not just an objective problem but an interactional event in which the legislator is involved[1360]. Thereby it is less about such by the legislature proclaimed goals, for example such mentioned in the above drafts, but rather it is to refer to the effect of a law, thus its function[1361]. Basically, according to the here followed view, the basic premise that the legitimacy of a law cannot be reasoned with its function, but with its necessity to protect a valid legal good; and that idea must be maintained. Yet, accordingly, especially in the case of hate crime it applies that 'symbolic legislation' is a comparative term, "which is a more or less and not an either or"[1362]. Insofar it is considered that hate crime legislation cannot constitute purely symbolic law, but actually could comply with the legal good doctrine and its precepts. If it is clear that hate crime are message crimes[1363], the damage which is caused by such can only be captured by a counter message (sent by the legislator). The removal/elimination of the misanthropic message which was sent into the social atmosphere through the committal of a hate crime could be addressed by the legislator when applying an explicit hate crime law, not only due to its symbolic effects – such a function might apply to average crimes – but by

1357 BT-Drs. 17/11061, p. 5.

1358 Jennes/Grattet, Making Hate a Crime, 2001, p. 3; Schneider, Internationales Handbuch der Kriminologie, Band 2, p. 326

1359 Schneider, Politische Kriminalität: Hassverbrechen, Fremdenfeindlichkeit im internationalen Kontext, Kriminalistik 2001, p.26.

1360 Hassemer, Symbolisches Strafrecht und Rechtsgüterschutz. in: NStZ, 1989, pp.553 -592 (533).

1361 Hassemer, Symbolisches Strafrecht und Rechtsgüterschutz. in: NStZ, 1989, pp.553 -592 (555).

1362 Hassemer, Symbolisches Strafrecht und Rechtsgüterschutz. in: NStZ, 1989, pp.553 -592 (556).

1363 Füllgrabe, Hassverbrechen, Kriminalistik, 2004, pp. 391-397 (394); Schneider, Politische Kriminalität: Hassverbrechen, Fremdenfeindlichkeit im internationalen Kontext, Kriminalistik 2001, p. 26; Schneider, Kriminologie der Hassdelikte. Konzeptionen, Ursachen, Vorbeugung und Kontrolle, in: Bewährungshilfe, 2003, p. 115, 117; Schneider, Hasskriminalität: Eine neue kriminologische Deliktskategorie, JZ, 2003, pp. 497-504 (498); Schneider, Hass- und Vorurteilskriminalität in: Grafl/Medigovic, (eds.): Festschrift für Manfred Burgstaller, 2004, pp. 553-568, p. 555; Singer, Erfassung der politsch motivierten Kriminalität, in einem neuen Definitionssystem mit mehrdimensionalen Analysemöglichkeiten, p. 34; Wallace, Victimology, 1998, p. 216.

recognizing the distinct nature of hate crime[1364] it is assumed that the damage which has been caused by the sent message of a hate crime would be eliminated by an encounter through legislative action. Thus the application of a hate crime law serves the recover of losses. Otherwise the harmful message, which is sent by a hate crime, remains to linger in the social atmosphere and continue to poison the climate.

After all it is recognized that a norm is symbolic only in the dimensions in which the latent functions outweigh the manifest functions[1365]. But, with a hate crime law it is not about symbolic effects only, nor is it feared that potential effects of such a law could occur which are not welcome[1366], the priority of a legal hate crime device clearly lies on addressing until yet not addressed harms to legal goods[1367]:

Accordingly, it must especially be referred on the impact of a law on the social problem and its suitability for solution. In 2008, the German Federal Government was still of the opinion that "the suppression of crimes of racist, xenophobic or other human-despising motives is an important task of the constitutional state" and that "[...] these acts [...] must be pursued consistently, and become appropriately punished"; yet, it was questioned whether the "proposed amendments to the Penal Code are necessary and appropriate to achieve these goals"[1368]. As disscussed, the legal Committee recommended that the Federal Parliament rejects the current legislative proposal of 2012[1369]. However, even opinions that oppose to the conceptualization of an independent construct of hate crime admit that hate crime laws at least in such cases could be a sufficient tool to combat this sort of crime in which the particular motivation is actually not taken into account by the current law[1370]. The opponents of amendments of the German criminal law mostly argue precisely with the existing legal possibility for (severe) punishment of hate crimes[1371], therefrom it is questioned, whether such a possibility, expressly, whether the particular motivation of hate crimes according to the current law is, in fact, taken into account. The reference to a theoretical possibility without appropriate reliable practical implementation or installed safety measures in case of non-implementation is not enough to assume that hate crimes are, in

1364 Hate crimes have a symbolic character, by the performance of an offense it constitutes a "public statement" (Martin, Investigating Hate Crimes: Case Characteristics and Law Enforcement Responses. Justice Quaterly 13, 1996, pp. 455-480, p. 467).

1365 Hassemer, Symbolisches Strafrecht und Rechtsgüterschutz. in: NStZ, 1989, pp.553 -592 (556).

1366 A norm is symbolic in the partial aspect in which it is expected that those by the norm addressed goals will not be achieved due to its application, instead rather other circumstances, which are not designated in the law itself, will be realized. (Hassemer, Symbolisches Strafrecht und Rechtsgüterschutz. in: NStZ, 1989, pp.553 -592 (556)).

1367 Hate crimes cause far more damage than other un-, or otherwise motivated acts, this was early known in the U.S. (Levin/Mc Devitt, Hate Crimes, 1993; Herek/Berril, Herek Berill, 1992) and is acknowledged in Germany in the present day as well. (Schneider, Internationales Handbuch der Kriminologie, Band, pp. 297-338 (298)).

1368 Appendix 2 to BT-Drs. 16/10123, "statement by the Federal Government", p.11.

1369 BT-Drs. 17/11061, dated Ocotber 17, 2012.

1370 Jacobs/Potter, Hate Crimes: Criminal Law & Identity Politics, 2001, p. 90.

1371 Lehmann, in: "Public Hearing of the Legal Committee of the German Bundestag on 06/13/2012 to so-called Hate Crime", p.1.

fact, offense- and guilt appropriately penalized in Germany. Except for provisions relating to murder and the hereto related established jurisprudence[1372], the suspicion emerged that the condemnation of such acts is inadequately expressed in legal practice[1373].

9. Comparison of the German Drafts with American Laws on Hate Crimes

Because of the different problem solving and distinct framework conditions, these German approaches are comparable with U.S. implementations only in partial aspects. It is noticeable that the idea of burdening the decision of whether to, and if so, to what degree a sentence enhancement is deserved for a hate crime perpetrator in the entirety on the judiciary, as it is currently the case in Germany, and as it is shall mainly be kept up in the future, according to the aimed at amendments, would not reach the compelling concept of the U.S. penal system. The U.S. legal regulating technique for the general treatment of hate crime motives in the prosecution process corresponds roughly to such according to the German dealings with the offense of murder under specific aggravating circumstances[1374]. Similar as it is constituted in the U.S., this legal regulation technique in collaboration with judicial handlings in the context of penalizing the murder offense ultimately led to an assumed constant penal-aggravating recognition of such motives in cases of murder; whereas regarding other offenses, where the specific German way of legally recognizing hate crime motives during the sentencing process in accordance with the extent of judicial discretion that is in force (Section 46 Penal Code) is followed, an aggravated punishment due to recognizing such motives as reasons for crime committal during the criminal trial can not be assured.

Changes of the current handling in Germany are related to the decision whether the penal law should consider the relevant motives in the offense level or only in sentencing.

There is an agreement in the legislative efforts mentioned above where at least to the extent that a fundamental consideration of the hate crimes motives in the context of criminal liability has to legitimately be made in any respective criminal case in whatever form, and this (eventually) must be expressed by the legislature. While the German intentions, in accordance with U.S. reasoning, also request an aggravated sentence for hate crimes, their aim turns out essentially more unspecific and unclear: so does the current proposal of 2012 name less clear what characteristics are to be protected, and try to avoid expressing the aimed at problem by hiding behind a general description: "inhumanity", instead of giving voice to a clear naming the problem.

1372 View hereto Chapter 4, D., 1. Judicial Recognition of Bias-Motivation in Homicide.

1373 This can be partly recognized through independent studies (Glet, Sozialkonstruktion und strafrechtliche Verfolgung von Hasskriminalität in Deutschland, 2011, p. 231; Krupna, Das Konzept der Hate Cirmes in Deutschland, pp. 171 et seqq.) and through the report by Human Rights Watch (Die Reaktion des Staates auf "Hasskriminalität" in Deutschland, Human Rights Watch-Hintergrundpapier, Dezember 2011). But most criticizable is the fact that no approved data, according the judicial assessment of the motive in trial, exists in Germany.

1374 View hereto Chapter 4, D., 1. Judicial Recognition of Bias-Motivation in Homicide.

10. Conclusion Legal Dealing with Hate Crime

The legislature, so far, has not established a regulation for hate crimes, but leaves the handling to the courts according to the precepts codified in Section 46 Penal Code. Due to the lack of explicit codification that hate crime motivations must be considered as an aggravated circumstance when determining the individual sentence, the task to adequately consider such proportionate to the offender's increased culpability remains completely to the sane judgment of the court. Besides the fact that the sentencing decision is truly discretionary, including all uncertainties of personal choices, the absence of an express stipulation could be acceptable if the task of the judiciary to acknowledge every hate crime as an aggravating fact when imposing the sentence in practice would be verifiable handled in a satisfactory manner, thus bias motivations are actually taken into account as aggravating facts during the imposition of the sentence in each relevant judicial proceeding[1375].

D. Judicial Dealing with Hate Crime

The following refers to the way hate crimes - even though this term does not exist in the legal environment - are supposed to be addressed according to the actual effective penal law.

1. Judicial Recognition of Bias-Motivation in Homicide

Section 211 Penal Code - murder under specific aggravating circumstances - refers to murder cases which reveal a particularly reprehensible character of the offender[1376]. Hate and bias as motives for the killing of another human being are considered as despicable motivations and therefore subsumed under Section 211, Paragraph 2, 1st group, Variant 4 Penal Code as so called "base motives"[1377]. A motive, which according to general ethical valuation is placed at the lowest level, driven by unrestrained selfishness and therefore is particularly reprehensible and contemptible, is considered to be a reprehensible motive according to this Section[1378]. This refers to bias motives of a hate crime - as decided by the Supreme Court since 1999 in solidified jurisdiction[1379]. Previous xenophobic bullying in conjunction with the admission

1375 For dogmatic deficits, which go along with following this way of letting the respective court at trial determine the measure of punishment for the committal of a hate crime in the individual case, view Chapter 4, D. 3. Hate Crime in the Light of Section 46 Penal Code.

1376 Wessels/Hettinger, Strafrecht BT I, p.31, marginal no. 86; Küpper, Strafrecht BT 1, p. 10, marginal no. 31.

1377 "Niedrige Beweggründe" – The offender acts because of a specific motive, which is considered to be in particular reprehensible. While the first three explicitly named motives in Section 211, Paragraph 2, 1st group the reprehensibleness is presupposed, in variant 4 - which applies to hate crimes - the reprehensibleness has to still be specifically examined and can not be automatically assumed (Küpper, Strafrecht Besonderer Teil 1, 2000, p. 12); however, due to jurisdiction of the supreme court (e.g. BGH January 12, 2000 - StB 15/99, marginal no. 9), the reprehensibleness can be assumed - nowadays - regarding the committal of a hate crime without putting too much effort into justification.

1378 BGHSt 3, 132; NJW 69, 2292; Maurach/Schröder/Maiwald, Strafrecht BT I, p. 45, § 2 III, B. 1. e), marginal no. 37.

1379 BGH NStZ 1999, pp. 129 et seqq. (The fact that courts qualify hate crime motives as in particular reprehensible proves the general consent of their nature among the judiciary. But the fact must be noted that it has been agreed that the killing of another constituting a hate crime constitutes 'murder under specific aggravating circumstances' (Section 211) instead of just 'murder' (Section 212) not before 1999.

of the offender that he was angry at the foreign victim are enough to determine and assure the existence of the motive[1380]. The jurisdiction and parts of the legal scholars consider the features of the murder offense of the first and the third Group of the Section 211, Paragraph 2 Penal Code, thus the such for hate crime relevant base motives, not as specific debt characteristics, but as characteristics which are part of the subjective facts of wrong, hence the motives of the perpetrator are recognized as constituent elements of an offense[1381]. According to the opponent legal scholars[1382] though, the murder features of Section 211, Paragraph 2, 1st group, consequently the bias motives of a hate crime offender, are rooted in the guilt, therefore constitute specific culpability characteristics, because they directly and exclusively indicate the special wickedness of the motivation[1383]. Therefore, if one follows this latter opinion of the German literature, hate-, and bias motives are considered - in respect of the murder offense - as features of culpability[1384], possibly in the form of "characteristics of cast of mind"[1385]; whereby bias motives according to their subsuming under Section 211, Paragraph 2, 1st group, Variant 4 Penal Code are categorized as particular contemptible. Unlike in the majority of the other German criminal offense, this legal standard is more focused on the offender's personality. This refers to the recognition of the concept of a substantial guilt term, according to which not only the sum of

---

This late acknowledgement of the despicable nature of hate crime proves that the question whether the perpetrators of hate crimes are worth of special judicial attention, thus whether such crimes are valid to cause the imposition of aggravated sentence does not go without saying – yet, this is purported by the statement of Lehmann, when it is stated that "a xenophobic, racist or anti-Semitic embossed motivation, which is expressed in a criminal offense, will regularly be taken into account as an aggravating factor, based on the value of the Basic Law and the experiences of German history". (Statement of Lehmann, in: "Public Hearing of the Legal Committee of the German Bundestag on 06/13/2012 to so-called Hate Crime", p.1). If this specific severity of hate crime was not acknowledged evenly and reliably to murder offenses before the year of 1999, even though there is a particular Section (Section 211 Penal Code) which hints at such an understanding, it may not be assured that this understanding, which insofar has only been determined for murder offenses, applies equally and uniformly to violent offenses in the present day.

1380 BGH NStZ 1999, p. 129.

1381 Maurach/Schröder/Maiwald, Strafrecht BT I, p. 38, § 2 III, A., marginal no. 23 with further references; Wessels/Hettinger, Strafrecht Besonderer Teil I, 2011, p. 32, marginal no. 92 with further references to: BGHSt 1, 368, 371; Arzt/Weber, Strafrecht BT, § 2, marginal no. 29, 32; Kühl, Strafrecht AT, § 20, marginal no. 155; Jähnke, in: LK StGB, eleventh Edition, marginal no. 46 Vor § 211; Otto, Jura 94, 141; Horn, in: SK-StGB, § 211, marginal no. 3, 20.

1382 Wessels/Beulke, Strafrecht AT, marginal no. 422; Lenckner/Eisele, in: Schönke/Schröder, StGB, Vorbem. § 13, marginal no. 122 with further references; critical: Küper, Prävention und gerechte Zurechnung. Überlegungen zur normativen Kontrolle utilitaristischer Strafbegründung, in: ZStW 104, (1992), 569, 574 et seqq.

1383 Wessels/Hettinger, Strafrecht Besonderer Teil I, 2011, p. 33, marginal no. 93.

1384 Only motives which are not based on a reference point in the legally determined area of wrong but which can be deduced directly and exclusively from the situational facts, which are linked to the area of culpability, can be termed as real culpability features. Such real culpability features can be attributed to hate crime, but one has to differentiate: the particular way of committal and the evocation of specific impact on the victim is partially assigned to the area of wrong (view for example the outcome of hate crime committal in the context of bodily injury, view hereto the discussion in Chapter 4., G., 1. 1.6., 1.6.1., 1.6.1.5. Sections 223; 224; 226 Penal Code). Since the factors from which a particular motivation can be inferred differ with hate crimes, it reveals that the crime increasing facts partly belong to the area of wrong, and partly to the area of culpability. Therefore, the motives of hate crimes are not to be consistently viewed as features of culpability, but partly are to be regarded as features of wrong. (Differentiating opinion, according to: Jescheck/Weigend, AT, p. 472, § 42 II 3. a); Schmidhäuser, Strafrecht AT, p. 247; Lenckner/Eisele, in: Schönke/Schröder, StGB, Vorbem. § 13, marginal no. 122; Wessels/Beulke, Strafrecht AT, marginal no. 137; Langer, Sonderverbrechen, pp. 346 et seq.).

1385 "Gesinnungsmerkmale".

the subjective reasons are considered for attribution, but also a deplorable lack of righteous mind of the offender is taken into account, whereby culpability becomes an increasable factor[1386]. In the German criminal law special culpability characteristics have always been used to define crime (penalty reasoning or penalty excluding culpability characteristics) or to graduate (criminal aggravating or mitigating culpability characteristics) the punishable area[1387]. Referring to graduation one must note that in the criminal dogmatic it is generally taken for granted that the culpability can have different degrees, for example, the motive or the economic situation of an offender, or a provocation or any other emotion can influence the degree of culpability[1388]. Whereas the different degrees of culpability usually play a role in the practice of sentencing (according to Section 46 Penal Code), with regard to the murder offense the increase of culpability is stipulated in the statutory norm; therefore it's higher level is pre-recognized through the legislator. Determining the higher degree of culpability in the statutory facts of the offense might lead to a more stringent allover recognition of such in a judicial process in practice according the relevant trial[1389]. This idea occurs from the fact that the regulation technique implemented in Section 211 Penal Code already necessarily requires the examination of the motive in order to subsume the act under the correct offense type, thus a consideration of the motives for committing the crime is not just legally imperative, but essential to be able to prosecute an accused for the right offense. Since no judge has the gift of looking into the mind of an offender, and therefore the in Section 211, Paragraph 2, 1st group established characteristics can not be determined directly, the knowledge results from drawing a conclusion from the external circumstances of the act[1390]. Culpability features therefore require certain - with the proper means of a process ascertainable - external situations[1391]. The peculiarity of the murder offense is that the motives of the hate crime offenders are in fact directly, although circumscribed as "base motives", stated in the facts of the offense[1392]. Whereas, although here it is left to the judge to pick out those facts and circumstances which from the design of the individual case of the act

1386 Jescheck/Weigend, Lehrbuch des Strafrechts AT, p. 470, § 42 I 2; p. 472, § 42 II 3. a).

1387 Jescheck/Weigend, Lehrbuch des Strafrechts AT, p. 472, § 42 II 3. a).

1388 Similarly, different culpability levels result from the commission of intent (as the stronger culpability level) and negligence (as the lighter culpability level). (Kern, Grade der Rechtswidrigkeit, ZStW, 1952, 64, p. 255).

1389 Therefore, reasoning the recognition of the aggravating nature of these motives by referring to the judicial handlings during homicide cases is not very meaningful. Due to the distinct regulation technique, an equalization of the judicial handling applying to Section 211 Penal Code and its "recent" jurisdiction of acknowledging hate crime motives as "specific aggravating circumstances" in the case of homicide to such judicial handlings surrounding Section 46 Penal Code must not occur. The precepts arising from the jurisdiction according homicide do not prove that these motives are already considered as aggravating circumstances during sentencing in general, i.e. regarding the punishment of offenses apart from homicide.

1390 Maurach/Schröder/Maiwald, Strafrecht BT I, p. 45, § 2 III, B. 1. e), marginal no. 37; BGH NStZ 93, 183; Jescheck/Weigend, AT, p. 472, § 42 II 3. a).

1391 BGHSt 18, 102 (107); Jescheck/Weigend, Lehrbuch des Strafrechts AT, p. 472, § 42 II 3. a).

1392 Schmidhäuser in the context of general attitude´s characteristics and their peculiarity that "moral- unworthy mental behavior" is specified in the objective elements of fact. (Schmidhäuser, Gesinnungsmerkmale, p. 217; Schmidhäuser, Strafrecht AT, p. 455).

enable him to draw a conclusion towards the required motive[1393], it is noteworthy that here, in the area of homicide, where the legal regulation technique is different from such of other offenses, the recognition of a bias motive as aggravated facts is judicial established and thereby implemented in the practice of German courts[1394]; whereas in the area of violent crimes and other offenses the judiciary might not necessarily consider such[1395]. But, even though the killing of others because of bias towards race, ethnic origin, nationality, and the further is penalized by means of statutory enhancement according to homicide, this enhancement does not go beyond the general enhancement established in Section 211 Penal Code which, in the case of killing another person out of certain base motives is applied in several distinct criminal murder cases, all such named in this section. Therefore, the killing because of other base motives, such as, for instance, greed or envy, is equated in terms of punitive action with such for hate crimes. While some of the American literature assume that the motivations of a hate crime offender are more condemnable than the exampled motivations of greed and envy and therefore are ought to be punished distinct from each other, the principal recognition of hate crime motives as base motives by German courts reveals the basic unified opinion of legal scholars in Germany that hate crime motives are particularly despicable and the penalty which is to be imposed shall be legitimately enhanced. For that purpose, this standard specifies the maximum penalty of up to 25 years. Yet, it is not clear, whether the legal technique in the overall code provides for the implementation of this unified acknowledgement.

If criminal offenses against certain victim groups are not even recognized as racist, xenophobic or homophobic, etc. - because there aren't any legal facilities for the verifiable and compelling investigation of the bias motivation - such can not lead to a penal-aggravating consideration of the motive at the end of trial. Whereas, according to the killing of another human being, these legal facilities due to the special regulation technique in combination with the nowadays settled case law exist in practice might exist, such are missing in other areas of the law, because the usual regulation technique which is applied in reference to other offenses is different with the result that the proper recognition of the hate crime motivations of a perpetrator during trial is uncertain[1396].

1393 Jescheck/Weigend, Lehrbuch des Strafrechts AT, p. 472, § 42 II 3. a).

1394 "A killing by reason of 'xenophobia' is to be considered as a base motivation in the sense of Section 211 Penal Code." (BGH January 12, 2000 - StB 15/99, marginal no. 9).

1395 For clarifications refer to the following Chapter 4., D., 2. Judicial Recognition of Bias-Motivation Apart from Homicide; Chapter 4, D. 3. Hate Crime in the Light of Section 46 Penal Code; and Chapter 4., D., 4. Litmited Verifiability of Judicial Sentencing Practice.

1396 Keiser in: "Public Hearing of the Legal Committee of the German Bundestag on 06/13/2012 to so-called Hate Crime", p. 2; Herzog, in: Mohr/Molthagen, Friedrich-Ebert-Stiftung, Der Aufstand der Zuständigen, Was kann der Rechtsstaat gegen Rechtsextremismus tun?, Ergebnisse einer Konferenz der Friedrich-Ebert-Stiftung am 20. März 2007, pp. 32.33; Refer to the findings of Human Right Watch, Die Reaktion des Staates auf „Hasskriminalität" in Deutschland, Dezember 2011; and such of Glet Sozialkonstruktion und strafrechtliche Verfolgung von Hasskriminalität in Deutschland, 2011, Chapter. II. „Hasskriminalität im Prozess der Strafverfolgung" , p. 186-244; and Krupna, Das Konzept der „Hate Crimes" in Deutschland, 2009.

2. Judicial Recognition of Bias-Motivation Apart from Homicides

A xenophobic-, racist-, or anti-Semitic motivation expressed through the committal of a criminal offense - in the light of the value of the Basic Law and the experiences gained due to the German history - must always be considered as an aggravating factor[1397]. However, the current legal situation in Germany does not provide hate crime offenses that purport to do so. The individual perpetrator of such an act who acts because of hate against race, Jews, homosexuals, or other forms of bigotry or bias-related hate, and thereby kill, bodily injures persons or damage property is punished according to the same standards as the one, whose acts are based on other emotions, such resulting from personal relationships and conflicts. The distinct fact that a hate crime victim at the time of the attack is inoffensively, rather contributed nothing to the emerged tort-situation, because he and the perpetrators have never met before[1398], so that the victim neither incurred the perpetrator's hatred, nor could he be able to expect such[1399], since the criminal assault occurs purely because of personal prejudices of the offender against the victim's personified qualities, is not explicitly considered by the German penal law, neither in the constituent elements of facts, nor in legislation addressing the sentencing level. Thus, the difference between treating someone unfavorably because of previous contact between human beings and treatment of someone, because he is of a certain race or because of personal characteristics associated with race (such as hair texture, skin color, or certain facial features), beliefs, sexual preferences and further subjective characteristics is however, recognized by the legislator[1400], but no difference is made in the current law established in the Penal Code. It is partly agreed upon the fact that not only the culpability of a hate crime perpetrator is increased, but also, the wrongs committed by perpetrators of hate crimes are considered to be greater than those committed by offenders who are not motivated by bias[1401]. It is also undisputed in the German criminal law, that "[t]he level of culpability [...] primarily depends on the severity of the personally realized wrong"[1402]. In that regard, due to the lack of a separate offense for hate crimes, the greater wrong of a hate crime act is not acknowledged by the legislature in the offense level. Due to the same fact

1397 Statement of Lehmann in: "Public Hearing of the Legal Committee of the German Bundestag on 06/13/2012 to so-called Hate Crime", p. 1.

1398 (Perry, In the Name of Hate, p. 29) It is not compelling for the establishment of a hate crime that offender and victims indeed are strangers to each other or, have never met. Surely, perpetrator and victim could be from the same area or have met in the past, decisive is only that the emotions of the perpetrator, which led to the attack on the victim, did not occur from the personal relationship to the victim, but that the victim was selected due to certain features which caused the perpetrator to view the victim as a representative of a group and him to be inferior and have no or a least right to exist and the attack on the victim therefore is committed for the symbolic reason of harming an entire group of humans.

1399 View hereto: Chapter 4., G., 1.1.1. Human Dignity of the Immediate Victim; moreover Herzog, in: Mohr/Molthagen, Friedrich-Ebert-Stiftung, Der Aufstand der Zuständigen, Was kann der Rechtsstaat gegen Rechtsextremismus tun?, Ergebnisse einer Konferenz der Friedrich-Ebert-Stiftung am 20. März 2007, p. 28.

1400 Proved by the repetitive legal initiatives, view: Chapter 4, C. Legal Dealing with Hate Crime, and the here presented draft bills.

1401 Drs. 577/00; Chapter 4, C., 6. Draft Bill of Brandenburg Drs. 577/00, dated September 26, 2000.

1402 BGHSt 10, 38; Fischer, § 46 StGB, marginal no. 6.

the increased culpability, which reasons a penalty[1403], is legally not considered either. A punishment therefore ranges in the frame of punishment established for the general, not hate-motivated, base offense which sentence refers to the relevant underlying criminal behavior only. But in any case, the increased culpability of a hate crime offender is to be taken into account during sentencing in accordance with Section 46 Penal Code, so that at least the culpability, which is relevant in the individual case[1404], is considered in the context of sentencing[1405] - and thereby, the offenders of hate crime could possibly be punished severe.

3. Hate Crime in the Light of Section 46 Penal Code

The definition of "culpability", used in Section 46, Paragraph 1 Penal Code, refers to the individual, specific action related culpability - to the culpability, which is relevant in the individual case[1406]. Unlike the culpability, which reasons a penalty - which in its basic meaning is limited towards the affirming or denial of the perpetrator's criminal liability for the caused wrong - the culpability, which is relevant in the individual case, is accessible for judicial quantification[1407], since it is agreed upon the fact that the concrete penalty must be imposed according to the individual culpability in the range of the penal frame, which is provided abstractly, in reference to the committed offense[1408]. This quantification is mainly based on the degree of the indebted wrong of the individual action committed by the offender and its outcome[1409]. Thus, in reference to the individual culpability of the offender when committing a hate crime the sentence could be adjusted upward in the range of the once for the base offense set up penal frame, since such is principally sufficient when aiming at purely punishing the underlying criminal behavior. These so-called sentencing rates, according to which the degree of culpability of a perpetrator must be defined in order to precisely determine his individual penalty, are established in Section 46 Penal Code. Such states:

"Principles of sentencing

1403 "Strafbegründungsschuld".

1404 "Strafzumessungsschuld".

1405 There are not just distinct degrees according the culpability, but also lighter and heavier degrees of wrong. This has a practical effect on the culpability, since, among other things, such depends on the wrong: "The culpability weighs, ceteris paribus, the heavier, the larger the negative value of wrong is." In particular, the increasing ability of the wrong has a direct impact on the culpability, which reasons penalty, therefore it is incorrect to acknowledge the degrees of culpability only in the sentencing doctrine. (Kern, Grade der Rechtswidrigkeit, in: ZStW 64, (1952), p. 255; 260 with reference to: Nowakowski, Schweiz. Z. f. Straft. 65. Jahrg. 1950, p. 301(304).

1406 Radtke, in: MK, Vorbem. §§ 38 et seqq., marginal no. 15 with further references; Statement of Radtke in: "Public Hearing of the Legal Committee of the German Bundestag on 06/13/2012 to so-called Hate Crime", p. 6.

1407 Radtke, Schuldgrundsatz und Sicherungsverwahrung. Freiheitsgarantien im zweispurigen Sanktionensystem, in: GA 2011, 636 (pp. 640 et seqq.); Radtke, in: MK, Vorbem. §§ 38 et seqq. marginal no. 15 with further references; Statement of Radtke in: "Public Hearing of the Legal Committee of the German Bundestag on 06/13/2012 to so-called Hate Crime", p. 6.

1408 Statement of Radtke in: "Public Hearing of the Legal Committee of the German Bundestag on 06/13/2012 to so-called Hate Crime", p. 6.

1409 Statement of Radtke in: "Public Hearing of the Legal Committee of the German Bundestag on 06/13/2012 to so-called Hate Crime", p. 6.

(1) The guilt of the offender forms the basis for sentencing. The effects of the sentence, which can be expected for the offender's future life in society, shall be taken into account.
(2) When sentencing the court shall weigh the circumstances in favor of and against the offender. Consideration shall in particular be given to
the motives and aims of the offender;
the attitude reflected in the offence and
the degree of force of will involved in its commission; the degree of the violation of the offender's duties;
the modus operandi and the consequences caused by the offence to the extent that the offender is to blame for them;
the offender's past, his personal and financial circumstances;
his behavior after committing the offense, particularly his efforts to restitute for the harm caused by him, as well as the offender's efforts to reconciliate with the victim.
(3) Circumstances which are already statutory elements of the offense must not be considered[1410]."

Thereby the sentencing principles of Section 46 Penal Code in form of a guideline for courts complement the valuation scale, which the statutory law already has established by determining the penal frame, which constitute the basis for sentencing this specific offense type[1411]. According to Paragraph 2, Sentence 1, the court must weigh circumstances in favor of and against the offender. These are on the one hand aspects of the inner relationship of the perpetrator to his act, on the other hand circumstances of the offense; finally external facts, which are necessary for assessment, must be included in the weighing process[1412]. Reasons for mitigation- and aggravating circumstances therefore are not to be easily compared with each other, but they must be evaluated according to their importance and their seriousness. This can lead to a mutual compensation[1413]. Which circumstances plead for, or against the offender, are not determined by the law, such provide solely an enumeration of facts, which may come into consideration, but such is not complete[1414]. This is because the legal doctrine of Section 46 Penal Code assumes that "there could hardly be a sentencing fact, which in any imaginable case simply and solely have either a criminally aggravating or mitigating effect on punishment"[1415] - hate crimes therefore, represent a case, which is not covered by Section 46 Penal Code: The bias motive does not constitute a circumstance, which can be formulated ambivalent[1416], yet, it does not fit into the dogmatic of Section 46, Paragraph II Penal Code. By Section 46 Penal Code the justness in the individual case shall be secured, which is why

1410 Section 46 Penal Code.
1411 Stree/Kinzig, in: Schönke/Schröder, StGB, § 46, marginal no. 2.
1412 Fischer, StGB, § 46 StGB, marginal no. 25.
1413 Stree/Kinzig, in: Schönke/Schröder, StGB, § 46, marginal no. 6.
1414 Fischer, StGB, § 46 StGB, marginal no. 21.
1415 Stree/Kinzig, in: Schönke/Schröder, StGB, § 46, marginal no. 6.
1416 Without reference to hate crime: Lackner/Kühl, StGB, § 46, marginal no. 32.

motives are not expressly named as aggravating facts, since in such a case the aggravate recognition of such would be imperative – whatever the circumstances in the individual case may be. For the same reason the "aims of the perpetrator" are not specified either. If one keeps in mind that in a violent hate crime the perpetrator commits an act not in the background of a personal dispute or relationship with the victim, but un-induced[1417], "by attack on the physical integrity of the victim [he wants to] express a basic decision of condemnation of the otherness"[1418], it is obvious, that this sort of motivation constitutes a sentencing fact, which "in any imaginable circumstance"[1419] must weigh aggravating. Consequently, there is no room for discretion in the sentencing practices in terms of the fundamental aggravating demerit of a hate crime. However though - according to the legal design of the law - the evaluation of whether hate crime motives are of importance for assessing the penalty and in what proportion such weigh to other facts is up to the court's judgment[1420]. This results from the fact that such in Paragraph 2 named facts for penalty assessment constitute the factual base for the weighing process of sentencing, by solely providing assistance for the court to fulfill its task of quantifying the culpability, which is relevant in the individual case, enabling such to hereinafter impose the individual penalty. After the relevant aspects for assessing the penalty are fully investigated, according to Section 244, Paragraph 2 Code of Criminal Procedure, Section 46 Penal Code provides a discretionary scope regarding the entire assessment process, which can be divided into the following: With the assistance through exemplarily named facts in Section 46 Penal Code, on the basis of a fully enlightened crime scene, the judge at trial shall be able to determine the value of the aspects regarding the point, whether such weigh for or against the perpetrator in the concrete case, and to what dimension such weigh in the one or the other direction[1421]. After a court determined the relevant facts and their value in the respective case, based on the guidelines in Section 46 Penal Code, such then must weigh the once determined facts against each other at its own discretion. Finally the inclusion of the case in the severity scale of the penal frame, stated for the concrete offense must be done[1422]. However, these steps provide plenty of scope for legitimately imposing either an enhanced penalty for a hate crime offender or even a mitigated penalty, based on other circumstances subsumable in Section 46 Penal Code. Thus, according to the current law and its practice of enhancing the penalty for hate crimes according to Section 46 Penal Law, the offenders may be punished severe in cases in which a judge

1417 "Un-induced" in the sense of a lack of provocation and emotions, which have been formed on the basis of a prior contact between perpetrator and victim.

1418 BR-Drs. 26/12 (decision) March 2, 2012, p. 1.

1419 Extraction of the quote, cited in regard to footnote 1414 (Without reference to hate crime: Stree/Kinzig, in: Schönke/Schröder, StGB, § 46, marginal no. 6).

1420 Without reference to hate crime: Stree/Kinzig, in: Schönke/Schröder, StGB, § 46, marginal no. 6.

1421 Streng, in: NK-StGB, § 46 marginal no. 123 (Bulletpoint 3. in the there stated "five-phase-model" followed by the doctrine of the phases of penal assessment) - with further references.

1422 The practical implementation of Section 46 Penal Code however, shall reveal two basic types of procedure: either according to a deliberative review of the most important factors, or by a more emotionally-intuitive approach. The achieved decision probably will not result in a significant difference in adherence to following the one or the other type. Streng, in: NK-StGB, § 46 marginal no. 124.

according to Paragraph 2, Sentence 1 decides that the hate crime motivation is to be considered as an aggravating fact in this specific case and he also gives such an importance to the motivation during his sentence assessment that as a result, other, for instance, mitigating facts, are outweighed by the bias motivation so that in the end an enhancement of penalty can be adjudged at all. Since the motivation did not play a role during the entire trial, in which it is about determining the facts of the statutory law, it is already questionable whether the court at all becomes aware of such in order to implement it in the valuation at the end. While Section 244, Paragraph 2 Code of Criminal Procedure rules that "[i]n order to establish the truth, the court shall, *proprio motu*, extend the taking of evidence to all facts and means of proof relevant to the decision", it - in practice - depends on the court at trial, whether the concrete hate motivation becomes relevant in the individual case, this if the judge decides that the motivation is relevant to his decision. The most intruding point to this handling is that the bias motivation of a hate crime offender must, in any case, be considered aggravating, not is there a possibility to choose whether such could not weigh aggravating, nor must it be up to the consciousness of a court to decide whether such might be compensated by circumstances in favor of the offender[1423]. There is no possibility for a mutual compensation of hate crime motives through other facts which surround the act, so a possibility must not be legally provided[1424]. Anyway, according to the German legal order and their dogmatic the question whether a hate crime shall be punished severe is to be answered by the respective court at trial according to the specific case, and this applies even though, discretion in relation to the principal aggravation of penalty for such offenses must not exist legitimately.

This leads to the question whether the German judicial system closes the gap regarding a clear legal ruling of aggravated sentences for hate crimes by generally taking the bias motive of a hate crime offender into account when constituting the individual sentence, and namely consider such as an aggravating factor pursuant to Section 46 Penal Code with the result that in the end the motive and the therefore enhanced culpability of an offender in practice is principally punished severe - which then also is pronounced in the judgment. Thereby, the evaluation of hate crimes would be left to the judiciary, which, for instance, through consolidated jurisdiction, could lead to the

1423 Special attention must be paid to the fact that courts tend to compensate hate crime motives with alcohol-related disinhibition of an offender in case a blood alcohol content is detected at the time of committing the offense. Thus, the alcoholization of an offender leads to elimination of the hate crime motive during the sentencing process. In judicial practice it even occurs that an order for the withdrawal of prosecution for a hate crime is explained with the reason that the offense has been committed in connection with an alcohol-related disinhibition of the offender. (Glet, Sozialkonstruktion und strafrechtliche Verfolgung von Hasskriminalität in Deutschland, 2011, p. 214 case no. 67; 77; p. 215, case no. 81, p. 220). And this applies, even though a hate crime is not committed because of an "alcohol-related disinhibition" but because of a highly questionable basic attitude of the offender towards his fellow men. (Glet, Sozialkonstruktion und strafrechtliche Verfolgung von Hasskriminalität in Deutschland, 2011, p. 221, case no. 5).

1424 For further explanation view Chapter 4, G., 1., 1.6., 1.6.1., 1.6.1.6.; c) Hate Crime motives are different and Chapter 4, G., 2., 2.3., 2.3.4. Hate Crime motives are to be differentiated from such exemplary named in Section 46 Penal Code.

stringent aggravating recognition of hate crime motives. The regulation of hate crimes would be moved from the legislative to the judicial responsibility[1425].

While the principal demand of considering the motives and aims of an offender when assessing the individual penalty is stated in Section 46, in connection with Section 244, Paragraph 2 Code of Criminal Procedure, the following examines how this principal precept would correctly be followed by every court during the sentencing of a hate crime perpetrator:

According to Section 46, Paragraph 2, Sentence 2 Penal Code "the motives and aims of the offender" are to be considered when assessing the penalty with regard to the inner relation of the offender to the committed act, the circumstances of crime committal, and further to external facts[1426]. With regard to the inner relation of the offender to his criminal act, therefore the bias- and hate motive of a hate crime may be considered as an aggravating fact by a court, but could also be compensated in the "dogmatical correct" way, according to Section 46 Penal Code, in the context of the overall scene through a different direction of assessment by the court focusing on mitigating facts, as stated above. Also it is referred to "the attitude reflected in the offense"[1427], which plays a role in hate crime offenses, because such are commonly committed by aggravating modalities, for instance, an increased brutality und recklessness of the offenders can be revealed when committing the statutory elements of fact[1428]. In addition, an excess of the normal level of threatened evil, connected to the committal of menacing, which is usually also committed with most violent offenses must be included. Since the harming of further legal goods must be considered aggravating[1429], also the inhuman,

1425 Referring the example of Section 211 Penal Code, which in the context of homicides considers aggravating subjective circumstances and therefore enhances the temporary imprisonment to life sentence (which in Germany is limited to 25 years of imprisonment), it is seen that the German law mentions so-called aggravating subjective motives but does not suggest racial hatred, nor hostility to foreigners, nor similar hate crime constituent features, instead rather let the judiciary decide that racial hatred is a special aggravating murder feature which is to be categorized as a low motive, for this decision the judiciary required several years. (According the matter that a general shift of the final evaluation of the act takes place through Section 46 Penal Law, view: Schönke/Schröder, § 46 StGB, marginal no. 6). This applies, even though, in the past, the intention to kill in the case of hate crime prosecution (particularly in regard to xenophobic arson offenses) was denied formulaic. Initially the intention to kill was denied and the defendants were punished for assault resulting in death (Section 227 Penal Code) instead of murder (Section 211 Penal Code), even though the victim, Amadeu Antonio Kiowa Angolans, was attacked with knives and baseball-bats and one of the offenders jumped on his head at the end of the killing attack (view judgment in12/05/1993, LG Frankfurt/Oder). Profound with respect to the change in direction of the judicial handling/court dealings according hate crime, which in the past paid little or illegitimate attention to hate crime motives to now finally acknowledging these kind of motives as base motives (in the meaning such gains in Section 211 Penal Law) view Seehafer, Strafrechtliche Reaktionen, 2003, pp. 34-39.

1426 Fischer, StGB, § 46, marginal no. 25.

1427 The "way of committal" is referred to such facts which surround the act or otherwise characterizes it (BGHSt 37, 154 [with note of Grasick, JZ 91, 933]; Fischer, StGB, § 46, marginal no. 32). With the "mind reflected in the act" it is not referred to a general attitude of the offender, but to the mind reflected in the concrete single criminal act, such points outward through the way of committal, meant is: crude, malicious, unscrupulous, cruel, ruthless. (Fischer, StGB, § 46, marginal no. 26).

1428 Since the perpetrators consider their victims as lower regarding their social value and deny their right to exist (at least in the (German) society), the perpetrators are more violent at any rate during the attack. This can be reasoned already due to such in their actions inherent destruction-, or expulsion thoughts. This already increased brutality is often multiplied by the use of additional equipment, for instance, through the use of combat boots.

1429 NStZ – RR 00, 104; Fischer, StGB, § 46, marginal no. 25.

humiliating expression, which surrounds the conduct, must at least be considered, as these corresponding expressions establish the offense of insult[1430], by fulfilling the respective legal criteria[1431]. It is questionable, whether these aspects during the consideration of a hate crime and its typically associated further violation of several legal goods is considered on the level of sentencing or whether such fades on the competition level. Those, in a legal process considered, but subordinately treated offenses, yet such which are at least partially consumed on the competition level, precisely are those typical features, by which a hate crime act becomes clearly visible to the outside[1432], and therefore should be recognized with special attention by a court. However, such must be considered as aggravating facts, since, exemplified by the also committed offenses of insult and menacing, such constitute the outer substance of the despicable and damage-intensifying motive and thereby constitute an own and independent criminal value; after all, through such, the overall harm is increased by additionally dehumanizing the victim; increasing the amount of threat towards the individual victim, it's group and the overall population[1433]. These effects of an act on the victim or third parties can be attributed as aggravating, if indebted by the perpetrator - which means if such, in the mean of type and severity could have been predicted and for which the offender can be accused[1434] - in reference to hate crimes those are even sought by the respective offenders[1435]. Further previous life and convictions of an offender should be considered at sentencing[1436], because in cases, in which a motive is apparently undiscoverable, the focus in the trial of convicted hate crime offenders is more securely drawn to such motives[1437]. Moreover, those external facts which do not surround the respective criminal act can be considered as well, if such reveal a connection to the offense, or enable the court to draw conclusions to an increased culpability[1438]. Therefore, for instance, legitimate statements of opinions prior to the act, suggesting a xenophobic attitude of the offender and are lived out in the following in a criminal manner must be considered[1439]. Further the masking as an expression

1430 Sections 185, 186, 187 StGB.

1431 The aim of a hate crime offender is to harm the victim in his dignity and debase it as a representative of an - in the eye of the perpetrator - inferior group in order to equally harm the whole group.

1432 According to a study "the expressed xenophobic and racist remarks during crime committal play a decisive [...] at judicial level". (Glet, Sozialkonstruktion und strafrechtliche Verfolgung von Hasskriminalität in Deutschland, 2011, p. 234).

1433 Subsumption according Fischer, StGB, § 46, marginal no. 25.

1434 Fischer, StGB, § 46, marginal no. 34.

1435 One must restrictively take the protection area of the relevant standard into account. According the offense of assault, for example, such is established for the protection of the physical integrity of the actually attacked victim only, and not for the protection of the integrity of "group members". This fact reveals the limitations of the established penal framework which is not geared to the specifics of hate crimes.

1436 Fischer, StGB, § 46, marginal no. 37; 38.

1437 This is why the judicial data storage in case of hate crimes is important; with such information on convicted hate crime offenders the focus could be more securely drawn to such motives during trial.

1438 NStZ 01, 87; Fischer, StGB, § 46, marginal no. 32.

1439 "A general attitude of the offender, his character and his convictions, which did not affect the specific criminal action, must not be taken into consideration". (BGH MDR 1980, 240; BayObLG NStZ 1982, 288 with note Bruns; Theune, in: LK, StGB, § 46, marginal no. 94; cf. BGH NJW1982, 2264 et seqq.). Regarding the wording of Section 46, Paragraph 2, Sentence 2 Penal Code: "the attitude reflected in the offense" , it is recognized that "it becomes clear that the belief that the accused holds, must not be used

of criminal intent[1440] can be subsumed to Section 46 Penal Code, so for instance, the wearing of combat boots or clothing typical for this sort of perpetrator could be justifiable considered as a fact, relevant for assessing the individual culpability, such, especially, if the equipment comes into use during crime committal.

According to the above attempted subsuming of typical features of hate crimes under the generally held sentencing rule of Section 46 Penal Code, a more severe punishment of these offenses - with the necessary information about the nature of these offenses, and the knowledge concerning the specific dimension of wrong realized by these acts - seems, with adequate referral and limited in scope, already applicable under the current design of criminal law. However, applicable and compelling demanded by law, is a theoretical difference, which - for the reason of legitimacy - would have to be compensated in practice. A real actual lack of the current law to address the particular motivation can only be assumed, if such in the end of the prosecution process in fact would not be taken into account - although they must be, according to legitimate criminal understanding. Then, it is that also the need for criminal action could be normatively assigned, especially since even opinions that oppose to the conceptualization of an independent construct of hate crime have assigned that at least in such cases hate crime legislation might help to solve the problem, in which the particular motivation by the current law in fact is not taken into account[1441]. Whereas the problem as such is existent in Germany, even though a direct conclusion from the above presented data to the true existence of the problem can only be assumed, and the lack of expressive legal implementation has just been illustrated, the following examines the practical handlings of hate crimes by the courts. If courts, in a satisfactory manner, apply the not expressly stipulated law in a sufficient way, for instance, by already imposing a stringent adjusted[1442] penalty on hate crime offenders according to the current law, the actual legislation, despite the formal lack of expressing such crimes expressly in the Penal Code, might be legitimate in its actual form and moreover sufficient to combat hate crimes. Less the formal design of the law, but also its actual application and its results are decisive for the legitimacy of the actual legal situation. However, the suspicion occurred that courts, in sentencing practices, hardly discuss hate crimes, yet hate-, and bias- motives are not (always) taken into account adequately[1443]. Therefore, in the following the handlings of hate crimes by the judicial branch with regard to the current precepts established in the Penal Code are examined.

---

against him in isolation from an actual criminal event". (Statement of Lehmann in: "Public Hearing of the Legal Committee of the German Bundestag on 06/13/2012 to so-called Hate Crime", p.1).

1440 Fischer, StGB, § 46, marginal no. 30.

1441 Jacobs/Potter, Hate Crimes: Criminal Law & Identity Politics, 2001, p. 90.

1442 Adjusted refers to the imposition of an aggravated penalty - led by the assumption that the motives of hate crimes legitimately are to be considered during trial and as a result must lead to severe punishment.

1443 Statement of lawyer Keiser in: "Public Hearing of the Legal Committee of the German Bundestag on 06/13/2012 to so-called Hate Crime", p. 2.; Refer to the findings of Human Right Watch, Die Reaktion des Staates auf „Hasskriminalität“ in Deutschland, Dezember 2011.

4. Limited Verifiability of Judicial Sentencing Practice

It is questionable , whether there is just no data available which statistically illustrates the sentence practice of the judiciary according to hate crimes, so that the number of convictions or the sentence imposed is just remained unknown, or if no data exists because courts hardly consider such base motives. Pursuant to Section 244 Paragraph 2 Penal Code, the Court of criminal procedure, "must extend the taking of evidence, ex officio, to all facts and evidence which are of importance to the decision in order to establish the truth"; however, what the court deems relevant for a decision is up to judicial discretion[1444]. So if certain motives are taken into account in the sentencing process - pursuant to Section 46 Penal Code - is not verifiable. The question therefore remains, whether the legal precepts in the context of hate crimes lead to an unreserved, aggravating consideration of the motivations in judicial decisions in practice - in all respective criminal cases. Statistically, it is not covered, how often racist, xenophobic or other motives are considered for sentencing purposes according to Section 46, Paragraph 2 Penal Code, nor at all, which motives are taken into account[1445]. In this regard, there have been several requests on the part of the legislature to apply for a legal study to examine the actual practice of judicial handlings[1446]. In order to examine the actual practice of the judicial branch one would refer to published decisions, which expressly mention hate crime circumstances[1447]. The exact number of verdicts of such a kind is not determined, but an initial indication for a possible not sufficient consideration of the respective motives could be the fact that the search for such did not lead to very many penal decisions, from which it could be concluded that the motive of a hate crime perpetrator is taken into account by every German court[1448]. According to the finding of an investigation

---

1444 In the written reasons for the judgment only those circumstances are mentioned which were taken into consideration when the sentence was formed. According to Section 267, Paragraph 3, Sentence 1 Code of Criminal Procedure only those circumstances shall be cited which have been decisive for the purposes of determining the penalty, i.e. more precisely, those which the trial court has considered to be decisive for the specific case. If a judge is of the opinion that certain motives can be neglected or outweighed by other circumstances and does not affect the degree of penalty of the offender, the hate crime motives as such, will never be mentioned in the verdict. (Statement of lawyer Keiser in: "Public Hearing of the Legal Committee of the German Bundestag on 06/13/2012 to so-called Hate Crime", p. 3).

1445 Human Right Watch, Die Reaktion des Staates auf „Hasskriminalität" in Deutschland, Dezember 2011, p. 22; for available data refer to: Glet Sozialkonstruktion und strafrechtliche Verfolgung von Hasskriminalität in Deutschland, 2011, Chapter. II. „Hasskriminalität im Prozess der Strafverfolgung", p. 186-244; and Krupna, Das Konzept der „Hate Crimes" in Deutschland, 2009.

1446 BT-Drs. 17/8796 Proposal of Bündnis 90/Die Grünen.

1447 In statement of Keiser in: "Public Hearing of the Legal Committee of the German Bundestag on 06/13/2012 to so-called Hate Crime", pp. 2 et seqq.

1448 For demonstration of the declaration that racial and other forms of hate crime are regularly evaluated as an aggravating circumstance by German courts, the Federal Ministry of Justice submitted an incomplete list of 23 spoken sentences from the period of 1995 to 2009 to Human Rights, in which racist, xenophobic, anti-Semitic and right-wing extremist motives were included as aggravating circumstances under Section 46 Penal Code in the verdict. While these data unambiguously demonstrate that racist, as well as other motives, are sometimes considered in the imposition of the penalty, it is not possible to draw the conclusion from 23 cases over a period of 14 years that such factors are generally taken into account by the courts. (Human Right Watch, Die Reaktion des Staates auf „Hasskriminalität" in Deutschland, Dezember 2011, pp. 24,25). Similar assessment of Keiser: It, in any case, is indisputable, "that in this way [of referring to published verdicts] only a few examples could be found for the consideration of various inhuman motives". (in: "Public Hearing of the Legal Committee of the German Bundestag on 06/13/2012 to so-called Hate Crime", p. 2).

regarding the legal treatment of hate crime, it was found that in some cases the motive of the act was not considered in the negotiation of a case[1449], or that even if the presence of such a motive for crime committal was detected, the prosecutor did not consistently demand that such is considered in sentencing according to the precepts of Section 46 Penal Code[1450]. In addition, it is stated that "even if evidence of hatred as a motivation for an offense was present during the trial, the judge did not always take such into account at sentencing"[1451]. The allegation that "the justice is blind in the right eye"[1452] could find a substantiated basis in the assertion that the rate of successfully solved politically motivated violent crimes is below average[1453].

However, from (incomplete) empirical data, a conclusion towards a real, practical deficit according the application of Section 46 Penal Code - and the therefrom drawn precept that the motives of hate crime offenders "usually" do not weigh as aggravating facts during sentencing -, nor towards illegitimacy of the current judicial practice can be drawn; neither can the contrary be proven[1454]. This is based on imponderables, for instance, on contentual vague variables, and the therewith associated possibilities for defining of the police[1455], and the non-comprehensive publication of judgments, etc. Solely the indication exists that the courts, although they already must extend the investigation to such circumstances which are relevant for the determination of the legal consequence of the criminal act according to Section 160, Paragraph

---

1449 Human Right Watch, Die Reaktion des Staates auf „Hasskriminalität" in Deutschland, Dezember 2011, p. 23, with reference to interviews of Human Rights Watch.

1450 Human Rights Watch, p. 23, with reference to interviews of Human Rights Watch.

1451 Human Rights Watch, p. 23, with reference to interviews of Human Rights Watch.

1452 Scholzen, Rechtsextremismus, Gefahr erkannt, Gefahr gebannt?, in: Kriminalistik, 2001, pp. 314-316 (315).

1453 "Hate crimes are considered a non-major offense category; they are overlooked or judged as trivial or as not "real" crimes [...]; "In mild cases, nothing happens" ; (Schneider, Kriminologie der Hassdelikte. Konzeption, Ursachen, Vorbeugung und Kontrolle, in: Bewährungshilfe, 2003, p. 119; idem, Politische Kriminalität: Hassverbrechen, Fremdenfeindlichkeit im internationalen Kontext, Kriminalistik 2001, p. 25; cf. to: "The Detection rate, even in regard to arson attacks, is below the average [...]", "[...] mostly enlightened cases are stopped due to insignificance; even severe hate crimes are called "sins of youth" and are punished by probation without conditions [...]". (Friedman, Toleranz. in. Bundeskriminalamt (ed.): Rechtsextremismus, Antisemitismus und Fremdenfeindlichkeit, 2001, pp. 15- 24 (19); Kubink, Fremdenfeindliche Straftaten, 1997, pp. 93, 95, 153, 155, 164, 246.

1454 A sanctioning weakness, especially a high penalty waiver would, however, have a devastating impact on victims and perpetrators. Whereas a poor success rate in solving and prosecuting criminal behavior always has negative effects on society one must keep the particular nature of hate crime in mind. Hate crimes are usually committed in the name of the majority of the population to oppress minorities. Catch-phrase: "majority against minority" . (Singer, Erfassung der politisch motivierten Kriminalität. In einem neuen Definitionssystem mit mehrdimensionalen Analysemöglichkeiten, Kriminalistik 2004, pp. 33, 34 - even though in the here followed opinion hate crime laws intent to protect all groups equally). Therefore, in the case of hate crime, a poor detection rate has not only negative effects on the willingness of the victim to file a crime report, because he thinks the society supports the acts of the offender, but moreover the misguided reaction to the primary victimization leads to far more damage regarding the so-called secondary victimization than it would do in the case of an ordinary crime: The perpetrator feels encouraged in his assumption that the society secretly and in reality supports his behavior. The confirmation of this assumption promotes relapse. In addition, a lapse reaction of the justice system increases the fear of the crime victims and has a negative impact on the total damage of society. (Schneider, Politische Kriminalität: Hassverbrechen, Fremdenfeindlichkeit im internationalen Kontext, Kriminalistik 2001, p. 25; Schneider, Kriminologie der Hassdelikte. Konzeption, Ursachen, Vorbeugung und Kontrolle, in: Bewährungshilfe, 2003, p. 120).

1455 Radtke, in: "Public Hearing of the Legal Committee of the German Bundestag on 06/13/2012 to so-called Hate Crime", p. 5.

3 sentence 1 Penal Procedural Law, might put their main focus on objective facts and thereby neglect base motivations during their investigations[1456]. It is not known for sure, but it indicates, that in the moment in which it is to the responsibility of the courts to examine the background of an offense and thereby, in the context of taking evidence, further to enlighten the causal factors of a situation without the necessary sensitivity for the detection of evidence according such, not always easy to recognize, motives, the main priority in the context of sentencing is not given to hate- and bias motivations[1457].

5. Conclusion

The real attitude of the judiciary towards crimes committed because of bias- and hate-motivations becomes obvious in the context of jurisdiction surrounding verdicts relating to murder offenses. Whereas in the past the judiciary more often failed to react to hate crimes[1458], and from that time encountered allegations, such as the judiciary would punish xenophobic and extreme right-wing perpetrators of violence crimes insufficiently[1459]; and, according to their tradition, the German courts are "blind on their right eye"[1460], these valuations changed with the precepts of the arson attack in Moelln[1461]. Courts from then on were significantly more willing to affirm a killing intent in the case a hate crime offender burns a building to harm certain minorities[1462], yet, in the case of arson the killing intent of a perpetrator in terms of potential victims is assumed on a more regular basis[1463]. This now followed opinion is

1456 Judicial handlings which neglect the existence of a hate crime motive during trial and finally during the assessment of penalty in turn have a negative impact on the work of the police according the detection of hate crime. "We also know that the motivation of the police is strongly influenced by the [...] feedback given from the judiciary and that an alleged lack of interest of the judicial branch leads to demotivation by the police". (Herzog, in: Friedrich-Ebert-Stiftung, Der Aufstand der Zuständigen, Was kann der Rechtsstaat gegen Rechtsextremismus tun?, Ergebnisse einer Konferenz der Friedrich-Ebert-Stiftung am 20. März 2007, p. 33).

1457 It is not howsoever "complicated" to investigate a hate crime. View FBI guidelines in footnote 1249 for how to detect motives; moreover, there is a repertoire of reference points, whether such being more unusual: tattoos of the defendant (Glet, Sozialkonstruktion und strafrechtliche Verfolgung von Hasskriminalität in Deutschland, 2011, p. 229, case no. 90) or the almost always expressed slurs of the perpetrator during committing the act, and most notably the motive is revealed by the selection of the victims. Anyhow, motives already must play a role during every crime investigation. Therefore, nothing else would apply to a hate crime law.

1458 The killing intent had been denied in a stereotyped manner in the context with right-wing extremist fire bombings, and, curiously, from the political motivation of the defendants, out of all things, the argument for the limitation of their intent derived. (LG Duisburg AZ: 14 Js 411/91: So "it is hardly included in the intentions of a political perpetrator that instead of solidarity with the committed act, the population feels compassionate with the victims. But, exactly that is what was to be expected, if people were killed or children excruciatingly burned"), quoted by Frommel, KJ 1994, 323, p. 337, according to: Seehafer, Strafrechtliche Reaktionen, 2003, p.34, footnote 264.

1459 Wieland, Bürgerrechte und Polizei, Cilip 44, 1993, pp 24, 26; Jahn (1998), p. 23: "laxity"; Frehsee, 1993, p. 161 "great toleration"; Vinke, 1981; Seehafer, Strafrechtliche Reaktionen, 2003, p.34.

1460 Seehafer, Strafrechtliche Reaktionen, 2003, p. 34; Frommel, KJ 1994, pp. 337 et seqq.; Müller-Münch, 1998, pp. 8 et seqq.

1461 Seehafer, Strafrechtliche Reaktionen, 2003, p. 34.

1462 Conclusion of Seehafer, Strafrechtliche Reaktionen, 2003, p. 34, based on: BGH NStZ 1994, 584; BGH NStZ-RR 1996, 35 et seq.; BGH 4 StR 105/95, DVJJ-J 1994, 359; Neubacher, Fremdenfeindliche Brandanschläge, 1998, p. 381.

1463 Internal instructions of the state attorneys general to the public prosecutor led to above illustrated change according the legal penalization practice in reference to arson attacks. The instruction demanded to from now on consider homicides when investigating arson attacks. This was necessary to galvanize the courts

correctly formed whenever one refers to the nature of hate crimes: such are directed against people “whose human dignity and right to exist is denied by the perpetrator“[1464]. While this clear understanding of wrong-increasing content is obvious to the judiciary - after all, at least became so in recent years - in the context of homicide, and this may be reasoned with the special status and regulation technique of this offense in the German law due to its recognition of subjective motives as constituent elements, the specialty of Section 211 Penal Code, however, can not capable explain, why these motivations in the context of personal injury, on a sudden, happen to sometimes not play a role during the practical implementation of the precepts stated in Section 46 Penal Code. This can only be reasoned with unknowingness on behalf of the judiciary[1465] - due to the lack of expression in the current Penal Law to consider hate crimes motives as aggravating facts[1466]; with a lack of interest for true indulging into the matter; maybe sometimes reasons due to internal structures, such as overwork or temporal facts[1467] play a role, so that the adoption of a judgment without the need for justifying an enhanced penalty, since due to not imposing a penal enhancement a separate reasoning in the judgement is not required, is simply too tempting.

Anyway, based on empirical statistics one is not able to ask for normative changes in law. Normative changes are solely necessary if due to the current law the aggravating content of a hate crime is legally not considered which leads to the practical result of a not considered and therefore legally unsolved criminal matter. The coverage of this matter by legal device must be necessary in order to preserve the welfare of a peaceful society. While it is indicated that the assumed severe content of hate crimes is - at least not always - taken into account by the respective court, the following aims at examining what this finding implies for the normative side of the law and, in connection herewith, examine whether there is a need for legal action.

---

regarding the proper sentencing of xenophobic arson attacks. (Neubacher, 1998, p. 112) Since, this was the reason what led to the appropriate change in judicial sentencing of hate crimes committed through arson attacks, the need for a means of interpretation seems to be required in the area of judicial dealings with hate crimes.

1464 Seehafer, Strafrechtliche Reaktionen, 2003, p. 35; Frommel, KJ 1994, 323, pp. 323, 342.

1465 It is noted that a concrete indication that the respective particularly reprehensible motivations of hate crime is actually considered as a special criminal aggravating factor can not be drawn from the commentarial literature, which explains the current version of the law, and is often used by a judge to resolve a case. Therefore, even in the case of unknowingness regarding the principal reprehensibility of such motives, a court will not gain the necessary knowledge if referring to the usual literal material, used for legal interpretation. (Konrad, in his statement to: "Public Hearing of the Legal Committee of the German Bundestag on 06/13/2012 to so-called Hate Crime", pp. 4, 5.). With regard to "unknowingness", it must be referred to footnote 230 and the fact that internal instructions of the State Attorney General to the public prosecutor have been necessary for the respective courts to value the true nature of hate crimes. Such finally led to the changed handlings of the courts according arson attacks.

1466 "In the internal prosecution guidelines it must be made clear that opportunity settings in hate-motivated acts are not eligible in generally." (Herzog, in: Friedrich-Ebert-Stiftung, Der Aufstand der Zuständigen, Was kann der Rechtsstaat gegen Rechtsextremismus tun?, Ergebnisse einer Konferenz der Friedrich-Ebert-Stiftung am 20. März 2007, Forum Berlin, p. 33).

1467 Mohr/Molthagen, in: Friedrich-Ebert-Stiftung, Der Aufstand der Zuständigen, Was kann der Rechtsstaat gegen Rechtsextremismus tun?, Ergebnisse einer Konferenz der Friedrich-Ebert-Stiftung am 20. März 2007, Forum Berlin.

E. Parenthesis

To complete the presentation of the German perspective and a possible need for legislative changes according to hate crimes resulting from German criminal law doctrine, it must be illustrated briefly, whether the need for legal change already follows from European law.

1. European Criminal Law Initiatives

The European Union is a confederation of sovereign states[1468], therefore the power to regulate the sector of criminal law in a Member State - considering the "in particular sensitive area of democratic self-determination in criminal- and criminal procedure provisions"[1469] - in principal completely remains in the competency of each state's legislature. However, it must be recognized that the Modification Agreement of Lisbon, signed on December 13th, 2007 by the twenty-seven Member States, entered into force on December, 1st 2009, "vastly"[1470] expanded the legitimation of the European Union to become involved in the area of criminal law by providing legal possibilities[1471] for harmonizing the criminal law of the Member States[1472].

1.1. Demands of ECRI for Fighting Hate Crime

The European Commission against racism and intolerance (ECRI) is an institution of the Council of Europe, composed of independent members. Its aim is to combat racism, xenophobia, anti-Semitism and intolerance at a pan-

---

1468 Detterbeck, Öffentliches Recht, 2011, p. 500, marginal no. 1103.

1469 BVerfG, 2 BvE 2/08 vom 30.6.2009, Absatz-Nr. (1 - 421), 358; (http://www.bverfg.de/entscheidungen/es20090630_2bve000208.html).

1470 Mansdörfer, Das europäische Strafrecht nach dem Vertrag von Lissabon - oder: Europäisierung des Strafrechts unter nationalstaatlicher Mitverantwortung, in: Strate, HRRS, Heft 1/2010, 11. Jahrgang, (11-23), p. 11; (http://www.hrr-strafrecht.de/hrr/archiv/10-01/index.php?sz=6#_ftn7); BVerfGE NJW 2009, 2267, 2287, marginal no. 352 with note of Terhechte, EuZW 2009, 724; Schorkopf, EuZW 2009, 718; with further information on what this judgment of the BVerfG implies for the area of German Criminal Law, view: Ambos/Rackow, ZIS 2009, 397; Heger, ZIS 2009, 406; Folz, ZIS 2009, 427; Schünemann, ZIS 2009, 393.

1471 The justification of European interference determined in Article 83, Section 1, Subparagraph 1 AEUV, cites certain, not conclusive, areas of criminal law in which criminality "according to its nature or impact of the offense or because of a special need" provides such a cross-border dimension, and therefore necessitates that the crime is fought on a common European basis. (BVerfG, 2 BvE 2/08 vom 30.6.2009, Absatz-Nr. (1 - 421), 359; (http://www.bverfg.de/entscheidungen/es20090630_2bve000208.html).

1472 Since 2009, the European Union has the competence to approximate criminal provisions of the Member States if necessary for legal issues regarding the safety in the European Union, according to Article 67, Section 3 AEUV. However, the use of this competence by the European Union requires a special justification in order to transfer sovereignty in this sensitive area (BVerfG, 2 BvE 2/08 vom 30.6.2009, Absatz-Nr. (1 - 421), 358; (http://www.bverfg.de/entscheidungen/es20090630_2bve000208.html). The competence expansion is not connected to an "overall authorization for a global harmonization of criminal law" (Mansdörfer, Das europäische Strafrecht nach dem Vertrag von Lissabon - oder: Europäisierung des Strafrechts unter nationalstaatlicher Mitverantwortung, in: Strate, HRRS, Heft 1/2010, 11. Jahrgang, pp. 11-23 (12); (http://www.hrr-strafrecht.de/hrr/archiv/10-01/index.php?sz=6#_ftn7); for more detailed information view: Frisch, GA 2007, 250, 271 et seq.), nor must these powers, granted to the EU, lead to the fact that there will not remain any substantial scope for action to the Member States. (According the problems regarding the through Lisbon newly provided responsibilities of the EU and its danger for the preservation of sovereignty to Member States, view: Mansdörfer, Das europäische Strafrecht nach dem Vertrag von Lissabon - oder: Europäisierung des Strafrechts unter nationalstaatlicher Mitverantwortung, in: Strate, HRRS, pp. 11-23 (12); (http://www.hrr-strafrecht.de/hrr/archiv/10-01/index.php?sz=6#_ftn7); BVerfG NJW 2009, 2267, 2274, marginal no. 249, 252, 253; 2287, marginal no. 352 et seqq.; BVerfG NJW 2009, 2267, 2274, marginal no. 253).

European level with focus on human rights[1473]. "One of the pillars of ECRI's work programme is its country-by-country approach, whereby it analyses the situation as regards racism and intolerance in each of the member States of the Council of Europe and makes suggestions and proposals as to how to tackle the problems identified"[1474]. As early as in 2000[1475] the ECRI demanded all EU states to ensure that the criminal law expressly and concrete address racism and xenophobia[1476]. In the second country report on Germany, ECRI recognized that "Germany is a society in which serious incidents of racially motivated violence occur"[1477], and determines that "the existing legal framework and policy measures have not proven to be sufficient to effectively deal with or solve these problems"[1478]. ECRI recommends to the German authorities that further action is to be taken to combat racism, anti-Semitism, xenophobia and intolerance in a number of areas. These recommendations cover, inter alia, the need to ensure that the legal framework aimed at combating these phenomena is adequate and effective; with regard to the field of criminal law it was demanded that actions must take place in order to improve the enforcement of criminal legislation aimed at racist and anti-Semitic crimes. In 2002, it was demanded that the law must provide for an independent specialized body to combat racism and racial discrimination in certain forms, otherwise the law should provide that, for all criminal offenses not specified in a substantive law, racist motivations constitute an aggravating circumstance[1479]. Accordantly, the Council Framework decision of 28 November 2008 on combating certain forms and expressions of racism and xenophobia by means of criminal law rules that Member States shall take the necessary measures to ensure that racist and xenophobic motivation is considered an aggravating circumstance, or, alternatively that such motivation may be taken into consideration by the courts in the determination of the penalties[1480]. German penal law, however, lacks an explicit provision which states that racist motivation should be considered as a specific aggravating circumstance when determining the penalty for the relevant offenses; with

1473 European Commission against racism and intolerance, Second Report on Germany, adopted on 15 December 2000, p. 3 – Foreword.

1474 European Commission against racism and intolerance, Second Report on Germany, adopted on 15 December 2000, p. 3 – Foreword.

1475 A first international signal to constitute instrument in order to ban xenophobic attacks reached the federal government of Germany in 1963, which was sent by the Sub-Commission of the Human Rights Commission (CERD), which issued a Declaration on the "Elimination of All Forms of Racial Discrimination". (Resolution 1904 (XVIII) of November 20, 1963, Centre of Human Rights, Human Rights – A Compilation of International Instruments (1988), p. 52; for further information on the theme view: Better implementation of international commitments in Germany according racial- and xenophobic hate, view: Partsch, EuGRZ 1994, 429 et seqq.

1476 European Commission against racism and intolerance, Second Report on Germany, adopted on 15 December 2000, p. 3 - Foreword.

1477 European Commission against racism and intolerance, Second Report on Germany, adopted on 15 December 2000, p. 4 - Summary.

1478 European Commission against racism and intolerance, Second Report on Germany, adopted on 15 December 2000, p. 4 - Summary.

1479 Furthermore: "The law should provide for effective, proportionate and dissuasive sanctions for the offenses" (European Commission against racism and intolerance, General Policy Recommendation No. 7 on national legislation to combat racism and racial discrimination, adopted on 13 December 2002, p. 8).

1480 Council Framework decision 2008/913/JHA of 28 November 2008 on combating certain forms and expressions of racism and xenophobia, Article 4 "Racist and xenophobic motivation".

regard there to, the consensus of EU Ministers recommended on November 28, 2008 that, according to Article 4 of the Framework Decision of the European Union, Germany "shall continue to work towards the incorporation of a specific provision into its domestic criminal legislation to ensure that ethnic, racial, or religious hatred is taken into account as a criminal aggravating factor in criminal proceedings"[1481]. Moreover, in 2009 again it is stressed[1482] that German authorities shall make "specific provision in the criminal law for racist motivation for ordinary offenses to constitute an aggravating circumstance". Even though ECRI´s conclusions on the implementation of earlier recommendations in 2012[1483] do not refer to criminal legislation, based on the last demand in 2009 and the precepts of Article 4 of the Council Framework decision[1484], it must be said that Section 46, Paragraph 2 Penal Code, includes a general regulation according to which the aims and the motives of the offender must be taken into account when assessing the penalty, thus the second variant of the framework decision could be considered to be implemented in the German penal law[1485]. However, if pointing to the fact of "ensuring" of an aggravating consideration of the respective motive in criminal proceedings, it is to be mentioned that precisely such an "ensuring" may not be guaranteed by the current general regulatory practice. In Germany solely such facts must be mentioned in the written judgment, which at all were part of the sentencing considerations[1486]. Therefore, a judge only cites such circumstances which he considered to be constituent for sentencing and proven for the particular case. Thus, whether a hate crime motive was taken into account sufficiently, it is neither actually verifiable, nor is such verifiable by the judicial appeal stages. If it applies that, in the case of an illegitimate consideration of a respective motive a legal possibility of correction is not provided, in other words, a judicial non-consideration of motives is possible due to a missing verifiability by higher courts, the German law at least does not guarantee that bias motives are fully elucidated in criminal proceedings. An obligation to guarantee the investigation of bias motives is said to already

1481 Statement made of the Committee of the United Nations for the Elimination of Racial Discrimination at its 73rd Session in 2008 in the part regarding Germany with reference to Para. 26, according Konrad in: "Public Hearing of the Legal Committee of the German Bundestag on 06/13/2012 to so-called Hate Crime", p. 7.

1482 "ECRI strongly recommends that the German authorities make specific provision in the criminal law for racist motivations for ordinary offenses to constitute an aggravating circumstance, taking account of the recommendations contained in ECRI's General Policy Recommendation No. 7 on national legislation to combat racism and racial". (ECRI Report on Germany, (4th monitoring cycle), adopted on 19 December 2009, p. 14).

1483 ECRI conclusions on the implementation of earlier recommendations in respect of Germany, adopted March 23rd, 2012.

1484 Article 4 of the Council Framework decision 2008/913/JHA of November 28th, 2008 on combating certain forms and expressions of racism and xenophobia states: "For offenses [...] Member States shall take the necessary measures to ensure that racist and xenophobic motivation is considered an aggravating circumstance, or, alternatively that such motivation may be taken into consideration by the courts in the determination of the penalties."

1485 So considered by: Keiser, ZRP 2010, 46 et seqq.

1486 According to Section 267, Paragraph 3, sentence 1 Code of Criminal Procedure only such circumstances are to be mentioned in a verdict, which for the purpose of determining the penalty have been considered to be decisive by the respective court. (Keiser, in: "Public Hearing of the Legal Committee of the German Bundestag on 06/13/2012 to so-called Hate Crime", p. 3).

occur from the command of equality in accordance with Article 3, Section 3 Basic Law, and not least from the prohibition of discrimination, Article 14 ECHR[1487], and its interpretation by the European Court of Human Rights[1488]. However, an express legal wording, implemented in Section 46, Paragraph 2 Penal Code – as recommended in by ECRI for Germany in 2009[1489] - would not lead to a change regarding the uncertainty based on lacking verifiability. Because of the dogmatics of Section 46 Penal Code, an implementation into this law can not lead to a legally verifiable order of considering certain motives as aggravating facts during sentencing. The legal assessment of penalty would still remain to the discretion of the respective court, this, despite an express inclusion of the demand to consider certain motives as aggravating facts. A decision would remain reversible only in the case that the reasons which led to the verdict are not stated, or just an overall lack of reasoning is provided[1490]. A circumstance, which is relevant for determining the individual sentence in the concrete case, however, does not become constituent and thus mentioned in the verdict through the fact that such is listed by name as an example in the law, but only if and when it specifically played a role in the case at issue and is considered to have been decisive when determining the individual punishment[1491].

Whereas an expressive naming of hate crime motives in the framework of Section 46, Paragraph 2 Penal Code surely could lead to a signal for courts, which then would have to deal with such in the base norm for general penalty assessment outlined specifically mentioned criteria during investing the actual fact; moreover a strengthening of the victims[1492], as well as value-based signals[1493] towards the perpetrators would be sent, but - due to the specific German legal practice and its establishment of legal decisional scopes surrounding the judicial dealings in accordance with Section 46 Penal Code - a guarantee through common constitutional control mechanism, "that ethnic,

1487 Keiser, in her statement to: "Public Hearing of the Legal Committee of the German Bundestag on 06/13/2012 to so-called Hate Crime", p. 9, with reference to the following verdicts: EGMR, verdict of May 31, 2007 -40116/02 Secic/Kroatien; view, especially in regard to the investigation of potentially racist motives, EGMR (Grand Chamber), verdict of July 6, 2005 – 43577/98 and 43579/98 Nachova et al../Bulgarien; cf. EGMR, verdict of March 4, 2008, Stoica v. Romania, Application No. 42722/02.

1488 ECRI Report on Germany, (4th monitoring cycle), adopted on 19 December 2009, p. 14; Keiser, in her statement to: "Public Hearing of the Legal Committee of the German Bundestag on 06/13/2012 to so-called Hate Crime", p. 8; with reference to: Weiß, in: Sieber/Brüner/Satzger/v. Heintschel-Heinegg (eds.), Europäisches Strafrecht, 2011, § 25, 424; Stoltenberg, ZRP 2012, 120.

1489 After acknowledging that "Section 46 Penal Code contains a list of circumstances to be taken into account in sentencing offenders, which include the motives and the aims of the offender. [But, however] [r]acist motivations are not explicitly listed as an element to be taken into account as a specific aggravating circumstance in sentencing." ECRI "[...] recommended that the German authorities explicitly provide in law that racist motivations constitute an aggravating circumstance for all offenses. (European Commission against racism and intolerance, 4th Report on Germany, adopted on 19 December 2008, p. 13).

1490 Stree/Kinzig, in: Schönke/Schröder, -StGB, § 46 marginal no. 65.

1491 Keiser, in: "Public Hearing of the Legal Committee of the German Bundestag on 06/13/2012 to so-called Hate Crime", p. 6.

1492 Highlighted as a positive side effect of explicit wording by Konrad, in his statement to: "Public Hearing of the Legal Committee of the German Bundestag on 06/13/2012 to so-called Hate Crime", pp. 8, 9.

1493 Herzog, ZRP 2001, pp. 393, 397.

racist, or religious based hatred is considered as an aggravating circumstance in the legal process" [1494] is still not provided.

These issues are addressed in the following. Moreover, several possibilities to implement legal devices in the German Penal Code which could ensure the aggravating consideration of hate crime motives are analyzed according to precepts of dogmatical practicability.

1.2. Demands of the OSCE for Fighting Hate Crime

The Organization for Security and Co-operation in Europe (OSCE)[1495] follows a "comprehensive approach to security that encompasses politico-military, economic and environmental, and human aspects"[1496]. The human dimension refers to the protection of human rights and fundamental freedoms[1497]. Germany, one among the fifty-six member states, agreed in 2003[1498] "to consider enacting or strengthening, where appropriate, legislation that prohibits discrimination based on, or incitement to hate crimes [...]"[1499]. In 2009, the participating states were yet again asked to "[e]nact, where appropriate, specific, tailored legislation to combat hate crimes, providing for effective penalties that take into account the gravity of such crimes"[1500]. The OSCE describes crimes "motivated by intolerance towards certain groups in society" as hate crimes and emphasizes that "such crimes have the potential to divide societies, and to "create cycles of violence and retaliation" and therefore promote for an explicit and active combat against such offenses, emphasizing that criminal laws are important in the fight against racism, xenophobia, anti-Semitism, and violence based on intolerance and discrimination towards "race, color, sex, language, religion, political or other opinion, national or social origin, property, birth or other status"[1501], in general towards the howsoever specified "others" in society[1502]. The OSCE leaves the criminal embodiment in order to capture hate crimes to its Member States and only provide a guide, to which the states are able to orientate themselves in order to adopt appropriate criminal legislation according to their specific requirements[1503]. Based on the provided precepts, the OSCE demand the enactment of specific hate crimes law, but do not significantly choose the establishment of substantive laws over penalty enhancement laws or over a

1494 Excerpt from Article 4 of the Framework Decision.
1495 http://www.osce.org (accessed: January 2012).
1496 http://www.osce.org/who (accessed: January 2012).
1497 OSCE/ODIHR, Hate Crime Laws- A practical guide, 2009, p. 7.
1498 In Maastricht the Ministerial Council meeting was held on December 2nd, 2003.
1499 Permanent Council Decision No. 621 "Tolerance and the Fight Against Racism, Xenophobia and Discrimination".
1500 In Decision No. 9/09, second day of the Seventeenth Meeting, MC (17) Journal No. 2, Agenda item 8, of the Ministerial Councils Meeting of the Organization for Security and Co-operation in Europe, held on December 2nd, 2009 in Athens on the subject "Combating Hate Crimes" the Ministerial Councils provided several aspects in encoring the Member States to actively address Hate Crimes, with one of them referring to legal obligations. (http://www.osce.org/cio/40695 - accessed: January 2012).
1501 Decision No. 621 of the Permanent Council. Tolerance and the fight against racism, xenophobia and discrimination (PC. DEC/621 from July 29, 2004); (view at: http://www.osce.org/pc/35610).
1502 OSCE/ODIHR, Hate Crime Laws- A practical guide, 2009, pp. 5, 7.
1503 OSCE/ODIHR, Hate Crime Laws- A practical guide, 2009.

combination of approaches[1504], however, the disadvantage of the German way of implementing a penalty enhancement for hate crimes is illustrated with regard to the fact that the court's decision to enhance the penalty on the basis of a bias motive is not part of the public record, which, in addition to the here stated problems of unverifiability of judicial dealings, lead to the consequence that a criminal history of the accused cannot be used to determine whether he or she has a past history of hate crimes[1505], which is an important piece of information, since – in case – such could help investigation authorities to draw their focus on the search for such motives in a future prosecution process.

The OSCE and the conclusion of agreements of the participating member states do not create legally binding norms and principles. They are solely political commitments and not legal enforceable so that the German legislator must not follow these precepts[1506]. However, the sole political agreements made among the member states of the OSCE may serve as a basis for legally binding standards, so occurred when the Member States of the Council of Europe signed the enactment of the Framework Convention for the protection of National Minorities on February 1st, 1995 into force, which based on a set of standards for the protections of minorities drafted by the OSCE earlier[1507].

2. Conclusion

The illustrated international obligation could require the establishment of a substantive law if the general rule in Section 46, Paragraph 2 Penal Code which enables the possibility to consider motives and which is applicable to hate crimes motivations, is not sufficient to address hate crime. The question whether a general norm, which does not explicitly list hate crime motivations as an element to be taken into account as a specific aggravating circumstance in sentencing, is sufficient to criminally address hate crimes is crucial for the decision whether the Penal Code requires the implementation of a specific hate crime norm. According to European measurements, a particular concern lies in the fact of the absence of an explicit reference to racist motivations in the German Penal Code. Such a reference should expressly mention these motives as an aggravating circumstance for ordinary offenses which contribute to this phenomenon; since without such a norm neither police nor prosecutors nor judges have any explicit legal basis on which to look beyond extremist motivations in their investigations, the charges they bring or the judgments they deliver[1508]. A failure to take the racist motivation of an offender into

1504 OSCE/ODIHR, Hate Crime Laws- A practical guide, 2009, pp. 32 et seqq.

1505 OSCE/ODIHR, Hate Crime Laws- A practical guide, 2009, p. 36.

1506 Office for Democratic Institutions and Human Rights, Politically binding commitments; (http://www.osce.org/odihr/43676 (accessed in: January 2012)).

1507 Such took place when human right violations increased in the early 1990´s and the OSCE reacted to this phenomenon by drafting a set of regulations to protect minorities. These only political binding standards where then insofar transformed into legally binding rules due to the fact that the Council of Europe in Strasbourg agreed on standards for the protection of minorities which wear initially drafted by the OSCE in the field of minority protection. (http://www.osce.org/odihr/43676 (accessed in: January 2012); http://www.coe.int/t/dghl/monitoring/minorities/1_AtGlance/PDF_H%281995%29010_FCNM_ExplanReport_en.pdf (accessed in: January 2012); http://conventions.coe.int/Treaty/en/Treaties/html/157.htm (accessed in: January 2012).

1508 ECRI Report on Germany, (4th monitoring cycle), adopted on 19 December 2009, pp. 8, 14.

account in the current legal (prosecution) practice may leave Germany at risk of breaching the European Convention on Human Rights; thereby the attention of the German authorities is drawn to the consistent case law of the European Court of Human Rights in this field[1509]. Furthermore, the lack of review of the effectiveness of the existing criminal law provisions in the areas of hate crimes is considered to be apprehensive[1510]. Insofar the European institutions alleged considerable concern of the current law, stating that racism could be understood only in its strongest forms, and in particular as a manifestation of right-wing extremism and thereby less obviously extreme manifestations of racism tend to be neglected as such in the criminal process, with the result that some racist offenses are not treated as such at all[1511]. The necessity to enact hate crime legislation in Germany therefore could result from international obligations; the answer depends on the following findings whether such laws could be legitimized by criminal precepts.

F. Brief Review

Before beginning with the eligibility check one is reminded of the different hate crime statutes effectuated in the United States which impose penalties for hate and bias-motivated criminal behavior.

Hate/bias crime legislation takes many forms and often specifies a number of different governmental objectives[1512]. One of them is the competence of governmental agencies to gather information about the relative number of hate- and bias-motivated offenses committed in their jurisdiction in specified time periods[1513]. The main impact, however, refers to the criminal law sector and the here enacted legislation that contains sentencing enhancement statutes that authorize or require the enhancement of criminal penalties when already criminally-prohibited actions are performed as a result of offenders' hatred or bias against a victim, based on his race, ethnicity, religion, gender, disability, or sexual preference, etc. All means combined result in the American Hate and Bias Crime concept. This concept, how it is followed in the United States, is the embrace of phenomenon's as xenophobia, anti-Semitism and right-wing radicalism which are put into a wider social context in order to make out the theoretic basic mechanism as an approach to solve the problem associated with such phenomenon[1514].

1509 ECRI Report on Germany, (4th monitoring cycle), adopted on 19 December 2009, p. 14 with reference to: Šečić v. Croatia, Application No. 4357740116/02, 31 May 2007, § 67; Anguelova and Iliev v. Bulgaria, Application No. 55523/00, 26 July 2007, § 115; view also EGMR, verdict of 4 March 2008, Stoica v. Romania, Application No. 42722/02.

1510 ECRI Report on Germany, (4th monitoring cycle), adopted on 19 December 2009, p. 13.

1511 ECRI Report on Germany, (4th monitoring cycle), adopted on 19 December 2009, p. 14.

1512 Hurd/Moore, Punishing Hatred and Prejudice, Illinois Public Law and Legal Theory Research Papers Series, No. 03-17, 2003, p. 5.

1513 Such a piece of law is established by the Hate Crime Statistics Act, 28 U.S.C. § 534 (HCSA); view Chapter 3, D., 1., 1.2. Hate Crime Statistic Act of 1990.

1514 Schneider, Internationales Handbuch der Kriminologie, Bd. II, p. 298.

The majority of hate crime laws represent itself as penalty enhancement laws, without differentiation whether such present itself as aggravating statutes of an existent law[1515], special aggravating legislation[1516], or just as aggravating assessment of penalty[1517]. In the U.S. the jury or the judge is able to find the defendant guilty of a hate crime, if it becomes evident beyond a reasonable doubt during trial that the inner context between the specific motivation and the action as it is established in the hate crime norm manifests itself in the committed offense[1518]. Whenever such motives of the offender become subject to trial and prove to be relevant for committing the respective crime, this fact will lead to the imposition of the enhanced penalty according to the application of the respective hate crime regulation. The frequent case is that the jury determines those statements of facts which constitute a hate crime, thus decides whether the relevant motivation was causally to commit the crime. The judge in accordance to this determination applies the enhanced penalty provided for a hate crime. The extent of the increase is either left to the judge or the relevant hate crime enhancement stipulates an automatic penalty increase[1519]. Statutes constituting the aggravation of a previously enacted law are usually freestanding in the formal sense only[1520]; this applies - according to the German understanding - if they protect the same legal good as the "base" offense does. In this case - to the German understanding - they therefore are to be considered as penalty enhancement laws. Frequently they just determine an aggravating assessment of penalty in case the discussed offense constitutes a hate crime; regardless of the manner used, the result is always the enhancement of penalty.

Pure, i.e. real hate crime statutes are considered as "true" new legislation, if referring to the criminalization of behavior that haven´t been punished yet, but due to its bias relation become penalized. Other than usual hate crime offenses which are based on a previously punished behavior, these norms refer to previously unpunished behavior which evidence racist motives; thus the committal of the act can be explained for only one reason: that is the bias motivation of the perpetrator that causes additional damage. Insofar there are two types of legislation considered as pure hate crime laws in the United States:

1. Civil Right laws - punishing the by bias-motivated interference with the free exercise of rights.
2. Intimidation statutes - punishing harassing, intimidating, mostly menacing behavior, which by the bias component (due to behavior manifesting a racial-, religious-, or any other reference) becomes

1515 "Qualifizierende Tatbestände".
1516 "Besonders schwere Fälle".
1517 "Strafzumessungsregeln".
1518 Wisconsin v. Mitchell, 113 S. Ct. 2194 (1993); view Chapter 3, F. The Standards set by the U.S. Supreme Court.
1519 Aydin, Die strafrechtliche Bekämpfung von Hassdelikten, p. 96.
1520 Lawrence, The Punishment of Hate: Towards a Normative Theory of Bias-Motivated Crimes, 93 Michigan Law Review, 1994, pp. 320 et seqq. (p. 326, footnote 20).

harassing at all[1521] (cross burning laws; fighting words acts; mask wearing laws)[1522].

Therefore, three different modes of imposing penalties upon a hate crime offender, all increasing the penalty in comparison to the penal imposed for non-motivated crimes: Statutes which solely increase the scale of punishment, penalty enhancement laws, Civil Right Laws that protect the exercise of Civil Rights, and so-called real/pure hate crimes laws that punish previously unpunished behavior due to its additional damage, usually it is referred to intimidating/harrassing/menacing effects caused by the offender´s motivation. However, with regard to the need of a cause of threat in substantial hate crime laws called intimidation statutes, it is important to consider that it must be enough if the prima facie evidence has an intent to intimidate a person or a group of persons. This reversal of the burden of proof, referring to the intent of the perpetrator to intimidate his victim, proves that within such laws it is about sanctioning the racist activity.

The American way of justifying hate crime legislation and the thereby included enhanced punishment of hate crime offenders is mainly based on the following criminal law theories[1523]:

1. the equality thesis, which views hate crime legislation as a means of evenly distributing the "state-produced good" of protection against crime[1524];
2. the expressive theory of punishment, which argues that the criminal law can and should be used as a tool for expressing society's commitment to the norm against prejudice[1525];
3. the greater wrongdoing thesis, which postulates that a hate crime increases the harm caused towards the immediate attacked victim due to an intensification of the psychological and/or physical harm, but additional not only harm its immediate victim (as all crimes do), but

---

1521 In those states where intimidation or menacing statutes are enacted, hate crime intimidation statutes would be based on such and therefore would be considered as penalty enhancement laws instead of pure/substantive hate crime laws.

1522 These laws are the constitutional most questioned, since they must not interfere with the First Amendment of the Constitution, however they don't, if they constitute fighting words acts. Fighting words refer to such expressed opinions "which are likely to make the person to whom they are addressed commit an act of violence" . Fighting words are not protected by the First Amendment, because, like other unprotected categories (for example, defamation, obscenity, etc.) they are not an exposition of ideas but clearly harassing. (View footnote 1057; Silver/Stein/Surman/Thompson; Fighting Words, at: http://www.bsos.umd.edu/gvpt/gvpt339/fightingwords.html - accessed 2011/09/09).

1523 Kim, Hate Crime Law and the Limits of Inculpation, Nebraska Law Review, 2006, Vol. 84, pp. 846-894 (848).

1524 Harel/Parchomovsky, On Hate and Equality, 109 YALE L.J., 1999, pp. 507 et seqq. (509); Kim, Hate Crime Law and the Limits of Inculpation, Nebraska Law Review, 2006, Vol. 84, pp. 846-894 (848).

1525 Kahan, The Anatomy of Disgust in Criminal Law, 96 Mich. Law. Rev., 1998, pp. 1621, 1641 ("We expect punishment to voice our moral outrage, in addition to protecting us from harm and imposing deserved suffering."); Kim, Hate Crime Law and the Limits of Inculpation, Nebraska Law Review, 2006, Vol. 84, pp. 846-894 (848).

causes greater injury to the victim's community and society at large[1526]; and

4. the culpability thesis, which posits that hate crime offenders are more blameworthy than offenders who commit crimes without the hateful motive[1527].

Similar to these theses the American legislature frequently provided reasoning prefixed to the actual hate crime law which describes the function of hate crime legislation and the understandable aim of combating hate crime[1528].

However, the question of the function and meaning of a sentence must be distinguished from the question of its justification[1529]. Whereas from all the above stated theories the quite understandable purposes for enhanced criminal punishment becomes evident, the answer whether the penal norms, which are established to achieve these aims, are legitimate is missing. This must be answered, according to this understanding, by referring to the Harm Principle if justifying in accordance to American standards, whereas in Germany the legal good doctrine must be used as a tool to determine and limit the legitimate ambit of criminal norms[1530]. Whether hate crime legislation is legitimate according to the Harm Principle is to be questioned by American scholars, the following will examine whether hate crime legislation could be legitimized according to the German dogmatical understanding of criminal law according to the precepts of the legal good doctrine. Thereby the findings proclaimed by the above mentioned theories are partially addressed in brief at the appropriate point. Therefore, the German perspective of criminal law is based on U.S. legitimation grounds for justifying U.S. hate crime legislation in order to evaluate whether such could be legitimately implemented in the German Penal Code in similar ways[1531].

Motives - except in such offenses in which they are explicitly established[1532] - usually are considered according to Section 46 Penal Code: by the judge in the context of assessing a sentence[1533]. Basically, the relationship between criminal law and the legal value which protection is aimed at is in the focus of

---

1526 Lawrence, Punishing Hate, 2003, pp. 39-44. (The main source for the American scholarly, non-empirical illustration of greater harms associated with hate crimes).

1527 Lawrence, Punishing Hate, 2003, pp. 58–61 - who explains that the hate crime offender (he calls them Bias Crimes) is more culpable because of his motive under either consequentialist or deontological theories of punishment); Lawrence, The Punishment of Hate: Toward a Normative Theory of Bias-Motivated Crimes, 93 Mich.L.Rev., 1994, p. 343.

1528 NY State Penal Code § 485.00; Wash. Rev. Code § 9A.36.078.

1529 Jescheck/Weigend, Strafrecht AT, p. 66. For additional information on the differentiation between the function of law and its justification view Chapter 4, C., 8. Symbolic Reasoning of Hate Crime Law.

1530 Hirsch, in: Hefendehl/v. Hirsch/Wohlers, Die Rechtsgutstheorie, p. 14.

1531 For methodological explanations view Chapter 1, D., 2. The Functional Method of Comparative Law.

1532 "[...] out of rawness" Section 17 No. 2 a) TierSchG; "[...] with the intention of [...]" Section 242 Paragraph I StGB; "[...] who kills a person for pleasure, for sexual gratification, out of greed or otherwise base motives, [...]" or "[...] in order to facilitate or to cover up another offense [...]" Section 211 Paragraph II, 1st. und 3rd. group.

1533 "[...] consideration shall in particular be given to the motives and aims of the offender; the attitude reflected in the offense and the degree of will involved in its commission [...]" Section 46 Paragraph II sentence 2 variant 1.-4 StGB.

the German discussion regarding the justification of a standard[1534]. In this approach, the question in regard to the ambit of criminal law, asking whether hate crime norms, thus whether an action which is connected to a hateful or biased motive of the offender, may legitimately be punished by expressive norms which must be enacted by the German legislator, leads the examination; thereby the focus in particular is drawn towards violent crimes (offenses against life Sections 211, 212 Penal Code; offenses against the person Sections 223 et seq. Penal Code), criminal damage (Sections 303, 304 et seq. Penal Code), and criminal arson offenses (Sections 306 et seq. Penal Code). To answer the basic question, if American hate crime statutes would stand up to German legitimation standards, the examination must consider constitutional aspects, the legal policy of Germany and criminal dogmatic precepts. In the end it is ascertainable whether hate crime statutes can be legitimized by precepts of legitimate punishment, according to German criminal scholars.

G. Eligibility Check of Hate Crime Legislation according to German Criminal Law Doctrine

According to the dogmatic of the German Penal Code the following possibilities come into account for implementing an aggravated sentence for hate crime offenses:

1. One could establish an independent specialized body of hate crime law which imposes a mandatory additional penalty to all criminal behavior that is motivated by racism, xenophobia and the further. This own body of law could either refer to already established offenses in the Penal Code and determine a separate penal frame in case such are motivated by hate crime motivations, or circumscribe previous punished behavior and connect such to the hateful or biased motive of the perpetrator.
2. Further, a sentence enhancement could be implied mandatorily by the enactment of aggravating exemplified rules, which would have to be connected to the several respective offenses established in the Penal Code.
3. Finally, a general enhancement of penalty for hate crime offenses could be achieved not through the order of law but by the legally voiced will of the legislator directed to courts that such shall in general consider certain motives as an aggravating fact when imposing the penalty. This, however, is not a legally established penalty enhancement. It would be up to the court at trial to implement the penal

1534 Solely in the context of non-result-constituted offenses the relationship between a criminal norm and the evil that such want to punish plays the central role (otherwise it is about the protection of a legal good). Similar to this it is handled in the hate crime debate in the United States, in which the question of the increased penalization is set in relation to the increased amount of evil which a hate crime brings in comparison to its un- or otherwise motivated counterpart.

aggravation. Such a sentencing order could be implemented in one of the two ways:

a) By legally enacting a subparagraph to the general sentencing guideline of Section 46, Paragraph 2 Penal Code, which expressly states that hate crime motivations shall be taken into consideration by the court at trial when imposing the individual penalty of the offender. Or by

b) the creation of a true mandatory order in a new norm in the general part of the Code, which as a special sentencing rule is applicable to all offenses codified in the following special part of the Code. Such could specify that the discretionary power of the judge is limited towards the fact that hate crime motives must imperatively be considered as a specific aggravating circumstance when determining the penalty for the relevant offense in any case.

The first variant constitutes a substantive norm. Such either protects a legal good which is not protected by a previous norm yet, or protects an already protected legal good against a "new" direction of attack.

If one thinks about substantive norms against hate crime as they are adopted in the U.S., as for example cross-burning laws, and reflect upon parallel legislation in Germany, one quickly acknowledges that in any case cross-burning laws as they are established in the U.S. are not required in Germany. The historical significance is lacking; the historical experience of lynching does not play a role in Germany, therefore, these sort of acts are neither used to threaten certain groups of people, nor - if committed - may they be rarely capable of imposing a likewise significant impact on groups of people who are living in Germany. A statutory counterpart to American substantive hate crime legislation - especially with regard to American mask-wearing legislation, for example, could be the criminal prohibition of wearing combat boots and bomber jackets - that at least in the case of being worn as a combination. This idea occurs from the fact that this type of clothing, if worn in public, has a clear meaning content (in the meaning of an outward exposure of a racist attitude) and objectively triggers an actually given, legitimate feeling of threat in parts of the population in Germany. By the enactment of such legislation, a behavior (the wearing of certain clothes) would become a criminal prohibition that without the - for everyone identifiable and outwardly become known - hate and bias motivation would not be punishable. This applies because it would not be threatening, thus without the expressed motivation such behavior would not cause any infringement of third parties. However, for the German region there are no further approaches of enacting such a sort of laws. The criminal prohibition of wearing certain items of clothing seems too specific[1535]. At least

1535 The next step would be to think about prohibiting the wearing of certain clothing from certain manufacturers in public. This results from the idea that the wearing of certain brands, those that visibly show the manufacturer's name or logo and contain the letters NSDAP and are known to be supported by the neo-Nazi scene (i.e. the brand: consdaple), as well as the wearing of combat boots and clean-shaved heads in combination with certain garments of those brands that are obviously attributable to that scene in the case of canceling the combination of combat boots and bomber jacket, a clear fear-inducing, message-sending signal to parts of the population by wearing certain clothes is not recognizable. Unlike in the case of the burning of crosses for the U.S., where cross burning behavior is clearly harassing[1536], such behavior - for instance, the wearing of certain clothes - can not be clearly defined for the German region. However, the public use of certain symbols or slogans - as an example for a substantive hate crime Law - is prohibited by German Penal Law[1537]. This in turn, leads to the fact that the wearing of certain clothes in a specific manner is prohibited by the threat of punishment[1538].

The second variant refers to a sentence enhancement law which increases the penalty for behavior punished in the respective base offense. The third variant is not a true penalty enhancement law, but a rule applying to courts when determining the sentence and stipulates that a court at trial shall or must consider the relevant motives as aggravating facts when imposing the penalty. These possibilities are discussed below neutrally, and their suitability is evaluated in the end in a summary discussion.

1. The Enactment of a Substantive Norm to Punish Hateful and Bias-Motivated Criminal Behavior

The first variant of a substantial hate crime law requires the legitimate protection of a legal good; further the punishment of behavior due to a "new" direction of attack on an already protected legal good comes into consideration. Questionable is, what legal good is aimed to be protected by a substantive hate crime norm; or which already protected legal good is in need to be further protected due to an independent mode of attack realized by a hate crime committal. In case, previously unprotected legal goods are detected, and their protection legitimates a new hate crime norm, it must be evaluated how solution-pointing a new, own substantive law implemented into

---

(Master Race Europe or Pit Bull) could lead to climate-damaging signals. However, according to the here taken approach, specific hate crime legislation intends to protect the immediate victim against attacks on his human dignity and to protect the society by protecting the public peace. At least, the aggravating violation of the human dignity of the immediate victim can not be recognized in the case that, e.g. Nazis, wear clothes that reveal obvious statements to the public, because the fact of simply wearing particular clothes in public do not form an attack against an individual, but an attack on an undefined collective. But a hate crime requires both components: the attacks on the immediate victim´s human dignity and the public peace. Yet, the wearing of such clothes can be condemned because of the aimed at tharassing or menacing impacts on third parties. Criminal prohibitions though, would - at least - find their limitations on the legitimizing level of necessity.

1536 "[...] cross burning is clearly intimidation." (De Vries, High Court Upholds Cross-Burning Ban, CBSNews, May 7, 2009; view Chapter 3, D., 2., 2.2., 2.2.3., 2.2.3.1., b), aa) Cross Burning Legislation.

1537 Section 86a, Paragraph 1 Penal Code stipulates: "Whosoever [...] domestically distributes or publicly uses symbols of one of the parties or organizations [...] or produces, stocks, imports or exports objects which depict or contain such symbols for distribution or use in Germany or abroad in a [certain] manner [...] shall be liable to imprisonment not exceeding three years or a fine." Paragraph 2 clarifies: "Symbols within the meaning of subsection (1) above shall be in particular flags, insignia, uniforms and their parts, slogans and forms of greeting. Symbols which are so similar as to be mistaken for those named in the 1st sentence shall be equivalent to them."

1538 The wearing of a sweatshirt of the brand "CONSDAPLE" under a half-open jacket, leaving only NSDAP readable, is punishable – it is not punishable to wear this brand if the shirt is worn without a jacket (i.e. if the brand is readable in its entirety). (LG Neuruppin, judgment February 17, 2010 - 14 NS 146/09; likewise: OLG Hamm, decision October 10, 2003 - 2 Ss 407/03).

the German Penal Code would be compared to the implementation of aggravating subparagraphs, or to the imposition of a general rule addressing the mode of sentencing, or compared to a mandatory regulation which constrain a court to enhance the sentence if it detects that hateful or biased motives were relevant for the committal of a crime.

1.1. Possible Goods Protected by a Hate Crime Law

A starting point for legitimating severe or additional penalties for hate- and bias-motivated criminal behavior is to clarify whether hate crimes violate a legal good which is not harmed by the committal of the relevant base offense. In case it is aimed at protecting several legal goods by just one norm, one must valuate the proportion of the desired protection. Despite the varied phrasing which is used by the different American states in order to define the required conditions for enhancing criminal penalties for hate crimes, one is able to draw on the summary of general precepts: hate crimes are criminal offenses directed against person and property. The offender either selects his target due to his bias (discriminatory selection model[1539]), or attacks such because of his racial animus (racial animus model[1540])[1541]. Questionable is whether - based on the multitude of U.S. hate crimes statutes - it is possible to detect the goods which are protected by these diverse laws. At least, it could be possible to define a narrow circle of goods which are protected by these diverse laws if all hate crimes as such inhere something specific, criminally relevant and harmful, which independent from the committal of the particular base offense (that may be, for instance, personal injury or criminal property damage) harms the same legal good(s), and, after all, the protection of these goods necessitates and legitimates the punishment of these sorts of behavior. The existence of this specific "something", which is inherent in every hate crime, independent from the form of criminal behavior, could be assured if every hate crime has the same specific, delimitable and definable effect on the

1539 "The "discriminatory selection model" of bias crimes defines these crimes in terms of the perpetrator's discriminatory selection of his victim. Under this model, it is irrelevant why an offender selected his victim on the basis on race. It is sufficient that the offender did so." (Lawrence, The Punishment of Hate, Michigan Law Review 320-381, 1994, p. 326; Lawrence, Punishing Hate, pp 29 et seqq.). The discriminatory selection model of bias crimes has received particular attention because it was a statute of the model that was upheld by the Supreme Court in Wisconsin v. Mitchell 508 U.S. 476, 476 (1993).; view Chapter 3, F. The Standards set by the U.S. Supreme Court.

1540 "The "racial animus model" of bias crimes defines these crimes on the basis of the perpetrator's animus for the racial or ethnic group of the victim and the centrality of this animus is the perpetrator's motivation for committing the crime." "Race" in "racial animus" is used by Lawrence inclusively, not exclusively, to encompass motivation based not only on the race, but also the color, ethnicity, religion or national origin or even gender and sexual orientation of the victim. (Lawrence, The Punishment of Hate, Michigan Law Review 320-381, 1994, p. 326; Lawrence, Punishing Hate, pp 29 et seqq.; 34). For examples of legislation which meet the category "racial animus model" view Cal. Penal Code §§ 422.6, 422.7, 422.75, and 1170.75 (prohibiting hate crimes committed because of the victim's gender); D.C. Code Ann. § 22-4001; Ill. Ann. Stat. CH. 38, 12-7.1(a); Iowa Code Ann. § 729A.1; Mich. Comp. Laws Ann. § 750.147b; N.H. REV. STAT. Ann. § 651:6.I(g); N.D. Cent. Code § 12.1-14-04; Vt. Stat. Ann. tit. 13, § 1455; W. VA. Code § 61-6-21; WASH. REV. Code Ann. §9A.36.080(1).

1541 Moreover there are Civil Right Laws which aim at the protection of the enjoyment of the Basic Rights of everyone; numerous individual state laws which combat hate crime and xenophobic harm. Such laws are based on the specific individual needs of a government and its area, for instance, laws against cross burnings, against the wearing of masks or hoods in public, against the violation of graveyards and churches and so on.

external society. This effect can be constituted by the endangerment of a legal good or by violating it. Due to an assumed commonality of all hate crimes, hate crimes are examined in general. The main focus though, is turned towards violent crimes and property damage, including in particular arson offenses. The premise of an overall view is that each bias-motivated act, which is considered a hate crime, causes an effect towards the individual attacked victim, or/and towards the entire harmed group, or/and towards society at large that, set in comparison to the relevant base offense,

a) is able to be differentiated from such effects caused by the base offense; and,
b) by taking the effect towards the attacked individual or towards a wider group of population into account, might not "just" significantly enhance the wrongfulness compared to the base offense, but perhaps, as the case may be, even violate further legal goods, which protection is not, or insufficient fulfilled by criminal norms previously established in the German Penal Code.

The verification of a hate crime norm must take place by answering the following series of questions: Which legal good is protected by a hate crime statute; followed by the question whether such is worthy of legal protection, which answer mainly depends on the general configuration of the relevant good and also on such reason, whether the protected good indeed is infringed through a hate crime[1542] (which must be evaluated by concrete measuring of harm) and in addition, whether such is not yet protected sufficiently by the punishment of the underlying behavior, thus by previously established norms.

Since the legal good is to be distinguished from the object of attack[1543], all personal, by hate crime violated interests can possibly constitute a legal good which requires protection by a hate crime norm. But, the protection of such goods is usually already aimed at by norms which punish the respective behavior only. Detached from the concrete object of attack one has to ask which goods are violated through hate crimes which are not protected by criminal law yet, and constitute a sufficient social reality[1544], according to the understanding of the German legal good doctrine, in order to be considered as violable and worthy of protection to the extent that the legislator may legitimately interfere with the rights of the hate crime perpetrator and, according to the proportionality principle, is able to decide that the aim of protecting these goods outweighs the liberty rights of the perpetrator.

In order to discover such legal goods which are affected by hate crimes in a demarkable way it is necessary to dunk into the nature of these acts.

1542 Roxin, Strafrecht AT I, § 2, p. 20, marginal no. 21.
1543 Using the example of Section 212 Penal Code it shall be explained that the object of action is the human, but protected legal good is "life". See also Section 242 Penal Code: action object is the thing that becomes stolen, the protected legal good, yet, is the ownership.
1544 Wohlers, Deliktstypen des Präventionsstrafrechts, p. 220.

The assertion that is substantiated by numerous studies in the U.S.[1545], and is recognized in Germany as fixed[1546], is that hate crimes are a source of greater harms. The impact of hate crimes is studied on two different levels: (i) the impact of bias crimes on the specific victim(s) of the crime; and (ii) the broader impact of bias crimes on the "target" group, that is, the racial group of which the victim is a member, and (iii) on the general community[1547].

Irrespective of the truthfulness these studies[1548], the following illustrates how hate crime in fact differ from parallel crimes and why this distinction could make a crucial difference in our criminal law.

In German criminology there are two distinct concepts followed to penetrate the character of hate crimes. One concept considers hate crimes as traditional offenses which are motivated through hate towards the victimized person (offender related concept)[1549]. According to the other concept hate crimes are considered as legal infringements of its own species which cause special damages to victim- and society (victim related concept)[1550]. A hate crime is not solely determined by a biased offender motivation. The main purpose of the concept of hate crime is not to impose harsher punishment on the prejudice oriented personality of perpetrators and on their prejudiced attitudes and values[1551]. “Such a one-sided offender-orientation is obsolete”[1552]. Hate crimes are directed against the “being” of the victim, against his race, religion, his ethnicity[1553]. That is why they are characterized by objective criteria, which

1545 Weisburd/Levin, On the Basis of Sex: Recognizing Gender-based Bias Crimes, 5 Stan. L. & Pol. Rev., 1994, pp. 21 et seqq.; Kelly/Louza/Reeves/Garrison/Adams/Burns, Hatred in Georgia: A Chronology and Analysis of Hate Activity, 1993 - who finds that hate crimes are more brutal, more serious – the possibility that hate Crimes turn out to be murder is more likely and yet these acts are taken less seriously (study based on hate crime against people who are perceived to be gay); Garnets/Herek/Levy, Violence and victimization of lesbians and gay men: Mental health consequences in: Herek/Berill (eds.) Hate Crimes: Confronting Violence Against Lesbians and Gay Men, 1992, pp. 207-226; Bard/Sangry, The Crime Victim's Book, 1979; Uhl, Hate Crime: Prevalence and Impact in an Urban College Population, UMI Dissertation Services, Ann Arbor, Michigan 1996, pp. 16, 18 et seqq., (61); Lawrence, The Punishment of Hate: Towards a Normative Theory of Bias-Motivated Crimes, 93 Michigan Law Review, 1994, pp. 320 et seqq. (343); Acknowledged by New York's legal findings, stating: "[Hate Crimes] inflict on victims incalculable [...] emotional damage." (New York Penal § 485.00 Legislative findings). So also Ehrlich, who noted in his study that the victims of hate crime incidents have suffered more than the victims of parallel incidents. (Ehrlich, The Ethnoviolence Project: Final Narrative Report of the National Survey of Prejudice and Violence in the United States (1992); cited after Uhl, Hate Crime: Prevalence and Impact in an Urban College Population, UMI Dissertation Services, Ann. Arbor, Michigan, 1996, pp. 21 et seqq.; affirmed by the U.S. Supreme Court that found that "[...] bias crime are more likely to inflict distinct emotional harm on their victims". (Wisconsin v. Mitchell, 113 S. Ct. 2194, 2201 (1993).

1546 E.g. Appendix to BR-Drs. 577/00, pp. 5 et seqq. (View the reasoning of the legislative initiatives to amend the current Penal Code in order to sufficiently address hate crimes, partly provided in Chapter 4, C., Legal Dealing with hate crime, and the here provided draft bills discussed in headings No. 2-6).

1547 Lawrence, The Punishment of Hate, Michigan Law Review 320-381, 1994, p. 327; Lawrence, Punishing Hate, pp. 39 et seqq.

1548 View hereto the following Chapter 4, G., 1.1.1. The Human Dignity of the Immediate Victim.

1549 Schneider, Internationales Handbuch der Kriminologie, Bd. 2, pp. 298 et seqq.

1550 Schneider, Internationales Handbuch der Kriminologie, Bd. 2, pp. 298 et seqq.; with respect to the American origin of these concepts, e.g., Perry, In the Name of Hate: Understanding Hate Crime, 2001, p. 19.

1551 Schneider, Kriminologie der Hassdelikte. Konzeption, Ursachen, Vorbeugung und Kontrolle, in: Bewährungshilfe, 2003, p. 117; in contrary, argued by Seehafer, Strafrechtliche Reaktionen, 2003, p. 69, in regard to footnote 517.

1552 Schneider, Kriminologie der Hassdelikte. Konzeption, Ursachen, Vorbeugung und Kontrolle, in: Bewährungshilfe, 2003, p. 117.

1553 Tolmein, ZRP, 2001, pp. 315,316.

describe the behavior of perpetrators[1554] and the motive of the offender. Crucial is the social significance of the behavior for the uninvolved public[1555] and this is palpable, but this, however, derives from the motivation.

This approach moreover leads to the "practical" advantage that a court precisely must not only orient itself towards the motivation of an offender, which in a particular case makes the prosecution very difficult[1556] and subjective[1557], due to the fact that the motivation is a vague term, and perpetrators seek for excuses to hide their true motives during the prosecution process[1558]. "For the detection of a hate crime it is rather - as with any political offense - about the social importance and the effect of the offender's behavior for the uninvolved audience, it is about the external circumstances of the victimization and in particular about the status of the victim"[1559]. Therefore, external facts and objective indicators, such as the identity of the victim, are important[1560].

A hate crime is characterized by the fact that such is mainly committed to set a symbolic message, it is aimed at sending a harmful effect towards the identity and the existence of persons with certain features, and therefore the individual attacked victim is simply used as a tool, used as an example by being portrayed "as a symbol of hate, enemy and impersonalized, faceless hate object"[1561]. Ultimately, the hate is turned towards the greater target behind the attacked victim[1562]. Hence, such acts are committed against persons or property, whatever harm suits the offender to transfer his symbolic message. Due to that, without further examination, two legal goods, which might be harmed in a different mode, or in a more intensive way through the comittal of a hate crime, are revealed: on the one hand the human dignity according to the direct attacked victim comes into mind, but also the human dignity in terms of the broader target community of the immediate victim could be affected; on the other hand, the effects put on society at large point to an affection of the legal good of public peace. With that said, the "human dignity" and the "public peace" as the legal goods, which are de lege ferenda protected by a hate crime norm, are to be examined for their suitability to constitute a legitimation base for a substantive hate crime statute.

1554 Schneider, Kriminologie der Hassdelikte. Konzeption, Ursachen, Vorbeugung und Kontrolle, in: Bewährungshilfe, 2003, p. 117.

1555 Schneider, Kriminologie der Hassdelikte. Konzeption, Ursachen, Vorbeugung und Kontrolle, in: Bewährungshilfe, 2003, p. 117.

1556 Morsch, The Problem of Motive in Hate Crimes: The Argument Against Presumptions of Racial Motivation; Journal of Criminal Law and Criminology 82, 1991, pp. 659-689.

1557 Jacobs, The Emergence and Implications of American Hate Crime Jurisprudence, in: Kelly/Maghan (eds.): Hate Crime, pp. 150-176.

1558 Schneider, Kriminologie der Hassdelikte. Konzeption, Ursachen, Vorbeugung und Kontrolle, in: Bewährungshilfe, 2003, p. 117.

1559 Schneider, Kriminologie der Hassdelikte. Konzeption, Ursachen, Vorbeugung und Kontrolle, in: Bewährungshilfe, 2003, p. 117.

1560 Wallace, Victimology, 1998, pp. 214-216; Schneider, Kriminologie der Hassdelikte. Konzeption, Ursachen, Vorbeugung und Kontrolle, in: Bewährungshilfe, 2003, p. 117; View hereto FBI guidelines, footnote 1249.

1561 Schneider, Internationales Handbuch der Kriminologie, Bd. 2, 2009, pp. 297-338, (299).

1562 Hatecrimes therefore are rightly referred to as symbolic crime. (Schneider, Hasskriminalität: eine neue kriminologische Deliktskategorie. In: Juristische Zeitung 58, pp. 497-504, (497)).

1.1.1. Human Dignity of the Immediate Victim

The outward manifestation of a hate crime motive could generate a certain impact on the victim which is not generated by the relevant parallel offense[1563]. Assuming that the gravity of an offense is determined by the amount of wrong and the offender's guilt[1564] findings in American science aim at proving that hate crime harms the victim and other members of the group to which the victim belongs beyond the physical injury which results from the concrete action[1565]. These numerous studies[1566] are mainly based on mental suffering, thus psychological harms, which indeed are difficult to measure. While the overall more brutal approach also leads to higher losses, but these in its core may be already covered by established criminal law, so possibly do not require and legitimate the establishment of a separate offense category for hate crime[1567], the change in psychological distress associated with these distinct external effects of hate crime are not (expressly) covered by the current law. hate crimes are said to "give rise to a heightened sense of vulnerability beyond that normally found in victims [...]. hate crime victims suffer deep psychological harm and the feelings of threat exceed the harm ordinarily experienced by victims[1568]. "The victims [of bias crimes] tend to experience psychological symptoms such as depression or withdrawal, as well as feelings of anxiety and helplessness and a profound sense of isolation"[1569]. This has been affirmed by the U.S. Supreme Court that found that "[...] bias crimes are more likely to inflict distinct emotional harm on their victims"[1570].

Those, who criticize these thesis which acknowledges the cause of greater harm, claim that these studies do not sufficiently conclude that the victims of

1563 Acknowledging New York's legal findings, stating: "[Hate Crimes] inflict on victims incalculable [...] emotional damage." (New York Penal § 485.00 Legislative findings).

1564 According to the American wrongfulness-culpability hypothesis two elements describe the severity of an offense, the offender's guilt and the damage caused to a society. (Michael Moore, The independent Moral Significance of Wrongdoing, 5 J. Contemp. Leg. Issues 237 (1994); Aydin, Die strafrechtliche Bekämpfung von Hassdelikten, pp. 102 et seq.).

1565 Lawrence, The Punishment of Hate: Towards a Normative Theory of Bias-Motivated Crimes, 93 Michigan Law Review, 1994, pp. 320 et seqq. (343); Aydin, Die strafrechtliche Bekämpfung von Hassdelikten, pp. 122 et seqq.

1566 Weisburd/Levin, On the Basis of Sex: Recognizing Gender-based Bias Crimes, 5 Stan. L. & Pol. Rev., 1994, pp. 21 et seqq.; Kelly/Louza/Reeves/Garrison/Adams/Burns, Hatred in Georgia: A Chronology and Analysis of Hate Activity, 1993 - who finds that hate crimes are more brutal, more serious – the possibility that hate crimes turn out to be murder is more likely and yet these acts are taken less seriously (study based on hate crime against people who are perceived to be gay); Garnets/Herek/Levy, Violence and victimization of lesbians and gay men: Mental health consequences in: Herek/Berill (eds.) Hate Crimes: Confronting Violence Against Lesbians and Gay Men, 1992, pp. 207-226; Bard/Sangry, The Crime Victim's Book, 1979; Uhl, Hate Crime: Prevalence and Impact in an Urban College Population, UMI Dissertation Services, Ann Arbor, Michigan 1996, pp. 16, 18 et seqq., (61).

1567 View hereto Chapter 4, G., 1.7.1.3. Sections 223; 224; 226 Penal Code.

1568 Lawrence, Punishing Hate, 2003, p. 61.

1569 Lawrence, The Punishment of Hate: Towards a Normative Theory of Bias-Motivated Crimes, 93 Michigan Law Review, 1994, p. 343.; So also Ehrlich, who noted in his study that the victims of hate crime incidents have suffered more than the victims of parallel incidents. (Ehrlich, The Ethnoviolence Project: Final Narrative Report of the National Survey of Prejudice and Violence in the United States (1992); cited after Uhl, Hate Crime: Prevalence and Impact in an Urban College Population, UMI Dissertation Services, Ann. Arbor, Michigan, 1996, pp. 21 et seqq.; view hereto also: Aydin, Die strafrechtliche Bekämpfung von Hassdelikten, pp. 112-130 (117)).

1570 Wisconsin v. Mitchell, 113 S. Ct. 2194, 2201 (1993); Aydin, Die strafrechtliche Bekämpfung von Hassdelikten, p. 113.

hate crime really suffer higher (emotional) losses than victims of similar offenses that were not motivated by prejudiced hate[1571]. It is therefore concluded that these studies lack the sufficient comparison to the effects of non-Hate-Crimes[1572]. The diagnostically conclusiveness might affect such empirical material in regards to the extent of the harm displayed, but one can not deny the cause of an extra dower to the immediate victim and its community[1573]. The reason why the demonstration of the increase in damage in the case of hate crime committal compared to the damage that is caused by comparable non-hate crime conducts is difficult, is because the arguments are mainly based on psychological effects of the immediate victim, its community and on impacts on society, which are difficult to measure. Furthermore, serious violent crimes seem to simply just always have a great effect on victims, regardless of the offender´s motivation. But, if it is about less serious offenses, like intimidation and harassment or simple assault, one might be able to more easily understand that the effects of hate crime are more severe on the victims than such of comparable acts that are not motivated by hate[1574]. Even opponents agree that even though otherwise motivated crimes can also be very brutal and severe, in the case of minor crimes one could accept the argument of a greater harm[1575]. Whereas the "loss of vandalism is insurable, and if not insured, is suffered in terms of time and money or both, if that vandalism is bias-motivated, the defacement might take the form of swastikas on the home of a Jewish family or racist graffiti on the home of an African-American family. The harm here is not a mere nuisance"[1576].

In agreement with the core of such studies that demonstrate the distinct impact of hate crimes on society and the opinions discussed in extensive literature[1577]

1571 Jacobs/Potter, Hate Crimes: Criminal Law & Identity Politics 82, Oxford, 1998, pp. 82,83; A follow-up study showed that in line with Jacobs/Potter a comparison between victims of hate crime and victims of other serious parallel crimes did not reveals increased suffering and distress of hate crime victims. Hate crimes victims were even claimed to suffer less severe injury, because "a major difference in the emotional response of hate violence victims appears to be the absence of a lowered self esteem. The ability of some hate violence victims to maintain their self esteem may be associated with their attribution of responsibility for their attacks to the prejudice and racism of others". (Barnes/Ephross, The Impact of Hate Violence on Victims: Emotional and Behavioral Responses to Attacks, 39 Soc. Work ,1994, pp. 257,250).

1572 Dillof, The Importance of Being Biased, Michigan Law Review, Vol. 98, p. 1684.

1573 Further criticism of hate crime legislation is usually pointed towards the questioned constitutionality of these laws. (view hereto: Gellman, Stick and Stones can put you in Jail, but can Words increase your Sentence?, Constitutional and Policy Dilemma of Ethnic Intimidation Laws 39, Ucla L. Rev., 1991, pp. 333 et seqq.).

1574 This idea is followed likewise by Bell, Jeannine, Policing Hatred: Law Enforcement, Civil Rights, and Hate Crime, New York, 2002, University Press; "In less serious cases, however, the hate-motivation obviously makes a difference. This would also be an easy conclusion of common sense." (Aydin, Die strafrechtliche Bekämpfung von Hassdelikten, p. 121).

1575 Jacobs/Potter, Hate Crimes: Criminal Law & Identity Politics 82, Oxford, 1998, pp. 84-85; Aydin, Die strafrechtliche Bekämpfung von Hassdelikten, pp. 121, 122.

1576 Lawrence, Punishing Hate, 2003, p. 61.

1577 Lawrence, Punishing Hate, p. 40, 63; with reference to: Melinda Henneberger, "For Bias Crimes, a Double Trauma" , Newsday, 113 (Jan. 9, 1992); N. R. Kleinfield, "Bias Crimes Hold Steady, But Leave Many Scards" , New York Times, A - 1 (Jan. 27, 1992); Brian Levin, "U. S. Supreme Court Upholds Stiffer Sentences for Hate Crimes" , Intelligence Report, 166 (sept. 1993); Joan Weiss, "Ethnoviolence: Impact upon the Responce of Victims and the Communtiy", in Bias Crime: American Law Enforcement and Legal Response, pp. 182, 183 (1993); see also Joan C. Weiss, Howard J. Ehrlich, Barabara E. K. Larcon, "Ethnoviolence at Work", 18 Journal of Intergroup Relations, p. 18 (Winter 1991 - 1992) – according to this study of violence in the workplace it was found that victims of bias – motivated violence reported a

which deal with those findings and also assume that hate crimes harm the victim and other members of the group to which the victim belongs beyond the physical injury caused by the concrete action[1578], it is understood that a hate crime harms the immediate victim more severe than a crime that is motivated otherwise, but in any case differently[1579]. In German literature the reasons are explained as follows: Victims of hate crimes are more traumatized because hate crimes are message crimes[1580]. This circumstance makes the victim feeling, unlike it is with other crimes, as if the threat is far from over after the completion of attack, and further attacks may follow in the future[1581]. This has two psychological consequences: From the theory of "learned helplessness" and with respect to depression research it shows that a cause that is everlasting, thus always may occur again, triggers more depression and feeling of helplessness than a one-time-only occurring cause[1582]. Secondly, violence that is unpredictable is especially intimidating[1583]. The victim of a hate crime can not change in order to not be victimized again[1584]. A respective avoidance behavior will not protect one from further attacks[1585]. Thus, logically, the ever-present sense of threat is differently from such of an accidential victimization, which can be explained by being in the wrong place at the wrong time. "It is one thing to avoid the park at night, because it is not safe. It is quite another to avoid certain neighborhoods because of one´s race"[1586].

---

significantly greater level of negative psychological symptons than did victims of nobias- motivated violence. The German literature acknowledges these U.S. findings: Füllgrabe, Hassverbrechen, Kriminalistik, 2004, pp. 391-397; Aydin, Die strafrechtliche Bekämpfung von Hassdelikten in Deutschland und in den Vereinigten Staaten von Amerika, 2006, pp. 112-130; Schneider, Politische Kriminalität: Hassverbrechen, Fremdenfeindlichkeit im internationalen Kontext, Kriminalistik 2001, pp.21-28; Schneider, Politische Kriminalität, in: R. Sieverts/H.J.Schneider (eds.), Handwörterbuch der Kriminologie, 2. Auflage, 5. Band, Berlin, New York, 1998, pp. 589-624 (590); Schneider, Kriminologie der Hassdelikte. Konzeptionen, Ursachen, Vorbeugung und Kontrolle, in: Bewährungshilfe, 2003, pp. 115 et seqq.; with further references to European literature: Garofalo, James, Hate Crime Victimization in the United States, in: Robert C. Davis/Arthur J. Lurigio/Wesley G. Skogan (eds.), Victims of Crime, 2. Edition, 1997, pp. 132-145 Thousand oaks, London, New Delhi: Sage (pp. 141, 142); Martin, Susan E., Investigating Hate Crimes: Case Characteristics an Law Enforcement Responses. Justice Quaterly 13, 1996, pp. 455-480 (470).

1578 Lawrence, The Punishment of Hate: Towards a Normative Theory of Bias-Motivated Crimes, 93 Michigan Law Review, 1994, pp. 320 et seqq. (343); Aydin, Die strafrechtliche Bekämpfung von Hassdelikten, pp. 122 et seqq.

1579 All in all, it is concluded that the social-psychological effects of hate crime are more severe. A victimization by a prejudiced filled criminal act must be more hurtful than a victimization by other vilifications because the human dignity of the victim is attacked by a concrete attack on his identity. ("Bias crimes thus attack the victim not only physically, but also at the very core of his or her identity [...]." (Lawrence, The Hate Crime Project and its Limitations: Evaluating the Societal Gains and Risk in Bias Crime Law Enforcement, Legal Studies Research paper No. 216, 2006, p. 2).

1580 Füllgrabe, Hassverbrechen, Kriminalistik, 2004, pp. 391-397 (394).

1581 Füllgrabe, Hassverbrechen, Kriminalistik, 2004, pp. 391-397 (394).

1582 Füllgrabe, Kriminalpsychologie – Täter und Opfer im Spiel des Lebens, 1997; Füllgrabe, Hassverbrechen, Kriminalistik, 2004, pp. 391-397 (394).

1583 Füllgrabe, Amok, Report Psychologie, 27, Nr. 11/12, November/Dezember 2002, 2002a, pp. 694-703; Füllgrabe, Hassverbrechen, Kriminalistik, 2004, pp. 391-397 (394).

1584 Defensive behavior changes including such as staying home more often, trying to become "less visible," or moving to another neighborhood, may only lead to a very limited success; since the reason for attack belongs to the victims inner self, and the attacked characteristics are simply not (completely) hideable.

1585 Even opponents of hate crime legislation agree that "[i]ndeed, it is deeply disconcerting to be the target of "random" violence." (Dillof, The Importance of Being Biased, Michigan Law Review, Vol. 98, 2000 p. 1683).

1586 Lawrence, Punishing Hate, 1999, p. 40.

While it is agreed in any case that surely the motive has a direct and important bearing on both, the dangerousness and the blameworthiness of an act[1587], it is assumed in the following that hateful bias motives of criminal acts harm the legal good of the human dignity of the victim deeper than otherwise- or unmotivated criminal acts. Thus, the degradation of the victim is so deep and the vulnerability is so omnipresent that the victim of a hate crime suffers greater psychological trauma than a victim of a parallel offense[1588].

The statement that the nature of damages sustained by a bias crime exceeds the harm caused by a parallel crime is traceable if one considers the true means behind a hate crime. The selective choice of a specific person takes place for the reason of imposing a special greatness of harm on huge parts of society[1589]. Whether empirical data, which quite comprehensible prove such effects of stigmatization and deeper psychological damages of hate crime victims, is reliable or not is irrelevant for the normative requirement of legal changes. Yet, the legal requirement of the behavior having a significant impact on a legal good must be traceable, and therefore these studies at least provide good starting points. An impact on a legal good must result in particular from the hateful or biased behavior of the offender; a distinct external form of the behavior in question could occur through its connection to the perpetrator's motive.

Usually the origin of victimization by physical assault, attempted homicide, or an arson attack lies in relationships[1590]. Perpetrator and victim had to do with each other in some kind of way in their past[1591]. Then a situation occurs, to which development both sides, perpetrator and victim, contributed their part[1592]. It is different in the field of hate crimes, perpetrator and victim have never met or had any contact[1593]; the victim is attacked without warning signs, because of who he/she is[1594]. The victim did not in any way contribute to the occurred situation; consequently he/she cannot make any chances in order to not get into a similar situation again. Due to the fact that the victim adheres

1587 Motives could be considered as "further intentions" (Murphy, Jeffrie G., Bias Crimes: What Do Haters deserve?, 11 Crim. Just. Ethics 21, 1992).

1588 Weisburd/Levin, On the Basis of Sex: Recognizing Gender-based Bias Crime, 5 Stan. L. & pol. Rev., 1994, pp. 21, 25.

1589 The highly symbolic effect of such an act can be increased by the choice of a special victim, for instance a famous person, which is considered by the offender as a special suitable victim in order to harm an entire part of society due to causing far reaching threat and anxiety. (Pointed hustle against a well known Soccer Player, Gerald Asamoah, in order to cause agitation. The perpetrator was found guilty of "Incitement to hatred", according to Section 130 Penal Code (May 19, 2009; OLG Stuttgart, 2 Ss 1014/09)).

1590 Perry, In the Name of Hate, p. 29.

1591 Herzog, in: Mohr/Molthagen, Friedrich-Ebert-Stiftung, Der Aufstand der Zuständigen, Was kann der Rechtsstaat gegen Rechtsextremismus tun?, Ergebnisse einer Konferenz der Friedrich-Ebert-Stiftung am 20. März 2007, p. 28.

1592 Herzog, in: Mohr/Molthagen, Friedrich-Ebert-Stiftung, Der Aufstand der Zuständigen, Was kann der Rechtsstaat gegen Rechtsextremismus tun?, Ergebnisse einer Konferenz der Friedrich-Ebert-Stiftung am 20. März 2007, p. 28.

1593 Perry, In the Name of Hate, p. 29.

1594 Schneider, Internationales Handbuch der Kriminologie, Bd. 2, pp. 298 et seqq.; Herzog, in: Mohr/Molthagen, Friedrich-Ebert-Stiftung, Der Aufstand der Zuständigen, Was kann der Rechtsstaat gegen Rechtsextremismus tun?, Ergebnisse einer Konferenz der Friedrich-Ebert-Stiftung am 20. März 2007, p. 28; (http://library.fes.de/pdf-files/do/04878.pdf).

something unchangeable[1595], for instance, because he is an "alien, black, homosexual, derelict or cripple"[1596], he risks the increased danger of being victimized by this certain type of acts[1597]. The bias-motivated hate, even if turned towards a specially selected victim for the purpose of victimizing him or her, it is not pointed against the individual person, but against the embodiment of such what the offender hates because of his bias; thus a race, a sexual orientation, a religion, etc. As opposed to the perpetrators of other crimes, perpetrators of hate crimes are more likely to be strangers to their victims, having focused exclusively on the victim's race, not his individual identity[1598]. "This fungibility of victims to the bias-motivated criminal is so integral to the [Hate] Crime that California considers it a critical element for identifying bias crimes"[1599]. This results from the fact that the perpetrator does not aim at harming the individuality of a certain person, but because he wants to get rid of his symbolic message stating that the existence of certain people is not tolerated in society. Through such enlightened instrumentalization of a person for the purpose of implementing one´s own undemocratic ideology in the respective society, one detects a violation of the human dignity of the victimized person which does not go along with usually committed violent crimes. Thus, hate crimes inflict a palpable effect on the legal good of human dignity which is not considered in the usual sentencing process, nor covered by an average norm, which was created by the legislature, whom of course not had this special nature of a hate crime and its therefrom resulting effects towards the human dignity in mind. Due to the fact that the offender of a hate crime primarily aims at depriving the Human dignity from the victim (and wide parts of society) because he believes the by him chosen people are ranking below him and are to be degraded, he - in order to enforce his view on society

---

1595 Keyword: "Ideological orientation and victim vulnerability are the main characteristics of hate crimes". (Schneider, Kriminologie der Hassdelikte. Konzeption, Ursachen, Vorbeugung und Kontrolle, in: Bewährungshilfe, 2003, p. 117).

1596 Herzog, in: Mohr/Molthagen, Friedrich-Ebert-Stiftung, Der Aufstand der Zuständigen, Was kann der Rechtsstaat gegen Rechtsextremismus tun?, Ergebnisse einer Konferenz der Friedrich-Ebert-Stiftung am 20. März 2007, p. 28; (http://library.fes.de/pdf-files/do/04878.pdf).

1597 The specifics of this certain type of acts relate to the caused modified external harms, and to the fact that they willingly identify themselves to the outside world by certain signs.

1598 Studies reveal that approximately sixty percent of all crimes are committed upon strangers, whereas over eighty-five percent of the victims of hate crimes are strangers to their perpetrators. (Lawrence, The Punishment of Hate, Michigan Law Review 320-381, 1994, supra note 81, at pp. 350 et seq. based on: Goodstein, Black Youth Acquitted in Hasidic Jew's Slaying in Crown Heights Riot, Washington Post, Oct. 30, 1992, at A3 ("killing of Yankel Rosenbaum in Crown Heights was committed by a mob which was looking to exact vengeance against a "Jew" for the accidental vehicular killing of a black child by a Hasidic Jew"); The Effects of Hate: A Partial List of Hate Crimes Reported Across the Country in Recent Months, Det. Free Press, Jan. 18, 1993, at 8A ("two white men were arrested for trying to set fire to two black women; two Korean American businesses were firebombed in Chicago; an Asian teenager was beaten to death for telling two skinheads he hated Nazis; a Hispanic man killed two black men because his ex-girlfriend had dated black men; a group of black men raped and murdered a white women because she was white; three white men were arrested for setting ablaze a black man who was on vacation in New York City). Even the cross burning in R.A.V. was directed not at the victim family qua individuals but rather as an African-American family who have moved into a previously all-white neighborhood." (R.A.V., 112 S.Ct at 2538); Lawrence, Punishing Hate, supra note 45, at p. 39.

1599 "In California, gender based violence may be classified as a bias crime if the prosecution can show that the defendant was indifferent to the identity of the individual victim and committed the crime as an attack against all women". (Lawrence, The Punishment of Hate, Michigan Law Review 320-381, 1994, pp. 350, 351).

- does such, by on the one hand clearly announcing this message by committing the crime, and on the other hand exploits the victim for the purpose of sending this message in a manner which a behavior unconnected to the relevant motivation could not realize. The violation of the human dignity through a hate crime represents such a different quality that it can not be equated with the "ordinary" violation of the human dignity which is accompanied by every criminal relevant violent behavior. This overall neglecting of the individuality of the victim by the perpetrator finds its outburst in the procedures of committing the crime. By looking into German books of precedents it reveals itself that the way of how hate crimes are committed and the manners how the perpetrators treat their victims in comparison to perpetrators not being motivated by bias, such offenses are committed with the aim of literally annihilation: "it is about torching"; "hunting"; "people are crushed and grounded with boots"; slaughtered"; "perpetrators target at throats of humans with knifes"; allover, hate crimes are about "banishing", "culling" – or whatever terms may be used in the scene"[1600]. Correctly it is concluded that the ways of how these offenses are committed, the perpetrators aim at terror, it is aimed at achieving an effect which goes beyond the harm towards the attacked individual victim but also reaches the entire group of people who shares the characteristics of the victim which got attacked. "According to the description of committal of the criminal act in the relevant judicature, with regard to the course of events, these acts are characterized by a complete denial of the victim's individual right for respect", the perpetrators aim at "terror and humiliation", thereby violate the human dignity in its core[1601].

Therefore it is decisive that according to hate crimes which are directed against the person, the interference into a legally protected sphere of the victim constitutes an instrumentalization of the concrete person. The individual is treated as a mere object, human beings are means to an end[1602]. Beside the "ordinary" degradation of the victim which goes along with any physical criminal attack, the victimization through a hate crime additionally violates the human dignity of the immediate victim due to the utilization of him/her by the perpetrator to send his dehumanizing message. By this, the victim of a hate crime attack is not only degraded in his personality due to dehumanized treatment, which clearly goes along with every physical or psychical attack, but

1600 Herzog, in: Mohr/Molthagen, Friedrich-Ebert-Stiftung, Der Aufstand der Zuständigen, Was kann der Rechtsstaat gegen Rechtsextremismus tun?, Ergebnisse einer Konferenz der Friedrich-Ebert-Stiftung am 20. März 2007, p. 29.

1601 Herzog, in: Mohr/Molthagen, Friedrich-Ebert-Stiftung, Der Aufstand der Zuständigen, Was kann der Rechtsstaat gegen Rechtsextremismus tun?, Ergebnisse einer Konferenz der Friedrich-Ebert-Stiftung am 20. März 2007, pp. 28, 29. This goes along with findings that proclaim that hate crimes are more brutal, more violent and the victims are more likely to be hospitalized after an attack compared to such violent attacks where the perpetrator was not motivated by bias. (Schneider, Hassverbrechen, p. 76; Lawrence, Punishing Hate).

1602 In accordance with the jurisprudence of the Supreme Court (BVerfGE) regarding the principle of human dignity according to which it is contradictory to subordinate a human being completely for one´s own interests and therby make him to a mere object of one´s own action (rule applies to the state as addressee). BVerfGE 5, 85, 204; BVerfGE 7, 198, 205; BVerfGE 27, 1, 6; BVerfGE45, 187, 228; BVerfG, NJW 2004, 999, 1001; Becker, Menschenbild des Grundgesetzes, p. 91.

due to the extra dower[1603] contained in the crime, forcing the victim to receive the message of denial of his right to exist. This added message, which the offender willfully sends, gives the hate crime the specific character, differentiating it from the parallel base offense, thus transforming it to a hate crime by violating an additional legal good, the human dignity of the attacked victim in this specific form.

1.1.2. Human Dignity of the Victim's Community

The harms suffered by the immediate victim in regard to its dehumanization and humiliation experienced through a hate crime attack are said to be suffered by other members of the victim's target group, thus by those, who share the characteristic that prompted the defendant to target the immediate victim[1604]. Therefrom it is stated that "this additional harm of a personalized threat felt by persons other than the immediate victims of the bias crime differentiate a bias crime from a parallel crime [...]"[1605]. Whereas proponents of hate crime legislation argue that hate crimes are different because they are aimed at groups and not just at individuals[1606], this information, whether true or not, leads German jurists to search for possibly affected legal goods, which could in particular be violated through the hateful or biased motivated committal of a criminal act and for impairments of legal goods which go beyond those belonging to the immediate victim. The ordinary criminal statute, enacted to combat violent crimes, focuses on the protection of the legal goods of the immediate victims[1607]. The protection does not refer to members of the victim's group[1608]. These further victims, the members of the target group, therefore are not included in the scope of criminal protection by previously enacted norms. The general nature of a hate crime reveals that the harm caused to the immediate victim occurs for the main reason of sending a message that humans who share specific characteristics of the immediate victim are not welcome in society. Therefore, all those who are addressed by crime committal receive this dehumanizing message. So regardless the

1603 Hate crime victims have been more closely compared to rape victims by the fact that the physical harm associated with the crime is less significant than the powerful accompanying emotional sense of the attack, i.e. the psychological violation is greater than it is with parallel offenses. (Weiss, Ethnoviolence: Impact Upon the Response of Victims and the Community, in Bias Crime: American Law Enforcement and legal response, 1993, pp. 174, 182; Lawrence, The Punishment of Hate, Michigan Law Review 320-381, 1994, p. 352).

1604 "Members of the target community of a bias crime experience that crime in a manner that has no equivalent in the public response to a parallel crime. The reaction of the target community not only goes beyond mere sympathy with the immediate bias crime victim, but exceeds empathy as well. Members of the target community of a bias crime perceive that crime as an attack on themselves directly and individually." (Lawrence, Punishing Hate, pp. 41 et seq.; with reference to: Minow, Making all the difference: Inclusion, exclusion, and American Law, (1990), 221.

1605 Lawrence, Punishing Hate, p. 41.

1606 "Crimes motivated by invidious hatred toward particular groups not only harm individual victims but send a powerful message of intolerance and discrimination to all members of the group to which the victim belongs." (New York Penal § 485.00 Legislative findings).

1607 See e.g. Section 223 Penal Code, the protected good is the psychical and physical well of the immediate victim (Eser/Sternberg-Lieben, in: Schönke/Schröder, StGB, § 223, marginal no. 1.).

1608 In part, the consequences for surviving dependents are at least considered during sentencing, so in homicides. (BGH NStZ/Mü 85, 161, NStZ 93, 385; Eser/Sternberg-Lieben, in: Schönke/Schröder, StGB, § 223, marginal no. 19).

question of empirical fact, if people who share the characteristic of attack really suffer more vicarious psychic injury in response to hate-motivated crimes than they do in response to otherwise-motivated crimes, the attack towards the human dignity of all members of society who share the features of the immediate victim, and to which the hate of the offender was drawn during the attack, has become affected through the message included in this criminal act. Therefore, it is not the question, whether such vicarious suffering exists at all; neither is it about the similar question of whether such exists to a significantly greater degree in groups targeted by hate crimes than it does in groups which have been victimized in distinct various "unbiased" ways in general, but it is the cognition that due to the hateful or biased motive of the offender the effects reaches out to legal goods which protection was not considered during the establishment of the ordinary offense, thus these offenses do not aim at covering these different type of effects. However, the question occurs whether the legal good of human dignity is capable of generalization, or whether it rather earns its legal good constituting character through the reference to the individual. Article 1 Section 1 Basic Law, which contains not only a normative statement about the importance of human dignity as "the highest legal value in the constitutional order"[1609], but also, acknowledge the protection of such as a fundamental right of the individual, reveals that such is established as a personal right of the individual[1610]. In terms of crimes against absolute individual rights, the construction of a collectively assigned good that has to be distinguished from an - in the end - protected individual good, makes little sense[1611]. This actual individual good would assert its independence, even though the nature of the fundamental right of human dignity requires the individual reference. Abstract nouns must not constitute a legal good if in reality it is about protecting the individual, protecting its dignity and emphasizing its right of existence in this society[1612]. Therefore, the creation of two legal goods, the human dignity of the immediate victim as one legal good which is to be distinguished from the human dignity of the target community as another legal good, has no content. The protection of the human dignity of the immediate attacked victim as: "dignity of man", is one task to consider in the framework of hate crime Laws. Summarizing, the legal good "dignity of man" concerning the individual - not the collective - comes into consideration in order to legitimize U.S. hate crime statutes according to the German perspective.

1609 BVerfGE 6, 32, 41; BVerfGE 45, 187, 227; Maihofer, Rechtsstaat und menschliche Würde, p. 9: "Fundamental norm of our Constitution and basic norm of our legal order as such"; Hörnle, Grob anstößiges Verhalten, pp. 116, 117.

1610 Hörnle, Grob anstößiges Verhalten, pp. 116, 117.

1611 Hörnle, Grob anstößiges Verhalten, p. 93.

1612 Roxin, Strafrecht AT I, § 2, pp. 13, 14 marginal no. 1; p. 16, 20, marginal no. 21.

1.1.3. Public Peace

Hate crimes are assumed to inflict a palpable harm on society at large[1613]. This is based on findings that hate crimes may spread fear and intimidation beyond the immediate victims and their friends and families who share the racial characteristics with the victim[1614]. Therefore, hate crimes could violate a collective legal good which is previously un- or insufficiently protected. This would be the case if a hate crime in general violates a good whose integrity is a concern of the overall population of society. Therefore it is questionable, which concerns hate crimes could affect which belong to the rectified, integrated interest of the society[1615].

One idea of a de lege ferenda to be protected legal good refers to the fact that hate crime could possibly increase the danger to the peace in society by threatening the general public[1616]. As mentioned above the victims of hate crimes are attacked without a warning. While it is deeply disconcerting to be the target of "random" violence, the cause of exactly this feeling is aimed at to be created within the target community by a hate crime offender and which is achieved by the committal of a hate crime. Since a hate crime attack is unforeseen it signifies that the value of life as such is questioned[1617]. Just anyone can be victimized who inheres a feature hated by the perpetrator. In consequence of this social-psychological threat and pressure of randomness an increase of fear of crimes occurs among those who possess the characteristics which define them as potential future immediate victims, i.e. the target community. This facilitated climate of threat and fear among the target community will, at some point, spill over to the society at large[1618]. Therefore, the public peace, which according to the German meaning is understood as the enabling of a free development of the individuality[1619] of all citizens by providing the consciousness of general safety and the universal respect for human rights in a society[1620], could possibly be endangered in particular through the committal of a crime which is connected to the hateful or biased motive of an offender.

1613 "Hate crimes do more than threaten the safety and welfare of all citizens. [...] They [...] tear at the very fabric of free society." (New York Penal Law § 485.00 Legislative findings).

1614 See, e.g., Ellias, The Politics of victimization 116 (1986); Karmen, Crime Victims: An Introduction to Victimiology 262-263 (2d Ed. 1990); Levin/Mc Devitt, supra note 3; Kelly/Tennant, supra note 3, at 26; Matsuda, supra note 6, at 2330-2331.

1615 Especially in German criminal law there are several criminal norms that protect legal goods which do not protect the direct-individual sphere of individual persons. (Wohlers, Deliktstypen des Präventionsstrafrechts , p. 213).

1616 As assumed by the Federal Supreme Court in: BGH January 12, 2000 - StB 15/99.

1617 In dependence on AE - Leben; GA 2008, 193, where it is stated that an act constitutes a threat to the general public if it expresses outside effects in the way that any citizen could possible be victimized because it indicates that the legal value of (human-) life as such is questioned. By that the fear of crime in society increases.

1618 To assure the protection of minorities - as members of the society - and to assure the protection of their rights and freedoms to an equal level with those of the majority forms an integral part of the protection by hate crime laws. As seen in the U.S., in the long term, solely the guarantee of safety for all members of society secures national peace.

1619 Article 2, Section I Basic Law.

1620 Jescheck/Weigend, Lehrbuch des Strafrechts AT; 1996, § 1 I. 2, p. 3.

The other idea refers to the symbolic message sent by a hate crime offender when committing his criminal act. By evoking the feeling that people with certain characteristics are potentially victimized due to their being, a climate of intolerance and exclusion is provoked. If this "symbolic group harming"[1621], which the perpetrator aims at when committing a hate crime, is answered by legislative counteractive symbol meaning due to the application of specific legislation, this harming effect could be captured by compensation. Since hate crimes are considered as "message crimes"[1622], specific laws could send a powerful signal for victims and communities that such crimes are not tolerated[1623], and thereby manage to express that the ideas sent into the national sphere by the perpetrator are not consented by the overall majority, thereby a hate crime law could serve the preservation of the existing climate[1624].

Since hate crime therefore could have the above considered harmful effects on a societal, thus collective, good, expressly by injuring or endangering the public peace[1625], the public peace could be the legal good which requires protection by hate crime legislation in its partial aspect which is in particular affected through the committal of a hate crime.

1.2. Priority of Protected Legal Goods

The human dignity, codified in Article 1 Basic Law[1626] is the highest individual right in the German Basic Order[1627]. The human dignity refers to the "intrinsic value of human beings"[1628], which is the value that constitutes a human element in virtue of his personhood[1629]. This dignity is part of every person, without regard to his characteristics[1630]. The human dignity is inviolable, thus

---

1621 Keiser, ZRP 2010, p. 46.

1622 Schneider, Hasskriminalität: Eine neue kriminologische Deliktskategorie, JZ, 2003, pp.497-504 (498).

1623 "We see that hate crime laws are working because they send a powerful signal not just to the perpetrator and the victim, but to the community". (Stachelberg in: Lynch and Stachelberg, Hate Crime Laws, Morning Show on C-SPAN's Washington Journal, March 13, 2012).

1624 View hereto Chapter 4, C., 8. Symbolic Reasoning of Hate Crime Law; and Chapter 4, G., 1.5. Legitimacy of a Hate Crime Norm in Regard to the Protected Partial Aspect of Public Peace.

1625 This results from the idea that "Hate crimes [...] tear at the very fabric of free society. [...] Hate crimes can and do intimidate and disrupt entire communities and vitiate the civility that is essential to healthy democratic processes". (New York Penal § 485.00 Legislative findings); View also the Assumption of the Federal Supreme Court in: BGH January 12, 2000 - StB 15/99: Hate Crimes, which are repeatedly committed in Germany, "disturb the peaceful cohabitation of Germans and foreigners severely; further they generate a general climate of fear and intimidation in public, especially among those in the Federal Republic of Germany living foreigners, by causing serious, the inner safety impairing doubts, whether the security forces are sufficiently capable and determined of protecting foreign residents".

1626 Article 1 Basic Law [Human dignity – Human rights – Legally binding force of basic rights] demands the following: "(1) The Human dignity shall be inviolable. To respect and protect it shall be the duty of all state authority. (2) The German people therefore acknowledge inviolable and inalienable human rights as the basis of every community, of peace and of justice in the world. (3) The following basic rights shall bind the legislature, the executive and the judiciary as directly applicable law."

1627 Sachs, Verfassungsrecht II, 2002, p.166, marginal no. 2; Epping, Grundrechte, 2009, p. 257, marginal no. 581 "exceptional position" – translation of "Sonderstellung"; Roxin, Strafrecht AT 1, § 2, marginal no. 8, p. 16; BVerfGE 6, 32; pp. 36, 41 Human dignity as "fundamental constitutive principle" of the Constitution - translation of "tragendes Konstitutionsprinzip".

1628 Sachs, Verfassungsrecht II, 2002, pp.167, marginal no. 8; Epping, Grundrechte, 2009, pp. 262, marginal no. 593.

1629 BVerfGE 30, 1 Leading Sentence 6.

1630 BVerfGE 96, 375, p. 399; BVerfGE 115, 118, p. 152.

cannot be taken from anyone; solely the claim to respect the human dignity, which derives from it, is injured by an "undignified" behavior[1631]. Therefore, the human dignity is an individual right of every person of society and "[t]o respect and protect it shall be the duty of all state authority". Since as mentioned, the claim to respect such might be injured by the "undignified" behavior which constitutes a hate crime, the punishment of a perpetrator could be legitimate due to him violating constitutional precepts. However, the addressee of this constitutional demand is the government, not the individual[1632]. In the original meaning the Basic Rights serve as protection against governmental intervention into the sphere of personal freedom of the individual (Article 1 Section 3 Basic Law)[1633]. The commandment, to respect the human dignity, at first sight, does not apply between individuals in the non-federally regulated area.

Basic Rights in general are merely to be respected by the public sector as the addressee of the Constitution, the government must not deny constitutional rights to an individual; an anchored criminal offense committed by the individual in case of him violating a constitutional precept can not be assumed in general according to German legal understandings. Constitutional values, which must be followed by the government, are not to be moved one-on-one into the relation between individuals in order to adopt an automatic criminal offense in the case of non-compliance; therefore constitutional guidelines must not be equally observed by individuals among each other[1634].

Principally, in order to punish behavior by criminal law, a criminal norm must provide the facts for a legitimate intervention into the basic right of the actor, codified in Article 2, Section 1 Basis Law. In order to restrict the freedom of action (Article 2 Section 1 Basic Law) of the perpetrator, the constitutional precepts must be recognized by the criminal legislator as protectable value-bearing states[1635], which have a sufficient outer substance; this assures the reference to a legal good when justifying criminal law. Therefore, pure, discriminatory acts of individuals do not violate the basic right barrier "rights of others" in Article 2, Section 1 Basic Law, unless made criminal due to the precepts of the legal good doctrine. The pure reference to constitutional demands lacks the justification for a norm and a restriction of the right of

1631 BVerfGE 87, 209, p. 228; BVerfGE 109, 133, p. 150; Epping, Grundrechte, 2009, p. 262, marginal no. 593.

1632 A so called "direct-effect-on-third-parties" of the Basic Rights of the German Constitution was once demanded of the Federal Labour Court (BAGE 1, 185/193 et seq.; BAGE 48, 122/138 et seq.: The change in importance of the fundamental rights among the development of a liberal- towards the today social-constitutional state, speaks "for the direct and legal binding effect towards individuals of such fundamental rights, which are indispensable for the transport fields for the legal community among each other in a liberal and social community"; but as a result, the German jurisprudence pronounced against such a direct effect on third parties. (Pieroth/Schlink, Grundrechte, pp. 46, 47, marginal no. 190 – 191).

1633 Beside the classic defensive function of the Basic Order, further rights in form of claims against the government are acknowledged to occur from the Constitution and its contained Basic Rights. (Epping, Grundrechte, view table of content and p. 139).

1634 The decisive reasons for punishment cannot derive from civil or public law standards, and also not from the constitution. (Hörnle, Grob anstößiges Verhalten, p. 73).

1635 Di Fabio, in: Münz/Dürig, GG, Art. 2 marginal no. 44; Kunig, in: von Münch/Kunig, GG, Art. 2 marginal no. 20; Pieroth/Schlink, Staatsrecht II, marginal no. 385; Hörnle, Grob anstößiges Verhalten, p. 72.

freedom of action (Article 2 Section 1 Basic Law) of the handling person would not be legitimate[1636].

It is disputed, whether a direct horizontal effect of Article 1, Paragraph 1 Basic Law towards third parties can be acknowledged, such could commit individuals to respect Article 1, Paragraph 1 Basic Law between each another[1637]. It is widely recognized that the claim to respect the human dignity also exists between individuals among themselves[1638], which is based on the special status[1639] of Article 1 Basic Law in the Constitution, and results from the in Article 1 Basic Law enshrined duty of the legislature to protect such. According to this, a human dignity-injurious behavior of private parties would be prohibited already according to the Constitution[1640]. Obtaining the status as "the highest legal value"[1641], would be contradictory, if individuals were not be able to rely on Article 1, Paragraph 2 Basic Law as a personal right[1642]. If individuals would not be compelled to comply with Article 1 Basic Law, they also would not have the right to be protected against actions exercised by another. Therefore, a pure state binding approach would be contrary to the idea of a comprehensive protection of the human dignity, therefore the commandment to respect the human dignity also applies to relationships between individuals[1643].

For the reliability of criminal prohibitions, however, the decision of this dispute is irrelevant, since acts which violate the human dignity violate the basic right barrier "rights of others", codified in Article 2, Paragraph 1 Basic Law, therefore a base for legitimate penal law, which limits the freedom of action of the perpetrator, is at hand either ways[1644].

Nevertheless, for the sake of completeness, the opposite view is represented in order to examine the full legitimative scope of hate crime legislation. The opponent view, which refuses a direct horizontal effect of Article 1, Paragraph 1 Basic Law, argues that the governmental duty for protection, according to Article 1 Basic Law, solely requires that the actual effectiveness of the fundamental right is ensured and guaranteed[1645]. To address the relations between private parties the legislator therefore must enact specific norms

1636 Hörnle, Grob anstößiges Verhalten, p. 118.

1637 For this purpose: Klinge, Todesbegriff, Totenschutz und Menschenwürde, p. 235; Against this: Stern, in: FS for Scupin, p. 636; Hörnle, Grob anstößiges Verhalten, p. 118.

1638 Hörnle, Grob anstößiges Verhalten, p. 118.; Epping, Grundrechte, 2009, p. 257, marginal no. 581.

1639 The special status derives from the position of the fundamental right which is organized at the tip of the Constitution as well as from the special protection that is obtained from the principles of Article 1 Basic Law by the so-called eternity guarantee of Article 79, Section 3 Basic Law. (Epping, Grundrechte, 2009, p. 257, marginal no. 581).

1640 BVerfGE 115, 189, p. 199; Kunig, in: v. Münch/Kunig, GG, Art. 1, marginal no. 27 with further references; Epping, Grundrechte, 2009, p. 257, marginal no. 581.

1641 BVerfGE 6, 32, 41; BVerfGE 45, 187, 227; Maihofer, Rechtsstaat und menschliche Würde, p. 9: Article 1, Section 1 Basic Law as the "fundamental norm of our Constitution and basic norm of our legal order as such".

1642 Hörnle, Grob anstößiges Verhalten, p. 117; Ipsen, JZ 2001, p. 991.

1643 Epping, Grundrechte, 2009, p. 257, marginal no. 581; BVerwGE 115, 189, p. 199; Kunig, in: Münch/Kunig, GG, Art. 1, marginal no. 27 with further reference; dissenting: Sachs, Verfassungsrecht II, 2002, p.167, marginal no. 7.

1644 Hörnle, Grob anstößiges Verhalten, p. 118.

1645 Epping, Grundrechte, 2009, p. 143, marginal no. 337.

which address the individual. This duty for protection, however, primarily refer to the legislature regarding the creation of civil law[1646], but in order to completely comply to this demand (established in Article 2, Section 1 Basic Law in conjunction with Article 1, Section 1 Basic Law), the legislature also needs the option of criminal law. So, while the government is obligated to ensure the protection of the fundamental right of human dignity against interference by third parties by the installment of appropriate safeguards, it is basically free to choose the means for doing so. Anyhow, because of the high value of the human dignity, a - compared to regular standards - more stringent intensity of governmental duty for protection can be assumed[1647].

In respect to hate crimes, the requirement for the enforcement of this legal obligation, i.e. the protection of the human dignity against impariment, could be even stricter than usual. Based on the idea that a hate crime offender violates the right of respect for the human dignity of a victim beyond the degree of violation which goes along with the committal of every violent crime[1648], due to the fact that he primarily aims at expressing his denial of this right verbally and physically, one could anchor a special demand for the legislator to protect the human dignity against hate crime attacks. But even if one acknowledges the fact of a very intense violation of the claim to respect for the right of human dignity through the interfering behavior of private parties through the committal of a hate crime, and moreover admit that this form of a more intense injury has not been criminally covered yet, the decisional scope of the legislature regarding of what instruments to use to protect the human dignity against hate crimes shall remain; the legislature may therefore continue to choose between different possible solutions. However, in no case may an additional, not yet criminally recognized, impairment of the human dignity through the conduct of third parties be legally ignored. The three elements of the attack on human dignity (core area of the personality, classifying one as an inferior being, denying one's right to life as an equivalent individuality)[1649] are realized by the commission of a hate crime. Therefore, hate crimes are clearly demarkable from ordinary (violent) crimes, since they provide the necessary specific negative aspects of violating the human dignity to a level, which the violation of general personal rights do not achieve: The "object formula", introduced by the Federal Constitutional Court, states that "the guarantee of human dignity protects every person against being exposed to a treatment that challenge his quality as a subject in general, and makes him a mere object of [state]

1646 Oeter, AöR 119, 1994, p. 529, pp. 537 et seq.

1647 Sachs, Verfassungsrecht II, 2002, p. 173, marginal no. 32. This more stringent obligation of the legislator can be drawn from the expressive demand in the constitution that requires the legislator to protect the human dignity. (BVerfGE 64, 274, 278; Kunig, in: von Münch/Kunig, GG, Art. 1 marginal no. 27 et seq.; Höfling, in: Sachs, GG, Art. 1, marginal no. 38 et seq.; Dreier, in: Dreier, GG, Art. 1 Abs. 1, marginal no. 135 et seqq.; Sachs, Verfassungsrecht II, B I, marginal no. 31 et seqq.; Starck, JZ 1981, 459; Taupitz, NJW 2001, pp. 3435 et seq.; Peglau, Schutz des allgemeinen Persönlichkeitsrechts, pp. 50 et seqq.; Hörnle, Grob anstößiges Verhalten, p. 118).

1648 An enhanced obligation of the legislature to protect the human dignity against violation in general, is assumed by: Sachs, Verfassungsrecht II, 2002, p. 173, marginal no. 33.

1649 View Chapter 4, G., 1. 1.1., 1.1.1. Human Dignity of the Immediate Victim.

action"[1650]. According to this, the claim to respect the human dignity of an individual is injured when, in principle, his validity claim is denied in a grossly contemptuous manner[1651]; that the perpetrators of hate crimes exactly do such by the realization of already criminally codified behavior, and thereby, in addition to the already punished violation of a legal good, realize a further violation of the human dignity due to this different and psychically and physically more intense way of attack[1652], which accrues due to connecting the criminal behavior to the motive with its specific meaningful content - as explained above - is clearly ascertainable[1653]. The fact that the victim is a human subject is not only "challenged in principle"[1654] or arbitrarily disregarded by a hate crime perpetrator, but outright denied[1655], due to the basic treatment

---

1650 BVerfGE 96, 375, p. 399; BVerfGE 115, 118, p. 152; Positively expressed: Men must always remain to be the purpose of handling - not the mean. (Sachs, Verfassungsrecht II, 2002, p.168, marginal no. 10).

1651 BVerwGE 93, 56 et seqq. shows, but in a different (non-hate crime) case, a victim-treatment, which is understood to be in precisely harming the human dignity and, however, is typical for hate crime acts, since for the perpetrators of these acts it is never about a target of higher-priority (e.g. obtain booty), but always about setting a degrading example: In this case, a lieutenant had taken a soldier captured, tied him up, and repeatedly verbally threatened him with death and humiliated him by sadistic and sexual innuendo in front of other soldiers. The Federal Administrative Court acknowledged a deliberate degradation of the victim to an "object" for the purpose of "demonstration" of the intrinsic superiority and power, therefore, considered a blatant violation of the human dignity, which is guaranteed by Article 1, Section 1 Basic Law and which stipulates the inviolability of the respect of this most fundamental right. (Epping, Fundamental Rights, 2009, p. 265, footnote 37). The deliberate degradation of the victim to an "object" is associated with the commission of a hate crimes; after all, besides the sending of a message, this is a major goal of the perpetrators. Implemented in the message sending activity is, equally fundamental, a "demonstration" of superiority and self-power, hence a hate crime offender try to bring out his superiority over other humans.

1652 Lawrence, Punishing Hate, p. 40, 63; with reference to: Melinda Henneberger, "For Bias Crimes, a Double Trauma" , Newsday, 113 (Jan. 9, 1992); N. R. Kleinfield, "Bias Crimes Hold Steady, But Leave Many Scards" , New York Times, A – 1 (Jan. 27, 1992); Brian Levin, "U. S. Supreme Court Upholds Stiffer Sentences for Hate Crimes", Intelligence Report, 166 (sept. 1993); Joan Weiss, "Ethnoviolence: Impact upon the Responce of Victims and the Communtiy", in Bias Crime: American Law Enforcement and Legal Response, pp. 182, 183 (1993); see also Joan C. Weiss, Howard J. Ehrlich, Barabara E. K. Larcon, "Ethnoviolence at Work" , 18 Journal of Intergroup Relations, p. 18 (Winter 1991 - 1992); Füllgrabe, Hassverbrechen, Kriminalistik, 2004, pp. 391-397; Aydin, Die strafrechtliche Bekämpfung von Hassdelikten in Deutschland und in den Vereinigten Staaten von Amerika, 2006, pp. 112-130; Schneider, Politische Kriminalität: Hassverbrechen, Fremdenfeindlichkeit im internationalen Kontext, Kriminalistik 2001, pp. 21-28; Schneider, Politische Kriminalität, in: R. Sieverts/H.J.Schneider (eds.), Handwörterbuch der Kriminologie, 2. Auflage, 5. Band, Berlin, New York, 1998, pp. 589-624 (590); Schneider, Kriminologie der Hassdelikte Konzeptionen, Ursachen, Vorbeugung und Kontrolle, in: Bewährungshilfe, 2003, pp. 115 et seqq.; with further references to European literature: Garofalo, James, Hate Crime Victimization in the United States, in: Robert C. Davis/Arthur J. Lurigio/Wesley G. Skogan (eds.), Victims of Crime, 2. Edition, 1997, pp. 132-145 Thousand oaks, London, New Delhi: Sage (pp. 141, 142); Martin, Susan E., Investigating Hate Crimes: Case Characteristics an Law Enforcement Responses. Justice Quaterly 13, 1996, pp. 455-480 (470).

1653 View Chapter 4, G., 1. 1.1., 1.1.1. Human Dignity of the Immediate Victim.

1654 BVerfGE 30, 1, pp. 25 et seqq.

1655 The human dignity must be considered as violated if a person has been degraded by a treatment not just to a mere object, but also has been exposed to "a treatment that principally puts its subject quality into question, or that the treatment in the particular case constitutes a gratuitous disregard for the dignity of man. It therefore has [....] to be an expression of contempt for the value which corresponds to a human by virtue of his being a person, so, in this sense, constitutes a "contemptuous treatment". (BVerfGE 30, 1, pp. 25 et seq.). This general, however by the government to be caused, injury must (even without the final settlement of the dispute regarding a direct horizontal effect of Article 1 Basic Law) obtain a considerable criminal weight even if committed by a private party as well in case of a multi-potentiated intensity of disregard of the human dignity in the way it takes place through the treatment realized by a hate crime. In any case, the protection of the fundamental right of human dignity must be guaranteed towards third parties by appropriate safeguards, which have to be established by the state, thus the legislator (criminal liability arises from the violation of the "rights of others" according to Article 2, Section 1 Basic Law). Due to the doubling of the conditions a tightened, over the regular standards intensified protection duty of the legislator occurs (Sachs, Verfassungsrecht II, 2002, p. 173, marginal no. 32). In reference to hate crime

of certain people as inferiorly[1656], an additional human-dignity injuring effect must be admitted[1657]. The message sent by the respective degrading mode of treatment is emphasized through the fact that the action takes place only because of an assumed inferiority of the victim. The sum of evils gives such an act the special victim-degrading content[1658].

The human dignity as an individual right serves for the justification of criminal prohibitions in general[1659] and therefore could serve as justification for hate crime legislation in particular, since the general higher interference with the human dignity through hate crime committal has not been legally recognized in previous enacted offenses for the punishment of un- or otherwise motivated criminal acts.

While in this opinion it is assured that hate crimes violate the human dignity of the immediate victim greater than unmotivated criminal acts which do not express the xenophobic message of the denial of one´s right to exist during the attack, it must, however, be acknowledged that the principal protection of the human dignity, at least in parts, has been taken into account by the legislature when it enacted previous norms which serve for the protection of individual goods of the victims. Therefore, the part of the legal good of public peace which precisely is affected through the committal of a hate crime could be the prevailing legal good, which requires protection through hate crime legislation.

If focusing on the most prevailing protection object of a hate crime norm it comes to mind that the core of hate crime legislation is to preserve the actual, for all livable climate[1660]; this is a collective good of the society. This includes the fact that "every person belonging to a national minority shall have the right to freely choose to be treated or not to be treated as such and no disadvantage shall result from this choice or from the exercise of the rights which are connected to that choice" [1661]. Moreover, "[P]ersons belonging to

---

due to the increased intensity of the violation of the entitlement to respect human dignity by the interfering behavior of the perpetrators, the scope of the legislator does indeed exist (the legislature may therefore continue to choose between different options), but in no case must it leave the additional impairment of the human dignity through the biased criminal behavior of others go unnoticed. In the field of hate crimes the requirements of the enforcement of this legal duty could be more strict than it is usual the case according its protection duties. (Likewise expressed in general for violations of the human dignity by Sachs, Verfassungsrecht II, 2002, p. 173, marginal no. 33).

1656 Jarass, in: Jarass/Pieroth, Art. 1 marginal no. 12.

1657 According to which, in the context of hate crimes, it is undoubtedly about a very serious and fundamental equality violation. Due to the seriousness of the offense the human dignity, or more precisely, its claim to respect, is violated. ("Very serious and fundamental equality violations can violate the human dignity" - Epping, Grundrechte, p. 299, marginal no. 602).

1658 While the mere insulting or degrading does not touch the human dignity, the protection area is already damaged by a severe insult (BVerfGE 30. 173, p. 214.; BVerfGE 102, 347, p. 367). Therefore, a hate crime, in any case, injures the very core of the human dignity to its greatest.

1659 BVerfGE 64, 274, 278; Kunig, in: von Münch/Kunig, GG, Art. 1 marginal no. 27 et seq.; Höfling, in: Sachs, GG, Art. 1, marginal no. 38 et seq.; Dreier, in: Dreier, Art. 1 Abs. 1, marginal no. 135 et seqq.; Sachs, Verfassungsrecht II, B I, marginal no. 31 et seqq.; Starck, JZ 1981, 459; Taupitz, NJW 2001, 3435 et seq.; Peglau, Schutz des allgemeinen Persönlichkeitsrechts, pp. 50 et seqq.; Hörnle, Grob anstößiges Verhalten, p. 116.

1660 Acknowledging New York's legal findings, stating: "Current law does not adequately recognize the harm to public order and individual safety that hate crimes cause." (New York Penal § 485.00 Legislative findings).

1661 Framework Convention for the Protection of National Minorities, Section I, Article 3, No. 1.

national minorities may exercise the rights and enjoy the freedoms flowing from the principles enshrined in the [respective constitutional and national legal [...] framework [...] individually as well as in community with others."[1662] And the legislator must make sure that these written rights are realized in the respective society. If the legislator does not serve for the realization of democratic standards throughout the national society, revolt, turmoil and national strife occurs, the peaceful co-existence in a nation becomes endangered. The protection of public peace, according to the German understanding, means that the free development of the individuality of all citizens is enabled by providing the consciousness of general safety and the universal respect for human rights in a society[1663]. Due to the widespread impacts of hate crime, which go beyond such affecting the immediate victim and which is uncommon for parallel crimes, from a legal point of view, the legal good of "public peace" is prevalently to be protected by a hate crime norm.

Summarized, it is considered that hate crime legislation, on the foreground, intends to serve the protection of the public peace. Yet, a weighty protection of the human dignity must result from such a penal provision as well. Whether the public peace is the sole legal good of a criminal norm depends on the relevant standard[1664]. In the context of hate crimes, as stated, it is not the only legal value, but beside the protection of the human dignity as an individual right of the attacked victim, the primary legal good which protection could be required by a hate crime norm. In the following it must be examined whether the protection of this legal good could legitimize the enactment of a criminal norm in the German Penal Code.

1.3. Legitimacy of Hate Crime Legislation according to the Legal Good Doctrine

In the following it is examined, whether the legal good, filtered from the ones discussed and considered as de lege ferenda protected by criminal law, is a concern which legitimately could be protected by criminal hate crime norms according to German legal requirements.

To understand whether the German legislature could be obliged to enact hate crime legislation, it is necessary to draw on basic precepts according legitimacy of criminal law and the existence of criminal provisions[1665]. The right of the legislator to punish in general is codified in Article 74 No. 1 Basic Law. This constitutional norm determines that criminal law is a part of the concurrent legislative power and thereby clarifies that the existence of legal punishment is

1662 Framework Convention for the Protection of National Minorities, Section I, Article 3, No. 2.

1663 Jescheck/Weigend, Lehrbuch des Strafrechts AT; 1996, § 1 I. 2, p. 3.

1664 Fischer, Die Eignung, den öffentlichen Frieden zu stören -Zur Beseitigung eines "restriktiven" Phantoms, NStZ 1988, 159 (163): Whereas the prevailing opinion considers public peace as the only protected legal good in Section166 and Section 140 No. 2 Penal Code the opinions vary regarding Section 130 Penal Code. In Section 126 Penal Code public peace is considered to be the primarily protected legal good among other threatened goods. (With reference to: Lackner/Kühl, StGB, § 130, marginal no. 1, with further references: Preisendanz, § 130 marginal no. 1; Rudolphi, § 130 marginal no. 1; opposing: Fischer, StGB, § 130 marginal no. 2, 3).

1665 Wessels/Beulke, Strafrecht AT, pp. 1, 2, marginal no. 4; BVerfGE 51, 324, 343, BVerfGE 88, 203, 257.

constitutionally presumed[1666]. By that though, it does not derive how behavior must be designed in order to be legitimately punished by the legislator, nor if it must be punished in order to meet constitutional precepts. This relates to the question of the substantive content of criminal behavior[1667]. Such is to be answered by taking the task of criminal law into account[1668]. The general purpose of criminal law is to ensure the peaceful co-existence among the citizens of the respective nation[1669]. Therefore, the task of criminal law is to prevent socially damaging behavior[1670]. As the controversy regarding the definition of the task of criminal law has been illustrated above[1671], the following proceeds on the prevailing opinion that the task of criminal law is the subsidiary protection of legal goods[1672]. The public peace is a collective good, in order for it to be affected, concerns that are an interest of the entire population of the society must be touched[1673]. Whether public goods are sufficient to legitimate criminal law is highly in question[1674]. For answering whether the public peace is able to legitimate a hate crime norm it must be referred to the precepts drawn from the legal good doctrine.

1.3.1. Precepts of the Legal Good Doctrine

State sanctions have the task to protect basic liberties. Liberties are an expression of a human society project[1675]. In order to assure a free living and the preservation of the constitutional guaranteed liberty rights of the individual the literature aims at limiting the ability of the penal legislature to punish human behavior. Accordingly the penal legislature must only enact legitimate norms. And the legitimation strategy is based on the protection of legal goods. Thus, according to this understanding, the protection of a legitimate legal good authorizes legal prohibitions and the ability to clearly indicate this legal good is a necessary precondition for the legitimacy of a penal norm[1676]. The offense is based on the norm and the norm is based on the legal good[1677].

The basic understanding of the German legal good doctrine and the legitimation of criminal norms has been illustrated above in more details, with the result that neither a distinction between individual- and universal legal goods, nor the requirement to a certain material content of the protected legal

---

1666 Roxin, Strafrecht AT I, p. 13, § 2, marginal no. 1.
1667 Zipf, Kriminalpolitik, 1980, pp. 106 et seqq.; Roxin, Strafrecht AT I, § 2, p. 13, marginal no. 1.
1668 Roxin, Strafrecht AT I, § 2, p. 13, marginal no. 1.
1669 Jescheck/Weigend, Lehrbuch des Strafrechts, § 1 I. 1, p. 2.
1670 Roxin, Strafrecht AT I, § 2, pp. 13, 14, marginal no. 1; § 2, p. 20, marginal no. 21.
1671 View Chapter 2, D., 4., 4.2. Purpose of Criminal Law according to the German Penal Theory.
1672 Roxin, Strafrecht AT I, pp. 13, 14, § 2, marginal no. 1.
1673 There are several criminal norms which protect legal goods that do not protect the direct-individual sphere of individual persons in German criminal law. (Wohlers, Deliktstypen des Präventionsstrafrechts, p. 213).
1674 View Chapter 2, D., 2., 2.1, 2.1.3. Individual- and Collective Goods.
1675 Zabel, Kriminologische Aspekte des modernen Rechtsgüterschutzes, Monatsschrift für Kriminologie und Strafrechtsreform, 2009, pp. 395-412 (395).
1676 Zabel, Kriminologische Aspekte des modernen Rechtsgüterschutzes, Monatsschrift für Kriminologie und Strafrechtsreform, 2009, pp. 395-412 (395); Jäger, Strafrechtsgesetzgebung und Rechtsgüterschutz, pp. 20 et seqq. Roxin, Strafrecht AT I, § 2, marginal no. 9 et seq, 42; Worms, Bekennntnisbeschimpfung, pp. 68 et seqq.
1677 Zabel, Kriminologische Aspekte des modernen Rechtsgüterschutzes, Monatsschrift für Kriminologie und Strafrechtsreform, 2009, pp. 395-412 (395).

good is able to clearly determine what goods are legitimately to be protected by criminal law[1678], it is, after all, solely known that within the precepts of the prevailing German legal good doctrine one follows the system critical precepts and therefore must call for a legal good which has a "certain" content of tangibility[1679]. Whereas more precise criteria to describe the term legal good are missing, the answer to the question, whether a legislator is legitimately authorized to consider the public legal peace as the main concern to be protected by hate crime legislation and the human dignity of the individual as the secondarily protected good - according to the German legal good doctrine with its system-critical point of view - depends on the extent to which goods, which do not have a physical palpable content, can be considered to be legitimately protected by a criminal norm and whether one acknowledges that collective legal goods, compared to individual legal goods, may be worthy of criminal protection as well. By that, it is searched for an answer whether or not the protection of the "public peace" in particular and the "human dignity" in the subordinated sense serve as legitimate criminological criterions for the legislator to punish offenses which are motivated by animus against particular human characteristics. This primarily depends on the degree of palpability which is demanded for a legitimately protected legal good. If one approves the requirement of tangibility as a limiting factor of the term legal good, at least terms of high universality can not be considered to be rightfully protected by a criminal norm[1680]. Actually, neither the human dignity, nor the public peace could be viewed as interests legitimately worth of criminal protection[1681]. While, after all, the human dignity of the specificly attacked victim is a highly individual legal good and its protection by criminal law is undisputedly acknowledged[1682], the criminal protection of the legal good public peace is not just debatably in terms of its intangible content, but also in spite of being a collective good. However, it is necessary to protect certain intangible and societal goods, if the functioning of society depends on their preservation[1683]. The individual as a socialized being can only achieve and maintain his individual goods in community with others, thus in societal institutions which require the functioning of societal and governmental systems[1684]. Insofar it is not satisfying to limit the ambit of criminal law to substantial, tangible or bodily legal goods only, since it is not possible to encompass all interests which are essential to life in a governmental society as the sum of all gathered concrete physical objects[1685]. And the protection of those "social conditions necessary

1678 View Chapter 2, D., 2., 2.1., 2.1.5. Intermediate Summary.
1679 Wohlers, Deliktstypen des Präventionsstrafrechts, p. 220.
1680 Wohlers, Deliktstypen des Präventionsstrafrechts, p. 225; Grützner, Die Sanktionierung von Submissionsabsprachen, p. 435.
1681 Wohlers, Deliktstypen des Präventionsstrafrechts, pp. 225, 226; Köhler, Strafrecht AT, p. 33; Grützner, Die Sanktionierung von Submissionsabsprachen, p. 435.
1682 View Chapter 1.4. Legitimacy of a Hate Crime Norm in Regard to the Protected Human Dignity.
1683 Hörnle, Grob anstößiges Verhalten, p. 97.
1684 Hefendehl, Kollektive Rechtsgüter, p. 77.
1685 "The life of a citizen in today's political and social constitution is not solely defined by his individual sphere of freedom, but by the functioning of society and state supply systems. On a regular basis, the interests of the individual can no longer directly mediatize themselves, but develop only with institutional bodies." (Anastasopoulou, Deliktstypen, p. 42 – with reference to Hefendehl, Kollektive Rechtsgüter, pp. 75 et

for the constitutional status and freedom of the individual citizen“[1686], as the prerequiste of a social community, is essential for human beings due to their living in a social community. As an aim of the community collective goods therefore seem worthy of criminal protection. Accordingly, a limitation of the legitimate ambit of criminal law to substantial and individual legal goods only, according to a system-critical understanding, must not take place. As a result, the protection of the public peace as an object for legitimating a hate crime norm can not be excluded, nor can the human dignity.

The public peace, as a legal good worthy of protection, could be excluded from the circle of legitimately protectable goods when considering that the concept of legal goods aims at determining the punishability of behavior with regard to the socially harmful effects associated with this behavior[1687]. Similar to the precepts of the Harm Principle, behavior therefore shall only be evaluated as punishable if a concrete substantial damage to a legal good is attributable to such[1688]. So, if it is stated "that the specific function of criminal norms protecting supra-individual, thus collective goods precisely lies in the protection of certain governmental or societal interactions which do not provide an individual substantial or touchable object, as it characteristically can be found within concrete objective individual legal goods, and which if harmed, reveals itself in an almost indefinable, however, elusive disorganization of problem-specific outcome“[1689], it must be said, that whenever this outcome is harmful and palpable, the (supra-individual) good which protection is aimed at, gains some measure of shape, thus substance and therefore is legitimately worth protecting[1690]. So, in fact, it is not about the substantial embodiment of legal goods but about their ability to be impaired[1691].

It is to remind oneself that it is significant that legal goods, which are protected by norms established in the German Penal Code, usually precisely are not protected in their entirety[1692] - with the exception of some constituted legal goods which protect the personal domain, for instance, life and physical integrity[1693]. Hence, also supra-individual interests are protected in selective areas, for instance, the human dignity is protected against several forms of interference (for example in Section 86 Penal Code "Dissemination of propaganda material of unconstitutional organizations; in Section 86a Penal Code penalizing the use of "symbols of unconstitutional organizations";

seqq.; Müssig, Rechtsgüterschutz, p. 155 et seq.; Wohlers, Deliktstypen des Präventionsstrafrechts, p. 226; Grützner, Die Sanktionierung von Submissionsabsprachen, p. 435).

1686 Müssig, Rechtsgüterschutz, p. 42; Rudolphi, in: SK-StGB, Vorbem. § 1 marginal no. 2.

1687 Wohlers, Deliktstypen des Präventionsstrafrechts, p. 223.

1688 According to the theory of social harmfulness it does not depend on the damaging success of the individual act, but it is to generalize: the general suitability of an act to cause harm to a legal good must decide on the harmfulness of an action. (Amelung, Rechtsgüterschutz, p. 388; Müssig, Rechtsgüterschutz, pp. 63 et seq.).

1689 Amelung, Rechtsgüterschutz, p. 356; Stratenwerth, in: Lenckner-Festschrift, p. 377 (385 et seqq.); Wohlers, Delitkstypen, p. 224; Grützner, Die Sanktionierung von Submissionsabsprachen, pp. 435, 436.

1690 Cf. Wohlers, Delitkstypen, p. 226; Amelung, Rechtsgüterschutz, p. 199.

1691 Wohlers, Delitkstypen, p. 225; Worms, Bekenntnisbeschimpfung, pp. 65, 82.

1692 Maiwald, in: Maurach-Festschrift, p. 9 et seq.; Grützner, Die Sanktionierung von Submissionsabsprachen, p. 423.

1693 Wohlers, Delitkstypen, p. 226.

Section 166 Penal Code penalizing the "Defamation of religions, religious and ideological associations"; Section 168 Penal Code criminalizing the "Desecration of graves etc.; moreover the human dignity is protected against acts like libel and slander, established in Section 185 Penal Code ("Insult")); based on these facts, it is not protected in the entirety, but in parts.

So, whenever a criminal statute protects a supra-individual good in clearly demarkable parts, it does not seem reasonable to exclude an actual possibility of interference with such, whenever it is determinable that a behavior is relevant to a measurable injury and it is possible to assess the need to protect the respective "interaction – context"[1694] it seems reasonable to consider the protection of this part[1695]. At least if the legal good, which is set up for criminal protection, is based on an "empirically ascertainable substrate of concrete interactional causal relations and courses of action"[1696] – in this case, its worthiness of protection can not be denied from the outset[1697]; because such a legal value is essential "to our constitutional society and therewith also for the constitutional position and freedom of the individual citizen and thus [must be considered] as an valuable social functional unit"[1698]. With that, a supraindividuell legal good like the public peace would serve as a criterion for legitimating a norm if it would somehow achieve shape in a physical-causally violate able object[1699]. Insofar it is questionable to what extent the legal good of public peace is capable of impairment in order for deciding whether it may be legitimately protectable by a hate crime norm.

Of course, in spite of individual liability of criminal law, a sufficient outline of the protected matter, especially regarding supra-individual legal goods, is essential for legitimating criminal law[1700]. This outline, thus the limit of a necessarily to be required tangibility of supra-individual legal goods, however, may not be drawn by the requirement of a certain tangibility of the protected legal good. The general question, which in broad aims at clarifying the extent to which goods that do not draw on a basic point of reference are able to be included into the circuit of legitimately criminal protected legal goods, can be answered insofar that at least in such cases in which a legal good can be concretized in so far that an interference with it is reasonably noticeable - thus harmful effects on society are perceivable - an exclusion of the protection of such goods can not be reasoned by a lack of substantial content[1701]. Accordingly, a legal good is understood as a legally protected abstract value of

1694 Grützner, Die Sanktionierung von Submissionsabsprachen, p. 436; Wohlers, Deliktstypen des Präventionsstrafrechts, p. 227.

1695 Grützner, Die Sanktionierung von Submissionsabsprachen, pp. 435, 436.

1696 Tiedemann, Tatbestandsfunktionen, p. 211.

1697 Wohlers, Deliktstypen des Präventionsstrafrechts, p. 226; Grützner, Die Sanktionierung von Submissionsabsprachen, pp. 435, 436.

1698 Rudolphi, in: FS for Honig, p. 164, 166; Rudolphi, in: SK-StGB, vor § 1 marginal no. 8; Müssig, abstrackte Rechtsgüter, p. 41; Anastasopoulou, Deliktstypen, p. 12.

1699 Grützner, Die Sanktionierung von Submissionsabsprachen, p. 435; Wohlers, Deliktstypen des Präventionsstrafrechts, p. 224 et seqq.

1700 Wohlers, Deliktstypen des Präventionsstrafrechts, p. 225.

1701 Grützner, Die Sanktionierung von Submissionsabsprachen, p. 436.

the social order whose preservation is an aim of the community[1702]. The legal good of public peace could, insofar, serve as a possible legitimate base for justifying a substantive hate crime law considering the German criminal law doctrine if it is determinable in which clear demarkable area such is harmed through the effects of hate crimes. And moreover, this clear demarkable area is an area, which protection is important not just for the immediate or indirect attacked victims, but equally important for the entire society.

In summary, it can be stated that the German legal good doctrine provides a clear outline of what is to be protected legitimately by criminal law, however this is not to be equated with the tangibility of a protected good. Public peace or the human dignity as so categorized non-substantial goods can not be excluded from the circle of possible legal goods which serve for the legitimation of a criminal norm by the German legal doctrine in general. With regard to hate crime legislation it is considered that the protected object of public peace is able to provide a sufficient outline of the protected matter in order not to be excluded as an object for legitimizing a hate crime norm a priori. If it actually serves as a legitimation object for a criminal hate crime provision depends on whether it is determinable in which clear demarkable part the public peace is harmed through hateful and biased motivated criminal behavior and whether it can be comprehensibly illustrated how the criminal protection of this partial area is important for the entire society and not just for the immediate victimized part of the population.

Whether the protection of the public peace as legal good of a hate crime norm finally serves as a legitimation object for a criminal provision depends on constitutional precepts according to the nature of legal goods and according to the jurisdiction regarding the legitimacy of norms. Ultimately, the degree of recognition of the legal good "public peace" in the German literature is to be considered as well, which acknowledges the public peace as a legitimate goodworthy of criminal protection. Finally, the answer depends on the direction of attack and the thereon based configuration of the offense. This again depends on the measurability of the concrete harm, and therefore touches the American doctrine for the legitimation of norms, by turning the view towards the harmful effects of criminal behavior.

1.3.2. Legitimization of Hate Crime Legislation according to the Social Theory

Not all harm caused to a legal good should allow the legislator to punish its causing behavior, but only such which in addition is socially detrimental[1703]. Behavior is considered as socially detrimental whenever it is derogatory to the solving of the basic problems of a social system and its constant mindset[1704].

1702 Zabel, Kriminologische Aspekte des modernen Rechtsgüterschutzes, Monatsschrift für Kriminologie und Strafrechtsreform, 2009, pp. 395-412 (395); Jescheck/Weigend, Lehrbuch des Strafrechts AT, § 26 I.

1703 Amelung, Rechtsgüterschutz, pp. 350 et seqq.; Hassemer, Einführung in die Grundlagen des Strafrechts, 1990, p. 25; BVerfGE 45, 187 (254); Amelung, Rechtsgüterschutz, p. 387.

1704 Amelung, Rechtsgüterschutz, pp. 361, 387; Anastasopoulou, Deliktstypen, pp. 12 (13) et seqq.

Therefore, the legal good doctrine is further developed to a "theory of social harmfulness"[1705]. Within such an opinion, the creation of an offense represents the random case, in which the dysfunctional behavior has been codified in order to solve the basic problems of a society[1706]. Unfortunately, if a behavior has such negative effects on society it can only be determined according to an ex post view, because the detrimental effects of an act must unfold itself on society, which naturally takes time[1707].

Actually, such a time period has been given to the U.S. society; and this ex post view indicates that the acceptance of hate crimes for several decades - even though the underlying criminal act as such has always been punishable by criminal law - led to, or rather maintained, inequalities in social, economical, judicial and allover conditions for particular groups of society, leaving the society split until nowadays, and accordingly caused harm to collective goods; thus, such social detrimental effects of hate crimes towards society seem to exist. However - if at all - this would apply to the U.S. society and not to the German society[1708]. By all ambiguity - the term "socially detrimental" does not serve clear criteria whether hate crimes statutes, protecting the legal good of public peace, lies within the legitimate ambit for the legislator to be enacted or not. It implies certain relevance for determining the legitimacy of enacted criminal law by not legitimizing the criminalization of just unmoral and offensive behavior[1709], and thus limits the ambit of criminal law insofar that the legislator must not be able to punish undamaging behavior. According to the here followed assumption, which states that the respective behavior harms the human dignity and in addition must have effects beyond the conflict between the perpetrator and his victim, thus extends the personal sphere, after all, harms society at large, it cannot be advised to wait in order to be able to take required measurements in an ex post view.

1705 Anastasopoulou, Deliktstypen, p. 12; Hassemer, Einführung in die Grundlagen des Strafrechts, 1990, p. 25.

1706 Amelung, Rechtsgüterschutz, pp. 361, 386 et seq.

1707 Kasper, Erheblichkeitsschwelle, p. 23; Knowing whether a certain behavior is socially detrimental requires "empirical knowledge"; according to: Hassemer, Einführung in die Grundlagen des Strafrechts, 1990, p. 25.

1708 Not only hate crimes, but also the legal system constituting inequalities, led to differences among citizens according to race, religion and the further. Hate crimes, however, contributed to help maintain inequalities by threatening minorities in order to keep them from claiming their legal rights established in theory. Restrictively to this argumentation it must be mentioned that the problem of U.S. hate crimes in the first instance is the lack of actual imposing sentence for the already punishable underlying criminal behavior according certain sorts of hate crimes. The just theoretical penalty enacted for hate crimes by solely punishing the so called underlying behavior of, for instance, physical assault or property damage - committed through, for example, drawing a swawistica on one´s house - was frequently not prosecuted de jure. Nevertheless, the argument of hate crimes having a diametrical effect on society cannot be countered, because a non punishment of the underlying base offense, thus of the plain criminal act, can precisely only take place because the motive of the perpetrator which caused him to commit a criminal act is either neglected, accepted or even supported, all because it was not sufficient proscribed to be unlawful in public and legal ways and this pre-eminently was expressed by the legal system (in its potential educational function) for a too long time due to not making clear that not just offenses as such, but also hate-motivated offenses are not tolerated. Such examples of legally and socially accepted criminal behavior due to bias are said to exist today: The attack towards a homosexual male because of his sexual orientation, is likely to be not prosecuted and considered as less harmless than the same (harm wise) attack towards a straight male for other reasons.

1709 Wohlers, Deliktstypen des Präventionsstrafrechts, pp. 226 et seqq.; Kasper, Erheblichkeitsschwelle, p. 24; Müller-Dietz, Strafe und Staat, p.18.

After all, some necessary[1710] empirical knowledge is also available for the legislator to know how to establish a norm. The alleged harm refers to the personal goods harmed by the commission of a hate crime, which are not the physical injuries of the punished underlying behavior, but the harm towards the human dignity; when referring to hate crimes against property the discussion is usually held around feelings of threat, but also in this case, most of all, the human dignity of the victim is injured[1711]; the second - here relevant - requirement is the burden put on society. hate crimes leave a society in divisiveness, threat, anger and feelings of revenge occur, the pluralistic element of a democratic society is violated, which, sooner or later - becomes palpable. Thus, the fulfillment of the requirements of the theory of social harmfulness in regard to hate crime could possibly be verifiable. Whereas, an ex post view according the American society is able to refer to the societal state before the enactment of hate crime legislation compared to the climate of society today since such legislation has been widely enacted, such could serve empirical data and knowledge according the suitability of these norms, in connection with the detection of combated injuries[1712]. Nevertheless, nothing is said about the value content of such examinational data with regard to the German society. Therefore, the "theory of social harmfulness" - considering the empirically recordable harmful effects of hate crimes towards society - could approve the legitimacy of hate crime statutes, however only towards the American society.

1.3.3. Legitimization of Hate Crime Legislation according to Constitutional Provisions

Since neither the system critical function of the legal good doctrine, nor influences of a positivistic dimension of the theory could answer completely whether the legal good of public peace is considered to be legitimately protected by a criminal norm and therefore in its concrete formation legitimize a hate crime norm, it is referred to the German Constitution in order to find answers whether such is to be protected in this specific formation by German criminal norms. As in general illustrated above, the system critical function of the legal good doctrine is not to be limited to the discussion about what aims a legislator has when enacting a respective statute, moreover it is considered to be a tool in order to verify the legitimacy of criminal legislation by inspecting if the norm actually truly protects a legal good worthy of legislative protection[1713]. Any review of the constitutionality of a criminal norm which restricts the fundamental rights of an individual admittedly begins with the question of the

---

1710 Hassemer, Einführung in die Grundlagen des Strafrechts, 1990, p. 25.

1711 View Chapter 4, G., 1., 1.1., 1.1.1 Human Dignity of the Imemdiate Victim; Chapter 4, G., 1.2. Priority of Protected Legal Goods.

1712 Stachelberg states: "Hate crime laws are working at the local, state, and federal level"; based on the finding that hate crime commission rates are as low as they have never been, therefore the public peace in the U.S society seems protected by these laws. (Winnie Stachelberg in: Timothy Lynch and Winnie Stachelberg, Hate Crime Laws, Morning Show on C-SPAN's Washington Journal, March 13, 2012).

1713 It is opined that there are legal norms that do not protect legal goods. (Roxin, Strafrecht AT I, § 2 marginal no. 13-49; Hefendehl, Mit langem Atem: Der Begriff des Rechtsguts - Oder: Was seit dem Erscheinen des Sammelbandes über die Rechtsgutstheorie geschah - GA 2007, pp. 1-14 (4)).

legitimate aim of the legislature, but this aim can certainly be narrowed in the sense that the legislator is not free to choose any desired public good for protection, but only the protection of a recognized legal good may be regarded as a constitutionally legitimate aim of penal law[1714]. To determine what such a recognized legal good is, this constitutional orientated approach attempts to find an answer by referring to the Basic Law[1715]. In order to determine what behavior must, may, or must not be punished, the Constitution, as the highest value order of society, is predestined to provide precepts what is to be made punishable. Since, if one distinct the legitimate goal of the legislator for enacting a norm from the legitimacy of a norm as such, necessarily the criteria, which constitute a legal good, must be brought into the legal good doctrine from the outside, which then must be incorporated[1716]. And these outer, normative precepts which are requested in order to evaluate the legitimacy of a norm could derive from no other than the basic order, which is the epitome of the normative identity of the respective society and also binding for the criminal legislator[1717]. If one considers the task of the legal system to be the establishment of sufficient conditions for an individual to be able to unfold himself in a by the Basic Law guaranteed liberal way, consequently the criteria for exercising this penal power must as well be found in the constitution[1718].

Lifting the discussion according the legal good doctrine in criminal law to the constitutional level[1719] seems apparent in order to find answers in a superior, more basically matter, especially the connection of these approaches to a concrete societal model[1720] seems promising for the here relevant matter, in which two different societies are compared to each other. "After all, the society that is to be protected from harm, is not an abstract coexistence of unconnected individuals, but it is always a constituted society with a particular institutional structure that is more or less defined by policy decisions of a Constitution"[1721]. In connection with the jurisdiction of the German Federal Constitutional Court, the Constitution could finally serve normative criteria to determine what is to be made criminal according to German criminal law doctrine and therefore answer the question about the need to adopt a hate crime standard in German criminal law.

1.3.3.1. Constitutional Obligation to enact Hate Crime Penal Law

1714 Stuckenberg, Grundrechtsdogmatik statt Rechtsgutslehre, pp. 653 – 661 (656).

1715 Amelung, Rechtsgüterschutz, § 12, pp. 258-329 (308); Wohlers, Deliktstypen des Präventions-strafrechts, p. 241.

1716 Stratenwerth, Strafrecht AT, § 2, p. 29, marginal no. 15 et seqq.; Jakobs, Strafrecht AT, 2/22; Wohlers, Deliktstypen des Präventionsstrafrechts, p. 229.

1717 Wohlers, Deliktstypen des Präventionsstrafrechts, p. 241.

1718 Appel, Verfassung, pp. 388, 450, 454, 486 et seqq.; Wohlers, Deliktstypen des Präventionsstrafrechts, p. 253.

1719 Grützner, Die Sanktionierung von Submissionsabsprachen, pp. 445 et seqq.; Wohlers, Delikstypen des Präventionsstrafrechts, pp. 241 et seqq.

1720 Rudolphi, in: SK-StGB, Vor § 1 marginal no. 7 et seq.; The question about the legitimate ambit of criminal norms can be answered only in regard to a concrete social conception – Wohler, Delikstypen des Präventionsstrafrechts, p. 253.

1721 Amelung, Rechtsgüterschutz, § 12, A, p. 308.

The legitimate ambit of criminal norms, with regard to legal goods worthy of criminal protection, could be further determined by the possibility of constituting a penalization commandment. Even though the constitution - beyond Article 26 Basic Law - does not lay down rules what to penalize[1722], the German criminal literature dealt with several decisions of the German Federal Constitutional Court[1723] examining the question, if and if so, according to which requirements must the legislator penalize behavior harming legal goods[1724]. Therefore, it is to find out, whether the constitution obliges the German legislator to punish[1725] hate crimes.

In a recent decision[1726] it was made clear that the legislator is authorized to decide what behavior is to be made punishable. It is obvious that without danger to an effective life protection, the enactment of penal law can only be mandatory if it is necessary to prevent a serious impairment of "elementary" or "fundamental" values[1727]. Questionable remains, when and in which cases such an impairment, and according to which values, such is to be assumed[1728], in order to know, when the German legislature must enact criminal law for the protection of goods. Since the determination of what is to be considered as an "elementary" or "fundamental" good already requires evaluation, and considering the already enacted alternative public peace protecting devices, a reasonable constitutional obligation for the German legislator to enact hate crimes laws by limiting the legislator's power of discretion to zero can not be concluded in general[1729], thus not for the protection of the legal good of public peace by a hate crime statute. A constitutional obligation to criminally protect certain legal goods can hardly reach wider than to the need of protecting such goods and rights which are explicitly named within the constitutional order, such are merely the classical goods of life, freedom and physical integrity[1730]. An obligation of the legislature to protect certain legal goods, i.e. a so-called concretised constitutional protection duty, does not apply, because of the legislature´s considerable amount of discretion according to decide what is worthy of legal protection, and according to decide by what means a potential protection is to be achieved[1731].

1722 Wohlers, Deliktstypen des Präventionsstrafrechts, p. 244.

1723 BVerfGE 39, 1, (46 et seqq.); 46 160, (164 et seqq.); 88, 203 (257 et seqq.); Wohlers, Deliktstypen des Präventionsstrafrechts, p. 243.

1724 Roxin, Strafrecht AT I, § 2 marginal no. 36 et seqq. with further references; Wohlers, Deliktstypen des Präventionsstrafrechts, p. 253

1725 BVerfGE 120, 224 (241); BVerfGE 27, 18 (30); BVerfGE 80, 244 (255) with further references; BVerfGE 90, 145 (173); BVerfGE 96, 10 (25 et seq.); Grützner, Die Sanktionierung von Submissionsabsprachen, pp. 440, 441.

1726 BVerfGE 120, 224.

1727 Roxin, Strafrecht AT I, § 2 marginal no. 37; Rudolphi, in: SK-StGB, Vorbem. § 1 marginal no. 1; Wohlers, Deliktstypen des Präventionsstrafrechts, p. 243.

1728 Wohlers, Deliktstypen des Präventionsstrafrechts, p. 243.

1729 Paulduro, Verfassungsgemäßheit, p. 149; Wohlers, Deliktstypen des Präventionsstrafrechts, p. 244; Grützner, Die Sanktionierung von Submissionsabsprachen, p. 442.

1730 Tiedemann, Verfassungsrecht, p. 188; Wohlers, Deliktstypen des Präventionsstrafrechts, p. 244; Grützner, Die Sanktionierung von Submissionsabsprachen, p. 442.

1731 Wohlers, Deliktstypen des Präventionsstrafrechts, p. 243.

Yet, since a hate crime is considered to be a threat to the public peace, one could refer to the public peace being established as a constitutional value according to Article 20, Section I Basic Law by bringing the argument forward that the public peace is based on such grounds of a social democracy that is endangered by bias-motivated attacks. However, the legal good of public peace in its concrete formation, how it is considered to be endangered by a hate crime[1732], lacks an express and concrete establishment within the Basic Law. Insofar, the collective good public peace, in its concrete formation how it could be protected by a hate crime law, lacks a concrete base in the constitution, the base for an obligation for its governmental protection consequently - also - cannot be found in the Constitution[1733].

The obligation of an enactment of an explicit norm to punish the violation of the public peace through the committal of a hate crime could only derive from constitutional precepts if the Constitution predetermines "clear, fundamental benchmarks" stating which values are to be protected by serving the "basic societal image"[1734]. Insofar, the constitutional determined aim of a multicultural society with the equal existence of 'the other' can be clearly inferred from the German Federal Constitution[1735]. Therefore, one may reasonably ask, if not behavior being injurious to this aim, as in message sending through violence, must be made punishable.

The requirements of the enforcement of a legal duty to enact a law could be even stricter in the field of hate crimes than it is usually the case with other protection duties. This applies when referring to the value of the human dignity, which is considered to be protected by a potential hate crime norm as well. It is assumed that a hate crime law would not just protect the legal good of public peace, but also the legal good of human dignity decisively[1736]. This leads to the idea that the legislator's freedom of what to punish could be restricted to a higher degree than it is the case towards the punishment of behavior which harms less valued legal goods. So it is questionable whether the basically existent legal scope of the legislator to enact norms, which mainly aim at the protection of the legal good of public peace, could be restricted in the case of hate crime legislation due to the additional protected legal good of the human dignity. After all, the human dignity is not just explicitly named in the constitutional order but the legislator is moreover explicitly addressed to protect such[1737]. Even though a norm enacted to protect the public peace may only be legitimized in regard to the legal good public peace, the presence of the human dignity as an additional aspect of legitimating a hate crime norm must not be ignored, since this same norm would actually aim at protecting the

1732 View hereto Chapter 4, G., 1.5.3. Result: Meaning Content Possessed by the Public Peace in a Hate Crime Norm.

1733 Without regard to hate crime: Wohlers, Deliktstypen des Präventionsstrafrechts, p. 244.

1734 Rudolphi, in: SK-StGB, Vor § 1 marginal no. 7 et seq.; Grützner, Die Sanktionierung von Submissionsabsprachen, p. 446.

1735 Article 1, 3, 4, 20 Basic Law.

1736 View hereto: Chapter 4, G., 1.2. Priority of Protected Legal Goods.

1737 "To respect and protect [the human dignity] shall be the duty of all state authority." - Article 1, Para-graph 1, Sentence 2 Basic Law.

human dignity and the public peace side by side. However, this approach does not lead to any other result. Whereas a constitutional obligation to criminally protect the legal good human dignity against any kind of infringement, thus also against hate crime attacks, exist[1738], the legislator is ought to decide how he fulfills his duty to protect it. As long as the legislature does not leave the additional impairment of the human dignity through biased criminal behavior unnoticed, he is free in choosing the instruments to protect it[1739].

Only general conditions, such as basic democratic values are provided to the legislature to decide on the legality of penalization[1740]. Here the legal good public peace does not solely refer to securing the constitutional ideal of an equal society, but it is based on such ideals of the democtratic society which secure the inner peace in general. Therefore, the question of what criteria let the above supra-individual good of public peace appear to be so worthy of protection that the freedom-impairing effects of penalization, caused by the protection of selective areas of the public peace, are outweighed against the freedom of action of the individual within the evaluation process, remains; especially because the underlying negative effects of hate crime on society are already covered by criminal law in parts.

If the Constitution does not serve binding prerequisites what to punish[1741], no precise precepts can be drawn from such regarding the question of what behavior generally must be made criminal[1742]. If the legislator does not have the obligation to penalize certain societal-harming behavior, one is not able to detect an obligation to protect special, singled out parts of the constitutional ordered society in concrete forms; namely, the public peace as a legally protectable good of hate crimes. However, even though the Constitution does not serve a clear obligation to punish certain behavior, it could serve an "action orientation" for the legislator[1743] which enables one to make out whether the public peace could be protected explicitly by a penal norm with respect to its concrete partial area that is affected through the committal of a hate crime.

1.3.3.2. Constitutional Criteria to Legitimize Hate Crime Penal Law

Since the German Basic Law serves no clear obligation of what the criminal legislator must punish in order to maintain a peaceful co-existence of human

---

1738 The existence of an obligation for criminalization in order to protect the human dignity can be assumed, based on the precepts of Article 1, Section 1 Basic Law, according to which the government must not only respect the human dignity, but provide for its protection. - View hereto: Chapter 4, G., 1.2. Priority of Protected Legal Goods, especially footnote 1646. (BVerfGE 64, 274, 278; Kunig, in: von Münch/Kunig, GG, Art. 1 marginal no. 27 et seq.; Höfling, in: Sachs, GG, Art. 1, marginal no. 38 et seq.; Dreier, in: Dreier, Art. 1 Abs. 1, marginal no. 135 et seqq.; Sachs, Verfassungsrecht II, B I, marginal no. 31 et seqq.; Starck, JZ 1981, 459; Taupitz, NJW 2001, pp. 3435 et seq.; Peglau, Schutz des allgemeinen Persönlichkeitsrechts, pp. 50 et seqq.; Hörnle, Grob anstößiges Verhalten, p. 118).

1739 View hereto: Chapter 4, G., 1.2. Priority of Protected Legal Goods, especially footnote 1646.

1740 Sternberg-Lieben, Rechtsgut, Verhältnismäßigkeit und die Freiheit des Strafgesetzgebers, in: Hefendehl/von Hirsch/Wohlers, Die Rechtsgutstheorie, 2003, pp. 65-88, p. 79; Wohlers, Deliktstypen des Präventionsstrafrechts, p. 248.

1741 Amelung, Rechtsgüterschutz, p. 369; Wohlers, Deliktstypen des Präventionsstrafrechts, p. 245.

1742 Grützner, Die Sanktionierung von Submissionsabsprachen, p. 443 – with respect to competition law.

1743 Wohlers, Deliktstypen des Präventionsstrafrechts, p. 245; Grützner, Die Sanktionierung von Submissionsabsprachen, p. 445.

beings within society, it might be that the Basic Law could at least serve an orientation for the legislator to decide what individual or supra-individual goods seems suitable to be punished legitimately[1744]. Thereby it could be answered whether the legislature is ought to punish hate crimes autonomously from the respective base offense. The starting point of this approach of justifying criminal prohibition by referring to the Constitution is the idea of the democratic state[1745]. Based thereon, the state is considered to be allowed to exercise its criminal jurisdiction for the purpose of ensuring an unendangered coexistence among all citizens[1746].

The Constitution which addresses the legislator and therefore the criminal legislator merely sets a guiding principle, according to which the legislator may orientate himself when enacting norms on the sub constitutional level and thereby implements rules that support those ideals determined in the Constitution[1747]. Anyhow, how a legislator obeys these constitutional supportive rules, by enacting explicit norms or by establishing norms that gives priority to other important legal goods, but include the protection of the here relevant legal goods at least in parts, is up to his decision. Therefore, the decision that, for instance, the plain offense of causing bodily harm by dangerous means (Section 224 Penal Code) is sufficient for penalizing a hate-motivated physical attack on a homosexual because of his sexual orientation, would have to be acknowledged, if it is argued that the human dignity of the victim as well as the public peace is adequately valued within a prosecution according to Section 224 Penal Code and moreover the protection served by this norm is sufficient to defend the legal order. This discretionary decision of the legislator would not be assailable, especially if acknowledging the fragmentary nature of criminal law. While an advocate of hate crime legislation could argue against this decision by stating that the attack on the human dignity is much severe if performed by a hate crime offense and the harm caused is not equivalent to such caused by an un-bias-motivated offense, and the public peace hazardous potential (due to message sending effects) of a motivated physical assault in form of a hate crime is not considered on the objective level of the already punished offense (Section 224 Penal Code), it becomes clear that the legislator would be authorized to enact hate crime legislation if he wanted to. He must not, but he could. Since a clear "action directive" to the legislator, of what he may regulate by means of criminal law,

---

1744 So called "criminally politic guidelines" Roxin, Strafrecht AT 1, § 2, p. 18, marginal no. 12, with further references to: Sternberg-Lieben, Rechtsgut, Verhältnismäßigkeit und die Freiheit des Strafgesetzgebers, in: Hefendehl/von Hirsch/Wohlers, Die Rechtsgutstheorie, 2003,pp. 65-88, p. 79: "criminally political signalization"; Schünemann, in Hefendehl/von Hirsch/Wohlers, 2003, p. 137: "normative directive"; Wohlers, Deliktstypen des Präventionsstrafrechts, pp. 245 et seqq.; Grützner, Die Sanktionierung von Submissionsabsprachen, p. 445.

1745 Amelung, Rechtsgüterschutz, § 12, A, p. 309.

1746 Amelung, Rechtsgüterschutz, § 12, A, p. 309.

1747 "Even in the realm of the constitutional protected freedom sphere of the Individual one can not draw on directly implementable action directives of the Constitution." (Wohlers, Deliktstypen des Präventionsstrafrechts, p. 247).

does not derive from the Constitution[1748], the legislator, after all, is constitutionally authorized to punish hate crime separately.

1.3.3.3. Constitutional Restriction to enact Hate Crime Penal Law

Since a benchmark for verifying the legitimacy of the legal good of public peace as a supra-individual good as such[1749] and therefore in the context of hate crimes, also in particular with regard to the Constitution has not been found, a conversely attempt is made[1750], in order to find devices within the Constitution, which argue against a criminalization for the reason of protecting supra- individual goods in general, thus the public peace in particular[1751]. Whereas the approach of positively determinating behavior that is to be made punishable according to the Constitution failed, precisely, the question whether there is a necessity to explicitly address public peace harming hate crimes by the German Penal Code is still unsolved, it is to find out whether the Constitution serves certain criteria in order to be able to determine what sort of behavior is not to be made punishable by the legislature.

In this approach it is, in contrast, not aimed at determining what legal goods are worthy of criminal protection, but it is tried to exclude such legal goods which obviously are not elementary enough to be protected by criminal law, since, in such cases, the structure of the respective criminal norm is not in accordance with the value judgments of the Constitution[1752]. Moreover, it is less about the tangibility or the sufficient material content of a legal good, but about enriching the legal good doctrine with normative constitutional basics and thereby narrowing the legislator's competence of punishing[1753.] The difference between the American approach to the within here followed approach is the change of perspective. Whereas the American criminal scholars likewise ask what exactly is harmed, they also refer to the question whether the relevant behavior is to be acknowledged as a legitimate reason for legislative penalizing action. The question is, however, not answered by referring to the sufficient value of the harmed something, but by referring to the punished behavior to then ask whether such belongs to a constitutional guaranteed private sphere in which the legislator is not authorized to interfere, it is. Thereby the answer is provided by referring to constitutional values, such as liberty values. A crucial point within the U.S. verification process is that

---

1748 Wohlers, Deliktstypen des Präventionsstrafrechts, p. 247.

1749 Due to the political freedom of the legislature and the lack of possibility to find a valuation criterion from the constitution, a benchmark to determine the legitimate from the illegitimate legal goods can not be found. (Sternberg-Lieben, Rechtsgut, Verhältnismäßigkeit und die Freiheit des Strafgesetzgebers, in: Hefendehl/von Hirsch/Wohlers, Die Rechtsgutstheorie, 2003, pp. 65-88, p. 79).

1750 "negative exclusionary function" - Hefendehl, Mit langem Atem: Der Begriff des Rechtsguts - Oder: Was seit dem Erscheinen des Sammelbandes über die Rechtsgutstheorie geschah - GA 2007, pp. 1-14 (p. 4); Grützner, Die Sanktionierung von Submissionsabsprachen, p. 445.

1751 Wohlers, Deliktstypen des Präventionsstrafrechts, pp. 249, 250; Roxin views the systemcritical content of the legal good doctrine which restricts the right of the legislator to punish. By considering constitutional precepts he comes up with clear outlined boundaries for the enactment of legal penal norms. (Roxin, Strafrecht AT I § 2, p. 18, marginal no. 12).

1752 Otto, Rechtsgutsbegriff, p. 15; Appel, Verfassung, pp. 66, 199, 330, 331; Wohlers, Delikstypen des Präventionsstrafrechts, p. 250.

1753 Wohlers, Deliktstypen des Präventionsstrafrechts, p. 250¸ Grützner, Die Sanktionierung von Submissionsabsprachen, pp. 445, 446.

punishment must not affect certain areas of constitutional guaranteed personal freedom. If it turns out that a protected interest is infringed by behavior that belongs to such an area, a governmental intervention is illegitimate[1754], a punishment of this behavior not acceptable, and thereof a norm stating such a competence would be illegitimate. Therefore, ultimately not the content of a norm according the protected good is examined, but it is rather important to view if the legislator interferes with a respective behavioral area which is constitutionally protected against governmental interference.

In contrast, with the here followed constitutional based (German) approach, it is not asked whether certain behavior can be acknowledged as a sufficient reason for punishment[1755], but if it affects sufficient weighty living-conditions, which are necessary for human existence and therefore must legitimately be protected with means of criminal law[1756]. According to that, the right of the legislature to adopt a criminal provision does not only refer to the protection of a sufficient tangible legal good, but to the need to raise a social condition as a protected subject of a criminal standard, because this "is necessary for the constitutional position and the freedom of the individual citizens and for our social life according to the constitution"[1757]. After that, the legislator is not free in his decision what he wants to protect. All social realities, "which are not necessary for our social life according to the Constitution" may not be raised to be protected goods of criminal norms[1758]. Only behavior that is “socially harmful in a special way“ and its prevention is “particularly urgent“ may be punished[1759]. Therefor it is conceded that the protection of collective goods, as it would be the case when protecting the public peace, is legitimate only in so far as it proves to be necessary to secure the precepts for a free development of the citizens[1760.] If *Roxin* defines legal goods as "all conditions or determination of goals that are necessary for the free development of the individual, the realization of his fundamental rights and the functioning of the state system which is built on these visional goals"[1761], he thus concludes from that, that the description of legislative goals does not yet fulfill the legal criteria of a legitimate legal good[1762]. Nor is sufficient a purely symbolic purpose[1763]. Thus, as already shown, goals of hate crime legislation like "a racism-free society" and from this deriving a "right to be spared from discrimination" would

1754 As an example Wohlers mentions the realm of private life (Wohlers, Delikstypen des Präventionsstrafrechts, p. 254).
1755 Wohlers, Deliktstypen des Präventionsstrafrechts, p. 254.
1756 Wohlers, Deliktstypen des Präventionsstrafrechts, p. 254.
1757 Rudolphi, in: SK-StGB, Vor § 1 marginal no.5; Grützner, Die Sanktionierung von Submissionsabsprachen, p. 446.
1758 Rudolphi, in: SK-StGB, Vor § 1 marginal no.5; Grützner, Die Sanktionierung von Submissionsabsprachen, p. 446.
1759 Wohlers, Deliktstypen des Präventionsstrafrechts, p. 246 with further references; Paulduro, Verfassungsgemäßheit, pp. 126 et seqq.
1760 Wohlers, Deliktstypen des Präventionsstrafrechts, p. 251; Grützner, Die Sanktionierung von Submissionsabsprachen, p. 447.
1761 Roxin, Strafrecht AT I § 2, p. 18, marginal no. 14.
1762 Roxin, Strafrecht AT I § 2, p. 18-19, marginal no. 14; Grützner, Die Sanktionierung von Submissionsabsprachen, p. 447.
1763 View hereto Chapter 4, C., 8. Symbolic Reasoning of Hate Crime Law; Roxin, Strafrecht AT, marginal no. 40, p. 26.

not be considered to justify the existence of a norm, and could, regardless of the legally protected content, due to the lack of answering the question of whether the incriminating behavior affects the peaceful coexistence of people and whether harm is caused at all, not reason the existence of a norm[1764]. Another implication of the presented concept is that the immorality or ethical reprehensibility of a behavior can not justify criminal punishment, as long as such does not impair the prerequisites for peaceful coexistence[1765]. Therefore, the reprehensibility of a hate crime act is not enough to ask for penalties that are severe than the already established penalties for the respective base offense[1766]. Instead, a reference point for enhanced penalties is the specific additional impairment of a peaceful coexistence, which is caused by the distinguishing criterion that differentiates the hate crime from the underlying base offense.

The behavior of the perpetrator when committing a hate crime must, according to its specific outward form[1767], affect the freedom and security - not necessarily of the individual, but of the generality - in an additional, intolerable way.

The legal protection of goods of the generality is subject of a still uncompleted critical discussion[1768], but not because their legitimacy as a legal good protected by a norm is controversial, rather the misuse of the term is discussed[1769]. Such a misuse is to be assumed especially, if the punished behavior actually does not cause any harm[1770]. If hate crimes causes harm, e. g. to the public peace and the human dignity of the individual, that is not caused by the respective base offenes, the legislature is authorized to punish hate crimes if such a penal norm is essential to protect these goods and the interference with the right of freedom of the perpetrator is neccessary for an effective protection of the said goods[1771].

1764 According to the precepts set in: Roxin, Strafrecht AT I § 2, pp. 18 et seqq.

1765 Roxin, Strafrecht AT I § 2, p. 19, marginal no. 17 with further references: Hefendehl, Kollektive Rechtsgüter im Strafrecht, 2002. p. 52; Krey, AT/1, § 1 marginal no. 12 et seq.

1766 Roxin, Strafrecht AT I § 2, p. 20, marginal no. 37

1767 The specific outer form obtained by such crimes results already through their message sending content. As a result, the public peace in the partial aspect of the existence of a pluralistic society is affected, which is not the case when offenses are motivated by other dispositions. Furthermore, the motive lead to a modified, more brutal, and dehumanizing way of offense committal and thus cause greater psychological and physical harm towards the attacked victim, which further continues to cause revenge-related violence of the addressed group and thereby leads to further to be discussed potential harms towards the generality, for instance, by stimulating revenge-related actions a peaceful climate could be endangered etc. This occurs in addition to the already caused breach of the public peace through the message sending effect of hate crimes.

1768 Wohlers, Deliktstypen des Präventionsstrafrechts, 2000; Hefendehl, Kollektive Rechtsgüter im Strafrecht, 2002; Anastasopoulou, Deliktstypen, 2005.

1769 Roxin, Strafrecht AT I, § 2, p. 17, marginal no. 10.

1770 Roxin, Strafrecht AT I, § 2, p. 17, marginal no. 10.

1771 Without regard to hate crime: Wohlers, Deliktstypen des Präventionsstrafrechts, p. 241, with further references.

1.3.4. Jurisdiction of the Federal Constitutional Court

The Federal Constitutional Court opposes an independent legal good doctrine and its aim to draw limits for the legislator to enact penal law[1772]. Such a critical function of this doctrine is remarkably said to be in contradiction to the fact that it is the responsibility of the democratically elected legislature to determine which interests are worthy of criminal protection and therefore to adjust penal norms to social developments[1773]. According to this concept of criminal law such indeed serves the protection of legal goods – but what constitutes a legal good, is decided by the legislature[1774]. The Federal Constitutional Court does not limit the scope of criminal legislation by requiring that a legal good must present a specific solid content, must originate from individual sources or even be established expressly in the Constitution. Rather, it says "[i]t's basically up to the legislator, to determine the area of criminal activity. He is free in deciding whether he wants to protect a particular legal good which protection appears worthy to him to be protected precisely by means of criminal law and how he wants to implement it"[1775]. Thus, the Federal Constitutional Court refuses to decide what values it basically deems worthy of protection and which not. Contrary, it emphasizes the discretionary power of the legislature with at the same time requiring that the criminal law is to be used to protect legal goods only "[...] if a certain behavior beyond its prohibition is socially harmful to a special degree, and intolerable for the organized coexistence of people, its prevention, therefore, is very urgent"[1776], whereas the latter requirement in connection with the discretionary power of the legislature appears to be a hollow phrase. The principal eligibility of criminal protection of nearly any valuable good becomes apparent when it is emphasized that a penal provision is solely illegitimate if it "would not be consistent with the provisions of the Constitution and the unwritten constitutional principles and with basic choices of the constitutional law [...]."[1777] Thereby it becomes clear that the Federal Constitutional Court, in principle, consideres any standard to be legitimate, as long as the legislator does not enact a penal norm to aim at a purpose, which is disapproving from the outset[1778]. The Federal Constitutional Court views no substantive benchmark in a system critical legal good theory which could be capable of

1772 Penal norms cannot be derived from the criminal legal good doctrine, according to: BVerfGE 120, 224 (241); BVerfGE 50, 142 (162); Grützner, Die Sanktionierung von Submissionsabsprachen, pp. 448, 449; They eligibility rather must derive from the constitutional order as such. (BVerfGE 27, 18 (30); BVerfGE 80, 244 (255); BVerfGE 90, 145 (172, 173); BVerfGE 96, 10 (25 et seq.); BVerfGE 92, 277 (326); BVerfGE 96, 10 (25); BVerfGE 27, 18 (30); BVerfGE 73, 201 (212); BVerfGE 45, 272 (289); BVerfGE 51, 60 (74).

1773 It is basically up to the legislator to determine punishable behavior by taking the particular situation into account. (BVerfGE 120, 224 (241, 242); Critical here to: Cornils, ZJS 2009, 87 et seqq.; Greco, ZIS 2008; 234 ff; Hörnle NJW 2008, 2085 et seqq. Noltenius, ZJS 2009, 15 et seqq.

1774 Murmann, GK Strafrecht, 2011, § 8 III. 1., p. 20, 21, marginal no. 14; For the inconsistency of the argumentation view: Noltenius ZJS 2009, 16; Roxin, StV 2009, 545.

1775 BVerfGE 50, 142 (162); BVerfGE 120, 224 (240); BVerfGE 27, 18 (30); BVerfGE 80, 244 (255); BVerfGE 90, 145 (173); BVerfGE 96, 10 (25 et seq.); BVerfGE 73, 201 (212); BVerfGE 45, 272 (289); BVerfGE 51, 60 (74).

1776 BVerfGE 120, 224 (240).

1777 BVerfGE 27, 18 (30); BVerfGE 80, 244 (255) with further references; BVerfGE 90, 145 (173); BVerfGE 96, 10 (25 et seq.).

1778 BVerfGE 120, 224 (242); BVerfGE 96, 10 (23).

limiting the legislator's legislative and regulatory competence[1779]. As a result the Federal Constitutional Court deals with the prevailing opinion of criminal jurisprudence, according to which the validity check of a norm must start with the question whether the norm protects a legal good, but refuses to acknowledge the existence of legal goods which preside over the positive law[1780]. Anyhow, the power of the legislature could not be narrowed by invoking on "alleged legal goods, existent or recognized by entities beyond the legislature"[1781]. Rather, a legal good theory which due to its system-critical understanding aims at instructing the legislature of what is to be considered as worthy of criminal protection and therefore of what is to be considered as a legitimate legal good capable of legitimating a norm, stands in contradiction to the constitutional order, according to which it is basically the task of the democratically elected legislature to determine the area of criminal law, by stipulating on a binding basis which behavior, in accordance to the particular situation, is to be made criminal[1782].

Instead, based on criminal purposes, the goods worthy of protection are to be determined in accordance to social needs[1783], which ultimately makes criminal provisions a product of social development[1784]. Therewith, according to the Federal Constitutional Court, any criminal norm is legitimate, if the legislator with its establishment follows "purposes that constitutionally are not objectionable and, at least in their entirety, legitimize the restriction of personal freedoms"[1785]. With that, in the opinion of the Federal Constitutional Court, the limits of the scope of criminal law can solely be found within the Constitution itself. However, as illustrated, not even the Constitution clearly demonstrates these limits. Thus, as a result, the Federal Constitutional Court refuses to take a stand on the question, and to examine, whether a norm - as specifically called for - has been enacted as a "device of last resort in order to protect legal goods"[1786], and solely takes a watchdog function with regards to the constitutionality of a norm, which then is to be assumed, if the legislator does not aim at an illegitimate purpose from the outset. With regard to the legal good of public peace, this means that a general exclusion of certain goods from criminal protection, from the perspective of jurisprudence, cannot be assumed; in particular supra-individual goods or general rights can be

---

1779 In line with: Lagodny, Strafrecht vor den Schranken der Grundrechte, 1996, p. 143 et seqq., 536; Appel, Verfassung und Strafe, 1998, p. 390; Appel, KritV 1999, p. 278 (286 et seqq.); Müller-Dietz, in: Gedächtnisschrift für Heinz Zipf, p. 123 (132); Hörnle, Grob anstößiges Verhalten, 2005, pp. 11 et seqq.; Of other opinion: Roxin, Strafrecht, AT I, § 2 marginal no. 27, 86 et seqq. with further references) stated in: BVerfGE 120, 224 (241 et seq.).

1780 Hörnle, NJW 2008, 2085.

1781 Hörnle, NJW 2008, 2085.

1782 BVerfG, 2 BvL 8/02 vom 29.6.2004, Absatz-Nr. (1-50), 45 (http://www.bverfg.de/entscheidungen/lk20040629_2bvl000802.html - accessed 2011/09/09); equal to: BVerfGE 90, 145 (172, 184); BVerfGE 27, 18 (29 et seq.); BVerfGE 39, 1 (46); BVerfGE 88, 203 (257); BVerfGE 120, 224 (241 et seq.).

1783 BVerfGE 45, 187 (253).

1784 Similar: BVerfGE 120, 224 (221).

1785 BVerfGE 120, 224 (243).

1786 BVerfGE 120, 224 (240).

impaired to the same extent as individual legal goods. Community values moreover, are already affected by abstract dangers[1787].

1.3.5. Result

Neither the legal good doctrine in its system-critical function, nor the social doctrine, nor the Constitution in connection with the jurisprudence of the Federal Constitutional Court is suited to withdraw a legislator's competence to protect the legal good public peace by a hate crime norm. As a result, the German legislature is solely not allowed to aim a priori illegitimate purposes, which are unconstitutional targets. According to the Supreme Courts opinion, the main focus of evaluating the legitimacy of a norm is to lie on the legislator's intent when enacting a norm; and the legislator finds the limit of the ambit of criminal law solely within the Constitution, in Article 1 Section 3 Basic Law. Anyhow, the main coinciding precepts of the system-critical function of the legal good doctrine, for instance, the exclusion of the criminal protection of just moral interest are to be upheld[1788].

Therewith, in the end, the legislator must decide whether he adjudges a legal content to the public peace and how he ranks this value in the constitutional order of values. The above remarks, which lead to the conclusion of a criminal protection of the collective legal good public peace, must be carefully justified. The protection of collective legal goods can not be excluded in general, however, certain institutions may only be criminally protected insofar they are essential for human beings. Since it is impossible to answer the question whether the legal good of public peace is generally suitable to legitimize a norm, this can only be answered specifically, with regard to its content which requires protection by a hate crime norm.

1.4. Legitimacy of a Hate Crime Norm in Regard to the Protected Human Dignity

The protection of the human dignity as a legal good to legitimate criminal legislation is as controversial as the legal good of public peace. But this criticism is often due to the fact that the human dignity is cited blankly to justify criminal norms without the demonstration of a thorough actual injury of the human dignity which makes the need for a norm understandable. Therefore, the misuse of its legal protection is problematic - not the legitimacy to protect it[1789]. If it is truly and comprehensible violated nothing precludes its legitimate criminal protection. In the case of hate crime it is clearly demonstrated that the dignity of the immediate victim is deeply violated and this violation derives in particular from the victimization by the biased and hate-motivated criminal attack, which causes increased stigmatization and there from further resulting

1787 BVerfGE 28, 175 (188).

1788 "A submission of crime policy under an assumed primacy of constitutional law would ultimately cut any criminal scientific and legal debate about the proper design of the criminal justice system."(Sternberg-Lieben, Rechtsgut, Verhältnismäßigkeit und die Freiheit des Strafgesetzgebers, in: Hefendehl/von Hirsch/Wohlers, Die Rechtsgutstheorie, 2003,pp. 65-88, p. 79).

1789 In a different respect: Roxin, Strafrecht AT I, § 2, p. 17, marginal no. 10.

psychological harmful impacts. All in all, the violation of the human dignity through a hate crime is so obvious, since the perpetrator precisely negates this outstanding major individual good during his attack, that the legitimation of a hate crime law, which is based on the legal protection of the human dignity, requires no further detailed examination.

1.5. Legitimacy of a Hate Crime Norm in Regard to the Protected Partial Aspect of Public Peace

Whether the public peace could serve as a legal good worthy of protection by a hate crime norm depends on which part of the public peace is affected by the harmful action. Likewise, the conceptual meaning of the public peace depends on its affected partial aspect. Without reference to a concrete subject it is impossible to determine the exact content of the legal good public peace, rather it encompasses many areas whose inviolated state is necessary for the wholesomeness of a society.

If one views the legal good of public peace in respect to a hate crime norm it can be seen that the purpose of such a norm is to protect society from those harms which precisely occur from biased motivated criminal behavior, clearly expressed, by addressing those kinds of harms which concern the entire population and which are not sufficiently addressed by already established base offenses. Insofar, the "additional" harm which is caused by a hate crime and which does not relate to individual damages enables one to determine in which partial aspect the legal good public peace is indeed affected and requires protection by a hate crime law.

The key aspect of working out those yet unprotected aspects, which underpin the legitimacy of this legal good and its need to be legally protected, lies in the dissociation of individual and collective damages. For defining the public peace one may only draw on such damages which are not congruent with those of the individual, since for the protection against such harms, which affect an individual good, solely the protection of this immediate individual good comes into question to legitimate a norm; whereas the criminal protection of the legal good public peace is just capable of legitimating the prevention of harms of collective entities[1790].

1.5.1. Ambiguity and Heterogeneity of the Legal Good Public Peace

The public peace as a collective legal good, in the meaning how it is acknowledged in the German Penal Code in several norms, is generally divided in an objective element and a subjective element. According to the prevailing opinion the objective part is described as "a state of general legal certainty", accompanied by "the subjective awareness of the population to live in peace and tranquility"[1791]. This definition is based on the fundamental understanding that the legal order of the society shall assure a co-existence of

1790 Hörnle, Grob anstößiges Verhalten, p. 93; Hefendehl, Kollektive Rechtsgüter, pp. 73 et seqq.
1791 Fischer, StGB, § 126, marginal no. 3; BGHSt 16, 56; BGHSt 29, 27.

individuals without fear of each other and "maintain the trust among the population of an at least not negligible number of persons in the continuance of this state"[1792]. The public peace is disturbed if a general concern of the population in the FRG, or at least among a not inconsiderable number of people[1793], occurs[1794]. Several scholars have already complained the vagueness and imprecision of the term "public peace"[1795]. With that said it is necessary to determine very closely which meaning is attributed to the public peace in order to qualify such as an independent legal good which is based on collective interests[1796]. It is important that the public peace in its content whose protection is aimed at by a hate crime norm does not represent the sum of individual interests of the victimized group, but refers to a state which justifies a transition to independence, thus in legitimate manners - indeed - refers to the collective[1797].

1.5.1.1. Meaning of the Objective Part of Public Peace in a Hate Crime Norm

There are different meanings ascribed to the objective part of the legal good of public peace. It is important to find out which acknowledged conceptual meaning of the public peace is suitable to legitimize a hate crime norm in accordance to these available apprehensions.

a) General Legal Safety

The objective part of the public peace is often circumscribed with "a condition of general legal safety"[1798]. According to this definition the objective part of public peace is equalized with the "adherence to legal orders"[1799], therefore the public peace is considered as a ´social condition in which no offenses are committed´. Yet, this semantic content does not serve for the construction of an own substantial good, rather "public peace", according to this understanding, lacks an own meaningful content[1800]. In this literal sense, the term "public" is understood, by jurisdiction and by penology, "as the unlimitedness of addressees"[1801]. By such means the public peace is understood as the protection of the sum of the already legally protected individual assets. Therefore, a norm protecting the public peace kind of

1792 Lackner/Kühl, StGB § 126, marginal no. 1.

1793 With the number of persons it is referred to a "part of the population" in the meaning imputed to it by Section 130 Penal Code, i.e. "the group of people needs to be of some relevance in numerical terms" (LK-StGB, § 130m, marginal no. 27; Lenckner/Sternberg-Lieben, in: Schönke/Schröder, StGB, § 130 marginal no. 3).

1794 Fischer, StGB, § 126, marginal no. 3; BGHSt 46, 36; BGHSt 46, 212, 219.

1795 Fischer, Die Eignung, den öffentlichen Frieden zu stören - Zur Beseitigung eines „restriktiven" Phantoms, NStZ, 1988, (159), p. 162; Schroeder, Straftaten gegen das Strafrecht, p.12.

1796 For the investigation of possible meaning levels in the abstract, see: Hörnle, Grob anstößiges Verhalten, pp. 90-108.

1797 Hörnle, Grob anstößiges Verhalten, p. 92.

1798 Von Bubnoff, in: LK-StGB, § 126, marginal no. 8; Lackner/Kühl, StGB, § 126, marginal no. 1.

1799 Fischer, Die Eignung, den öffentlichen Frieden zu stören - Zur Beseitigung eines „restriktiven" Phantoms, NStZ 1988, 159 (163).

1800 Wohlers, Deliktstypen des Präventionsstrafrechts, p. 270; Hörnle, Grob anstößiges Verhalten, p. 93; Schroeder, Straftaten gegen das Strafrecht, p. 12.

1801 Fischer, Die Eignung, den öffentlichen Frieden zu stören - Zur Beseitigung eines „restriktiven" Phantoms, NStZ 1988, 159 (161); with reference to. BGH, NJW 1987, 1898 and OLG Düsseldorf, NJW 1986, 2518.

double-protects what is already protected by every other penal norm which refers to individual goods: The "[s]ubstantive content of "peace disturbance" is therefore the breach of any [criminal] norm."[1802]

The concept of the construction of a collective good termed "public peace" which refers to a state of "general legal safety" leads nowhere[1803]. Thus, there must be a different understanding of the semantic content addressed by the term "public peace"; an understanding that allows a distinction to goods of the individual and which is moreover meaningful and important to be protected by a criminal norm. The construction of a legal good which is to be differentiated from individual goods may make sense for cases in which offenses are directed against classical collective belongings[1804]. A major, seriously damaging condition for societal institutions can be caused by an attribute that not simultaneously cause damage towards concrete individuals. Hence, the harm caused to the societal facilities by the relevant behavior is not congruent to such caused to the individual persons[1805]. This is assumed to be the case in the committal of a hate crime: the harm caused to the immediate victims and it's larger community is not congruent with the harm which is caused to the entire population, because in this opinion it is considered that the people which do not share the characteristic which is attacked by a hate crime perpetrator also suffer a loss[1806].

In order to concretize what this damage to the public is and by that counteract the liquefaction of the legal good term "public peace" it is important to find out below which part of the public peace is in concrete affected by a hate crime and thereby receive the answer to the conceptual understanding of "public peace" which it would adopt in a hate crime norm.

b) Protection of Public Peace to Preserve the Current Social Climate

Another understanding of public peace provided by the literature is the "protection of the current climate in society". In this conceptual meaning of the objective condition of public peace it is aimed at maintaing the current societal climate[1807] with respect to different aspects.

aa) Prevention of Vigilante Justice

A danger to the legal good public peace is viewed in the creation of a condition in which it is feared that people try to eliminate harming behavior by themselves if there is no (adequate) criminal sanction to prevent it[1808]. In other

1802 Fischer, Die Eignung, den öffentlichen Frieden zu stören - Zur Beseitigung eines „restriktiven" Phantoms, NStZ 1988, 159 (161), NStZ 1988, p. 161; Hörnle, Grob anstößiges Verhalten, p. 93; Hassemer, Theorie und Soziologie, p. 59; Fischer, GA 1989, p. 445, 451; Schroeder, Straftaten gegen das Strafrecht, p. 12; Wohlers, Deliktstypen des Präventionsstrafrechts, p. 270; Junge, Schutzgut des § 130, p. 49 et seq.; Stegbauer, Der Straftatbestand gegen die Auschwitzleugnung – eine Zwischenbilanz, NStZ 2000, p. 283; Amelung, in: Hefendehl/von Hirsch/ Wolters (eds.), pp. 172 et seq.

1803 Hörnle, Grob anstößiges Verhalten, p. 93.

1804 Hefendehl, Kollektive Rechtsgüter, pp. 73 et seqq.; Hörnle, Grob anstößiges Verhalten, p. 93.

1805 Hörnle, Grob anstößiges Verhalten, p. 93.

1806 Schneider, Politische Kriminalität: Hassverbrechen, Fremdenfeindlichkeit im internationalen Kontext, Kriminalistik, 2001, pp.21-28 (24).

1807 Von Bubnoff, in: LK-StGB, § 125, marginal no. 41.

1808 Hörnle, Grob anstößiges Verhalten, pp. 106 et seqq.

words, if an expressive appreciation of the legislature in terms of condemning a behavior is missing, the citizens take the law into own hands, this fact interferes with the public peace of the society[1809]. In case of a frequent committal of offenses which affect victims quite intense, the prevention of uncontrolled punitive activities may be an aspect which could be involved in the decision whether or not to criminalize a behavior[1810]. As a prerequisite for such social developments, it is said that individuals must be harmed who in consequence are driven to actions of self-protection[1811]. Logically necessary the victims of a hate crime attack feels driven to self-protection measures in a more intense way than such facing harm arising from relationship conflicts, since the attack of a hate crime perpetrator is in no way explainable and therefore cannot be emotionally accepted. This sort of vigilantism could occur in the case of frequent hate crime commission, especially also by the revolt of engaged citizens who want to maintain their current pluralistic social structure and disagree with the message which is sent by the perpetrator. In terms of the dual nature of hate crime, which simultaneously addresses both, the victimized group and all those who disagree with the by force revealed mindset and aims of the perpetrator, this precept, the drivenness of those who are affected, seems quite likely to become fulfilled.

However, the question rises, whether already isolated types of these hateful attacks are capable to motivate individuals to form such problematic organizations of self-protection and form of vigilantism, or if such a militia is likely to occur only in case of a frequent commission[1812] of hate crimes over a long lasting period of time. In other words,it is questioned, if the committal of a hate crime must achieve a particular numerical magnitude and damage-prone extent before such could be classified as "disturbing the peace". This may be left unanswered since this concept of the legal good public peace is considered inappropriate - as elobarated below[1813].

bb) Prevention of Revenge Related Activity

The fact that a larger number of victims feels threatened by one hateful and biased act increases the risk of joint countermeasures, so that already due to group dynamics the risk of revenge defense-related activities is increased. Since revenge conditioned behavior should naturally decrease once the revenge-causing behavior is punished explicitly and thereby the idea of atonement of the sacrificial victim circle is taken into account in a noticeably way, victims would not have to feel themselves called to (more) or less irrational emotion-driven retaliation-activities (anymore).

Therefore, it would be theoretically conceivable that the adoption of a hate crime standard, which perceives “climate protection” by placating revenge, is likely to achieve the specific target at issue.

1809 Rudolphi, in: SK-StGB, Vorbem. § 166 marginal no.3.
1810 Hörnle, Grob anstößiges Verhalten, p. 106.
1811 Hörnle, Grob anstößiges Verhalten, p. 106.
1812 Hörnle, Grob anstößiges Verhalten, pp. 106, 107.
1813 Chapter 4, G., 1., 1.5., 1.5.1., 1.5.1.1., c) Incited Climate.

cc) Exchangeability of Victims

The public peace is disturbed by the special way of committal of hate crimes: "open or latent violence potentials are created which prevent coexistence [of humans with different ethnics, beliefs etc.] without fear for their personal safety and belongings, [...] and therefore undermine the confidence in the public safety of the attacked victims groups"[1814]. Such created agitation can not be limited to a certain area of society, the negative climate affects society as a whole. Even people who do not share the attacked characteristics are threatened since they might become victimized if mingling with such individuals who are addressed by hate crimes[1815]. The fungibility of victims to the hateful biased motivated criminal is so integral to hate crime that courts have looked to it as a critical element for identifying hate crimes[1816.] The committal of a hate crime serves the evocation of fear within certain segments of the population, but beyond these thereby individual affected legal goods harm the societal climate due to the evocation of unreasonable and unforeseeable victimization.

dd) Prevention of Intergroup Relations

If a minority is victimized through a hate crime the entire community to which the victim belongs feels victimized and isolated[1817], moreover develops feelings of hate and revenge towards all members in society which share the characteristics defining the offender, therefore they feel authorized to defend themselves in case the "perpetrator's kind" does not serve for the appropriate justice through the respective legal system. This fact leads to the finding that hate crimes spark intergroup relations and thereby harm the fabric of society[1818] and so destroy the public peace. Furthermore, the victims and its community withdraw themselves from society and thereby cause further harms to the entire population[1819].

1814 BGHSt 16, 56; BGHSt 29, 26; Lenckner/Sternberg-Lieben, in: Schönke/Schröder, StGB, § 130, marginal no. 10.

1815 Also refer to Chapter 4, G., 1., 1.1., 1.1.2. Human Dignity of the Victim´s Community.

1816 E.g., in a Californian case the court relied on the defendant's indifference to the personal selection of the victim as persuasive evidence of bias motivation. See People v. Baker, 5 Cal. Rptr. 2d 372, 378-379, opinion superseded by 28 Cal. Rptr. 2d 794 (Cal. 1994).

1817 Martin/Chase, Hate Crimes, in: Lukenbill/Peck (eds.) Encyclopedia of Criminology and Deviant Behavior. Band 2: Crime and Juvenile Delinquency, 2001, pp. 254-257 (255).

1818 Hate crimes "disturb the peaceful cohabitation of Germans and foreigners severely; further they generate a general climate of fear and intimidation in public, especially among those in the Federal Republic of Germany living foreigners, by causing serious, the inner safety impairing doubts, whether the security forces are sufficiently capable and determined of protecting foreign residents". (BGH January 12, 2000 - StB 15/99). Also cf. Lawrence, Punishing Hate, pp. 39 et seqq. (40)): Racism in particular puts an unwelcome dent in the harmonious functioning of society.

1819 The social consequences of hate crime are harmful to the society at large due to the following: the victims have lost confidence in their fellow human beings. They withdraw themselves from the community. They have severe interpersonal difficulties. Victims of hate crime are said to suffer from the posttraumatic stress disorder: The thoughts of victimization return persistently, therefore they have a decreased interest in interpersonal contacts, hold themselves back in isolation and develop feelings of distance to others (Schneider, Kriminologie der Hassdelikte. Konzeption, Ursachen, Vorbeugung und Kontrolle, in: Bewährungshilfe, 2003, p. 24; Lawrence, Punishing Hate, pp. 39 et seqq.). The economic, social and political damage caused by the fact that parts of the population no longer participate in the social life and isolate themselves compromises the entire nation. Whereas some withdrawal reaction of victims of violent crime is typical, a hate crime victim exceeds the isolation which victims of usual violent crime do. The bias

ee) Incited Climate

In accordance with the established case law and legal scholars which view the objective condition of the "disturbed public peace" as a climate in which potential perpetrators could be stirred up to commit crimes[1820] the public peace could be hurt by the commission of hate crimes due to the fact that hate crimes create a "psychological climate" which stimulates the commission of crime in that other potential hateful and biased perpetrators imitate the perpetrators. The adoption of a hate crime standard must be suitable to "prevent the described social psychology state[1821], regardless of further effects"[1822]. Since a hate crime announces the readiness of the offender to commit incalculable further offenses such are in particular suitable to create the willingness of the threatened group to commit revenge related offenses towards the "offender – kind". The so by a hate crime created substantiated ubiquitous preparedness for aggression not only generates respective fear, but could violate the public peace due to "poisoning the societal climate" for all members of society. Considering this finding, a specific ability of impairment of the public peace in the sub-field of "climate change" could be acknowledged.

c) Intermediate Summary

The problem with reasoning a hate crime norm with the above illustrated climate changes is that the description of harm does not refer to a specific climate and its changes, but the core of the preventable evil are these potentially later, as part of the climate change, committed criminal offenses[1823] or likely to arise (victim's) behaviors, which then cause further damage. So it is in fact not the preservation of the existing climate which is the content of a

---

crime victim's injury will exceed that inflicted harm upon the parallel victim. "This [results] from the far greater occurrence of depression, withdrawal, anxiety, and feelings of helplessness and isolations among bias crime victims than [it] is ordinarily experienced by victims." (Lawrence, Punishing Hate, pp. 40, 63; with reference to: Henneberger, "For Bias Crimes, a Double Trauma" , Newsday, 113 (Jan. 9, 1992); Kleinfield, "Bias Crimes Hold Steady, But Leave Many Scards" , New York Times, A – 1 (Jan. 27, 1992); Levin, "U. S. Supreme Court Upholds Stiffer Sentences for hate crimes", Intelligence Report, 166 (Sept. 1993); Weiss, "Ethnoviolence: Impact upon the Response of Victims and the Community", in Bias Crime: American Law Enforcement and Legal Response, pp. 182, 183 (1993); see also Weiss/Ehrlich/Larcon, "Ethnoviolence at Work" , 18 Journal of Intergroup Relations, p. 18 (Winter 1991 - 1992) - according to this study of violence in the workplace it was found that victims of bias-motivated violence reported a significantly greater level of negative psychological symptoms than victims of non-bias-motivated violence.

1820 Hate crimes "create an imitation effect in individuals with a right-wing attitude, who consider the violent struggle against foreigners as necessary to preserve the national identity of Germans, resulting in an increasingly harder to controllable danger, especially since certain parts of the population show understanding for anti-foreigner violence and show their solidarity with the perpetrators". (According to: BGH January 12, 2000 - StB 15/99; BGHSt 29, 26, 28; BGHSt 34, 329, 331; OLG Celle, NStZ 1997, 495, 496; Rudolphi, ZRP, 1979, 220; Hörnle, Grob anstößiges Verhalten, pp. 94 et seqq.).

1821 "Incitement to crime" is to be understood in the meaning of a "social-psychological phenomenon". (OLG Celle, NStZ 1997, 495, 496).

1822 Hörnle, Grob anstößiges Verhalten, p. 94.

1823 The finding that feelings of rage and revenge felt by members of the victimized group due to a hate crime attack are capable of causing intergroup relations which again have destructive effects on the fabric of society, reveals that this refers to harms, which are caused by the perpetrator of a hate crime only indirectly. This raises the question of the offenders liability; the answer is circumvented by referring to the protection of a collective interest. (Hörnle, Grob anstößiges Verhalten, p. 94).

legal good called "public peace", but it is about the prevention of possible future crimes and behaviors[1824].

If the aim of a hate crime law would be to prevent crimes which eventually could be committed in the future, it would represent a norm that supports existing criminal law standards[1825] by accelerating the legal protection for traditional individual legal goods[1826]. Such an accelerated protection could be necessary if one acknowledges that the "incited climate", as result of hate crime committal, causes these expected violent acts. This could apply in both ways, potential imitators also commit hate crimes and hate crime victims commit acts of revenge or in form of exaggerated self-defense. The emergence of an incited climate by a hate crime committal is easily comprehensible since – in opposite to the usual criminal act against traditional individual legal goods[1827] which is usually committed as a purposive-rational action[1828]– neither a hate crime as such nor an act of revenge of the hate crime target group is based on a pragmatic background. These acts are solely built on uncontrolled, criminally lived-out motives and thereby generated emotions within the population.

The risk of harm for several individual legal goods is sufficient to legitimize punishment reasoned with a disturbance of the public peace if it is likely that this imminent harm will occur[1829]. Further, it must not be certain which individual goods are likely to be violated by an attack as long as there is no doubt according the risk of injuries for the respective victims due to a concrete dangerous situation since it is usually not predictable what course such events take[1830]. In order to legally penalize behavior which constitutes these hazardous risks, a norm is established as a non-result-constituted offense. If a norm protects a collective legal good which is connected to an individual legal good and therefore simultaneously accelerates the protection for this individual good, the matter of "accountability of harmful consequences of a dangerous act" requires increased attention[1831]. This raises the question of how likely it is that the perpetrator's behavior leads to a certain type of crime at a later point, and whether these future events are part of the perpetrators previous actions.

1824 Sternberg-Lieben, Schranken der Einwilligung, pp. 389 et seqq.

1825 Junge, Schutzgut des § 130 StGB, pp. 72 et seqq.; Sternberg-Lieben, Schranken der Einwilligung, pp. 389 et seqq.; Schroeder, Straftaten gegen das Strafrecht, p. 211; Hörnle, Grob anstößiges Verhalten, p. 95.

1826 Junge, Schutzgut des § 130 StGB, pp. 72 et seqq.; Fischer, Öffentlicher Friede, pp. 533 et seqq., 609 et seqq.; Fischer, Die Eignung, den öffentlichen Frieden zu stören - Zur Beseitigung eines „restriktiven" Phantoms, NStZ 1988, 159 ff; Fischer, GA, 1989, pp. 450 et. seq. The objective part of public peace is not an independent legal good but solely paraphrases the (fore field-) protection of legal goods of individuals or the society which are already protected by other criminal norms, likewise the subjective public peace is not an independent legal good, but a benchmark of the society to grant protection under criminal law; (cf. Sternberg-Lieben, Schranken der Einwilligung, pp. 389 et. seq.; p. 389, supra note 276, with more detailed information and further references). Norms protecting the climate are flanking norms which only support norms for the protection of individual legal goods or provide the guarantee of their protection. (Jakobs, ZStW 97, 1985, pp. 751, 773 ff; Hörnle, Grob anstößiges Verhalten, p. 95).

1827 For instance, larceny, robbery, etc.

1828 Hörnle, Grob anstößiges Verhalten, p. 108.

1829 Hörnle, Grob anstößiges Verhalten, p. 95.

1830 Hörnle, Grob anstößiges Verhalten, p. 95.

1831 Hörnle, Grob anstößiges Verhalten, p. 96.

Considering the above, the establishment of a non-result-constituted offense might not be the best solution to combat hate crimes and its constituting respective criminal behavior. This applies even more if it is possible to determine the specific damage to a legally recognized collective good. In fact, the establishment of a non-result-constituted offense in order to criminally combat hate crimes is senseless if it is possible to establish a norm as a result-constituted offense, because this configuration is more promising to achieve the respective aims. The question of the necessary causal connection between the hateful and biased motivated act of the offender and the danger for a legal good would be avoided if one rest on the possibility of protecting a collective legal good like "public peace" and at the same time refers to possible harms in the future for legitimating penalty. Due to including a subjective motive into criminal liability as it occurs in the context of punishing hate crimes, it is precisely essential to clarify the relationship between the incriminating behavior, which is based on this motive, and the goods of others which require protection in the design of a law.

The same applies with respect to so-called secondary damaging effects towards victims, whose initial trigger is the hate crime act. For instance, in terms of the here relevant potential impacts on the social climate, which preservation is a collective good, one must identify the causal relationship between the initial harmful criminal behavior and the damaging result. In this case, the primary damage, which is the one caused to the individual victim, is in the foreground. The secondary damage that occurs to the collective may step back when reasoning hate crime norms. The damage caused to a person who is part of the community may ultimately always affect the community as a whole which results from the fact that the community is based on the individual and the individual is in dependence of society, which is the reason why the transition between individual and collective goods is fluent. The point is that individual losses which likewise have an impact on the community are not considered as damages of the collective.

Accordingly, by protecting the public peace it must not be about the veiled protection of individual goods. This applies even if protecting the public peace actually results in an useful acceleration of protecting individual legal goods due to an accompanied support of primary standards. Since hate crimes are said to spark intergroup conflicts and thereby affect the existing climate, it is convenient to enact a legal norm for the protection of the status quo. However, such only serves the protection of the legal good public peace if it actually protects a collective good against violation in a comprehensible way and does not, in reality, just serve the protection of individual goods which already are protected by criminal law by accelerating their protection. In order not to give a hate crime norm the form of a 'flanking standard', nor to design it as a non-result-constituted offense, a hate crime norm must be based on a legally protected content which itself is concretely affected through the conjunction of the motive to criminal behavior.

d) Protection of a Tolerant Climate to Maintain the current Multi-Cultural, Pluralistic Form of Society

In this conceptual meaning of the objective condition of public peace it is aimed at the preservation of the current climate by maintaining a minimum level of tolerance in society[1832]. According to the specific nature of a hate crime it is assumed that such not only generate a certain change of climate, which possibly lead to crime committal or other societal damaging behavior in the future, but it actually changes the level of tolerance within a nation in the moment of its committal. Therefore, a legal norm, which protects the legal good public peace in the meaning that is addressed here, protects a minimum level of tolerance in society. The protection serves for the preservation of a "climate, in which individual parts of the population are neither made to intellectual unprotected batches and pariahs of society, nor become otherwise excluded, and this applies regardless of whether a latent danger potential is created or not."[1833] According to this, the public peace is affected in its subregion of a "harmonious co- and side by side living of citizens"[1834], irrespective of the essence of their personality. The understanding of the "harmonious coexistence of people"[1835] as an object of a norm implies that the norm aims at protecting all members of society, regardless of race, sex, religion, sexuality, or their origin as community. If conditions, such as tolerance and the prevention of exclusion and the harmonious co-and side-by-side living, are possible to be considered as worthy of protection regardless of the creation of potential hazards for individual goods, the argument that a legal good named public good is superfluous, because it is solely based on the threat of ordinary individual legal goods, is invalidated. This applies, because the "tolerant or harmonious coexistence" clearly is a subject of a collectively shared interest[1836]. The evidence for the collectivity of this good can be provided by referring to the chosen example of *Hörnle*: "for an isolated individual, living on an island, this legal good would be meaningless, while the other human interests, such as to survive, his physical integrity and the preservation of freedom of movement, etc. would remain"[1837]. Intolerance and exclusion as such are preventable evils which necessitate the construction of an independent legal good[1838]. The actual tolerant and democratic climate is a condition of life, emerged through the modern socialization[1839].

Precisely, the prevention of a loss of tolerance enables the protection of all further individual goods. Accordingly, the public peace in its here to be

1832 Lenckner/Sternberg-Lieben, in: Schönke/Schröder, StGB, § 125, marginal no. 41.
1833 Lenckner/Sternberg-Lieben, in: Schönke/ Schröder, StGB, § 126 marginal no. 1.
1834 Von Bubnoff, in: LK-StGB, § 125 marginal no. 41; view also: Renzikowski, GS for Meurer, p. 188; Hörnle, Grob anstößiges Verhalten, p. 96.
1835 Wehinger, Volksverhetzung, p.83; Hörnle, Grob anstößiges Verhalten, p. 96.
1836 Hörnle, Grob anstößiges Verhalten, pp. 96, 97.
1837 Hörnle, Grob anstößiges Verhalten, p. 97.
1838 Lenckner/Sternberg-Lieben, in: Schönke/ Schröder, StGB, § 126 marginal no. 1 et seqq.
1839 "The concept of the legal good [...] requires the [...] installation of living conditions of the modern socialization, thus mainly such of universal interests, into the system of the legal goods." (Hassemer, in: Hefendehl/ von Hirsch/Wohlers (eds.), Die Rechtsgutstheorie, 2003, p. 64).

protected part can be considered as a "real" collective legal good[1840]. It does not only serve the free development of many persons, but also protects fundamental functional conditions of social coexistence, whose negation in the specific case would cause a profound shock to the collective consciousness and at the same time induces danger to a variety of different, from the outset not to be determined, individual legal goods. With such an understanding of the “universal/collective good” public peace, the sustainable bridge to the "true" goods of the individual people is established[1841].

1.5.1.2. Meaning of the Subjective Part of Public Peace in a Hate Crime Norm

In its subjective content, the public peace is defined as "the subjective consciousness of the people to live in quiet and peace"[1842]. This requires "the faith of the people, at least of a not inconsiderable number of persons, in the continuance of this state."[1843] “With the guarantee of the inviolability of the law and the herein lying protection of individual and supra-individual goods, the state creates a piece of elementary physical and psychological security, thus the freedom of citizens.”[1844] A state would be discredited as a guarantor of the legal order and safety of citizens if it would not fulfill its original purpose and if it would let the sense of security of its citizens be affected unlimitedly[1845]. The protection of legal peace ultimately encourages the confidence of the public society in the societal system, without this confidence the existence of the democratic state is not possible in the long run[1846].

So, if it is about the maintenance of the public confidence in the governmental ability to serve its purpose, the question raises how to define “public” in this context. In accordance to *Fischer*, "public" in this context is not a descriptive term but a normative evaluative term, "public" refers to public interests, in terms of "general interest", which is not the sum of the individual interests of the citizens, but in truth consists of the moral precepts of the legislator, because the subjective public peace does not reflect the emotional state of the majority of people, but ultimately reflects the legitimacy of the criminal law itself[1847]. Accordingly, in the context of the subjective part of the public peace, the punishability would be made to a legal criterion of an offense[1848]. This assumption of a purely normative meaning of the term "public peace" is

1840 Anastasopoulou, Deliktstypen, p. 304.

1841 "The concept of the legal good should be realistically". The legal good doctrine must manage to find the proper relationship between protecting ´real´ (individual) goods and abstract conditions. (Hassemer, in: Hefendehl/ von Hirsch/Wohlers (eds.), Die Rechtsgutstheorie, 2003, p. 64).

1842 Fischer, StGB, § 126, marginal no. 3; BGHSt 16, 56; BGHSt 29, 27.

1843 Lackner/Kühl, StGB,§ 126, marginal no. 1

1844 Sternberg-Lieben, Schranken der Einwilligung, p. 390; with reference to Arzt/Weber, LH 5, marginal no. 23.

1845 Sternberg-Lieben, Schranken der Einwilligung, p. 390; with reference to Arzt/Weber, LH 5, marginal no. 23.

1846 Sternberg-Lieben, Schranken der Einwilligung, p. 390.

1847 Fischer, Die Eignung, den öffentlichen Frieden zu stören - Zur Beseitigung eines „restriktiven“ Phantoms, NStZ 1988, 159 (164).

1848 Fischer, Die Eignung, den öffentlichen Frieden zu stören - Zur Beseitigung eines „restriktiven“ Phantoms, NStZ 1988, 159 (164).

allegedly not based on the lack of empirical measurability of psychological damage[1849], but on the fact that the solving of difficulties, which go along with measuring such social psychological effects[1850], is avoided in practice on a regular basis[1851] by letting the plain ability of an act disturb the public peace be sufficient to legitimate punishability[1852]. This means that in fact not the disturbance of the public peace, but its integrity must be proved[1853]. However, it is rather necessary to reveal which damage an offender causes by his behavior.

Regardless to this, whenever it is referred to a subjective loss of confidence of the public in the existence of social security, it is not about a collective legal good, but about the sum of individual interests[1854]; and therefore such must not be captured by the legal good of public peace in its meaning of a collective good. A collective legal good in the meaning of "public trust" may not be recognized. An understanding of the subjective part of the public peace, which in the end is only the description of the worthiness of punishability of the conduct in question[1855], is to be refused. Rather, “public”, as in "public peace", is to be considered as a supportive adjective of the already determined objective part of the public peace, thus as being a legal good of the ‘public’ community.

1.5.2. Current Protection of Public Peace by the German Penal Code

The current German penal law protects the legal good public peace in a number of norms, yet, depending on the norm, it has several distinct meanings. The pure suitability to interfere with the public peace[1856] is protected in Sections 126, 130, 130a, 140 No. 2, 166 and 241 Penal Code[1857]. The view stating that a disturbance of the public peace lies in the creation of a psychological climate in which potential perpetrators are stirred up to commit crimes usually refers to cases in which certain behaviors arouse hatred (Section 130 Penal Code)[1858]. The aspect of a tolerant climate is protected by Sections 166 et seq. Penal Code. The prevention of vigilante justice usually plays a role in the justification of criminal prohibitions directed against the disturbing of funerals and the desecration of graves, dead silence, etc.

1849 In regard to the difficult measurability of such social psychological states, refer to: Rudolphi, ZRP, 1979, p. 221; Streng, in: FS for Lackner, p. 514 et seq.; Hörnle, Grob anstößiges Verhalten, p. 102.

1850 Fischer, Die Eignung, den öffentlichen Frieden zu stören - Zur Beseitigung eines „restriktiven“ Phantoms, NStZ 1988, 159 (164).

1851 Hefendehl, Kollektive Rechtsgüter, pp. 291, 292.

1852 Hörnle, Grob anstößiges Verhalten, p. 103.

1853 Fischer, Die Eignung, den öffentlichen Frieden zu stören - Zur Beseitigung eines „restriktiven“ Phantoms, NStZ 1988, 159 (161) based on: OLG Düsseldorf, NJW 1986, 2518.

1854 "A social-empirically "public" subjective legal peace is a majority of the protected object enshrined in Section 241 Penal Code; the mere reproduction of such does not provide a new quality [for it to become an independent collective good]." (Fischer, Die Eignung, den öffentlichen Frieden zu stören - Zur Beseitigung eines „restriktiven“ Phantoms, NStZ 1988, 159 (163)).

1855 Fischer, Öffentlicher Friede und Gedankenäußerung, 1986, p.530 ff, 607; Fischer, Die Eignung, den öffentlichen Frieden zu stören - Zur Beseitigung eines „restriktiven“ Phantoms, NStZ 1988, 159 (163).

1856 If the pure suitability to interfere with the public peace is considered as sufficient to establish a criminal norm, such is formed as a non-result-constituted offense.

1857 Sternberg-Lieben, Schranken der Einwilligung, p. 389.

1858 BGHSt 29, 26, 28; OLG Celle, NStZ 1997, 495, 496; Hörnle, Grob anstößiges Verhalten, p. 94.

(Sections 167a, 168 Penal Code)[1859]. The variant of public trust is consistently recognized by the legislature through penalizing behavior which appears disturbing or threatening; for instance, the public incitement to crime (Section 111 Penal Code), the rewarding and approving of offenses (Section 140 Penal Code) and the breach of the public peace by threatening to commit offenses (Section 126 Penal Code) are established to maintain public confidence in the rule of law. Accordingly, a clarification of the meaning of "public peace" cannot be drawn from the established law and its conceptual acknowledgement.

Nevertheless, the extensive use of this legal good to establish penal law does not weigh against the general possibility to legitimize criminal norms. However, it is necessary to clearly determine its meaning in respect to the relevant issue in order to be able to legitimately punish its violation.

1.5.3. Result: Meaning of Public Peace in a Hate Crime Norm

The damage that is caused to social facilities, i.e. the societal system, can be subdivided - in dependence on the damaged object - into different sorts of disturbances of the public peace. One primarily thinks of hate crimes injuring structures like the constitution and the democracy, but particularly the actual degree of tolerance within the pluralistic society is affected. The already partially punished behavior of a hate crime violates or endangers an already legally recognized legal good of the individual; the connection between the respective motive and the thereon based action which objectifies itself in the broadcast of a message further injures an additional value-bearing state. This value-bearing state is the actual degree of tolerance. The level of tolerance forms an independent value that is worthy of protection because the multi-cultural, pluralistic society in its present form can not exist if the actual content of tolerance is changed, i.d. diminished, or even eliminated.

Consequently, it is recognized that hate crime laws neither aim at protecting the democratically order as such, nor do such legislation aim at guaranteeing a compromised protection of the public peace in society against all kinds of threats. The aim of hate crime law is to abolish criminal acts based on prejudiced animus against a particular group of people, thus parts of the society, because such acts in consequence of their inherent motive (which finds expression in the criminal act) send a specific harm enforcing message and thereby modify the actual, constitutional protected societal climate.

It is not about the possibility of these crimes sparking racial conflicts and retaliation[1860] or that such incite further perpetrators to imitate a criminal behavior in the future, but about the fact that by its committal the level of tolerance in society is modified; thus the tolerant climate in the society is actually violated, even though its integrity is essential to the existence of a German multi-cultural society.

1859 Hörnle, Grob anstößiges Verhalten, p. 94.

1860 Iganski, Hate Crime hurts more, American Behavioral Scientist, Vol. 45, No. 4, December 2001, pp. 626-638 (630).

Since this climate changing potential of hate crimes is based on (criminal) acts and not on opinions[1861], a clear objective fact is identifiable for a clearly defined harmful impact. Racial- (religious-, gender- and further-) hate, incarnated in criminal acts, harms the tolerant climate and thereby demarks a specific aspect of societal threat which hinders a peaceful co-existence of all citizens. Therefore, a hate crime norm protects the functional capability of society in a specific partial section (tolerant climate) against a specific form of interference (violating the requirement of acceptance and the permissiveness of foreign beliefs, practices and customs, thus abolishing the recognition of equal rights of different individuals).

Since, the general suitability of the public peace as a legal good of a criminal norm has been determined above, its specific meaning in respect to a hate crime norm and the indeed effect on its concrete partial region is acknowledged as well.

1.6. Hate Crimes and "Worthiness of Punishment"[1862]

When establishing a new penal norm it must be examined whether a behavior is considered to be "worthy of punishment"[1863] and whether it "necessitates punishment"[1864] because only if the behavior reaches a certain level of reprehensibility and its punishment is required, the enactment of a penal norm to prohibit it, may be established[1865]. A just unwanted, annoying impairment of a "legal good" does not legitimate to enact a criminal norm[1866]. Since the enforcement of punishment is a serious limitation of freedom, the personal development and the dignity of the punished, the constitutionally guaranteed freedom, the imperative to respect the dignity of an individual, but even the principle of proportionality requires that punishment is only imposed as a reaction in areas where it is essential to ensure peace by law[1867].

Whereas insofar it has been determined that the public peace in its concrete form may be worth to be protected by criminal law, it is to find out whether the bias-motivated behavior in question contradicts the principles of a peaceful coexistence to such an extent that it is worthy to be counteracted with penalty. This relates to the question of the extent to which criminal law can be legitimately used to protect the public peace[1868]. Just because it is in principle possible to protect a particular affected area of this legal good against bias-motivated acts, it is still not clear to what extent this legal good may be criminally protected against the specific conduct at issue; this refers to the

1861 The legislature will not criminalize bigoted thoughts. This applies to the U.S. legislature and likewise to the German legislature: The principles established by the Court in the case Wisconsin v. Mitchell, 508 U.S. 476, 485 (1993) rule that a hate crime law is aimed at conduct (not expression). Conduct is neither protected by the First Amendment U.S. Constitution, nor by Article 5 German Basic Law.

1862 View Translation Index.

1863 View Translation Index.

1864 View Translation Index and Chapter 1.7. Necessity of Punishment.

1865 Otto, ZStW 96 (1984), 339, p. 347, supra note 19.

1866 Otto, ZStW 96 (1984), 339, p. 347.

1867 Otto, ZStW 96 (1984), 339, p. 347.

1868 Jescheck/Weigend, Lehrbuch des Strafrechts AT, pp. 49 et seqq.

determination of the "worthiness of punishment". Behavior can only be considered as "worthy of punishment" if it involves a degree of social danger or harmfulness that is suitable to significantly endanger the social conditions in society[1869]. The answer to the question whether the interference in question constitutes such a serious violation of legal goods, is composed of two components[1870], the "disvalue of the result"[1871] and the "disvalue of the act"[1872] of the respective behavior[1873]. While the "disvalue of the result" is dependent on the value that is attributed to the attacked legal good by the society[1874], the "disvalue of the act" determines the social demerit of the act and its abjection[1875].

1.6.1. Disvalue of the Result

It is questionable whether the securing of a pluralistic society due to protecting the legal good public peace can be considered as a value that is important enough to be protected by a criminal norm and legitimizes the punishment of the respective biased criminal behavior. The answer depends on the importance which the affected conceptional good has for the social coexistence. This again can be determined with viewing in the constitutional value system of the respective society[1876]. The higher the rank of a legal good in this value system is, the more likely it is that significant hazards or injuries will appear which are worthy to be punished[1877]. The lower the rank is, the more it will be appropriate to classify only certain impairments of that legal good to be "worthy of punishment", namely such which are due to a particular level of social worthlessness[1878].

A collective good that relates to the maintenance of the current state of a multicultural, pluralistic society by protecting the actual degree of tolerance is an independent good of the highest rank, if this condition of the actual society is essential for the achievement of all further security interests[1879]. This fact would make it a right of the society as a collective. Such a right, if related to individual goods would meet the content of a right in accordance with Article 2,

1869 Jescheck/Weigend, Lehrbuch des Strafrechts AT, pp. 50, 51.
1870 Grützner, Die Sanktionierung von Submissionsabsprachen, p. 463.
1871 View Translation Index.
1872 View Translation Index.
1873 Roxin, Strafrecht AT I, § 10, p. 321, marginal no. 88; Otto, ZStW 96 (1984), 339, p. 348; also: BVerfGE 39, 42 et seqq.
1874 "The value of the legal good can not be equated with the value of the material damage which the offender inflicts, but it is about the importance that the affected ideational interest has for the co-existence of the community". (Jescheck/Weigend, Lehrbuch des Strafrechts AT, p. 51).
1875 The affirmation of worthiness of punishment of a behavior contains a social-ethical condemnation. (Otto, ZStW 96 (1984), 339, p. 346); Grützner, Die Sanktionierung von Submissionsabsprachen, p. 463.
1876 The Basic Law embodies especially in its bill of rights objective an "objective order of values". (Otto, ZStW 96 (1984), 339, p. 347; with reference to: BVerfGE 7, 205; 21, 372; 35, 114; 37, 65; 39, 41).
1877 Otto, ZStW 96 (1984), 339, p. 347.
1878 Otto, ZStW 96 (1984), 339, pp. 347, 348.
1879 Papageorgiou; Schaden und Strafe, pp. 151 et seqq. with reference to von Humboldt, Ideen zu einem Versuch, die Grenzen der Wirksamkeit des Staates zu bestimmen, 1851; Hörnle, Grob anstößiges Verhalten, pp. 76 et seqq.

Section 1 Basic Law[1880]. With that the idea of Feinberg's "welfare interests" receives attention in the German discussion according to which it is less a matter of political discretion of what makes a decent base for the life of every member of society, but rather the clear recognition that any discretionary decision is only enabled because of the underlying and sustaining foundation, which is the current form of society. Likewise as the current form of society only enables a discretionary decision of the legislator, the protection of each individual good ultimately depends on the overriding existence of the collective legal good public peace and its partial region of a tolerant climate, which - as a social condition - is guaranteed by the Basic Law.

The basic concept of a pluralistic society is that there are different mindsets in society and it is legitimate and even desirable that they are articulated and represented - this applies until the point where a mindset, by being acted out, in particular violates this respective basic concept. Pluralism implies a tolerant climate. Pluralism is the undisputed aim of a democratic society[1881] and therefore constitutes an overriding concern as a collective interest of all. The preservation is important to the overall population that is also to the part of the population against whom the incendiary and prejudice motivated act is not directed. This is because the functioning of a modern immigration society depends on equal protection of all members of society and equal realization possibilities for all societal members. A for others negatively vested intolerant climate therefore must turn out negatively even for those who are not directly victimized by an act[1882], i.e. for those who assume not to be in risk of certain sorts of hate crime attack or do not belong to the addressed group or a similar group which is in risk of hate crime attacks, because an unstable climate, marked by inequalities, means that even people who are not directly attacked may not be able to realize their rights. Germany, as an immigration's society, based on an autonomous life design, can not accept intolerant behavior that crosses the line to criminal behavior due to connecting a misanthropic message to a criminal act and thereby attacking the society in its current form. Therefrom it attests itself that the public peace in its here relevant aspect is a good of maximum value. The current existence of the society in its pluralistic form requires the preservation of the current tolerant climate, which therefore is determined to be such a weighty collective good that its preservation is indispensable.

So if it is undisputed that the legal good public peace makes up a value for society and moreover it is agreed that such is an overly high value, it must further be answered whether a criminal offense is required to protect the public peace in the variant "tolerant, pluralistic coexistence". To ensure that the relationship between the motive and the act can legitimately be punished

1880 By the commission of a hate crime the interest in a tolerant coexistence turns into a security interest and can therefore be qualified as a right in accordance to Article 2, Section 1 Basic Law; and therefore is capable of creating a commandment for criminalization. (Based on the precepts of Hörnle, Grob anstößiges Verhalten, p. 100).

1881 Schneider, Internationales Handbuch der Kriminologie, Bd. 2, 2009, pp. 297 et seqq.

1882 Based on the idea of Hörnle, Grob anstößiges Verhalten, p. 98.

separately, it is crucial that precisely the connection damages the plural society. Whereas the collective good of a tolerant climate is worth being protected due to its degree of value, the demerit of the violating behavior connected to a motive must provide enough criminal disvalue in order to be punishable.

1.6.2. Disvalue of the Act

Since the required "disvalue of the result" is awarded to the violation of the public peace's constituting part of a tolerant, pluralistic climate, the assessment of punishability of a behavior further requires the determination of the social unworthiness and the reprehensibility established in the act, summarized: the determination of the "disvalue of the act"[1883]. It is therefore necessary to clarify the extent of the content of wrong of a hate crime act. Therefore, one must address and evaluate the wrong, which is attributed to a biased motivated commission of a criminal act, in order to justify the criminalization of this behavior. This applies by referring to the hate crime act, instead of referring to the plain - i.e. underlying - criminal behavior, in order to evaluate whether it increases the wrong, compared to the pure base offense. Basically, the design and formation of the mind of a perpetrator must not constitute a social misconduct[1884]. While all opinions must be approved by the legal system, the inside remained formation of an attitude of a perpetrator is not relevant, in so far hate crime acts do not constitute a peculiarity. However, as stated, in terms of hate crime legislation it is about capturing criminal behavior which conflicts with constitutional aims[1885]. The political attitude of the hate crime offender is insignificant for determining the disvalue of behavior, but crucial is the the circumstance of acting out one´s own desire or views - which is the ideal of a society freed from strangers - and by this action not solely expressing one´s own political aim, but giving one´s inner formed destination a piece of reality.

Therefore, it is not about the existence of unpleasant motives of perpetrators, but about the fact that ideologies active-combatively exclude conflicting beliefs and manifestations from society by committing criminal behavior[1886]. Thus, the inner (in principle irrelevant) motive is objectified in actions and thereby obtains criminal importance by violating the public peace in its partial aspect of tolerance. The tolerance precept is being thwarted - which is not the case if an act is committed unlinked to the motives in question; consequently, the disvalue of the act is subsumable enlarged towards an otherwise- or unmotivated act that is captured by the respective parallel offense. It is in particular reprehensible to link punishable behavior to the broadcast of certain

1883 Otto, Strafwürdigkeit und Strafbedürftigkeit als eigenständige Deliktskategorien? Überlegungen zum Deliktsaufbau, in: Gedächtnisschrift für Horst Schröder, Stree/Lenckner/Cramer (eds.), 1978, pp. 53 et seqq.; p. 55.

1884 The offender however is never blamed for his mindset as such, but only for the crime which is characterized by his mindset. (Wessels/Beulke, Strafrecht AT, p. 149, marginal no. 401).

1885 "No one pretends that actions should be as free as opinions". (J. Mill, 1859).

1886 Cf. Wohlers, Deliktstypen des Präventionsstrafrechts, p. 274.

messages in order to infiltrate the legal good public peace, which is indispensable for a social order and is orientated towards the idea of tolerance and equality. Such behavior reveals a level of social disvalue which is significantly lower compared to a mere violation of individual goods. The social disvalue of such a behavior - that is giving one´s own ideology an expression by connecting it to a criminal act - evidences wrong-enhancing features, which are reflected in an increased "disvalue of the act"[1887].

1.6.3. Intermediate Result

The attack action includes, precisely because of the connection between the motive and the thereon based behavior of the offender, an unsurpassed social unworthiness, which expresses itself in the contempt of all democratic values. Thereby it is to refer to the expressive dimension of hate crimes[1888], which degrades the individual attacked victim to a despicable creature whose right to exist, based on his affiliation, is deprived[1889], and thereby violates already protected individual legal goods deeper in several ways[1890] and in addition violates, unconnected from such already protected personal legal goods of the immediate victim and its community: the public peace, which in its specific form that is addressed by a hate crime, is not yet protected, in other words, the form of attack which a hate crime causes to the public peace is not yet penalized by the Penal Code.

This concrete reprehensible behavior with its distinct character, due to it being connected to the specific hateful- and biased motive of the offender, enhances the allover content of unworthiness, such of the result and such of the act. The "disvalue of the result" occurs from the value of a tolerant climate as an indispensable part of our societal system. In conjunction, yet not prevalent when discussing the protection of the public peace alone, the additional element of an increased impairment of the dignity of the directly affected victims pushes the whole to the peak. The "disvalue of the act" regarding the conduct at issue must be awarded due to its above described modified typology based on the connection between motive and action. Thus, as a result, the aspect of "worthiness of punishment" - is given in order to affirm the differentiable content of wrong to a hate crime.

1.7. Necessity of Punishment

The legitimacy of punishing behavior, which meets the requirements set by the precepts of being "worthy of punishment", further requires an explanation

---

1887 Eser, in: Schönke/Schröder, StGB, § 211, marginal no. 6.

1888 View hereto: Chapter 4, C., 8. Symbolic Reasoning of Hate Crime Law.

1889 Hörnle, Grob anstößiges Verhalten, p. 272.

1890 Even though the harmful way of crime committal based on external facts is partly captured by previous norms (view Chapter 4, G., 1., 1.6., 1.6.1., 1.6.1.5. Sections 223; 224; 226 Penal Code), the particularly humiliating treatment of the victim increases the infringement of the personal "legal good" human dignity to a noteworthy different dimension compared to the behavior which is addressed in the relevant norms which punish the non-, or otherwise motivated counterparts. (View hereto: Chapter 4, G., 1.1.1. Human Dignity of the Immediate Victims and Chapter 4, G., 1.2. Priority of Protected Legal Goods).

regarding the practical necessity of the use of criminal law[1891], and thus the need to clarify the issue of when there is a need for criminal sanctioning of concrete behavior[1892]. Not just any reprehensible behavior may be punished, it is important that its punishment is necessary to protect a legal good against it. Moreover, only if specific institutions are indispensable for humans and their societal being, the use of criminal law may be applied for their protection[1893]. While the "penalty deserving" element of punishment is largely determined by the rating of the social harmfulness of a behavior, the "necessity of punishment" primarily captures the purpose element of governmental punishment[1894]. It commands that if other, less serious interventions than the penalization of behavior are similar promising or at least seem to lead to an equal success are available, the priority must be granted to such[1895]. Accordingly, there must be no equally appropriate, less restrictive measures available which are capable to protect the public peace in the concrete by a hate crime attacked aspect in order for a hate crime norm to be legitimate. However, the legislator in this aspect has a discretionary power concerning the assessment whether other means seem similar promising; just as he has the prerogative of assessment for the evaluation and the way of designing a law[1896].

1.7.1. Necessity of Punishment with regard to Previously Established Criminal Norms

According to the fragmentary protection against hate crimes by applicable law the question raises whether an explicit additional regulation is necessary to combat hate crime. It might be that the reach of the following sections established in the German Penal Code are sufficient to protect the German society, thus, sufficient to protect the public peace against hate crimes.

1.7.1.1. Necessity of a Hate Crime Law with regard to the Existence of certain Criminal Norms

The following provides a brief examination of legal norms which could already capture hate crime in part. The following presentation raise no claim to completeness, but shows selective examples of criminal norms only. There are far more norms which could be examined in more details in regard to their capability of capturing hate crimes (especially Section 130 Penal Code, but also Section 303 Penal Code). However, it is clear that neither one of the

---

1891 Grützner, Die Sanktionierung von Submissionsabsprachen, p. 417.

1892 Hörnle, Grob anstößiges Verhalten, p. 23; Otto, Grundkurs AT, § 1, marginal no. 50.

1893 This follows from the principle that criminal law should be used as a tool of "last resort" to protect "legal goods", according to which a certain behavior beyond being prohibited must also be unbearably socially harmful and its prevention for the orderly coexistence of people therefore must be particularly urgent (BVerfGE 90, 145, 172; BVerfGE 39, 1 (47); Jeschenk/Weigend, Lehrbuch des Strafrechts AT, p. 3; BVerfGE 120, 224, (240); BVerfGE 27, 18, 30; BVerfGE 96, 10, 25 et seqq.; Hörnle, Grob anstößiges Verhalten, p. 104).

1894 Otto, ZStW 96 (1984), 339, p. 384.

1895 Otto, ZStW 96 (1984), 339, p. 384.

1896 BVerfGE 88, 203, 262.

exemplified norms, nor further unmentioned sections of the Penal Code are capable of addressing the entire criminal content of hate crimes.

Sections 125, 125a Penal Code could at least address certain forms of hate crime and therefore one could assume that an additional explicit norm to penalize hate crimes would be superfluous. These criminal norms punish a group dynamic act of violence and thereby protect the legal good public security[1897] in combination with threatened personal goods[1898] by forwarding the protection for legally recognized personal goods[1899]. These standards can capture hate crimes in only those cases where acts, constituting the offense of Section 125, Paragraph 1 Penal Code, are directed against persons who are attacked as representatives of a group of people, "because this kind of violence does not only interfere with the sense of security of the immediate victim, but with a huge number of people and therefore leads to a threat to the public safety"[1900]. Whereas this standard is able to address specific hazards of hate crimes before they actually occur[1901], i.e. before a violation of a specific legal good has taken place, it is not nearly suitable to capture hate crimes in general. Due to the various forms of hate crimes, the wrong of such acts such can not be covered by Sections 125, 125a Penal Code in its entirety.

Section 130 Penal Code, overwritten with “Incitement to Hatred“, states the following in its Paragraph 1:

> *“Whosoever, in a manner capable of disturbing the public peace incites hatred against segments of the population or calls for violent or arbitrary measures against them; or assaults the human dignity of others by insulting, maliciously maligning, or defaming segments of the population, shall be liable to imprisonment from three months to five years.”*

When examining whether this offense is capable of capturing hate crimes, Alternative 1 of Section 130, Paragraph 1 Penal Code, which punishes incitation, i.e. stimulation, or encouraging others, deserves special attention. The elements of this offense require an act which has an impact on the emotions and the mindset of the addressee, it must be objectively suitable and subjectively intended - in the meaning of a goal-directed action - to generate or increase a hostile attitude of the recipient that goes beyond the mere rejection or contempt towards the respective section of the population[1902]. Insofar, it can be acknowledged that Section 130, Paragraph 1 Penal Code is valuable to address partial aspects of hate crime, but it is not suitable to provide an overall coverage of such criminal acts which are determined in several base offenses (causing bodily harm, murder, libel, etc.), but are linked to the respective

1897 Maurach/Schröder/Maiwald, Strafrecht BT II, § 60 I, marginal no. 4; Schäfer, in: MK-StGB § 125, marginal no. 19.

1898 Schäfer, in: MK-StGB, § 125, marginal no. 1.

1899 Krupna, Das Konzept der Hate Crimes in Deutschland, pp. 103 et seq.

1900 BGH 29th April, 2004 – 4 StR 43/04 - NStZ 2004, 618; Rudolphi/Stein, in: SK-StGB, § 125, marginal no. 12; Fischer, StGB, § 125, marginal no. 9; Krupna, Das Konzept der Hate Crimes in Deutschland, p. 104.

1901 Cf. Krupna, Das Konzept der Hate Crimes in Deutschland, pp. 103 et seqq.

1902 Krupna, Das Konzept der Hate Crimes in Deutschland, p. 141; Fischer, StGB, §130, marginal no. 8.

motive and therefore contain the public peace violating content of injuring the tolerant and pluralistic state of the current society. The general additional indivual and environmental harming aspect of a hate crime, regardless of the underlying criminal act, is not encompassed by Section 130 Penal Code.

Sections 185 et seq. Penal Code are designed for punishing defamation offenses. The legal good of Section 185 Penal Code refers to the honor of the victim or the victimized group of people[1903]. hate crimes, as discussed, hurt more deeply, yet not only violate the honor of the victims, but they violate the constitutional guaranteed, and governmentally to be protected human dignity of the immediate victim and his group members. Therefore, Section 185 Penal Code is not capable of embracing the content of wrong realized by a hate crime act[1904].

1.7.1.2. Section 211 Penal Code

As mentioned above, the murder offense, codified in Section 211 Penal Code, is a specially formed norm due to the fact that the mental elements of the offense state subjective motives as penalty enhancing features. There is a dispute between the legal literature and the German jurisprudence, if the (subjective) characteristics listed in Section 211 Penal Code only aggravate the manslaughter offense established in Section 212 Penal Code, or whether the murder offense forms a separate offense with an own, i.d. enhanced, content of wrong[1905]. Regardless of this dispute, the killing of a human being (Section 212 Penal Code) because of racial hatred, xenophobia, or similar hate crime motives is subsumed under the subjective element referred to as "base motives" in Section 211 Penal Code, therefrom the killing of another because of such a motive is punished more severely compared to the killing of someone because of motives that are not mentioned by Section 211 Penal Code. This is a Supreme Court ruling[1906], so that it can be assumed that within the framework of murder the investigation of such motives, relevant for hate crime, in fact takes place during the criminal prosecution process when solving an offense. This necessary involvement with the motives of an offender in the case of murder already results from the criminally codified need of a correct classification of the offense to either Section 212 (if the perpetrator was not motivated by Hate Ceime motives) or to Section 211 Penal Code (if the perpetrator was motivated by hate crime motives), which requires the prior determination of a legally mentioned motive that initiated the respective

1903 Lenckner/Eisele, in: Schönke/Schröder, StGB, §§ 185 et seqq., marginal no. 1 et seqq.5 et seqq.; SSW – StGB/Sinn, § 185, marginal no. 3, 6.

1904 A hate crime attacks the human dignity, not the honor of a victim. For the distinction, thus the greater degree of violation of the human dignity footnote 1650 (Chapter 4, G., 1. 1.2. Priority of protected Legal Goods).

1905 The opinion in literature considers the murder offense as a dependent modification of Section 212 Penal Code, i.e. as a aggravation of the "ordinary" killing offense (while Section 216 Penal Code forms the mitigating case of Section 212 Penal Code). The Supreme Court, however views in Sections 211, 212, 216 Penal Code autonomous offenses with own facts of wrongfulness. (Wessels/Beulke, Strafrecht AT, p. 27, marginal no. 69, 70; BGH 1, 368; 22, 375).

1906 Killing only because of the victim´s membership to an ethnic, political, or social group (BGH, NStZ 04, 89); because of racial hatred (BGHSt 18, 37); because of xenophobia (BGH NStZ 94, 124).

criminal action. However, this need is not met for other offenses, regarding hate crimes in particular. This reveals a lack of distinction between the severity of the wrong caused by a hate crime compared to such caused by un-motivated crimes. In the context of homicide the specificity of defamatory hate acts is not expressly taken into account by the Penal Code either. But by consolidated jurisprudence in recent years, the entire judiciary now[1907] realized that through the prejudiced motives of the perpetrator the killing of another represents an act whose disvalue cannot be outweighed with other motives or circumstances accompanying the act, but modifies the type of crime. In literature it is followed that a hate crime constitutes an attack on the human dignity[1908] because such a motive calls the moral value of an individual or group in question and thereby denies their right of social existence[1909]. And such a motive is considered to be based at "the lowest level and it is, in any circumstances, morally comprehensible".

It is unclear to what extent the harmful effects on the here addressed legal good public peace are recognized when a homicide in the form of a hate crime is punished in accordance to Section 211 Penal Code[1910]; although the legal good public peace does not play a role in the field of Section 211 Penal Code and its function of increasing the penalty in case of hate crime commission in the form of killing. In the case of committing murder in accordance with these aggravating facts, Section 211 Penal Code imposes the maximum penalty which is constitutionally permissible. Therefore, if a hate crime is punished due to Section 211 Penal Code additional harmful effects which relate to collective legal goods could not change the imposed penalty. The specific wrong of a hate crime is not expressly recognized as an aggravating circumstance by this law, but according to the possibility of subsuming hate crime motives under the wording of "base motives" and today's actual judicial application, hate crimes, in the case of killing offenses - in practice - are criminally recognized and according to their additional wrong- and culpability increasing content[1911] are punished more severely compared to the killing of a person because of other, less repulsive, motivations. However, the base motives of hate crime offenders do not lead them to commit murder offenses only, far more offenses which qualify as hate crime are committed. These criminal cases require an adequate consideration of the distinct character of bias-motivated behavior as well. Section 211 Penal Code does not serve for the encompassment of the difference between a hate crime and a crime unless it is a delict of homicide. Thus Section 211 Penal Code itself is not capable of solving the problem of hate crime alone.

1907 View hereto: Chapter 4, D., 1. Judicial Recognition of Bias-Motivation in Homicide.

1908 Stegbauer, Der Gesetzentwurf zur Bekämpfung von "Hate Crimes", NJ 2008, 108; Tolmein, ZRP, 2001, 315, p. 319.

1909 Werle, Völkerstrafrecht, p. 269, marginal no. 665.

1910 The central legal value of the murder offense is "life". It is a dependent modification of Section 212 Penal Code, i.e. an aggravation that punishes the murderer with life imprisonment. The imposition of this penalty is just only if it is guaranteed that it is applied only to murder cases with particularly reprehensible character. (Wessels/Beulke, Strafrecht AT, p. 26, 27, 31).

1911 View hereto Chapter 4, G., 1.7.1.4. a) Hate Crime Motives: Part of the Wrong or the Culpability.

1.7.1.3. Sections 223; 224; 226 Penal Code

The offenses of Sections 224 et seqq. Penal Code require objective facts in order to aggravate the penalty compared to the one stated in Section 223 Penal Code. Motives and subjective intents of a perpetrator when committing physical assault are not taken into account in the context of enhancing the penalty frame in regard to the base offense determined in Section 223 Penal Code. If one wants to consider hate crimes in the context of bodily injury as an aggravating factor, such is only possible by referring to the particular form of committal (Section 224 Penal Code), or the cause of a severe result on the victim (Section 226 Penal Code).

The external facts, which are typical for violent hate crimes, could be addressed by these norms and consequently be punished more severely than the base offense that is determined in Section 223 Penal Code[1912]. hate crimes are said to be more brutal than their unmotivated counterparts, which is due to the motive[1913]. With a hate crime attack the victim is considered as an "enemy" who is dehumanized. This process of dehumanization takes place by the perpetrator´s denial of the victim´s human qualities and thereby increases his aggression[1914]. Thus, the offender has a very deep potential for violence[1915]. After all, due to his motive, he wants to cause harm up to the victim´s destruction[1916]. These intensified harmful results of a criminal hate crime act could be addressed by Sections 224 et seqq. Penal Code.

hate crimes are often committed with weapons or dangerous tools (Section 224, Paragraph 1, No. 2 Penal Code) which are suited to bring the victim in mortal danger (Section 224, Paragraph 1 No. 5 Penal Code) and due to the frequent way of hate crime perpetrators acting jointly with another (Section 224, Paragraph 1, No. 4 Penal Code) these facts are considered as aggravating factors so that some hate crimes could be punished severe due to their way of execution[1917]. The type, design and the criminology related

1912 "The disvalue of the act lies in the manner of the attack towards the action object." (Jescheck/Weigend, AT, p. 51; with reference to: Gallas, Einheit und objektiver und subjektiver Merkmale" , in: Bockelmann FS, pp. 156 et seqq.).

1913 This is confirmed at two levels: Hate crimes are more violent than other crimes; a crime which is committed with a bias motivation is more likely to be an assault than an otherwise-, or unmotivated crime (Levin/Mc Devitt, Hate Crimes. The Rising Tide of Bigotry and Bloddshed, 1993, pp. 11,12; Lawrence, The Punishment of Hate: Towards a Normative Theory of Bias-Motivated Crimes, 93 Mich. L. Rev. 1994, p. 342). The second point refers to the fact that hate crimes are often committed by more than one perpetrator, thus by groups (Levin/Mc Devitt, Hate Crimes. The Rising Tide of Bigotry and Bloddshed, 1993, p. 16).

1914 Füllgrabe, Hassverbrechen, Kriminalistik, 2004, pp. 391-397 (392).

1915 Füllgrabe, Hassverbrechen, Kriminalistik, 2004, pp. 391-397 (392); with reference to Zimbardo 1991.

1916 Cunneen, Hysteria and Hate: The Vilification of Aboriginal and Torres Strait Islander People, in: Cunnen/Fraser/Tomsen (eds.): Faces of Hate. Hate Crime in Australia, pp. 137-161, 1997; Schneider, Kriminologie der Hassdelikte. Konzeptionen, Ursachen, Vorbeugung und Kontrolle, in: Bewährungshilfe, 2003, pp. 116, 117.

1917 In reference to the dehumanizing objectification of the victim in order to express one´s own undemocratic reprehensible mindset, hate crime perpetrators in general act more brutal and despicable during the commission of a criminal violent act compared to the proceedings of perpetrators who are not driven by comparable motives. (Descriptions of attacks which support this thesis are provided by: Herzog, in: Mohr/Molthagen, Friedrich-Ebert-Stiftung, Der Aufstand der Zuständigen, Was kann der Rechtsstaat gegen Rechtsextremismus tun?, Ergebnisse einer Konferenz der Friedrich-Ebert-Stiftung am 20. März 2007, pp. 28, 29). Acccordingly, the "disvalue of the act" is substantially increased, thus the way of typology of committing such acts involves an increased seriousness of the event[1918].

Several findings aim at proving that the attacked victim of a hate crime suffers more, not just physically, but psychically[1919]. Whereas the increased psychical effects - which result from the enhanced violation of the human dignity - are not covered by current law, the increased physical result may be captured since such is the result of the different way of crime committal (addressed by Section 224 Penal Code), or it becomes obvious in a serious result, which then may be addressed by Section 226 Penal Code[1920]. Therefore, with the current design of the law, some violent hate crime cases, due to their crime-typical way of commission, already lead to the application of an increased penalty frame – but without the consideration of subjective. Nevertheless, hate crimes which are not committed in the punishment-enhancing manner specified in Section 224 Penal Code or do not cause results stated in Section 226 Penal Code are unrecognized by the law, even though they cause an increased damaging result to the psychological health of the victim and his human dignity and moreover cause far reaching effects towards the legal good of public peace.

Moreover, the pure objective design of these laws do not capture the targeted group of offenders selectively enough, it is constituted to address a wide range of behaviors which is unconnected to the wrong at issue.

Whereas aggravating statutes, which are based on Section 223 Penal Code, are suitable to address the in general more brutal committal of hate crime by punishing such for hate crime common interaction with peers and the use of objects to achieve increased harm and also are capable of addressing certain

committing a hate crime could be considered as an aggravating factor according to Section 224 Penal Code.

1918 Hörnle, Grob anstößiges Verhalten, p. 272.

1919 The psychological damages which are caused by a hate crime attack are worse than physical damage. The victims put their own value in question, they internalize the social stigma which is associated with becoming a victim, they are ashamed of themselves for being weak, they suffer from depression, insomnia, anxiety, nightmares, headaches, crying spells, restlessness, - summarized hate crime victims suffer more than victims of other crimes. In other words, the damages caused by a hate crime exceed such of un-, or otherwise motivated parallel behavior. (Schneider, Politische Kriminalität: Hassverbrechen, Fremdenfeindlichkeit im internationalen Kontext, Kriminalistik 2001, pp.21-28 (24)). "Minority victims of bias crimes therefore experience the attack as a form of violence which manifests racial stigmatization and its resulting harms. Stigmatization has been shown to bring about humiliation, isolation and selfhatred. An individual who has been racially stigmatized will often be hypersensitive in anticipation of contact with other members of society whom he sees as "normal" and will even suffer a kind of self-doubt that negatively affects his relationships with members of his own group. The stigmatized individual may experience clinical symptoms such as high blood pressure or increased use of narcotics and alcohol. The defensive behavior changes included such items as staying home at night more often, watching children more closely, trying to be "less visible", or moving to another neighborhood." (Lawrence, The Punishment of Hate: Towards a Normative Theory of Bias-Motivated Crimes, 93 Mich. L. Rev. 1994, p. 343 with references to Richard Delgado, Words That Wound: A Tort Action for Racial Insults, Epithets, and Name-Calling, 17 HARV. C.R.-C.L. L. REV., 1982, pp. 133 et seqq. (136-137); Gordon W. Allport, The Nature of Prejudice 480, 1954, pp. 148,149; Erving Goffman, Stigma 7-17, 1963, pp. 130-135; Robert M. Page, Stigma, 1984). For more information view Chapter 4, G., 1.1.1. Human Dignity of the Immediate Victim; and Chapter 4, G., 1.2. Priority of Protected Legal Goods.

1920 Almost three quarters of all hate attacks cause psychical injuries. In 30% of the cases the victim requires hospital care. (Levin/Mc Devitt, Hate Crimes, pp. 65-114 (111); Lawrence, Punishing Hate, p. 39; Levin/McDevitt, Hate Crimes, pp. 11, 12).

harmful results which are usually based on the overall more brutalness of the hate crime offender, the particularly humiliating treatment of the victim which increases the infringement of the personal legal good human dignity compared to its otherwise- or unmotivated counterparts for which the Sections 223 et. seqq. Penal Code are designed, is legally not recognized. Furthermore, the noteworthy different dimension of harm on the collective is not addressed.

1.7.1.4. Section 46 Penal Code

hate crimes are currently considered to be recognized in the judicial arbitrary decision in which the judge, based on the penalty frame which is served for the parallel offense, according to Section 46, Paragraph 2 Penal Code must consider the motives of an offender in order to determine the individual culpability of the offender[1921].

a) Hate Crime Motives: Part of the Wrong or the Culpability of an Offense

The distinction between wrong and culpability is an essential characteristic of a sophisticated criminal justice system and of a refined dogmatic[1922]. Whether the motives of an offender belong to culpability or to the wrong of an offense is disputed[1923]. It is assumed that hate crime offenders - due to their motives - increase the unworthiness of an act due to their generally more brutal way of committing the crime, which is based on the fact that their acts are intended to achieve humiliation in the victims and the abolition of beings[1924]. This is a matter which refers to the disvalue of the act, because it primarily concerns the demerit of committal and only indirectly allows conclusions about the attitude of the offender[1925], and therefore indeed increases the content of wrong of hate crimes compared to the content of wrong of the relevant base offense. It therefore must be recognized as part of the wrong of a hate crime, if the xenophobic and similar attitude of the offender manifests itself in the nature and severity of the attack[1926]. It is important to be understood that the main fact what makes a crime to a hate crime is not the motive alone[1927], but the relation

1921 View Chapter 4, D., 2. Judicial Recognition of Bias-Motivation Apart from Homicide; and 3. Hate Crime in the Light of Section 46 Penal Code.

1922 Hörnle, Das Unwerturteil und der Schuldvorwurf, in: Hefendehl, Empirische und dogmatische Fundamente, pp. 105-134, (105).

1923 Welzel, Das Deutsche Strafrecht, 1969, p. 62 – who considers such as part of wrong; Wessels/Beulke, Strafrecht AT, p. 158; Wessels/Hettinger, Strafrecht BT I, p. 33 – who considers such as part of the culpability; Schmidhäuser, Strafrecht AT, p. 106, Roxin, Strafrecht AT I, § 10, marginal no. 71 et seqq., and Jescheck/Weigend, Lehrbuch des Strafrechts AT, p. 244 who follows the here adopted differentiated view.

1924 View hereto: Chapter Chapter 4, G., 1.1.1. Human Dignity of the Immediate Victim; and Chapter 4, G., 1.2. Priority of protected Legal Goods.

1925 Wessels/Beulke, Strafrecht AT, p. 158, marginal no. 422.

1926 View hereto: Section 225 Penal Code, where the element of "rawness", (in the meaning of brutalness) which refers to the abuse of the victim and is considered to be a part of the wrong of the offense, is fulfilled if the raw attitude of the offender manifests in the nature and severity of the attack. (BGHSt 25, 277; Wessels/Beulke, Strafrecht AT; p. 158, marginal no. 422).

1927 Even though such is stated by e.g. Seehafer, Strafrechtliche Reaktionen, 2003, p. 69. In this work, a purely subjective view is opposed, it is considered that the Hate-motivation is of most importance for categorizing a crime as a hate crime. This work does not set the course in favor of a purely objective concept. In the first instance, it depends on the motivation, which - only if it is existent - leads to specific objective effects.

between the inner motive and its outer effects. Even if one purely focuses on the motive one must recognize that due to this motive further enhancing wrong circumstances radiate. Whereas the generally more brutal and humiliating practice of hate crime offenders - at least in parts - is addressable by the current law[1928], the culpability features of hate crimes are not yet expressly recognized by law. It is argued that a hate crime motive is a real feature of guilt, a hate crime though constitutes an own content of wrong if it is expressed by criminal handlings. It is acknowledged that a motive is a real feature of guilt if it exclusively - and not merely - constitutes a reflection of wrong, if it is identifiable to be at the lowest standing and if it reveals the reprehensible attitude of the perpetrator[1929]; but, since the hate crime motive expresses itself in an increased disvalue of the act, it as such also increases the wrong of an act.

Anyway, even if one considers the hate crime motive as a true culpability feature, i.e. reasons the required penalty increase with the motive per se, this sounds reasonable if purely basing one´s argumentation on the inner mindset of the offender of a hate crime. The motive can be categorized as a characteristic of culpability, if the distinction of a hate crime to an otherwise motivated crime is solely based on the motive[1930] - yet, this concept is to be rejected[1931]. Hate crimes are rather distinguished by objective criteria as well[1932]. If one denies these external effects of hate crime one would have to identify a hate crime solely by the prejudice motivation of an offender, which would make the determination in a particular case extremely difficult and subjective[1933]; moreover the recognition policies - such as published by the FBI[1934] would bear any reasonable content, since they are based on outer facts, which have external effects and not solely on inner mindsets of perpetrators.

1928 View Chapter 4, D., 2. Judicial Recognition of Bias-Motivation Apart from Homicide; and 3. Hate Crime in the Light of Section 46 Penal Code.

1929 Wessels/Beulke, Strafrecht AT, p. 158, marginal no. 422.

1930 View: Seehafer, Strafrechtliche Reaktionen, 2003, p. 69.

1931 View hereto: Chapter 4, G., 1.1. Possible Goods protected by a Hate Crime Law; Chapter 4, G., 1.7.1.4. a) Hate Crime Motives: Part of the Wrong or of the Culpability of an Offense.

1932 In order to identify a hate crime one must refer to the external circumstances of victimization and in particular to the status of victim. External objective indicators are the identity of the victim, cultural differences between offender and victim, the crime structure and the crime scene and time, written and verbal comments, gestures and signs, symbols with which the offender supports his criminal behavior, left behind letters at the crime scene, threatening phone calls, the seemingly entirely missing motive, the missing connection between the victim and the offender, etc. Every crime must be examined in order to enlighten the facts and circumstances which constitute a hate crime – but this is nothing unusual, such an examination takes place during the prosecution of every crime, however concerning hate crimes, the prosecution authorities must pay attention to distinct facts of which one needs to be aware. (Schneider, Politische Kriminalität: Hassverbrechen, Fremdenfeindlichkeit im internationalen Kontext, Kriminalistik 2001, pp.21-28 (22); Schneider, Kriminologie der Hassdelikte. Konzeption, Ursachen, Vorbeugung und Kontrolle, in: Bewährungshilfe, 2003, p. 117; FBI-guidelines, view footnote 1249).

1933 Schneider, Kriminologie der Hassdelikte. Konzeption, Ursachen, Vorbeugung und Kontrolle, in: Bewährungshilfe, 2003, p. 117.

1934 View footnote 1249.

Most importantly, hate crimes are further distinguishable by their different social impact in the external world[1935]. As illustrated above, a hate crime contains wrong increasing elements, since the disvalue of the result is increased in case of the committal of a hate crime in comparison to an unmotivated or otherwise motivated counterpart, that is because a hate crime violates the public peace in addition to those in either way violated individual legal goods and beyond violates the individual good of human dignity more deeply.

b) Culpability Addressed in Section 46 Penal Code and the Influence of the Bias Motive

Like the content of wrong of an act is determined in accordance to the "disvalue of the act" and the "disvalue of the result", the content of culpability is determined by the disvalue of the attitude in reference to the concrete committal of crime[1936]. This determination is accomplished by two steps: In the first instance, culpability is measured towards the relevant act, it therefore is based on the committed wrong, which is done by the legislature when enacting a norm. In the second instance, the measurement refers to the individual perpetrator, such is done by the judge at trial. This second step is necessary because penalty must be an "equitable culpability compensation"[1937].[1938] This is because the legal condemnation of wrong refers to a certain behavior in general, whereas the accusation of culpability refers to the individual guilt of the perpetrator, which content is based on the respective condemnation of the general wrong[1939]. The principle of human dignity in Article 1, Paragraph 1 Basic Law forbids "ejecting a blanket-punishment" without respecting the individual offender[1940]. In the end of the prosecution process the individual culpability of the offender in respect to his committed wrong must be recognized in the imposed penalty. This precept is fulfilled by enabling a decisional scope to a judge whom must, in regard to the individual accused, impose the relevant sentence by basing his decision on the sentence frame which has been provided by the legislature. The offender, however, is never blamed for his mindset as such, but only for the crime which is characterized

1935 Schneider, Politische Kriminalität: Hassverbrechen, Fremdenfeindlichkeit im internationalen Kontext, Kriminalistik 2001, pp.21-28 (22); Schneider, Kriminologie der Hassdelikte. Konzeption, Ursachen, Vorbeugung und Kontrolle, in: Bewährungshilfe, 2003, p. 117; These different external effects of hate crime are considered by the U.S. legislature as well, which reasons their hate crime legislation with the following: "The intentional advocacy of unlawful acts by groups or individuals against other persons or groups and bodily injury or death to persons is not constitutionally protected when violence or civil disorder is imminent, and poses a threat to public order and safety, and such conduct should be subjected to criminal sanctions." (SB27By Senator Dial; RFD Judiciary; Rd 1 07-FEB-12; A Bill to be entitled an Act to amend Section 13A-5-13, Code of Alabama 1975, relating to hate crimes; to impose additional penalties for the crimes of arson, burglary, or criminal mischief in any degree when committed against religious property.).

1936 BVerfGE 50, 125, 133; BVerfGE 25, 269, 286; BVerfGE 45, 187, 260; BVerfGE 50, 2, 12; Wessels/Strafrecht, Strafrecht AT, p. 149, marginal no. 401.

1937 Own translation of "gerechter Schuldauslgeich".

1938 Fischer, StGB, 2001, §46, marginal no. 3.

1939 Hörnle, Das Unwerturteil und der Schuldvorwurf, in: Hefendehl, Empirische und dogmatische Fundamente, pp. 105 – 134, (121).

1940 Seehafer, Strafrechtliche Reaktionen, 2003, p. 84; Torka, Nachtatverhalten und Nemo tenetur; 2000, p. 33.

by his mindset[1941]. A characteristic feature of a motive that is realized in the act realized and affects the culpability is the hostile and indifferent attitude of the offender towards the behavioral norms of law[1942]. Due to the handlings in judicial penal assessments, it is in general consented that culpability is divisible in different degrees[1943]. The culpability of similar violent acts can not be differentiated unless one recognizes such facts by which the offender was motivated[1944]. Therefore, culpability can be divided by considering with which casualness an offender negates a norm[1945]. An increase of culpability is reasoned with the finding of whether an offender violates a "legal good" with the idea of such being unjustifiably protected; or he considers that a legal good is legitimately protected, but in his opinion this protection has a substantial less ranging claim to validity; summarized: the common criterion to evaluate the increased degree of culpability is to examine the extent of casualness of the offender when violating a legal good and the way how an offender lowers a legal good, this expresses itself in his motivation[1946]. According to this, "[...] who kills, violates and criminally acts because of racist and racial- or otherwise similar biased motives, is blameworthy in terms of the highest degree of culpability, because he negates the right of equivalent of a certain group of humans, negates the right of existance of others, their quality of being a human subject entirely, thus negates the "legal good" to the highest possible amount casualness"[1947]. The difference therefore is that "the other person is not attacked because of particular motives resulting from a distinct particular [personal] conflict (- for instance - envy, [hate, rage]), but simply because he exists and that [in the eyes of the offender] must not be"[1948]. This shows that a hate crime offender committing what ever criminal offense violates the respective "legal good" in a particular extremely degrading and lowering manner. The culpability of a hate crime offender is higher than such of the offender of the respective parallel crime[1949]. This could be determined in the law.

1941 Wessels/Beulke, Strafrecht AT, p. 149, marginal no. 401.

1942 Wessels/Beulke, Strafrecht AT, p. 149, marginal no. 400; "The more hostility towards a law can be revealed from the act, the more sustained is the criminal charge". (Torka, 2000, p. 35).

1943 Kern, Grade der Rechtswidrigkeit, ZStW, 1952, p. 255.

1944 Köhler, Zur Abgrenzung des Mordes, GA 1980, p. 138.

1945 Köhler, Zur Abgrenzung des Mordes, GA 1980, p. 138.

1946 Köhler, Zur Abgrenzung des Mordes, GA 1980, p. 138.

1947 Köhler, Zur Abgrenzung des Mordes, GA 1980, p. 138.

1948 Köhler, Zur Abgrenzung des Mordes, GA 1980, p. 138. (Köhler cites the motive of greed as one of the most evil motives.) In Chapter 4., G., 2., 2.3., 2.3.4. Hate Crime motives are to be differentiated from such exemplarily named in Section 46 Penal Code, it is illustrated, why a hate crime motive is to be differentiated from other so called "low motives", which in its core is based on the fact that a hate crime motive cannot be outweighed by particular external circumstances, whereas "greed" can. (View hereto - unrelated to hate crime but in general - Paeffgen, Habgier und niedrige Beweggründe, GA 1982, p. 269).

1949 The degree of culpability of a hate crime offender is higher than the degree of culpability of an offender who commits the similar offense without the respective motivation. This is explained by the idea that a hate crime is more likely to cause harm than its unmotivated counterpart. Hate crimes are considered to be more blameworthy than parallel crimes because they violate the "most deeply held tenets of our legal system and culture". By that, hate crimes are considered to represent an increased degree of blameworthiness, even though motives are principally not able to increase the wrong of a criminal act. (Lawrence, The Punishment of Hate: Towards a Normative Theory of Bias-Motivated Crimes, 93 Michigan Law Review, 1994, pp. 364 et seq.) Yet, it is agreed that the level of culpability has a determining influence on the gravity of an offense. Therefore, it can be assumed that a hate crime increases the total level of

The culpability which is addressed in Section 46 Penal Code, however, only refers to the individual realized culpability, not to the culpability which stands in conjunction to the committed wrong (that is the culpability, which reasons a penalty)[1950]. But, a penalty must be appropriate to blame[1951]. Thus, the dimension of the culpability blame must be determined in regard to the violated legal good and the way of how the act is committed, thus in regard to the manifested unworthiness in the act[1952]. Therefore, without citing any reasons the penalty must comply with the penalty that is established for a certain type of wrong[1953]. This reveals that if hate crime constitutes a different type of wrong, the existing penalty frames of ordinary offenses are not made to capture the changed culpability of a hate crime offender, since they were composed for the wrong which is caused by an unmotivated or otherwise motivated behavior. A court has the competence to only emanate from the "unmodified" culpability, which reasons a penalty included in the frame of the respective base offense to then only adjust the culpability, which is relevant in the individual case; therefore if a ruling for hate crime takes place in Section 46 Penal Code, it must be assumed that the culpability, which reasons a penalty is the same in a hate crime as it is in the ordinary crime. This could be the case if the content of wrong is the same in a hate crime as it is in a otherwise motivated crime; this assumption, however, is not followed, since it is assumed that hate crime modifies the wrong of an act, to which the culpability is connected[1954].

Since it is not about the theoretical establishments in a legal order but about its practical effects, it could be that Section 46 Penal Law, howsoever, is sufficient to captures hate crime. Neglecting the fact of hate crimes constituting a different crime type, and therefore also the culpability which reasons a penalty is modified, a hate crime could be addressed by a court in its arbitrary decision by imposing a penalty for a hate crime which is attached to the upper edge of the penal frame that is established for the respective base offense. The legislature, when it established the penal frame for punishing the respective behavior, did not consider the distinct nature of hate crime motives. Therefore it is questionable, if hate crime motives could be recognized sufficiently by the penal frame of the ordinary offenses. Since such a penal frame is orientated towards the underlying behavior, but offers a width range to adjust the penalty upward for whatever emerging gravity, this is strongly believed. After all, at least such by the respective norm addressed behavior is basically congruent. The answer to this question is irrelevant since, due to the current design of

---

wrongfulness of a crime. (View hereto: Chapter 4, G., 1.7.1.4. a) Hate Crime Motives: Part of the Worng of the Culpability of an Offense).

1950 Today, it is agreed that the culpability, which reasons a penalty is not identical to the culpability, which is relevant in the individual case. (Stree/Kinzig, in: Schönke/Schröder, StGB, § 46 marginal no. 9a; Lackner/Kühl, StGB, § 46, marginal no. 23; Schäfer, Praxis der Strafzumessung, 2001, marginal no. 226; Roxin, Strafrecht AT I, § 19, marginal no. 50 et seqq.; Seehafer, Strafrechtliche Reaktionen, 2003, p. 84).

1951 Stree/Kinzig, in: Schönke/Schröder, StGB, Vorbem. §§ 38, marginal no. 13; with further references.

1952 Wessels/Beulke, Strafrecht AT, p. 149, marginal no. 401; BVerfGE 50, 125, 133; BVerfGE 25, 269, 286; BVerfGE 45, 187, 260; BVerfGE 50, 2, 12.

1953 Stree/Kinzig, in: Schönke/Schröder, StGB, Vorbem. §§ 38, marginal no. 18a.

1954 Refer to the previous section a) Hate Crime Motives: Part of the Wrong or the Culpability of an Offense.

Section 46, Paragraph 2 Penal Code, hate crime motives must not even compulsively lead to an increased punishment when starting from the mid of the sentence range established for the parallel offense, therefore, it can hardly be assumed that such at all leads to an increased sanction in any imaginable case, thus - in every respective case - leads to the maximum sentence provided by the established penal frames. Section 46 Penal Code refers to a judicial arbitrary decision, in which the judge, based on the penalty frame which is served for the parallel offense, according to Section 46, Paragraph 2 Penal Code, must consider the motives of an offender in order to determine the individual culpability of the offender[1955]. Thereby hate crime motives are included in the overall value assessment were a judge pays attention to several circumstances which surround the crime committal and the offender as a person to an even degree. Therefore, the judge - according to Section 46, Paragraph 2 Penal Code - is ought to outweigh a recognized hate crime motive by other mitigating facts[1956] and in the end does not increase the punishment, or even lower it in regard to the penal frame which is set for the parallel offense. Due to the lack of coercion or the lack of security regarding the enhancement of the penalty for hate crime committal in general, the question of adequacy of the existing penalty frames, if one starts off at a high position for imposing the penalty, is unimportant. The norm which governs the higher attachment of penalty is missing.

c) Hate Crime Motives are Different

Finally, Section 46 Penal Code is not considered to be sufficient to address hate crimes because the hate crime motives are different from such in Section 46 Penal Code stated features. hate crime motives are not on the same level as such in Section 46, Paragraph 2 Penal Code named facts for assessing the penalty, so they may not be inclined in this overall assessment process[1957]; thus can not be recognized and captured by Section 46, Paragraph 2 Penal Code. hate crime motives are part of the abstract determination of the unworthiness of the overall crime.

Hereby the question arises what causes the prejudice motive in a hate crime to deserve severe punishment in the abstract, whereas other motives always require an examination of the surrounding facts and happenings, which lead to the respective motive, in order to qualify it as low. It is often asked what distinguishes the motive of hatred in a hate crime perpetrator from the other so-called "low" motives, such as revenge or greed. Why is it that the committal of physical assault motivated by a bias motive is worse than such motivated by greed? Well, a hate crime assault differs from such motivated by revenge

1955 View Chapter 4, D., 3. Hate Crime in the Light of Section 46 Penal Code.

1956 View Chapter 4, D., 3. Hate Crime in the Light of Section 46 Penal Code.

1957 The positive about such an implemented wording into Section 46 Penal Code stating "the need of a penalty-increasing consideration of Hate Crime motives" is that the courts attention would be led to an increased knowledge and correct handling of the legal authorities who are responsible for law enforcement. (View Chapter 4, C. Legal Dealing with Hate Crime). However, this refers to the function of a legal establishment and not to its dogmatic legitimacy. (View Chapter 4, C., 8. Symbolic Reasoning of Hate Crime Law).

already because such action is usually the result of personal relationships, the contribution of the victim and the consequences of the victimization therefore are different, but the basic question remains.

The jurisdiction consideres a motive as low if, in the case of homicide, it is despicable and considered to range at the deepest level, which is determined by a general moral intuition[1958]. There should be a huge disproportion between the motive and the induced action. This relational concept unfortunately does not imply what is the common feature[1959] of the killing and the motive, in other words, what is the difference between the killing motivated by hunger and such motivated the desire for chocolate[1960]. As a result, this leads to the consequence that motives cannot be rated in isolation of further facts[1961]. It is therefore considered that there are no low motives per se[1962]. Such are always in a context of incitement, in the context of actions and success which enables to assess their (social) value[1963]. Thus hatred is not per se to be classified as low, but only if it is based on a low cast of mind[1964].

Here comes the exception of hate crime motives into play[1965]. This is the only motivational area in that a performance-oriented rating is superfluous. hate crime motives are always based on a low mentality. There is no conceivable case in which the motive of racial-, religious- and similar hateful bias in connection with the commission of a criminal act could have a relativizing effect.

Many motives are socially ordinary[1966], therefore the violent realization of such is already prohibited due to their banality[1967]. Yet these motives only serve as a starting point for the rating and the benchmark for the measurability of "low" is their social ruthlessness[1968]. But the setting of this benchmark is impossible for hate crimes. Because it is based on the idea that there is an area in which the offender recognizes the other as "you", as a person whom he incorporates in that structure of motivation and intentionality[1969]. A hate crime though, lies in a region that lacks an area of tension between the motive and these social-ethical oriented control forces. The attacker recognizes his victim as a completely depersonalized being[1970]; the victim's human quality is blocked

1958 BGHSt 3, 132 et seq.; this interpretation has been criticized by the literature, because it is confusing, see: Woesner, NJW 1978, 1025 (1026); Woesner, NJW 1980, 1136, (1138).

1959 Das Tertium Comparationis.

1960 Paeffgen, Habgier und niedrige Beweggründe, GA 1982, p. 266.

1961 Paeffgen, Habgier und niedrige Beweggründe, GA 1982, p. 266.

1962 Paeffgen, Habgier und niedrige Beweggründe, GA 1982, p. 266.

1963 Schmidhäuser, Gesinnungsmerkmale, p. 277; Paeffgen, Habgier und niedrige Beweggründe, GA 1982, pp. 266, 267.

1964 Eser, NStZ 1981, 383, 385; with reference to BGH 2 StR 453/79 from February 29th, 1980.

1965 For additional information refer to Chapter 4, G., 2., 2.3., 2.3.4. Hate Crime motives are to be differentiated from such exemplary named in Section 46 Penal Code.

1966 Jakobs, Niedrige Beweggründe beim Mord, NJW, 1969, pp. 489 et seqq. (490).

1967 So it would be in the case of greed or for the satisfaction of the sexual instinct. (Paeffgen, Habgier und niedrige Beweggründe, GA 1982, p. 267).

1968 Paeffgen, Habgier und niedrige Beweggründe, GA 1982, p. 269.

1969 Paeffgen, Habgier und niedrige Beweggründe, GA 1982, p. 269.

1970 Füllgrabe, Hassverbrechen, Kriminalistik, 2004, pp. 391-397 (p. 392, with reference to: Zimbardo 1991); Chapter 4, G., 1., 1.1., 1.1.1. Human Dignity of the Immediate Victim; and Chapter 4, G., 1., 1.2. Priority of protected Legal Goods).

out[1971]. This, after all, allows the offender to objectify the victim. While the adjectivization "low" usually is a social rating act and the required netting of various enhancing and mitigating value components theoretically enables one to find the middle on which these values neutralize each other[1972], this neutralization correctly must not occur for the bias motive. Nevertheless, this possibility for such exists due to the legal granting of judicial discretion and the statutory scheme of considering hate crime motives in the context of Section 46 Penal Code.

Even if one looks at the motive alone, bias motives are "low"[1973]. While not the ambition, curiosity, hatred, etc., is socially unworthy as such, but rather the non-mastery of these tendencies, insofar as they have socially damaging effects in the concrete, can be determined as socially (un-)worthy in regard to their social consequences[1974], the prejudice hatred in contrast is already socially unworthy as such[1975]. The non-mastery of this tendency does not only result to be socially harmful in the specific case, but always result to be so. Even if following the basic valid assumption that "first the interaction of the motive with the intentionality that sees the criminal outcome and predicts the secondary consequences - or at least can do so, which is able to survey the environment and thereby as it is, is capable of reacting to the motive; [thus] only this total [...] [provides] a rating substrate for a social ethical evaluation"[1976] one comes up with the same, only proper social and ethical rating of a bias motive being - unlike in the case of other hatred, revenge, anger and greed - invariably and always low. The reprehensibility of the motive per se, as well as a reprehensible relation between ends and means can be always affirmed.

As a result, the acting based on such a motive is always socially hostile, whether an act leads to homicide or to property damage. So, if such an innately negative disvalue can be assigned to a hate crime motive, and it is assured that such a motive reveals hostility to the requirements of the community, it's acting out is invariably unworthiness-increasing.

The answer to the question why the attack of an offender against a foreign victim, which is motivated by the prejudiced hatred of the offender is to be punished more severely than the similar attack on a victim which is based on other motives is: Because the prejudiced hate motive - unlike other motives - is per se low, therefore the culpability, which reasons the criminal penalty and

1971 "The characteristic of hate crime is the symbolic damage of a victim; these acts are directed against the way of being of the victims; victims are understood as enemies, depersonalized faceless hate objects". (Schneider, Kriminologie der Hassdelikte. Konzeptionen, Ursachen, Vorbeugung und Kontrolle, in: Bewährungshilfe, 2003, p. 115).

1972 Paeffgen, Habgier und niedrige Beweggründe, GA 1982, p. 269.

1973 "Low" is understood in its meaning, it experiences within the homicide offense. (View Chapter 4, D., 1. Judicial Recognition of Bias-Motivation in Homicide).

1974 Paeffgen, Habgier und niedrige Beweggründe, GA 1982, p. 267.

1975 Paeffgen, who says that there are intentions, which have a negative social value and as an example for social hostility cites the killing of others, who are of a different opinion or race. (Pfaeffgen, Habgier und niedrige Beweggründe, GA 1982, p. 268).

1976 Paeffgen, Habgier und niedrige Beweggründe, GA 1982, p. 267.

personal guilt of the offender is increased. Moreover it leads to higher damages for the attacked individual victims as well as to an entire segment of the population and to society at large. As illustrated above, legitimate legal dealings with hate crimes depend on the realized wrong, the hereto connected culpability, which reasons penalty and the individual culpability (which is assessed by the respective court at trial). So the content of any hate crime could be addressed by Section 46 Penal Code if hate crimes would be differentiated from their un- or otherwise motivated counterparts only by means of the degree of the individual culpability, linked to the individual offender. If this is considered to be the case, thus hate crimes motives are facts which are substantial comparable to other attitudes of an offender, they are valid to be outweighed by mitigating circumstances which are also addressed in Section 46, Paragraph 2 Penal Code[1977]. The respective court at trial then would have to, in any case[1978], consider such motives as penalty enhancing facts to then be able to erode them by other circumstances. This handling however, is not guaranteed by the current substantive and prosecution law.

Yet, since hate crime motives are not considered to be valid to be included in the overall assessment process of the court, thus they are not valid to be outweighed by further, the offense or the attitude of the offender surrounding facts, Section 46 Penal Code is not capable of addressing the different criminal nature of hate crimes and their offenders and therewith does not accomplish the need to protect the public peace by itself. One cannot pretend that hateful bias motives are worse than other low motives[1979], but one has to realize that a hateful bias motive is always, in any situation reprehensible, and this trait distinguishes it from other motives which can only be assessed as reprehensible with certainty if one includes the outer context.

d) Result According the Reach of Existing Standards

All of these above illustrated norms, and several more[1980], recognizes the phenomenon of hate crimes in partial aspects by addressing certain features which constitute a hate crime but either limit them to a certain kind of act or to a certain kind of perpetrator and thereby do not provide the capacity to establish hate crime as a distinct delinquency category in order to cover all of its key criteria and according to that adjust the punishment. Section 46, Paragraph 2 Penal Code which in general refers to the motives and aims of the offender, the attitude reflected in the offense and the degree of force of will

1977 Such as other aims and motives of the offender; the offenders prior history, his personal and financial circumstances; and more, view hereto: Section 46, Paragraph 2 Penal Code.

1978 Since neither are hate crime motives expressed as generally aggravating circumstances in Section 46 Penal Code, nor is there any data to check if such motives in fact are taken into account sufficiently when imposing a penalty, nor are their any forms of control in such cases when hate crime motives are not taken into account in legitimate manners - due to a limited verifiability of discretionary decisions by the Court of Appeals – Section 46 Penal Code does not seem capable of addressing the hate crimes safely. (View hereto: View Chapter 4, D., 2. Judicial Recognition of Bias-Motivation Apart from Homicide; and Chapter 4, D., 3. Hate Crime in the Light of Section 46 Penal Code).

1979 Aydin, Die strafrechtliche Bekämpfung von Hassdelikten, p. 98.

1980 See also Sections 86a, 90, 90a; 125, 125a; 127; 129, 129 a; 131 Penal Code.

involved in its commission could seem to criminally capture the motive of hate crime offenders, but due to equalizing hate crime motives with other motives and facts such cannot bring the required criminological effect, moreover further mentioned lacks, such as verifiability, consistency and the undetermined degree of how penalty must be adjusted to a hate crime motive lead to the result that Section 46 Penal Code is not valid to address hate crime in the here aimed at entirety. In summary, Section 46 Penal Code is not a proper basis for dealing with hate crime, neither when considering normative aspects, nor when considering practical aspects.

e) Necessity with Regard to the German society

Criminal law is known to be only one of many instruments of social control[1981]. Noting that a particular legal standard, even in case of an overall legitimate adoption, is only one possible solution of a problem the question relating to hate crime occurs whether a comprehensive control system which takes the interests of the public into an adequate account, exists as a milder alternative solution.

Whether other regulations are available, which make the use of criminal law appear unnecessary must be assessed in regard to the relevant society. The German and the American society have the same ideas about the equality of human beings based on their similar constitutions. Anyway both countries adjust to the problem with different engagement and distinct concepts. Questionable with regard to this is whether a possible different societal base necessitates hate crime legislation for the one country, whereas the other society does not (yet) have the need for such laws.

Certain incidents which were mentioned earlier[1982] show that the German society has a problem with hate crimes. If the problem requires the necessity of criminal regulation is a decision which must be taken by the legislature. Certain facts surrounding hate crime attacks, like when the entire inhabitants of a town applauded and supportively affirmed the committal of hate crimes[1983]; or certain voicing of opinions from the center of the population after a man (Alberto Adriano), who was from Mozambique, was killed[1984]; and such after Guben Omar Ben Noui has been rushed to death[1985], could suggest that the German society has a problem with hate crimes and the hereto linked

1981 Haffke, Die Legitimation des staatlichen Strafrechts, in: FS for Claus Roxin, pp. 955-975 (958 et seq.).

1982 View Chapter 4, A. Historical Background of Hate Crime in its Social and Criminal Political Context (Brief Overview), especially marginal no. 354.

1983 View the example of Rostock-Lichtenhagen; The arson attacks on asylum centers in Germany gained worldwide publicity. (Schneider, Foreigner as Perpetrators and as Victims in Germany, in: Schneider/Holyst (eds.): Euro Criminology; Band 8/9; pp. 95-108.

1984 Some citizens stated: "There has been a right scene in Dessau for many years, which is up to mischief in the city". But others said: "That guy (Alberto Adriano) should have known that he cannot run-around there at night" said a woman from Dessau. Others even said in their city and in the state of Saxony-Anhalt there are too many foreigners in general, even though the statistics at the time show that the proportion of foreign population, according to the Federal Statistic Office in 1997 was just 1.8 percent in this state. (Scholzen, Rechtsextremismus, Gefahr erkannt, Gefahr gebannt? in: Kriminalistik. 2001, pp. 314 – 316 (316).

1985 Scholzen,: Rechtsextremismus, Gefahr erkannt, Gefahr gebannt?. in: Kriminalistik. 2001, pp. 314-316 (316).

lowering of tolerance in society. If one views the handlings of legal authorities when it comes to penalizing certain hate crime attacks[1986], it can be assumed that the German society requires a penal law to call a halt to current legal dealings in order to maintain the current climate.

When one considers that the U.S. society is ahead of the German society in so far that social phenomena with a certain time lag usually come to Germany[1987] and that through migration, Europeanization, and globalization the harmful effects on the public peace will increase[1988], since the German society will become more heterogeneous and more multicultural just as the American society already is, the legislator could include the fact that hate- and bias-motivated crime will take on greater significance[1989].

1.7.2. Intermediate Result

In so far it can be noted that neither from the doctrine of the legal good nor from such in conjunction with the constitutional value system one can draw a general statement regarding the question of the limitation of the legitimate ambit of criminal law in relation to the protection of supra individual goods. The Basic Law embodies "objective values", especially in its bill of rights, in which the main social ethical decisions have received the rank of constitutional decisions.[1990] The “worthiness of punishment” depends on the priority which is given to a “legal good” within this value system. Insofar the “disvalue of the result” and the “disvalue of the act” determine the “worthiness of punishment” of a behavior[1991]. Due to the specific value content of a tolerant climate for the existence of German society, hate-motivated criminal behavior needs to be qualified as “worthy of punishment”. Since no milder means which promise equal success of protecting the collective legal good public peace against hate crime could be detected, the behavior constituting hate crimes “necessitates punishment”. With that said, hate crimes are - irrespective of the degree of wrongfulness of the respective base act, that is, irrespective of whether the behavior constitutes a violent offense or a criminal property damage - to be penalized explicitly.

1986 Nur vier Randalierer kamen ins Gefängnis, Die Zeit, 25/2002, June 13, 2002 - 14 p.m.; Lausberg, Michael, Die extreme Rechte in Ostdeutschland, pp. 60 et seqq. (65).

1987 For example the term "hate crime" appeared in the U.S. first, which was in the early 80s (1985 – view footnote 1061); 20 years later it was established in Germany (view footnote 1185 - used as a working definition by the police) (cf. Bleich/Hart, Quantifying Hate: The Evolution of German Approaches to Measuring ‘Hate Crime’, German Politics, 2008, p. 63).

1988 McLaughlin, Eugene, Hate Crime, in: Eugene McLaughlin/John Muncie (eds.), The Sage Dictionary of Criminology, p. 136.

1989 Schneider, Kriminologie der Hassdelikte. Konzeptionen, Ursachen, Vorbeugung und Kontrolle, in: Bewährungshilfe , 2003, p. 116.

1990 Hereto: BVerfGE 7, 205; BVerfGE 21, 372; BVerfGE 35, 114; BVerfGE 37,65; BVerfGE 39,41; Otto, ZStW 96 (1984), 339, p. 347.

1991 Hereto: BVerfGE 39,42 et seqq.; Hillenkamp, Vorsatztat und Opferverhalten, 1981, pp. 174 et seqq.; Otto, ZStW 96 (1984), 339, p. 348.

1.8. Characterization of a Hate Crime Law

Since the respective legal goods are found to be worthy of legal protection, the legitimacy of the norm further depends on the structure of the offense[1992]. It must be determined in which form criminal protection may be granted to a legal good, thus which scope should a norm have and against which form of attack shall a norm protect a legal good. The way of implementing the protection results in the systematic differentiation between result-constituted offenses[1993] and non-result-constituted offences, whereas the latter are further divided into abstract and concrete conduct offenses[1994]. As illustrated above[1995], these different crime types are relevant to the inclusion and the interpretation of a penal provision.

The core of an offense is the wrong committed by the perpetrator[1996]. The effects that results from the legally defined action forms the basis for the classification in either a result-constituted offense or in a non-result-constituted offense[1997]. Divided into these categories, crimes which are constituted by an abstract endangerment for the attacked object are considered as non-result-constituted offenses, i.e. pure conduct crimes. With the action object it is referred to the concrete subject, which is addressed by the relevant behavior[1998]. Questionable therefore is, whether an offense which punishes hate crimes would have to be categorized as a result-constituted offense or as a pure conduct crime. This is said to be determinable by examining whether the harmful outcome of an act, labeled as result, can be felt in a spatially and temporally separate injury or threat to the action object[1999]. In order to categorize an offense to one of these crime types one must not refer to the effect of an act towards the protected "legal good" but to the harm caused towards the object of attack[2000]. In opposite to "result" in this context, the violation of a "legal good" refers to the relation between the criminally determined behavior and the claim of respect for a value, which is attributed by a criminal norm[2001]. Correctly, the harm caused towards the object of attack can be distinguished from the interference with the protected legal good, since the object of attack and the legal good protected by a norm are not the same. With "action object" it is referred to the concrete subject, which is addressed by the relevant behavior[2002], thus to the immediate attacked victim. As

1992 Wohlers, Rechtsgutheorie und Deliktsstruktur, GA, 2002, pp. 15-20 (20.).
1993 Krey, Deutsches Strafrecht, p. 151, marginal no. 183.
1994 Wohlers, Rechtsgutheorie und Deliktsstruktur, GA, 2002, pp. 15-20 (pp. 17 et seqq.).
1995 View Chapter 2, C., 3.4.2 Classification of Offenses, especially marginal no. 173 et seqq.
1996 Jescheck/Weigend, Lehrbuch des Strafrechts AT, § 26 II. p. 260.
1997 Jescheck/Weigend, Lehrbuch des Strafrechts AT, § 26 II, 1 a), b) p. 260, 263.
1998 Wessels/Beulke, Strafrecht AT, marginal no. 8; Stratenwerth, Strafrecht AT I § 8, marginal no. 11; Otto, Grundkurs AT, § 1 marginal no. 42; Jescheck/Weigend, Lehrbuch des Strafrechts AT, § 26 I 4, pp. 259 et seq.
1999 Jescheck/Weigend, Lehrbuch des Strafrechts AT, § 26 II, 1 c) p. 263.
2000 Jescheck/Weigend, Lehrbuch des Strafrechts AT, § 26 II, 1 c) p. 263.
2001 Lenckner/Eisele, in: Schönke/Schröder, StGB, Vorbem. 9 vor § 13; Jescheck/Weigend, Lehrbuch des Strafrechts AT, § 26 II, 1 c) p. 263.
2002 Wessels/Beulke, Strafrecht AT, marginal no. 8; Stratenwerth AT I § 8, marginal no. 11; Otto, Grundkurs AT, § 1 marginal no. 42; Jescheck/Weigend, Lehrbuch des Strafrechts AT, § 26 I 4, pp. 259 et seqq.

illustrated[2003], a hate crime norm moreover refers not only to the human dignity of the immediate victim but also to the protection of the current structure of society, in which a certain minimum of tolerance is existent, thus the relevant legal good of public peace. Since it is understood that a "legal good" is not an abstract appearance, but a real, changeable subject the dispute regarding the distinction between the object of the act and the protected legal good has no further relevance for the now following classification of the hate crime offense, because if one searches for the real object, which is protected by a hate crime standard, one therefore may also come up with the current existence of the social climate. As a point of substantial reference one therefore must draw on the climate in its current form.

1.8.1. Differentation of Injury Torts and Non-Result-Constituted Offenses

It is questionable, whether the legal good, which is to be protected by a hate crime norm, is impaired in its integrity (injury offense) or just endangered (offense of endangerment)[2004]; the answer depends on the intensity of the effect on the legal good[2005]. Thereafter the public peace may be affected only by certain hate crime acts.

1.8.1.1. Sensational Features as Supplementary Elements of Criminal Liability

The current form of society requires a tolerant climate, without such it is not able to exist in its pluralistic form. Influences which generate a xenophobic and further bias-based climate, violate the tolerance component. The question is how a hate crime norm must be constituted in order to preserve this tolerant element of the climate.

It is acknowledged that a hate crime is suitable to violate the legal good public peace in case of its accumulation and its sending of exemplary effects[2006]. This refers to the classification criteria for particular hate crime cases used by the jurisdiction of the Attorney General (*Generalbundesanwalt*). The Attorney General is competent to prosecute those hate crimes which have a tangible impact on the internal security of the Federal Republic of Germany, further when they are capable of providing a signal effect to generate potential copycats and if they affect the appearance of the Federal Republic of Germany[2007]. Since, due to that, a hate crime case requires a "special significance", it is questioned, whether the here addressed general hate crime act must provide a certain magnitude or severity in order to be valid to violate the public peace[2008]. Such a magnitude could refer to an increased accrual of

2003 Chapter 4, G., 1.2. Priority of Protected Legal Goods.
2004 Roxin, Strafrecht AT I, § 10, marginal no. 122 et seqq.; Wessels/Beulke, Strafrecht AT, marginal no. 25 et seqq.
2005 Jescheck/Weigend, Lehrbuch des Strafrechts AT, § 26 II, 2, p. 263; with further references.
2006 The General Attorney at Bundesgerichtshof, Prosecution because of a right-wing extremist arson attack in Jessnitz. Press release 4/2002, January 28, 2002.
2007 The General Attorney at the Bundesgerichtshof, Press release 2000 in the case Eggesin.
2008 According to Section 120, Paragraph 2, no. 1-3 Courts Constitution Act, the General Attorney takes over the prosecution because of the special significance of the case.

hate crime acts or a special severity of a single act. At least, the need of a certain frequency of committed hate crime acts in order for such to be considered as violating the public peace seems to be required[2009]. Thus, for an act to be considered to be qualified to cause a negative change to the current climate it must be a repeated offense. The frequency of hate crimes is determinable in numbers, served by the above illustrated statistical data. Questionable is, whether the true public peace endangering effect is ascertainable by published numbers, or rather by certain significant societal negative changes, which are only measurable in an ex post view. Certain negative effects - which are recognizable in the present and in this case lead to the required hazardous effect towards the public peace and legitimate a norm, established as an injury tort in order to protect the "legal good" public peace - could, at least according to such a precept, definitely be acknowledged to the U.S. Church Arson Prevention Act[2010]. This law was a reaction to an increase of church burnings and arson of places of religious worship that serve predominantly African-American congregations in the early 90s. This law contains provisions increasing the sentencing for damaging places of worship. The Congress found that destruction and vandalism of places of worship "[...] pose a serious national problem"; and that "[...] changes in Federal law are necessary in order to deal properly with this problem"[2011]. Therefore, the aspect of a certain prevalence of hate crimes and the therefrom resulting special effects on society due to the frequency such acts is fulfilled. Sensational arson attacks in form of church burnings are committed in Germany as well. Such acts occurred in Erfurt in April, 20th 2000 and in Düsseldorf in October, 2. 2000 which due to their recurrence could constitute a danger to the "legal good" of public peace and therefore legitimate a new statute comparable to the American Arson Act; however both cases could not be confirmed to be motivated by bias and hate towards certain groups. Anyhow, between 2001 and 2011 in Germany at least 219 hate crimes were committed against Mosques and other religious facilities[2012].

The idea of determining the demerit of certain acts by an accumulation or their recurrence is not profitable. Not even the pure suitability of an attack to violate a legal good can be reduced to its ability of being publicly visible[2013]. Therefore, the idea of basing the need for a statute on the circumstance of a high prevalence of hate crimes is rejected. The result of an individual act may not be measured by its frequent occurrence. The damage caused by a high incidence of acts must be broken down to the individual act. If, after so doing, a harmful effect is still obvious, it must be admitted that each single hate crime

2009 "The [...] right-wing extremist violence act was due to the accumulation of xenophobic attacks and the exemplary effect of such riots suitable and capable of affecting the internal security of the Federal Republic of Germany" (The General Attorney at the Bundesgerichtshof, Prosecution because of a right-wing extremist arson attack in Jessnitz. Press release 4/2002, January 28, 2002. (http://www.generalbundesanwalt.de/prnt/showpress.php?newsid=74 - accessed 2011/09/09).

2010 110 Stat. 1392 Public Law 104-155-July 3, 1996.

2011 Church Arson Prevention Act of 1996 18 USC 247 note; Sec. 2 "Findings".

2012 BT-Drs. 17/9523 "Small request of the left fraction to the Bundestag".

2013 Von Bubnoff, in: LK-StGB, § 130, marginal no. 4.

act causes harm to the public peace. Whether each single hate crime actually harms the public peace must be found out in dependence on the nature of hate crime by referring to the respective society.

Since it is assumed that not the accumulation, but the single hateful or biased act undermines the public peace, it is questionable whether the single hate crime must provide a special quantitative requirement in order to affirm the need of an increased combat of this sort of crime. The gravity of a hate crime act, which is increased compared to other unmotivated acts of this kind, would therefore be a necessary prerequisite for criminalization. An interference with the legal good of public peace is indisputable admitted for certain hate crime acts. This admission seems to depend on the specific sensational character of an act: A threat to the national peace is legally affirmed when the hate crime was committed "[...] solely to realize the right-wing extremist criminal ideology of the perpetrator who wanted to contribute his part to free [his town] from foreigners"; because the demand of "foreigner-free zones" - which the perpetrator expressed through crime committal - creates a climate of fear and intimidation[2014]. This, however, refers to cases in which a hate crime obviously exceeds the amount of "natural" interference with a peaceful co-existence which goes along with any form of crime. In these cases, the impact on the public peace exceeds the usual impact to such an extent that it automatically evokes extra legal recognition or criminal involvement in order to protect the constitutional guaranteed living of the people. Accordingly, it is questioned whether the protection of the public peace against xenophobic and similar attacks might be required only in cases in which it is possible to filter out particularly dangerous forms of hate-motivated acts. It could be assumed that the public peace is only violated in such cases where a hate crime is investigated by the Attorney General[2015]. A typical feature of a hate crime violating the legal good of public peace could be seen in such circumstances which create a latent danger of an eminently large and numerous victimization. With that it could be thought of some hate crimes being suitable to violate the national public peace, while others are not. Being guided by the requirements of Sections 120, 142 a Courts Constitution Act, the Attorney General is able to make a use of his authority if an act, according to its surrounding circumstances, is suitable to endanger the national safety of Germany and the criminal case involves a specific gravity[2016]. The competency of the Attorney General was affirmed "if a hate crime is committed to harm the national fabric of society or its constitutional texture"[2017]. This was said to be the case if an offender attacks a victim "solely in order to affect him or her as a member of a

2014 The General Attorney at the Bundesgerichtshof, Prosecution because of a right-wing extremist arson attack in Jessnitz. Press release 4/2002, 28 January 2002. (http://www.generalbundesanwalt.de/prnt/showpress.php?newsid=74 - accessed 2011/09/09).

2015 View hereto: Section 120 Courts Constitution Act.

2016 According to Section 120, Paragraph 2, no. 3a Courts Constitution Act.

2017 The General Attorney at the Bundesgerichtshof, Rechtsextremismus. Karlsruhe, 2000. (http://www.generalbundesanwalt.de/prnt/rechts.php - accessed 2011/09/09)

national, racial, religious or ethnical group"[2018]. This, however, is the element of every hate crime.

Even lacking a noticeable frequent committal, one single hate crime is considered to be capable of containing a "special significance"[2019]. However, it is unclear what requirements are necessary to constitute "the special significance"[2020]. In contrary to depending on a certain numerical occurrence of sensational cases, it is referred to the nature of a single hate crime, which is able to harm the very fabric of society. Assuming that every hate crime fulfills what is determined to arise the competence of the Attorney General, which is to put a concrete bias related impact on the internal climate of the Federal Republic of Germany, broadcasts a signal to potential copycats, and also hurts the appearance of the Federal Republic of Germany towards those states that are connected to Germany by common values[2021], a single hate crime act provides that "special significance" to violate the public peace. Considering this, the General Attorney assumed his authority in several hate crime cases in the last years[2022]. All cases had in common that they were considered to threaten the national peace of the German society due to the so called secondary harms accruing from hate crimes which violate the legal good public peace. In 2000 a hate crime was committed by three German people who injured a Mozambican citizen in Dessau who died after the attack due to the severity of these injuries[2023]. According to the prosecutor the perpetrators attacked their victim because of hate towards all aliens living in Germany. It was stated that the victims were attacked "as representative for a group that is hated by the offenders and that these acts are committed against the value judgment of the German Basic Order which is based on tolerance towards human being of diverse races, languages and religious and political views" and that these acts "generate a climate of fear and intimidation" among foreign fellow citizens"[2024]. Due to that statement all hate crimes acts are considered to provide a demerit which - in addition to such which is addressed by the penalty of the respective parallel offense - is constituted by a despicable high

2018 The General Attorney at the Bundesgerichtshof, Rechtsextremismus. Karlsruhe, 2000. (http://www.generalbundesanwalt.de/prnt/rechts.php - accessed 2011/09/09)

2019 According to Section 120, Paragraph 2, No. 3a Courts Constitution Act, the General Attorney takes over the prosecution of a hate crime because of the special significance of the case.

2020 Footnote 2017.

2021 Der Generalbundesanwalt beim Bundesgerichtshof, Rechtsextremismus. Karlsruhe, 2000. (http://www.generalbundesanwalt.de/prnt/rechts.php - accessed 2011/09/09).

2022 Attack in Eggessin, August, 22nd 1999, The General Attorney at the Bundesgerichtshof, Prosecution by the General Attorney in the case "Eggesin". Press release 1/2000, 29. January 2000.; The General Attorney at the Bundesgerichtshof, Prosecution because of a right-wing extremist arson attack in Jessnitz. Press release 4/2002, 28 January 2002; The General Attorney at the Bundesgerichtshof, General Attorney takes over investigation in the case Dessau. Press release 16/2000, 21. June 2000.

2023 The General Attorney at the Bundesgerichtshof, General Attorney takes over investigation in the case Dessau. Press release 16/2000, 21. June 2000.

2024 The General Attorney at the Bundesgerichtshof, General Attorney takes over investigation in the case Dessau. Press release 16/2000, 21. June 2000. Likewise the American opinion defends the need of pure hate crime laws when it is explained that "the motivation of the bias-crime offender violates the quality principle, one of the most deeply held tenets in our legal system and out culture". (Lawrence, Punishing Hate, p. 61; similar sentiments pp. 38-39, 75).

unworthiness. This particular additional unworthiness is valid to generate additional penalties and, besides, to harm the legal good of public peace.

1.8.1.2. Frequency and Severity are no Criminality Prerequisites

Frequency and severity of acts as a complementary element of punishability is not required. A hate crime norm does not aim at protecting the social climate in general. Neither is it about the concrete endangerment of the social climate[2025], nor about the realization that these acts typically are dangerous to the public peace in its conceptual entirety, but about the fact that a real loss occurs to the element of tolerance in its currently existing form in society, due to the respective criminal behavior. The value that is attributed to a tolerant climate in the German society is outstanding high, since it is a necessary prerequisite for everyone's individual life planning. Such, from personal goods to be distinguished tolerant climate, builds the foundation that is required by everyone for his howsoever individually crafted livelihood[2026]. Thereby the good, which is protected by a hate crime standard, builds the frame condition that must exist to enable the realization of all other individual lifestyles. So the public peace, in its here to be protected partial aspect, creates the physical and material conditions and provides such circumstances which support the specifically human capacity for an autonomous organization of the social environment[2027]. Whether the individual in concrete actually values the protection of a tolerant climate is not important, it is enough that this typically is a prerequisite for further life plans[2028]. Considering the important function of a tolerant climate, the preservation of such is essential. The existence of a climate, which enables a tolerant co-existence, is particularly affected by the hateful and biased content of hate crime, regardless of its dimension. Neither a uniqueness of criminal behavior in relation to its incomparability, its impressive power, its sensational strength, nor an excessive damage production or a specific sensational moment of an act is required to breach the public peace. Even if one does not necessarily view a single hate crime act, for example, one with a comparable lower content of wrong as a threat to the constitutionally protected pluralistic society and therefore not as a socially dangerous or harmful behavior which exceeds the harms caused by the respective base offense and therefore does not consider a need to punish such an hate crime act more severely, this opinion would solely require to make a decision in how far the legislator must limit the scope of a hate crime standard towards certain public or sensational acts which creates a damage of higher significance; but it does not lead towards a rejection of the in principle

2025 An offense of endangerment is based on the fact that the danger in the individual case has actually came into appearance. (Wessels/Beulke, Strafrecht AT, marginal no. 28).

2026 Based on Kleinig´s and Feinberg´s idea of welfare interests, who acknowledge collective interests, and in case such are violated, consider that it is justified to speak of 'harm'. (Feinberg, Harm to Others, pp. 31 et seqq.; Kleinig, American Philosophical Quarterly 15 (1978), pp. 28 et seqq.); summarized in Hörnle, Grob anstößiges Verhalten, p. 75; and adapted for this purpose.

2027 With regard to the description of welfare interests: Feinberg, Harm to Others, pp. 37 et seqq.; Kleinig, American Philosophical Quarterly 15 (1978), pp. 30 et seqq.; Hörnle, Grob anstößiges Verhalten, p. 75.

2028 With regard to the description of welfare interests: Kleinig, American Philosophical Quarterly 15 (1978), p. 31.

changed criminality of a hate crime. If one holds the opinion to solely punish such hate crime acts severe where the offender´s behavior already reveals an above-average high degree of wrong, the therewith expected following problems in terms of determining a demarcation would have to be solved. The intruding idea of just capturing those acts which are constituted by an increased wrongfulness[2029] cannot be approved, if acknowledging that the public peace is injured by the commission of any hate crime[2030]. Rather, it must be recognized that the required unworthiness of result can be awarded to every hateful or biased motivated act[2031]. There might be a difference in the created amount of loss, but every hateful or biased criminal act reduces the current tolerance level in society, not necessary is its abolishment, the reduction is enough. The objectification of the motive of the offender through a hate crime committal results in a violation of tolerance which stands in contrast to the pluralistic structure of society. A high number of injuries of this kind would ultimately lead to the destruction of the pluralistic society form, thus – in the long run - transform the current societal climate. Destruction is not necessary for the entry of the result, the single injury suffices.

Each crime that is detectable as a racist, religious, homophobic, etc. crime, thus has been committed because of the corresponding motivation, sends out a message that violates the tolerant climate of a pluralistic society. Therefore, such a crime contrasts with the essential preservation of the tolerant and social physical environment. The violation of the public peace must be awarded to a hate crime[2032] because each single act constitutes itself as a combative expression which abolishes the acceptance and permissiveness of foreign beliefs and certain appearances and thereby changes the actual climate; thus, in general, presents itselves more than just a challenge to society. Each hate crime act is a declaration against the recognition of equal rights of different individuals and so bit by bit actually reduces tolerance in society. By that criminal behavior, which expresses the respective hateful bias-motive, objectifies the violation of the societal climate.

Questionable remains if the effects caused by these concrete behaviors rationally assessable harms the integrity of the public peace. That the

2029 As it done with Section 130 Penal Code, which addressed only such acts which provide an increased content of wrong. (Bubnoff, in: LK-StGB, § 130, marginal no. 16).

2030 View hereto: Chapter 4, G., 1.8.1.2. Frequency and Severity are no Criminality Prerequisites.

2031 The special dimension of the disvalue of the result can be already considered to lay in the fact that the victim is not victimized accidentally, but simply views himself to be provided with the special humiliation that he was under attack because he is the way he is. (Tolmein, ZRP 2001, pp. 315, 316).

2032 Violent hate crime offenses; property damage, including arson offenses and, in addition, further potential violent acts, as described in existing standards, are equally to be involved when punishing hate crime behavior. Even if basing the term violence on the assumption of a narrow designation concept, beside killing and injuring, also coercion would have to be taken into account. Furthermore, an increased disvalue of the result must be acknowledged to the offense of insult if committed in the form of a hate crime. Less harmful offenses, such as libel, may be involved, since hate crime constitute an attack on the human dignity, that means not 'just' towards the honor of a person, which is protected by libel. Whenever a hateful biased-motivated criminal behavior constitutes an enhanced attack on the human dignity (of the immediate victim) and, furthermore, constitutes an attack towards the public peace by affecting the current tolerant and pluralistic climate in society, it may be acknowledged that the additional individual and environmental harmful content of a hate crime that is not found in the same unmotivated crime is worthy of punishment.

measurability of "social psychological phenomenon"[2033] causes difficulties is well known[2034]. Since a hate crime law solely aims at protecting the functioning of society by abolishing bias related harm, thus harm caused to the specific area of the public peace, empirical measuring of the harmful relevance of hate crimes and an evaluation of the worthiness of protection of identified characteristics, described as affected interactional relations, seems basically possible. So a comprehensible validation of possible interference and damage does not seem impossible in all aspects[2035]. In order to prove this sort of universal harm, several studies have been undertaken and empirical measuring took place in order to evaluate the effects of hate crimes on society[2036]. Through the commission of a hate crime, the public peace is affected only in the partial aspect of tolerance in the respective society, whose preservation is an interest of the community[2037]. This partial aspect, i.e. the degree of tolerance in the society is negatively affected not through the already punished act as such, but in addition due to the connection of criminal behavior to the hateful or biased motive of the perpetrator. This connection has a sufficient external content, in order to constitute a punishable fact. This harmful content of the connection between the motive and the criminal act turns outward and objectifies itself in the message sent towards the entire society. Therefore, related to the specific motive of the perpetrator, which he outwardly expresses, it is to assume that only such specific motives which contain the ideal of the perpetrator to expel certain people from society causes to harm the public peace in this respective specific region, which relates to the current form of society. With that, the public peace is in particular affected in the area of tolerance; and the unimpaired degree of tolerance is essential for the existence of a "pluralistic, multicultural society"[2038]. This affected region is a value which protection is important to the entire society. As a result, whenever a criminal behavior sends the harming message, it actually violates the public peace in its here addressed region.

1.8.2. **Intermediate Result**

The harm caused towards the public peace is difficult to measure[2039]. Therefore, the design of a legal standard of a non-result-constituted offense is convenient. According to the here adopted meaning of the legal good of public peace, this collective good is based on the existence of a multicultural

2033 OLG Celle, NStZ 1997, pp. 495, 496.
2034 "In a judicial context, however, it is impossible to make valid statements according social-psychological conditions". (Hörnle, Grob anstößiges Verhalten, p. 102; with further references to: Wandres, Auschwitz-Leugnen, p. 217; Hefendehl, Kollektive Rechtsgüter, p. 292; regarding the difficult measurability of such social-psychological states, view: Rudolphi, ZRP, 1979, p. 221; Streng, FS for Lackner, p. 514 et seq.).
2035 In order to meet the requirements of the legal good doctrine in its critical function and the here followed understanding, a comprehensible validation of possible interference can not be excluded from the outset. (Wohlers, Deliktstypen des Präventionsstrafrechts, p. 227).
2036 Iganski, Hate Crime hurts more, American Behavioral Scientist, Vol. 45, No. 4, December 2001, (626-638).
2037 The preservation of a collective good must be an interest of the community. (Jescheck/Weigend, Lehrbuch des Strafrechts AT, § 26 I 2, pp. 257 et seqq. - with further references).
2038 Cf. Schneider, Internationales Handbuch der Kriminologie, Bd. 2, p. 326 - who acknowledges the fact that hate crime violates the "pluralistic, multicultural society".
2039 Hörnle, Grob anstößiges Verhalten, p. 102

pluralistic society, which requires a certain degree of tolerance. The degree of tolerance of society is harmed by the commission of any hate crime, a hate crime must not result in a certain enhanced intensity or increased loss, nor is the degree of tolerance "at risk" only in terms of an accumulation of hate crimes, but it is violated by any biased motivated act. According to the conceptual distinction between injury and destruction, it becomes clear that the realization of a violation is already fulfilled with the committal of the hate crime act that triggers the desired result. Therefore there is no need for a (complete) destruction or abolition of the current content of tolerance in a society in order to comply with conditions of an offense which is designed as a result constituted offense. Sufficient is the always same specific external shape of a hate crime: through the message sent into society, the tolerant climate is violated in concrete, and for this form of violation, the violation of goods of the individual does not matter. If an offense, in accordance with its content, its nature and its specific circumstances, is designed to constitute itself as a manifestation of xenophobic criminal behavior, which is to be determined by an overall assessment, such damages the tolerant climate.

1.9. Summary According a Separate Offense

It has been shown that the transition of the violation of an individual good to the detriment of the entire society is fluent. Whereas one hate crime harms the human dignity of a plurality of human beings, due to its changed mode of attack and due to an increased dehumanization based on the expressed motive, and therefore this attack towards an entire group of people is worthy to be condemned, the attack towards the entire society appears to be even more dangerous. hate crimes give the inhuman mind of the offender's an expression by attacking a being in order to demonstrate his secondariness according to the population's mind; the offenders not only voice, but directly realize their will of eradicating certain groups of people from society, at least they make sure that the attacked know that they are not welcome in society. Thereby the rights of the actual attacked and also such of the particular groups are violated, and separated from such, the legal good of the tolerant co-existence receives an independent value, which is affected by the commission of these offenses[2040]. The recognition of this value arises from the fact that the circle of the concerned must be drawn beyond the immediate attacked group: A tolerant climate is important for the entire population, that is for the part of the population against whom the inciting or defamatory action is not directed. As a result, the public peace, in a closer to be described subregion, is violated by the commission of a hate crime act. The protection of this sub-region could be achieved by a penalization of the inner connection between motive and crime, which emerges to the outside in form of a symbolic message and unfolds its damaging effects in the society. It is assumed that the public peace in its concrete form is the main legal good which has such a value content that the Penal Code must provide for its protection against hate crime.

2040 Hörnle, Grob anstößiges Verhalten, p. 98.

1.10. Prerequisites of Penalization of Hate Crime

The offense character is constituted by the fact that the perpetrator intentionally or knowingly commits the offense to use it as an activity directed against the existence of a tolerant climate[2041], or could have known that his criminal behavior harms the tolerant climate as the attacked partial aspects of the public peace. The climate violating intent can be objectively determined by the aforementioned indications[2042].

1.10.1. Objective Constituent Elements of a Norm

There are two different variants in question in order to form the objective part of an offense: Either the hate crime norm refers to existing standards and its objective facts, or the objective part of the offense describes acts which are previously established in other offenses. In particular, an encompassment of murder, physical assault, property damage, threat, and insult must be considered. A reference to existing standards is uncommon to German legal dogmatics since this would cause an unnecessary duplication of offenses, which leads this new offense to become an issue on the offense level of competition[2043]. The description of acts which are previously established in other offenses is more valuable, since this is a known procedure, e. g., from the enactment of the stalking section[2044].

However, both possibilities of forming the objective part of a hate crime norm lead to difficulties when defining a common penalty frame while also meeting the requirements of definiteness (Article 103 Basic Law), because of the fact that distinct acts would have to be addressed by only one norm, i.e., the entire range of offenses against the physical integrity to also property damaging offenses would have to be captured in a single norm.

Furthermore, the objectification of the motive is required to form a hate crime. The external part of the inner motive must emerge from beneath. This already

---

2041 Based on the description in relation to offenses endangering the democratic state (Sections 90, 90a Penal Code) used by: Hörnle, Grob anstößiges Verhalten, p. 255; and on the description in relation to offenses endangering the democratic state (Sections 87, 88, 89, 90b) Penal Code used by: Backes, Rechtsstaatsgefährdungsdelikte, pp. 169 et seqq.

2042 View hereto: FBI-guidelines footnote 1249, which serve objective criteria by which a hate crime is recognizable.

2043 The committal of several offenses of the same type by one act ultimately leads to an encompassment of all offenses during the legal appraisal in order to impose only one comprehensive penalty for all acts.

2044 Also in the offense of stalking the manifestations of a criminal act are diverse and compassed in one offense. The offense of stalking Section 238 Penal Code circumscribes an overall behavior, which is constituted by many different partial acts, and reveals a clear proximity to Section 239 Penal Code and to coercion, established in Section 240 Penal Code. (Seiler, § 238 StGB – Analyse und Auslegung des Nachstellungstatbestandes, 2010, pp. 17 et seqq.; Mitsch, Der neue Stalking Straftatbestand im Strafgesetzbuch, NJW 2007, 1237, 1238). Moreover, detectable stalking acts commonly perform other offenses such as the utterance offenses (insult, slander, libel, Section 185-192 Penal Code); threat (Section 241 Penal Code); assault (Section 240 Penal Code), physical assault (Sections 223 ff Penal Code); vandalism (Section 303 Penal Code); trespass (Section 123 Penal Code); sexual assault (Sections 178 Penal Code); and computer crimes, such as Section 202 a, 303 a and b Penal Code. Nevertheless, a legislative gap has been identified, which was to be closed by the enactment of this offense.

results from the fact that a hate crime is perceptible, because in this case a certain message is sent towards society which violates the tolerant climate[2045].

1.10.2. Protected Characteristics

The motto of the American legislation is that "whenever hatred or bias against certain sections of the population become noticeable within a society, these sections are to be incorporated in the protection by hate crime legislation"[2046]. This becomes evident by the numerous and distinct characteristics which are protected by American state laws.

It is correct that the decision of what characteristics would have to be protected by a hate crime norm de lege ferenda must be made with regard to the needs of the respective country, however, not all that indiscriminately. A decision of what characteristics would have to be protected by German law must be based on a proper assessment of a number of factors, which are named in the following.

1.10.2.1. Immutable or Fundamental Characteristics

A hate crime hits the core of the human personality, because hate crimes target an aspect of a person's identity that is unchangeable or fundamental to a person's sense of self. This aspect must not only be exclusive to him individually, but to him and an entire group of people[2047]. A group is defined as a plurality of people, who are linked by shared characteristics and thereby contrast to the general population, and also feel that way themselves[2048]. This refers to the necessary factor of a characteristic to be a "marker[2049] of group identity"[2050]. Not all immutable or fundamental characteristics are markers of group identity[2051]. Therefore, at this point, it should be noted that only such characteristics qualify as being worthy of protection which are generally accepted as group characteristics.

If referring to the features of immutability or fundamentality, it must be stressed that fundamentality can erode immutability. There are a few characteristics which are changeable, but are nevertheless fundamental to a person's sense of self[2052]. This precept becomes understandable when referring to the nature

---

2045 Sometimes this is more obvious (in case of letter of confession; the use of racist symbols; slurs and language used during committing the act, etc.), sometimes an act is not recognizable as a hate crime at first sight. An act which is not recognized as a hate crime instantly, is still suitable to harm the public peace, since the knowledge of its true nature already affects the climate.

2046 Quotation or words to that effect by Stachelberg, in: Lynch and Stachelberg, Hate Crime Laws, Morning Show on C-SPAN's Washington Journal, March 13, 2012.

2047 It is crucial that there are several potential victims who, based on their same identity, are selected by a perpetrator and chosen to be a target.

2048 LK, § 220a, marginal no. 9.

2049 "Marker" refers to the aspect which is attacked by a hate crime perpetrator. Such markers are usually evident, such as skin color, but must not be.

2050 OSCE/ODIHR, Hate Crime Laws: A Practical Guide, 2009, p. 38.

2051 View the example provided by OSCE/ODIHR : "[...] blue eyes may be described as an immutable characteristic, but blue-eyed people do not usually identify together as a group, nor do others see them as a cohesive group, and eye color is not typically a marker of group identity." (OSCE/ODIHR, Hate Crime Laws: A Practical Guide, 2009, p. 38).

2052 OSCE/ODIHR, Hate Crime Laws: A Practical Guide, 2009, p. 38.

of hate crime as an identity crime[2053], which is what renders it different from ordinary crimes[2054]. With regard to the attack towards the human dignity of the people it has been determined above that the particularly harmful content of a hate crime is characterized by the fact that with the attack the core of the personality of the victim is addressed, hate crime is an action directed against people who are at risk of victimization because they are what they are. Human dignity is the "intrinsic value of man"[2055], which is the value of a person which belongs to him by the virtue of his being a person[2056]. This dignity belongs to everyone, without regard to his characteristics[2057].

According to the formula for the demarcation of human dignity and honor, established by the Federal Constitutional Court to determine whether an act touches the core of human existence[2058], the human dignity is violated when essential defining properties of a certain strength and duration are attacked. This formula is to use for determining the characteristics which are in need to be included in a law[2059]. Despite not unchangeable, but because of its fundamental nature, therefore worthy of protection, for example, is 'religion'. Even though it is possible to change one's religion, it is a widely-recognized marker of group identity that a person should not be forced to surrender or conceal[2060]. Likewise, a certain strength and duration, and because of its fundamental content, homelessness is to involve as a characteristic in the protection. Despite that this is not an unchangeable characteristic in every respect, it is an aspect that at least cannot be doffed off from one day to the next through the will of the concerned person and, above all, constitutes a part of the identity of the victim and presents itself as a markable group characteristic.

Acts that are aimed at marginal aspects of the personality image only, neither violate the victims' groups in the essence of their personality, nor do they touch the public peace as a social institution in its, by a hate crime norm protected, subregion. Not to be incorporated in the protection of a standard therefore are professionals, athletes, and politicians. An act that infringes the personal area, which is marked by an occupational position[2061], regularly does not harm the human dignity[2062] and therefore an attack towards such a characteristic is also

2053 View Chapter 3, B. Emergence of the Hate Crime Concept in the USA.

2054 OSCE/ODIHR, Hate Crime Laws: A Practical Guide, 2009, p. 38.

2055 Sachs, Verfassungsrecht II, 2002, p.167, marginal no. 8; Epping, Grundrechte, 2009, p. 262, marginal no. 593.

2056 BVerfGE 30, 1 Leading sentence 6.

2057 BVerfGE 96, 375, p. 399; BVerfGE 115, 118, p. 152.

2058 BVerfGE; NStZ 2001, 26, 27 et seq.; BVerfG, NJW 2001, 2957, 2959.

2059 Thus, the distinction of groups worthy of protection from such less worthy of protection must apply according to the formula used for the demarcation of the human dignity and honor. The distinction between mere defamation and violations of the human dignity applies according to the Federal Constitutional Court on whether a violation touches the core human existence. (For the formula of the Federal Constitutional Court to distinct violation of honor from such of the human dignity, view: Höfling, in: Sachs, GG, Art. 1, marginal no. 16).

2060 OSCE/ODIHR, Hate Crime Laws: A Practical Guide, 2009, p. 38.

2061 Lenckner/Eisele, in: Schönke/Schröder, StGB, § 130, marginal no. 7; von Bubnoff, in: LK-StGB, § 130, marginal no. 26; Rudolphi, in: SK-StGB, § 130. marginal no. 7; Giehring, StV 1985, p. 30, 34; Hörnle, Grob anstößiges Verhalten, p. 125.

2062 BGHSt 36,38,90; OLG Frankfurt, NJW 1989, 1367, 1369; KG, NJW 2003, 685, 686.

not to be qualified as a hate crime in the here acknowledged sense, because the core of the personality cannot be equated with the "core area of the self-chosen identity"[2063]. Although, a group identity can be defined by a professional position, moreover this is or can be attacked, the attack of such features does not correspond to the here followed understanding of hate crime and the therefore necessary factor of fundamentality[2064].

A hate crime is distinguished in that the perpetrator chooses the characteristics which he attributes to the victim as the trigger[2065] for his behavior, he therefore rejects to accept the victim and his group members as equal human beings with the same basic rights and responsibilities in the community[2066]; these traits, if influenceable by the victim, doffable at any time, and which are self-selected, do not require the protection of a hate crime standard, because they are neither essential nor constitutive for the persons fundamental being; therefore, an attack cannot bear equal serious consequences, compared - for instance - to such against the race or the disability of a human being.

This limitation is supported by the establishment of a connection to the primarily protected legal good of public peace. hate crimes are usually about the targeted victimization to deliver a message. In their form as message-bearer they violate the public peace in its partial aspect of a tolerant climate and affect the constitutional "institution pluralism", respectively. The drastic consequences, which are based on the message character of a hate crime, must occur in form of a violation of the public peace. These effects require that the offender manifests his mind - the rejection of the victims as equal beings - supposedly representing the opinion of the majority/society through criminal behavior. By the circumstance that the offender makes the victim believe that he is the voice of society, not just the victim groups are affected by assuming that the society does not approve their being, but the society is affected in its current pluralist existence[2067]. These acts are usually committed out of the middle of the population[2068]. The broadcast of such a message fails, for instance, regarding violent football clashes, although the area of the tolerant climate is affected at least in some way in a broad understanding, the constitutionally protected society is not damaged in its specific plural form. The

2063 Hörnle, Grob anstößiges Verhalten, p. 125.

2064 Because such an attack only violates the honor of a human, but does not violate the human dignity. (Lenckner/Eisele, in: Schönke/Schröder, StGB, § 130, marginal no. 7; von Bubnoff, in: LK-StGB, § 130, marginal no. 26; Rudolphi, in: SK-StGB, § 130. marginal no. 7; Giehring, StV 1985, 34; Hörnle, Grob anstößiges Verhalten, p. 125).

2065 The reason for his behavior is his hateful bias against the characteristics which he attributes to certain persons.

2066 OLG Tröndle/Fischer, § 130, marginal no. 12; Lenckner/Eisele, in: Schönke/Schröder, StGB, § 130, marginal no.6.

2067 To protect the "legal good" of the public peace, according to a democratic belief, the principle of equality is to be upheld high and the constitutional status quo must be maintained.

2068 Currently there is no specific sports team in Germany, whose members are knowling attacked in order for the team to be eliminated. If there are hateful attacks on members of sport teams, these attacks usually occur from warring teams, so it is about criminal activities of sport members among themselves, yet do such acts arise from the middle of society. After all, there is no particular victimized group identifiable

total population is not injured by disputes among members of certain sports clubs in the here relevant section of the public peace.

While an affection to a football league may form a group identified marker, such does not reach the core of the personality of someone (missing fundamental factor), and does not touch the multi-cultural society in its present pluralistic existence (lack of impairment of the protected legal good). Therefore, it is necessary that the acts are directed against characteristics that shape the human dignity and which, in the event of an attack, affect the universal legal good of public in its here relevant area.

1.10.2.2. Social and Historical Context

The process of determining which characteristics are to include requires an inclusion of current social problems as well as potential historical oppression[2069] and discrimination[2070]. "Characteristics that have been the basis for past attacks should be included, as should characteristics that are the basis for contemporary incidents"[2071]. Statistics could be included to reveal the generally most victimized groups of a country. Basically, the most vulnerable minorities are those that due to superficial features are easily attributable to a specific group, this refers to the past and to nowadays. Due to the easy recognition, an increased, clearly visible dislike from the center of the population may occur easier. At least if referring to Germany, xenophobia is arguably one of the most common motives for hate crimes; from the perspective of the offender certainly also the easiest choice to harm society by spreading his xenophobic opinion with the selection of a victim who has visible foreign features (skin color, hair texture) since there is no need to deal with the closer identity of the attacked person[2072]. Moreover, this is the most convenient form of disturbing the public peace, because at any time some kind of potential victim is clearly available. There is no effort required in order to identify a target if a perpetrator purely bases his hate on visual criteria. If now adding the facilitating circumstance of such cases in which the victim is chosen because he is a "foreigner", which is the fact that "foreigners" obviously are weaker victims due to their lowered legal defense, based on a lack of language, support, etc., it becomes clear which particular groups necessitate the balancing mechanism of a special law.

With regard to Germany's Nazi past and the right-wing extremist background of many offenses at issue, groups that were victims of the Nazis and -

2069 "The characteristics that ought to be included are those that implicate societal fissure lines – divisions that run deep in the social history of a culture". (Lawrence, Enforcing Bias-Crime Laws without Bias: Evaluating the Disproportionate-Enforcement Critique, Journal of Law & Contemporary Problems, Vol. 66, 2003, p. 49).

2070 OSCE/ODIHR, Hate Crime Laws: A Practical Guide, 2009, p. 38.

2071 "Because criminal law attempts to deal with social issues, a legislature considering enactment of a hate crime law must understand just what those issues are." (OSCE/ODIHR, Hate Crime Laws: A Practical Guide, 2009, p. 38).

2072 A hate crime offender holds a distance to his victims; he considers them as enemies, as depersonalized "faceless" hate objects. (Schneider, Politische Kriminalität: Hassverbrechen, Fremdenfeindlichkeit im internationalen Kontext, Kriminalistik 2001, pp.21-28 (21).

remarkably again - are the mostly attacked nowadays[2073] must be included. Accordingly, further characteristics such as disability[2074], sexual orientation[2075] and homelessness[2076] must be protected in addition to the main characteristics that are connected to the basic problem of xenophobia, which are: race[2077], ethnicity/national origin[2078], and religion[2079]. The inclusion of the mentioned characteristics are in line with legally already recognized characteristics of discrimination[2080], which confirms a certain general, legally officially assumed recognition of their risk to be endangered.

1.10.2.3. Excluded Characteristics

Circumlocutions as "human dignity" and "parts of the population" must not be used in the wording of a law. Such unspecified paraphrases do not name the problem and therefore will not be able to address it. The protection of a legal good which aims at tolerance, equal respect and therefore is orientated against discrimination, is however, "precisely communicatively negated by such [non-specific formulations]: It could also include the discriminated groups, but it must not - it especially does not impart the message that it is about countering violent discrimination against vulnerable groups[2081]". hate crime laws protect all people equally, therefore also too concretized and narrow designations, e.g. "Buddhists", "women", or "people of color" should not be

---

2073 Tolmein, Strafrechtliche Reaktionsmöglichkeiten auf rassistisch motivierte Gewaltdelikte, ZRP 2001, p. 318.

2074 Bias against disability is understood according to the American understanding "[a] preformed negative opinion or attitude toward a group of persons based on their physical or mental impairments/challenges, whether such disability is temporary or permanent, congenital or acquired by heredity, accident, injury, advanced age, or illness". (U.S. Department of Justice, Hate Crime Data Collection Guidelines, 1999, p. 2).

2075 Bias against sexual orientation is understood according to the American understanding "[a] preformed negative opinion or attitude toward a group of persons based on their sexual attraction toward, and responsiveness to, members of their own sex or members of the opposite sex, e.g., gays, lesbians, heterosexuals." (U.S. Department of Justice, Hate Crime Data Collection Guidelines, 1999, p. 3).

2076 For instance, this historical background of Germany, that is interwoven in the social history of the German culture, could allow an exception to the rule that no concrete characteristics are to be included in a law, since hate crime legislation protects every being equally. In this case, a German law could address the Jewish belief as a part of the characteristic 'religion' explicitly. This exception may apply especially since anti-Semitism is still present nowadays. (For the inclusion of characteristics based on the history of a nation view in general: (Lawrence, Enforcing Bias-Crime Laws without Bias: Evaluating the Disproportionate-Enforcement Critique, Journal of Law & Contemporary Problems, Vol. 66, 2003, p. 49).

2077 According to the American understanding, bias against race is defined as a "preformed negative opinion or attitude towards a group of persons who possess common physical characteristics, e.g., color of skin, eyes, and/or hair; facial features; etc., genetically transmitted by descent and heredity which distinguish them as a distinct division of humankind, e.g., Asians, blacks, whites." (U.S. Department of Justice, Hate Crime Data Collection Guidelines, 1999, p. 3).

2078 According to the American understanding, bias against ethnicity/national origin is defined as a "preformed negative opinion or attitude toward a group of persons of the same race or national origin who share common or similar traits, languages, customs, and traditions, e.g., Arabs, Hispanics." (U.S. Department of Justice, Hate Crime Data Collection Guidelines, 1999, p. 2).

2079 According to the American understanding, bias against religion is defined as a "preformed negative opinion or attitude toward a group of persons who share the same religious beliefs regarding the origin and purpose of the universe and the existence or nonexistence of a supreme being, e.g., Catholics, Jews, Protestants, atheists." (U.S. Department of Justice, Hate Crime Data Collection Guidelines, 1999, p. 3).

2080 Compare to: Coalition agreement between the Social Democrats (SPD) and Bündnis 90/Die Grünen, Art. VI Nr. 6.; Act to reduce discrimination against lesbians and gays from. 22. 12. 1997 (GVBl LSA, 1072); Tolmein, Strafrechtliche Reaktionsmöglichkeiten auf rassistisch motivierte Gewaltdelikte, ZRP 2001 Heft 7, p. 318.

2081 Tolmein, Strafrechtliche Reaktionsmöglichkeiten auf rassistisch motivierte Gewaltdelikte, ZRP 2001, p. 317.

included in the text of the law, to not meet the misunderstanding that white, male Protestants could be excluded from the protection of such a law. Correctly, these exemplified characteristics would generally, in accordance with their scope, refer to religion, gender and race. Logically necessary a hate crime standard is more rarely to be applied for the protection of a white male Protestant[2082], but precisely this very fact confirms its rightful necessary enactment. Until a norm is not equally often applied for the combat of acts against any group, it evidences the existing threat to pluralism and therefore its necessity.

1.10.2.4. Implementation Issues

Since legislators and policymakers are likely to be from majority communities, the question of current and past discrimination and victimization can be effectively represented by non-governmental organizations, ombudsmen, and community groups representing minority communities[2083]. Thus, the U.S. concept was also helped to be developed by civil right organizations[2084]. Whereas original state functions - such as the legal solving of social problems - must, of course, be assumed by the government, especially in the area of right-wing extremism the resistance must arise from the people of the society - and it must not be left solely to the legislator[2085]. This, however, was accomplished in the U.S. by the efforts of organizations such as the ADL, SPLC, and the CDR[2086]; therefore in Germany the opinions of similar organizations are to include in the legislator's assessment when enacting a norm, since being directly affected, such are able to evaluate the necessities of protection for a certain area to their perception, which could be the Opferperspektive e.V.; Lesben- und Schwulenverband in Deutschland (LSVD) e.V.; Association of foreigners; Central Council of Jews in Germany; and others.

1.10.2.5. The Protection of Persons Affiliated with Principal Hate Crime Victims

Some crimes are committed against individuals because of their connection with a particular group. Some hate crime victims are chosen not because they share a particular protected characteristic themselves, but because of their association with others who do[2087]. It is opined that persons affiliated or associated with a group that shares a protected characteristic can easily be overlooked as a category to include in hate crime laws[2088]. However, the

2082 One of the most popular hate crime cases in the U.S. was about a hate crime attack, committed by a black person against a white male. (Wisconsin gegen Mitchell 6508 U.S. 476 (1993).

2083 OSCE/ODIHR, Hate Crime Laws: A Practical Guide, 2009, p. 39.

2084 View hereto Chapter 3, B. Emergence of the Hate Crime Concept in the USA.

2085 With societal organizations influencing the hate crime concept in the USA it is opposedly considered that lobbyists are taken over tasks of the government, thus the legislature does not fullfill its original function anymore. (Seehafer, Strafrechtliche Reaktionen, 2003, p. 46, with reference to: Grumke, 2001, p. 92.

2086 Anti Defamation League; Southern Poverty Law Center; Center for Democratic Renewal; view hereto Chapter 3, B. Emergence of the Hate Crime Concept in the USA.

2087 The United States legislation pays particular attention towards hate crimes directed at interracial couples and families. (RCW 9A.36.078 Malicious harassment - Finding).

2088 OSCE/ODIHR, Hate Crime Laws: A Practical Guide, 2009, p. 39.

protection of those persons who are not attacked because of their specific own way of being must not be included in a hate crime law according to the here followed perception. The reasoning for including persons who are attacked because of mingling with certain beings could be explained with the aim of these laws to protect the public peace. Yet, these targets are not chosen because of incorporating a fundamental, unchangeable characteristic, but because of their relationship to certain persons who are the true targets of such an attack. Therefore, the additionally required aggravated attack towards the human dignity of the immediate victim cannot be acknowledged to be as deep as it is if one is directly attacked because of his own fundamental and unchangeable characteristics, that is because of his own way of being. Moreover, the characteristic of “a connection” or “relationship” to an actually addressed person, thus to a person who actually “consists” of a respective characteristic, can be dropped at any time; hence, neither is it unchangeable nor fundamental of one’s own self. In the end, a hate crime is an attack to a person’s self and to society at large - not either one. The victim who is attacked because of his relationship to the actual target, lacks the individual concern which makes up the specific form of attacks towards the human dignity.

Beside that, further included considerations of reasoning hate crime legislation, e.g. the vulnerability of certain victims and the omnipresent threat based on the fact of being "different" in the eye of hate crime offenders, are contrary to the inclusion of persons who are attacked because of their affiliation with a person who possess characteristics which are protected by a hate crime law. By following this opinion, the strong piece of circumstantial evidence that the offender and the victim are of different origin, share different religious beliefs, etc. can be upheld as an important indicator for the committal of a hate crime[2089].

2089 The first mentioned objective evidence that the crime was motivated by bias“ according to the U.S. federal guidelines is the circumstance that "the offender and the victim were of different race, religion, disability, sexual orientation, and/or ethnicity/national origin. For example, the victim was black and the offender was white". (View: U.S. Department of Justice, Hate Crime Data Collection Guidelines, 1999, pp. 4 et seq. and footnote 1249 of this dissertation).

1.10.2.6. Conclusion

The violation of human dignity as an additionally legal good which is violated by a hate crime act must be incorporated during the characterization of the protected groups. The acts must be directed against the victim's way of being[2090]. The commission must show its nature of being a message transmitter, which violates the pluralistic element of the societal order that is the tolerant climate. Since just marginal personality traits are not to be protected, in view of the current situation in the FRG and incorporating its historical events, the following characteristics are to be explicitly mentioned in a law: race; ethnicity/national origin/nationality; religion; disability, sexual orientation; homelessness.

1.10.2.7. Defining the Motive in Regard to Consequential Differences

According to the American concept there are two conceptions of a hate crime. One is the "racial animus model" according to which the offender acts out of hatred or hostility towards a particular characteristic of the victim; or targets property associated with people who share that characteristic, such as a church, place of worship or private property. Crimes hereto are defined on the basis of the perpetrator's animus for the characteristic of the victim and the centrality of this animus is the perpetrator's motivation for committing the crime[2091]. The other conception refers to the "discriminatory selection model" according to which a law only requires that the offender intentionally selected the victim because of a certain protected characteristic which the victim inhered [2092]. The difference between these two models is important. Established according to the discriminatory selection model a law is broader because it reaches those offenders who did not act because of hostility, but selected their victims based on stereotyped information achieved from their bias[2093]. Thus the court at trial must not prove the hate of the accused, which makes a law enacted according to the discriminatory selection model easier to apply. If "hate" is a legal requirement of an offense, the respective law enforcement authorities would have to make an assessment of an offender's mental state, which is inexpedient[2094]. Furthermore, a law based on the discriminatory selection model addresses the kind of harm that hate crime laws are intended to prevent in a trustier way. What matters is that a victim has been chosen because of an immutable or fundamental aspect of his identity, this is covered by a law that is established in the manner of the discriminatory selection model.

2090 So-being of the victim.

2091 Lawrence, The Punishment of Hate, Michigan Law Review 320-381, 1994, p. 326; Lawrence, Punishing Hate, pp 29 et seqq.; 34. View also: OSCE/ODIHR, Hate Crime Laws: A Practical Guide, 2009, pp. 46 et seqq.

2092 The "discriminatory selection model" of bias crimes defines these crimes in terms of the perpetrator's discriminatory selection of his victim. Under this model, it is irrelevant why an offender selected his victim on the basis on race. It is sufficient that the offender did so." (Lawrence, The Punishment of Hate, Michigan Law Review 320-381, 1994, p. 326; Lawrence, Punishing Hate, pp 29 et seqq.).

2093 OSCE/ODIHR, Hate Crime Laws: A Practical Guide, 2009, p. 48.

2094 OSCE/ODIHR, Hate Crime Laws: A Practical Guide, 2009, pp. 49 et seq.

If choosing the conception of a law in accordance with the discriminatory selection model, the degree of xenophobic and other discriminatory mindset[2095] and its relation to crime committal must be carefully defined. Although there is a popular conception of a "typical" hate crime, in which the offender is motivated purely by hatred of the victim's group, but sometimes the motives behind hate crimes are far more complex. In addition to general problems in proving the motive, hate crimes often present special questions of the prevalent motive, whenever an offender has more than one reason for acting[2096]. The problem to determine the hate crime motive therefore occurs when it turns out that due to its complexity it is not clear whether such is conductive. In U.S. case law, a number of courts have adopted the requirement that the bias motive must be a "substantial factor" behind the offense[2097]. Incidental use of racist language is generally not considered sufficient. The substantial motive requirement, however, does not exclude the possibility of multiple motives. Another common wording, acceptable for a German law, is such according to which a hate crime act was motivated in whole or in part by hateful bias[2098]. What would reduce the effect of a law is a precept that requires that the biased motive must be (overly) dominant[2099].

1.10.2.8. Drawn Precepts of the Racial Animus- and the Discriminatory Selection Model for Implementation

It is important to solely reach true hate crimes only, therefore it is important that the bias motive is in the center of the conception of the perpetrator. Thus, the offender must attack the victim solely or at least in parts because of the victims true or perceived group membership, this conception should, in the meantime, automatically include his bias-related animus against a respective characteristic. Insofar, if a certain person is attacked because of his inherent characteristics solely because these characteristics lead to a simplification of committing the previously aimed at goals of the offender, thus the purpose of crime is not the group hate but the committal of the crime as such, the offender just chooses a certain victim type, because – due to his bias – he assumes to easier reach his goal, this attack is not to be considered as a hate crime. If an offender aims at committing the crime "burglary", he thinks about who is rich and where the rich live. With that he possibly draws on his bias assuming that Jews are rich. Thus, he aims at attacking Jews, whereas obviously his true aim is to attack the rich, which is a characteristic, which is decisive for his crime committal (burglary)[2100]. hate crime legislation is not intended to punish

2095 The lines between motivation and attitude are blurred and for the largely theoretical; the Federal Supreme Court parallelizes the assessment of the motive with the assessment of the mindset/attitude. (Gerkan, 1998, p. 50, supra note 25; Seehafer, Strafrechtliche Reaktionen, 2003, p. 77, supra note 582).

2096 OSCE/ODIHR, Hate Crime Laws: A Practical Guide, 2009, pp. 53 et seqq.

2097 With that said, those motives are to be identified and assessed which gives the conduct its character.

2098 It must be sufficient for the categorization of a crime as a hate crime, if the hate crime motive as one of a bundle of motives gives the criminal act its character due to its clarity.

2099 "The danger of such a requirement is that it is very difficult, in respect of mixed motives, to calculate exact proportions or percentages." (OSCE/ODIHR, Hate Crime Laws: A Practical Guide, 2009, p. 54).

2100 Similar examples can be found in: Aydin, Die strafrechtliche Bekämpfung von Hassdelikten, 2006 and Lawrence, Punishing Hate - Bias Crimes under American Law, 2003.

the wrong of such kind of criminal motivated acts. The sense and purpose of hate crime laws is to combat xenophobic related harm to society. Therefore, if a victim has characteristics (e.g. being Jewish) which does not trigger the crime, but solely creates the decision to commit an already planned crime by choosing a specific victim type, this committed crime is not a hate crime. Therefore, the "racial animus model" is more suitable to address only this type of harm that would not have occurred without the motivation of the perpetrator; precisely these yet unconsidered "side-effects" - but only these - may be captured and duly penalized. It is essential to distinguish hate crime from other violent crimes. Not every violent crime is a hate crime; it is a hate crime only in case it is motivated by animus towards a particular group of people. A violent crime which is committed by a perpetrator who hates the individual victim, but not an entire group of people, or is motivated by the need for robbery or a break in, is not a hate crime.

The question whether each rape of a woman, committed by a male offender, constitutes a hate crime, is to be answered in a similar way. If it is not assumed that the offender selected the victim because of her gender but because of his sexual impulses, the gender is not the leading motive for crime committal and therefore the victim is not adjudged a symbol status, rape is not a hate crime in the here followed understanding[2101]; what, however already derives from the fact that women are not to be incorporated as protected characteristic in the German society.

1.10.2.9. Unimportant Error in Persona

An offender may also select the victim because of a mistaken belief about the victim's membership in a particular group. For example dark haired people are attacked because they are assumed to be Muslim[2102]. For the same reasons, "mistakes of fact", i.e. mistaken belief about the victim's actual identity, should not prevent an offense being categorized and prosecuted as a hate crime. It must depend on whether the offender intentionally selected this particular victim because of hate crime bias[2103]. Therefore, a common wording of U. S. hate crime law refers to an offense which was motivated by the victim's

2101 Considering the opinion in literature that rape or sexual offenses committed against women constitutes a hate crime because of the brutal exercise of power of the male offender in order to tyrannize the, in his eyes, weaker gender and therefore the weak/fragile women is chosen to be victimized solely because of her weakness, it is to say that pervy behavior against the weaker victim maybe qualifies to penalty enhancement according the vulnerable victim, but not fulfills the requirements for constituting a hate crime. Precisely because women could be considered as weaker, this factor can be seen as a fact which simplifies the already decided idea of crime committal of the offender, in other words, women solely are considered as a suitable crime object. Of course, sexual violence against women reveal discrimination, humiliation and lowering of the female gender, but this usually is not based on hate or animus towards the female gender in general (hate crime), but it is motivated by the venereal desire of sexual violent crimes.

2102 In the United States, following the terrorist attacks of September 11, 2001, a wave of "backlash" crimes occurred against Muslims. Included among the victims were Sikhs, Hindus, and Latinos because the offenders thought they were Muslim. ("We are not the Enemy: Hate Crimes Against Arabs, Muslims, and Those Perceived to be Arab or Muslim after September 11", Human Rights Watch, November 2002, p. 33; OSCE/ODIHR, Hate Crime Laws: A Practical Guide, 2009, p. 50.

2103 OSCE/ODIHR, Hate Crime Laws: A Practical Guide, 2009, p. 48.

characteristic or because of his or her perceived membership in a minority group[2104]. This is a valid wording in order to capture all hate crimes.

1.10.2.10. Conclusion

If a hate crime law requires the victim to actually be a member of the protected group, the hate crime law will not capture the categories of crimes mentioned above. A hate crime law must be drafted in terms of the offender's motives and, most important according to the social importance which a hate crime has in the outside world. As described, hate crimes are characterized by objective criteria, which describe the behavior of the perpetrators. The social significance which this behavior has for the uninvolved public is the crucial fact; irrelevant therefore is a victim's actual status. Failure to include all categories of victims would weaken the value of a hate crime law and undermine effective enforcement. Therefore, hate crime laws should also penalize those who attack others on the basis of their perceived legally protected characteristic of the victim.

In some crimes, the very nature of the attack shows that it was motivated by bias. In other cases, the bias motive is less immediately apparent and will require further investigation. This further investigation, however, is no reason to argument against the legal hate crime concept. In every crime the prosecutor must investigate the motive and the circumstances of the crime. According to the objective evidence of the common hate crime committal the identification of a motive rarely is as simple as it can be during a hate crime investigation. Moreover, it is common practice in German law that the aggravations of laws are formulated in the specific section because of certain intentions of the perpetrator[2105]. The intention to cause an accident; to enrich oneself; or to harm the other is a subjective inner driving momentum of the perpetrator, which verifiability is compelling for punishability[2106]. Any so implied difficulties of proof did not keep the legislator from once establishing these aggravating statutes, nor do they hinder an effective implementation of such. Even according the murder subjective characteristics - that unlike hate crime characteristics are even partly vague ("base motives") - , the Federal Constitutional Court has no objections in terms of their legitimacy to justify punishment[2107]. Also in literature it is assumed that the socio-ethical attitude of an offender can be objectified[2108] and an attitude which shows a

---

2104 Even if the offender was mistaken about the victim´s membership in a certain group, the offense is still a bias crime because the offender was motivated by bias against the group. (View "Note" of the official federal guidelines of determining a Hate Crime in the USA. (Hate Crime Data Collection Guidelines of the Federal Bureau of Investigation, revised October 1999, p. 2).

2105 An enhancement of penalty is imposed, if the perpetrator of physical assault (Section 223 Penal Code) intentionally or knowingly causes certain consequences by his act (Section 226, Paragraph 2 Penal Code). Also refer to: Section 244, Paragraph 1, No. 1 b Penal Code; Section 250, Paragraph 1, No. 1 b Penal Code; Section 90, Paragraph 3, Variant 2 Penal Code; Section 90 a, Paragraph 3 Penal Code.

2106 View hereto - however of opposing opinion: Seehafer, Strafrechtliche Reaktionen, 2003, p. 74.

2107 BVerfGE 54, 100, 112; BVerfGE 45, 187, 262 et seqq., 269.

2108 Otto, ZStW 83, 1971, pp. 39, 44, 45.

misconception of values is clearly perceptible and possible to be determined[2109].

Especially for hate crimes, due to the difficulty that the criminality depends partly on the inner attitude of the offender and a judge therefore is faced with the task of determining a state of mind of the perpetrator, there are clear external circumstances which enable a conclusion towards the inner driving force of an offender[2110]. Therefore, the legislator and the following casuistic would have to provide precepts that describe the kind of evidence that can be used to establish the bias motive and possibly impose restrictions.

2. Further Possibilities of Explicit Implementation of Hate Crime Legislation

2.1. Aggravated Statute

A further possibility to establish aggravating hate crime legislation for certain previously established offenses in accordance with the German dogmatic is to enact aggravating statutes, which refer to a respective base law, i.e. the statute which addresses the counterpart crime. A new penalty frame is imposed for an act by final legislative determination due to adding altering facts towards an already existing law[2111]. If one of the cases which are determined in the aggravating norm comes about, the judge must impose the altered sentence[2112]; therefore the judge has no choice between applying and not applying the modified case law (so-named criminal cause for change)[2113]. This alteration can either change the character of the offence from a misdemeanor to a crime[2114], or just generally shift the penalty frame[2115]. An aggravating statute refers to the modified amount of wrong in comparison to the respective base offense, or to the changed culpability[2116]; however, an aggravation statute enhances the contentual demerit of an act which is already made criminal in a previous law. In the current law aggravating statutes are usually applicable in cases of serious crime effects[2117]. Accordingly, if an offender commits, for instance, physical assault, deprivation of liberty, or an arson crime and he thereby causes the death or recklessly causes the death

2109 Schmidhäuser, Gesinnungsmerkmale 1979, p. 115.
2110 View hereto: FBI-guidelines for outer signs of the presence of an inner hate crime motivation in footnote 1249 of this work.
2111 Sections 224, 244, 250, 260, 315 Paragraph 2 Penal Code.
2112 BGHSt 32, 332 et seqq.
2113 Stree/Kinzig, in: Schönke/ Schröder, StGB, Vorbem. §§ 38 et seqq. marginal no. 43.
2114 Sections 226; 315, Paragraph 2 Penal Code.
2115 Section 244, Paragraph 1, No. 1-3 Penal Code.
2116 Moreover both may coincide. (Stree/Kinzig, in: Schönke/ Schröder, StGB, Vorbem. §§ 38 et seqq. marginal no. 42a).
2117 Sections 176a, Paragraph 1, No. 3, Variant 1 and Variant 2; 176 b; 178; 221, Paragraph 3; 221, Paragraph 2, No. 2; 225, Paragraph 3, No. 2; 226, Paragraph 1, No.1-3; 227, Paragraph 1; 231, Paragraph 1; 235, Paragraph 4, No. 1, Variant 3; 235, Paragraph 5; 236, Paragraph 4, No. 2; 239, Paragraph3 No.2 and Paragraph 4; 239a, Paragraph3; 239b, Paragraph2 in conjunction with 239a, Paragraph 3; 251; 250, Paragraph 2, No. 3a; 306b, Paragraph 1; 306c; 307, Paragraph 3; 308, Paragraph 2; 309, Paragraph 2 and Paragraph 3; 309, Paragraph 3; 312, Paragraph 3 and Paragraph 4; 314, Paragraph 2 in conjunction with 308, Paragraph 3; 314, Paragraph 2 in conjunction with 308, Paragraph 2; 315, Paragraph 3, No. 2; 316a, Paragraph 3; 316c, Paragraph 3; 318, Paragraph 3 and Paragraph 4; 330, Paragraph 2, No. 1 and No. 2; 330a, Paragraph 2 Penal Code.

of the victim, the legislator obeys a minimum punishment which a court must not undercut[2118]. Also the specific way of committing a crime may enhance the penalty due to the modified content of wrong in an act; Section 224 Penal Code which refers to the base offense of physical assault in Section 223 Penal Code enhances the penalty if causing bodily harm to others by dangerous means, for instance, if the offender uses a weapon or other dangerous instrument; acts jointly with another; or uses methods that pose danger to life. However, these aggravating statutes mostly refer to external facts, whereas with hate crimes the inner motive enhances the wrong of an offense[2119]. The content of wrong of an act is determined according to its unworthiness of act and its disvalue of the result[2120]. The increase of wrong in a hate crime is based on the fact that the motive of the offender leading him to commit the crime causes a different, far worse result than it would, being committed without the specific hate or biased motive. According to the underlying understanding of hate crime, originally based on American findings[2121], hate crimes present a criminal behavior, which wrongfulness is relatively upgraded to all otherwise motivated criminal behavior. hate crimes contain a larger content of wrong compared to ordinary crimes because such do not just attack the physical integrity of the attacked victim but violate further legal goods[2122]. There is a considerable increase in the threatening of the event when the victim is confronted with an offender who is recognizable driven from xenophobic motives[2123]. Moreover it is to refer to the expressive dimension of hate crimes[2124]. Therefore, the individual attacked victim is degraded to a despicable creature who's right to exist, based on his affiliation, is deprived[2125]; the special dimension of the disvalue of the result can be already considered to lay in the fact that the victim is not victimized accidentally, but simply sees himself provided with the special humiliation that he was under attack because he is the way he is[2126]. Humans are harmed in representative of an entire part

2118 "imprisonment of not less than three years" in Section 227, Paragraph 1, and in Section 239, Paragraph 4 Penal Code; "imprisonment [...] not less than ten years" in Section 306 c Penal Code. In case of hate crime connected to arson it must be kept in mind that the perpetrators, however not recklessly cause a victims death, but intentionally aims at such. (BGH NStZ-RR 1996, 35; BGH NStZ 1994, 584).

2119 If one assumes that Section 211 Penal Code is an own form of crime as the judiciary does, i.e. not just constituting aggravating fact of Section 212 Penal Code, the following does not refer to Section 211 Penal Code. The main opinion in literature views Section 211 Penal Code as an aggravating statute referring to Section 212 Penal Code. With regard to the opinion held by the prevailing literature, Section 211, Paragraph 2, first and third group Penal Code examplifies in an unique manner of how inner subjective motives are capable of changing the content of wrong in relative to the base offense. However, Section 211 Penal Code is an exception in the overall dogmatics of the German Penal Code. View hereto: Chapter 4, D., 1. Judicial Recognition of Bias-Motivation in Homicide.

2120 Wessels/Beulke, Strafrecht AT, p. 45, p. 149, recital 401.

2121 View hereto Chapter 4, G., 1.1.1. Human Dignity of the Immediate Victim.

2122 View hereto: Chapter 4, G., 1.1. Possible Goods protected by a Hate Crime Law.

2123 Hörnle, Grob anstößiges Verhalten, 1999, p. 272; Seehafer, Strafrechtliche Reaktionen, p. 68.

2124 Hate crimes are message crimes, "because they do not only severely traumatize the immediate victim, but send damage - signals also to by - victims, friends, family members, to the victims group (the hated minority), to the by-victims groups (other hated minorities), to the state of law and to the pluralistic society." (Schneider, Hass- und Vorurteilskriminalität in: Grafl/Medigovic, (eds.): Festschrift für Manfred Burgstaller, 2004, pp. 553-568, p. 555).

2125 Hörnle, Tatproportionale Strafzumessung, p. 272.

2126 Tolmein, ZRP 2001, pp. 315, 316.

of society[2127] and the attack at all is committed in order to stir up anxiety to excite the public[2128] and to spread fear and terror among the addressed[2129]. While therefore a hate crime reaches further legal goods not just such highly personal interests of the individually attacked, the motive of attack as such directly leads to an increased wrong, which proves the need to consider hate crime as an own, i.e. different, crime category[2130]. The fact of attacking a human being solely because of assigning him certain features that one hates or dismisses, not just proves one´s despicable character, but attributes a special dimension of wrong to this kind of behavior[2131]. So it is dogmatically well justified to implement several aggravating statutes to especially violent crime offenses, which enhance the penalty for the killing; or the physical attack; and the further, in case the offender committed the crime due to his racial, religious, ethnic, national, etc. biased and hateful motive. One must not forget about criminal property damages[2132]. This would lead to quite a few more norms which would have to be organized in the special part of the German Penal Code.

In favor of the enactment of aggravating statutes, in order to address hate crimes by codified penal law in this mentioned manner, are the facts that hate crime laws in the main describe factual features which have already been described by existing norms. Likewise, hate crimes are also directed against legal goods of highly personal interests that are already in parts protected by these other laws. A norm now enhancing the penalty for the same already punished act is to be considered in accordance with the German legal dogmatic as an aggravation statute. Once the existence of a bias motive is proven, further judicial assessment according the baseness would not need to be exercised; since it would be taken into account generally due to the law that demands that hate crimes are a different type of crime than the underlying base offense with an increased content of wrong- and guilt. A judgment about the degree of wrong or culpability according a hate crime must not be failed in the particular case, since it is neither a matter of the particular personality of a concrete offender, nor a matter of the concrete situation of attack, but a matter of this sort of crime in general, which *always* constitutes an increased wrong and an *always* increased guilt of the respective offender who commits the

2127 LG Potsdam, 26.5.2000, 26 Ns 29/00.

2128 This again refers to the violation of further "legal goods", independent of such harmed personal goods of the attacked victim. (View hereto: Chapter 4, G., 1.5. Legitimacy of a Hate Crime norm in Regard to the Protected Partial Aspect of Public Peace). Moreover, in the long term, hate crimes are able to destroy the reputation of the FRG, which in turn has a negative impact on foreign affairs and external economical issues. (BGH ZRP 2001, 1359, 1363; Seehafer, Strafrechtliche Reaktionen, 2003, p. 70; "Such [...] committed horrifying acts of violence against foreigners harm [...] also the international reputation of the FRG." (BR-Drs. 564/00; attachment p. 1).

2129 BGH NStZ 1994, 584.

2130 Schneider, Internationales Handbuch der Kriminologie, Bd. 2, p. 326

2131 Because of the motives, which are based on the depriving the victim, the offender of a hate crime subjectively realizes a higher degree of wrong. (Seehafer, Strafrechtliche Reaktionen, p. 69).

2132 Whereas "loss of vandalism is insurable, and if not insured, is suffered in terms of time and money or both, if that vandalism is bias-motivated, the defacement might take the form of swastikas on the home of a Jewish family or racist graffiti on the home of an African – American family. The harm here is not a mere nuisance." (Lawrence, Punishing Hate, p. 61).

crime. Therefore, a hate crime would not be left to be a part of the individual judicial evaluation process. The uniformity of applying the law, in case of a hateful biased motive revealing itself in a criminal form, would be secured. The downside is, whenever it turns out in retrospect that the motive did not exist, a miscarriage of justice would be the result. However, this ultimately does not weigh against the legitimate use of this technique to incorporate hate crime in the German Penal Code; after all, the following of correct litigation practices must be assumed.

2.2. Implementation of Aggravated Exemplified Rules

The legislature could further restrict the range of judicial discretion by adding an aggravating case to the basic type of an offense instead of enacting a new substantive norm[2133].

The legislator constricts the width of the judicial discretionary power by adding aggravating (or privileging) cases to an offence on various occasions[2134]. These are circumstances which would usually have a role in the process of determining the correct sentence through the judge[2135]. The determination of aggravating or privileging cases by statutory law occurs in the following legal mode: A law illustrates the most important cases when to alter a sentence, but the provided listing is not intended to be complete. The listed possibilities constitute rules for determining the sentence, but they do not change the statement of facts. If the precepts of an exemplified case are fulfilled the sentence shall be imposed in accordance with the relevant altered sentence frame. However, with the ruling example technique the judge is able to verdict in compliance with an exemplified case though he does not have to. The indicative effect of the circumstances determined in such a section can be compensated by mitigating circumstances. According to this dogmatical manner the legislator could implement rules stating that "an enhanced penalty usually[2136] is to impose if the offender acts out of bias against a person or group because of his race, religion, ethnic, nationality, disability, homelessness" in the special part of the German Penal Code. Such pieces of legislation would have to be incorporated into the relevant base offense in order to have the effect of an "especial severe case", which leads to the imposition of an enhanced penalty. This method of constituting a penal enhancement for certain severe cases of already otherwise punished behavior is a common way used in the German Penal Code to adjust the penalty to a modified content of wrong of a behavior. Increased harmful effects and dangerous ways of committal are objective criteria which enhance the penalty compared to the respective base offense. However, also subjective criteria are valued legitimatle in order to change the penalty, for instance, "[a]n especially

2133 Stree/Kinzig, in: Schönke/Schröder, StGB, Vorbem. §§ 38, marginal no. 42a.
2134 Penal-aggravating and -mitigation reasons.
2135 Stree/Kinzig, in: Schönke/ Schröder, StGB, Vorbem. §§ 38 et seqq. marginal no. 52.
2136 Translation of "in der Regel" - "as a rule".

serious case typically occurs if the offender acts by reason of gross self-seeking"[2137]; or "acts for the reason of profit-seeking"[2138].

In favor of the implementation of an especially serious case connected to several respective offenses established in the special part of the Penal Code in case that the offense is a hate crime weighs the fact, that a broad legislative recognition of hate crimes by the German Penal Code would take place due to applying this method. It would be made clear that the motive as a fact is valid to enhance the penalty compared to otherwise motivated acts. It would be legally determined that such offenses "usually" realize a greater wrong and the court at trial would at least be conducted by the legislature of how to punish such a crime.

The important fact that a judge must not apply the aggravating rule, he only may; weighs against such a technique; if the overall cause of event leads him to the decision that other mitigating facts outweigh the hate crime motive, he must not punish an offender according to the hate crime ruling example. Thus, the aggravating hate crime rule could be undermined by other so called privileging-facts which surround the crime scene. This circumvention possibility leads to a precarious legal practice in general[2139] and enables the possibility to ultimately not punish a biased or hateful motivated crime as a hate crime. It is important to consider that the classification of an aggravated or privileged case does not have to be quoted in a judgment[2140]. Within this manner the review of an aggravated or privileged case by the next higher court takes place only considering whether the reason stated to confirm the delivered judgment make sense at all. A verdict is only repealed if it lacks to provide essential facts or considerations which led to the judgment in its entirety, i.e. lacks justification[2141]. The appeal court therefore eventually would not object to the non-application of the hate crime ruling. This is a huge deficit in case of deciding for the use of this technique in order to address hate crimes by law. Opposed hereto, the implementation of such aggravating statutes would state a clear penalty frame, which must be applied by a court, and they also would make sure that the offender knows that he is accused of a hate crime and not of, for e.g., physical assault[2142].

A legal ruling based on the lack of a compelling need for criminal enhancement should be avoided to address hate crimes. The method of exemplified rules must resign against the possibility of implementing aggravating statutes, because of its observed counter-productivity according the here pursued goal of an assured, uniform, aggravating consideration of

2137 Section 264, Paragraph 2, No. 1, Variant 1 Penal Code.
2138 Sections 283a, sentence 2, No.1 Penal Code; Section 283d, Paragraph 3, sentence 2 No. 1 Penal Code; Section 330, Paragraph 1, sentence 2, No. 4 Penal Code.
2139 Seehafer, Strafrechtliche Reaktionen, p. 82; Callies, NJW 1998; pp. 929, 932.
2140 Stree/Kinzig, in: Schönke/ Schröder, StGB, Vorbem. §§ 38 et seqq. marginal no. 50
2141 Stree/Kinzig, in: Schönke/Schröder, StGB, § 46 marginal no. 65.
2142 Seehafer, Strafrechtliche Reaktionen, p. 82.

such base motives in the entire criminal procedure, which must have an impact on the level of criminal punishment[2143].

2.3. The Enactment of a Rule for Judicial Penalty Assessment

In order to capture the increased culpability[2144] of hate crimes it is suggested to implement a rule in Section 46 Penal Code which states that a consideration shall particularly be given to "particularly inhumane, racist or xenophobic" motives[2145]. The idea behind implementing an express wording into Section 46 Penal Code, which states states "the need of a penalty-increasing consideration of hate crime motives", is that the court´s attention would be led to an increased knowledge and correct handling[2146]. However, this refers to the function of a legal establishment and not to its dogmatical legitimacy[2147]. Speaking of dogmatic:

2.3.1. Scope of Culpability that Could be Addressed by such a Regulation Technique

The culpability which is addressed in Section 46 Penal Code refers to the individual realized culpability only, not to the culpability which stands in conjunction to the committed wrong (which is the culpability, which reasons a penalty)[2148]. This reveals that if a hate crime constitutes a different type of wrong, the penalty frames of ordinary offenses are not made to capture the changed culpability of a hate crime offender, since they were composed for the

---

2143 The same finding refers to the similar dogmatical way of enhancing penalties by simply changing the frame of penalty withhout changing the facts of the base offense. This applies by enacting neutral elements that require judicial filling in in order to determine when to refer to the milder and when to the more severe penalty frame. Within this manner it is the way choice of the judge to decide on which circumstances surrounding the act he lays his focus, and therefore it is for him to decide, in which conditions he views the offense to constitute an aggravating case. His position therefore is no other, than if the legislator would simply enhance the sentence frame of the base offence. (Difference between named and unnamed cases (Transl. "benannte und benannte Fälle"; Stree/Kinzig, in: Schönke/ Schröder, StGB, Vorbem. §§ 38 et seqq. marginal no. 46).

2144 The lack of a victim-offender relationship; the fact that the victim has not only given no relevant reason, but no cause for the offender's attack; and, moreover, became victimized because of an unchangabel feature and everyone who carries this feature is interchangeable with any other person who - in the view of the attacker - carries this certain feature which triggered the attack, reveals an overall threat to the population; and, furthermore, the objectified use of people as a tool to implement one´s own unconstitutional, antidemocratic thoughts into reality proves a significant disvalue of the act of a hate crime. Further, the thereon based dimension of will when committing such an offense, increases the culpability which reasons penalty. (View hereto: Chapter 4, G., 1.6. Hate Crimes and "Worthiness of Punishment").

2145 For instance, view BR-Drs. 458/08; for detailed illustration and the manner of how this rule is intended to work, view Chapter 4, C. 3. Draft bill of Mecklenburg-Vorpommern Drs. 759/00, dated November 16, 2000, et seq. of Chapter C.

2146 BT-Drs. 759/00, p. 4, view Chapter 4, C. 3. Draft bill of Mecklenburg-Vorpommern Drs. 759/00, dated November 16, 2000,

2147 The positive about such an implemented wording into Section 46 Penal Code stating "the need of a penalty-increasing consideration of hate crime motives" is that the courts attention would be led to an increased knowledge and correct handling; however, this refers to the function of a legal establishment and not to its dogmatic legitimacy. (View Chapter 4, C., 8. Symbolic Reasoning of Hate Crime Law).

2148 Today, it is agreed that the culpability, which reasons a penalty is not identical to the culpability, which is relevant in the individual case. (Stree/Kinzig, in: Schönke/Schröder, StGB, § 46 marginal no. 9a; Lackner/Kühl, StGB, § 46, marginal no. 23; Schäfer, Strafzumessung, marginal no. 226; Roxin, Strafrecht AT I, § 19, marginal no. 50 et seq.).

wrong which is caused by an unmotivated or otherwise motivated behavior[2149]. A court, however, has the competence to only emanate from the "unmodified" culpability, which reasons a penalty in order to adjust the culpability, which is relevant in the individual case. Therefore, if a ruling of hate crimes takes place only in Section 46 Penal Code, it must be assumed that the culpability, which reasons a penalty, is the same in a hate crime as it is in the ordinary crime, this assumption, however, is not followed, since it is agreed that hate crimes modify the wrong of an act, to which the culpability is connected.

2.3.2. Legislator's Duty of Providing the Abstract Penal Frame in Regard to the Type of Crime

It derives from the principle of culpability that the legislator must fix the minimum and maximum punishment so that the possible debt levels of a type of crime can be met[2150]. Insofar, facts and legal consequences must be coordinated[2151]. The substantial importance of all sentence altering aspects are the same, whether they are taken into account by the legislator to enact a modification of the sentence frame of the base offence or by the judge in order to impose the concrete sentence. It is always either degrees of wrong or of culpability which must be detected, and none is to be considered by either the judge or the legislator only[2152]. However, the legislature is more independent and separate from the individual case and from the personality of the defendant, freed of personal opinions the legislature is most able to imply abstract regulations, which is why the legislator must set the frame for punishment. Therefore, whenever it comes to crucial, fundamental facts of high priority, at least the frame concerning the specific type of offense must be set by an abstract, independent, impartial legislator, since decisions of an individual differ from case to case. It constitutes a lack of legal regulatory burdening the court with the decision of adjucating the extent of the general wrong and the overall debt of a hate crime in general, i.e., unrelated to the particular act in question. Without setting up the frame of penalty (providing the maximum- and the minimum limit and therewith serving the points for orientation within sentencing[2153]) a consistent legal practice in relation to acts that are motivated by a hate crime motive seems rarely possible.

Since hate crimes are currently considered to be punished by a pure judicial arbitrary decision, based on the penalty frame which is served for the parallel offense, even though they constitute a different crime type[2154], it is revealed that even a correct consideration of the motive by a court would possibly not meet the overall increased dimension of wrong of such crimes; moreover the question regarding the general degree of punishment, which the offenders of

2149 View hereto: Chapter 4, G., 1.7.1.4. a) Hate Crime Motives: Part of the Wrong or the Culpability of an Offense.
2150 Stree/Kinzig, in: Schönke/Schröder, StGB, Vorbem. §§ 38, marginal no. 25.
2151 Stree/Kinzig, in: Schönke/Schröder, StGB, Vorbem. §§ 38, marginal no. 25.
2152 Stree/Kinzig, in: Schönke/ Schröder, StGB, Vorbem. §§ 38 et seqq. marginal no. 52.
2153 Stree/Kinzig, in: Schönke/ Schröder, StGB, Vorbem. §§ 38 et seqq. marginal no. 42.
2154 View Chapter 4, G., 1., 1.1. Possible Goods protected by a Hate Crime Law, especially at marginal no. 433.

this different type of crime deserve, would not be answered by such an insertion into Section 46 Penal Code.

2.3.3. Hate Crime Enhancement - a Decision of a Court drawn in Equity and Good Conscience

The current handling does not serve any verifiability, nor can be assured that the punishment imposed on a hate crime offender is increased in comparison to the punishment of an offender who committed a parallel crime[2155]. A literal reference to hate crime in Section 46 Penal Code would not provide any regulatory content and it would not lead to a culpability appropriate punishment of hate crimes.

An amendment of Section 46 Penal Code is not a true penal enhancement due to the dogmatics of this norm[2156]. The enhancement of punishment in accordance with the culpability of the offender remains to be an individual decision of a court drawn in equity and good conscience, thus such brings all the intricacies personal decisions bring[2157]. Whether explicitly stated or not, it will still be up to the consciousness of a judge to value the hate motive as an aggravated fact. Moreover, the possibility to verify the just imposition of sentence through a higher court is restricted[2158]. Furthermore, due to the suggested insertion, it remains unclear to what dimension such an aggravation must lead in order to meet the increased wrong and the increased culpability of an offender who committed a hate crime. The need to determine a penalty frame cannot be fulfilled through the legislator by reference to the penalty frame of another category of offenses.

2.3.4. Hate Crime Motives are to be Differentiated from Such Exemplarily Named in Section 46 Penal Code

Hate crime motives are not on the same level as the other facts which are named in Section 46 Penal Code for assessing the penalty; thus they may not be inclined in this overall assessment process[2159]. They are a part of the abstract determination of the unworthiness of the overall crime, which is increased und not accessible to balancing. Especially this unworthiness cannot be outweighed by such mitigating facts stated in Section 46, Paragraph 2 Penal Code which are, for e.g., other motives and aims of the offender; the degree of the violation of the offenders duties; the offenders prior history, his personal and financial circumstances; etc. In contrary, once the new base

---

2155 View Chapter 4, D., 2. Judicial Recognition of Bias-Motivation Apart from Homicide; and 3. Hate Crime in the Light of Section 46 Penal Code.

2156 Chapter 4, D., 3. Hate Crime in the Light of Section 46 Penal Code.

2157 Bruns StrZR 87 et seqq.

2158 According to Section 267, Paragraph 3, Sentence 1 Code of Criminal Procedure only such facts must be stated in a verdict which were decisive for the imposed penalty. Therefore, a verdict can be reviewed considering the misuse of discretionary power, but not according to justness. (BGH VRS 21, 54; Zipf, Strafmaßrevision, pp. 164 et seqq.).

2159 For the reason why such must not be inclined in the judicial evaluation process of Section 46 Penal Code view the explanation provided in Chapter 4, G., 1.7.1.4. b) Culpability addressed in Section 46 Penal Code and the Influence of the Bias Motive.

offense to penalize a hate crime is set, all these facts are to be considered, but by drawing from a modified, thus enhanced, sentence frame which captures the increased wrong and the enhanced culpability of a hate crime as a base, from which the evaluation process of Section 46 Penal Code may start off[2160].

2.4. Implementation of an Extra Rule in the General Part of the Penal Code

The enactment of an extra rule, organized in the general part of the Penal Code, which mandatorily rules that hate crime motives are to be acknowledged as penalty-increasing facts of the committal of any crime determined in the following special part of the Code, is a further possibility to implement a new hate crime norm[2161]. Such a compelling and binding arrangement, which refers to the court at trial and which implies that the penalty - in case the respective crime determined in the special part of the Penal Code turns out to be a hate crime - must be increased, would be a new dogmatical way of restricting the decisional scope of a court. This way of addressing the court to consider hate crime motives as aggravating facts - independent from such in Section 46 Penal Code stated mitigating facts - seems promising to lead to an indeed aggravating consideration of hateful motives in the verdict. Each court would have to clearify in every trial, concerning every offender, if such motives played a role during the prosecution process. The insertion of an additional section, apart from Section 46 Penal Code, would legally determine that the possibility of assessing these motives, in the form of mitigating them through other circumstances which surrounded the crime, is not provided. A mutual interaction between this new section and Section 46 Penal Code could be established by referring to Section 46 Penal Code when it comes to the act. The focus would not solely be laid on the offender, but from such back to the act and its criminal content[2162]. This scheme would meet several points: not just the culpability, which is relevant in the individual case, would be addressed, but also the culpability, which reasons a penalty, would be captured due to the perspective drawn towards the act and its constituting wrong. Thereby a general penalty enhancement of hateful and biased motivated acts, based on their overall higher demerit of the result and the act, and correspondingly, the increased wrong and the integral culpability could be legally embraced.

Furthermore, it is suggested to draw a connection between a hate crime norm and the Criminal Procedure Law. This could be achieved by the fact that the effects of a substantive law directly reflects on the procedural side of the law due to the fact that a judge must comply to certain handling operations. This would be a legal mechanism, which, however, in the previous law, i.e., in the

2160 For the reason why hate crime motives are not on the same level, therefore unable to be included in the overall assessment procedure of the court view Chapter 4, Chapter 4, G., 1.7.1.4. c) Hate Crime Motives are Different; and Chapter 4., G., 2.3.4. Hate Crime motives are to be differentiated from such exemplarily named in Section 46 Penal Code.

2161 Idea based on the concept of Tolmein, ZRP, 2001, pp. 315 et seqq.

2162 Seehafer, Strafrechtliche Reaktionen, p. 101; Tolmein, ZRP 2001, p. 315.

current design of the law, is not represented. For this purpose, the attention is drawn to Section 267, Paragraph 3, Sentence 1 Code of Criminal Procedure which stipulates that " [t]he criminal judgment shall further specify in its reasons the penal norm which was applied and shall set out the circumstances which were decisive in assessing the penalty."

It is suggested that, regardless of whether the motives for determining the punishment according to the respective court´s opinion have been "decisive" for the purpose of "assesing the penalty" or not, they must - once they played a role in the legal process and are considered to have been existent at the time of committing the offense - be stated in the operative part of the judgment. For instance, in case the victim was physically attacked because of the offender´s hateful bias against a legally protected characteristic and due to the attack lost his sight in one eye (Section 226 Penal Code), the verdict would not be allowed to read as follows: "The defendant is condemned to three years in prison for aggravated assault according to Section 226, Paragraph 1, No. 1; Paragraph 2 Penal Code", but it would have to be quoted as follows: "The defendant is condemned to three years in prison for aggravated assault because of hateful bias against the [exemplarily:] religion of the victim according to Section 226, Paragraph 1, No. 1; Paragraph 2 Penal Code". A circumvention or a non-examination of the existence of such motives would be more difficult, because as soon as they are mentioned at any point in the legal process, or cited by witnesses, the existence or non-existence would have to be examined concretely.

Moreover, this would lead to a changed rule-exception-relation, which complicates a disregard of the motives during a judge's sentencing process, due to the following fact: A judicial reasoning effort would not *only* be required in the verdict in case the penalty is increased due to the existence of the respective motive in accordance to Section 267, Paragraph 3, Sentence 1 Code of Criminal Procedure; 46 Penal Code, but it would rather afford a considerable justification effort to reason why - despite the existence of such hateful bias motives - the penalty was *not* increased[2163]. The citation of further mitigating facts and circumstances, established in Section 46 Penal Code, would - according to this opinion - not be enough to neutralize a corresponding

2163 In the main, this regulation corresponds to the stipulation set in Section 267, Paragraph 3, Sentence 3 Code of Criminal Procedure, according to which, in the case of legally determined aggravated exemplified rules, "[t]he judgment shall also indicate the reasons why a particularly serious case is deemed not to exist when the prerequisites generally applying to such a case pursuant to the penal norm are fulfilled". The implementation of a rule in the General Part of the Penal Code to encompass hate crimes could rule that the judgment must indicate in its reasoning why an aggravating penalty is not imposed if the existence of a hateful bias motive is fulfilled. This includes two necessary steps: as soon as the respective motive plays a role at trial, a courts must examine the existence of such motives. The outcome of this examination regarding the involvement of bias motives for crime committal would have to be noted and moreover it must be justified in the reasoning of the court. Even more extensively, one could consider whether the content of the regulation of Section 267, Paragraph 3, Sentence 2, Alternative 2 Code of Criminal Procedure is to be applied mutatis mutandis in particular to hate crimes, with the result that the reasons for the judgment must indicate why the initial during trial discussed existence of a hateful bias motive could not be proved; even though the presecutor of the victim filed for a hate crime in the first place during the hearings. After all, a way to enshrine a once in trial discussed hate crime motive in the reasoning of the court must be found.

hate crime motive with the result of not increasing the penalty. As a result, the scope of unverifiable discretionary power of a judge in the context of sentencing hate crimes would be significantly limited.

A further considerable fact of an implementation of the represented exemplary legal solution is that in the case of a persistent hate crime perpetrator, subsequent courts - in case of indications or the supposed total lack of a motive - could investigate in the direction of hate crime, thus examine whether the respective crime possibly constitutes a hate crime. This applies due to the fact that a hate crime, if mandatorily noted in the verdict, becomes part of the criminal record of the respective perpetrator.

3. Final decision

In summary, the culpability and the wrong of hate crimes are higher than such of the respective parallel crime[2164]. A blanket-penalty-enhancement for hate crimes can be justified from general positive aspects: The actions are designed to address a multitude of victims and intimidate the society at large[2165]. This must become a feature of the sentence.

The communicative significance of the condemnation of wrong is different from such which arises from the condemnation of culpability[2166], because the disvalue-judgment of wrong is directed not only to the perpetrator, but also to the victim. With the condemnation through a verdict, the victim is confirmed that he has been wronged and that he was not obliged to tolerate or accept the behavior of the offender[2167], and that the society does not agree with the mindset of the offender.

An express inclusion in Section 46 Penal Code is redundant since hate crime motives *can* be considered as an aggravating factor during sentencing already. What is missing is a legal mechanism that these particular motives *actually are* considered as aggravating facts beyond doubt, in each respective case. The enactment of a substantive criminal offense seems constitutionally problematic because of the required width of the penal frame which is constituted to capture various offenses with a distinct content of wrong. The addressee of such a norm could not precisely foresee the legal consequences which result from his behavior (Article 1 Basic Law, Section 1 Penal Law). Moreover, this penal law encompasses those behavioral acts which have already been addressed by other norms, with the aim of appreciating the additional violation of legal goods and correspondingly increase the imposed penalty.

2164 View Chapter 4, G., 1.7.1.4. a) Hate Crime Motives: Part of the Wrong or the Culpability of an Offense; View Chapter 4, G., 1.1. Possible Goods protected by a Hate Crime Law; Chapter 4, G., 1.6 Hate Crimes and "Worthiness of Punishment" .

2165 BR-Drs. 759/00, p.4.

2166 Hörnle, Das Unwerturteil und der Schuldvorwurf, in: Hefendehl (ed.), Empirische und dogmatische Fundamente, pp. 105 – 134, (105 et seqq.).

2167 Hörnle, Das Unwerturteil und der Schuldvorwurf, in: Hefendehl (ed.), Empirische und dogmatische Fundamente, pp. 105 – 134 (109).

This purpose can be fulfilled likewise in a better way at the appropriate place. While the increased wrong that is established by a hate crime, due to the particular way of committal, is already partially covered by the current law, the violation of additional legal goods and the generally increased wrong, and the always increased culpability is not considered by the current law and therefore reasons the enactment of aggravating statutes. Whereas aggravating exemplified rules comply to this purpose only insufficiently - and due to the general uncertainty which is associated with regard to their application[2168] - the enactment of aggravating statutes is the best dogmatic tool to capture an until yet legally unrecognized criminal content of hate crimes[2169].

4. Summarizing Aspects

What should be achieved by the implementation of a new regulation in the German Penal Code:

- A hate crime must, in any case, be prosecuted due to public interest[2170].
- Hate crime motives must not be a part of the general penalty assessment process because in no case may they be outweighed by so considered otherwise mitigating facts[2171].
- The hateful or biased motive must always be taken into account when prosecuting an offense[2172].
- The evidence that a hateful and biased motive led to the committal of crime must in any case lead to an enhanced penalty in comparison to the penalty imposed for the base offense.
- The conviction of a hate crime must become part of the record.

2168 The adoption of a particularly serious case occurs only, but "not always in the presence of aggravating ruling example." (Callies, NJW 1998, 929, 930; Seehafer, Strafrechtliche Reaktionen, pp. 82 et seq.; supra note 630; with further references to critical opinions in regard to Article 103 Basic Law.

2169 It is absolutely essential to include changes in the area of juvenile criminal law. The juvenile criminal law in Germany focuses on education, instead of punishment. However, juvenile sentences may at least not be imposed so low that the degree of guilt becomes "trivialized", which was ruled precisely in the area of hate crime committed by juvenile offenders. (BGH NStZ-RR 1996, 120; Seehafer, Strafrechtliche Reaktionen, p. 95). Therefore, it remains incomprehensible why "even severe hate crimes, are called "youthful sins", which are punished with probation without any further restrictions". (Friedman, Toleran, in: Bundeskriminalamt (ed.), Rechtsextremismus, Antisemitismus und Fremdenfeindlichkeit, pp. 15- 24).

2170 Drs. 17/9345, view Chapter 4, C., 6. Draft Bill of the federal Council Drs. 17/9345, dated April 18, 2012.

2171 According to the above findings, it is simply unlawful if - for instance - a court rules during it´s assessment process that the alcohol intake of an offender outweighs his hateful and biased motive with the result that an even lower penalty is imposed on a hate crime offender than it is usually imposed on a sober offender who 'only' commits the respective base offense. That means, the mitigating fact of an offender being drunk while committing a crime leads courts to nullify his hate crime motive, which must be prevented. (For general handlings of the prosecution authorities (puplic prosecutor and court) view: Glet, Sozialkonstruktion und strafrechtliche Verfolgung von Hasskriminalität in Deutschland, 2011, pp. 211 et seqq. (p. 214, case no. 67; p. 215, case no. 81; pp. 219 et seqq. (220)).

2172 This starts with the detection of the police (where the non-inclusion of facing facts that the crime might be a hate crime must lead to a dereliction of official duty); and goes over to the prosecutor, who must include such by the police detected motives in the criminal charge; and ends with the judge who must acknowledge the wrong and culpability increasing features of the act and adjust the imposition of penalty to the respective degree.

German Abstract

Criminal Law dealing with hate crimes - functional comparative law - Germany vs. USA

Die vorliegende Dissertation befasst sich mit einer rechtsvergleichenden Analyse des strafrechtlichen Umgangs mit so genannten „Hate Crimes" in Deutschland und den USA. Der Begriff „Hate Crimes" steht für Delikte, die sich nicht nur durch ein besonderes Tatmotiv, nämlich den Hass auf das Anderssein anderer, auszeichnen, sondern gerade durch ihre veränderte soziale Bedeutung in der Außenwelt. „Hate Crimes" werden nicht nur alleine durch eine vorurteilsbehaftete Tätermotivation bestimmt, sondern sind auch durch objektive Kriterien gekennzeichnet. „Hate Crimes" haben eine über die eigentliche Tat hinausgehende, andere soziale Bedeutung, nicht nur für die unmittelbar angegriffenen Opfer, sondern für das unbeteiligte Publikum und damit für die gesamte Gesellschaft.

Die vorliegende Dissertation möchte einen Beitrag in Bezug auf die aktuelle Diskussion leisten, bei der es um die Frage geht, ob auch in Deutschland die Notwendigkeit besteht, die Begehung von „Hate Crimes" mit Strafe zu bedrohen und ob diese Deliktsform ausdrücklich im Strafgesetzbuch als Straftatbestand verankert werden sollte. Die Dissertation widmet sich dieser Frage allerdings von einem neuen, bisher noch nicht betrachteten Blickwinkel, indem sie im Wege der funktionalen Rechtsvergleichung mögliche Erkenntnismöglichkeiten aus der gegenwärtigen strafrechtlichen Behandlung von „Hate Crimes" in Deutschland und den USA untersucht.

Die Arbeit geht der Frage nach, ob die aktuelle Ausgestaltung des Strafrechts in Deutschland hinreichend geeignet ist, einen Menschen mit rechtlichen Mitteln davon abzuhalten, einen anderen Menschen aufgrund bestimmter Merkmale dieses Menschen, anzugreifen. Sie wählt dabei die Methode der funktionalen Strafrechtsvergleichung als Weg zur Beantwortung der beschriebenen Frage (Kapitel 1). Das Funktionalitätsprinzip basiert auf der Annahme, dass eine Gesellschaft dem Recht Probleme aufgibt, die von der Rechtsordnung der jeweiligen Gesellschaft gelöst werden. Ausgangspunkt der funktionalen Rechtsvergleichung ist das zu untersuchende Sachproblem selbst in Gestalt des tatsächlichen Bestehens in der jeweiligen Gesellschaft. Es ist das konkrete Problem der Vergleichsländer, frei von jeglicher Einbindung in einen rechtlichen Rahmen, zu analysieren. Um eine Rechtsvergleichung vornehmen zu können, muss das konkrete Problem um dessen rechtliche Lösung es geht, im Wesentlichen gleich sein. Stellt man also fest, dass das Problem der Begehung von „Hate Crimes" in Deutschland und den USA zumindest ähnlich ist, ist es Aufgabe der Rechtsvergleichung zu untersuchen, wie das Problem in der fremden im Vergleich zur hiesigen Rechtsordnung gelöst wird. Die funktionale Rechtsvergleichung kann auf diese

Weise für die Frage nach einer rechtspolitischen Notwendigkeit und Legitimation von Änderungen des Strafgesetzbuches zur Bekämpfung von „Hate Crimes“ in Deutschland durch den Blick auf das Vergleichsland - die USA - einen Erkenntnisgewinn bieten. Sie kann zugleich dem U.S.-amerikanischen Leser die Gedanken des deutschen Strafrechts zu der gegenwärtigen Behandlung des Problems in den USA sowie eigene Gedanken der deutschen Rechtswissenschaft und des Gesetzgebers nahe bringen.

Die USA wurden bewusst als Vergleichsland gewählt. Die USA verfügen - als Begründer des Konzepts „Hate Crimes“ - über einen großen Erfahrungsschatz in Bezug auf die Pönalisierung dieser Deliktsform. Die USA muss sich als bewusstes Einwanderungsland seit jeher - wie kein anderes Land - damit auseinandersetzen, das Nebeneinander unterschiedlichster multiethnischer Gruppen zu vereinen. Es verwundert nicht, dass in den USA das Bedürfnis nach einer Bekämpfung von Delikten basierend auf Missachtung oder Verachtung des jeweils anderen als erstes als gesellschaftliches Problem aufkam. Die USA sind historisch dafür bekannt, dass fremdenfeindliche, hassmotivierte Taten ein verbreitetes Phänomen sind. Die Bundesrepublik Deutschland befindet sich ebenso auf dem Weg ein Einwanderungsland und damit eine multikulturelle Gesellschaft zu werden. Die deutsche Geschichte weist ähnliche Beispiele für eine fremdenfeindliche Viktimisierung auf, auch wenn die geschichtlichen Hintergründe jeweils unterschiedlich sein mögen. Auch ein vergleichbarer Zivilisationsgrad sowie die politische Organisation und die Verfassungen beider Länder sprechen für eine Vergleichbarkeit des zu untersuchenden sozialen Problems.

Nachdem die Arbeit die grundsätzliche Vergleichbarkeit des sozialen Problems der Begehung von „Hate Crimes“ in Deutschland und den USA bejaht, stellt sie dar, welche grundsätzlichen rechtlichen Konzepte und rechtlichen Rahmenbedingungen in den USA sowie in Deutschland bestehen und eine theoretische Basis für mögliche Reaktionen auf „Hate Crimes“ bieten. Hierbei wird am Rande auf gesellschaftliche und historische Gegebenheiten eingegangen (Kapitel 2). Nach der Darstellung der Methodik, der politischen Grundsätze und der Rechtssysteme der beiden zu vergleichenden Länder, widmet sich die Arbeit der Darstellung der gegenwärtigen U.S.-amerikanischen Gesetzeslage im Umgang mit „Hate Crimes“ (Kapitel 3). Das Rechtssystem der USA kennt diese Diskussionen seit Jahrzehnten und hat sowohl auf Bundes- als auch auf Landesebene durch die Einführung von Straftatbeständen reagiert. Die „Geburtsstunde“ des in den USA bestehenden Konzepts der „Hate Crime“ Gesetzgebung wird in dem Civil Right Act von 1964 gesehen. Gleichwohl erfolgte die erste namentliche Bezeichnung eines „Hate Crime“ Gesetzes als solches, erst 1990, mit dem in Kraft treten des Hate Crimes Statistic Acts. Die USA beschäftigt die Bewältigung des Problems einer gesetzlichen Normierung des Schutzes gegen „Hate Crimes“ durch die ausdrückliche Erfassung dieser Delikte im Gesetz somit bereits seit mehreren Jahrzehnten. Nicht zuletzt aus diesem Grund stößt man bei der Recherche nach Materialien und Erkenntnissen einer strafrechtrechtlichen Bekämpfung von „Hate Crimes“ in Wissenschaft, Rechtsprechung und legislativen Vorhaben wie auch implementierten Präventionsmaßnahmen der USA auf einen großen Erfahrungsschatz im rechtlichen Umgang mit derartigen Delikten.

Mag auch das gesellschaftliche Problem der Begehung von „Hate Crimes“ in gewisser Weise vergleichbar mit der gesellschaftlichen Situation in den USA sein, die gegenwärtige Gesetzeslage ist es nicht (Kapitel 4). In dem deutschen StGB existiert ein mit der U.S.-amerikanischen Gesetzgebung - unabhängig von den unterschiedlichen Strukturen der Rechtssysteme - vergleichbarer Sondertatbestand zur Erfassung von „Hate Crimes“ gegenwärtig nicht. Diskussionen um die Einführung eines entsprechenden Sondertatbestands gibt es in Deutschland bereits seit dem Anfang des neuen Jahrtausends. Aufgrund des Fehlens eines entsprechenden Rechtssatzes hier zu Lande darf nicht auf einen rechtsfreien Raum für Verhaltensweisen, die als „Hate Crime“ eingestuft werden könnten, geschlossen werden. Die Arbeit untersucht daher, ob die aktuelle deutsche Rechtsordnung das Problem der „Hate Crimes“ nicht mit bereits bestehenden Normen des Strafgesetzbuches hinreichend lösen kann und vielleicht sogar löst.

Die Dissertation plädiert nicht für die Einführung eines entsprechenden Sondertatbestands oder eine härtere Bestrafung von bestimmten vorurteilsorientierten Täterpersönlichkeiten und vorurteilsbestimmten Einstellungen und Werten. Sie untersucht vielmehr die sozialen Auswirkungen derartiger Delikte, wobei auf die Beeinträchtigungen des individuellen Opfers, des speziellen Opferkreises und des pluralistischen Gesamtgefüges eingegangen wird und die Störung des öffentlichen Friedens untersucht wird. Die Arbeit unternimmt dabei den Versuch, die Legitimation und Grenzen der strafrechtlichen Bekämpfung von „Hate Crimes“ zu untersuchen. Hierzu überprüft sie nicht nur, inwieweit die bestehenden Strafgesetze entsprechende Verhaltensweisen bereits hinreichend mit Strafe bedrohen, sondern auch die Frage, dem Schutz welchen Rechtsguts ein derartiger Sondertatbestand dienen würde und ob es für diesen Schutz eine legitime Grundlage gibt. Die Arbeit möchte auf diese Weise einen weiterführenden dogmatischen Beitrag zu der kontrovers diskutierten Frage leisten, ob die gegenwärtige Ausgestaltung des deutschen Strafrechts „Hate Crimes“ in geeignetem Maß sanktionieren kann, oder ob eine Änderung des deutschen Strafgesetzbuches zur Sanktionierung hass- oder vorurteilsmotivierter Delikte erstrebenswert ist.

Die Arbeit ist in englischer Sprache verfasst, um nicht nur dem deutschsprachigen Raum einen Erkenntnisgewinn zu ermöglichen. Sie möchte zugleich dem englischsprachigen Leserkreis das Angebot unterbreiten, von den in Deutschland geführten Diskussionen und dem Umgang mit „Hate Crimes“ zu profitieren. Auf diese Weise bietet die Dissertation nicht nur Lesern beider Jurisdiktionen die Möglichkeit wechselseitig voneinander zu lernen und Erkenntnisse bezüglich des strafrechtlichen Umgangs mit „Hate Crimes“ zu gewinnen, sondern gewährt auch dem gesamten englischsprachigen Ausland einen Einblick in die dogmatischen Gedanken des deutschen Strafrechts zu der Pönalisierung von „Hate Crimes". Die Arbeit löst auf diese Weise die Einbahnstraße einer ausschließlichen Verwertung der U.S.-amerikanischen Erkenntnisinteressen bezüglich „Hate Crimes" in Deutschland auf und bietet durch den englischsprachigen Ansatz einen international verwertbaren Beitrag zu dem strafrechtlichen Umgang mit „Hate Crimes".

Bibliography

Abel, Richard L.	Law as Lag: Inertia as a Social Theory of Law, 80 Michigan Law Review, 1982, pp. 785 et seqq.
Achenbach, Hans	Historische und dogmatische Gundlagen der strafrechtssystematischen Schuldlehre, in: Abhandlungen zur rechtswissenschaftlichen Grundlagenforschung, Juristische Fakultät München, Münchner Universitätsschriften, 1974
Adler, Freda Mueller, Gerhard O. Laufer, William	Criminology and the Criminal Justice System, 6th Edition, 2007
Althoff, Martina	Die soziale Konstruktion von Fremden-feindlichkeit, Wiesbaden, 1998
Amar, Akhil Reed	The Bill of Rights: Creation and Reconstruction, Yale, 2000
Ambos, Kai	Erste Überlegungen zu den Konsequenzen des Lissabon
Rackow, Peter	Urteils des Bundesverfassungsgerichts für das Europäische Strafrecht, in: Zeitschrift für Internationale Strafrechtsdogmatik (ZIS) 2009, pp. 397 et seqq.
Ambos, Kai Steiner, Christian	Vom Sinn des Strafens auf innerstaatlicher und supranationaler Ebene, in: Juristische Schulung (JuS) 2001, pp. 9 et seqq.
Amelung, Knut	Rechtsgüterschutz und Schutz der Gesellschaft, Frankfurt a.M., 1972 ("Rechtsgüterschutz")
Anastasopoulou, Ioanna	Deliktstypen zum Schutz kollektiver Rechtsgüter, Munich 2005, ("Deliktstypen")
Andenaes, Johannes	Punishment and Deterrence, University of Michigan Press, 1974

Appel, Ivo	Verfassung und Strafe. Zu den verfassungsrechtlichen Grenzen staatlichen Strafens, Berlin, 1998 („Verfassung“)
Aronson, Elliot	The Social Animal, 1991,
Arrigo, Bruce A.	Criminal Behavior: A Systems Approach, 4th Edition, Northwestern University, 2006
Arzt, Gunther Weber, Ulrich	Strafrecht. Besonderer Teil. LH 5, Bielefeld, 1982 (“LH 5“)
Avenarius, Hermann	Die Rechtsordnung der Bundesrepublik Deutschland, Bonn, 3rd Edition, 2001
Aydin, Öykü Didem	Die strafrechtliche Bekämpfung von Hassdelikten in Deutschland und in den Vereinigten Staaten von Amerika, 2006
Backes, Otto	Rechtsstaatsgefährdungsdelikte und Grundgesetz, Cologne, 1970 (“Rechtsstaatgefährdungsdelikte“)
Badura, Peter	Staatsrecht - Systematische Erläuterung des Grundgesetzes für die Bundesrepublik Deutschland, 4th Edition, Munich 2010 („Strafrecht“)
Baldus, Volker	Hate Crime: Gesetze zur effektiven Bekämpfung von Rechtsextremismus und Fremdenfeindlich-keit in Deutschland?, 2003
Baratta, Alessandro	Jenseits der Strafe – Rechtsgüterschutz in der Risikogesellschaft, in: Festschrift für Arthur Kaufmann, 1993, pp. 393 et seqq.
Bard, M. Sangry, D.	The Crime Victim’s Book, 1979
Barkan, Steven E.	Criminology: A Social Understanding, 5th Edition, Los Angeles, 2011 (“Criminology”)
Barnes, Arnold Ephross, Paul H.	The Impact of Hate Violence on Victims: Emotional and Behavioral Responses to Attacks, 39 Soc. Work, 1994, pp. 247 et seqq.

Bartol, Curt R.	Criminal Behavior: A Psychological Approach, 9th Bartol, Anne M. Edition, New York, 2010
Baumann, Jürgen Weber, Ulrich Mitsch, Wolfgang	Strafrecht. Allgemeiner Teil: Ein Lehrbuch, 11th Edition, 2003 ("Strafrecht AT")
Bell, Jeannine	Policing Hatred: Law Enforcement, Civil Rights, and Hate Crime, New York University Press, 2002
Bernstein	The Oxford International Encyclopedia of Legal History (Editor in Chief: Stanley N. Katz), Vol. 2, 2009, pp.147 et seqq.
Bierling, Ernst Rudolf	Juristische Prinzipienlehre, Vol. 1 (1894) and Vol. 2 (1898), ("Strafrecht AT")
Binding, Karl	Die Normen und ihre Übertretung: Eine Untersuchung über die rechtmäßige Handlung und die Arten des Delikts. Normen und Strafgesetze, Vol. 1, Normen und Strafgesetze, 1965 ("Binding I")
Bleich, Erik	Hate Crime Policy in Western Europe: Responding to Racist Violence in Britain, Germany, and France, in: American Behavioral Sc., Vol. 51, No. 2, 2007, pp. 149 et seqq.
Bleich, Erik Hart, Ryan K.	Quantifying Hate: The Evolution of German Approaches to Measuring 'Hate Crime', German Politics, 17:1, 2008, pp. 63 et seqq.
Bockelmann, Paul	Strafrecht, Allgemeiner Teil, 4th Edition, Munich, 1987 ("Strafrecht AT")
Volk, Klaus Bogdan, Michael	On the Value and Method of Rule-Comparison in Comparative Law, in: Mansel, Heinz-Peter (ed.), Festschrift für Erik Jayme, Vol. 2, Munich, 2004, pp. 1233 et seqq.
Brooke, James	Witnesses Trace Brutal Killing of Gay Student, in: New York Times, Published: November 21, 1998

Bruns, Hans-Jürgen — Anmerkung zu BGH, Beschluß vom 13.9.1976 - BGHSt 27, 4 et seqq. (§ 46 StGB) in: Juristische Rundschau 1977, pp. 146 et seqq.

Bruns, Hans-Jürgen — Strafzumessungsrecht. Allgemeiner Teil, 1967 (“StrZR“)

Buckland, William Warwick
McNair, Arnold Duncan
Lawson, Frederick Henry — Roman Law & Common Law - A Comparison in Outline, 2nd Edition, 1952

Butler, Judith — Haß spricht - Zur Politik des Performativen, Berlin 1998, pp. 67-97

Cappeletti, Mauro — A General Introduction, in: Capeletti, Mauro/ Seccombe, Monica/ Weiler, Joseph: Integration through Law, Europe and the American Federal Experience Band 1, Vol. 1, Berlin/New York, 1985, pp. 1 et seqq.

Chakraborti, Neil
Garland, Jon — Hate Crime: Impact, Causes and Responses, 2009

Chandler, Ralph C.
Enslen, Richard A.
Renstrom, Peter G. — The Constitutional Law Dictionary, Vol. 2: Governmental Powers, 1987

Coester, Marc — Das Konzept der Hate Crimes aus den USA unter besonderer Berücksichtigung des Rechts-extremismus in Deutschland, 2008 (“Hate Crimes“)

Conklin, John E. — Criminology, 11th Edition, 2011 (“Criminology”)

Corwin, Edward S. — The Constitution of the United States of America: Analysis and Interpretation, Washington D.C., 1952

Cunneen, Chris	Hysteria and Hate: The Vilification of Aboriginal and Torres Strait Islander People. In: Chris Cunnen/David Fraser/Stephen Tomsen (eds.): Faces of Hate. Hate Crime in Australia, pp. 137-161, 1997; Annandale/NSW Hawkins
Dannemann, Gerhard	Comparative Law: Study of Similarities or Differences? in: Reimann, Mathias/ Zimmermann, Reinhard (eds.): The Oxford Handbook of Comparative Law, 2006
De Cruz, Peter	A Modern Approach to Comparative Law, 1993
De Cruz, Peter	Comparative Law in a Changing World, 1999
Degenhart, Christoph	Staatsrecht I, Staatsorganisationsrecht, 27th Edition, Munich et. al., 2011
Detterbeck, Steffen	Öffentliches Recht, Basislehrbuch zum Staatsrecht, Verwaltungsrecht und Europarecht mit Übungsfällen, 8th Edition, 2011 ("Oeffentliches Recht)
De Vries, Lloyd	High Court Upholds Cross-Burning Ban, CBS News, May 7, 2009, view at: http://www.cbsnews.com/2100-280_162-548121.html
Dharmapala, Garoupa	Penalty Enhancement for Hate Crimes: An Economic Analysis, Georgetown University Law Center, Working Paper Series in Business, Economics, and Regulatory Law Working Paper No. 268644, 2001, p. 5.
Dillof, Anthony M.	Punishing Bias: An Examination of the Theoretical Foundations of Bias Crime Statutes, Northwestern Law Review 91 (4), (1997), pp. 1015-1081

Dillof, Anthony M. — The Importance of Being Biased, Michigan Law Review, Vol. 98, No. 6, 2000 Survey of Books Related to the Law, May, 2000, pp. 1678-1703

Dölling, Dieter
Duttge, Gunnar
Rössner Dieter — Gesamtes Strafrecht: StGB, StPO, Nebengesetze: Hand Kommentar (citation: HK GS-author), 2011

Dollinger, Bernd,
Raithel, Jürgen — Einführung in die Theorien abweichenden Verhaltens, 2006

Dral, Christy H.,
Phillips, Jerry J. — Commerce by Another Name: The Impact of United States v. Lopez and United States v. Morrison; Tennessee Law Review 68, 2001, pp. 605 et seqq.

Dubber, Markus D. — Einführung in das US-amerikanische Strafrecht, Munich, 2005

Dubber, Markus D. — Policing Possession: The War on Crime and the End of Criminal Law, Journal of Criminal Law and Criminology 91 (2001), p. 829

Dubber, Markus D. — Comparative Criminal Law, in: Reimann, Mathias/Zimmermann, Reinhard (eds.), The Oxford Handbook of Comparative Law, 2006, p. 1319

Edge, Ian — Comparative Law in a Global Perspective, London, 2000

Ehrlich, H. J. — The Ethnoviolence Project: Final Narrative Report of the National Survey of Prejudice and Violence in the United States (1992)

Eisenberg, Ulrich — Kriminologie, Munich, 2005

Elias, Norbert — Über den Prozess der Zivilisation, 1939

Enneccerus, Ludwig
Nipperdey, Hans Carl — Allgemeiner Teil des Bürgerlichen Rechts, Tübingen, 1959/60

Epping, Volker — Grundrechte, 4th Edition, Berlin, Heidelberg 2010

Eser, Albin — Funktionen, Methoden und Grenzen der Strafrechtsvergleichung, in: Albrecht, Jörg/ Dünkel, Frieder/ Kerner, Hans-Jürgen/ Kürzinger, Josef/ Schöch, Heinz/ Sessar, Klaus / Villmow, Bernhard (eds.), Festschrift für Günther Kaiser, Band II, Berlin 1998, pp. 1499 et seqq.

Eser, Albin — Die Tötungsdelikte in der Rechtsprechung zwischen BVerfGE 45, 187 und BGH-GS SZ 1/81, IV, in: Neue Zeitschrift für Strafrecht (NStZ) 1981, pp. 383 et seqq., 429 et seqq.

Feinberg, Joel — Harmless Wrongdoing the Moral Limits of the Criminal Law, Michigan Law Review Volume: 88, Issue 6, (1990), pp. 1415-1429

Feinberg, Joel — The Moral Limits of the Criminal Law, Vol. 1: Harm to others, 2nd Edition, Oxford University Press, 1987 ("Harm to others")

Feinberg, Joel — The Moral Limits of the Criminal Law, Vol. 2: Offense to Others, Oxford University Press, 1985 ("Offense to others")

Feinberg, Joel — The Moral Limits of the Criminal Law, Vol. 3: Harm to Self, Oxford University Press, 1986

Feinberg, Joel — The Moral Limits of the Criminal Law, Vol. 4: Harmless Wrongdoing, Oxford University Press, 1988

Feldman, Richard — Contextualism and Skepticism, in: Tomberlin, James E. (ed.), Philosophical Perspectives Vol. 13, Epistemology, Oxford, 1999

Feuerbach — Lehrbuch des gemeinen in Deutschland gültigen peinlichen Rechts, 11th Edition, 1832, Giessen

Fischer, Thomas — Das Verhältnis der Bekenntnisbeschimpfung (§ 166 StGB) zur Volksverhetzung (§ 130 StGB), in: Goltdammer's Archiv (GA) 1989, pp. 445 et seqq.

Fischer, Thomas	Öffentlicher Friede und Gedankenäußerung: Grundlagen und Entwicklung des Rechtsguts „öffentlicher Friede, insbesondere in den §§ 126, 130, 140 Nr. 2, 166 StGB ("Öffentlicher Friede")
Fischer, Thomas	Strafgesetzbuch: StGB und Nebengesetze, 59th Edition, Munich 2012
Fischer, Thomas	Die Eignung, den öffentlichen Frieden zu stören - Zur Beseitigung eines "restriktiven" Phantoms, in: Neue Zeitschrift für Strafrecht (NStZ) 1988, pp. 159 et seqq.
Folz, Hans-Peter	Karlsruhe, Lissabon und das Strafrecht - ein Blick über den Zaun, in: Zeitschrift für Internationale Strafrechtsdogmatik (ZIS) 2009, pp. 427 et seqq.
Friedman, Michel	Toleranz. in. Bundeskriminalamt (ed.): Rechtsextremismus, Antisemitismus und Fremdenfeindlichkeit, 2001, pp. 15 et seqq.
Frisch, Wolfgang	Wesentliche Strafbarkeitsvoraussetzungen einer modernen Strafgesetzgebung, in: Eser, Albin et. al. (eds.) Von totalitärem zu rechtsstaatlichem Strafrecht, 1992, pp. 201 et seqq.
Frommel, Monika	Fremdenfeindliche Gewalt, Polizei und Strafjustiz, in: Kritische Justiz, 1994, pp. 323 et seqq.
Füllgrabe, Uwe	Kriminalpsychologie - Täter und Opfer im Spiel des Lebens, Frankfurt: Edition Wötzel 1997
Füllgrabe, Uwe	Amok, Report Psychologie, 27, Nr. 11/12, November/Dezember 2002, 2002a, pp. 694-703
Füllgrabe, Uwe	Hassverbrechen, Kriminalistik, 2004, pp. 391-397
Gardner, Martin R.	The Mens Rea Enigma: Observations on the Role of Motive in the Criminal Law Post and Present, 1993

Garner, Bryan A. — Black´s Law Dictionary, 9th Edition, 2009

Garnets L.
Herek, G.M.
Levy B. — Violence and victimization of lesbians and gay men: Mental health consequences in: Herek, G.M./Berill, K.T. (eds.) Hate Crimes: Confronting Violence Against Lesbians and Gay Men, 1992, pp. 207-226

Gellman, Susan — Sticks and Stones Can Put You in Jail, but Can Words Increase Your Sentence, UCLA Law Review 39, (1991), pp.333-396

Gerstenfeld, Phyllis B. — Hate Crimes: Causes, Controls, and Controversies, Thousand Oaks, 2004

Giehring, Heinz — Pazifistische radikale Kritik als Volksverhetzung?, in: Strafverteidiger (StV) 1985, pp. 30 et seqq.

Glendon, Mary Ann
Gordon, Michael W.
Osakwe, Christopher — Comparative Legal Traditions, West Publishing, Vol. II: The Civil Law Tradition, MN, 1994 ("Comparative Legal Traditions")

Glet, Alke — Sozialkonstruktion und strafrechtliche Verfolgung von Hasskriminalität in Deutschland, 2011

Grasmann, Günther — Die römisch-germanische Rechtsfamilie, in: David, Rene/Grasmann, Günther (eds.), Einführung in die großen Rechtssysteme der Gegenwart, 2nd Edition, Munich, 1988, pp. 125 et seqq.

Grattet, Ryken
Jenness, Valerie — The Birth and Maturation of Hate Crime Policy in the United States, American Behavioral Scientists 45, 2001, pp. 668 et seqq.

Graziadei, Michele — The Functionalist Heritage, in: Legrand, Pierre/Munday, Roderick (eds.), Comparative Legal Studies: Traditions and Transitions, Cambridge, 2003, pp. 101 et seqq.

Goehrs, O. — Der Rechtsfrieden als besonderes Rechtsgut im modernen Strafrechtssystem und seine

Stellung im geltenden Reichsstrafrecht, Strassburg, 1900

Großfeld, Bernhard | Kernfragen der Rechtsvergleichung, Tübingen, 1996

Grützner, Thomas | Die Sanktionierung von Submissionsabsprachen, Eine Untersuchung der bestehenden Möglichkeiten zur Bekämpfung von Sub-missionsabsprachen unter besonderer Berück-sichtigung des § 298 StGB, Göttingen, 2002

Günther, Hans-Ludwig | Die Genese eines Straftatbestands, in: Juristische Schulung (JuS) 1978, pp. 8 et seqq.

Gutteridge, Harold C. | Comparative Law, An Introduction to the Comparative Method of Legal Study & Research, 2nd Edition, Cambridge, 1949

Hacking, Ian | Was heißt „soziale Konstruktion“? Zur Konjunktur einer Kampfvokabel in den Wissenschaften, Frankfurt, 1999

Haffke, Bernhard | Die Legitimation des staatlichen Strafrechts zwischen Effizienz, Freiheitsverbürgung und Symbolik, in: Schünemann, Bernd (ed.), Festschrift für Claus Roxin zum 70. Geburtstag am 15. Mai 2011, Berlin, 2001

Hagen, Frank E. | Introduction to Criminology: Theories, Methods and Criminal Behavior, 7th Edition, Chicago, 2010

Hassemer, Winfried | Darf es Straftaten geben, die ein strafrechtliches Rechtsgut nicht in Mitleidenschaft ziehen?, in: Hefendehl, Roland/Hirsch, Andrew von/Wohlers, Wolfgang (eds.), Die Rechtsgutstheorie, Legitimationsbasis des Strafrechts oder dogmatisches Glasperlenspiel? Baden-Baden, 2003, pp. 57 et seqq.

Hassemer, Winfried | Theorie und Soziologie des Verbrechens: Ansätze zu einer praxisorientierten

Rechtsgutslehre, 1973 ("Theorie und Soziologie")

Hall, Jerome — General Principles of Criminal Law, 1947

Harel, Alon
Parchomovsky, Gideon — "On Hate and Equality", Yale Law Journal 109 (3), 1999, pp. 507 et seqq.

Hasenstab, Dan — Is Hate a Form of Commerce? The questionable constitutionality of federal "hate crime" legislation, St. Louis University Law Journal 45, 2001, pp. 973 et seqq.

Haselbach, Dieter — Multikulturelle Apartheidpolitik oder liberaler Pluralismus?, in: Kommune. Forum für Politik, Ökonomie und Kultur, 15. Year., No. 4 1997, pp. 15 et seqq.

Hassemer, Winfried — Symbolisches Strafrecht und Rechtsgüterschutz. in: Neue Zeitschrift für Strafrecht (NStZ), 1989, pp.553 et seqq.

Hassemer, Winfried — Einführung in die Grundlagen des Strafrechts, 2nd Edition, Munich, 1990

Hay, Peter — Civil Law, in: Smelser, Neil J./Baltes, Paul B., International Encyclopedia of the Behavioral and Social Sciences, pp. 1865 et seqq., Amsterdam, 2001

Hay, Peter — The Law of the United States, Munich, 2010

Hefendehl, Roland — Kollektive Rechtsgüter im Strafrecht, 2002 ("Kollektive Rechtsgüter")

Hefendehl, Roland (ed.) — Empirische und dogmatische Fundamente, kriminalpolitischer Impetus - Symposium für Bernd Schünemann zum 60. Geburtstag, Cologne, 2005

Hefendehl, Roland (ed.) — Mit langem Atem: Der Begriff des Rechtsguts - Oder: Was seit dem Erscheinen des Sammelbandes über die Rechtsgutstheorie geschah -, in: Goltdammer´s Archiv für Strafrecht (GA), 2007, pp. 1 et seqq.

Hefendehl, Roland (ed.) | Der fragementrische Charakter des Strafrechts, in: Juristische Arbeitsblätter (JA) , 2011, pp. 401 et seqq.

Hegel, Georg Wilhelm Friedrich | Grundlinien der Philosophie des Rechts, Suhrkamp paperback Edition, 5th Edition, 1996

Heger, Martin | Perspektiven des Europäischen Strafrechts nach dem Vertrag von Lissabon, Eine Durchsicht des (wohl) kommenden EU-Primärrechts nach dem Vertrag von Lissabon, in: Zeitschrift für Internationale Strafrechtsdogmatik (ZIS) 2009, pp. 406 et seqq.

Heinrich, Bernd | Strafrecht Allgemeiner Teil, Vol. 1, 2nd Edition, 2009 ("Strafrecht AT")

Heller, Kevin J., Dubber, Markus D. | The Handbook of Comparative Criminal Law, Stanford, 2011

Henneberger, Melinda | "For Bias Crimes, a Double Trauma", Newsday, 1 13, January 9, 1992

Herek, Gregory M. Berill, Kevin | Hate Crimes - Confronting Violence Against Lesbians and Gay Men, 1992 ("Hate Crimes")

Herrmann, Joachim | Strafrechtsreform in den Vereinigten Staaten, in: Kaiser, Günther/Vogler, Theo (eds.), Kolloquium Strafrecht und Strafrechtsvergleichung, Freiburg, 1975, pp. 25 et seqq.

Herzog, Felix | Verbieten, bestrafen, wegsperren. Öffentlicher Anspruch und gesetzliche Wirklichkeit in der Auseinandersetzung mit dem Rechtsextremismus, in: Mohr, Irina/Molthagen, Dietmar, Friedrich-Ebert-Stiftung, Der Aufstand der Zuständigen Was kann der Rechtsstaat gegen Rechtsextremismus tun?, Ergebnisse einer Konferenz der Friedrich-Ebert-Stiftung am 20. März 2007, Berlin, 2007, pp. 23-34

Herzog, Felix | Präimplantationsdiagnostik - im Zweifel für ein Verbot?, in: Zeitschrift für Rechtspolitik (ZRP) 2001, pp. 393 et seqq.

Hessick, Clarissa B. Motive's Role in Criminal Punishment, Southern California Review, Vol. 80, 2006, pp. 89 et seqq.

Hickok, Eugene W. The Bill of Rights: Original Meaning and Current Understanding, Virginia, 1991

Hirsch, Andrew von Der Rechtsgutsbegriff und das "Harm Principle", in: Hefendehl, Roland/Hirsch, Andrew von/Wohlers, Wolfgang (eds.), Die Rechtsgutstheorie, Legitimationsbasis des Strafrechts oder dogmatisches Glasperlenspiel? Baden-Baden, 2003, pp. 13 et seqq.

Hirsch, Andrew von Der Rechtsgutsbegriff und das „Harm Principle", in: Goltdammer's Archiv (GA) 2002, pp. 2 et seqq.

Hirsch, Andrew von The Offense Principle in Criminal Law: Affront to Sensibility or Wrongdoing, King's College Law Journal, 2000, pp. 82 et seqq. ("The Offense Principle in Criminal Law")

Hörnle, Tatjana Das Unwerturteil und der Schuldvorwurf - Inhalte und Adressaten, in: Hefendehl, Roland (ed.), Empirische und dogmatische Fundamente, kriminologischer Impetus; Symposium für Bernd Schünemann zum 60. Geburtstag, Cologne et. al., 205, pp. 105 et seqq. ("Das Unwerturteil und der Schuldvorwurf")

Hörnle, Tatjana Offensive Behavior and German Penal Law, in: 5 Buffalo Criminal Law Review (2002), pp. 255 et seqq.

Hörnle, Tatjana Grob anstößiges Verhalten - Strafrechtlicher Schutz von Moral, Gefühl und Tabus, Frankfurt am Main, 2005 ("Grob anstößiges Verhalten")

Hörnle, Tatjana Tatproportionale Strafzumessung, Berlin, 1999

Hohmann, Olaf — Das Rechtsgut der Umweltdelikte: Grenzen des strafrechtlichen Umweltschutzes, Frankfurt a.M., 1991

Holzberger, Mark — Offenbarungseid der Polizeistatistker - Registrierung rechtsextremistischer Straftaten. Bürgerrechte & Polizei/CILIP (68/1), 2001

Honig, Richard M. — Die Einwilligung des Verletzten, Vol. I: Die Geschichte des Einwilligungsproblems und die Methodenfrage, Mannheim et. al., 1919 ("Einwilligung")

Honsell, Heinrich — Römisches Recht, 7th Edition, Berlin, 2010

Honsell, Heinrich — In fraudem legis agere, in: Medicus, Dieter/Seiler Hans Hermann (eds.), Festschrift für Max Kaser zum 70. Geburtstag, Munich, 1976, pp. 111 et seqq.

Hufen, Friedhelm — Staatsrecht II: Grundrechte, 3rd Edition, Munich, 2011

Human Right Watch, — Hintergrundpapier, Die Reaktion des Staates auf „Hasskriminalität" in Germany, 2011

Humboldt, Wilhelm von — Ideen zu einem Versuch die Gränzen der Wirksamkeit des Staats zu bestimmen, Breslau, 1851

Hurd; Heidi M.
Moore, Michael S. — Punishing Hatred and Prejudice, Illinois Public Law and Legal Theory Research Papers Series, No. 03-17, November 18, 2003

Iganski, Paul — Hate Crime hurts more, American Behavioral Scientist, Vol. 45, No. 4, December 2001, pp. 626 et seqq.

Ipsen, Jörn — Staatsrecht I: Staatsorganisationsrecht, Munich, 2011

Israel, Jerold H.
Kamisar, Yale
Fave, Wayne R. — Criminal Procedure and the Constitution. Leading Supreme Court Cases, and La Introductory Text, St. Paul, 1995 Edition ("Israel/Kamisar/La Fave 1995")

Jacobs, James B. — The Emergence and Implications of American Hate Crime Jurisprudence, 1993

Jacobs, James B.
Potter, Kimberly — Hate Crimes: Criminal Law & Identity Politics 82, Oxford, 1998

Jacobs, James B.
Potter, Kimberly — Hate Crimes: A Critical Perspective, in: Tonry, Michael (ed.): Crime and justice: A review of research, Chicago, 1997

Jäger, Herbert — Strafgesetzgebung und Rechtsgüterschutz bei Sittlichkeitsdelikten, Stuttgart 1957 ("Rechtsgüterschutz")

Jakobs, Günther — Niedrige Beweggruende beim Mord und die besonderen persönlichen Merkmale in § 50 Abs. 2 und 3 StGB, Neue Juristische Wochenschrift (NJW), 1969, pp. 489 et seqq.

Jakobs, Günther — Strafrecht als Mittel des umfassenden Klimaschutzes, in: Zeitschrift für die gesamte Strafrechtswissenschaft (ZStW) 97 (1985), pp. 751 et seqq.

Jakobs, Günther — Strafrecht - Allgemeiner Teil. Die Grundlagen der Zurechnungslehre, 2nd Edition, Berlin, 1993

Jakobs, Günther — Staatliche Strafe: Bedeutung und Zweck, 2004

Jakobs, Günther — Rechtsgüterschutz? Zur Legitimation des Strafrechts, Ed. Nordrhein-Westfälischen Akademie der Wissenschaft und der Künste, 538. Sitzung am 5. September 2012

Jareborg, Nils — Criminalization as Last Resort (Ultima Ratio), Ohio State Journal of Criminal Law, Vol. 2, 2005, pp. 521 et seqq.

Jauering, Othmar — Wann ist das Grundgesetz in Kraft getreten, in: Juristenzeitung (JZ) 1989, pp. 615 et seqq.

Jenness, Valerie
Grattet, Ryken — Making Hate a Crime: From Social Movement to Law Enforcement, 2001 ("Making Hate a Crime")

Jeschek, Hans-Heinrich
Weigend, Thomas — Lehrbuch des Strafrechts, Allgemeiner Teil, Berlin, 1996

Jescheck, Hans-Heinrich
Ruß, Wolfgang
Wilms, Günther — Strafgesetzbuch, Leipziger Kommentar, Großkommentar Vol. 1 (§§ 1 - 31 StGB), 11th Edition, Berlin/New York, 2003

Jescheck, Hans-Heinrich
Ruß, Wolfgang
Wilms, Günther — Strafgesetzbuch, Leipziger Kommentar, Großkommentar Vol. 4 (§§ 80 – 145d StGB), 11th Edition, Berlin/New York, 2005

Joecks, Wolfgang et. al. — Münchener Kommentar zum Strafgesetzbuch ("MK"), Vol. 1: §§ 1 – 37 StGB, 2nd Edition, Munich, 2011

Johnson, Dennis W. — The Laws that Shaped America, 2009

Jones, Dionne — Racially Motivated Violence: An Empirical Study of a Growing Social Problem, National Urban League Report, May 1989

Junge, Iris — Das Schutzgut des § 130 StGB, 2000

Kahan, Dan M. — The Anatomy of Disgust in Criminal Law, 96 Michigan Law Review 1998, pp. 1621 et seqq.

Kahn-Freund, Otto — Comparative Law as an Academic Subject, The Law Quarterly Review 82, University of California, 1966, pp. 40 et seqq.

Kaiser, Günther — Kriminologie Ein Lehrbuch, Heidelberg, 1996

Kamba, Walter Joseph — Comparative Law: A Theoretical Framework, International and Comparative Law Quarterly 23, 1974, pp. 485 et seqq.

Kamisar, Yale
Wayne R.
Israel, Jerold H.
King, Nancy J. — Modern Criminal Procedure: Cases, LaFave, Commentsand Questions, 9th Edition, St. Paul, 1999 ("Kamisar/ La Fave/ Israel/ King 1999")

Kant, Immanuel — Metaphsysik der Sitten, Rechtslehre, Ed. Vorländer, 3rd Edition, 1919

Kasper, Bernd — Die Erheblichkeitsschwelle im Bereich des Umweltstrafrechts, Freiburg, 1997 ("Erheblichkeitsschwelle")

Kaufmann, Armin — Strafrechtspraxis und sittliche Normen, in Juristische Schulung (JuS) 1978, pp. 361 et seqq.

Keiser, Claudia — Öffentliche Anhörung des Rechtsausschusses des Deutschen Bundestages am 13.06.2012 zur sog. Hasskriminalität; Gesetzentwurf BT-Drs. 17/8131 vom 14.12.2011 Gesetzentwurf BT-Drs. 17/9345 vom 18.04.2012; Aufnahme menschenverachtender Tatmotive als besondere Umstände der Strafzumessung; Antrag BT-Drs. 17/8796 vom 29.02.2012; Vorurteilsmotivierte Straftaten wirksam verfolgen ("in: "Public Hearing of the Legal Committee of the German Bundestag on 06/13/2012 to so-called Hate Crime")

Kelly, P.
Louza, M.
Reeves, W. B.
Garrison S.
Adams, S.
Burns, N. — Hatred in Georgia: A Chronology and Analysis of Hate Activity, 1993.

Kern, Eduard — Grade der Rechtswidrigkeit, in: Zeitschrift für die gesamte Strafrechtswissenschaft (ZStW) 64, (1952), pp. 255 et seqq.

Kim, Janine Young — Hate Crime Law and the Limits of Inculpation, Nebraska Law Review, 2006, Vol. 84, pp. 846 et seqq.

Kimball, Emily — Hate-Crimes Bill Would Expand Federal Jurisdiction, in: Richmond Times; Published: June 13, 2009

Kischel, Uwe — Vorsicht, Rechtsvergleichung!, in: Zeitschrift für Vergleichende Rechtswissenschaft (ZVglRWiss) 104 (2005), pp.10 et seqq.

Kleinfeld, N.R. „Bias Crimes Hold Steady, But Leave Many Scars,“, New York Times, January 27, 1992, p. Al.

Kleinig, John Crime and the Concept of Harm, American philosophical Quaterly, 15 (1), 1978, pp. 27 et seqq.

Köhler, Michael Über den Zusammenhang von Strafrechtsbegründung und Strafzumessung, erörtert am Problem der Generalprävention, Heidelberg, 1983

Köhler, Michael Strafrecht, Allgemeiner Teil, 1997 (“Strafrecht AT“)

Köhler, Michael Zur Abgrenzung des Mordes. Erörtert am Mordmerkmal „Verdeckungsabsicht“, in: Goltdammer's Archiv (GA) 1980, pp. 121 et seqq.

Konrad, (Generalstaatsanwalt) Öffentliche Anhörung des Rechtsausschusses des Deutschen Bundestages am 13.06.2012 zur sog. Hasskriminalität; Gesetzentwurf BT-Drs. 17/8131 vom 14.12.2011 Gesetzentwurf BT-Drs. 17/9345 vom 18.04.2012; Aufnahme menschenverachtender Tatmotive als besondere Umstände der Strafzumessung; Antrag BT-Drs. 17/8796 vom 29.02.2012; Vorurteilsmotivierte Straftaten wirksam verfolgen ("in: "Public Hearing of the Legal Committee of the German Bundestag on 06/13/2012 to so-called Hate Crime")

Kotulla, Michael Deutsche Verfassungsgeschichte - Vom Alten Reich bis Weimar (1495 - 1934), Berlin, 2008

Kratsch, Dietrich Aufgaben- und Risikoverteilung als Kriterien der Zurechnung im Strafrecht, in: Festschrift für Dietrich Oehler, Cologne, 1985, pp. 65 et seqq. (“Festschrift für Dietrich Oehler“)

Kratsch, Dietrich Verhaltenssteuerung und Organisation im Strafrecht. Ansätze zur Reform des strafrechtlichen Unrechtsbegriffs und der

Regeln der Gesetzesanwendung, Berlin, 1985 ("Verhaltenssteuerung")

Kratsch, Dietrich — Unrecht und Prävention - eine Replik, in: Goltdammer's Archiv (GA) 1989, pp. 49 et seqq.

Kratsch, Dietrich — Prinzipien der Konkretisierung von abstrakten Gefährdungsdelikten - BGHSt 38, 309, in: Juristische Schulung (JuS) 1994, pp. 382 et seqq.

Krey, Volker — Deutsches Strafrecht, Vol. 1, Grundlagen, Tatbestandsmäßigkeit, Rechtswidrigkeit, Schuld, 3rd. Edition, 2008 ("Deutsches Strafrecht")

Krey, Volker — Deutsches Strafrecht, allgemeiner Teil: Studienbuch in Esser, Robertsystematisch-induktiver Darstellung, 2011 („Deutsches Strafrecht")

Krüger, Christine — Rechte Gewalt als Vorurteilskriminalität, Bewährungshilfe, 2011, pp. 161 et seqq.

Krüger, Christine — Zusammenhänge und Wechselwirkungen zwischen allgemeiner Gewaltbereitschaft und rechtsextremen Einstellungen. Eine kriminologische Studie zum Phänomen jugendlicher rechter Gewaltstraftäter, Mönchengladbach, 2008

Krupna, Karsten — Das Kozept der "Hate Crimes" in Deutschland; Eine systematische Untersuchung der riminalitätsform, der strafrechtlichen Erfassungsmöglichkeiten de lege lata und der Verarbeitung in der Strafrechtspraxis, Marburg Univ. Diss., 2009; Frankfurt am Main, 2010

Kubink, Michael — Rechtsextremistische und fremdenfeindliche Straftaten, in: Zeitschrift für Rechtspolitik (ZRP) 2002, pp. 308 et seqq.

Küper, Wilfried — „Besondere persönliche Merkmale" und „spezielle Schuldmerkmale", in: Zeitschrift für die gesamte Strafrechtswissenschaft (ZStW) 104 (1992), pp. 559 et seqq.

Kunz, Karl-Ludwig — Prävention und gerechte Zurechnung. Überlegungen zur normativen Kontrolle utilitaristischer Strafbegründung, in: Zeitschrift für die gesamte Strafrechtswissenschaft (ZStW), Volume 98, Issue 4, (1986), pp. 832 et seqq.

Kunz, Karl-Ludwig — Kriminologie, Bern, 2008

La Fave, Wayne R.
Israel, Jerold H. — Criminal Procedure. Constitutional Limitations, 5th Edition, St. Paul, MN, 1991 ("La Fave/Israel, 1991")

La Fave, Wayne R.
Israel, Jerold H. — Criminal Procedure. Constitutional Limitations, 6th Edition, St. Paul, MN, 1992 ("La Fave/Israel, 1992")

Langer, Winrich — Das Sonderverbrechen. Eine dogmatische Untersuchung zum Allgemeinen Teil des Strafrechts, Berlin, 1972 ("Sonderverbrechen")

Lausberg, Michael — Die extreme Rechte in Ostdeutschland 1990-1998, Marburg, 2012

Law, John — 'Introduction: Monsters, Machines and Sociotechnical Relations in: A Sociology of Monsters: Essays on Power, Technology and Domination, London, New York, 1991, pp. 18 et seqq.

Lagodny, Otto — Das materielle Strafrecht als Prüfstein der Verfassungsdogmatik, in: Hefendehl, Roland/Hirsch, Andrew von/Wohlers, Wolfgang (eds.), Die Rechtsgutstheorie, Legitimationsbasis des Strafrechts oder dogmatisches Glasperlenspiel?, Baden-Baden, 2003, pp. 83 et seqq.

Lagodny, Otto — Strafrecht vor den Schranken der Grundrechte, Tübingen, 1996

Lambert, Edouard — Conception générale et défintion et défintion de la science du droit compáre, Procès-verbaux des seánces et documents, Congrès international de droit comparé I (1905), 26, printed in: Zweigert, Konrad/Puttfarken, Hans-Jürgen (eds.), Rechtsvergleichung, Darmstadt, 1978

Larenz, Karl — Methodenlehre der Rechtswissenschaft, 6th Edition, 1991, pp. 257 et seqq.

Lawrence, Frederick M. — Punishing Hate - Bias Crimes under American Law, 2003 ("Punishing Hate")

Lawrence, Frederick M. — Enforcing Bias-Crime Laws without Bias: Evaluating the Disproportionate-Enforcement Critique, Journal of Law & Contemporary Problems, Vol. 66, 2003, pp. 49 et seqq.

Lawrence, Frederick M. — The Punishment of Hate: Towards a Normative Theory of Bias-Motivated Crimes, 93 Michigan Law Review, 1994, pp. 320 -381

Lawrence, Frederick M. — The Hate Crime Project and its Limitations: Evaluating the Societal Gains and Risk in Bias Crime Law Enforcement, The George Wahsington University Law School, Public law and Legal Theory Working Paper No. 216, 2006

Lehmann, Jens — Öffentliche Anhörung des Rechtsausschusses des Deutschen Bundestages am 13.06.2012 zur sog. Hasskriminalität; Gesetzentwurf BT-Drs. 17/8131 vom 14.12.2011 Gesetzentwurf BT-Drs. 17/9345 vom 18.04.2012; Aufnahme menschenverachtender Tatmotive als besondere Umstände der Strafzumessung; Antrag BT-Drs. 17/8796 vom 29.02.2012; Vorurteilsmotivierte Straftaten wirksam verfolgen ("in: "Public Hearing of the Legal Committee of the German Bundestag on 06/13/2012 to so-called Hate Crime")

Levin, Brian — "U.S. Supreme Court Upholds Stiffer Sentences for Hate Crimes", Intelligence report, 4-5, September 1993

Levin, Jack.	The rising tide of bigotry and bloodshed Hate Crimes, McDevitt, Jack 1993 ("Hate Crimes")
Levin, Jack	America's War on Those Who are Different, Oxford, McDevitt, Jack 2002 ("America's War")
Liszt, Franz von	Der Zweckgedanke im Strafrecht, in: Strafrechtliche Aufsätze und Vorträge, Vol. 1, 1905, Berlin, pp. 126 et seqq.
Lackner, Karl Kühl, Kristian	Strafgesetzbuch: StGB - Kommentar, 27th Edition, Munich, 2011
Lösche, Peter	Merkmale der Präsidialdemokratie, in: Bundeszentrale für politische Bildung (ed.), Informationen zur politischen Bildung, Heft 283, Politisches System der USA, 2008
Maiwald, Manfred	Zum fragmentarischen Charakter des Strafrechts, in: Festschrift für Reinhart Maurach zum 70. Geburtstag, Schroeder, Friedrich-Christian/Zipf, Heinz (eds.), Karlsruhe, 1972, pp. 9 et seqq.
Markesinis, Basil	Rechtsvergleichung in Theorie und Praxis: Ein Beitrag zur rechtswissenschaftlichen Methodenlehre, Munich, 2004
Marx, Michael	Zur Definition des Begriffs >Rechtsgut< Prolegomena einer materialen Verbrechenslehre, Munich, 1972
Maroney, Terry A.	The struggle against Hate Crime: Movements at a crossroads, New York University Law Review 73 (2), 1998: pp. 564 - 620
Massey, Douglas Denton, Nancy	American apartheid: segregation and the making of the underclass, 1993
Maurach, Reinhard Zipf, Heinz	Strafrecht, Allgemeiner Teil, Teilband 1, 8th Edition, 1992 ("Strafrecht AT")
Maurach, Reinhard Schroder, Friedrich-Christian Maiwald, Manfred	Strafrecht, Besonderer Teil, Teilband 2, Straftaten gegen Gemeinschaftswerte, 9th Edition, 2005 („Strafrecht BT I")

Maurer, Hartmut	Staatsrecht I, 6th Edition, 2010
McLaughlin, Eugene	Hate Crime, in: Eugene Mc Laughlin/John Muncie (ed.), The Sage Dictionary of Criminology, London, California, New Delhi, 2006
Michaels, Ralf	The functional method of comparative law, in: Reimann, Mathias/Zimmermann, Reinhard (eds), The Oxford Handbook of Comparative Law, Oxford 2008
Mill, John Stuart	On Liberty, Boston, 1859
Mill, John Stuart	Über die Freiheit, Stuttgart, 1988
Mill, John Stuart	On Liberty and other Writings, Collini, Stefan (ed.), Cambridge University Press, 1989
Miller, Gale Holstein, James A.	Constructionist Controversies: Issues in Social Problems Theory, 1993
Miller, Gale, Holstein, James A.	Rethinking Victimization: An international approach to Victimology, 1990
Mitsch, Wolfgang	Der neue Stalking-Tatbestand im Strafgesetzbuch, in: Neue Juristische Wochenschrift (NJW) 2007, pp. 1237 et seqq.
Momsen, Carsten Rackow, Peter	Die Straftheorien, in: Juristische Arbeitsblätter (JA), 2004, pp. 336 et seqq.
Monk, Linda R.	The Bill of Rights: A User's Guide, 2004
Monroe, Merlinus Goodman	Hate Crimes in Georgia, October 16th, 2010 (view at: http://www.merlinusmonroe.com/2010/10/16hate-crimes-in-georgia)
Moore, Michael	The independent Moral Significance of Wrongdoing, 5 J. Contemp. Leg. Issues 237 (1994)

Morris, Aldon D.	The Origin of the Civil Rights Movement: Black Communities Organizing for Change, 1986
Morsch, J.	The Problem of Motive in hate Crimes: The Argument Against Presumptions of Racial Motivation; Journal of Criminal Law and Criminology 82, 1991, pp. 659 et seqq.
Müller-Dietz, Heinz	Strafe und Staat, 1973
Müller-Gugenberger, Christian	Die römisch-germanische Rechtsfamilie, in: David, Rene/Grasmann, Günther (eds.), Einführung in die großen Rechtssysteme der Gegenwart, 2nd Edition, Munich, 1988, pp. 79 et seqq.
Müssig, Bernd J. A.	Schutz abstrakter Rechtsgüter und abstrakter Rechtsgüterschutz: Zu den materiellen Konstitutionskriterien sog. Universalrechtsgüter und deren normentheoretischem Fundament: am Beispiel der Rechtsgutsbestimmung für die §§ 129, 129a und 324 StGB, Hamburg, 1994 („Rechtsgüterschutz“)
Naucke, Wolfgang	Strafrecht: Eine Einführung, 10th Edition, Frankfurt, 2002 (“Strafrecht“)
Nelken, David	“Towards a Sociology of Legal Adaption?“, in: Nelken, David/Feest, Johannes (eds.), Adapting Legal Cultures, Oxford, 2001, pp. 7 et seqq.
Neubacher, Frank	Fremdenfeindliche Brandanschläge. Mönchengladbach, 1998
Neumayer, Heinz	Grundriß der Rechtsvergleichung, in: David, Rene/Grasmann, Günther (eds.), Einführung in die großen Rechtssysteme der Gegenwart, 2nd Edition, Munich, 1988, pp. 1 et seqq.
Newton, Michael Newton, Judy Ann	Racial and Religious Violence in America: A Chronology, 1991
Oetker, Friedrich	Rechtsgüterschutz und Strafe, in: Zeitschrift für die gesamte Strafrechtswissenschaft (ZStW) 17 (1897), pp. 565 et seqq.

Otto, Harro — Grundkurs Strafrecht, Allgemeine Strafrechtslehre, 7th Edition, Berlin, 2004 ("Grundkurs AT")

Otto, Harro — Die strafrechtliche Bekämpfung unlauterer Einflußnahmen auf öffentliche Versteigerungen durch Scheinangebote, in: Neue Juristische Wochenschrift (NJW) 1979, pp. 681 et seqq.

Otto, Harro — Konzeption und Grundsätze des Wirtschaftsstrafrechts (einschließlich Verbraucherschutz), in: Zeitschrift für die gesamte Strafrechtswissenschaft (ZStW) 96 (1984), pp. 339 et seqq.

Otto, Harro — Strafwürdigkeit und Strafbedürftigkeit als eigenständige Deliktskategorien? Überlegungen zum Deliktsaufbau, in: Stree, Walter/Lenckner, Theodor/Cramer, Peter (eds.), Gedächtnisschrift für Horst Schröder, 1978

Paeffgen, Hans-Ulrich — Einmal mehr - Habgier und niedrige Beweggründe, in: Goltdammer's Archiv (GA) 1982, pp. 255 et seqq.

Papageorgiou, Konstantinos — Schaden und Strafe. Auf dem Weg zu einer Theorie der strafrechtlichen Moralität, Baden Baden, 1994, ("Schaden und Strafe")

Partsch, Karl-Josef — Neue Maßnahmen zur Bekämpfung von Rassen- und Fremdenhaß, Bessere DurchführuNg der internationalen Verpflichtungen Deutschlands, in: EuGRZ 1994, pp. 429 et seqq.

Paulsen, Monrad G. — Grundzüge des amerikanischen Strafprozesses, in: Zeitschrift für die gesamte Strafrechtswissenschaft (ZStW) 77 (1965), pp. 141 et seqq.

Pearlman, Terrylynn — Sanctioning Bias Crime. A Public Perspective, El Paso, 2008

Peek, George S.	Where are we going with federal Hate Crime Legislation? Congress and the politics of sexual orientation, Marquette Law Review, 85 (2001), pp. 537 et seqq.
Perry, Barbara	In the Name of Hate: Understanding Hate Crimes, 2001
Perry, Barbara	Where do we go from here?, Internet Journal of Criminology (IJC), 2003
Perry, Barbara	Hate and Bias crime, New York/London, 2003
Platsas, Antonios E.	The Functional and the Dysfunctional in the Comparative Method of Law: Some Critical Remarks, Electronic Journal of Comparative Law 12.3, December 2008
Pfahl-Traughber, Armin	Ursachen rechtsextrem motivierter Gewalt, in: Kriminalistik, 2004, pp. 38 et seqq.
Piek, Sarah	Die Kritik an der funktionalen Rechtsvergleichung, in: Greifswalder Halbjahresschrift für Rechtswissenschaft (GreifRecht), 2009, pp. 84 et seqq.
Pound, Roscoe	The Formative Era of American Law, 1938
Price, A. W.,	Contextuality in Practical Reason, Oxford, 2008
Rabel, Ernst	Aufgabe und Notwendigkeit der Rechtsvergleichung, Rheinische Zeitschrift für Zivil- und Prozessrecht, 13, 1924, pp. 279 et seqq.
Radin, Max	Handbook of Roman Law, 1927
Ramsey	in: Katz, Stanley N. The Oxford International Encyclopedia of Legal History, Vol. 2, 2009,
Radtke, Henning	Schuldgrundsatz und Sicherungsverwahrung. Freiheitsgarantien im zweispurigen

Sanktionensystem, in: Goltdammer's Archiv (GA) 2001, pp. 636 et seqq.

Radtke, Henning — Öffentliche Anhörung des Rechtsausschusses des Deutschen Bundestages am 13.06.2012 zur sog. Hasskriminalität; Gesetzentwurf BT-Drs. 17/8131 vom 14.12.2011 Gesetzentwurf BT-Drs. 17/9345 vom 18.04.2012; Aufnahme menschenverachtender Tatmotive als besondere Umstände der Strafzumessung; Antrag BT-Drs. 17/8796 vom 29.02.2012; Vorurteilsmotivierte Straftaten wirksam verfolgen ("in: "Public Hearing of the Legal Committee of the German Bundestag on 06/13/2012 to so-called Hate Crime")

Rawls, John — Eine Theorie der Gerechtigkeit, Höffe, Otfried (ed.), Berlin, 2006

Reichard, Michael — Die Behandlung fremdenfeindlicher Straftaten im deutschen Strafrecht: Eine tatbestands- und strafzumessungsbezogene Analyse, Hamburg, 2008

Reichel, Peter — Vergangenheitsbewältigung in Deutschland, Die Auseinandersetzung mit der NS-Diktatur von 1945 bis heute, Munich, 2001

Reimann, Mathias — The Oxford Handbook of Comparative Law, Oxford,/Zimmermann, Reinhard (eds.), 2006

Reitz, John — How to do Comparative Law, American Journal of Comparative Law 46, 1998, pp. 617 et seqq.

Renzikowski, Joachim — Toleranz und die Grenzen des Strafrechts, in: Gedächtnisschrift für Dieter Meurer, 2002, pp. 179 et seqq. ("GS for Meurer")

Rescher, Nicolas — Welfare: The Social Issue in Philosophical Perspective, University Press of Pittsburgh Press, Pittsburgh, 1972

Rheinstein, Max — Einführung in die Rechtsvergleichung, 1987

Riedel, Marc — Criminal Violence: Patterns, Causes, and

Welsh, Wayne N. Prevention, Oxford University Press, 2010

Robinson, Paul H. "United States", in: Heller; Kevin J./Dubber, Markus D. (eds.), The Handbook of Comparative Criminal Law, Stanford, 2011, pp. 563 et seqq.

Rogers, John M. International Law and United States Law, 1999

Rönnau, Thomas Grundwissen -Strafrecht: Erfolgs- und Tätigkeitsdelikte, in: Juristische Schulung (JuS) 2010, pp. 96 et seqq.

Roxin, Claus Strafrecht Allgemeiner Teil, Band I: Grundlagen. Der Aufbau der Verbrechenslehre, 4th Edition, Munich, 2006

Roxin, Claus Rechtsgüterschutz als Aufgabe des Strafrechts?, in: Hefendehl, Roland (ed.), Empirische und dogmatische Fundamente, kriminalpolitischer Impetus, Symposium für Bernd Schünemann zum 60. Geburtstag, 2005, pp. 135 et seqq.

Roxin, Claus Täterschaft und Teilnahme, Hamburg, 1963

Roxin, Claus Zur Entwicklung der Kriminalpolitik seit den Alternativ-Entwürfen, in: Juristische Arbeitsblätter (JA) 1980, pp. 545 et seqq.

Rudolphi, Hans-Joachim Die verschiedenen Aspekte des Rechtsgutsbegriffs, in: Barth, Eberhard et. al. (eds.), Festschrift für Richard M. Honig zum 80. Geburtstag am 3. Januar 1970, 1970, pp. 151 et seqq. ("FS for Honig")

Rudolphi, Hans-Joachim 'Notwendigkeit und Grenzen einer Vorverlagerung des Strafrechtsschutzes im Kampf gegen den Terrorismus,' in: Zeitschrift für Rechtspolitik (ZRP) 1979, pp. 220 et seqq.

Rusch, Arnold F. Methoden und Ziele der Rechtsvergleichung, in: Jusletter 13 February 2006

Sachs, Michael	Verfassungsrecht II - Grundrechte, Berlin, Heidelberg 2003
Sachs, Michael	Grundgesetz Kommentar, 6. Edition, 2011
Saucier, D.A. Brown, T. L. Cawman, A.J.	Effects of Victim´s Characteristics on attitudes toward Hate Crimes, in: Journal of Interpersonal Violence 21, Mitchell., R.C. 2006, pp. 890 et seqq.
Schäfer, Gerhard	Praxis der Strafzumessung, Munich, 2001
Scheffler, Uwe	Körperverletzung aus niedrigen Beweg-gründen? in: Neue Justiz (NJ) 2001, pp.13 et seqq.
Schetsche, Michael	Wissenssoziologie sozialer Probleme. Grundlegung einer relativistischen Problemtheorie, 2000
Schmallenger, F.	Criminology Today, 2004, Upper Saddle/River/NJ
Schmidhäuser, Eberhard	Strafrecht, Allgemeiner Teil, Studienbuch, 2nd Edition, 1984 ("Strafrecht AT")
Schmidhäuser, Eberhard	Gesinnungsmerkmale im Strafrecht, Stockstadt, 1958
Schmidt, Rolf	Strafrecht, Allgemeiner Teil, 11th Edition, 2012 ("Strafrecht AT")
Schneider, Hans Joachim	Hass- und Vorurteilskriminalität. In: Grafl, Christian/ Medigovic, Ursula (eds.): Festschrift für Manfred Burgstaller, 2004, Wien, Graz, pp. 553-568
Schneider, Hans Joachim	Foreigners as Perpetrators and as Victims in Germany, in Schneider, Hans Joachim/ Holyst, Brunon (eds.), EuroCriminology, Band 8/9, Lodz University Press, 1995, Wien, Graz
Schneider, Hans Joachim	Hassverbrechen, in: Schneider, Hans Joachim (ed.), Kriminologie für das 21. Jahrhundert:

	Schwerpunkte der internationalen Kriminologie; Überblick und Diskussion, Münster, 2001, pp. 70-90
Schneider, Hans Joachim	„Kriminologie der Hassdelikte. Konzeption, Ursachen, Vorbeugung und Kontrolle" in: „Bewährungshilfe – Soziales – Strafrecht – Kriminalpolitik", 2003
Schneider, Hans Joachim	Haßverbrechen - Eine neue kriminologische Delikts-kategorie, in: Hirsch, Hans Joachim/Hofmanski, Pietr/Plywaczewski, Emil W./Roxin, Claus (Eds.): Neue Erscheinungsformen der Kriminalität in ihrer Auswirkung auf das Straf- und Strafprozeßrecht, 1996, pp. 271 et seqq.
Schneider, Hans Joachim	Hasskriminalität: eine neue kriminologische Delikts-kategorie, in Juristenzeitung (JZ), 2003, pp. 497 et seqq.
Schneider, Hans Joachim	Politische Kriminalität, in: Sieverts, Rudolf/Schneider, Hans-Joachim (eds.): Handwörterbuch der Kriminologie. Vol. 5, Berlin et al., 1998, pp. 589 et seqq.
Schneider, Hans Joachim	Politische Kriminalität: Hassverbrechen, Fremdenfeindlichkeit im internationalen Kontext, in: Kriminalistik 2001, pp. 21 et seqq.
Schönke, Adolf Schröder, Horst	Strafgesetzbuch: StGB - Kommentar, 28th Edition, Munich, 2010
Scholzen, Reinhard	Rechtsextremismus, gefahr erkannt, gefahr gebannt?, in: Kriminalistik 2001, pp. 314 et seqq.
Schroeder, Friedrich-Christian	Die Straftaten gegen das Strafrecht, Berlin, 1985
Schünemann, Bernd	Geleitwort, p. VII, in: Dubber, Markus D., Einführung in das US-amerikanische Strafrecht, Munich, 2005

Schünemann, Bernd — Kritische Anmerkungen zur geistigen Situation der deutschen Strafrechtswissenschaft, in: Goltdammer's Archiv (GA) 1995, pp. 201 et seqq.

Schünemann, Bernd — Spät kommt ihr, doch ihr kommt: Glosse eines Strafrechtslehrers zur Lissabon-Entscheidung des BVerfG, in: Zeitschrift für Internationale Strafrechtsdogmaitk (ZIS) 2009, pp. 393 et seqq.

Seehafer, Silvia — Strafrechtliche Reaktionen auf rechtsextremistisch/ fremdenfeindlich motivierte Gewalttaten - Das amerikanische „hate crime“ Konzept und seine Übertragbarkeit auf das deutsche Rechtssystem, 2003. („Strafrechtliche Reaktionen“)

Seiler, Matthias — § 238 StGB: Analyse und Auslegung des Nachstellungstatbestands, Saarbrücken, 2010

Silver, Ethan
Stein, Ari
Surman, Tony
Thompson — Fighting Words, view at: http://www.bsos.umd.edu/gvpt/gvpt339/fightingwords.html

Seelmann, Kurt — Rechtsgutskonzept, „Harm Principle“ und Anerkennungsmodell als Strafwürdigkeitskriterien, in: Hefendehl, Roland (ed.), Die Rechtsgutstheorie - Legitimationsbasis des Strafrechts oder dogmatisches Glasperlenspiel?, 2003, pp. 261 et seqq.

Seher, Gerhard — Liberalismus und Strafe: Zur Strafrechtsphilosophie von Joel Feinberg, Berlin, 2009

Siegel, Larry J. — Criminology - Theories, Patterns + Typologies, 11th Edition, Belmont/CA, 2011 ("Criminology")

Simester, P.
Hirsch, Andrew von — Rethinking the Offense Principle, Legal Theory, Vol. 8, 2002, pp. 269 et seqq.

Sina, Peter — Die Dogmengeschichte des strafrechtlichen Begriffs "Rechtsgut", 1962

Singer, Jens Peter — Erfassung der politsch motivierten Kriminalität. In einem neuen Definitionssystem mit mehrdimensionalen Analysemöglichkeiten, in: Kriminalistik 2004, pp. 32 et seqq.

Sitomer, Curtis J. — New Civil Rights Thrust: Aid for Victims in: Christina Science Monitor, April 5, 1983

Söllner, Alfred — Einführung in die römische Rechtsgeschichte, 5th Edition, Munich, 1996

Somló, Felix — Juristische Grundlehre, Michigan, 2nd Edition, University of Michigan, 1927

Stächelin, Gregor — Strafgesetzgebung im Verfassungsstaat: Normative und empirische materielle und prozedurale Aspekte der Legitimation unter Berücksichtigung neuerer Strafgesetzgebungspraxis, Berlin, 1998 ("Strafgesetzgebung")

Winnie Stachelberg — Interview of Timothy Lynch (Cato Institute Criminal Jusitce Project Director) and Winnie Stachelberg (Center for American Progress/External Affairs, Senior Vice President), Hate Crime Laws, in: Morning Show on C-SPAN's Washington Journal, March 13, 2012

Stegbauer, Andreas — Der Gesetzentwurf zur Bekämpfung von „hate crimes", in: Neue Justiz (NJ) 2008, pp. 108 et seqq.

Sternberg-Lieben, Detlev — Die objektiven Schranken der Einwilligung im Strafrecht, Tübingen, 1997 („Schranken der Einwilligung")

Stoltenberg, Klaus — Verpflichtung der Ermittlung und Berücksichtigung rassistischer Motive bei der Strafzumessung, in: Zeitschrift für Rechtspolitik (ZRP) 2012, pp. 119 et seqq.

Stolle, Peter | Öffentliche Anhörung des Rechtsausschusses des Deutschen Bundestages am 13.06.2012 zur sog. Hasskriminalität; Gesetzentwurf BT-Drs. 17/8131 vom 14.12.2011 Gesetzentwurf BT-Drs. 17/9345 vom 18.04.2012; Aufnahme menschenverachtender Tatmotive als besondere Umstände der Strafzumessung; Antrag BT-Drs. 17/8796 vom 29.02.2012; Vorurteilsmotivierte Straftaten wirksam verfolgen ("in: "Public Hearing of the Legal Committee of the German Bundestag on 06/13/2012 to so-called Hate Crime")

Stegbauer, Andreas | Der Straftatbestand gegen die Auschwitzleugnung - eine Zwischenbilanz, in: Neue Zeitschrift für Strafrecht (NStZ) 2000, pp. 281 et seqq.

Stratenwerth, Günter | Zum Begriff des „Rechtsguts", in: Eser, Albin/Schittenhelm, Ulrike/Schumann, Heribert (eds.), Hat die deutsche Strafrechtssystematik eine europäische Zukunft?, Festschrift für Theodor Lenckner zum 70. Geburtstag, Munich 1998, pp. 377 et seqq.

Stratenwerth, Günther | Strafrecht Allgemeiner Teil I. Die Straftat, 6th Edition, Kuhlen, Lothar Munich 2011 („Strafrecht AT")

Stree, Walter; Lenckner, Theodor; Cramer, Peter, Eser, Albin | Gedächtnisschrift für Horst Schröder, Munich 1978

Streng, Franz | Das Unrecht der Volksverhetzung, in: Küper, Wilfried et.al (eds.), Festschrift für Lackner zum 70 Geburtstag am 18. Februar 1987, Berlin, 1987, pp. 501 et seqq. ("FS für Lackner")

Stuckenberg, Carl-Friedrich | Grundrechtsdogmatik statt Rechtsgutslehre. Bemerkungen zur heutigen Diskussion von Strafe und Staat, in: Goltdammer's Archiv (GA) 148 (2011), pp. 653 et seqq.

The Oxford English Dictionary | Vol. 8 (VIII), Second Edition, Oxford, 1989

Tiedemann, Klaus — Tatbestandsfunktionen im Nebenstrafrecht, Tübingen, 1969 ("Tatbestandsfunktionen")

Tilch, Horst
Arloth, Frank — Deutsches Rechts - Lexikon, Vol. 3, Q-Z, 3rd Edition, Munich, 2001

Tolmein, Oliver — Neue strafrechtliche Reaktionsmöglichkeiten auf rassistisch motivierte Gewaltdelikte, in: Zeit-schrift für Rechtspolitik (ZRP) 2001, pp. 315 et seqq.

Tolmein, Oliver — Öffentliche Anhörung des Rechtsausschusses des Deutschen Bundestages am 13.06.2012 zur sog. Hasskriminalität; Gesetzentwurf BT-Drs. 17/8131 vom 14.12.2011 Gesetzentwurf BT-Drs. 17/9345 vom 18.04.2012; Aufnahme menschenverachtender Tatmotive als besondere Umstände der Strafzumessung; Antrag BT-Drs. 17/8796 vom 29.02.2012; Vorurteilsmotivierte Straftaten wirksam verfolgen ("in: "Public Hearing of the Legal Committee of the German Bundestag on 06/13/2012 to so-called Hate Crime")

Torka, Ronald — Nachtatverhalten und Nemo tenetur, Eine Untersuchung über die Grenzen „zulässiger Verteidigung" und die Relevanz des Nemo-tenetur-Prinzips bei der Strafzumessung selbstbegünstigenden Nachtatverhaltens gem. § 46 Abs.2 StGB. Berlin, 2000

Trüg, Gerson — Lösungskonvergenzen trotz Systemdivergenzen im deutschen und US-amerikanischen Strafverfahren, Tübingen, 2003

Tschaggelar, Christopher A. — Hate Crimes und Hasskriminalität: Neue Erscheinungsformen von Gewaltkriminalität unter besonderer Berücksichtigung des Attentates von Zug, 2003

Uhl, Anthony Gary — Hate Crime: Prevalence and Impact in an Urban College Population, UMI Dissertation Services, Ann Arbor, Michigan 1996

Vito, Gennaro F.
Maahs, Jeffrey R. — Criminology – Theory, Research and Policy, 3rd Edition, London, 2012, ("Criminology")

Vogel, Joachim — Strafrechtsgüter und Rechtsgüterschutz durch Strafrecht im Spiegel der Rechtsprechung des Bundesverfassungsgerichts, in Strafverteidiger (StV) 1996, pp. 110 et seqq.

Voigt, Rüdiger — Globalisierung des Rechts. Entsteht eine „dritte Rechtsordnung"?, in: Voigt, Rüdiger (ed.), Globalisierung des Rechts, Baden-Baden, 2000

Von Münch, Ingo
Kunig, Philip — Grundgesetz Kommentar Band 1: Präambel bis Artikel 69, 6th Edition, 2012

Von Münch, Ingo
Kunig, Philip — Grundgesetz Kommentar Band 2: Artikel 70 bis 146, 6th Edition, 2012

Wallace, Harvey — Victimology, 1998, pp. 214-216

Wandres, Thomas — Die Strafbarkeit des Auschwitz-Leugnens, Berlin, 2000 ("Auschwitz-Leugnen")

Wassermann, Rudolf — Reihe Alternativkommentare, Kommentar zum Strafgesetzbuch, Vol. 1 (§§ 1- 21 StGB), Neuwied 1990 ("AK-StGB/author")

Watson, Alan — Legal Transplants: an approach to comparative law, University Press of Virginia, 1974

Watson, Alan — Legal Transplants and European Private Law, Vol. 4.4, in: Electronic Journal of Comparative Law, (December 2000)

Watts — Aggressive Youth Cultures and Hate Crime Skinheads and Xenophobic Youth in Germany, American Behavioral Scientist December 2001 vol. 45 no. 4, pp. 600-615

Wehinger, Markus — Kollektivbeleidung – Volksverhetzung: Der strafrechtliche Schutz von Bevölkerungsgruppen durch die §§ 185 et seqq. und § 130 StGB", Munich, 1994 ("Volksverhetzung")

Weiss, Joan C. — Ethnoviolence's Impact Upon And Response of Victims And the Community, in: Kelly, R.:Bias Crime, pp. 174 et seqq.

Weiss, Joan C.
Ehrlich, Howard J.
Larcon, Barbara E.K. — "Ethnoviolence at Work", 18 Journal of Intergroup Relations, 1991

Wengler, Wilhelm — Die Anpassung des englischen Rechts durch die Judikatur der Vereinigten Staaten , in: Dölle, Hans (Ed.), Festschrift für Ernst Rabel, Band I: Rechtsvergleichung und internationales Privatrecht, Tübingen, 1954, pp. 39 et seqq.

Weinberg — in: Katz, Stanley N. (ed.), in: The Oxford International Encyclopedia of Legal History, Vol. 2, 2009, pp. 255 et seqq.

Weisburd, Bennet
Levin, Brian — On the Basis of Sex: Recognizing Gender-based Bias Crimes, 5 Stan. L. & Pol. Rev., 1994, pp. 21 et seqq.

Welzel, Hans — Das deutsche Strafrecht, Eine systematische Darstellung, 11th Edition, Berlin, 1969

Welzel, Hans — Das Gesinnungsmoment im Recht, in: Festschrift für Julius von Gierke, Berlin, 1950, pp. 290 et seqq.

Werle, Gerhard — Völkerstrafrecht, 2nd Edition, Berlin, 2007

Werner, Olaf
Häberle, Peter
Kitagawa, Zentaro
Saenger, Ingo — Brücken für die Rechtsvergleichung – zugleich: Festschrift für Hans G. Leser zum 70. Geburtstag, Tübingen, 1998

Wessels, Johannes
Beulke, Werner — Strafrecht Allgemeiner Teil: Die Straftat und ihr Aufbau, 41th Edition, Heidelberg, 2011 ("Strafrecht AT")

Wessels, Johannes — Strafrecht Besonderer Teil 1: Straftaten gegen

Hettinger, Michael — Persönlichkeits- und Gemeinschaftswerte, 35th Edition, Heidelberg, 2011 ("Strafrecht BT I")

West, Henry R. — Mill´s case for liberty, pp. 22 et seqq. in: Ten, C. L. (ed.), Mill´s On Liberty, Cambridge, 2008

Will, Michael — Das Common Law, in: David, Rene/Grasmann, Günther (eds.), Einführung in die großen Rechtssysteme der Gegenwart, 2nd Edition, Munich, 1988, pp. 431 et seqq.

Wittig, Petra — Rechtsgutstheorie, Harm Principle und die Abgrenzung von Verantwortungsbereichen, in: Hefendehl, Roland/Hirsch, Andrew von/Wohlers, Wolfgang (eds.), Die Rechtsgutstheorie, Legitimationsbasis des Strafrechts oder dogmatisches Glasperlenspiel? Baden-Baden, 2003, pp. 239 et seqq.

Woesner, Horst — Grundgesetz und Strafrechtsreform, in: Neue Juristische Wochenschrift (NJW) 1966, pp. 1729 et seqq.

Woesner, Horst — Moralisierende Mordmerkmale, in: Neue Juristische Wochenschrift (NJW) 1978, pp. 1025 et seqq.

Woesner, Horst — Neuregelung der Tötungstatbestände, in: Neue Juristische Wochenschrift (NJW) 1980, pp. 1136 et seqq.

Wohlers, Wolfgang — Deliktstypen des Präventionsstrafrecht - zur Dogmatik „moderner" Gefährdungsdeliktes, Berlin, 2000 ("Deliktstypen")

Wohlers, Wolfgang — Rechtsgutstheorie und Deliktsstruktur, in: Goltdammer's Archiv (GA) 149 (2002), pp. 15 et seqq.

Wolter, Jürgen et. al. (ed.) — Systematischer Kommentar zum Strafgesetzbuch, Vol. 1, Allgemeiner Teil (§§ 1 - 37 StGB), 8th Edition, (SK-StGB-author)

Woods, Laurie — Sometimes it´s personal: Hate Crime Prosecution in California, 2008

Woodward, Comer V. — The Strange Career of Jim Crow, 3rd Edition, New York: Oxford University Press, 1974

Worms, Martin — Die Bekenntnisbeschimpfung im Sinne des § 166 Abs. 1 StGB und die Lehre vom Rechtsgut, Frankfurt, 1984 ("Bekenntnisbeschimpfung")

Wüst, Wolfgang — Die „gute Policey" im Rechtskreis. Zur frühmodernen Normensetzung in den Kernregionen des Alten Reiches, Vol. 1: Der Schwäbische Reichskreis, unter besonderer Berücksichtigung Bayrisch-Schwabens, Berlin, 2001

Zalman, Marvin — Crimininal procedure: Constitution and society, West Siegel, Larry J. Publishing, 1991, St. Paul, MN

Zernike, Kate — Jury Finds Spying in Rutgers Dorm Was a Hate Crime, The New York Times, N.Y. Region, March 16, 2012, view at: http://www.nytimes.com/2012/03/17/nyregion/defendant-guilty-in-rutgers-case.html?pagewanted=all&_moc.semityn.www

Ziercke, Jörg — Lagebild extremistischer Kriminalität in Deutschland, in: Extremistische Kriminalität, 2006, pp. 61 et seqq.

Zipf, Heinz — Die Strafmaßrevision: eine strafrechtssystematische Untersuchung über den systematischen Aufbau der Strafzumessung und ihre Revisibilität im Erwachesenen- und Jugendstrafrecht, Munich 1969 ("Strafmaßrevision")

Zipf, Heinz — Kriminalpolitik, Heidelberg, 1980

Zoller, Elisabeth — Congruence and Proportionality for Congressional Enforcement Powers: Cosmetic Change or Velvet Revolution?, Indiana Law Journal 78, 2003, pp. 567 et seqq.

Zweigert, Konrad Kötz, Hein	Einführung in die Rechtsvergleichung, 3rd Edition, Tübingen, 1996
Zweigert, Konrad Kötz, Hein	An Introduction to Comparative Law, Oxford, 1998

SCHRIFTEN ZUM STRAFRECHT UND STRAFPROZESSRECHT

Herausgegeben von Manfred Maiwald und Carsten Momsen

Band 1 Christian-Peter Frees: Die steuerrechtliche Selbstanzeige. Zur kriminalpolitischen Zweckmäßigkeit des § 371 AO. 1991.

Band 2 Norbert Joachim: Der Hörensagenbeweis im Strafverfahren. 1991.

Band 3 Alfred A. Göbel: Die Einwilligung im Strafrecht als Ausprägung des Selbstbestimmungsrechts. 1991.

Band 4 Karl-Heinz Vehling: Die Abgrenzung von Vorbereitung und Versuch. 1991.

Band 5 Heiko Hartmut Lesch: Das Problem der sukzessiven Beihilfe. 1992.

Band 6 Dirk Schwerdtfeger: Besondere persönliche Unrechtsmerkmale. 1992.

Band 7 Stefan Göhring: Polizeiliche Kontrollstellen und Datenverarbeitung. § 163 d StPO und novellierte Polizeigesetze der Länder zwischen Strafverfolgung, Gefahrenabwehr und vorbeugender Straftatenbekämpfung. 1992.

Band 8 Werner Kemper: Horizontale Teilrechtskraft des Schuldspruchs und Bindungswirkung im tatrichterlichen Verfahren nach der Zurückverweisung. §§ 353, 354 Abs. 2 StPO. 1993.

Band 9 Ovvadias Namias: Die Zurechnung von Folgeschäden im Strafrecht. 1993.

Band 10 Jan Zopfs: Unfallflucht bei eindeutiger Haftungslage? Unverzüglichkeitsgebot und Wahlmöglichkeit in § 142 Abs. 2 und 3 StGB. 1993.

Band 11 Stefan Hiebl: Ausgewählte Probleme des Akteneinsichtsrechts nach § 147 StPO. 1994.

Band 12 Ralf Krack: List als Straftatbestandsmerkmal. Zugleich ein Beitrag zu Täuschung und Irrtum beim Betrug. 1994.

Band 13 Henning Radtke: Zur Systematik des Strafklageverbrauchs verfahrenserledigender Entscheidungen im Strafprozeß. 1994.

Band 14 Bernd J. A. Müssig: Schutz abstrakter Rechtsgüter und abstrakter Rechtsgüterschutz. Zu den materiellen Konstitutionskriterien sog. Universalrechtsgüter und deren normentheoretischem Fundament – am Beispiel der Rechtsgutsbestimmung für die §§ 129, 129a und 324 StGB. 1994.

Band 15 Heinz Koriath: Über Beweisverbote im Strafprozeß. 1994.

Band 16 Burkhard Niepoth: Der untaugliche Versuch beim unechten Unterlassungsdelikt. 1994.

Band 17 Karsten Altenhain: Die Strafbarkeit des Teilnehmers beim Exzeß. 1994.

Band 18 Ina Walbaum: Schuldspruch in der Revisionsinstanz nach freisprechendem Urteil des Tatgerichts. 1996.

Band 19 Birgit Dalbkermeyer: Der Schutz des Beschuldigten vor identifizierenden und tendenziösen Pressemitteilungen der Ermittlungsbehörden. 1994.

Band 20 Thomas Hackner: Der befangene Staatsanwalt im deutschen Strafverfahrensrecht. 1995.

Band 21 Hartmut Loritz: Kritische Betrachtungen zum Wert des strafprozessualen Zwischenverfahrens. 1996.

Band 22 Heinz-Hermann Berghof: Therapie und Strafe im Betäubungsmittelrecht. Recht und Wirklichkeit der Behandlung Drogenabhängiger unter besonderer Berücksichtigung der §§ 35 ff BtMG. 1995.

Band 23 Oliver Mertens: Strafprozessuale Grundrechtseingriffe und Bindung an den Wortsinn der ermächtigenden Norm. 1996.

Band 24 Sönke Bahnsen: Das Akteneinsichtsrecht der Verteidigung im Strafverfahren. Dogmatische Grundlagen und Einzelprobleme im Lichte einer rechtsstaatlichen Verfahrensgestaltung. 1996.

Band 25 Dirk Schwieger: Der Vorteilsbegriff in den Bestechungsdelikten des StGB. 1996.

Band 26 Stephanie Meinecke: Die Auswirkungen von Verfahrensfehlern auf die Strafbarkeit nach den Aussagedelikten. 1996.

Band 27 Ute Lambrecht: Strafrecht und Disziplinarrecht. Abhängigkeiten und Überschneidungen. 1997.

Band 28 Carsten Momsen: Verfahrensfehler und Rügeberechtigung im Strafprozeß. Die Strukturen der Revisionsberechtigung unter besonderer Berücksichtigung des Begriffs "Rechtsnormen, die lediglich zugunsten des Angeklagten gegeben sind" in § 339 StPO. 1997.

Band 29 Ursula Epp: Die Abgeordnetenbestechung – § 108 e StGB. 1997.

Band 30 Bernd Scheiff: Wann beginnt der Strafrechtsschutz gegen kriminelle Vereinigungen (§ 129 StGB)? 1997.

Band 31 Ulrike Fontaine: Max Grünhut (1893-1964). Leben und wissenschaftliches Wirken eines deutschen Strafrechtlers jüdischer Herkunft. 1998.

Band 32 Claudia Keiser: Das Kindeswohl im Strafverfahren. Zur Notwendigkeit eines am Kindeswohl orientierten Umgangs mit minderjährigen Opfern und Zeugen, den Möglichkeiten de lege lata und den Erfordernissen de lege ferenda. 1998.

Band 33 Wiebke Schürer-Mohr: Erlaubte Risiken. Grundfragen des "erlaubten Risikos" im Bereich der Fahrlässigkeitsdogmatik. 1998.

Band 34 Stephan Voigtel: Zum Freibeweis bei Entscheidungen der Strafvollstreckungskammer. Eine Untersuchung zu ausgewählten Fragen des Beweisrechts im gerichtlichen Verfahren in Strafvollstreckungs- und Strafvollzugssachen. 1998.

Band 35 Volkmar Wißgott: Das Beweisantragsrecht im Strafverfahren als Kompensation der richterlichen Inquisitionsmaxime. Die Judikatur des Reichsgerichts zum strafprozessualen Beweisrecht. 1998.

Band 36 Susanne Merz: Strafrechtlicher Ehrenschutz und Meinungsfreiheit. 1998.

Band 37 Uwe Schlömer: Der elektronisch überwachte Hausarrest. Eine Untersuchung der ausländischen Erfahrungen und der Anwendbarkeit in der Bundesrepublik Deutschland. 1998.

Band 38 Michael Liedke: Die Vermögensstrafe gemäß § 43a StGB in ihrer kriminalpolitischen Bedeutung. 1999.

Band 39 Danja Domeier: Gesundheitsschutz und Lebensmittelstrafrecht. Zur Konkretisierung der Verkehrspflichten und ihrer Strafbewehrung, insbesondere mit Blick auf §§ 8 ff. LMBG. 1999.

Band 40 Ritva Westendorf: Die Pflicht zur Verhinderung geplanter Straftaten durch Anzeige. Eine kritische Betrachtung der §§ 138, 139 StGB im Kontext der Unterlassungsdelikte. 1999.

Band 41 Hans Theile: Tatkonkretisierung und Gehilfenvorsatz. 1999.

Band 42 Nicole Lange: Vorermittlungen. Die Behandlung des staatsanwaltschaftlichen Vorermittlungsverfahrens unter besonderer Berücksichtigung von Abgeordneten, Politikern und Prominenten. 1999.

Band 43 Tanja Gunder: Der Umgang mit Kindern im Strafverfahren. Eine empirische Untersuchung zur Strafverfolgung bei Sexualdelinquenz. 1999.

Band 44 Sven-Markus Thiel: Die Konkurrenz von Rechtfertigungsgründen. 2000.

Band 45 Jan Schlüter: Die Strafbarkeit von Unternehmen in einer prozessualen Betrachtung nach dem geltenden Strafprozeßrecht. 2000.

Band 46 Detlef Heise: Der Insiderhandel an der Börse und dessen strafrechtliche Bedeutung. Eine Untersuchung des neuen deutschen Insiderrechts speziell unter Bezugnahme auf die strafrechtstheoretischen und strafrechtsdogmatischen Grundlagen. 2000.

Band 47 Hermann Wichmann: Das Berufsgeheimnis als Grenze des Zeugenbeweises. Ein Beitrag zur Lehre von den Beweisverboten. 2000.

Band 48 Rainer T. Cherkeh: Betrug (§ 263 StGB), verübt durch Doping im Sport. 2000.

Band 49 Kristian Hohn: Die Zulässigkeit materieller Beweiserleichterungen im Strafrecht. Eine Untersuchung über Erscheinungsformen und Grenzen der Lösung beweisrechtlicher Probleme im materiellen Strafrecht. 2000.

Band 50 Malte Rabe von Kühlewein: Der Richtervorbehalt im Polizei- und Strafprozeßrecht. 2001.

Band 51 Donata Meinecke: Die Gesetzgebungssystematik der Versuchsstrafbarkeit von Verbrechen und Vergehen im StGB. 2001.

Band 52 Joachim Bock: Begriff, Inhalt und Zulässigkeit der Beweislastumkehr im materiellen Strafrecht. 2001.

Band 53 Gabriele Rose: Grenzen der journalistischen Recherche im Strafrecht und Strafverfahrensrecht. 2001.

Band 54 Wiebke Reitemeier: Täuschungen vor Abschluß von Arbeitsverträgen. Zum Verhältnis zwischen dem Straftatbestand des Betrugs und dem Anfechtungsrecht wegen arglistiger Täuschung (§§ 263 Abs. 1 StGB, 123 Abs. 1 Alt. 1 BGB). 2001.

Band 55 Peter Rackow: Das DNA-Identitätsfeststellungsgesetz und seine Probleme. 2001.

Band 56 Frank Zschieschack: Geiselnahme und erpresserischer Menschenraub (§§ 239a, 239b StGB) im Zwei-Personen-Verhältnis. 2001.

Band 57 Natascha Sëyfi: Das Sicherungsverfahren (§§ 413 - 416 StPO). 2002.

Band 58 Dirk Seiler: Die *Sperrwirkung* im Strafrecht. 2002.

Band 59 Dorothee Sydow: Die actio libera in causa nach dem Rechtsprechungswandel des Bundesgerichtshofs. 2002.

Band 60 Inga Metrikat: Die Unterbringung in einer Entziehungsanstalt nach § 64 StGB – Eine Maßregel im Wandel? Eine vergleichende, empirische Untersuchung zur Entscheidung des Bundesverfassungsgerichts vom 16.03.1994, BVerfGE 91, 1 ff. 2002.

Band 61 Sabine Caroline Bechtoldt: Die Erledigungserklärung im Maßregelvollzug des § 63 StGB. Eine empirische Untersuchung der Erledigungserklärung und zugleich rechtsdogmatische Erörterung ihrer Rechtskraftproblematik. 2002.

Band 62 Sandra Schulte-Nover: Strafrichter in Deutschland und England. Ein systematischer Rechtsvergleich im Hinblick auf die richterlichen Kompetenzen im Strafverfahren. 2003.

Band 63 Tim Schurig: Belehrung und Beratung des Beschuldigten über sein Aussageverhalten. Eine gemeinsame Aufgabe von Gericht und Verteidigung? 2003.

Band 64 Markus Laski: Die strafrechtlichen Bezüge des Bundes-Bodenschutzgesetzes. 2003.

Band 65 Gunnar Lüer: Die Versäumung im Berufungsverfahren. Das strafprozessuale Anwesenheitsprinzip im Spannungsfeld von autonomer Subjektstellung und öffentlichen Interessen am Beispiel des § 329 Abs. 1,2 StPO. 2003.

Band 66 Thomas Grützner: Die Sanktionierung von Submissionsabsprachen. Eine Untersuchung der bestehenden Möglichkeiten einer Bekämpfung von Submissionsabsprachen unter besonderer Berücksichtigung des § 298 StGB. 2003.

Band 67 Bettina Noltenius: Kriterien der Abgrenzung von Anstiftung und mittelbarer Täterschaft. Ein Beitrag auf der Grundlage einer personalen Handlungslehre. 2003.

Band 68 Bettina Kraft: Tendenzen in der Entwicklung des Jugendstrafrechts seit der Jugendgerichtsbewegung. 2004.

Band 69 Jessica Däbritz: Die Bestimmung strafbaren fahrlässigen Verhaltens in der Forschung am Beispiel ärztlicher Humanerprobungen. Ein Beitrag zur methodischen Ermittlung und inhaltlichen Bestimmung von Sorgfaltspflichten in der Humanforschung. 2004.

Band 70 Maike Steenbock: Über die Unfallflucht als Straftat. Eine kritische Untersuchung zum Zusammenhang der Strafbarkeit der Unfallflucht mit den Besonderheiten des Straßenverkehrs. 2004.

Band 71 Holger Mann: Beschleunigungspotential im Jugendstrafverfahren. 2004.

Band 72 Dorothee Krutisch: Strafbarkeit des unberechtigten Zugangs zu Computerdaten und -systemen. 2004.

Band 73 Heinz-Helmut Fuhrmann: Das Begehen der Straftat gem. § 25 Abs. 1 StGB. Unter besonderer Berücksichtigung der sogenannten "eigenhändigen" Delikte. 2004.

Band 74 Gerwin M. Moldenhauer: Eine Verfahrensordnung für Absprachen im Strafverfahren durch den Bundesgerichtshof? 2004.

Band 75 Dirk Busch: Konzernuntreue. Eine Untersuchung spezifischer Untreuestrafbarkeit innerhalb von Konzernverbindungen mit Aktiengesellschaften und Gesellschaften mit beschränkter Haftung. 2004.

Band 76 Mitsuru Iijima: Die Entwicklung des strafrechtlichen Unrechtsbegriffs in Japan. Eine kritische Betrachtung aus strafrechtsdogmatischer und rechtsphilosophischer Perspektive. 2004.

Band 77 Lena Barbara Kötter: Private Elemente in der Strafvollstreckung. Zur Privatisierung von Bewährungshilfe, Gerichtshilfe und gemeinnütziger Arbeit. 2004.

Band 78 Martin Maria Laufen: Der Wucher (§ 291 Abs. 1 Satz 1 StGB). Systematische Einordnung und dogmatische Struktur. 2004.

Band 79 Maike Aselmann: Die Selbstbelastungs- und Verteidigungsfreiheit. Ein Beitrag zu den Garantiewirkungen von Verfahrensrechten im Hinblick auf die Beweiswürdigung, Strafzumessung und Strafbarkeit des Beschuldigten im Strafprozess. 2004.

Band 80 Ingmar Wolf: Graffiti als kriminologisches und strafrechtsdogmatisches Problem. 2004.

Band 81 Misuk Son: Straftatfolgen im deutschen und koreanischen Strafrecht. Ein prinzipieller Vergleich. 2004.

Band 82 Matthias Saal: Die Beteiligung an einer Schlägerei (§ 231 StGB). Ein Plädoyer für die Streichung der schweren Folge. 2004.

Band 83 Michael Stüber: Die Entwicklung des Prinzips der Unmittelbarkeit im deutschen Strafverfahren. 2005.

Band 84 Patrick Gerberding: Das Rechtsmittelsystem im US-amerikanischen Strafverfahren. Eine rechtsvergleichende Betrachtung. 2005.

Band 85 Rouven Seeberg: Aufgedrängte Nothilfe, Notwehr und Notwehrexzess. 2005.

Band 86 Andre Knoerchen: Schadenswiedergutmachung über anwaltliche Schlichtungsstellen. Rechtsökonomische Analyse eines Modellprojekts. 2005.

Band 87 Andreas Quante: Sanktionsmöglichkeiten gegen juristische Personen und Personenvereinigungen. 2005.

Band 88 Gundula Momsen-Pflanz: Die sportethische und strafrechtliche Bedeutung des Dopings. Störung des wirtschaftlichen Wettbewerbs und Vermögensrelevanz. 2005.

Band 89 Klaus Kleinbauer: Rechtsmittelverzicht und Rechtsmittelzurücknahme des Beschuldigten im Strafprozeß. 2006.

Band 90 Manuel Fumagalli: Rechtsprobleme vorgeburtlicher Diagnoseverfahren. Die personenrechtliche Begründung von Pränataldiagnostik und Präimplantationsdiagnostik. 2006.

Band 91 Matthias Dann: Staatliche Tatprovokation im deutschen, englischen und schottischen Recht. Rechtsvergleichende Untersuchung unter besonderer Berücksichtigung europäischer und internationaler Entwicklungslinien. 2006.

Band 92 Shahryar Ebrahim-Nesbat: Die Herausbildung der strafrechtlichen Teilnahmeformen im 19. Jahrhundert. 2006.

Band 93 Christoph Paglotke: Notstand und Notwehr bei Bedrohungen innerhalb von Prozesssituationen. 2006.

Band 94 Sebastian Olk: Die Abgabe von Sacherklärungen des Angeklagten durch den Verteidiger. 2006.

Band 95 Bernadette Pape: Legalverhalten nach Sexualdelinquenz. Eine empirische Analyse der Delinquenzkarrieren nach Sexualstraftaten an Kindern. 2007.

Band 96 Uttam Das: Möglichkeiten der Angleichung materiellen Strafrechts zwischen England und Deutschland im Rahmen des Art. K 31 EUV. 2007.

Band 97 Dennis Miller: Die Beteiligung am Verbrechen nach italienischem Strafrecht. Ein Beitrag zur Geschichte und Gegenwart von Einheits- und Differenzierungsmodellen der strafbaren Beteiligung mehrerer Personen. 2007.

Band 98 Michael Nehring: Kriminelle und terroristische Vereinigungen im Ausland. Auslegung und Analyse des im Zuge der Terrorismusbekämpfung nach dem 11. September 2001 geschaffenen § 129b Strafgesetzbuch. 2007.

Band 99 Bernadette Berger: Das Gesinnungsmoment im Strafrecht. 2008.

Band 100 Peter Rackow: Neutrale Handlungen als Problem des Strafrechts. 2007.

Band 101 Simone Mölders: Bestechung und Bestechlichkeit im internationalen geschäftlichen Verkehr. Zur Anwendbarkeit des § 299 StGB auf Sachverhalte mit Auslandsbezug. 2009.

Band 102 Anke David: Die Entwicklung des Mordtatbestandes im 19. Jahrhundert. 2009.

Band 103 Arne Habenicht: Die Beteiligung an sexuellen Gewalttaten. 2009.

Band 104 Marwan Hamdan: Drittmittelforschung in der Medizin. Eine Gratwanderung zwischen strafbarer Vorteilsannahme und verfassungsgarantierter Forschungsfreiheit. 2009.

Band 105 Carl-Friedrich von Scherenberg: Die sozialethischen Einschränkungen der Notwehr. 2009.

Band 106 Andreas Poppe: Die Akzessorietät der Teilnahme. Eine kritische Analyse der dogmatischen Grundlagen. 2011.

Band 107 Jonathan Burmeister: Die schuldangemessene Bewertung von Ehrenmorden im deutschen Strafrecht. Differenzierte Schuldmerkmale auf Tatbestandsebene bei sonstigen niedrigen Beweggründen. 2011.

Band 108 Philipp Reinhold: Amtsträgerbestechung. Unrechtsgehalt und Grenzen der §§ 331 ff. StGB. 2011.

Band 109 Simone Reiß: Verbotsirrtum und Subventionsbetrug. Unter Berücksichtigung der Besonderheiten bei der betrügerischen Erlangung von EU-Subventionen. 2012.

Band 110 Johannes Altenburg: Die Unlauterkeit in § 299 StGB. Ein Beitrag zur Harmonisierung von Strafrecht und Wettbewerbsrecht. 2012.

Band 111 Christoph Skoupil: Handeltreiben mit Betäubungsmitteln. Strafbarkeitsvorverlagerungen vor und nach der Entscheidung des Großen Senats für Strafsachen vom 26.10.2005. 2012.

Band 112 Frederike Wewerka: Internal Investigations. Private Ermittlungen im Spannungsfeld von strafprozessualen Grundsätzen und Anforderungen eines globalisierten Wirtschaftsstrafverfahrens. Eine Problemanalyse unter besonderer Berücksichtigung des Falles Siemens. 2012.

Band 113 Lena Witzmann: Die gemeinsame Verhandlung. Eine Untersuchung des Öffentlichkeitsgrundsatzes, des Opportunitätsprinzips, des Anwesenheitsrechts und des Fairnessgrundsatzes im verbundenen Verfahren. 2012.

Band 114 Lea Boller: Der unbefugte Gebrauch von Kraftfahrzeugen und Fahrrädern – § 248b StGB. 2013.

Band 115 Nina Wadle: Privatisierung im deutschen Strafvollzug. 2013.

Band 116 Annik Lamshöft: Das Modell des vereinfachten Ablehnungsverfahrens. Ein Gegenentwurf zur strafprozessualen Fristenlösung des Bundesgerichtshofs. 2013.

Band 117 Christine Marie Shavers: Criminal Law Dealing with Hate Crimes. Functional Comparative Law. 2014.

www.peterlang.com

www.ingramcontent.com/pod-product-compliance
Ingram Content Group UK Ltd.
Pitfield, Milton Keynes, MK11 3LW, UK
UKHW021830100926
8556IPUK00004B/261

9 783631 642207